Rhetorical Criticism and Theory in Practice

Dann L. Pierce
University of Portland

Boston Burr Ridge, IL Dubuque, IA Madison, WI New York San Francisco St. Louis
Bangkok Bogotá Caracas Kuala Lumpur Lisbon London Madrid Mexico City
Milan Montreal New Delhi Santiago Seoul Singapore Sydney Taipei Toronto

McGraw-Hill Higher Education 

A Division of The McGraw-Hill Companies

RHETORICAL CRITICISM AND THEORY IN PRACTICE

Published by McGraw-Hill, a business unit of The McGraw-Hill Companies, Inc., 1221 Avenue of the Americas, New York, NY, 10020.

This book is printed on acid-free paper.

1 2 3 4 5 6 7 8 9 0 FGR/FGR 0 9 8 7 6 5 4 3 2

ISBN 0-07-250087-5

Publisher: *Phillip A. Butcher*
Sponsoring editor: *Nanette Kauffman*
Developmental editor II: *Jennie Katsaros*
Marketing manager: *Sally Constable*
Producer, Media technology: *Jessica Bodie*
Project manager: *Karen Nelson*
Production supervisor: *Susanne Riedell*
Coordinator of freelance design: *Mary E. Kazak*
Photo research coordinator: *Alexandra Ambrose*
Photo researcher: *Christine Pullo*
Cover design and illustration: *Donna Cambra*
Typeface: *10/12 Palatino*
Compositor: *GAC Indianapolis*
Printer: *Quebecor World Fairfield Inc.*

Library of Congress Cataloging-in-Publication Data

Pierce, Dann L.
Rhetorical criticism and theory in practice / Dann L. Pierce.
p. cm.
Includes index.
ISBN 0-07-250087-5 (soft cover : alk. paper)
1. Rhetoric. 2. Rhetorical criticism. 3. Communication. I. Title
P301.P473 2003
808—dc21

2002032133

www.mhhe.com

This book is dedicated to all my parents.

Preface

This is a most exciting time to be an undergraduate taking a communication course. Compared to 50 years ago, humans now have astonishing access to understanding how humans use language and other symbol systems to communicate to vast numbers of people. This recent knowledge gives you many choices. You can choose to delve into dangerous words that promoted the collapse of a decade of economic prosperity. You can gain the insights necessary to understand what would make anyone pay $5 million for a story. You can predict with reasonable accuracy the key words on which a Supreme Court case will pivot.

But you can only do those things if you are willing to invest the sweat, work, and energy necessary to understand how various language systems work in human communication. *Rhetorical Criticism and Theory in Practice* is devoted to helping you make that start.

This book began as a series of chapters I wrote for an Introduction to Rhetorical Criticism and Theory class I teach at the University of Portland. I discovered that most available textbooks were written for senior to grad-level students. While students in my classes were bright, they were not equipped to wade through the jargon and perspectives geared toward juniors, seniors, and graduate students. Experiences with students in those classes encouraged worthwhile changes in this book.

Most students in introductory rhetorical criticism and theory classes aim at careers in communication-related occupations, or pursue majors that will make significant use of insights available from quality communication classes. They need a solid foundation of understanding in the types of human communication they will most often encounter and use as working professionals. If you are such a student, this book is written particularly for you.

Plan of the Book

The opening chapters of this book are an introduction to rhetorical criticism as a primary means of accomplishing study of human public communication.

In each chapter, I focus on core ideas that act as a springboard into more sophisticated material. I know that talented teachers and students will build in impressive ways on the core ideas presented.

Chapter 1 sets the focus for the rest of the book by helping you to grasp why we so often ignore the implications of how messages are created. You will discover why the term "rhetoric" is an honored word from an ancient past that provides the basis for modern-day systematic investigations of the power of messages.

Chapter 2 introduces you to two types of criticism: popular criticism and analytic, academic criticism. While you likely read, hear, or use popular criticism already, the chapters of this book will give you direct access to powerful analytic criticism. Understanding *how* academic critics work and where you can find their insights will give you an intense resource for enhancing your awareness of how human communication works.

Chapter 3 coaches you on how to read an example piece of rhetorical criticism written by an accomplished scholar. Her insights will help you see what American presidents must do with language choices to make powerful public messages. While you will certainly learn some things about leaders and rhetoric, you will also learn an excellent system for quickly recognizing the setup of rhetorical criticism articles. With this awareness, you can find and use the discoveries available from formal, academic, analytic investigation of some of the most important messages to reach vital audiences. Knowing how to read rhetorical criticism will give you access to insights to how speeches, news, TV programs, films, or commercials among various types of messages connect (or fail to hook up) with intended audiences.

Chapter 4 changes the focus and allows you to learn how to approach, develop, and write rhetorical criticism. Geared specifically for undergraduates, this material starts with informal decisions and understandings we all use on a daily basis to gauge the potential and impact of messages. In stages we then move to more formal, systematic analysis that will encourage and enable you to write initial research studies seeking to better understand the power of messages created to produce influence.

Highlights: Chapters 1–4

- Communication, Culture, and Rhetoric (Finding Systematic Insight on Powerful Messages)
- Popular Criticism Contrasted with Analytic, Rhetorical Criticism
- Find the Gold: How to Read a Rhetorical Criticism Article
- How to Initiate, Setup, and Write Undergraduate Rhetorical Criticism
- Chapter Workshops
- Scrutinize Exercises

Chapters 5 through 8 focus on foundational areas of human communication: metaphor, narrative, visual messages, and language and ideology. Each of these chapters provides concentrated focus on important rhetorical criticism and theory discoveries in these key areas of human public communication. Materials you read and understandings you develop through these chapters will open many other doors to quality rhetorical criticism in areas you will pursue in the future.

Highlights: Chapters 5–8

- Metaphoric Rhetorical Analysis: Superior Tools of Analysis for Non-Literal Comparisons
- Narrative Rhetorical Analysis: Discovering How Stories Work
- Visual Rhetorical Analysis: Decoding Powerful Pictures and Images
- Language and Ideology: Finding the Rhetorical Power of Worldviews and Values
- Exemplar Journal Articles for Each Chapter
- Chapter Workshops
- Scrutinize Exercises

Chapters 9 and 10 complete the book by initiating careful consideration of what students and scholars can do with superior rhetorical criticism. Chapter 9, on rhetorical theory, presents you with insights into the purpose and development of rhetorical theories designed to better understand the power of public messages. The chapter also gives a rapid overview of the key theory terms you are most likely to encounter as you begin to use articles and books of rhetorical criticism and theory. Brief examples with each key theory term will help you in an initial understanding of pertinent theories. The chapter ends with an examination of the give and take between two outstanding rhetorical scholars who seek to improve and build superior rhetorical theory. Chapter 10 is devoted to your most likely use of existing rhetorical criticism. Gaining experience and insight through reading and writing rhetorical criticism will allow you to discover how highly talented rhetorical critics can provide you with in-depth insights on how (and more importantly *why*) some messages accomplish the persuasive purpose intended by rhetors (message creators) in our culture.

Highlights: Chapters 9–10

- Purpose of Rhetorical Theory Explained
- Rapid Access to Key Rhetorical Theory Terms and Examples
- Guided Example of Scholarly Exchange on Key Theory Issues
- How to Best Discover and Use Rhetorical Criticism Insights
- Exemplar Journal Articles for Each Chapter
- Chapter Workshops

Chapter Pedagogy

Chapters in this textbook often are interspersed with a variety of quick **exercises** designed to help undergraduates scrutinize the concepts and key terms under investigation. These exercises have been pre-tested in classes. They are intended to provoke substantial thought on your part as you learn ideas and analytic frameworks that will enhance your ability to create compelling messages.

Workshop sections appear at the end of each chapter. Use each of these areas to put your newfound skills, perspectives, and terms into action. Many of the workshop exercises are keyed to journal articles that accompany Chapters 3 and 5 through 10.

Resources for Instructors and Students

A complete Instructor's Manual and PowerPoint slides are available at the McGraw-Hill Online Learning Center at www.mhhe.com/pierce.

For students, the Online Learning Center contains interactive Self-Quizzes to reinforce key concepts from each chapter.

Acknowledgments

Talented reviewers examined this textbook at various stages and added their valuable perspectives, suggestions, and insights. Their help was most welcomed. I would like to thank:

Bohn D. Lattin
University of Portland

Celeste M. Condit
University of Georgia

Dan Coburn
Cascade College

Lois Einhorn
Binghamton University

Kathryn A. Wiss
Western Connecticut University

Trudy L. Hanson
West Texas A&M University

Monica Weis
Nazareth College

K. Charles Pearce
St Anselm College

Halford Ryan
Washington & Lee University

Mark A. Pollock
Loyola University Chicago

Timothy J. Brown
Buffalo State College

Ferald J. Bryan
Northern Illinois University

Gregory L. Dickinson
Colorado State University

Anthony B. Schroeder
Eastern New Mexico University

Without the help of these dedicated professionals, this book would have offered much less to students who will use it.

I value the teachers who responded to our nationwide questionnaire. Information about classes and degree programs proved very helpful in designing this book.

I am grateful to the exceptional crew at McGraw-Hill who encouraged this book to set sail. Nanette Kauffman and Jennie Katsaros saw promise in this project and helped from beginning to end. Karen Nelson, Sarah Watts, Christine Pullo, and Alex Ambrose each helped me discover the potential in each chapter. I am deeply appreciative of their talent and dedication.

I am thankful for the continuing support and encouragement of my department and campus colleagues at the University of Portland—especially to Carol Bruce. Members of the University of Portland Library staff did outstanding work (as they always do).

I also thank members of my weekly study group for their unwavering encouragement and reinforcement by entreaty.

My family provided daily support and encouragement throughout the writing and production of this book. Penny, Seanacey, and Brogan make each new day an enjoyment and challenge. I am sincerely grateful for their lives.

And finally: *eucharisteō to theō.*

Table of Contents

The Power of Messages

When was the last time you paid close attention to any part of human communication? Not just ordinary attention, but very close attention? If you are like many people, messages grab your attention only when someone uses words in a clever or unusual way. Or message making can demand your attention when you have to try to communicate with someone who doesn't speak your native language. Or, messages seize your awareness when one word becomes critical to the outcome of a social or business situation.

Do you think the word "Andrews" is worth very much? You might think it worth a great deal if that happens to be your family name. Or, if your name is Julie, and you have appeared in numerous Hollywood films, you might place a significant worth to such a word. Would you be interested in the word "Andrews" if it was worth $703,500? How about $1.5 million? The IRS said that "Andrews" was worth $1.5 million when a publisher printed a number of novels using the name of a dead novelist (V.C. Andrews). The Andrews estate appealed the IRS decision and a Federal District Judge ruled that the true value of the novelist's name was only $703,500.[1] What could make a name worth that much money? When any word, phrase, or expression gains currency and use in mass culture, it can be valuable, powerful, annoying, or dangerous (among other possibilities).

Do you keep track of how words and other language forms become focus points of power and dispute? If you are interested in a career as a communication professional, you must. Various people, institutions, interests, and groups vie for the right to control, use, or influence how language is presented to different audiences. Consider the case of wine "on the plate."

Once in Oregon a retired wine merchant found out how one word from a forbidden category substantially changed the outcome of an ordinary, but important, situation. He wanted to obtain specialized license plates

Scrutinize exercise

Since most license plates in Oregon are three letters followed by a space and three numbers, should the state ban the "XXX" series (for sexually explicit movie reference)? the "SAP" series (for personal embarrassment to the driver)? the "WAR" series (for pacifists)? Can you think of other three letter combinations that could cause trouble or negative reaction? Is public communication as seen on vanity plates worthy of state intervention? Do states regulate any other forms of public communication? Should the state have similar control over window decals and bumper stickers? Why?

that read: "WINE," "VINO," and "IN VINO." His application was denied because those words were related to alcohol, and requests for such plates are routinely turned down in Oregon. The former wine merchant argued that he sold wine for a living for 27 years and had held similar plates in California. The Department of Motor Vehicles did not budge in their refusal of the application, noting that all words related to sex, drugs, or alcohol are prohibited. The retired wine merchant filed a lawsuit to change Oregon DMV policy. As this book went to press, the Oregon State Supreme Court was scheduled to decide on this case. Do such cases deserve the attention of a state Supreme Court? What would *you* rule in this case?

Like the wine merchant, or the "Andrews" estate, we can live for weeks, months, or even years without paying careful attention to messages that have impact on our lives. Inevitably, however, some part of language or human message making will take on urgent importance for us.

In this book we will reverse our typical inattention. Instead, we will pay incredibly close attention to message making in terms of symbols, language, storytelling, communication, and rhetoric.

LANGUAGE AND LIFE

People in American culture sporadically *do* pay very close attention to language. You have probably seen bumper stickers that feature "LIFE" or "CHOICE" as key words used on the battleground of public persuasion. When reading or listening to such rhetoric, you are asked to make a decision—about words, about human behavior, about human values.

Some decisions you make have impact for years—in the case of a reelected president, eight years. Ronald Reagan was called many things during his two terms in office; he might have become known as the "great deregulator," the "great deficit fighter," or the "great gun runner"—but he did not. Instead, the media dubbed him the "Great Communicator" because of his recognized ability to connect by various messages with the American people.

Using a very different style, former president Bill Clinton also had the ability to connect with audiences, even at the height of political and legal troubles (much to the delight of his supporters and the anguish of his opponents). In the fall of 1996, two years after his party lost both houses of Congress (and two years before his impeachment scandal), Clinton was running for reelection against a well-respected World War II veteran. One political observer (under the headline: "Even Republican Operatives See Clinton as a Fearsome Genius") wrote what many others had observed about Clinton's skillful use of public communication:

> Clinton, like Franklin Roosevelt and Ronald Reagan, also views governing as a sort of permanent campaign for his ideas and initiatives. By contrast, Vice President Al Gore, his heir apparent, is a wooden speaker who often fails to connect with audiences in the same emotional way as Clinton.[2]

It is no accident that American presidents in the last 100 years are often judged on how well they communicate through the media with various groups within the United States. They now have entire staffs that work hard to control, shape, and guide how the president will speak or otherwise communicate with mass audiences.

The current White House communication staff of 42 people is directed by Karen Hughes. When the *Washington Post* profiled Hughes they noted:

> Hughes is one of the three most powerful aides in the White House, along with Chief of Staff Andrew H. Card Jr. and senior adviser Karl C. Rowe. . . . [S]he works in a West Wing office with a view of the White House residence and has been given broad authority by a president who puts a premium on image and tone. . . . Mary Matalin, the "Crossfire" co-host turned counselor to Vice President Cheney, says Hughes is "everywhere, into everything and indispensable." "Any public utterance of this White House—of whatever size, for whatever purpose—is her responsibility," Matalin says.[3]

Clearly the importance of creating and distributing political messages is not lost on members of an American White House staff—regardless of the political party in power.

Politicians, among other public figures, are often *only* known through the messages made for (or about) them. A few years ago, after flying into a major American city, I was picked up by a staff member of a person running for public office. The staff member was excited by the campaign, but was very upset about the way her candidate was being portrayed by his opponent in the election. She said, "if the voters could only see how many weekends and evenings [the candidate] has given up over the years to help people who would have been powerless, they'd know that [his opponent] is spreading vicious lies. If voters only knew what a great guy he is . . ." As we talked, the staff person came to a better understanding that voters in her state might *never* come to know the "real" person behind the candidate—and she didn't like it! I understood exactly how she felt; by the time a campaign reaches a national, state, or even city-wide level, the *direct* ways in which a voter can come to know about the qualities of a candidate are greatly reduced. We are left with voters only being able to "see" a candidate in TV ads, newspaper accounts, or debates. While late night hours are spent on pursuing the good of others (even at great personal expense) or other worthwhile activities, they often get lost in the jumble of messages that accompany a modern political campaign.

Since public messages to a mass audience can become so deeply important, you may wish to pay closer attention to language and its many different uses. Perhaps you *have* seen personally the impact of key messages on a community. Perhaps you have worked with a political campaign, a non-profit group attempting to get media coverage for an event, a school publication that received overwhelming attention due to one published article, or an institution that hopes a symbolic gesture will be understood and well received.

LANGUAGE AND CONTROVERSY

Clearly, values, understandings, life frameworks, and perspectives overlap, and at times clash, in modern life. Language is nearly always at the center of such overlaps (and clashes) in one way or another.

In January 1998, NASA ran afoul of traditional Navajo beliefs. The space agency rocketed the cremated remains of a planetary scientist to the moon as part of the Lunar Prospector mission.[4] In Navajo traditions, ceremonies, and stories, the moon is revered; it is understood to regulate life cycles. The disagreement received print and electronic media coverage. Said one columnist:

> What's next, NASA? Who ya gonna apologize to next? The Tlingits? The Aleuts? The Egyptians? The descendants of those moon worshippers in ancient Greece and Rome? And if the mission of the space agency has truly shifted from science to sensitivity, why stop there?
>
> Next time NASA desecrates the moon, it best consult with the Unitarians, the Moonies, and the Werewolves of London, lest any of 'em cry, "Sacrilege!"[5]

Navajo Nation president at the time, Albert Hale, saw the situation very differently:

> It is one thing to probe, to study, to examine and even for men to walk on the moon, but it is sacrilegious, a gross insensitivity to the beliefs of many Native Americans to place human remains on the moon.[6]

Do you think the placing of cremated remains of a scientist who studied the moon as part of his life work is an "honor" or "sacrilege"? Many entities—federal agencies, the president of the United States, tribal leaders and members, citizens, and family members of the dead scientist, among others—all have a stake in what words are used to describe this decision by NASA. In Chapter 8 we will investigate the specific power that words have to influence human belief and action.

NASA moved quickly to issue a public apology to the Navajo people.

Should all federal agencies or officials act to conform or change government decisions to minimize anger or wrongs perceived by groups within the culture served by the agency? On what basis should one group's "voice" be more powerful or influential than another's? If language, or key pivotal words such as "honor" or "sacrilege" can create cultural disagreement, can language also give us the means to resolve those disputes successfully? We will spend more time in Chapter 8 carefully investigating the limits and advantages of language to accomplish those sorts of tasks.

And since we've just been talking about a federal agency, we might do well to ask what is evoked in your mind when the words "federal" and "agency" get linked together. Are "federal agencies" good or bad? Desirable or undesirable? Can you trust them? Recognize that our understanding of what a "federal agency" is likely to do (or not do) is often set by public messages you and I have been given by our culture.

For instance, the movie *Wag the Dog* (released in December 1997) satirically portrays the planning, trickery, and deception that may go on when government officials give "information" to citizens. As thought-provoking as that movie might be, we must *also* realize that it (or any other movie) is also trying to persuade us, and should be held to strong standards of evaluation.

How often do *you* evaluate—in a careful way—messages that surround you? What advantage could such evaluation bring to your awareness of life? Are you manipulated to your disadvantage by those who create mass-media messages? Most of us would say "no." But, are we *really* sure that we *really do* withstand the efforts of thousands of people who spend billions of dollars to create messages designed to influence our behavior?

Scrutinize exercise

The next time you are in a supermarket shopping for standard items, try to reach three times in a row for the cheapest, generic store brand instead of brand name foods or products. What is your reaction? Could you easily put the generic items in your cart? Is your reaction based on messages you've received through the media about that food or product? Ad messages don't influence you, right? Right?!

Does it matter to you that the Coca-Cola company has a director of "experiential marketing" at its Atlanta headquarters? How about that she reportedly authorized hiring the services of a small Scottish ad firm (to the tune of tens of thousands of dollars above the normal Coke multi-million-dollar ad budget) in order to look for " 'out-of-the box' creative ideas" for her brand?[7] What kinds of messages might "experiential marketing" create? Are you prepared to understand the tactics of message creation and language use over the next ten years? Your eventual professional goals call for a "yes" answer from you—but how will you do it?

By what means would you analyze the tactics or expressions used by businesses or political groups? How would you probe the force or quality of messages created by your neighbors or by your school? This book and your ongoing study of rhetoric will help you to learn and develop a specific set of tools and skills. You will be able to accomplish careful, systematic analysis of vital messages given by the mass media in our culture with your rhetorical analysis tools.

AWARENESS OF LANGUAGE POWER

An old joke asks this question: "What do fish not know about?"

If we brainstorm, we recognize that most fish know nothing about a seemingly endless list of things: Elvis, elk hunting, the top of Mt. Everest, elevators, elves, and so on (and those are only some of the "E's"!). The "official" answer to the joke holds that fish don't know about water. Similarly, we live, breathe (swim?), and operate in a symbolic environment that is much as water is to a fish; we often pay no direct attention to our message habitat. Since fish can thrive or die based on the nature and relative quality of their habitat (water), we, too, must give careful attention to our habitat of messages—to not do so could imperil our lives or the lives of those we care about. Do you live in a healthy message environment?

Steven Covey, self-help-effective-habits guru, has claimed: "Communication is the most important skill in life."[8] He is joined by outplacement firms, Fortune 500 companies, and independent research firms that regularly discover this truth: businesses, agencies, institutions, and many other employers believe that communication skills are critical for desirable managers, executives, staff, and other employees. Many highly valued classes in Communication Studies in areas of small group communication, interpersonal communication, and conflict management speak directly to concerns about face-to-face communication.

We will discover that persons who have influence and control over mass-mediated messages deserve equal attention. They can have immediate and long-term impact on thousands or millions of people—sometimes with incredible speed.

Scrutinize exercise

The McDonald's scalding coffee case was settled in the mid-90s. Do you still see warning signs about hot coffee or other beverages? What other indications can you spot that restaurants or coffee shops are worried about possible scaldings? Legal "power terms" such as "wanton conduct" were not invented just for this hot coffee case. Where did they come from? Who gets to decide their real meaning or application? Should judges be trained in rhetoric as well as the law?

In February 1992, when an elderly woman burned herself with hot coffee from a McDonald's in New Mexico, few people took notice. But when news messages of her winning multi-million dollar lawsuit featured legal "power" terms such as "callous disregard," "willful, reckless, malicious, wanton conduct," and "punitive damages," signs warning of coffee temperatures and caution quickly went up at restaurants, cafés, and fast-food joints all over America. Certain words *can* carry enormous weight and power in our culture.

Do you know how, or on what basis, messages perform many different functions and tasks? If you seek to become a communication professional who creates or deals with mass media messages, it is your responsibility to know.

In this book you will learn a specific set of terms, perspectives, and sources of research. These tools will give you an initial entry into the important realm of rhetorical theory and criticism. You will learn how rhetorical critics and theorists develop knowledge and seek understanding about the power of messages in our culture. This "doorway" will enable you to go far beyond gut, or surface, responses and understandings concerning the power of verbal language, the power of storytelling, and the power of visual images that dominate public messages in our culture.

RHETORIC, RHETORIC, RHETORIC

One of the first ways we can move into a quick and useful awareness is through a better understanding (and use) of the term *rhetoric.*

If your only contact with the word *rhetoric* (or related words such as *rhetorical* or *rhetorically*) is through typical journalistic uses of the term, you could be forgiven for thinking that rhetoric is a negative or disreputable word, even a horrible one.

Let's examine the use of the term *rhetoric* in contemporary, popular writing.

From a news story about a White House official:

> In trying to hold the spending line, the 52-year-old Mr. Daniels [George W. Bush's budget director Mitchell Daniels, head of the White House Office of Management and Budget] boasts of having had more success than failure so far. He has held the administration's defense proposals below what some in the Pentagon wanted, and kept early spending bills in line. But even some of his friends worry that with his brash **rhetoric** along the way, he has alienated some of the very people he will need.[9]

In this use, the term *rhetoric* appears as a substitute for "talk" or "words." It designates how one person chooses to express himself with words and the possible response to that personal decision and style.

The next example comes from a news report about attempts at the state level to pass laws to help senior citizens with the cost of prescription drugs:

> Some retirees, such as Johnson, the former brewery worker in Vancouver, are tired of the debate [about government help to seniors for prescriptions].
>
> "They get up on the Senate floor and say that people are eating dog food to afford drugs," he said. "So they know that, but when does the **rhetoric** stop and when do they do something?"[10]

Quite similar in tone and use is this report about legislative competition in the U.S. Senate:

> Majority Leader Tom Daschle, from the farm state of South Dakota, is eager to move on agriculture assistance, which includes billions of dollars in direct payments to grain producers. But since taking the Senate helm, he has been buffeted by a series of Republican efforts to challenge his leadership. . . . And on a $60 billion-plus bill for the Transportation Department, Mr. Daschle faces a continuing filibuster over proposed safety rules for Mexican trucks, which are slated to be allowed to travel throughout the United States next year.
>
> The White House, stung by Mr. Daschle's recent criticism about the president's foreign-policy skills, jumped into the fray, accusing the Senate of "pursuing an isolationist path" on the issue.
>
> If the two sides can get past the **rhetoric,** there is hope for some compromise.[11]

These uses contrast rhetoric with action. Sometimes called "mere" rhetoric, this use suggests that some people talk, some people act, and that talking and action should *not* be confused with one another. This use of rhetoric is often adopted by those frustrated by what they see as too much talk and too little action.

The next example comes from an op-ed column concerning the evaluation of a mayor in a suburban community:

> The purchase of more than 70 acres of prime property that was zoned for development was complete when Mayor Dodds took office. Improving these parks was a commitment made in the 1998 bond. The purchase of these properties did more to slow growth in West Linn than any of the anti-growth **rhetoric** bandied about by Mayor Dodds.[12]

This use suggests that various advocates use different types of talk (in this case "anti-growth" talk); moreover, any array of public talking has certain recognizable themes or characteristics that form a subsegment of talk within a community's use of persuasive communication. Hence, one can easily find references to liberal or conservative rhetoric, feminist rhetoric, spiritual rhetoric, southern rhetoric, or progressive rhetoric (to name but a few) within cultural comment and argument in America.

Finally, this book review features a use of the term rhetoric that pulls together common elements from the others:

> Cullen Murphy's book *The Word According to Eve: Women and the Bible in Ancient Times and Our Own* provides an insightful overview of recent feminist religious scholarship. This work amounts to the fifth intellectual revolution in Bible history, disassembling the centuries-old male bias in biblical interpretation. (The first revolution is the origin of the Bible itself, followed by Christianity, then the Reformation, and, fourth, the application of the Reason of the Enlightenment to biblical interpretation.)
>
> The book suggests that, while political feminism may be stagnating in a morass of **rhetoric** and media sound bites, intellectual and spiritual feminism are far from dead.[13]

Rhetoric here is the term used to designate the condition that occurs when cultural talk, discussion, and disagreement become so noticeably tangled (and dysfunctional) as to stagnate and possibly die. This is not a pretty or desirable condition.

All of the popular, contemporary uses of rhetoric reviewed to this point have one underlying theme in common: rhetoric is used to designate those messages with which someone or some group disagrees or disapproves. Hence, whether applied to personal style, types of public argument, understandings of inaction, or unsavory conditions after much public debate, rhetoric becomes the term used by these writers to describe specific messages with which there is great disagreement. Hence, the word rhetoric gets used when people are upset with forms of human communication with which they disagree or disapprove. This use gives us an indirect signal that such rhetoric is perceived as powerful or potentially powerful. Indeed it is. Rhetoric has been the inspiration and location of informed talk about persuasion from ancient times through the present. A long list of scholars (including Isocrates, Plato, Aristotle, Longinus, Cicero, Quintilian, Augustine, Erasmus, Ramus, Locke, Hume, Sheridan, Campbell, Blair, Palmer, Willard, Richards, Burke, Weaver, Nichols, Perelman,

Olbrechts-Tyteca, Bryant, Black, Bitzer, Campbell, McGee, Gronbeck, Leff, Medhurst, Condit, and Daughton, to name but a few) have added to our understanding of how language and its use in communication have power in human community and actions.

Rhetorical studies have moved from Aristotle's musings about a speaker's credibility to Gronbeck's study of how negative political ads function. We've extended Erasmus's concern with peace in human communication to Condit's concern with cultural meaning and power exchange. Our sights were set by Isocrates on the political power of words and have been reset by Piccirillo on how televisual messages give "shape and form" to human social relationships.[14]

While you will get to know many of these people in your related reading, you should know that thousands of scholars have refined our awareness of the power of language and communication through rhetorical studies. This book is but a starting point in your own quest to understand and use language. Therefore, we will not be able to give any one (or set) of these wonderful scholars full coverage. We will, however, cover some of the most exciting findings about rhetoric from across the ages. Chapter 9 will give you an initial "toolbox" of rhetorical criticism and theory terms. With it, you will better understand existing investigations of communication, power, and language. Your understanding of how messages work will be greatly enhanced if you apply yourself to the intense study of how and why human communication works through messages. (If you watched snowboarding in the Winter Olympics, you know a rider doesn't get much air with only casual, partial practice.)

For reasons noted above, we will be using a much different approach to the term *rhetoric* than we typically find in news coverage or political commentary. We will use rhetoric to mean both the *use of* communication by people and the *study of* the use of communication by people. (Both of these definitions have long, ancient trails of use.)

Human **communication** is a process wherein one or more humans create a message (or messages) allowing meaning to be evoked and understood by one or more other humans. Communication so far as we know cannot occur without messages.

Adjust your mental software to recognize that throughout this book *rhetoric* (as a reference to the messages created by humans) and *rhetoric* (as a reference to the specific, systematic study of messages created by humans) will be used as positive, helpful terms.

Related terms such as *rhetorical, rhetorically, rhetor,* and *rhetorician* will also need to become part of your working vocabulary.

We will say that a message or an aspect of a message is **rhetorical** when it uses a recognizable strategy or form to encourage meaning making on the part of an audience member. Granted, some public messages may seem haphazard, or even stupid. Few public messages, however, seem incoherent; they employ language forms and tactics in more or less conventional ways.

Would you, as a national leader, ever deliberately attempt to offend an audience that was important to you? Doing so might seem, at first glance, foolish or random, but on reconsideration might show some discernable underlying purpose:

> During Bill Clinton's 1992 bid for the U.S. presidency, his campaign staff implemented a tactic which they described as "counter-scheduling." This entailed Clinton accepting invitations to attend campaign events with marginal or unpopular constituencies at which he would intentionally strike a discordant note—delivering a message that would offend his audience. Superficially that would appear to be bad manners and even worse politics. But Clinton was not concerned with his effect on his immediate audience so much as the broader middle-class audience watching from their living-room vantage point. . . . Instead of addressing issues designed to connect with his audience, Clinton availed himself of the opportunity to attack a black teenage Rap singer by the name of Sister Souljah who had made some provocative remarks around the time of the 1992 Los Angeles riots.[15]

Hence, any conventional use of language or its forms should allow us to make valid estimations about approaches to communication and persuasion.

We can also say that a message is **rhetorical** if it produces or encourages change, even if that change was never intended (or foreseen) by the message creator (rhetor).

So, long before the O.J. Simpson case splashed through the American media delivery system, Condit and Selzer analyzed the rhetorical messages in newspaper coverage of a murder trial in Topeka, Kansas. Their investigation revealed that information reported to people in Kansas was quite different from information shared within the courthouse during the trial. Condit and Selzer built on previous work by Bennett and Feldman as they discovered:

> . . . the social interpretation of reality, not the discovery of truth, is the operative force in the courtroom. . . . Prosecutors and defense attorneys are charged . . . not only with presenting the facts of the case—the elements of the story—but also with providing an interpretation of these facts—a narrative structure accounting for motive and purpose. (198)

Their research on the rhetorical dynamics of storytelling through journalistic practices shows how a professional norm of "objective reporting" may well prevent journalists from focusing on items presented in the trial that are convincing to the jury.

Condit and Selzer's analysis helps us better understand that competing versions of events offered within a trial may compel juries and regular citizens to use different story-making strategies. Hence, gauging the rhetorical dynamics of trial information as reported in the press is critical if we are to understand public outrage over certain verdicts.[16]

We will say that a message or an aspect of a message operates **rhetorically** when a recognizable strategy or form to encourage meaning making on the part of an audience member can be discovered.

Olson discovered that four famous paintings by Norman Rockwell were used rhetorically to motivate American citizens to support the war effort in World War II. His analysis revealed the specific tactics used within the paintings to create that motivation.[17] He revealed that Rockwell used "productive ambiguity" to create characters and settings that appeared familiar, but that would also encourage identification and response by many different types of American citizen. As Olson says: "Although Rockwell's meticulous attention to exact detail was well-known, perhaps not so well-known was his ability to omit detail so as to promote varied identifications" (16).

We will say that a person (or set of persons) who uses a recognizable strategy or form to encourage meaning making on the part of an audience member by creating a message is a **rhetor.** Again, we've learned from long experience and investigation that a strategy detected may or may not have been intended by the rhetor. For instance, I have investigated the work of America's most famous political cartoonist, Thomas Nast, and have discovered that we mold and influence certain cultural rhetors by how we celebrate their work.[18] My analysis revealed that writers and reporters describe political cartoonists in public messages as if they were special single combat warriors; their descriptions create firm expectations about the style and purpose of graphic political messages. Yet, writers and other rhetors likely never specifically *intended* to describe and promote a "fighting" profession.

We will say that a person who seeks to understand and interpret a message or an aspect of a message when it uses a recognizable strategy or form to encourage meaning making on the part of an audience member is a **rhetorician.**

In several senses we are all practical rhetoricians as we seek to understand how messages work so as to make better messages. Farrell sought to discover how producers and directors of ABC at the 1984 Winter Olympics acted as rhetoricians under pressure when the results of the Winter Games did not occur as expected.[19] The tactical decisions of these television rhetoricians reveal some of the strategies necessary when things do not go as planned. (Would you be willing to make on-the-fly critical message decisions with an audience of millions looking on?) Professor Farrell suggests that any commercial, televised Olympic Games is a spectacle that has "fragile narrative properties" (162). By this he notes that beer sellers, television networks, rabid sports fans, and over-optimistic announcers (among others) set the stage for expectations of athletic success by the United States when that success was by no means insured. Hence, when many American teams and individual athletes did less well than expected, Farrell's investigation reveals that sports reporters used "compensatory" rhetoric (including blaming the athletes, decrying political judging, blaming coaches, and highlighting the superior "emotion" exhibited by American competitors in previous Olympic games). His study demonstrates that careful analysis of statements, interview questions, network promos, and commercial spots can reveal the strategies broadcasters use when highly promoted expectations go unfulfilled.

Our path, then, will carry us to the work of rhetorical critics and theorists who take as their life's work the responsibility of understanding the persuasive and influential characteristics of messages created for public audiences.

This book is split evenly into four focus areas once we move beyond the basics in the opening chapters. We will investigate how metaphors (and other nonliteral comparisons) are critical to how we think and to how we perceive significant parts of life. Next, we will consider narrative as a primary way in which we structure information and life experiences. Then, we will look into visual images as forms of information and persuasion. Finally, we will examine how language use over a long period of time creates an inherited worldview.

We must remember that message challenges *always* come to rhetors with preexisting contours, requirements, and resources. A president of a large car company who must make a crucial public statement about a defective engine component cannot willy-nilly decide to deliver the message in haiku verse. Likewise, an attorney making the closing argument in a murder 1 trial must consider multiple constraints. Rulings by the presiding judge, education level of jury members, demonstrated facts of the case, and news coverage of similar cases in the recent past (among many other factors) must all be considered before she settles on the components of her rhetorical message.

These four focus areas have been selected because they are at the root or base of many different types of public messages that influence large audiences. Learning how these communication forms and tactics work will allow you to better understand important messages that you will want audiences to receive well. Various examples in the chapters and in the journal reading that accompanies most chapters will help remind us that rhetorical message characteristics do not operate in a vacuum. Instead, rhetors and rhetoricians must constantly work with constraints and opportunities presented by language use, political and economic conditions, audience expectations, physical circumstances, legal requirements, and cultural experience. Hence, before investigating these core areas of rhetorical criticism and theory we need to understand the places and conditions in which they occur.

OUR THREE WORLDS

We live in three very distinct, yet overlapping, "worlds." We live in a physical world, a social world, and a symbol world. We have to cope with conditions and attributes within each of these worlds every day.

Physical World

Our **physical world** has always provided us boundaries, resources, and challenges. In many ways we have "mastered" our physical environment. We now sail all oceans and dive beneath their surfaces, climb all mountains, drill deep into the earth's crust, fly for more than 16 hours in the air with hundreds of passengers, and escape the atmosphere and gravity of earth to explore space. We build buildings that tower into the sky, hide within mountains, stand over water, withstand earthquakes, and provide basic comfort in exceedingly harsh environments.

Our own bodies have become a testing ground for our ability to "explore" our own biological world with probes and imaging tools.

Our last century allowed us to understand that certain material resources, once available in abundance, are shrinking or damaged in the face of growing population and use.

Consequently, our physical world often reminds us that we have neither total nor adequate control of physical conditions. One hurricane, one deadly virus, one tsunami, or one ravaging fire can quickly remind us that all of our efforts, improvements, technologies, and skills are at times puny. Even in non-catastrophic situations, we sometimes realize that the physical world will only yield to certain kinds of influence. An article about contemporary blacksmiths made these observations about their craft:

> The simple joys of handwork explain much of blacksmithing's considerable attraction. The concentration necessary to draw, shape and twist a piece of metal is total. Hot metal can't be reasoned with or pleaded with. A meeting or a memo won't turn a lump of steel into a set of fireplace tools or a stand for your Norse drinking horn; only skill and determination will.[20]

While you cannot typically study to be a blacksmith in college, whole courses of study at the university level *are* devoted to better understanding the characteristics of our physical world, including metals. Whole professional lives are devoted to understanding and using physical resources and attributes of our physical world.

For instance, Dr. Norman Heglund has discovered how to carry over sixty pounds without breaking a sweat. He has studied women in Kenya since 1977. Some women there routinely carry heavy firewood on their heads over long distances and seem unaffected by the load. Dr. Heglund has discovered through biomechanical research that these talented women alter their gait and thereby use less energy when walking.[21]

Backpackers, freight workers, and others may well be very interested in this research in the characteristics of our physical world.

We must continue to find our way in our material environment. Most of us will live in a "built" physical environment most of our lives. What is the best way to do that? How will our perspectives and decisions change the physical world in which we live? What impact does rhetoric have upon the physical world? Remember the blacksmith! Words cannot actually shape hot steel. Words, however, do shape the blacksmith. Does the physical world have impact upon rhetoric? What are the physical conditions necessary for the creation of sounds and symbols used in human communication? Does rhetoric have much impact on our physical world?

Social World

Our **social world** gives us boundaries, resources, and challenges daily. We live in a social world unique to our culture and time, yet one deeply similar to social practices that have held sway in the human community for ages.

No human lives long without eating, yet the "proper" way to eat is built within our social world. An American visitor to South Korea discovered this:

> From the moment we arrived at Kimpo airport in Seoul we felt somewhat out of place. The scent of ginger and garlic sharply contrasted with the smell of antiseptic cleansers and fresh-brewed coffee more common in American terminals. . . . Our gracious guides immediately took us to eat one of their favorite foods. It looked very much like a snow cone in a bowl, so we could hardly wait to try it. Shaved ice, fruit juice, a spoon full of powered milk, and a smattering of jellied candy. And beneath the heaping mound? Surprise! A big scoop of black beans. We stirred our dishes valiantly and smiled.[22]

Family life provides us early context and training in what it means to be human (and a member of *our* family). Soon we are introduced to social contacts, norms, and expectations that extend far beyond our home. If you are a woman raised in a Kenyan village, would it seem normal to carry sixty-five pounds of firewood on your head for miles? If you are an American citizen, when, and how, did you learn what your citizenship means? Since 9/11 have you used any of your social relationships to re-explore what it means to be you?

Our ability to understand and use these relationships has a significant effect on us. It allows us happiness or finds us distraught, provides comfort for us or makes us problem-solve like crazy, offers us resources or makes us wonder why we were born.

Our social exchanges have many layers and different conditions. The fast pace of twenty-first century life has only made these exchanges more challenging, pain-filled, or exhilarating!

Social connections and expectations are often more or less flexible and changeable in different cultures. Those different cultures are now coming into greater and greater contact with each other because of advances in transportation and communication devices. Have you noticed that many commercial products are now packaged with labeling in two or three languages? When you see a window cleaner with designations in English, French, and Spanish, does it signal anything to you? If you have traveled in international, regional, or cultural settings other than your native country or region, you've probably noticed that people eat, play, or work at different hours from those familiar to you.

At minimum, if you are in a different city, your social connections and expectations are challenged simply because you are not "home." At maximum, if you are experiencing a different culture and language, your social connections and expectations can feel "out of place." If you are a French exchange student visiting in Chicago for a year, your host family may seem to eat much too quickly and informally most of the time. If you are an American exchange student visiting in Paris, it may seem as if far too much time is spent on food preparation and dining.

Hence, our social world often is the source of our greatest contentment and the root of our most maddening distractions. We know that to be human is to be in community, yet (especially in America) we've been taught to prize individuality and freedom. Our social training often guides and constrains our options for life choices.

We must continue to find our way in our social environment. Most of us will live in specific social environments most of our lives. What is the best way to do that? How will our perspectives and decisions change the social world in which we live? What influence does rhetoric have on our social world? What influence does our social world have on rhetoric?

Symbol World

Our **symbol world** gives us boundaries, resources, and challenges that stretch for ages: from a millennial past to the year in which we live to the moment in which you read this sentence. This whole chapter is devoted to helping us initially recognize the power, size, and influence of our symbol world. All cultures and societies use sounds and images passed on to them by earlier generations and individuals. Sounds and images, when combined, create languages. In turn, we use languages as we create a symbol world within which we work, eat, sleep, play, and plan. During a very small portion of our life (from birth to around 24 months) we know about our environment and social relationships in a very direct and physical way. Soon, however, our training in the use of language tools and habits allows us to manipulate words and images about time, space, and physical conditions.

We have, of course, in different places and cultures created very different symbol worlds. We need only to walk down a street (or *rue*, or *calle*, or *via*, or *rua*) in a city far from our own culture to be reminded how different symbol systems can seem confusing and challenging.

Within our own culture, wherever that may be, we can rightly expect to encounter minor differences. But we can anticipate great understanding and ability to use and exchange language in furthering our own goals and aspirations.

Hence, as we have already seen, our symbol world (when within our own culture) can seem "transparent" (as water is to fish) and not be an especially important concern. Yet, it does not take long before we encounter important problems which seem to have their origin in communication difficulties. Language, it seems, is like a car: we pay little attention to it until it falters or fails us.

We must continue to find our way in our symbol environment. We will all live in specific symbol environments all of our days. What is the best way to do that? How will our perspectives and decisions change the symbol world in which we live? We've noted that the specific use of our symbol world (and the study of that use) has been called *rhetoric*. We will continue to use the very best of rhetorical scholarship throughout this book to better understand how our symbol world works and interacts with our physical and social worlds.

FIGURE 1.1 **Our Three Worlds**
Physical, social, and symbol worlds overlap and have mutual influence in human communication.

Source: Pierce Communication

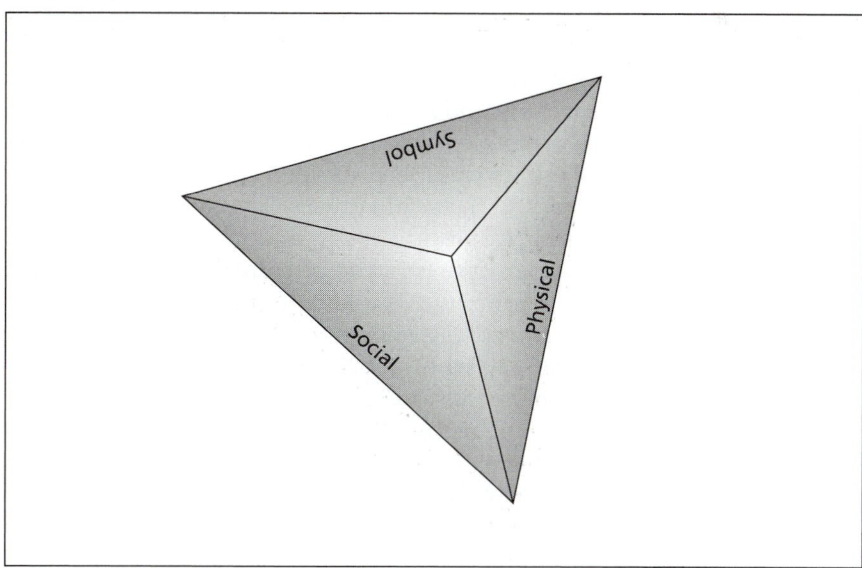

OVERLAP IN OUR THREE WORLDS

Although I've separated these three worlds for purposes of focus and emphasis, we occupy and use all three "worlds" at once. We have used our symbol world to describe, understand, and manipulate our physical world. Our physical world holds the constraints and possibilities that make our creation of symbols, words, and language possible. Our social world deeply influences how we use material resources to construct what some scholars call our "built" environment.

The reminders of the profound interaction between and among these three worlds everywhere surround us. In the movie *Hart's War,* a scene early in the film depicts American prisoners of war being strafed mistakenly by U.S. airplanes in a rail yard in Germany. In a desperate attempt to save lives, the soldiers line up in a formation that spells out P O W and is visible to the pilots. The strategy works and the fighters break off the attack. Here we find an example, albeit in a fictional story, of a manipulation of the physical world (bodies in a rail yard) to accomplish a symbol world goal (spelling an English letter acronym) to forestall death within a portion of the social world (conventions of treatment of prisoners of war). If the spelling of three letters using human bodies represents an essentially basic form of human communication, then a nefarious strategy in cyberspace may indicate a twenty-first century sense of complexity.

Wired magazine reports that clever deception within social conventions of cyber-activity may signal new levels of danger to computer users.[23] Most of us have become used to messages warning of destructive viruses that may threaten our computers. Likewise, some of us have followed instructions sent to help us remove or overcome a virus or potential virus. Some destructive hackers have taken advantage of this "routine" activity that rests at the intersection of our physical, social, and symbol worlds. They send a message warning the computer user that she or he must search out and remove a virus file. The file the user is instructed to remove is a component of the operating system of the computer. Hence, the harmful hacker (who has to send no clever code to invade the computer) in essence uses social conventions to trick a computer user into becoming their own "virus."

Somewhere between prisoners-of-war standing in a life-saving formation to save lives and a computer user being duped into wrecking their own computing system lies most of our concerns about public messages. We can see that rhetoric has profound impact on individuals and groups within our culture.

After some time in the Chapter 1 workshop, we'll investigate a character you may have met in your social world or symbol world (or both): the critic. We'll discover why well-written criticism could make or break you as a communication professional.

In this Chapter 1 workshop, we will probe in focused workshop exercises many of the concepts you discovered in this chapter. Work at a pace by assignment, or by choice, that allows these various insights to "sink in" at an even deeper level for you.

WHERE DID WE GET THESE WORDS?

Comedian (and protolinguist) George Carlin makes these observations:

> The words *Fire Department* make it sound like they're the ones who are starting the fires, doesn't it? It should be called the "Extinguishing Department." We don't call the Police the "Crime Department." Also, the "Bomb Squad" sounds like a terrorist gang. The same is true of *wrinkle cream.* Doesn't it sound like it causes wrinkles? And why would a doctor prescribe pain pills? I already *have* pain! I need relief pills.[24]

Following Carlin's lead, discover or think of at least 3 examples of titles or names that seem mismatched if understood literally. How did our word-based language arrive at some words that seem to make perfect sense and others that, on reflection, seem a bit goofy? How did we get words or word combinations that seem to make little sense? How much choice do you have over what you call things? Rhetoricians, philosophers, and others have pondered on these matters of language and meaning for centuries. Some hold that language is a prison over which we have little or no control. Others see language as an adaptable tool or instrument. Still others see language as an active tool of political and social oppression. Our language-specific chapters will help you decide on some of these age-old questions as well as learn some very cool characteristics of language.

BUMPER STICKER MESSAGING

Below you'll find a series of statements or questions seen on actual bumper stickers. Use these very brief messages as a launching point for considering how thinking, perspective, or reasoning get started from people sharing bits of language with each other.

If you saw this bumper sticker on a car:

Eat Dessert First, Life's Too Short

what would you think it means? Would adoption of this as a life stance or philosophy extend beyond dessert?

If you saw this bumper sticker on a pickup:

Women Want Me Fish Fear Me

what would you think about the person who put it on the pickup? Do you know anyone who would exhibit a message like this one? What response is called for toward this message?

If you saw this bumper sticker on a car:

This is not an abandoned vehicle

would you take it seriously? Would your interpretation change if the bumper sticker was on a new, bright blue BMW? What purpose might someone have for using a bumper sticker such as this?

If you saw this bumper sticker on a car:

I read your e-mail

would you take it seriously? Who would the intended audience be for this message? Could you believe this claim? Why or why not?

LEFT-HAND MEANING

Raise your left hand high in the air and gaze at your hand. When you've looked at it briefly, take a pen and paper and follow the remaining instructions.

Next, write a brief essay defining how you knew which hand to raise. How did you know it was your *left* hand (i.e., how would you explain it to someone who did not know of the concept of "left")?

Restrictions: You *cannot* use the opposite side of the body as a point of reference (e.g., "it's the hand opposite of my right hand"); you *cannot* rely on social convention or agreement (e.g., "that's what we decided to call it"); you *cannot* use argument by authority ("my mom told me to call it that"); and, you *cannot* use special personal characteristics (e.g., "it's the hand with two warts on it").

How did you go about this difficult task? What point of reference did you use to explain how "left" came to be the designation for one of your hands? In your class what were some of the different strategies for explaining "left" hand? Have you ever had something that was *very* clear and simple to you, but difficult to explain to someone else? Thinking again, specifically, about language, have you ever known a phrase or word you've known all your life that you cannot explain when you are asked about it? Try the next workshop on for size.

DOZEN? TWELVE?

How many are in a dozen? Twelve? Is twelve the same as a dozen? Are you sure?

Make two lists of things or phrases you remember that use "twelve" or "dozen."

Twelve	Dozen
Months in a year	Roses

Are the words "twelve" and "dozen" interchangeable? If they mean the same thing, why do we use "dozen" to talk about donuts and "twelve" to talk about inches in a foot? Can you think about any other pairs (or groups) of words that mean essentially the same thing, but are usually used only in certain areas of life or experience?

If you enjoyed these workshop investigations, you'll be interested to discover in our next chapter that some people spend nearly all of their time thinking, pondering, and writing about how language works. (OK, OK, not about whether we ate a dozen donuts, or 12 donuts, but about similar language matters that really do matter!)

Key Words

communication, *6, 10*
rhetoric, *7–10, 17*
rhetorical, *10, 11*
rhetor, *10, 12, 13*
rhetorician, *10, 12, 13*
physical world, *14, 18*
social world, *15, 18*
symbol world, *16, 18*

Endnotes

1. David Streitfeld, "Book Report," *Washington Post* 12 June 1994: X–15.
2. Glenn Kessler, "Even Republican Operatives See Clinton as a Fearsome Genius," *Buffalo News* 1 Sept. 1996, F–9.
3. Mike Allen, "Bush's Alter Ego," *Washington Post* [Weekly Edition] 02 April 2001: 6–7.
4. Enric Volante, "NASA Apologizes to Navajos for Flying Ashes to the Moon," *Oregonian* 14 Jan. 1998: A–17.
5. Steve Duin, "Sensitivity: The Final Frontier," *Oregonian* 15 Jan. 1998: D–1.
6. Michael Ellison, "Dreamer's Ashes End in Moon Dust," *The Guardian* [Manchester, England] 29 July 1999. <http://www.guardian.co.uk/Print/0,3858,3887592,00.html>
7. Christine Ferguson, "Scottish Company Wins Prestigious Coke Deal," *Business A.M.* 13 March 2002, Lexis-Nexis <http://web.lexis-nexis.com/universe/document?_m=e2750ebc57896ea89c8dfcbe5ce38362&_docnum=2&wchp=dGLSlS-lSlzV&_md5=d8dd18279f4e9da8bc602da1be7c8edb>
8. Steven Covey, *The Seven Habits of Highly Effective People* (New York: Simon and Schuster, 1989) 237.
9. Jacob M. Schlesinger, "The Enforcer: Bush Budget Director Jousts with Congress, and Big Fight Is Likely," *Wall Street Journal* 15 Aug. 2001: A–1. Emphasis added.
10. Joe Rojas-Burke, "Drug Pricing Side Effects Include Mild Confusion," *Oregonian* 12 Aug. 2001: A–1. Emphasis added.
11. David Rogers, "House Nears Patients' Rights Vote as Senate Haggles over Farm Bill," *Wall Street Journal* 31 July 2001: A–20.
12. Dee Burch, "Mayor, Council Must Unite Community, Solve Problems," *Oregonian* 9 Aug. 2001: C–10. Emphasis added.
13. Kathleen S. McFall, "Anthology Sums Up Feminist View of Bible," *Oregonian* 20 Dec. 1998: F–06. Emphasis added.
14. Mary S. Piccirillo, "An Isocratean Rhetoric of Rhetoric of Television," *Communication* 12 (1990): 1–18.
15. Malcolm McGregor, "Howard Reconciles the Cost of Conflict," *Australian Financial Review* 28 May 1997, 23.
16. Celeste Michelle Condit and J. Ann Selzer, "The Rhetoric of Objectivity in the Newspaper Coverage of a Murder Trial," *Critical Studies in Mass Communication* 2 Sept. 1985: 197–216.
17. Lester C. Olson, "Portraits in Praise of a People: A Rhetorical Analysis of Norman Rockwell's Icons in Franklin D. Roosevelt's 'Four Freedoms' Campaign," *Quarterly Journal of Speech* 49 (1983): 15–24.

18. Dann L. Pierce, "Cultural Molding of a Provocative Rhetor: Thomas Nast and Graphic Persuasion," *Journal of the Northwest Communication Association* 26 (Spring 1998): 47–62.
19. Thomas B. Farrell, "Media Rhetoric as Social Drama: The Winter Olympics of 1984," *Critical Studies in Mass Communication* 6 (1989): 158–182.
20. John Foyston, "Forging Art," *Oregonian* 17 Aug. 2001. [Arts & Entertainment Section] 5.
21. Otto Pohl, "Improving the Way Humans Walk," *NYT* 12 March 2002. <http://www.nytimes.com/2002/03/12/health/12HEAD.html>
22. Jeff W. Childers, Douglas A. Foster, and Jack R. Reese. *The Crux of the Matter* (Abilene, Texas: ACU Press, 2001) 31.
23. Gareth Branwyn, "Jargon Watch; Wetware Exploits," *Wired* March 2002, 54.
24. George Carlin. *Brain Droppings* (New York: Hyperion, 1997) 122.

A Tale of Two (Types of) Critics

Do you like critical people? You should. While being a "critical" (or especially an "overly critical") person is a negative aspect of interpersonal relations, we often use "critical" people to help us better understand and use many cultural products (including messages) created in twenty-first century life.

We know the reasons that may send us to see a doctor or an auto mechanic. Why do we "go see" or utilize the expertise of a critic? Critics play a key part in almost all of our lives. As a culture, we employ critics to save us money, time, and frustration. While we may not directly hire a critic to work for us, we indirectly (through the media and through universities) hire and support critics to process and evaluate many things and processes that take a considerable amount of expertise to understand.

In this chapter we will examine the similarities and differences between two very different types of critics. The first type of critic, one we'll call a popular critic, you will recognize immediately. We'll address the second type of critic later in this chapter; you will likely be unaware that this second "mystery" critic has any influence on your life. As a quick check, whose name is more recognizable to you: Karlyn Kohrs Campbell or

Scrutinize exercise

When you pay your stylist for a hair color change, what have you paid for? When you pay your dental bill, what have you paid for? When you spend $60-$70 to see a band play, what have you paid for? When you (and the rest of the people in your culture) pay for the writing, or televisual talking, of a critic, what have you paid for? Specifically, what good, or service, or benefit do we get from paying the salary of a popular critic?

Roger Ebert? Both are talented critics, yet you likely recognize one much more readily than the other.

A meal, CD, movie, novel, or painting has likely come to your attention through the writings or ramblings of a popular critic. We most often think of critics as associated with the arts or with fine food and wine. However, most *important* aspects of life have experts who serve to evaluate equipment or techniques associated with a hobby, event, or activity. Remember, we rely on such people because they save us time, money, effort, and frustration. After all, who wants to spend seven (or 10?) bucks on a movie ticket, or $250 on a new fly fishing rod, if the result is going to be less than pleasing?

Moreover, popular critics (or "area-experts") often add to our appreciation or enjoyment because their enhanced understanding or expertise allows insight to which we have no direct access. We might never think about key or telling aspects of certain areas or practices without their guidance. Depending on these critics often becomes second nature to us as we find their useful observations in various forms of electronic and print media.

Such critics will be easier for us to understand if we examine their purpose, audience, goals, and impact in American culture.

PURPOSE OF POPULAR CRITICS

The purpose of **popular critics** working in the areas of human interest and activity is to express informed preference or "taste." The hallmark of critics working in popular media is a sign or symbol of approval or disapproval. Hence, thumbs (up or down), stars (five to none), lights (green for go . . .), or ribbons (blue, etc.) are among the symbolic images popular critics use to express their preference or dislike. In fact, condensed movie reviews will often only feature a line or two about the film, but will prominently list or display the critic's judgment in one of these shorthand forms. Do you pay attention to these ratings? Would a three star movie rating send you to a movie while a two star rating for the same movie

Scrutinize exercise

What is the most unusual popular critic (or "area-expert") you can discover in a mass-media outlet? Remember that any publication, or program, reaching a large audience of interested people is considered "mass" for our purposes—even if "mass" audience means 1,632 people. Check with a friend who participates in an unusual hobby or sport to discover an "out of the way" critic. Bring a print or video example to class.

Scrutinize exercise

What popular critic have you read, or watched, who uses the tackiest symbols for expressing approval or disapproval? Bring a print or video example to class. Do you like absolute (e.g., thumbs up or thumbs down) ratings, or gradation ratings (e.g., one to five stars). Why? Do you read the written reviews of films, or rely on thumbs or stars? Do thumbs or stars, as systems, tell you the basis for the critic's evaluation? Do you care about the basis for the recommendation?

"Let me through! I'm a critic."

would find you at home watching *Seinfeld* reruns? Do you place much trust in such ratings?

To say that critics have a purpose of expressing taste is not to suggest that they have *no* basis for their judgments; on the contrary, many popular critics are highly educated, have deep insight into the area they critique, and have vast experience at their craft. Often sheer time or space constraints force popular critics who write or talk for the mass media to give us only a glimpse of their true expertise and insight.

For the most part, popular critics *do* explain their conclusions, but they often have to do so quickly and briefly.

Consider these claims by film critic David Denby:

> This new *Planet of the Apes* is a typical high-tech project, put together with extraordinary production skills and pathetic dramatic skills. Eager for authenticity, the filmmakers sent much of the cast to "ape school," but they forgot to teach themselves how to create a narrative structure that anyone could give a damn about.[1]

These are quick, forceful claims about a movie upon which producers spent millions of dollars. If David Denby were asked to give more substantial reasons for his evaluation about the lack of narrative structure in Tim Burton's *Planet of the Apes,* he, no doubt, has the talent and background to do so—just not in his review. In his *New Yorker* reviews he is allowed but a few hundred words to evaluate entire movies. Such severe restrictions do not lend themselves to thorough and systematic explanations about observations and evaluations of a movie. Given the substantial restrictions placed on popular critics as they express their views or taste preferences, it is fair for us to inquire as to the goal of those who bring us such popular critics (and criticism).

GOAL OF POPULAR CRITICS

While their personal or professional purposes might be many, the overarching goal of most popular critics (or at least the goal of their employers) is to make money for their newspaper, TV syndicate, or parent company (and perhaps themselves). No real shame here. Most of us don't object to a healthy monetary return for our efforts or work. But, we do well to remind ourselves that popular critics really *do* have to be "popular" to some significant degree or another. Some have suggested that the need to be popular and accepted leads to some less than straightforward evaluations on the part of certain popular critics. Nonetheless, the critic in American culture, much like any worker, must create money (for someone) by her or his skills and messages. Fickle audience attention or trust may have much to do with such operating norms for popular critics; the "audience" for such criticism is the next defining characteristic of these types of critics.

POPULAR CRITICS AND THEIR AUDIENCES

Popular critics seek large audiences. What critic wouldn't? Certainly movie critics seen on television seek large audience share much as any other TV program does. Food critics, no doubt, are not hated by their editor or publisher (or advertisers) if their reviews bring more readers to a newspaper. Hence, while the size of a critic's audience might vary from millions to thousands, the *desire* to engage more readers or viewers is shared by almost all popular critics. As a food critic, would you like to return to an elegant French restaurant three times, then slave over writing a brilliant review, only to discover your mother and best friend are your sole readers? Solidly popular critics in a number of media outlets have no such direct worries. Due to the large audience achieved by some popular critics, the impact of their work can have profound repercussions on the industry, product, or service they critique. Another type of "impact" is often desired by the group or company that publishes or broadcasts the work of their critic.

Popular critics no doubt have many purposes for their criticism. If pressed, they will suggest that they really wish to inform, contextualize, enlighten, tantalize, or provoke their audience members. However, if the enlightened, tantalized audience member does not yearn for more of the critic's work, that critic will soon be out of business. Let's shift our attention now to the impact of popular critics.

IMPACT OF POPULAR CRITICS

Finally, the popular critic is important due to the relatively immediate impact (upon publication or transmission) of his or her work. Hollywood studios, for instance, preview movies knowing well that positive critical reviews can boost opening weekend box-office returns. Likewise, a stinker film will often be kept under wraps with no critics allowed to preview it in the hope that some audiences can be lured into theaters by sheer force of marketing campaigns (and lack of negative reviews). The growth of the entertainment and leisure industries in the last 30 years has created many situations in which a critic can "make or break" a play, CD, or book.

So important are positive reviews that Sony corporation created phony positive quotations to run in ads for their summer 2001 films *A Knight's Tale* and *The Animal.* Sony marketing executives created an imaginary film critic they named "David Manning" by using blurbs from Manning reviews that had never been actually written or published. Engaging in a starkly unethical practice such as creating a fake film critic and quotations should remind us of the economic pressures felt by entertainment corporations.

Sony suspended two marketing executives early in June 2001 and signed an agreement with at least one state attorney general's office by early fall 2001, promising to only use actual quotes from real reviewers in future ads from their studio Sony Pictures Entertainment. If the studio breaks the agreement, "Sony could end up paying a $25,000 fine for each victim of marketing fraud. . . ."[2] Hence, the real and perceived power of popular critics is observed on both sides of the fence in our economic system.

Popular critics often moan that they are ignored—and they can be. Just consider these reviewer comments about films that were popular with audiences:

> *Titanic:* ". . . tells a tear-jerking but preposterous story of a love affair,"[3]
>
> *Twister:* "You want loud, dumb, skillful, escapist entertainment? "Twister" works. You want to think? Think twice about seeing it.";[4]
>
> *American Pie:* ". . . some raunchy nonsense that will prompt embarrassed laughter, but not a trace of wit."[5]

Just as often, however, popular critics have profound influence on the entertainment and lifestyle choices we make as an entire culture.

The popular critic looms large in the popular American cultural landscape. She or he can regularly produce great influence almost immediately after a specific critique is made available to a reading, viewing, or listening audience. Many such critics are well-trained and knowledgeable; even when we disagree with their views and taste, they give us a benchmark or point of decision-making reference. Popular critics of food, music, television, or movies typically seek to reach a substantial audience to whom they express their preferences or "taste" (their purpose in writing) in order to make money for their owner, media syndicate, or publication (their goal in writing).

Popular Critics

Purpose:	To Inform or Persuade by Expression of Informed Preference ("Taste")
Goal:	To Make Money for Their Publications or Stations or Syndicates
Audience:	Larger Is Better (in almost all cases)
Impact:	Substantial and Often Immediate

We'll turn our attention now from many different types of popular critics to a type of critic you may not know so well—at least directly.

This type of critic has impact on your life, but the recognizable impact is likely *so slight* that you know little or nothing about the analytic or rhetorical critic. Their lesser-known type of criticism is worthy of our attention, and we will examine it in relation to the same markers we have established for popular critics.

These critics also have a purpose, an audience, a goal, and a type of impact. As we will discover, however, they are quite different than their popular critic cousins.

PURPOSE OF RHETORICAL CRITICS

Analytic critics work under several names: rhetorical critic, culture critic, media critic, or ideological critic. (Although I am referring to all of these types of critics in this chapter, I will use the terms *rhetorical* critic and *analytic* critic as representatives.) All, however, seek to systematically understand the impact and influence of messages that reach public audiences, often through mass media outlets. Contemporary rhetorical or analytic critics have been investigating speeches, political and social movements, cultural trends, movies, TV programs, and many other types of public communication for over 85 years. Historical roots of such analysis and thinking about human influence and persuasion through messages reach back to ancient civilizations. Later in this chapter I'll reveal why one or two well-picked pieces of analytic analysis may be of greater worth to you than a couple hundred well written pieces of popular criticism.

Most analytic critics are academically trained in university programs (most often with a Ph.D. as a calling card for identification of their education in a specialized area of knowledge). They often belong to professional academic organizations that support their efforts and allow them mutual contact with each other, such as the National Communication Association (NCA), the Association for Education in Journalism and Mass Communication (AEJMC), the University Film and Video Association (UFVA), or the International Communication Association (ICA). The size and scope of these professional organizations can vary widely. NCA (the National Communication Association) has over 7,000 members and provides substantial variety in services and membership focus, whereas the Northern Oregon Rhetoricians Association (NORA) has fewer than two dozen members and supports those members in a much more focused way.

The purpose of an analytic critic is to create understanding, and, for some rhetorical critics, to express judgment about the discoveries their rigorous analysis has created. Analytic critics care deeply about the messages that have such provocative influence on you and me. They actively seek ways to better understand how such messages create meaning within both individuals and larger cultural groups or communities.

Whereas popular critics succeed by expressing informed "taste," rhetorical critics by desire and design cannot simply promote or persuade their readers to an informed preference. Instead, rhetorical critics and others are required to systematically explain and defend three things:

1. The necessity of their research, analysis, and criticism,
2. The means or method of their analysis, and,
3. The telling accuracy of their discoveries in analysis.

While we will investigate these three things through a specific example of rhetorical analysis in the next chapter, we can note here that popular critics are required to do none of these things (and if required, it would probably make for dull popular reading).

GOAL OF RHETORICAL CRITICS

The goal of rhetorical critics is to advance knowledge about human communication that reaches audiences with public messages (often mass-media messages).

Hence, rhetorical (and other analytic) critics are building a superior, careful awareness of public or mass-mediated messages by rigorous and thoughtful analysis. They examine deep within, around, and behind specific messages to understand how they tick. For instance, dropping nuclear bombs on Japan by the U.S. Armed Forces was one of the most important decisions of the twentieth century. How are we, now 50 years beyond those events, remembering those decisions and results? Can high quality rhetorical analysis better enable us to understand how messages have power to create awareness and meaning for us? Two recent analysis articles suggest: yes!

Taylor analyzed photographic realism in museum exhibits, and (in another article) Hubbard and Hasian Jr. investigated the controversy that accompanied the decision to display the *Enola Gay* (the name of the airplane flown by the crew who dropped an atomic bomb on Hiroshima) at the National Air and Space Museum.[6] Popular museum exhibits about profound historical decisions and events, it seems, are important enough to create substantial public controversy (especially when over eight million people a year visit the museum in question). When considerable controversy erupts over public messages (even museum exhibits) the overarching goal becomes clear. Talented rhetorical (or analytic) critics seek not only to help us understand the controversy or interesting message(s) at hand, but also to see where that understanding fits within a larger framework of knowledge about human communication and cultural persuasion.

For instance, Professor Taylor carefully examines the decisions and interactions of competing interest groups who disputed how we ought to *remember* the fiftieth anniversary of the bombing of Hiroshima and Nagasaki. He demonstrates that any complex convergence of our social, physical, and symbol worlds will present difficulties in picking the "appropriate," "accurate," or "right" pictures (out of hundreds or thousands available) to help people remember events in which most of them had no direct part. Any picture selected, labeled, positioned, and displayed with hundreds of other photos and objects necessarily contributes to favoring one story or another about the meaning of the event(s) being remembered. Some people within most cultures care deeply about how we remember key historical events. Taylor's careful critical analysis aids our understanding of this specific dispute, but also helps us anticipate the rhetorical dynamics that are likely to occur in similar public disputes in the future.

Likewise, Hubbard and Hasian explore the rhetorical exchanges of messages between, among, and about groups who cared about the *Enola Gay* exhibit at the National Air and Space Museum (including veterans, peace activists, museum curators, and politicians). As they found: "Despite 50 years of revision and historical research, the story of the *Enola Gay* remains unfinished—a work in progress of memory as much as history" (378). Dedicated rhetorical critics such as Hubbard and Hasian, who are willing to examine over 600 different messages to help us discover how we construct public, cultural memory, contribute to our knowledge about human communication that reaches audiences with public messages. In later chapters we'll see how other rhetorical critics are hard at work helping us tease out how we use messages to address vital concerns and situations we face.

AUDIENCES OF RHETORICAL CRITICS

Analytic critics also seek a profoundly different audience than the audience desired by popular critics. Whereas popular critics would typically be delighted to reach an ever-enlarging mass audience of interested people, analytic critics often seek to reach a very small, peer audience made up of critics and researchers who are also investigating influential mass media messages.

For instance, remember that the National Communication Association (NCA) has over 7,000 members. Of that total group of scholars and researchers, who are interested in many different aspects of human communication, perhaps only 3,500 are involved directly in the investigation of mass communication. Of that 3,500 perhaps 2,500 are engaged directly in the investigation of mass-media *messages* (as opposed to, say, other scholars who specialize in a specific interest area, such as government regulation of the media). Hence, a pool of only 2,500 possible readers may be available for a serious effort of analysis by a rhetorical critic. That pool of possible readers becomes further reduced if adjustments are made in total for specific interests in film, music, television, and so forth.

An analytic critic researches and writes to such a small number of people because of a number of restraints and conditions. The first restraint that restricts the audience for the rhetorical critic involves education and common working vocabulary. As mentioned earlier, most analytic critics have formal education (typically a Ph.D.) and unusual experience compared to many people in American culture. Their education provides them with insights, frameworks, words, and procedures unknown to typical citizens. This is just as true in other professions that require a high degree of education and expertise. Architects, surgeons, engineers, and microbiologists are constrained in how much, and how well, they can tell the rest of us about what they know. How they pursue their responsibilities and tasks is often a mystery to those of us who do not share their expertise. To fully understand the following statements, you would need to have used 8–12 years of your life learning the language and practices of microbiologists:

> I have reported that tachyzoites trigger the release from monocytes of the monokines, IL-12 and TNF-alpha, which elicit the release of IFN-gamma, most likely from NK cells. IFN-gamma primes the monocytes and up-regulates a number of cell surface receptors, including CD40, CD64, CD54, CD80, and MHC Class II, resulting in an antigen-presenting cell phenotype. IFN-gamma also induces the release of soluble factors that mediate inhibition of both mitogen-induced lymphocyte DNA synthesis and ADCC. These soluble factors do not include IL-10, TGF-B, nitric oxide, PGE2, lipoxygenase products, or TNF-alpha-induced mitochondrial-derived oxygen intermediates.[7]

Rhetorical critics are in much the same boat. While most would be delighted in sharing what they know (and are interested in) they can typically be fully understood by a very small number of similarly educated people.

Read the following statements, and recognize that you would need to spend 12–15 years of your life learning the language and practices of a rhetorical (or analytic) critic to make full sense and complete use of them:

> We are also not discussing the twentieth-century commodity produced in response to burgeoning industrialization in which the supply of particular goods (such as weapons) outstripped demand that Max Horkeimer and Theodor W. Adorno (1944/1988), and Guy DeBord (1983) examined. Nor are we discussing the commodities resulting from the efficiencies of Fordism and Taylorism. Nevertheless, we do not insist the process of the cipher is altogether new. Instead, we are suggesting that what may be at least contemporary about the cipher is the dislocation of the referent from any single material object.
>
> In fact, the cipher itself is the referent; products refer to it, and its existence depends on its relationship to a field of products. Hence, the cipher is an effect of the many images and discourses referencing it.[8]

Or these claims:

> The space of communicative praxis permits one to understand what others have called "public knowledge." In the argument that such knowledge occurs in discursive space, we get the view that it differs from the kind of knowledge promoted by scientism because it is understood according to the rules of its dissemination rather than the rules of its production. This ties the problem of knowledge firmly to discourse theory, making knowledge itself as much a topic of discourse theory as rhetoric or narrative. Arguments made thus far, however, do not speak to the need for a general theory of communicative praxis. More than anywhere in academic circles, discourse theorists resisted scientism, preserving the great traditions of antiquity—poetic, rhetoric, and dialectic—against the mad rush to methodize human knowledge. Treated as general perspectives on human life, these traditions have already funded such discourse-based alternatives to scientism as Burke's theory of dramatism, various theories of narrativity, and the evolving theory of rhetoric as "epistemic," a practical account of human inquiry.[9]

Which of these two set of claims and comments do you think are from an examination of the Disney film *Pocahontas?*[10]

Hence, just as structural engineers write to other structural engineers, art historians write to other art historians, and microbiologists write to other microbiologists, rhetorical critics write to other rhetorical critics.

The goal of analytic critics in reaching that relatively small peer audience is to advance arguments that promote superior research, theory, and understanding of public messages. In short, our knowledge and understanding about vital, often mass-mediated messages increases.

IMPACT OF RHETORICAL CRITICS

The process by which rhetorical criticism "officially" happens is laborious, slow, and arduous. Remember that the process and impact of **popular criticism** is very rapid—not so with criticism created in an academic framework.

Here is a quick overview of the interesting process that allows superior analytic or rhetorical criticism to reach an audience.

Rhetorical criticism, or any other type of analytic criticism, happens in three stages: pre-analysis, analysis, and post-analysis.

In the pre-analysis stage, analytic critics are in a "mulling" mode. They might be struck by how companies construct public responses when accused of illegal or unethical practices, or how the scene design in certain movie situations influences perception of certain political issues, or how people in a homeless shelter react violently to certain screen characters. Much like regular citizens, analytic critics have many of these small, interesting, curious responses to what they see and hear in public messages. The response to such pondering, or mulling over, of messages and perceived rhetorical strategies is usually either "Aha!" or "Hmmmm. . . ." If the "Aha!" response wins out, the critic is probably satisfied with the most immediate or plausible answer that comes to her or his mind. If the answer is less immediate, elusive, or unsatisfactory, the "Hmmmm . . ." response usually prevails. Some "Hmmm . . ." responses bother analytic critics so much that their minds become consumed with discovering or figuring out the answers to their curious questions about the public message(s). That condition leads to the second, or analysis, stage.

Analysis stage involves directly or indirectly posing a research question (RQ), developing or selecting a method of analysis, selecting of an artifact (or artifacts), and performing the actual analysis. (Again, these things will be covered in the next chapter in a case example of how to read and use an example of rhetorical criticism.) Accomplishing these tasks is challenging and difficult. From beginning to end (i.e., moving from pre-analysis mulling to full analysis) this process might take as little as six to eight months, or as long as five or more years.

Different critics use different means of working through the difficulties of establishing and accomplishing analytic criticism, but all typically address the items just mentioned.

Once the analysis has been accomplished and placed in formal written form (see Chapter 3 for the basis of that form), the rhetorical critic sends the analysis to the editor of a respected scholarly journal. A critic has a number of possible journals to which she or he might send an analysis. A few national or international journals commonly used by rhetorical or analytic critics include: *Critical Studies in Mass Communication* (CSMC), *Quarterly Journal of Speech* (QJS), *Journal of Communication* (JOC), *Media, Culture and Society* (MCS), and *Television and New Media* (TVNM). (See the end of the chapter for a longer list of journals that publish academic, rhetorical criticism.)

The editor of a journal performs an initial screening of the study submitted by the analytic critic and asks (among other pertinent questions): Has this research already been accomplished and published elsewhere? Is this research original and important? Does this research advance our knowledge of public or mass-mediated messages? Has this analysis been done wisely and with high quality methods?

If the research submitted to the editor passes his or her initial screening, the analysis is sent to three different anonymous reviewers or judges. These judges are often said to be "blind" because they do not know the name or identity of the analytic critic(s) who submitted the research for review; likewise the researcher(s) who performed the criticism does not know the reviewers selected by the editor to review the research. The blind review process is used to reduce, or eliminate, favoritism and to promote high quality research results.

Three judges, or reviewers, are used to create an automatic majority response to the submitted research. Reviewers can give the editor three possible responses:

1. Do not publish (i.e., the research is flawed or deficient),
2. Publish with substantial revision (i.e., the research is worthy, but needs additional work), or,
3. Publish with minor revision, or as is (i.e., this research is outstanding and needs to be published as soon as possible).

At least two of the three reviewers typically agree on the overall quality of the submitted research. Yet, the process is very rigorous with as low as seven out of 100 pieces of submitted research being approved for publication in a major scholarly journal.

While academic, analytic critics can be challenging to read, their work has become the foundation on which a superior understanding of human communication is being built.

The value of their work can be seen by adapting the meaning of this Gary Larson cartoon on the next page.

The hunters in this cartoon have indeed arrived at a key piece of information. Recognizing a vital spot on an important animal of prey would provide important information for hungry cavepeople. Much of human

THE FAR SIDE® By GARY LARSON

"We should write that spot down."

Rhetorical or Analytic Critics	
Purpose:	To Create Understanding by Creating Analytic Research that Advances Specific Arguments about Public or Mass-Media Messages
Goal:	To Advance Knowledge about How Public Messages Are Used in Human Communication
Audience:	Small Peer Audience
Impact:	Slow and Substantial

history concerning the use of communication has worked in a very similar way. By trial and error people have taken guesses, attempts, and improbable tactics and discovered when they typically do or do not work. Such trial and error would be a great basis for deciding on message strategy *if* the conditions of, and responses to, human communication remained uniformly constant. They don't.

Hence, a strategy that worked last year for an advertising firm may fizzle quickly in the wilting heat of newer circumstances or changed audience perceptions. Communication scholars in the past 30 years have begun to better understand the "why" behind the "what" or "how" of conventional practices in human public and interpersonal communication.

In reference to the Larson cartoon, knowing *where* to shoot an animal of prey is valuable knowledge for hungry people; better yet if you have the tools to investigate *why* that particular spot is vulnerable—or why a certain tool or weapon was able to reach the key spot. Rhetorical critics have been honing such tools and analysis perspectives for many decades now concerning public and mass-media messages.

Go back to your newfound awareness about the number of academic critics working to perform analysis on mass-media messages. Somewhere around 2,500 talented people have taken as their life's work the task of understanding the characteristics and functions of mass-mediated messages. How could you as a budding communication professional, or any professional who will extensively use public communication, put the discoveries of such fine folks to work?

Imagine this: Suppose you were the head of a racing team that wanted to win the Indianapolis 500. To win the most venerable auto racing event in America, you would have to design, build, and race a superb car against the very strongest competitors in the world. Further suppose that you discovered over 2,500 researchers hard at work all over the world on tasks *directly* related to the design of such a racing car. Specialists in aerodynamics, fuel formulas, tire compounds, driving tactics, and other key areas were working diligently to discover the secrets of those areas. Finally, suppose that you could have access to their discoveries by learning to find and read their research reports. Would you do so? Of course.

Consider this (you don't have to pretend): suppose you were a key communication professional working at an important firm or institution in the early 2000s. Your company or institution gained success by the impact of important messages (realize that this is absolutely true for everything from political campaigns to charity fundraisers to international diplomacy to beer companies). You discovered as a college student that over 2,500 researchers are hard at work all over the world on research tasks directly related to the design of mass-mediated messages. You learned how to find and read their research reports. You, and your company or institution, have benefited greatly from messages created by knowing the "why" behind the "whats" and the "hows" that your competitors are using. You are successful and happy.

If you like that possibility, let's spend some time in the Chapter 2 workshop, where we'll extend our understanding of who critics are and how they work. Then we'll turn to Chapter 3 and get started in learning how to read and use academic research.

In this Chapter 2 workshop, we will probe in focused workshop exercises many of the concepts you discovered in this chapter. Work at a pace by assignment, or by choice, that allows these various insights to "sink in" at an even deeper level for you.

WHO CRITIQUES THE CRITICS?

Find a magazine article or website or TV news magazine program that covers a well-known popular critic. Compare the content of the article to the chart on page 29. What purpose, audience, goals, and impact are covered in the article? Does the popular critic come off as a nice person? Bring a print or video example to class.

LET'S EAT!

Eat a late lunch at a neighborhood restaurant that has been reviewed in the local, regional, or national media (positive reviews will likely be framed and on highly visible walls). Talk with the owner or manager and ask what impact a review had on business. How accurate did the owner or manager think the review was? Do they advertise in the publication or on the station where the review appeared? Has the restaurant ever received a poor or negative review? How did the negative review impact business? Bring a brief report to class about the answers you receive. How is popular criticism of food similar or different from popular criticism of mass-media messages (e.g., TV shows, CDs, or movies)? Are sales, or paying restaurant customers, the only way to discern whether a popular critical review has any impact?

CRITICS, WHOM DO YOU KNOW?

Name five people who are popular critics in American culture. Name five people who are analytic critics in American culture. Why is it easier to name five of one than the other? If rhetorical critics wanted to become better known, what would be the best means or outlet to raise visibility? *Should* analytic criticism have wider popular appeal or visibility?

Popular Critics	Rhetorical Critics
David Denby	John Lucaites

FOLLOW THE CRITIC

You've learned in this chapter that academic, analytic, or rhetorical critics typically reach only a small, specialized, peer audience who has great interest in their analysis efforts. Ask your instructor or professor for a list of a dozen highly regarded rhetorical or analytic critics. Use those names in several Web search engines and popular press database searches. Can you find any trace of academic critics in *non-academic* media? Do you find articles, quotations, announcements, or what? You are experiencing one of the most likely ways of academic critics reaching another audience: the college textbook and classroom. Do you think the work of academic critics should be more widely available? Why or why not?

If you enjoyed these workshop investigations, you'll be interested to discover in our next chapter how an example of rhetorical criticism unfolds, and more importantly, how you can learn to read it for your own use. Buckle your mental seatbelts!

Key Words

popular critic, *24–25*
popular critical purpose, *25–27*
popular critical goal, *27*
popular critical audience, *27*
popular critical impact, *28–29*
rhetorical critic, *29–37*
analytic critic, *30*
rhetorical critical purpose, *29*
rhetorical critical goal, *31*
rhetorical critical audience, *32–34*
rhetorical critical impact, *34–37*
NCA (National Communication Association), *30, 32*
UFVA (University Film and Video Association), *30*
ICA (International Communication Association), *30*
AEJMC (Association for Education in Journalism and Mass Communication), *30*

Journals for Rhetorical and Analytic Criticism Articles

Argumentation and Advocacy

Asian Journal of Communication

Australian Journal of Communication

Canadian Journal of Communication

Communication

Communication Monographs

Communication Quarterly

Communication Studies

Critical Studies in Mass Communication

Discourse and Society

European Journal of Communication

Howard Journal of Communications

Journal of the American Forensic Association

Journal of Communication

Journal of Communication and Religion

Journalism Quarterly

Language and Communication

Media, Culture & Society

Nordicom Review

Philosophy and Rhetoric

Political Communication

Quarterly Journal of Speech

Rhetoric Review

Rhetoric & Public Affairs

Semiotica

Southern Communication Journal

Television and New Media

Western Journal of Communication

Women's Studies in Communication

Endnotes

1. David Denby, "The Current Cinema: Misanthropes; Apes and Teens," *New Yorker* 6 August 2001: 89.
2. "State, Sony OK Ban on Phony Reviews," *Oregonian* 14 Aug. 2001. E–4.
3. Malcolm Johnson, "Taking on Water; DiCaprio Dashing in Meticulous, Preposterous *Titanic*," *Hartford Courant* 19 Dec. 1997. D–1.
4. Roger Ebert, Review of *Twister. Chicago Sun-Times* <http://www.sun-times.com/ebert/ebert_reviews/1996/05/051003.html>
5. Colin Covert, "*American Pie* Aims for Crust, Comes out Half-baked," *Minneapolis Star Tribune* 9 July 1999. E–1.
6. Bryan C. Taylor, "The Bodies of August: Photographic Realism and Controversy at the National Air and Space Museum," *Rhetoric & Public Affairs* 1 (1998), 331–361; Bryan Hubbard and Marouf A. Hasian, Jr., "Atomic Memories of the *Enola Gay:* Strategies of Remembrance at the National Air and Space Museum," *Rhetoric & Public Affairs* 1 (1998), 363–385.
7. Jacqueline Y. Channon Professional Page, 24 Jan. 2000 <http://www.dartmouth.edu/~microbio/faculty/Channon.html>.
8. Kent A. Ono and Derek T. Buescher, "Deciphering *Pocahontas:* Unpackaging the Commodification of a Native American Woman," *Critical Studies in Mass Communication* 18 (2001), 27.
9. Michael Calvin McGee, "Against Transcendentalism: Prologue to a Functional Theory of Communicative Praxis," *Form, Genre, and the Study of Political Discourse.* Eds. Herbert W. Simons and Aram A. Aghazarian. Columbia, South Carolina: University of South Carolina Press, 1986. 123.
10. If you are a regular reader of endnotes, you would already know that the first set of comments from Ono and Buescher are part of an analysis of the film *Pocahontas.*

Chapter Three

Finding the Gold: Reading and Using Academic Rhetorical Research

How do rhetorical critics and other analytic researchers talk to each other? What can we expect when we read one of their articles? What is important in setting up an article containing solid rhetorical criticism? While you may not have jumped out of bed this morning asking these questions, you nonetheless need to have some starting pointers in how to read, understand, and use the research of rhetorical critics.

In the last chapter we investigated the difference between popular and analytic criticism. We also examined the typical process that leads to publication of an analytic study using the tools of rhetorical criticism and theory.

Once a study is published, it becomes available for use to *anyone who has access to it*—including you! Of course, peer academic critics are the people most likely interested in such writing, but in this chapter we'll discover the tools that will allow you to find the "gold" of each study.

Your ability to "decode" academic research can achieve for you rich rewards. As mentioned in our last chapter, typical practitioners might have to wait for years or decades for new, vital information to get to them. Until then, they are working with old—sometimes outdated—information or perspectives about communication factors and rhetorical strategies. They may not know the very best ways to reach a public or mass audience.

As a communication professional with a degree from a solid program of study, you'll have access to that information much faster than practitioners in your field who do not have academic degrees, or who never learned how to use key resources available to them. Either way, you win. Can you imagine an engineer, dentist, or landscape architect who would want to work on important projects using obsolete techniques, tools, or ideas? Of course not. As a working communication professional, you will want to use all of the tools, perspectives, insights, and knowledge available to you. Learning how to decode and use academic, analytic writing from rhetorical and cultural critics (among other sources) will go a long way toward making sure you are neither outmoded or behind your peers (or competitors).

In this chapter we will examine how a study from an academic journal works and why it provides new and essential information. We'll start with one from a venerable and vital academic journal (the first in our field). We will discover a set-up, or foundation, scheme that appears in the first few pages of most rhetorical criticism studies. If you learn how to spot these foundation points, you will be able to better anticipate the direction, focus, and potential worth of the study for *your* professional use.

JUSTIFICATION FOR STUDY (JFS) IN RHETORICAL CRITICISM

All academic critics must, early in a journal article, establish the *reasons* that the study is desirable, or necessary. Remember, they were originally writing these reasons to an editor and a series of unknown reviewers. Now, with the article published, they are making these statements of justification (i.e., reasons) to the readership of the journal (or book) in which the study is published. When they are giving these reasons (making scholarly arguments) we will say that they provide a **justification for the study (JFS).**

Years ago rhetorical critic Suzanne Daughton became interested in Franklin D. Roosevelt's speaking abilities. Since he was elected to four terms as president (and had an extensive career prior to the presidency), she had plenty of material with which to work. She knew, however, that one of his most important and admired speeches was his first inaugural address in 1933.

We will use Suzanne Daughton's study of FDR's first inaugural address to discover several examples of well-thought-out reasons as to why her study was pursued.[1] (You'll find a copy of her article at the end of this chapter.) She, like all rhetorical critics, had to give her readers valid, substantial reasons that anchored the worth and utility of her study. The basic JFS question: "Professor Daughton, why is this study necessary?"

We will start with one of her justifications for doing the overall study (JFS).

JFS #1:

> The situation in which Roosevelt took office in March 1933 made strong presidential leadership an immediate imperative. The United States was in the midst of the Great Depression, the Congress was divided, and the American people were confused and afraid. (427) [60]

Notice, as she recalls crisis conditions in America of 1933, Daughton tells her reader *why* this particular historical circumstance needed a strong, forceful message from a particular national leader: the president. Be aware, she is not yet talking about the speech itself, but about the conditions that may have made FDR's speech important and necessary. She is laying the groundwork for giving you one overall justification for doing this study (JFS).

Notice, also, that this particular reason from page 427 of her study (reprinted page 60 in this text) could be understood by most any person (communication scholar or not) interested in this era and crisis in American culture.

We will give one additional label to such a JFS—we will call it an **external JFS.** It serves as an external justification in that it would make sense to people in *and* out of academic circles. If you could give this explanation to an uncle in Omaha or a person sitting next to you on a cross-country plane trip, and have both understand it, you have discovered an external JFS.

By now, you have realized, cleverly, that if we can have external JFSs, we must be able to have **internal JFS**s. You are right. Here is an example:

JFS #2:

> FDR's first inaugural presents rhetorical critics and theorists with a prime example of a speech that used familiar and reassuring combinations of metaphor to transcend a particular (and recurring) rhetorical problem. Roosevelt's twofold task was to first calm, then activate the American people. . . . Together they present a rhetorical dilemma of trying to simultaneously quell anxiety and inspire economic vitality. (427) [61]

Scrutinize exercise

External JFSs:

Think of five different people you know well. Make sure that the five are of different ages and backgrounds. Reread example JFS #1. If you showed this JFS to each of those five people, would they be able to understand the reasons that Daughton uses to suggest that March 1933 was an important time in the history of the United States? If four of five (or all five) of your selected people could understand Daughton's reasons, you are likely looking at an external JFS. Such JFSs are understandable to many educated adults even if they have *not* had special training in rhetorical criticism.

Many different people, fields of study, or groups might have some interest in the economic, political, and cultural circumstances faced by FDR (hence the previous JFS example was called an *external* JFS). Reread this JFS #2. To whom does Daughton address this observation? Right! In this JFS, Daughton clearly addresses her comments to "rhetorical critics and theorists" and gives reference to a *type* of speech in which they might have interest (one that uses specific types of metaphors to deal with specific rhetorical or persuasion problems).

Here she talks to her peer professionals (rhetorical critics and other interested scholars) from the National Communication Association (NCA). Hence, she directs her reasons to an *internal* audience of peer critics and theorists who share her interest in important public messages that reach large audiences. Remember, when writing internal JFSs, rhetorical critics often use terms that only an insider (a peer critic or scholar) would use or understand. In our later chapters you will gain a working knowledge of some of the more useful and important concepts used by rhetorical critics and theorists.

Since you are now gaining the understanding necessary to "decode" such an academic analysis article, you place yourself in an important position to "overhear" the exchange between scholars working on the cutting edge of our field of study.

I am convinced that you (and people like you who want to become communication professionals) are primed to become incredibly important people in our culture and throughout the world. When I think of vital, crucial, important people, I tend to think of people like surgeons, scientists, national leaders, philosophers, teachers, attorneys, police officers, and so forth. Yet, none of those very important people can do their job without communication. Few of these VIPs have all of the funding, facilities, or support they might like to have to do the best job possible. To achieve the funding, facilities, and support they would like to have they must communicate with large audiences (or have someone do it for them). You may be the speech-writer who creates the speech that raises millions of dollars for the new wing of a hospital. You may be the video producer who creates the 30 second spots that help elect a reform candidate in a particularly difficult district. You may be the writer who creates an instructional book on a new game that starts a recreation revolution. You are as important as doctors, politicians, philosophers, and entertainers—perhaps more important. Your growing knowledge, practical skills, and insight can put you in a position to reach and help many people who need the ability to create better messages.

Again, you know that medical doctors, electrical engineers, and biochemists all want the most up-to-date information so they can make wise decisions. Should you want any less as a communication professional? Right! You should be as dedicated and concerned as professionals in other fields. Messages and communication are vital. Give yourself the best tools and knowledge possible.

Scrutinize exercise

Can you find five other JFSs in the first four pages of Daughton's article? Once you find them, can you decide if they are primarily *internal* JFSs (written to, and fully understandable by, peer scholars) or *external* JFSs (ones understandable to ordinary people)? Be ready to explain why you think one way or the other about one of her reasons for doing the study.

By providing both internal and external JFSs for her reading audience, Daughton builds a case for *why* writing this particular study on FDR's speech is necessary.

It takes some practice to find, understand, and identify the reasons that a rhetorical critic uses for developing a particular analytic study of persuasion in a culture. As you read more rhetorical and cultural criticism, you'll get better and better at finding and identifying the set-up elements of a given study.

JUSTIFICATION FOR ARTIFACT (JFA) IN RHETORICAL CRITICISM

Now that we know Suzanne Daughton has provided several JFSs as a foundation to her study, we can turn our attention to her justifications (reasons) for the importance of her artifact.

Before we can adequately talk about **justifications for artifacts** (JFAs), we must first decide what counts as an artifact for rhetorical critics.

Artifact. **Artifact.** Artifact. Hmmmm. Sounds like something Indiana Jones or Lara Croft might go after instead of something that would intrigue a scholarly critic working in her office or study. What *is* an artifact for a rhetorical critic? To answer that question, we have to examine the differences and similarities between communication, messages, and artifacts.

Communication

Communication is a process wherein one or more humans create a message (or messages) that allows meaning to be evoked and understood by one or more other humans. Communication so far as we know cannot occur without messages.

Message

The English word **message,** on the other hand, was developed through French from the past tense of a Latin verb that meant "to send away."

Indeed, when we exchange messages, we "send them away" to other people.

But, what do we "send away"? The answer to that question in interpersonal or small group communication can be as varied as a glance, a cleared throat, a scream, or a five minute lecture. But remember that rhetorical critics are most typically interested in public messages that reach large numbers of people (in our day and era most often through the mass media).

In mass media, we "send away" movies, CDs, TV and cable programs, books, flyers, speeches, websites, billboards, and many other types of messages. So a mass-media message is a grouping of sounds or images (or smells, if you want to count scratch-and-sniff ads) in a common code understood by the person (or persons) who create and send the sounds or images, and by the person who perceives and creates an understanding of the created communication.

Artifact

There's that word again. Artifact. Don't rhetorical critics study messages? No. They study artifacts. An **artifact** is a *tangible, retrievable* trace or recording of the original message. For an example, let's go back to Suzanne Daughton's interest in Franklin D. Roosevelt's public speaking. In the study she conducted, she had access to transcripts of the speech, audio tapes of the speech, and film of the speech. All of these forms are tangible (you can touch, hear, or see them) and they are retrievable (you can find them and carry them with you). Remember that as an active politician, Roosevelt gave hundreds of speeches during his career. So while he created and delivered hundreds of speeches (messages) we do not have artifacts (tangible and retrievable traces or recordings) for all of his speeches. Rhetorical critics *must* have access to some form of artifact to do their systematic analysis.

So to recap: Rhetorical critics seek to better understand persuasion within a selected culture that reaches large audiences. To do that, they have to investigate selected aspects of the communication that took place in key places or at key times by key people. To investigate cultural communication, they must seek times, places, people, and occasions when someone was trying to change someone else by using a type of message that would reach a large audience. Not all messages that reach mass audiences result in an enduring artifact.

For example, scholarly film critics know about many early, important films that they would love to analyze and better understand. Many of those early films have disintegrated, burned, or otherwise been ruined by unstable film stock that was unable to endure for more than a few decades. So while they know the movie (message) existed and had influence (by related records and notations), they no longer have any useful, tangible, retrievable form (artifact) of that message.

CHART 3.1
Messages, Artifacts, Communication

Public Messages	
A grouping of sounds or images or marks (or other encoding elements) in a common code understood by the person (or persons) who creates and sends the sounds or images, and by the person who perceives and creates an understanding of the created communication.	Examples: A TV commercial; a speech by a university president; a song on a CD; a political direct mail appeal; sky writing; a Hollywood movie; a speech by an ancient military leader.

Artifact	
A tangible, retrievable trace or recording of an original message.	Examples: FDR's First Inaugural Address; a video or DVD copy of *Top Gun;* an ad in the *Wall Street Journal* (with a frog and a fly) for Ernst and Young on 24 May 2001, B-3.

Communication	
A process wherein one or more humans create a message (or messages) that allows meaning to be evoked and understood by one or more other humans.	Examples: An audience watching a championship football game on TV; a congregation listening to a sermon; a crowd listening to an activist speaker at a rally.

Scrutinize exercise

Reread the examples under "Public Messages" in the chart above. How many of these messages would be likely to have an artifact (a tangible, retrievable record of the message)? How many types of mass-media messages automatically have an artifact?

So in relationship to justifying a study to her or his peer reading audience, a rhetorical critic also has to provide reasons for selecting and analyzing specific artifacts (tangible, retrievable forms of important messages). We'll call those reasons justification for artifacts JFAs.

We will designate each claim that gives a reason for the choice of critical focus on a message (or set of messages) as a JFA. JFAs are similar to JFSs and we will often find understandable overlap between the two. A JFA claim or statement, however, is about the specific, tangible form of the *message* analyzed by the critic, or about response or reaction to that message by audiences. JFAs are *not* about other cultural circumstances or conditions within which the message was created or used.

As we move back to Daughton's article we will see her claims about her selected artifact(s).

A couple of examples will serve to guide our understanding. The basic JFA question: "Professor Daughton, why was this specific speech important to study?"

JFA #1:

> Roosevelt's first inaugural, considered by many to be one of his best speeches, was important because it lived up to its rhetorical potential in a situation of crisis. (427) [61]

JFA #2:

> However, Campbell and Jamieson also include among their criteria that the inaugural [any presidential inaugural address] "achieves these ends through means appropriate to epideictic discourse, i.e., while urging *contemplation not action* . . ." (my [Daughton's] emphasis). In this, at least, Roosevelt's first inaugural adds a challenging footnote to that generalization. Due to the extraordinary social and economic circumstances under which he took office, Roosevelt emphasized the need for immediate, corrective action to overcome the banking crisis and begin the process of recovery from the Depression. (430) [63–64]

Each of the claims listed as JFAs above do focus on the message, but from two different vantage points. The first is an **external JFA** (i.e., one that many people could understand and in which they might have interest). The second is an **internal JFA** which strongly suggests how this speech may be quite different than the norm for presidential inaugural speeches. The second is an internal JFA because Daughton writes, primarily, to peer critics and theorists who are well acquainted with the work of Karlyn Campbell and Kathleen Jamieson. A novice reader, not knowing who Campbell and Jamieson are, may well wince at unknown phrases such as "functions performatively," or "epideictic rhetoric." Such discomfort clearly indicates that Daughton addresses here a peer professional audience and not a general audience: hence the designation of an *internal* JFA.

When you think about how to distinguish between an *internal* JFA and an *external* JFA, use the airline-seat test. If you spoke or read the JFA to a person you chanced to sit beside on a trip across the country, would that person understand the JFA? If so, the JFA passes the airline-seat test, and

Scrutinize exercise JFS and JFA

Find at least one more example of both a JFS and a JFA between pages 427 [60] and 430 [64] in the Daughton article on FDR. After finding as many JFSs and JFAs as possible (mark the margin of your copy of the article with the appropriate abbreviations), decide if each claim (or set of claims) has an *internal* or *external* characteristic. Be prepared to read JFA or JFS statements you find and be prepared to support your claim that they are either *internal* or *external* in focus. In other words, which kind of audience (academic peer professional or general) would best understand them?

you probably have an *external* JFA (one understood by many people). If not, you probably have an *internal* JFA (one meant for peer scholars).

Going back to Daughton's JFAs, most people who know even a little about the Depression or about FDR might well understand the claim she makes in the first JFA. When she suggests that the speech lived up to its "potential" in a crisis situation, most people can readily understand the claim. Hence, we discover an *external* JFA (one understood by *both* peer professionals of Daughton and by a more general audience).

As Daughton lays the groundwork for her study, she also begins a review of other pertinent studies. She indicates that her review will have four sections: The Civil Religious Tradition, The Holy War, The Presidential Inaugural, and The Metaphoric Focus. In each of these sections we will learn of the extensive background research that Daughton did to accomplish her study. She read and consulted with rhetorical critics, rhetorical theorists, historians, linguists, biographers, and philosophers who could either help her understand FDR and the Depression era or understand the importance of metaphors as a persuasive tool in presidential speeches. Moreover, she also worked with primary sources from the Depression era (e.g., newspapers, presidential papers, books).

Daughton's foundation, then, consists of a solid set of JFSs and JFAs, which when combined with a strong review of other pertinent studies place her in an excellent position to understand and analyze FDR's first inaugural address.

RESEARCH QUESTIONS (RQ) IN RHETORICAL CRITICISM

Such a firm foundation needs to support a quality research question. What was Daughton primarily trying to discover? We will not find her (or most rhetorical critics) directly stating a **research question (RQ),** but we can find statements that indicate the focus of her implied RQ. Consider this claim:

> Roosevelt, I will argue, resolved this dilemma by subtly blending metaphoric clusters—religious and military—into a single integrated image of holy war. (427) [61]

When she says "I will argue," Daughton indicates that FDR's need to simultaneously motivate the American people in two different directions is a focal point of her scholarly investigation and writing. She identifies his dilemma: "Roosevelt's twofold task was first to *calm*, then *activate* the American people" [Daughton's emphasis]. Either goal on its own would have been a challenge in such circumstances of national and international turmoil; together they presented a rhetorical dilemma of trying simultaneously to quell anxiety and inspire economic vitality" (427). A research question that reflects these focal points would read like this: "How did FDR deal with the dilemma of simultaneously trying to calm and activate the American people in his first inaugural address during the Great American Depression?"

Since her answer to that RQ deeply involved the power of metaphors, we can guess that this study would be of interest and worth to at least two groups of people:

1. Those interested in FDR and his presidency during the Depression, and,
2. Those interested in how a rhetor reached and influenced an important audience by the persuasive resources of metaphors.

We will pursue the second of those possible worthwhile sets of information by asking a simple question:

"After reading Suzanne Daughton's article on FDR's first inaugural address, what do we now know about metaphors and their use that we did not know before?"

We will examine pages 431 [65] to 440 [76] to answer that question and find the "gold."

METHOD IN RHETORICAL CRITICISM

Once you realize how the first few pages of a piece of academic, rhetorical criticism is set up (covering JFSs, JFAs, and stating or indicating a RQ), you are one step closer to being able to find the important discoveries within an article. One last stop before finding the "gold" addresses the **method** or tools the critic is using in her investigation.

A rhetorical or analytic critic is responsible to tell a peer audience member what means were used to accomplish the analysis. As she briefly explains her method of analysis, Daughton writes: "The present analysis is an attempt to add to [Halford Ross] Ryan's research by focusing on the duality of rhetorical objectives and their corresponding metaphoric clusters" (430). She tells us here that in examining FDR's speech, she knows that he had the difficult task of calming the American people, while at the same time getting them charged up to confront the difficulties of the Depression. Moreover, following the research of Ryan, she knows that FDR used military metaphors, and she recognizes that he used many instances of religious metaphoric phrases. Hence, her plan for examining the speech included finding clusters of military metaphors and clusters of religious metaphors as they addressed the two primary problems faced by President Roosevelt. Using theoretic understandings borrowed from Michael Osborn, Lakoff and Johnson, and Kenneth Burke about metaphors, Daughton then observes: "Thus, even if the linguistic choices that led to the metaphoric clusters in Roosevelt's speech were not always totally 'conscious' or 'deliberate,' the patterns of what is highlighted and what is hidden—and the resolution of their apparent contradictions—reveal the speaker's values, motives, and perspectives on leadership, and help explain the speech's reception" (431) [65]. Thus, she again indicates that her discovery of the clusters of metaphors in FDR's speech will help explain its power—even if FDR and his speechwriters did not deliberately set out to create such clusters.

Once a critic has established her or his JFS, JFA, RQ, and an explanation of method, the actual analysis and discoveries can be shared with readers. We will turn to Daughton's discoveries now.

Naturally we can expect to find some of the "gold" (insights, discoveries, understandings) of a rhetorical analysis in the formal conclusion of the article, chapter, or book. Indeed, Daughton offers her reader insights about the historical results of FDR's speech, about presidential inaugurals as a type of speech, and about the rhetorical power and tactics her analysis revealed. Here is an example of one of her insights from this study:

> But Roosevelt's joining of war imagery with religious imagery to form a larger unifying structure, a holy war, enabled him to invoke an historically powerful cultural archetype, take on the roles of military leader as well as religious leader, and call for action in a much more forceful manner than one usually finds in a presidential inaugural, thereby pushing at the recognized boundaries of the genre.[2]

As we look for insights that might translate back to message tasks faced by communication professionals, we can find at least three usable insights:

1. Types of metaphoric imagery (in this case, religious and military imagery) can be joined or fused in a specific message to harness the power of both types toward accomplishing a persuasive message goal. In other words, in spite of what your sixth grade composition teacher told you, some mixed metaphors can make a message powerful.
2. Metaphoric imagery can help a speaker take on certain kinds of social or political roles in a message.
3. Genres of messages (in this case a presidential inaugural address) can change by enlarging expected boundaries.

Obviously, to make maximum use of these insights, you need awareness of related details or perspectives; for instance, how many types of standard metaphoric imagery (other than military or religious images) are available? Chapter 5 on metaphoric analysis should help put you in contact with appropriate resources and information to begin the process of developing this baseline knowledge.

Let's try another discovery noted by Daughton:

> The dark side of these rhetorical moves [using both religious and military leader images in the speech] was, of course, that neither of the leadership roles Roosevelt adopted was ultimately compatible with a democratic system of government; in fact, both set the leader above the people in such a rigid hierarchy that the very act of questioning the leader is forbidden. [Political] Critics who dare to practice their First Amendment rights open themselves to charges of "blasphemy" in the religious realm and "mutiny" in the military setting. So while many American people may have embraced Franklin Roosevelt's strong leadership style out of desperation, critics then and later saw signs of an aristocratic, authoritarian mind-set that they found justifiably disturbing.[3]

Can we find other insights that might translate back to message tasks faced by communication professionals? At least three usable insights present themselves:

1. Metaphoric images, when played out to their logical or cultural conclusions, have implications through connections. Hence, invoking a "holy war" with a righteous purpose may eventually be connected to what our expectations are for a religious leader (or a political leader who poses as a religious leader through language choices).
2. Metaphoric images will have some recognizable relationship with cultural norms and expectations. What happens when a democratically elected leader starts acting and talking more like a king or a priest?
3. Audience members may accept metaphoric images in times of stress, turmoil, or panic that at other times they might not believe or allow.

Daughton offers many other insights and discoveries in her conclusion (making it a great place to locate and develop understandings about metaphors and rhetorical strategy in important public speeches). We will discover, however, that the "gold" of an academic article or rhetorical or cultural criticism can be found in places other than just the conclusion to an article. Remember that our basic question in reading and understanding an article like this is: "After reading the article, what do we now know about metaphors and their use that we did not know before?"

Let's move back to earlier in Daughton's research in this article and see what we can discover.

On page 427 [61] of her article, Daughton makes this claim: "Roosevelt, I will argue, resolved this dilemma by subtly blending metaphoric clusters—religious and military—into a single integrated image of holy war."

If we are interested less in the specifics of FDR, the Great Depression, or presidential rhetoric, and we have great interest in how to use language to persuade, how can we translate a claim such as this one to give us a better understanding of tools available to us? Try this translation:

Rhetors can subtly blend metaphoric clusters. Metaphors can help create a single integrated image.

Think of it this way: if usable, powerful metaphoric clusters exist in our language (ready for use), and if metaphors are powerful in reaching audiences, would it be wise to know which clusters work and which ones don't? In Chapter 10 we will look at an example of some clusters that did not work well for potential persuaders. Knowing, however, that metaphor clusters, such as military and religious clusters, exist gives you a working advantage over someone who is blank about the power of metaphors in public persuasion.

Let's look for another on-the-way insight (i.e., one not exclusively offered in the conclusion of the study). Says Professor Daughton:

"Michael Osborn has argued that attention to metaphor can 'permit a more precise focusing upon whatever values and motives are salient in society at a given time.'"[4] Our translation might be:

Rhetors can use metaphor to focus an audience's attention upon ideas and images that match commonly held values and motives in a society.

All kinds of communicators (speakers, writers, producers, directors, cinematographers, audio engineers, etc.) must think of ways to focus an audience's attention to indicate that certain parts of the message are of great importance and value. Metaphors (and other non-literal comparisons) are primary tools to use in oral and written messages.

So let's think of a situation in which you might use this insight. Suppose you were a speechwriter who needed to help a candidate craft a speech about a terrible public official. The speech would call for the removal of the head of a branch office of the INS (Immigration and Naturalization Service). Knowing that the action (removal, extraction, rejection, expulsion, replacement) called for was to get rid of someone, you might ask yourself: In this culture, what do we regularly wish to get rid of? Garbage comes to mind, but it might be a bit tough to justify calling a public official garbage (at least in some cases). We also regularly wish to get rid of dirt and grime (just check the sales figures for cleaners, cleansers, soaps, and cleaning tools in the United States). So we might start to think about a "cleaning" cluster of metaphors as one possibility. Indeed, upon reflection, we can think of many instances where getting rid of dirt was key to a metaphoric expression. In ancient times this judgment was expressed: "I will wipe Jerusalem as one wipes a dish, wiping it and turning it upside down."[5]

Wiping or cleaning a dish was a metaphoric image invoked to discuss getting rid of something undesirable. It is similar, in some ways, to this image of cleaning: "'Music washes away from the soul the dust of everyday living.'
–Leopold Stokowski[6]

In this case, we've probably all experienced being surrounded by dust (on a trip? on a hike? on a work crew?) and the joy of being able to wash it off. Is music really water? No. But Leopold Stokowski was smart enough to know that a well picked metaphoric image could help you think of music in that way.

So we have examples of getting rid of dirt from ancient to modern times, from religious disputes to ads for musical performance—but our job is to come up with an image that will fit a political or governmental situation. Can we find a working metaphor that will express the desire or necessity to get rid of some*thing?* Can that metaphor carry over and help us call for getting rid of some*one?*

We know that it is common for political campaigns to talk about "mudslinging" in a campaign. Do political figures also talk about getting rid of dirt, or mud? In the summer of 1994 Dan Rostenkowski, a famous political leader and elected official from Chicago, was indicted on federal charges of fraud and embezzlement. After he entered his plea of innocent in the courtroom, he said this on the courthouse steps: "I will wash away the mud splattered on my reputation."[7]

So a brief review of actual messages used in important situations suggests that getting rid of dirt, grime, dust, or mud is a desirable activity. So much so that the idea is used in language to support getting rid of other things (religious practices, the hassles of everyday life, or the accusations of a federal grand jury). Hence, you might be wise to think about using the resources of this cluster of metaphoric expressions to help your client.

So, finding the "gold" in observations, discoveries, and insights offered by rhetorical critics can provide you with rich resources for making day-to-day decisions about messages you may create. Your procedure for finding this "gold" should be:

1. Locate articles that address the types of tools you wish to know more about (e.g., metaphors, storytelling, persuasion, evidence), or locate articles that address message situations you may wish to know more about (e.g., presidential speeches, labor rhetoric, nuclear arms talks, advertising).

Scrutinize exercise

Brainstorm all of the ways you can think of to "clean" something. Brainstorm all of the things (mud, etc.) that might need to be cleaned off. Which of these might help get rid of the INS official mentioned on page 54? Which images or ideas of cleaning will be best for your client's speech? Why? Could you invoke or use another cluster of metaphoric images (other than cleaning) that would help express the necessity of getting rid of something (or someone)?

2. Read the articles using the foundational tools of identifying JFS, JFA, RQ, and Method.
3. Find the "gold." Examine the conclusion as well as the rest of the article for key observations, insights, and discoveries about the kind of message you want to create.
4. Translate the specific key observations, insights, and discoveries into general propositions that you can use directly.
5. Find the best way possible to include these insights into your message creation.

If you practice and develop your ability to recognize and use insights gained from the research and writing of rhetorical critics, you will have found a great resource.

If you like the sound of that, let's spend some time in the Chapter 3 Workshop, where we'll extend our understanding of how to find the critical "gold." Then we'll turn to Chapter 4 and we will get started in learning how to write rhetorical criticism.

Inaugural Speech of Franklin Delano Roosevelt
Washington, D.C.
March 4th, 1933

President Hoover, Mr. Chief Justice, my friends:

This is a day of national consecration, and I am certain that on this day my fellow-Americans expect that on my induction into the Presidency I will address them with a candor and a decision which the present situation of our people impels.

This is pre-eminently the time to speak the truth, and boldly. Nor need we shrink from honestly facing conditions in our country today. This great nation will endure as it has endured, will revive and will prosper.

So first of all let me assert my firm belief that the only thing we have to fear, is fear itself—nameless, unreasoning, unjustified terror which paralyzes needed efforts to convert retreat into advance.

In every dark hour of our national life a leadership of frankness and of vigor has met with that understanding and support of the people themselves which is essential to victory. And I am convinced that you will again give that support to leadership in these critical days.

In such a spirit on my part and on yours we face our common difficulties. They concern, thank God, only material things. Values have shrunk to fantastic levels: taxes have risen, our ability to pay has fallen, government of all kinds is faced by serious curtailment of income, the means of exchange are frozen in the currents of trade, the withered leaves of industrial enterprise lie on every side, farmers find no markets for their produce, and the savings of many years in thousands of families are gone.

More important, a host of unemployed citizens face the grim problem of existence, and an equally great number toil with little return. Only a foolish optimist can deny the dark realities of the moment.

And yet our distress comes from no failure of substance. We are stricken by no plague of locusts. Compared with the perils which our forefathers conquered because they believed and were not afraid, we have still much to be thankful for. Nature still offers her bounty and human efforts have multiplied it. Plenty is at our doorstep, but a generous use of it languishes in the very sight of the supply.

Primarily, this is because the rulers of the exchange of mankind's goods have failed through their own stubbornness and their own incompetence, have admitted their failures and abdicated. Practices of the unscrupulous money changers stand indicted in the court of public opinion, rejected by the hearts and minds of men.

True, they have tried, but their efforts have been cast in the pattern of an outworn tradition. Faced by failure of credit, they have proposed only the lending of more money.

Stripped of the lure of profit by which to induce our people to follow their false leadership, they have resorted to exhortations, pleading tearfully for restored confidence. They know only the rules of a generation of self-seekers.

They have no vision, and when there is no vision the people perish.

Yes, the moneychangers have fled from their high seats in the temple of our civilization. We may now restore that temple to the ancient truths.

The measure of that restoration lies in the extent to which we apply social values, more noble than mere monetary profit.

Happiness lies not in the mere possession of money, it lies in the joy of achievement, in the thrill of creative effort.

The joy, the moral stimulation of work no longer must be forgotten in the mad chase of evanescent profits. These dark days my friends will be worth all they cost us if they teach us that our true destiny is not to be ministered unto but to minister to ourselves, to our fellow men.

Recognition of that falsity of material wealth as the standard of success goes hand in hand with the abandonment of the false belief that public office and high political position are to be valued only by the standards of pride of place and personal profit, and there must be an end to a conduct in banking and in business which too often has given to a sacred trust the likeness of callous and selfish wrongdoing.

Small wonder that confidence languishes, for it thrives only on honesty, on honor, on the sacredness of obligations, on faithful protection, and on unselfish performance. Without them it cannot live.

Restoration calls, however, not for changes in ethics alone. This nation is asking for action—and action now.

Our greatest primary task is to put people to work. This is no unsolvable problem if we face it wisely and courageously.

It can be accompanied in part by direct recruiting by the government itself, treating the task as we would treat the emergency of a war, but at the same time, through this employment, accomplishing greatly needed projects to stimulate and reorganize the use of our great national resources.

Hand in hand with that, we must frankly recognize the over-balance of population in our industrial centers and, by engaging on a national scale in a redistribution, endeavor to provide a better use of the land for those best fitted for the land.

Yes the task can be helped by definite efforts to raise the values of agricultural products and with this the power to purchase the output of our cities.

It can be helped by preventing realistically the tragedy of the growing loss, through foreclosure, of our small homes and our farms.

It can be helped by insistence that the Federal, the State, and the local governments act forthwith on the demand that their cost be drastically reduced.

It can be helped by the unifying of relief activities which today are often scattered, uneconomical, unequal. It can be helped by national planning for, and supervision of, all forms of transportation and of communications and other utilities that have a definitely public character.

There are many ways in which it can be helped, but it can never be helped by merely talking about it. We must act; we must act quickly.

And finally, in our progress toward a resumption of work we require two safeguards against a return of the evils of the old order: there must be a strict supervision of all banking and credits and investments; there must be an end to speculation with other people's money, and there must be provision for an adequate but sound currency.

These my friends are the lines of attack. I shall presently urge upon a new Congress in special session detailed measures for their fulfillment. And I shall seek the immediate assistance of the 48 States.

Through this program of action we address ourselves to putting our own national house in order and making income balance outgo.

Our international trade relations, though vastly important, are, in point of time and necessity, secondary to the establishment of a sound national economy.

I favor as a practical policy the putting of first things first. I shall spare no effort to restore world trade by international economic readjustment, but the emergency at home cannot wait on that accomplishment.

The basic thought that guides these specific means of national recovery is not narrowly nationalistic.

It is the insistence, as a first consideration, upon the interdependence of the various elements in, and parts of, the United States of America a recognition of the old and permanently important manifestation of the American spirit of the pioneer.

It is the way to recovery. It is the immediate way. It is the strongest assurance that recovery will endure.

In the field of world policy, I would dedicate this nation to the policy of the good neighbor; the neighbor who resolutely respects himself and, because he does so, respects the rights of others—the neighbor who respects his obligations and respects the sanctity of his agreements in and with a world of neighbors.

If I read the temper of our people correctly, we now realize, as we have never realized before, our interdependence on each other: that we cannot merely take, but we must give as well, that if we are to go forward we must move as a trained and loyal army willing to sacrifice for the good of a common discipline, because without such discipline, no progress can be made, no leadership becomes effective.

We are, I know, ready and willing to submit our lives and our property to such discipline because it makes possible a leadership which aims at the larger good.

This I propose to offer, pledging that the larger purposes will bind upon us, bind upon us all, as a sacred obligation with a unity of duty hitherto evoked only in times of armed strife.

With this pledge taken, I assume unhesitatingly the leadership of this great army of our people, dedicated to a disciplined attack upon our common problems.

Action in this image, action to this end, is feasible under the form of government which we have inherited from our ancestors.

Our Constitution is so simple, so practical, that it is possible always to meet extraordinary needs by changes in emphasis and arrangement without loss of essential form.

That is why our constitutional system has proved itself the most superbly enduring political mechanism the modern world has ever seen. It has met every stress of vast expansion of territory, of foreign wars, of bitter internal strife, of world relations.

And it is to be hoped that the normal balance of executive and legislative authority may be wholly equal, wholly adequate to meet the unprecedented task before us. But it may be that an unprecedented demand and need for undelayed action may call for temporary departure from that normal balance of public procedure.

I am prepared under my constitutional duty to recommend the measures that a stricken nation in the midst of a stricken world may require.

These measures, or such other measures as the Congress may build out of its experience and wisdom, I shall seek within my constitutional authority to bring to speedy adoption.

But in the event that the Congress shall fail to take one of these two courses, in the event that the national emergency is still critical, I shall not evade the clear course of duty that will then confront me.

I shall ask the Congress for the one remaining instrument to meet the crisis—broad executive power to wage a war against the emergency as great as the power that would be given to me if we were in fact invaded by a foreign foe.

For the trust reposed in me I will return the courage and the devotion that befit the time. I can do no less.

We face the arduous days that lie before us in the warm courage of national unity, with the clear consciousness of seeking old and precious moral values, with the clean satisfaction that comes from the stern performance of duty by old and young alike.

We aim at the assurance of a rounded, a permanent, national life.

We do not distrust the future of essential democracy. The people of the United States have not failed. In their need they have registered a mandate that they want direct, vigorous action.

They have asked for discipline and direction under leadership. They have made me the present instrument of their wishes. In the spirit of the gift, I take it.

In this dedication of a nation, we humbly ask the blessing of God. May He protect each and every one of us. May He guide me in the days to come.

Metaphorical Transcendence: Images of the Holy War in Franklin Roosevelt's First Inaugural

Suzanne M. Daughton

> So first of all, let me assert my firm belief that the only thing we have to fear is fear itself—nameless, unreasoning, unjustified terror which paralyzes needed efforts to convert retreat into advance." To [Labor Secretary-designate] Frances Perkins, it was like a revival meeting. Roosevelt had seen and understood the spiritual need of all the people who had to be given purpose and direction. Despair was the greatest of sins, the contrary of hope, and Roosevelt was asking, "Do you believe?" You could see tears streaming down people's faces. Sitting next to her . . . [Roosevelt advisor] Ray Moley said, "Well, he's taken the ship of state and turned it right around.[1]

In an explanatory note appended to his First Inaugural Address, Franklin Delano Roosevelt wrote, "I sought principally in the foregoing Inaugural Address to banish, so far as possible, the fear of the present and of the future which held the American people and the American spirit in its grasp."[2] Roosevelt made this purpose clear early in the speech with his famous assertion about fear, a phrase which has achieved a measure of immortality for itself and its speaker because it was both timely and timeless.[3]

Banishing fear was no small task, nor was it the rhetor's only objective that day. The situation in which Roosevelt took office in March of 1933 made strong presidential leadership an immediate imperative. The United States was in the midst of the Great Depression, the Congress was divided, and the American people were confused and afraid.[4] Immediate reaction to the speech, while not unanimous, was overwhelmingly favorable:[5] the public and the press supported FDR's assertions that the corrupt practices of the "moneychangers" had caused the banking crisis.[6] Congress passed FDR's Emergency Banking Act on March 9, just five days after the inaugural address;[7] and shortly after the reopening of the banks, private citizens redeposited large quantities of previously hoarded

Source: *Quarterly Journal of Speech 79* (1993): 427–46

money.[8] It is clear, then, that Roosevelt's first inaugural, considered by many to be one of his best speeches,[9] was important because it lived up to its rhetorical potential in a situation of crisis. To a measurable extent, the first inaugural functioned rhetorically to achieve both the explicit purpose of allaying fear and the implicit purpose of creating public support for the new president and his policies.[10]

Beyond its historical significance, FDR's first inaugural presents rhetorical critics and theorists with a prime example of a speech that used familiar and reassuring combinations of metaphor to transcend a particular (and recurring) rhetorical problem. Roosevelt's twofold task was first to *calm,* then *activate* the American people. Either goal on its own would have been a challenge in such circumstances of national and international turmoil; together they presented a rhetorical dilemma of trying simultaneously to quell anxiety and inspire economic vitality. Roosevelt, I will argue, resolved this dilemma by subtly blending metaphoric clusters—religious and military—into a single integrated image of holy war.

THE CRITICAL FRAMEWORK: A REVIEW OF THE LITERATURE

The Civil Religious Tradition

Scholars, preachers, and politicians alike have long been aware that "the separation of church and state" is a mythic construct in American society, a national bedtime story that we tell ourselves in order to keep the twin monsters of Theocracy and Totalitarianism from our dreams.[11] One of the most obvious ways in which religion and politics merge in public life is through the presidential habit of rhetorically invoking the aid and blessing of a "Supreme Being," especially in solemn, ceremonial situations.[12] Robert Bellah describes what he sees as America's "civil religion,"

> a theme that lies very deep in the American tradition, namely the obligation, both collective and individual, to carry out God's will on earth. This was the motivating spirit of those who founded America, and it has been present in every generation since.[13]

Although the civil religion is not identical to any one faith or church, Bellah recognizes specifically Judeo-Christian influences. He writes, "Behind the civil religion at every point lie Biblical archetypes: Exodus, Chosen People, Promised Land, New Jerusalem, Sacrificial Death and Rebirth."[14] Many authors, before and since, have focused attention on this connection between the political and spiritual aspects of life in the United States, although the tradition of such linkages is far older than this country. Kenneth Burke writes about "Political Rhetoric as Secular Prayer,"[15] and devotes an entire book to *The Rhetoric of Religion.*[16] Roderick P. Hart catalogues the varieties and properties of "civic piety" in *The Political Pulpit*,[17] and John F. Wilson takes issue with the term "civil religion" but nonetheless acknowledges the existence and importance of what he refers to as "public religion."[18] In fact, Burke argues that borrowing between the secular and religious realms is linguistically unavoidable, since words

> have wholly naturalistic, empirical reference. But they may be used analogically, to designate a further dimension, the "supernatural" . . . [and] whereas the words for the "supernatural" realm are necessarily borrowed from the realm of our everyday experiences . . . once a terminology has been developed for special theological purposes the order can become reversed. We can borrow back the terms from the borrower, again secularizing to varying degrees the originally secular terms that had been given "supernatural" connotations.[19]

Thus, a critical focus on metaphor is especially appropriate. Certainly Burke would agree that while at times the term "civil religion" is used to refer literally to political events that have religious elements, such as prayer or invocation of the name of God, at other times "civil religion" becomes, itself, a metaphor, for it is a *way of seeing* certain political behaviors and persons in the terms, contexts, and roles normally associated with the religious realm, as when the president is described as the "high priest of our civil religion."[20]

Even without the lens of a metaphorical perspective, evidence of historical and contemporary blendings of religion and politics is common and plentiful. Phrases such as "In God We Trust," "one nation under God," and "I swear [on a Christian *Bible*] to tell the truth, the whole truth, and nothing but the truth, so help me God," have become so "natural" a part of the fabric of everyday life in the United States that they often go virtually unnoticed as "religious," being accepted as simply "American." Bellah notes that the United States Declaration of Independence justifies its rebellion against earthly authority (Great Britain) by appealing to a "higher law" that all people "are endowed by their Creator with certain inalienable Rights."[21] And a more recent example of such religious-political merging comes from Bill Clinton's speech accepting the Democratic nomination for president at the 1992 Democratic National Convention. Clinton called his approach "a *New Covenant*, a solemn agreement between the people and their government, based not simply on what each of us can take, but what all of us must give to our nation" (my emphasis).[22] Civil religion flourishes in American political rhetoric.

The Holy War

Although the idea of a holy war, or military crusade for religious purposes, certainly could be subsumed into civil-religious ideas, it is remarkable because of the *extreme* nature of its means and ends. When one invokes the image of a holy war, one implicates both civic and religious elements of society. The inverse, however, does not hold: "civil religion" is not necessarily focused on the military, so that politicians can and do claim that "God has favored our undertaking," without referring to soldiers or guns either metaphorically or literally.

This is not to say that such references cannot be naturalized: made mundane, conventional, and acceptable. The old standard, "The Battle Hymn of the Republic," after all, begins, "Mine eyes have seen the glory of the coming of the Lord. . . ." The long history of such mergings renders them familiar. In *The First Crusade and the Idea of Crusading*, Jonathan Riley-Smith notes that late-eleventh-century Pope Gregory VII enlisted scholars as research assistants, seeking justification for violence in defense of the Church.[23] Excerpts from the writings of St. Augustine showed that warfare was "approved of and even directly commanded by God, who could intervene physically on behalf of his chosen instruments of force."[24] This notion, that God (as the "Ultimate Weapon") could assist one's army in battle, encouraged confidence and reinforced belief in one's cause. England's "Lord Protector" Oliver Cromwell was one such leader who saw the seventeenth-century English revolution against the monarchy as endorsed by God. In his biography of Cromwell, Christopher Hill notes, somewhat dryly, that "cooperation with omnipotence was undoubtedly good for morale."[25]

The concept of a holy war has been invoked throughout the centuries by English-speakers on both sides of the Atlantic to justify or motivate "real" violence as well as to inspire dedication to battles that are "only" symbolic.[26] Far from being out of date or place, images of a holy war were vital to Franklin Roosevelt's rhetorical strategy in his first inaugural address.

The Presidential Inaugural

Karlyn Kohrs Campbell and Kathleen Hall Jamieson write that the presidential inaugural functions performatively, "evinc[ing] presidential leadership by the very fact of its delivery."[27] In many ways, Roosevelt's first inaugural address conformed to the generic pattern they describe: it served to "unify the audience," "rehearse shared values," "enunciate the political principles that will guide the new administration," and "demonstrate that the President appreciates the requirements and limitations of executive power."[28] However, Campbell and Jamieson also include among their criteria that the inaugural "achieves these ends through means appropriate to epideictic discourse, i.e., while urging *contemplation not action* . . ." (my emphasis).[29] In this, at least, Roosevelt's first inaugural adds a challenging footnote to that generalization. Due to the extraordinary social and economic circumstances under which he took office, Roosevelt emphasized the need for *immediate, corrective action* to overcome the banking crisis and begin the process of recovery from the Depression. As Halford R. Ryan concludes, "a contemplative inaugural in 1933 would have been inappropriate."[30] In answer to this need for action, then, Roosevelt demonstrated throughout his speech that he would provide direction as well as encouragement. In so doing, he enacted, rather than merely promised, leadership.

Despite its historical and rhetorical significance, critical studies of Roosevelt's first inaugural are surprisingly rare.[31] Halford Ross Ryan's 1979 essay on Roosevelt's use of three rhetorical techniques is perceptive and persuasive, and his book on Roosevelt as a rhetorical president stands as a thorough analysis of Roosevelt's style and technique in its various manifestations. Ryan points to Roosevelt's use of metaphor as a crucial strategy; his insightful analysis of the patterns of military metaphor informs this study, in which I seek to add to the critical understanding of that address and of the motivational implications of metaphor as a rhetorical strategy.

The present analysis is an attempt to add to Ryan's research by focusing on the duality of rhetorical objectives and their corresponding metaphorical clusters. Although there are obvious advantages to creating a sense of war-time urgency as a means of stimulating cooperative action—perhaps not least among them the opportunity to cast the "enemies" one faces in moral (ideologically "pure") rather than political (potentially suspect as "self-serving") terms—one might also expect military language to interfere with the rhetor's attempts to "allay fear," since images of war are normally far from reassuring.[32] But William Leuchtenberg argues persuasively that "the analogue of war" provided the American people a useful and ultimately positive way of seeing and attempting to understand the mystery of the depression.[33] In fact, Leuchtenberg notes that this analogue of war was especially useful for FDR in securing the passage of his New Deal programs.

It is possible that even had this not been the case, any potentially negative aspects of the war imagery would have been tempered ("saved") by the spiritual language the president used, and by the fact that the tradition of merging military and religious "voices" in public discourse rendered that rhetorical move both familiar and comforting. For not only did Roosevelt use *military* metaphors frequently in this address—metaphors which typically connote destructive activity: aggression, violence, savagery, bloodshed, division, death, and conquering—but he also employed a great deal of *religious* imagery as well, imagery that is often associated with peace, passive acceptance of earthly suffering (as in Jesus's "passion,"), an inward rather than an outward focus, nonviolence, and unity.[34] Although these metaphoric types may at first appear contradictory, the power and centrality of the civil-religious tradition in American public address makes their juxtaposition singularly unproblematic.

The Metaphoric Focus

Michael Osborn has argued that attention to metaphor can "permit a more precise focusing upon whatever values and motives are salient in society at a given time."[35] George Lakoff and Mark Johnson have pointed out that people cannot speak without using metaphor, and that much of what we normally consider "literal language" is based on metaphoric concepts.[36] They note that many metaphors form coherent clusters, or systems, around concepts such as "time is money" and "argument is war."[37] Lakoff and Johnson also call attention to the contradictory functions of metaphor, which both highlights and hides aspects of the concept under discussion:

> The very systematicity that allows us to comprehend one aspect of a concept in terms of another (e.g., comprehending an aspect of arguing in terms of battle) will necessarily hide other aspects of the concept . . . that are inconsistent with that metaphor . . . [such as] the cooperative aspects of arguing.[38]

Moreover, Kenneth Burke argues that for "metaphor" one could substitute the word "perspective," since a metaphor invites its receivers to view its subject anew, thus (re)producing perspective.[39] Thus, even if the linguistic choices that led to the metaphoric clusters in Roosevelt's speech were not always totally "conscious" or "deliberate," the patterns of what is highlighted and what is hidden—and the resolution of their apparent contradictions—reveal the speaker's values, motives, and perspectives on leadership, and help explain the speech's reception.[40] I turn next to the inaugural itself, and particularly to Franklin Roosevelt's use of war metaphor, in an attempt to extend Ryan's work.

FRANKLIN ROOSEVELT'S FIRST INAUGURAL ADDRESS

Military Metaphors

In his analysis of the first inaugural, Halford Ryan focuses on Roosevelt's use of the military metaphor as a method of garnering unified support.[41] Although Roosevelt's choice of precise and confident language conveyed the impression of him as a strong, committed leader throughout the address, the war imagery appeared only in certain sections of the speech. As Ryan notes, FDR planted the seeds of the military metaphor almost immediately, in perhaps his most famous statement.[42]

> So first of all let me assert my firm belief that the only thing we have to fear is fear itself—nameless, unreasoning, unjustified terror which paralyzes needed efforts to *convert retreat into advance.*
>
> In every dark hour of our national life a leadership of frankness and of vigor has met with that understanding and support of the people themselves which is essential to *victory.* (my emphasis, 271)

Ordinarily, such war imagery serves to add a sense of drama to the situation, inviting listeners' involvement. But this was no ordinary situation. Whereas Lyndon Johnson's "unconditional war on poverty" focused the national gaze on economic problems that may have previously been ignored,[43] the American people in 1933 hardly needed convincing: they knew that the national and international situation was serious and deserved their concern and attention. What they needed, instead, was a way of looking at their situation that would enable them to act, and to act productively. The metaphor of "depression" worked well here because a "depression" is a period of economic as well as psychological stagnation. Roosevelt capitalized on those dual possibilities; he had even hinted earlier at the connection between "mood" and economic state in his 1932 Commonwealth Club Address.[44] Just as common wisdom once held that war would save a country from its economic woes, war is the *conceptual* curative for such psychological resignation: whatever else it is, war is certainly active. The language of war promises that victory is possible through action and directs listeners to harness their frustration productively, by "fighting back." In a sense, then, Roosevelt's rhetorical task was the opposite of what Lyndon Johnson's would be 31 years later. Johnson sought to direct attention and energy to the problem of "unseen" poverty. David Zarefsky points out that Johnson's use of the war metaphor essentially doomed his program to failure; once the antipoverty effort had been cast into war-like terms, no compromises were possible. In war, one either wins or loses, and a war on poverty (like its rhetorical heir, the war on drugs) is inherently unwinnable. Franklin Roosevelt, on the other hand, was not facing a no-win situation. Instead, he was addressing the immediate crisis, providing people who were already suffering *as if* they were in the midst of war with an explanation that made fitting emotional sense. By metaphorically naming the depression a war, Roosevelt helped his listeners make sense of their pain and cast it as something temporary and addressable through combat.

Not surprisingly, the role Roosevelt assumed by using such formulations was that of military leader. Roosevelt's linguistic choices conveyed a firm, warlike resolve to triumph over adversity, encouraging listeners to unite (*again*, as Roosevelt said they had done at other crucial moments in the past) behind strong "military" leadership. Not only would the American people prevail over their enemies (economic adversity and its ally, fear) but they were at a crucial point where their efforts would be most needed and most effectively utilized to "convert retreat into advance."

A few moments later in the address, the president assured the American people that "our distress comes from no failure of substance. We are stricken by no plague of locusts. Compared with the perils which our forefathers *conquered* because they believed and were not afraid, we have still much to be thankful for" (my emphasis, 271). With the phrase "forefathers conquered," FDR reminded his audience that overcoming problems was part of their national heritage, and that if they wished to live up to the image they had of themselves as solid American citizens, they would not give up without a fight. Once Roosevelt had thus established his resolve and laid the grounds for optimism, however, such combative images were absent from the next segments of the inaugural, where he discussed the nation's economic and moral dilemma and the need for ethical changes to address this problem. Perhaps such matters of national character (or "soul") should be contemplated in peace and reverence. And, as Robert Ivie has noted, citizens are likely to view war as an immoral act unless the president establishes that the war has been "imposed on America by violation of her rights."[45]

FDR satisfied this last prerequisite by describing the corruption of the "unscrupulous moneychangers" (bankers who have mismanaged the savings of their depositors) and the economic crisis he charged them with creating (272). Once he had established that the actions he was advocating were defensive rather than offensive in nature, the war imagery gradually returned in Roosevelt's description of his plan of action, which occurred about midway through the speech. He recommended "treating the task as we would treat the *emergency of a war*" (my emphasis, 272). In summarizing his program, he said, "These, my friends, are the *lines of attack*," informing Americans that they were so morally justified in this war that they were now equipped to go on the offensive (my emphasis, 273), a possibility he alluded to in the early moments of his address: once rid of fear, Roosevelt said, the nation would be able to "convert retreat into advance" (271).

The military metaphors Roosevelt used up to this point in the inaugural asked his listeners to prepare themselves for an ordeal, rather than promising a quick end to their economic suffering. This suggestion could easily have been rejected by angry citizens tired of deprivation. But by visualizing this economic crisis as a war, Roosevelt paradoxically focused on positive aspects of the situation: rather than simply telling his listeners that economic recovery was "just around the corner," as Herbert Hoover had done, or asking them to "endure" their suffering passively (with the assurance that they would be rewarded in the hereafter), Roosevelt told them that they could, and indeed, must, take an active role in solving the crisis. By asking his audience to work harder with him, Roosevelt granted them a sense of control over events in their lives, and led them in visualizing movement toward the ultimate goal, an easing of the economic crisis.

The most strident use of military metaphor occurred two-thirds of the way through the speech, where it operated in conjunction with religious metaphor, establishing the moral righteousness of the attack. Because of the inseparability of the religious and military imagery in that section, I will first examine Roosevelt's religious imagery and then discuss its unification with military metaphor.

Religious Metaphors

The religious function of the presidential inaugural, in particular, has been recognized and documented.[46] Summarizing a portion of Bellah's essay, Fairbanks extends the metaphor of civil religion, in his description of the religious function of the inaugural: "Inaugural addresses can be considered the 'scriptures' of the civil religion, statements outlining the basic doctrines of the religion of the state."[47] And Campbell and Jamieson write:

> Inaugurals typically place the President and the nation under God, and this . . . is part of the process of acknowledging limits. By calling upon God, the President subordinates himself to a higher power. . . . It is only when the President is fully invested in office that he has the power and authority to place the nation "under God." For this reason, prayers or prayerlike statements occur near or at the end of inaugurals.[48]

Here again Roosevelt's first inaugural pushed at the boundaries of the generic pattern Campbell and Jamieson describe, by making use of religious language throughout the address.

Roosevelt set a religious, even prophetic, tone immediately and maintained it throughout the speech. By addressing his audience as "My Friends," much as a preacher might, and referring to the day as one of "national consecration," he created an expectation that the inaugural address would involve his listeners in a purifying, intimate, and holy relationship (271). FDR continued his use of religious language as he described the nation's economic problems: a "host" of citizens "toil" (Biblical language); "we are stricken by no plague of locusts" (Biblical allusion); "our forefathers believed and were not afraid" (Biblical language and idea: faith will sustain us); and "we have . . . much to be thankful for" (Biblical language and idea: giving God gratitude) (271). He assured the American people that "this great nation will endure as it has endured, will revive and will prosper" (271). Roosevelt presented himself as both priest and prophet, one who could see both the conscience of the nation and its future, implying that Americans would survive by following his lead and by virtue of their commitment to the national faith; to put the statement in military terms, Americans would be victorious because the American way of life was a just cause for which to fight, and hence the nation would be made stronger for its ordeal. America, battered but not beaten, would regain its strength and ultimately its full economic health ("revive and prosper" [271]). The religious language FDR used did not call upon listeners to be passive, to "Let Go, Let God"; instead, it was more along the activist lines of "God helps those who help themselves" (by "toiling," for example).[49]

In order to fight evil, however, one must first define it. In his first inaugural address, especially, Roosevelt was careful to distinguish himself from previous leaders who had tried and failed to solve the economic crisis. FDR contrasted his brand of leadership with the "false leadership" of the "moneychangers," thus associating himself with Jesus, who drove the moneychangers from the temple.[50] The bankers became clearly labelled as enemies, or even scapegoats (272).[51] Unlike the bankers, Roosevelt was able to recognize "the falsity of material wealth as the standard of success," and to know that happiness "lies in the joy of achievement, in the thrill of creative effort" (272). By defining the depression as the enemy and blaming it on human speculation and corruption, FDR separated the blame from the American people and from himself. The American people were not spiritually guilty (later Roosevelt would say, "The American people have not failed," 274); instead, they had been misled in the past by false leaders.

"Now," however, they had chosen Roosevelt as their spiritual leader. As one of his first tasks in this role, Roosevelt set limits on despair. His speech was replete with negatives as he strove to counteract the widespread loss of hope in Biblical terms and grammatical constructions: "We are stricken by no plague of locusts," (271), "they have no vision, and when there is no vision the people perish," and "happiness lies not in the mere possession of money" (272). The strong, direct nature of his speech created the impression of Biblical authority, and his insistence on the material (and hence, ultimately solvable) nature of the problem portrayed him as not only suitably solemn but justifiably confident as well. Paradoxically, Roosevelt had framed this material evil in moral terms. To the extent that listeners accepted this framing without questioning it, Roosevelt was then allowed to tell his audience that they were morally pure, that the bankers were morally reprehensible,[52] and that moral purity would triumph over physical adversity—a logically questionable conclusion, to say the least.

FDR's repeated reference to the bankers, who "have fled from their high seats in the temple of our civilization," and his conclusion, "we may now restore that temple to the ancient truths," contributed to the view of the American way of life as holy and America as the promised land for God's chosen people (272). Roosevelt's use of the term "restoration" was important, for it recalled the recurrent religious theme of regaining the paradise from which humankind had fallen (and again, the image of FDR-as-Savior appears, for the Psalmist writes, "he restoreth my soul").[53] "Restoration" is a more conservative term than "reform," which does not appear in the inaugural but did figure prominently in Roosevelt's campaign speeches.[54]

This conservative emphasis inherent in Roosevelt's stressing the word "restoration" rather than "reform" is emblematic of the inaugural's focus on the civil-religious merger (a familiar and reassuring set of symbols) rather than on the specifics of the potentially radical (and therefore threatening) nature of the New Deal programs Roosevelt was about to propose. Of course, the notion of reform was present even in the absence of the word itself, in Roosevelt's plan to "stimulate and reorganize the use of our great natural resources," and in his plans for the "unifying of relief activities" (272) and the "national planning for and supervision of all forms of transportation and of communications" (273). Politically, the stress on the concept of "restoration" (and possibly the neglect of the specific word "reform") reassured those who feared change by implying that the changes Roosevelt advocated would result in positive effects, such as healing and renewal. In effect, Roosevelt delivered a radical message in a conservative envelope.[55] While government involvement in economic life is a change that some would label "radical,"[56] Roosevelt announced that his program was based on the *good* tradition of unchanging values ("the ancient truths") rather than the "outworn tradition" of temporary solutions offered by his opponents (272). The implicit notion of *reform* allowed him to tie his program to an active vision of movement (through war) while the idea of *restoration* calls to mind the fundamental (Biblical and Constitutional, essentially conservative) truths on which any productive change must rest.

As keeper of the fundamental truths of the society, the spiritual leader serves as guardian of the nation's moral values. "Values have shrunken to fantastic levels," said Roosevelt, "taxes have risen, our ability to pay has fallen . . ." (271). Although from the context of that statement one is led to infer that Roosevelt meant primarily monetary values, the implication of lost moral value is present as well. The corrective to the situation would be in "the extent to which we apply social values more noble than mere monetary profit" (272). Restoration could not be accomplished without the application of the religious principles of personal sacrifice and soul-searching: the people had to recognize (and FDR implied that they had begun to do so, by rejecting the practices of the "moneychangers") "the falsity of material wealth as the standard of success" (272).

Roosevelt encouraged pride in the national faith. He depicted the promised land: an America of the future, leading and helping other nations. America must be a holy and compassionate nation, serving as an example to others by virtue of moral action. But before concentrating on America's role in world affairs, he cautioned, it was important to recognize the "interdependence" of the United States. Roosevelt said that America must be a "good neighbor" (which calls up associations with the parable of the "good Samaritan") respecting the "sanctity" of international agreements, but that this would be impossible until the "national house" has been put "in order" (273). So America could not assume leadership in world affairs until its national priorities were set.

Metaphorical Transcendence: The Holy War

Although quite different at first glance, the two main metaphoric clusters in the speech serve as a powerful source of rhetorical energy when used together. The two cluster themes, religion and war, encourage listeners to produce different responses for different goals. Religion (in some "pure" form, if not in practice) asks for trusting, perhaps even passive acceptance of God's laws, and promises a state of peace and calm; war asks for active combat (as well as obedience to orders) and promises a state of satisfaction in victory. War for religion's sake, or holy war, has long constituted part of our cultural vocabulary (as when we speak of someone "launching a righteous crusade"). The blending of military and religious voices into a holy war combines qualities of both concepts and asks listeners for unquestioning obedience and inspired, committed action for a morally satisfying victory over evil, which ultimately results in peace, both spiritual and physical.

By combining religious metaphor with military metaphor, Roosevelt took a strong rhetorical stand against the country's economic ills, in effect, declaring a "holy war" on the depression and on the practices of those he deemed responsible for the banking crisis.[57] Of course, the phrase "holy war" never appeared in the speech. But by using strong military imagery, as Ryan has demonstrated, and by adding religious metaphor to that military call, Roosevelt implicitly blessed the war he had declared. The power of his rhetorical achievement lies in its deftness: the valence of the discourse was such that it subtly invited the emergence of the *concept* "holy war," without having to make that phrase an obvious part of the message. Perhaps there exists a cultural taboo against blatantly using the phrase "holy war" in political discourse.[58] In any case, public discourse before and after the inaugural was replete with references to both the religious and the military themes, often used together in the same message;[59] frequently these references cast FDR as "the people's Messiah,"[60] blamed the nation's economic problems on collective or individual "sins,"[61] and expressed militant commitment to "the war" in which "we are enlisted."[62] Roosevelt did not invent the civil-religious tradition, nor did he invent the concept of a religious crusade, nor was he the first person to make such statements about the depression. What he did was to call upon two potent metaphoric clusters that were already in the public consciousness and, with the power of the presidency and its connotations of Commander-in-Chief and civil-religious leader behind him, he used those two sets of images together as a powerful motivating force. By speaking in the same metaphorical terms as his fellow citizens, he demonstrated his connection to the very real distress that they were feeling. By doing so *as president,* FDR showed that he had the authority and the expertise to summon and direct their energies into positive action for reform, thus giving people a sense of purpose and hope.

The conjunction of religious and war imagery enabled the president to promise *active* (military) and *moral* (religious) leadership in return for cooperation, sacrifice, and discipline (virtues valued in military as well as spiritual realms). As a result, Roosevelt's use of a *metaphorical, holy* (and implicitly *just*) war served to inspire courage and comfort rather than fear because it entailed fewer risks than a "real" war; not only was it a symbolic war requiring no one to die for his or her country, but more importantly, it carried with it a guarantee of success because "God is on our side." The patterns of metaphor within the speech functioned to install FDR as priest and commander-in-chief of a crusade against economic evil, to enlist the support of the Congress and the American people in that crusade, and ultimately, to inspire confidence in place of fear.[63]

The various images in the first inaugural worked together within the overall scheme of a just and holy war, in which the American form of government and way of life were the "holy land" for which the crusade was to be fought. The desperate nature of the banking crisis and Roosevelt's talk during the campaign of enlisting government to help the nation's economy combined to generate anticipation among his listeners that the new president would focus on changing the existing system—somehow. Obviously, while such uncertainty could potentially leave some listeners hopeful, others would be nervous and uneasy that FDR would attempt to expand his presidential power for personal gain.[64] So Roosevelt, especially, exemplifies a dilemma hinted at in Campbell and Jamieson's notion of "acknowledging limits" and "subordinat[ing] himself to a higher power"[65]: the new president had to strike a careful balance between portraying himself as a strong leader and assuring his listeners that he did not crave a dictatorship. While the majority of the inaugural was dedicated to the former purpose, in the last few minutes of his address, Roosevelt reassured Congress and the American people that although he intended a strong, active leadership, he would remain "within my constitutional authority" and would take action "under my constitutional duty" (274). He acknowledged both the limited nature of his authority and the power of the American people as demonstrated in their choice of him as "the *present* instrument of their wishes" (my emphasis).

Having already enacted his role as priest through the use of religious language and prophetic tone, Roosevelt assumed the stance of military leader as well, without casting off the priest's robe. He combined the moral virtue appropriate to a spiritual leader with the courage and strength of a military general by stating his willingness to "speak the truth . . . frankly and boldly" and by his refusal to "shrink from honestly facing conditions in our country today" (271). Roosevelt used unqualified language to enhance the image of himself as a man of action and faith (conviction): "my *firm belief*," "In *every* dark hour," "our difficulties . . . concern, thank God, *only* material things" (my emphasis, 271). In so doing, he kept the focus on himself with a frequent use of first person pronouns: "I am certain," "let me assert my firm belief," "I am convinced," (271), "I shall presently urge," "I favor," "I shall spare no effort" (273).

Approximately two-thirds of the way through the address, Roosevelt made his declaration of war on the depression more explicit. Ryan has pointed to the strong military imagery in this section of the speech; while the religious language is less obvious, Roosevelt assumed divine approval of the war by using the word "sacred," and by emphasizing selfless ideals in righteous, even sanctimonious, language. Just as a holy war is first and foremost a *war* with religious overtones, rather than a prayer meeting with militant overtones, a metaphorical holy war would be expected to follow the same pattern of emphasis: the main focus is on the activity of war, which is morally justified by some tinge (light or heavy) of religious sentiment. Holy wars, metaphorical or real, are therefore talked about in terms that are not so violent that they belie divine endorsement, nor so prayerful that they encourage "contemplation, not action." Thus, it is significant that the overall pattern of belief and behavior that Roosevelt here endorsed (submission to a higher moral authority for a greater good) is equally appropriate in military and religious contexts.

> If I read the temper of our people correctly, we now realize as we have never realized before our interdependence on each other, that we cannot merely take but we must give as well, that if we are to go forward we must move as a trained and loyal army willing to sacrifice for the good of a common discipline, because without such discipline no progress can be made, no leadership becomes effective. We are, I know, ready and willing to submit our lives and property to such discipline because it makes possible a leadership which aims at the larger good. This I propose to offer, pledging that the larger purposes will . . . bind upon us all as a sacred obligation, with a unity of duty hitherto evoked only in times of armed strife. With this pledge taken, I assume unhesitatingly the leadership of this great army of our people dedicated to a disciplined attack upon our common problems. (273)

Terms such as "sacrifice," "submit," "sacred obligation," "trained," "discipline," "pledge," "dedicated," "loyal," "common good," and "larger purpose," are equally at home in the convent or the barracks. In his dual role, made possible by the long civil-religious tradition, Priest and Commander-in-Chief Roosevelt enlisted the aid and cooperation of the American people, who had been given a chance to restore their faith and to join the crusade.

The word "if," with which he began, ("If I read the temper of our people correctly,") was a lonely qualifier, soon overpowered by the force of the statements that followed. In fact, at this point in the speech, since FDR had already demonstrated active leadership and an ability to speak words of comfort and confidence to the American people, the word "if" would only add to the strength of his assertions because of its surface humility: How could anyone be against unity, which was essentially what he was advocating? When he used "if" a second time ("if we are to go forward"), the effect was amplified: Who could wish to go back to the horrors of the past? With his program of unified forward motion (which, described in such abstract terms, was not open to debate), Roosevelt could succeed in enlisting virtually the entire nation in his holy war.

After Roosevelt had assured his audience that, in accordance with his leadership position, he would be faithful to the Constitution, one final war metaphor made an appearance (Ryan describes the following as a "stick" with which to threaten the Congress):[66]

> But in the event that the Congress shall fail to take one of these two courses, in the event that the national emergency is still critical, I shall not evade the clear course of duty that will then confront me. I shall ask the Congress for the one remaining instrument to meet the crisis: broad executive power to wage a war against the emergency, as great as the power that would be given to me if we were in fact invaded by a foreign foe. (274)

Although members of Congress may have felt intimidated by such a warning, in depicting the situation as a "national emergency" and his response as a "clear course of duty," FDR claimed the moral high ground by defining his potential action as motivated by public interest and appropriate to the situation.

CONCLUSION

Throughout his first inaugural, Roosevelt enacted his strong, active brand of leadership by using language that encouraged his audience to enlist with him in a holy war for the restoration of the American way of life. He reaped the benefits of both progressivism and conservativism by carefully distinguishing the "ancient truths" of his policies from the "outworn" traditions of his political opponents.[67] Not surprisingly, the "ancient truths" were those that, as Bellah and others have indicated, form the basis of a strong civil religious tradition. Roosevelt's justifications for his sometimes unprecedented actions were always tied to historical lessons: he declared himself ready to deal with unprecedented situations by using tactically unprecedented, but morally traditional, means. Roosevelt sought to portray his break with tradition as contiguous with the best traditions of forward-thinking American political life.

The favorable reaction to FDR's first inaugural has been credited with establishing the momentum for economic recovery by demonstrating the new president's leadership skills.[68] Certainly the presidential inaugural always enacts leadership to some extent, as Campbell and Jamieson have noted. But Roosevelt's joining of war imagery with religious imagery to form a larger unifying structure, a holy war, enabled him to invoke an historically powerful cultural archetype, take on the roles of military leader as well as religious leader, and call for action in a much more forceful manner than one usually finds in a presidential inaugural, thereby pushing at the recognized boundaries of that genre.

Ironically, because of the power and eloquence of his speech, Roosevelt risked embroiling himself in a deeper ideological controversy. The dark side of these rhetorical moves was, of course, that neither of the leadership roles Roosevelt adopted was ultimately compatible with a democratic system of government; in fact, both set the leader above the people in such a rigid hierarchy that the very act of questioning that leader is forbidden.[69] Critics who dare to practice their First Amendment rights open themselves to charges of "blasphemy" in the religious realm and "mutiny" in the military setting. So while many American people may have embraced Franklin Roosevelt's strong leadership style out of desperation, critics then and later saw signs of an aristocratic, authoritarian mind-set that they found justifiably disturbing. It is quite probable that such a blatant use of "crusade" imagery today would find even greater numbers of critics, especially among those who are already sensitized to (and concerned by) the powerful, and increasingly joined, appeal of the religious and political right.[70]

The dangers of war rhetoric—even if that war is metaphorical, and most certainly if that war is somehow sanctioned by the Almighty—should not be underestimated. The original idea of preserving the separate identities of the political and religious realms in American society may well have been to prevent such "holy wars," although the civil-religious tradition renders the concept so familiar (and the belief that God is on our side makes victory seem so inevitable) that crusades are attractive during times of uncertainty, offering as they do both moral certainty and comfort. But critics need to be watchful of how, where, when, and by whom the power of the civil-religious tradition is invoked. Many speakers attempt such mergers, only to fail badly with rhetoric that is hopelessly heavy-handed, resulting in public dismissal of their ideas. But when a talented and subtle rhetor, such as Franklin Delano Roosevelt, calls less blatantly upon the civil religion to justify certain policies in times of crisis, as he did in his first inaugural, critics and audiences alike must be certain to scrutinize the crusade they are being asked to support.

The range of voices and roles available to American presidents is wide, but the civil-religious blend of president with priest and commander-in-chief exerts a siren song simply by virtue of its potential power. The danger inherent in a skillful execution of the merging of civil and religious voices is an amplification of what Lakoff and Johnson noted, when they described the ways in which systems of metaphor simultaneously highlight certain aspects of the topic under discussion, and hide others. For civil religion offers not just a single metaphoric system, but a preconstructed template for rhetors. Roles, appropriate behaviors, scriptural and historical references all become available, springing immediately to life when one frames something as a "holy war." In fact, the script is so preset that it is self-justifying, and therein lie its seductive possibilities for rhetors (the search for arguments and convincing evidence is automatically over) and the very real dangers for listeners: neither religion nor the military encourages free, critical thought in its "laity" or "enlisted personnel" (namely, the vast majority of the American public).

The language of war, metaphorical or "real," dehumanizes the enemy and makes possible an unthinking, brutal "attack" on those who are somehow different. The Christian religion, in theory, encourages compassionate behavior. But when one adds religion to war, intolerance is the result. Moral certainty too often justifies trampling on the rights of those who do not share the crusader's ideals. To the extent that Franklin Roosevelt targeted the depression, or the *practices* of the bankers (rather than specific individuals themselves) for attack in his first inaugural, one can applaud his use of the metaphorical holy war to accomplish his aims. But the inherently undemocratic nature of the religious and military establishments lend themselves, in real life as well as in metaphorical depiction, to abuse. Speakers are well advised to call on these metaphorical clusters sparingly, and without dehumanizing the political opposition. Listeners and critics must be wary of those who claim simultaneously the powers of priest and commander-in-chief, for such concentration of power contains the seeds of both corruption and combustion.

Reading Endnotes

Suzanne Daughton is assistant professor of speech communication at Southern Illinois University, Carbondale. An earlier version of this essay was presented at The Speech Communication Association convention (November 1989). The author wishes to thank Professors Stephen E. Lucas, Kathleen H. Jamieson, and Roderick P. Hart for their helpful comments on earlier drafts of this essay.

1. Ted Morgan, *FDR: A Biography* (New York: Simon and Schuster, 1985) 375. See Franklin Delano Roosevelt, "First Inaugural Address, Washington, D.C., March 4, 1933," *Great Speeches for Criticism and Analysis,* ed. Lloyd F. Rohler and Roger Cook (Greenwood, Indiana: Alistair Press-Educational Video Group, 1988) 271–274. Citations from the inaugural are found in parenthesis in the text.
2. Franklin Delano Roosevelt, *The Public Papers and Addresses of Franklin D. Roosevelt,* ed. Samuel I. Rosenman, 1928–1936, 5 vols. (New York: Random House, 1938) 11:16.
3. Campbell and Jamieson describe great inaugural addresses as those that "address timely questions timelessly." Karlyn Kohrs Campbell and Kathleen Hall Jamieson, "Inaugurating the Presidency," *Presidential Studies Quarterly* 15 (1985): 405. Jamieson has spoken of "synecdochic moments" in a campaign or in a presidency which present an overarching theme, uniting and standing for the whole; she points out that "the only thing we have to fear is fear itself" has come to stand for the FDR presidency. Kathleen Hall Jamieson, "Synecdochic Moments," Lecture at the University of Texas at Austin, April 1988.
4. Rollins writes of the tension that filled the months between Roosevelt's election and the inauguration: "No period of transition had been so potently fateful since the country had waited through four

critical months for the inauguration of Abraham Lincoln." Alfred B. Rollins, Jr., *Roosevelt and Howe* (New York: Alfred A. Knopf, 1962) 366.

5. In *Franklin D. Roosevelt's Rhetorical Presidency*, Halford R. Ryan writes, "From all quarters came support for Roosevelt's bid for quasi-military leadership power, and that support was often couched in the president's infectious military imagery." See Halford R. Ryan, *Franklin D. Roosevelt's Rhetorical Presidency* (New York: Greenwood Press, 1988) 82, hereafter referred to as *Presidency*.

   James A. Hagerty reported on the reaction to the inaugural. "The immediate reaction to the address among leaders in Congress, even among the Republicans, was generally favorable." "Roosevelt Address Stirs Great Crowd," *New York Times* 5 March 1933: 3.

   The *Birmingham News-Age Herald*, like countless other papers, raved about the address: "Nothing that Mr. Roosevelt has said or done since his election, nothing that has happened in this country in many months, has held for the American people so much hope, so much encouragement, so much promise, as the words uttered by the new President in his inaugural address." Quoted in the *New York Times* 5 March 1933: 6.

   And private citizens across the country addressed letters to the editors of their local papers urging their fellow citizens to do everything in their power to assist the new administration in pursuit of its goals. For example, E. A. Condit of Montclair, N.J. wrote, "Before election I was 100 percent against Franklin D. Roosevelt; now I am 100 percent for him. His inaugural speech, I believe, showed him to be the leader which we sadly needed. . . ." *New York Times* 8 March 1933: 12.

6. The *New York Herald Tribune* reported on the inaugural, "His indictment of the money changers drew by far the greatest applause from a sober-minded audience," 5 March 1933: 2. Ryan quotes other reactions from the contemporary press and concludes that, "Various contemporary signs indicated that FDR struck a responsive rhetorical chord by utilizing his scapegoat technique. . . . Available evidence from the inaugural audience, from contemporary news-films and news-print media, and from later commentators suggests that FDR was successful in obtaining his end." Halford Ross Ryan, "Roosevelt's First Inaugural: A Study of Technique," *Quarterly Journal of Speech* 65 (1979): 142–3, hereafter referred to as "Study."

7. Many historians and biographers note the unusually frenzied passage of this first bill. Burns, among others, writes that House representatives shouted "Vote, Vote!" after only minutes of debate. He also quotes Bertrand Snell, the Republican floor leader, as saying, "The house is burning down, and the President of the United States says this is the way to put out the fire." See James MacGregor Burns, *Roosevelt: The Lion and The Fox* (New York: Harcourt, Brace and Company, 1956) 166–7.

8. Franklin Delano Roosevelt, *The Public Papers and Addresses of Franklin D. Roosevelt* 11:65–6. Many contemporary reporters cited the nationwide bank closings as a factor which contributed to the improvement in the national "mood," and they were quick to praise Roosevelt's decisive call for action to solve the banking crisis. One could hardly expect bank closings to inspire confidence in the midst of a depression without the promise of leadership that many saw in Roosevelt's inaugural. Arthur Krock reported on the inaugural for the *New York Times*, noting:

   > It was curious that a crowd so large . . . should have gathered in Washington today, matters of personal finance being what they were. But it was tremendous and it showed remarkable enthusiasm in view of the fact that thousands did not know where the cash was coming from to pay their hotel bills and get them home.
   >
   > But Americans always call upon their sense of humor on such occasions, and on every side there were jests about "rubber checks" and "no money from home." There seemed to be little use in worrying about it. The President was working on it, wasn't he? Some way out would surely be found . . .

   "Roosevelt Acts to End Bank Crisis," *New York Times* 5 March 1933: 3.
9. Ryan, "Study" 137. Campbell and Jamieson count it as one of the great inaugurals, 404.
10. Burns writes, "A dozen days after the inauguration a move of adulation for Roosevelt was sweeping the country. . . . A flush of hope swept the nation," 168. Davis contends, "And for this dissipation of gloom, this sudden focus of resurgent energies in the light of renewed optimism, the tone of the inaugural address and the image projected by the new President of the United States were largely responsible." Kenneth S. Davis, *FDR: The New Deal Years 1933–1937: A History* (New York: Random House, 1986) 34.
11. John F. Wilson notes that the "separation" of church and state was conceived by the founders to enable and empower both religion and government, rather than to build a wall that would be impervious to penetration from either side. See John Frederick Wilson, *Public Religion in American Culture* (Philadelphia: Temple University Press, 1979) 3–6.
12. Bellah, Hart, and Fairbanks note, from different perspectives, that the presidential inaugural has important functions in this civil religion (or civic piety). Hart notes that every inaugural but Washington's second includes some reference to the Deity. See Roderick P. Hart, *The Political Pulpit* (West Lafayette, Indiana: Purdue University Press, 1977) 70. See also James David Fairbanks, "Religious Dimensions of Presidential Leadership: The Case of Dwight Eisenhower," *Presidential Studies Quarterly* 12 (1982): 260–267, and Robert N. Bellah, "Civil Religion in America," *Daedalus* 96 (Winter, 1967): 1–21.

13. Bellah 5. (He notes that the phrase "civil religion" is, of course, Rousseau's.)
14. Bellah 18. In the course of his first inaugural, Roosevelt evoked nearly all of these archetypes, either specifically, or by allusion.
15. Kenneth Burke, *A Grammar of Motives* (Berkeley: University of California Press, 1945) 393–4.
16. Kenneth Burke, *The Rhetoric of Religion* (Berkeley: University of California Press, 1961).
17. Roderick P. Hart, *The Political Pulpit* (West Lafayette, Indiana: Purdue University Press, 1977).
18. John Frederick Wilson, *Public Religion in American Culture* (Philadelphia: Temple University Press, 1979).
19. Burke, *The Rhetoric of Religion* 7.
20. Hart notes that this metaphorical, rhetorical dimension of the term "civil religion" is the basis of Wilson's critique of it; Wilson and Hart both prefer "civic piety" instead, 32–39.
21. Bellah 6.
22. "Transcript of Speech by Clinton Accepting Democratic Nomination," *New York Times* 17 July 1992: A14. Clinton described his New Covenant as "based not simply on what each of us can take, but what all of us must give. . . ." Although the phrase is not an unusual one, the parallels with FDR's first inaugural here and elsewhere are interesting. FDR said "we cannot merely take, but we must give as well" (273). The echo became stronger a moment later in Clinton's address, when he criticized George Bush for:

    > . . . how he derides and degrades the American tradition of seeing and seeking a better future. He mocks it as "the vision thing." But just remember that the Scripture says: "Where there is no vision the people perish." (A14)

    FDR made the identical critique of the bankers, although he did not make his reference to "the Scripture" explicit: "They have no vision, and when there is no vision the people perish" (272).
23. See Jonathan Riley-Smith, *The First Crusade and the Idea of Crusading* (London: Athlone Press, 1986) 5.
24. Riley-Smith 5–6.
25. Christopher Hill, *God's Englishman: Oliver Cromwell and the English Revolution* (New York: The Dial Press, 1970) 288.
26. Several examples will illustrate. The first examples are of "actual" violence discussed in religious terms. In his "Boston Massacre Oration" of March 5, 1774, John Hancock said:

    > But I forbear, and come reluctantly to the transactions of that dismal night . . . when heaven in anger, for a dreadful moment, suffer'd hell to take the reins; when Satan with his chosen band open'd the sluices

> of New-England's blood, and sacrilegiously polluted our land with the dead bodies of her guiltless sons. . . .

In Ronald F. Reid, ed., *Three Centuries of American Rhetorical Discourse* (Prospect Heights, IL: Waveland Press, 1988) 102.

Biographer Martin Gilbert notes that in his famous "finest hour" speech of 1940, Winston Churchill needed "to raise the morale of the nation and to sustain it": "I expect that the Battle of Britain is about to begin. Upon this battle depends the survival of Christian civilisation." See Gilbert's *Churchill: A Life* (New York: Henry Holt and Company, 1991) 663.

As for metaphorical violence, a similar tradition exists. In May of 1840, shoemaker Samuel L. Boicourt concluded his "Confession of a Convert" (a religious metaphor for his own change in sympathies from Van Buren Democrat to Harrison Whig), with the following image:

> And now, sirs, I am going with the "log cabin dwelling-cider-drinker," to battle against those palace-dwelling, champaigne-drinking democrats, with full confidence that, under the humble banner of the log cabin, the nation is to be rescued from the dominion of the spoilers. It was under the banner of the infamous cross, sirs, that the world was redeemed from the devil and his imps—a banner assumed by the followers of our blessed Lord in commemoration of the ignominious treatment to which he had been subjected by his unholy scoffers and persecutors. (Reid 286)

And one of the most famous examples of such discourse is William Jennings Bryan's 1896 "Cross of Gold" speech, in which he made numerous religious allusions, such as the following:

> With a zeal approaching the zeal which inspired the Crusaders who followed Peter the Hermit, our silver Democrats went forth from victory unto victory until they are now assembled, not to discuss, not to debate, but to enter up the judgement already rendered by the plain people of this country. (Reid 601)

27. Campbell and Jamieson 401.
28. Campbell and Jamieson 394.
29. Campbell and Jamieson 394.
30. Ryan, *Presidency* 85.
31. Although many biographers and essayists mention the inaugural and discuss people's reactions to it, only two rhetorical criticisms of that address (careful analyses of the first inaugural as a rhetorical text) exist in print (one of which is a later expansion of the first). Halford Ross Ryan, author of both works, notes, "Although [several] rhetorical works on FDR are helpful, they do not explicate FDR's first inaugural nor its significance," "Study" 137.

32. Military language could potentially pose at least three kinds of rhetorical risks. Ryan addresses the first possibility, that FDR's warlike tone could fuel American fears of a Roosevelt dictatorship, and concludes that the public was generally unalarmed. See Ryan, *Presidency* 83 and "Study" 145–8.

    Second, and more literally, one might expect the American people to have been "gun-shy" after the first World War. Recent and painful memories of that war encouraged isolationist sentiment among the people and could have resulted in an aversion to the language of war, even when that language was clearly metaphorical. Morison, for example, discusses the sense of post-war disillusionment following World War I. See Samuel Eliot Morison, *The Oxford History of the American People* (New York: Oxford University Press, 1965) 885–6.

    And third, borrowing the language of war to talk about the current economic situation might be less-than-strategic for another reason. In *President Johnson's War on Poverty: Rhetoric and History*, David Zarefsky has illustrated that the rhetorical momentum of the military metaphor is both initially attractive, and ultimately self-destructive, for when the metaphorical war is against something so difficult to eradicate as poverty, the war is categorically lost, since war cannot be "partially" won (University, AL: University of Alabama Press, 1986).
33. Leuchtenberg writes,

    > In the months and years that followed the stock market crash of 1929, America searched for some way to make comprehensible what was happening. Sometimes people thought of the Great Depression as a breakdown of a system, sometimes as the product of the machinations of evil or stupid men, sometimes as the visitation of a plague like the Black Death. But from the very first, many conceived the depression to be a calamity like war, or more specifically, like the menace of a foreign enemy who had to be defeated in combat. Occasionally, the analogue of war was a general one, more often it referred specifically to World War I. . . .
    >
    > In addition to employing the metaphor of war to explain the meaning of the depression, the 1930's drew on the experience of the economic mobilization of World War I for instrumentalities to combat hard times. . . . In the New Deal years, the two strands [war and economic mobilization] were inseparable. (81–3)

    See William E. Leuchtenberg, "The New Deal and the Analogue of War," *Change and Continuity in Twentieth-Century America* John Braeman, Robert H. Bremner, and Everett Walters, eds., (Columbus, OH: Ohio State University Press, 1964) 81–143.
34. However, as Kenneth Burke notes, such distinctions often hold in image, more than in practice: "Though Christians have a record of much turbulent fighting, Christianity is a philosophy of peace," *A Grammar of Motives* 397.

35. Michael Osborn, "Archetypal Metaphor in Rhetoric: The Light-Dark Family," *Quarterly Journal of Speech* 53 (1967): 126. Rhetorical critics and theorists have increasingly focused on the analysis of metaphor in recent years. See for example, Michael M. Osborn and Douglas Ehninger, "The Metaphor in Public Address," *Speech Monographs* 29 (1962): 223–234; Edwin Black, "The Second Persona," *Quarterly Journal of Speech* 56 (1970): 109–119; Kathleen Hall Jamieson, "The Metaphoric Cluster in the Rhetoric of Pope Paul VI and Edmund G. Brown, Jr., *Quarterly Journal of Speech* 66 (1980): 51–72; Robert L. Ivie, "The Metaphor of Force in Prowar Discourse: The Case of 1812," *Quarterly Journal of Speech* 68 (1982): 240–253; and Robert L. Ivie, "Literalizing the Metaphor of Soviet Savagery: President Truman's Plain Style," *Southern Speech Communication Journal* 51 (Winter, 1986): 91–105.
36. See George Lakoff and Mark Johnson, *Metaphors We Live By* (Chicago: University of Chicago Press, 1980).
37. Lakoff and Johnson 7–9.
38. Lakoff and Johnson 10–13. In their first chapter, "Concepts We Live By," the authors hint at the potential dangers of war metaphor (or any metaphoric cluster, used in isolation): war metaphors, in particular, close off other interpretations of events that would be less competitive or less hostile, and more importantly, structure our actions and patterns of thought, 4.
39. *A Grammar of Motives* 503.
40. The fact that Roosevelt was not the exclusive author of the speech does not pose problems for this analysis. Ryan has established the degree to which Roosevelt contributed to the construction of the speech (see "Study" 138–140), but in any case, Roosevelt, like most presidents, would not say something with which he disagreed. Ryan's conclusion is mine, as well: "What follows, then, is based on the assumption that 'the President's speech is the President's speech.' " Ryan, "Study" 140, quotes Arthur Larson, *Eisenhower: The President Nobody Knew* (New York: Scribner's, 1968) 150.
41. Ryan also discusses two other techniques prominent in this speech: Roosevelt scapegoated the moneychangers and offered Congress a choice of the "carrot-and-stick." Ryan, "Study" 141–143 and 145–146.
42. See Ryan, *Presidency* 82.
43. See David Zarefsky's *Lyndon Johnson's War on Poverty: Rhetoric and History* (University, AL: University of Alabama Press, 1986).
44. In his campaign address to the Commonwealth Club in San Francisco (September 23, 1932), Franklin Roosevelt said, "It seems that things are in a rut, fixed, settled, that the world has grown old and tired and very much out of joint. This is the mood of depression, of dire and weary depression," 147. Ernest J. Wrage and Barnet Baskerville, eds., *Contemporary Forum: American Speeches on Twentieth Century Issues* (New York: Harper, 1962) 146–156.

45. Robert L. Ivie, "Presidential Motives for War," *Quarterly Journal of Speech* 60 (1974): 343.
46. Jamieson discusses the contribution of the sermonic form to the presidential inaugural and notes that religious elements are found in most inaugural addresses. See Kathleen M. Hall Jamieson, "Generic Constraints and the Rhetorical Situation," *Philosophy and Rhetoric* 6.3 (Summer, 1973): 162–170. Roosevelt's extraordinarily long tenure in office provides the critic with more data for comparison than is available for any other American president before or since: he delivered four inaugural addresses rather than one or two. Roosevelt's first inaugural is far more laden with religious metaphor and allusion than even his own later inaugural addresses, indicating that the language patterns he used were more in response to the immediate "rhetorical situation" than to generic constraints. For a discussion of the notion of "rhetorical situation," see Lloyd Bitzer, "The Rhetorical Situation," *Philosophy and Rhetoric* 1 (1968): 1–14.
47. Fairbanks 263. In addition to a scriptural function, Roosevelt's first inaugural exhibits a sermonic structure, intensifying the new president's role as religious leader. Roosevelt began with an assessment of the bleak external situation, then indicated that he would lead the nation in an examination of its problems with prevalent values and ethical practices (the sermonic parallel would be "the national soul"). Next Roosevelt outlined his views on the ethical principles necessary to guide the system in the future and then led his flock outward again with advice on the type of action and "right living" in the world community that would bring them salvation (economic and moral recovery) in the future. Roosevelt called attention to the ultimate benefits, the "higher purposes" to which such action would be directed. In the penultimate section of his speech, FDR appealed to "Biblical authority" by returning to "today's scriptural message" in the form of the United States Constitution. And in the final moments of his address, Roosevelt blessed his "congregation" and sent them out into the world to apply what they had learned.
48. Campbell and Jamieson 402–3.
49. This active and activist trend in religion also has its own history, which works particularly well in the civil-religious tradition. Robert Bellah writes, "As S. M. Lipset has recently shown, American religion at least since the early-nineteenth century has been predominantly activist, moralistic, and social rather than contemplative, theological, or innerly spiritual," 12. Bellah cites Seymour Martin Lipset, "Religion and American Values," Chapter 4, *The First New Nation* (New York, 1964).
50. See John 2:15.
51. Ryan discusses FDR's successful scapegoating of the moneychangers and the religious origins of the term "scapegoat," "Study" 141–3.

52. Roosevelt referred to "this great nation," and said,

    > the rulers of the exchange of mankind's goods have failed through their own stubbornness and their own incompetence, have admitted their failure and have abdicated. Practices of the unscrupulous moneychangers stand indicted in the court of public opinion, rejected by the hearts and minds of men. (271)

    In other words, the American people were morally superior to the Wall Street bankers, as shown by their recognition and rejection of the bankers' evil practices.
53. Psalm 23:3. Not coincidentally, Ernest Bormann calls the "restoration" fantasy type "one of the most venerable and powerful . . . in the history of American public address." See Ernest G. Bormann, "A Fantasy Theme Analysis of the Television Coverage of the Hostage Release and the Reagan Inaugural," *Quarterly Journal of Speech* 68 (1982): 136.
54. See, for example, Roosevelt, "Address to the Commonwealth Club," in Wrage and Baskerville. See also Morison 948.
55. I am indebted to an anonymous reviewer for this image.
56. Leuchtenberg notes that government involvement in economic life was justified by the analogy with World War I, 85.
57. In so doing, Roosevelt also fulfilled what Fairbanks has called the "religious dimensions of presidential leadership." While Fairbanks stresses the religious dimension and does not deal with the conjunction of religious and military leadership, his choice of Eisenhower as subject is interesting: Eisenhower, of course, was a popular military leader prior to his election as president. Fairbanks 260.
58. Viewers of the 1992 Republican National Convention were treated to Pat Buchanan's discussion of the "holy war" in which this nation was supposedly engaged; many rejected this view as melodramatic and divisive. Buchanan's characterization seemed especially doomed to failure because the war of which he spoke was a civil one, setting American citizens against one another, rather than against some common (external or inhuman) foe.
59. For example, in a letter dated the day *before* the inaugural, William C. Longstreet of Jersey City wrote to the editor of the (Republican) *New York Herald Tribune:*

    > Conditions at present cry for some sort of *faith*, some sort of hope. The press of our country should be the dominant factor in supplying this demand. We all are Americans, and let me say to you and your readers my belief in the *creed of an American* at this time is:
    >
    > 1. Confidence in the new Administration.
    > 2. Confidence in the Constitution of the United States.
    > 3. *Faith* in the American dollar.
    > 4. *Faith* in every banking institution in our country.

> We, as Americans, are at this time in a *bloodless war. Let not our soldiers run from the battle. Let us stand foursquare in the face of the enemy,* and if the bank where our money is on deposit closes, *we, as soldiers, have been wounded but not killed. Let us as soldiers in this war stand by our bank,* wherever it may be, *and if we are wounded we will recover, but don't let us retreat. The creed of an American,* established not by us but by our forefathers, hated and despised a *retreat.*

My emphasis, 6 March 1933: 10.

In a *New York Times* article entitled "Speech Wins Favor From Both Parties," Senator King is quoted as saying,

> It [the inaugural] is a great speech, full of courage and hope. While the President's statements were rather broad and general, there were back of them specific measures to be adopted against the *common foe.* It showed the courage of Andrew Jackson, the philosophy of Thomas Jefferson, the humanity of Lincoln and *courage of a great prophet.*

Emphasis mine, 5 March 1933: 6.

And several days after the inaugural, in a news article entitled "Spirit of Congress Grim in Bank Task," a *New York Times* reporter wrote,

> *It is trite to say that they [Congress] declared war, but it is nevertheless true that they hurled against the enemy of depression and despondency a weapon which they hoped would penetrate the subtle armor of an allegorical or Bunyan-like antagonist.* Congress hardly knew what was in the [Banking] bill they passed today. . . .
>
> They were glad to place the responsibility for action in the hands of one man [Roosevelt] . . . and showed in their demeanor their hope that the revolutionary means they were adopting would bring the country some *surcease from growing economic casualties.*
>
> Representative Steagull voiced this feeling when, with arms widespread and voice ringing through the large chamber of the house, he said:
>
> *"We rely on leadership whose face is lifted to the skies."*
>
> *It was a declaration of faith, almost a prayer,* and in it there was an unmistakable note of optimism. Whatever the outcome of today's action may be, it was taken with the belief that by that way, and no other, could confidence and *economic peace* return. . . .

My emphasis, 10 March 1933: 1.

60. Rabbi William F. Rosenblum said of the new president, "To the people he has become more than a political hero, more than a Chief Executive, more than a possible dictator. They see in him a *God-like messenger,* a darling of destiny, the man of the hour—*the Messiah of America's tomorrow.*" My emphasis, quoted in the *New York Times* 6 March 1933: 11.

    In a letter to the editor of the *New York Herald Tribune,* John Schaefer of Forest Hills, Long Island, praised the inaugural for its "thrilling evangelical tone." 8 March 1933: 10.

And Schlesinger quotes from one of the nearly half-million letters Roosevelt received in the days immediately following the inauguration, "People are looking to you almost as they look to God." See Arthur M. Schlesinger, Jr., *The Age of Roosevelt: The Coming of the New Deal,* 2 vols. (Boston: Houghton Mifflin Company, 1958) II:1.

61. Louis Surut, President of the Woolen Corporation of America, placed an ad in the financial section of the *New York Times,* which said in part:

> Confidence is called for. *Faith* is demanded. . . . There is no use *bewailing the sins of the past, either of omission or commission. . . .*
>
> The revival of America's confidence is a *sacred duty* which must be borne not alone by the statesmen but by the bankers, the industrialists and the working class, whether profitably engaged or unhappily unemployed. . . .
>
> It is for the new leaders to find the way. And for us to follow—not with doubt and misgiving—but with courage and confidence. That is the *loyal duty* we owe to the new administration. That is the *patriotic duty* we owe to the nation!

My emphasis, 6 March 1933: 23.

62. The *Omaha World Herald* editorialized,

> We are enlisted in a war, we Americans. It is a real war: a war for the preservation of ourselves, of our country, of our children's heritage. The call of the President of the nation summons us to his side—summons the humblest and weakest as well as the most powerful. It is a war that under his fearless leadership must be fought by all, for it is fought for all alike.

Quoted in the *New York Herald Tribune* 5 March 1933: 4.

63. Roosevelt's frequent use of religious and military language could have fed either a positive or a negative impression (that he was a strong, charismatic leader, or that he might have become too strong for the good of the country). However, there are other metaphoric clusters in the address. Roosevelt used the language of (1) legality ("the truth, the whole truth" [271] and "indicted in the court of public opinion" [272]), (2) light and dark (Roosevelt used the word "dark" to describe present conditions three times in the first third of the speech [twice on page 271, once on 272] and at the end of his speech described the future as positive, in light-associated terms: "clean," "clear," and "warm" [274]), (3) life and death (He linked the country's health to both war and religion: "terror," he said, "*paralyzes* needed efforts to convert *retreat* into *advance,*" [my emphasis, 271]; and "confidence *languishes,* for it *thrives* only on honesty, on honor, on the *sacredness* of obligations, on *faithful* protection, and on unselfish performance. Without them, it cannot *live*" [my emphasis, 272]), and (4) instrumentality (Roosevelt depicted the government and executive power as instruments to be used for the public good, and FDR himself

as the instrument the people had chosen to lead the nation: "our constitutional system has proved itself the most superbly enduring *political mechanism* the modern world has ever seen" [my emphasis, 274]; and "The people of the United States . . . have made me the present instrument of their wishes" [274]). These other metaphors, occurring in conjunction with the religious and military imagery, could serve to mitigate the negative interpretation by emphasizing FDR's subordination of himself and his purposes to a higher good (in the form of light, life, the United States justice system, and the American ideal of the leader leading by consent of the people).

64. Morison writes that Herbert Hoover, for one, later attributed the bank closings of March 4, 1933, to "fear" of New Deal radicalism, 949. Rollins describes the eve of the inauguration as "a time of testing, a moment of uneasy hope held carefully in check by skepticism learned of hardship," 364.
65. Campbell and Jamieson 402.
66. Ryan, "Study" 145–6.
67. Burns reprints a telling political cartoon from the era: it depicts a grinning FDR playing a violin marked "CONSERVATISM" while a saxophone labelled "BOLD POLICIES" waits by his side. A smiling Uncle Sam is seated in a comfortable chair, leaning forward and listening appreciatively. The caption, "A Master of Both Instruments," adds yet another dimension to the instrument image (see note 63). Burns cites Edwin Marcus, cartoon, *New York Times* 18 November 1934.
68. Rollins writes, "What Roosevelt did do, and with monumental success, was to preserve the faith which vague commitment or partial action might have shattered," 366. Schlesinger quotes Walter Lippmann: "At the beginning of March, the country was in such a state of confused desperation that it would have followed almost any leader anywhere he chose to go. . . . In one week, the nation, which had lost confidence in everything and everybody, has regained confidence in the government and in itself," 13.
69. This is not to say that societies that call themselves "democratic" do not go to war, or operate in a bureaucratic or hierarchical fashion. They do, of course. But the fundamental premise of democracy, that all people are created equal, is subverted somewhat when some people are, in Orwell's terms, "more equal than others." George Orwell, *Animal Farm* (New York: Harcourt Brace Jovanovich, [1946] 1960).
70. See note 58. See also, for example, Flo Conway and Jim Siegelman, *Holy Terror: The Fundamentalist War on America's Freedoms in Religion, Politics, and Our Private Lives* (New York: Dell Publishing Company/Delta, 1982).

In this Chapter 3 workshop, we will probe several of the ways you can recognize and use the "gold" of academic, rhetorical criticism. As part of this workshop, we will use Suzanne Daughton's rhetorical criticism of FDR's first inaugural address as a focal article. Read her analysis starting on page 60. Be careful to reconsider the JFS, JFA, Method, and RQ items (about which you learned in this chapter) that Daughton used to establish the need for her research.

Reread the chart on the next page (you'll recognize some of the quotations from the chapter discussion). See if you can notice how we moved from the original claim, insight, or discovery to the resulting "translation."

Next, use the blank chart on the following page to find more nuggets of "gold" in the article from your own reading. Be sure to keep track of the page on which you find the quotation and think about how you can best translate the insight or discovery to a practical translation you could use in preparing a message.

FINDING THE GOLD

Discovering Application Ideas and Knowledge in Analysis Articles

Example:

Daughton, Suzanne M. "Metaphorical Transcendence: Images of the Holy War in Franklin Roosevelt's First Inaugural." *Quarterly Journal of Speech* 79 (1993): 427–446.

(Page numbers in brackets indicate pages reprinted in this textbook.)

Quotation	Page	Translated Idea or Insight
"Roosevelt, I will argue, resolved this dilemma by subtly blending metaphoric clusters—religious and military—into a single integrated image of holy war."	427 [61]	Rhetors can subtly blend metaphoric clusters. Metaphors can help create a single integrated image.
"Ryan points to Roosevelt's use of metaphor as a crucial strategy[.]"	430 [64]	Rhetors can use metaphors as a strategic means of creating policy meaning for an audience.
"The present analysis is an attempt to add to Ryan's research by focusing on the duality of rhetorical objectives and their corresponding metaphorical clusters."	430 [64]	Rhetorical objectives can be achieved by use of metaphors and clusters of metaphors.
"Although these metaphoric types [military metaphors and religious metaphors] may at first appear contradictory, the power and centrality of the civil-religious tradition in American public address makes their juxtaposition singularly unproblematic."	430 [64]	Metaphors will be received and interpreted within a cultural matrix of existing values, ideas, and practices. Rhetors should create, or contemplate use of, metaphors with appropriate traditions and practices in mind.
"Michael Osborn has argued that attention to metaphor can 'permit a more precise focusing upon whatever values and motives are salient in society at a given time.' "	431 [65]	Rhetors can use metaphor to focus an audience's attention upon ideas and images that match commonly held values and motives in a society.
"George Lakoff and Mark Johnson have pointed out that people cannot speak without using metaphor, and that much of what we normally consider 'literal language' is based on metaphoric concepts."	431 [65]	Rhetor can investigate unnoticed metaphoric foundations of everyday language and messages for potential tools and tactics. People cannot consistently communicate without metaphors.
"Lakoff and Johnson also call attention to the contradictory functions of metaphor, which both highlights and hides aspects of the concept under discussion[.]"	431 [65]	Metaphors often hide as many aspects as they reveal. Rhetors should use this function of metaphor to create message advantages for themselves or their clients.

Use the chart on the next page to find, identify, and chart the potential advantage of other observations on metaphors that Daughton makes in this analysis.

Quotation	Page	Translated Idea or Insight

FINDING OTHER RHETORICAL CRITICISM GOLD

Pick one of the following articles of rhetorical criticism and use the blank chart on the next page to record your discoveries of rhetorical criticism gold.

Lessl, Thomas M. "The Galileo Legend as Scientific Folklore." *Quarterly Journal of Speech* 85 (1999): 146–168.

Bennett, W. Lance. "Storytelling in Criminal Trials: A Model of Social Judgment." *Quarterly Journal of Speech* 64 (1978): 1–22.

Sawhney, Harmeet. "Information Superhighway: Metaphors as Midwives." *Media, Culture & Society* 18 (1996): 291–314.

Foss, Sonja K. "Ambiguity as Persuasion: The Vietnam Veterans Memorial." *Communication Quarterly* 34 (1986): 326–340.

Article Citation:

Quotation	Page	Translated Idea or Insight

Key Words

Endnotes

1. Suzanne M. Daughton, "Metaphorical Transcendence: Images of the Holy War in Franklin Roosevelt's First Inaugural," *Quarterly Journal of Speech* 79 (1993): 427–446.
2. 439.
3. 439.
4. 431.
5. 2 Kings 21:13; B. M. Metzger and R. E. Murphy, eds. *The New Oxford Annotated Bible.* New York: Oxford University Press, 1991.
6. Avery Fisher Hall at Lincoln Center Ad, *New Yorker* 25 Dec. 1995, 93.
7. Hess, David. "Rostenkowski Quietly Pleads Innocent." *Oregonian* 11 June 1994. A-10.

Chapter Four

Writing Rhetorical Criticism: Your Analysis of Important Public Messages

As you become a fully capable communication professional, you will be able to take the insight derived from rhetorical critics and use it to your benefit. In the same way, however, you need to attain experience in actually doing the sort of analysis you've been seeing other rhetorical critics do.

Chapters throughout this book allow you to see highly skilled critics at work. Cloud's analysis of how Oprah Winfrey has become a potent media persona in American culture (Chapter 8), the Hardy-Short and Short analysis of the Yellowstone controversy (Chapter 5), and Lester Olson's analysis of visual messages created by one of America's most powerful rhetors (Chapter 7), among other articles, allow you to see how substantial the insights are from talented rhetorical critics. This chapter will start *your* steps toward doing rhetorical criticism in at least three ways.

First, we will discuss (from the perspective of performing the tasks) the building block elements of initial ideas and quick investigation. These starting blocks form the initiation point of both formal and informal rhetorical criticism. Second, we will discuss an intermediate form of rhetorical criticism that stretches your ability to interpret, with care, some of the main factors in several kinds of message artifacts. Finally, we'll cover how you can accomplish, at an undergraduate level, an initial study using rhetorical criticism. You'll learn step-by-step the procedure for initiating a formal, insightful study using some of the perspectives and theories you've been learning about in previous chapters. Let's get started.

INFORMAL RHETORICAL CRITICISM

If we knew perfectly how messages in human communication work, we would have little reason to do rhetorical criticism of any type. Since we are not yet at that stage of knowing and using perfect communication rules and strategies, almost everyone does informal rhetorical criticism (i.e., trying to figure out why certain messages seem to work wildly well, while others seem to bomb). You may remember that before we learn formal strategies for rhetorical analysis, we tend to learn by trial and error.

So many message makers in human culture (speakers, sign painters, singers, ad writers, designers, legislators, politicians, business execs, etc.) still make messages using only their accumulated experiences (trial and error) as a guide. No law states that you must be a skilled, knowledgeable rhetorician to be allowed to make a message that will reach a large public audience. (Maybe such a law would help the general quality of messages, however!)

You, nevertheless, are deciding to take a different path. As happened with engineers, pharmacists, and agribusiness people before you, the word has come home: systematic, careful study of *how* something works (whether bridges, chemical compounds, or seed germination patterns) allows you to approach the task with greater care and skill. Hence, your steps of attentive study will pay off for you because you will have the *basis* for making better decisions about what strategies to use when designing and using a message. Remember, at one time, *anyone* with the means could build a bridge, make a medicine, or grow crops. Anyone still can, but we tend now to leave those things to people who can do them exceptionally well using techniques based on years of careful study by scholars. We are making the same "move" in contemporary culture; people in our culture are deciding that if a political campaign, a $750,000 marketing budget, or a product launch depends on a message for success, maybe (just maybe!) we ought to have on board someone who actually knows how messages work. Thus, knowing how to evoke meaning through message creation is your learning task of the moment.

Let's note that almost all curiosity about messages and their attributes stems from wanting to know how meaning is created or evoked. We need to take that curiosity and route it to productive initial activities that help us unravel how a message may create meaning for most audience members who will decode it.

To start, let's find ways to examine the power of individual words used in their natural "habitat" by rhetors who wish to influence your behavior. A natural place to start such a search might be where we know focused persuasion using words in language is occurring. Let's try the want ads in a newspaper (hard copy or online) as a case example.

Look at 50 ads where each ad writer is trying to influence you to examine and then buy a car (from individuals, not dealers). We know persuasion is happening. We know the person would like for you (or anyone else) to respond to the ad. We know the rhetor (the classified ad writer) would like that response to be the sale of the vehicle. What rhetorical dynamics are likely to go on in such ads?

Can we learn anything from the rhetorical tactics we find there? Go online, or find a newspaper, and let's find out.

As you read over 50 classified car ads, what are some of the "trends" you notice in form, content, or function of these persuasive messages? For starters, we can notice that two of the major characteristics noted are make and model of the car. Why are these more important (and therefore featured more) than dividing the available cars up by the size of gas tank or by number of doors? We begin, even in a minor way, to see the "hegemony" of *form* in messages. Cars are listed by make, model, and year because "that's the way we do it" (i.e., that's the form we've long used based on experience and history). Yet, if gas tank size or number of doors were *more* important to you, the effort necessary to find that information would be much greater for you than for someone who was primarily concerned with year and manufacturer. Why should you have to work harder to get the information you want when shopping for a car? Hence, we begin to see that patterns of information form what may be an important conceptual doorway into how and why certain messages are the way they are. (Rhetorical critics call such investigations genre studies.) What other aspects of a classified car ad might help you better understand how or why they are persuasive?

As you read many such ads, you notice an interesting array of abbreviations and designations. EX, 4dr, V-Tech, 60K, 5spd, CD, PW, am/fm, 16V, studded snows, AT, air, PDL, bra, whls, m/roof, non-smkr, T-top, all opts, lthr, tow pkg, warr, alloys, snrf, always gar'd, PS, mags, trac, batt, and other designations appear in such ads. With a bit of work, some information digging, and some questions you could probably find what all of those designations mean (or perhaps you already know).

Examination of 50 ads, however, shows that a couple dozen abbreviations are the *most commonly used* when trying to sell a car. Once you know the "code," you can "get" the message. However, some members of your class (or family) would more quickly "get" the abbreviations than others. Why? Again, we must note that cultural training and language used go hand in hand. If someone you know does much buying or selling of cars, she or he would much more easily interpret the car ads than someone doing so for the first time. He or she would be at an advantage. Why, then, don't car sellers spell out the characteristics and advantages of their cars in much greater detail, and with no abbreviations? Why the alphabet soup of designations and abbreviations? Cost, of course, would be one prime factor. The shorter your ad, the less it costs to run. Messages, to large audiences, we then note, have some cost associated with their distribution or creation. So as informal critics, we should realize that the expense of making or distributing persuasive messages has something to do with the "code" or style of messages that rhetors use.

Finally, some classified car ads go beyond simple description (even with abbreviations) of what the car has to offer you. So words and phrases such as "super clean," "wrecked but runs/drives well," "runs great!," "very clean," "one owner," "nice," "Sharp!," "Loaded!," "pristine," "see to believe," (and my favorite) "collision free" show up amid the promises of automatic transmissions and alloy wheels. From Kenneth Burke we learn that often labels and words we use are "instruction books" about how we should respond to the thing or person (see Chapter 8 for details). Would you rather have an ordinary car or a "pristine" car? Would you rather spend 11K on a "very clean" SUV or on one that is "wrecked but runs/drives well"? So, over 50 ads you might notice which word promises (many a little bit more subjective than whether the car does or does not have a CD) seem to be most often used. Could we tell from a tally which characteristics rhetors *believed* would be more persuasive than others? In other words, do we find more promises of cars being "clean" or more of them being owned by a single person? Which appears more important to potential buyers? Here we can begin to notice that what we emphasize about something may tell us as much about the expected audience as about the message or the rhetor.

But, are you genuinely curious about car ads and how they create meaning? You might be, if you were the vice president in charge of classified ads at a major metropolitan newspaper where 30 percent of your ad revenue came from automobile ads. If not, however, we can take our quest for interesting perspectives that spring from communication curiosity in other directions.

Scrutinize exercise

What other parts of culture can you remember that have fairly simple, but important, strategies of influencing an audience with a persuasive message? Try grocery store ads, telemarketing appeals, or political ads (or other similar possibilities that seem interesting to you). Aim for a type of message close to your long-term professional career goals. First read, listen to, or watch the messages you've picked.[1] Take notes on characteristics or trends you notice in the messages. Also, write down anything you *don't* understand in terms, form, or function. Next, pose a series of questions similar to the ones we asked about classified car ads. What categories seem dominant? Are any specialized codes or message strategies used? What attributes of the product or service for sale seem most often mentioned? What factors (cost? purpose? audience?) might explain some of the tactics used? What implied word promises seem most important to the expected audience?

Bonus scrutinize exercise

Do the same exercise as the one above, only work in hard copy magazines that are at least 40 years old. Is it harder or easier to see trends and tactics? Why?

What other parts of culture can you remember that have fairly simple, but important, strategies of influencing an audience with a persuasive message?

Curiosity that leads to useful informal rhetorical criticism may take a number of different roads, but controversy or unusual performance in a message are two of the most promising possibilities. Let's look at controversy first.

On 12 January 2002 an AP wire story reported from New York:

> A statue based on the famous photograph of the flag-raising at the World Trade Center site is being criticized because the three white firefighters in the picture have been transformed into one white, one African American and one Latino.
>
> Some firefighters and their families say the 19-foot bronze is political correctness run amok and an attempt to rewrite history.
>
> The $180,000 sculpture is expected to be erected this spring at the Fire Department's Brooklyn headquarters in tribute to the 343 firefighters killed in the attack. It is based on the Sept. 11 newspaper photo of firefighters raising the U.S. flag on about 20 feet of rubble.[2]

As we think about this controversy, which is deeply important to those directly involved (as well as to others), we can point to how an informal analysis of this controversy may aid in helping those concerned to better understand the issues involved. We can put to use some of the visual rhetoric terms available from Chapter 7.

To start, we must note that we are discussing here images, and images of images that have different characteristics and functions as messages. Moreover, different audiences have different interests in how any of the images might be used. The original photograph was taken by "Tom Franklin of *The Record* of Bergen County, N.J." which is owned by the "North Jersey Media Group, which publishes *The Record* and holds the copyright [for the original photographic image]."[3] Many commentators saw in the picture a likeness to the famous Rosenthal picture of Marines raising a flag on Iwo Jima in World War II. In fact, one may speculate that this resemblance may have had much to do with the picture's appeal and its rapid reproduction in various mass-media messages.[4] How else might we see the meaning created in these multiple images?

In visual rhetorical analysis terminology, we would say that the original photograph was an iconic message as it was a direct representation of the actions and people in front of Tom Franklin's camera on September 11th. Moreover, you could note that the iconic message was set within a larger narrative framework which most people in the world (with access to media messages) knew about in the days following September 11th. Hence, as most audience members would interpret this message, it was also a narrative moment frozen in time by the resources of photography. What then are we to make of the proposed bronze statue?

The N.Y. Fire Department and the company commissioned the statue (they own the department headquarters building): " 'Given that those who died were of all races and all ethnicities and that the statue was to be symbolic of those sacrifices, ultimately a decision was made to honor no one in particular, but everyone who made the supreme sacrifice,' said Fire Department spokesman Frank Gribbon."[5] Hence, the sponsors of the statue want it to contain iconic elements that signal firefighters' work in the face of the 9/11/01 terrorist attack, but they want it to work as a symbolic message to honor all of the people who died in that work.

As a critic doing informal analysis, you might well be able to point out to the people and groups involved that they have a tangled set of manageable message strands, but that contain some trade-offs. You might suggest that the people sponsoring the statue understandably wish to utilize the emotional power (pathos) and historical memory of the original picture that was so widely reprinted; that is, they wish to employ some of the iconic message power captured in the photograph of that moment in American and world history. On the other hand, they rightly wish to produce a message (in the form of the statue) that honors more than 340 firefighters who all gave their lives in dedicated public service under unbelievable circumstances; they wish to produce a visual message that has a symbolic function. The trouble occurs, then, when those dual purposes result in different decoding strategies on the part of audiences who have concern with the situation and the images.

The three firefighters whose images appeared in the original photo (and their families) have some understandable concern about the iconic properties of the proposed statue. As the people who were, at that moment in history, in front of a camera raising a flag in tribute to their fallen comrades, they may well desire that the statue image be as accurate as possible. Yet, they would likely be in the forefront of people who would ask, or demand, that all firefighters and emergency personnel who responded on September 11th be honored in any proposed statue.

So what to do? As a rhetorical critic working on an informal analysis of the message properties of this controversy, you might well suggest that some important decisions need to be made. And, if made properly, the message issues that have frayed nerves and disrupted lives in this case could be avoided or bypassed. Hence, you might point out that the

Scrutinize exercise

Interview artists from a local art co-op or community who have done commissioned work for clients. Discover any challenges or difficulties that arose in the process of creating public artwork. Can you use terms and ideas from Chapter 7 to untangle a many-sided debate? If you have no local access to artists, look for news coverage of similar difficulties.

sponsors of the statue need to decide whether they think that historical, iconic accuracy is more important than the visceral power gained from using the image from the well-remembered photograph. Do the sponsors have a stronger wish to honor all fallen 9/11 firefighters, or to remember that particular historical moment? Are the sponsors limited to just one statue? Surely New York City isn't limited to one statue to help honor and remember the heroic efforts of that day—and beyond. Could not one statue mark with iconic, personal accuracy the flag raising done by the individuals whose images were captured and catapulted around the world? And, another statue that uses iconic firefighter characteristics, yet symbolically honors a variety of people types, could recall other heroic work done that terrible day. You may recognize that simply being able to untangle some of the message threads and functions involved in a controversy may allow the participants to think clearly about their options.

If controversy about messages is one viable place to discover resources for doing informal analysis, then unexpected performance is another. Let's look there.

The movie *The Sixth Sense* arrived in theaters across America when few people had heard of the writer/director M. Night Shyamalan. Yet, *The Sixth Sense* was one of the top two movies of 1999, with a formal marketing budget from Hollywood Pictures and Spyglass Entertainment that was a small fraction of the amount spent on films such as *Star Wars Episode I: The Phantom Menace* and *Toy Story II.* What made this movie so popular in a very unexpected way? Most popular critics and commentators (and average audience members by word-of-mouth) would cite the surprise ending. Yet many films employ a surprise at the end of the movie. What made this one special?

The narrative analysis ideas from Chapter 6 will allow you to venture an educated estimation about "how" the extreme surprise was created. We know that nearly all films play with the difference between story^{g} (story given) and story^{c} (story constructed) elements. In order to tell *any* tale that is more than two hours long from more than a single perspective, you must encourage the audience to supply appropriate story^{c} material. Hence, after a period of time we become so practiced at the process that

Scrutinize exercise

Go back and re-read five or 10 popular reviews of *The Sixth Sense.* All of the reviewers will make some prominent mention of the surprise twist in the film. How many take the trouble to hint as to *how* the strategy unfolds? Now that you know one key element of the strategy, could you duplicate the *strategy* (not_the content or characters) in a radio spot narrative form? In a comic strip? In a short story? How is the story[g] different in each of those cases?

we don't have our mental "guard" up. Putting the pieces of story[g] together that the director has provided us becomes "second nature."

So when we see *very little* of the Bruce Willis character's wife in *The Sixth Sense,* no alarm bells go off. We are content to watch the bulk of the story[g] material devoted to "Dr. Malcolm Crowe" and to the little boy "Cole" and his mother. It makes narrative sense to us because of our extensive training in decoding Hollywood-style films that tend only to pay attention to one, two, or three characters (well, if you don't count Robert Altman's films) in the story[g] material.

So, M. Night Shyamalan used our movie audience training to conceal one of the best ending plot twists in recent memory (or so box office figures suggest). We were so busy creating the unfolding story[c] between the psychiatrist and his patient that we failed to notice the very few glimpses we were given of the wife character. Of course, had scenes with the wife character been more plentiful, the mounting story[g] clues about her husband's absence would have eventually tipped us off as to his condition.

Of course, a detailed analysis of *The Sixth Sense* would uncover many other attributes and tactics that helped make this movie a great box-office success. Nevertheless, using your quick, at-hand skills and insights in informal criticism, you can discover interesting dynamics within successful narratives dangled before unsuspecting movie audiences. (Perhaps you can discover the *lack of* success elements for horrible films as well.)

Several informal ways in which you can incorporate parts of your rhetorical theory language into your examination and understanding of messages (on the fly) in your media environment have been suggested. The more you use, develop, and hone your abilities as a maker (or audience for) messages, the greater the chance that you'll reach better than average decisions about the range of possibilities (inventional strategies) open to you.

When you are in a grocery store produce area, do you appreciate having many choices or would you be satisfied with only two choices? All too many people who make messages for large audiences seem to be satisfied with minimal choices rather than the bounty that could be available with a bit of critical work and awareness.

Let's move now from informal, on the fly analysis using the tools, insights, and terms available in other chapters. Our next pause will be in the area of intermediate criticism (more formal than informal, less serious and involved than with detailed academic criticism).

INTERMEDIATE RHETORICAL CRITICISM

Sometimes popular critics, reporters, language observers, teachers, or even academic rhetorical critics, take a quick but semi-detailed look at how language is operating, or how it seems to signal something to us about the condition of our culture. When this happens we should be pleased that someone is (if even offhandedly) paying attention to matters of language, meaning power, and rhetorical potential.

Below you'll find reprinted a column written many years ago by a reporter whose "beat" included cultural observation. After you read the column, we can discuss how he opens the possibility for intermediate criticism.

❁

History in 3 Volumes

Portland's 1990–91 phone directory reflects lifestyles, community growth

Spencer Heinz

As another new year nears, the time seems right to celebrate some big news in this town.

Portland has become a city with a three-volume phone book.

The 1990–91: It is not just something to stand on to reach the upper shelves.

It is a cultural treasure. It holds a lot of names. They range from Aaben, Phuo and Phong to Darlene's Cut-N-Strutt. Especially when placed alongside the single volume from 20 years back, this US West Direct triple set tells as much as history books about a city and its creatures.

In 1970, the listings under "Attorneys" covered five pages. That was before they could advertise. As freed-up marketers, they cover 65 pages today.

In 1970, the Yellow Pages had just two names listed under "Social Workers." The list today is 89.

In 1970, the Yellow Pages devoted a half page to "Burglar." They touch seven pages today.

In 1970, the Yellow Pages listed 10 malls or shopping centers. More than a couple dozen are there today.

"It really is a reflection of the growth of the community," says Karen Colby, market manager for US West Direct. "Business growth and residential growth."

On the surface, the White Pages simply lists the names from A through Z. Spending longer with the book, though; reveals other levels. For example, it turns out to contain some of the major food groups.

Good citizens go by the last names of Fish, Bass, Trout, Salmon, Apple, Berry, Peach, Pear, Pickle, Hamburger, Salt, Pepper, Vodka, Gin and so on.

But the full value of the book is not in that alone.

Neither is it totally in the 14 pages of hair-care shops that fill the space for "Beauty." Their names represent a remarkable hunt for ways to say new things about hair. The result includes Affair With Hair, A Flair For Hair, The Hair Affair and the Hair Barn. The Hair Depot, Hair Bender, The Hair Dr. and Hair Force One. Hair Else, Hair Hunters, Hair on Broadway, Hair on Burnside, Hair Today, The Hair Tree, the Hair Zoo, L'Hair-Itage and Red Hot Hair.

In pioneer times, when people carried Bowie knives, such a list did not exist.

The value of this book, then, is to show how things have changed.

In 1970, the phone book had a single listing for "Limousine." Today, there are five pages.

A half-page for "Guns" has gone to nearly three.

Two and one-half pages for "Locks" is up to 13 now.

Back then, "Alcoholism" was three listings: it covered just 2 inches. Today, six pages do the job.

"Apartments" has gone from two pages to five; more people know the single life.

In 1970, "Consultants" was not a consolidated listing. Today, it holds eight pages.

"Dentists"—from five pages to 30.

"Garbage"—from 2¼ pages to eight.

"Physicians"—10 pages then, 63 now.

"Retirement"—from one to 10.

"The trends in the Yellow Pages," says Colby at the phone company, "reflect the trends in the community: that the population is aging, and that people are spending more on entertainment and free-time activities. The Yellow Pages is a reflection of the community."

It goes on from A to Z: From Abortion and Abrasives to Yogurt, Youth and Zoos.

Finally, after all these years, Portland has reached the status of a triple-volume city with attendant rights and privileges.

That has to amount to something.
It amounts to as much as a history book.

In 30 paragraphs Spencer Heinz comes to a very important intermediate claim about a 1990–91 phone directory. Far from believing it merely a repository for phone numbers and business information, he claims that it may be a "history book." In other words, without benefit of editors, blind reviewers, JFA's, or any other technical analysis apparatus, he has taken his interpretation to another level (one we'll call an intermediate level of rhetorical criticism).

Rhetorical criticism is taking place at an intermediate level (even if the "critics" don't use that designation for themselves or their activity) if they:

1. Make an arguable claim (or claims) about human messages with which another person can reasonably disagree.
2. Give an explicit or implicit reason for holding the claim.
3. Leave allowance for other points of (differing) view.
4. Make an interpretation of their discoveries that suggest why they may be important.
5. Are willing to share their claims and reasoning with an audience in a printed message.[6]

Let's examine how Spencer Heinz does those things in a very rudimentary form. First, he does more than simply make random observations about the (then new) phone book. He takes the trouble to contrast its internal messages with a similar book from 20 years before. Hence, a portion of his intermediate analysis is done by building parallel contrasts between the two books from a number of different category markers (e.g., social workers, beauty, apartments, dentists).

In each of these cases, he implicitly or explicitly makes a "leap" of judgment. For instance, after a series of parallel comparisons, he calls in an "expert witness" from the phone company: " 'It really is a reflection of growth of the community,' says Karen Colby, market manager for US West Direct. 'Business growth and residential growth.' "[7] Thus he goes beyond mere comparisons of differences. He makes claims about the critical value those contrasts might warrant.

Yet, we must notice that most of his observations can serve as enthymemes (see Chapter 9 for details) as they seem to reason to as yet unstated conclusions. So when Heinz informs you that "In 1970, the Yellow Pages devoted a half page to 'Burglar.' They touch seven pages today" he leaves readers to draw their own conclusions about the status of crime in the community based on this shred of message evidence. Similarly, he seems to take us on a bit of a history lesson when he calls attorneys "freed-up marketers" or points to how hair was cut before the availability of hair salons.

Heinz goes yet another step further in his embryonic analysis: he makes some critical judgments about the *value* of what he's discovered. So words such as "history," "reflection," "status," and "treasure" pop up in his writing and description about the new phone books. He's clearly making some interpretations that go beyond even his point-for-point "finds" between the 70s and the 90s.

Finally, he fulfills the last mark of an intermediate critic in that he shares his work in a formal way; it's printed in the newspaper for many to read. People could, if they so wished, take exception to his observations. They could write to his newspaper. They could call him on the phone (if they could find him in the book!). They could catch him on a downtown sidewalk and engage him in a spirited conversation. Did any of these things happen? (Well, we could check the letters to the editor for any groundswell of response, but the other possibilities might leave us out of luck.)[8] Nonetheless, because his observations and rudimentary arguments were printed in a tangible message source, we can still talk about them today. He meets the requirement to offer his interpretations to a larger audience in a tangible way.

Spencer Heinz, then, is "guilty" of writing a quick, intermediate form of rhetorical criticism. His form is not long. His rationale is not extensive. His argument structure is limited. His set up and review of other research is non-existent. Yet, he is accomplishing many of the same things at a much more plain level as we see professional, academic critics accomplish. It would be unfair to officially call Heinz a rhetorical critic, as he might well point out that he (as a newspaper feature writer) never intended to do "rhetorical criticism" in the first place. Yet, he helps us realize that *many* cultural observers, in a very informal way, reach in the direction of trying to find more than surface meaning in cultural message artifacts.

Let's jump from an updated phone book to some intermediate rhetorical analysis of visual, statistical, and material messages in Japan.

Quentin Hardy, a reporter for the *Wall Street Journal,* explains to his readers that economic experts need to find message value in out-of-the-ordinary economic indicators. In rapid order, he recounts how various economic analysts are using unconventional message information to decide whether or not Japan has emerged from an economic downturn:

Scrutinize exercise

Can you find at least three other instances in the brief article in which Heinz makes a clear claim about what his observations reveal? Do you agree with his interpretations (or that of others he cites)? Why? Can you think of alternative explanations for some of the changes he thinks he's discovered? (What if US West Direct had just doubled the size of their phone book sales staff in 1989?)

"Investors here want proof that Japan's long economic downturn is over. Problem is, lots of the official yardsticks, such as consumer prices and gross domestic product, are too slow and unreliable to suit private analysts."[9]

Although we must make allowances for the rules of a reporter being in force (rather than a feature columnist such as Spencer Heinz), we find Hardy reaching out to various "sub-critics" (research assistants?) to establish his case. So he finds one economic analyst looking at cab ridership, another at sales of bikinis, another at a baseball team's success, yet another the visual check of the speed of trucks driving (full = slow, empty = fast). In each case, including a "garbage gauge" (more garbage = more purchases), he suggests a level of plausibility problem for some of the "critics" of Japan's economy: "The [baseball] Giants are Japan's most popular team, she [a Bank of Tokyo analyst] notes, so their victory means more celebrations. 'Makes more sense than bikinis,' she says.' "

His lead in the journalistic story, however, is the thing that marks him as a real (if reluctant) intermediate critic: "How's Japan doing? Pretty well: Trucks are slower, it's hard to get a cab, and skin is in. Now all that is needed is more garbage."

Let's see how he stacks up against our five markers of an intermediate critic:

1. Make an arguable claim (or claims) about human messages with which another person can reasonably disagree.

   Hardy claims that the 1994 Japanese economy is on the rebound.

2. Give an explicit or implicit reason for holding the claim.

   He cites five different possible message indicators that have bearing on his claim (four of five support the claim).

3. Leave allowance for other points of view.

   Internally he certainly suggests that not all message indicators (e.g., the bikini index) are valid; externally he at least hints that even these attempts may be less than highly reliable; he indicates pressure: "investors want proof." He indicates strategy "shortcuts": "they look for ways to beat the outdated data." He suggests that some of the indicators may "sound like rubbish." He gives ample reason to disbelieve many of the claims.

4. Make an interpretation of their discoveries that suggest why they may be important.

   Again, the indicated desperation for information is noted. The length of Japan's commercial trouble is noted: "long economic downturn."

5. Be willing to share claims and reasoning with an audience.

   His article appears on the first page of a prominent section of a well-regarded newspaper.

Scrutinize exercise

If you were to measure or gauge the "health" of your campus, what are some untraditional markers of that good status (or lack thereof) that you might look for if you wished to be a non-traditional intermediate critic of campus "health"? Would it make any difference if you were seeking to discern the "wealth" of the campus instead of its "health"? How about the "pace" of your campus? What of the "charm"? How would you build your case and seek your evidence support? Where would you make your results public?

Does all of this make Quentin Hardy an intermediate rhetorical critic? In some ways, yes. Even though his reporter's tongue is deep in his cheek with puns throughout the article (and the headline is a touch non-serious: "If the Poky Truck Driver Wears a Bikini, Good Times are Here"), he is addressing how serious economic professionals are grasping for meaning "straws" in an attempt to gauge the status of a major world economy for their clients. Some articles you may find about people who do deep investment (exploitation?)[10] in un- or underdeveloped countries will indicate that similar "real world" indicators are used to gauge valid investments.

We've seen then that different forms of casual analysis can take place in precincts of life far from careful, systematic academic rhetorical analysis. Yet we can see (especially with intermediate criticism) that even casual, on-the-fly criticism has *some* connections with deeper, more thoughtful criticism. Informal criticism (such as our discussion of critique of *The Sixth Sense* or of classified car ads) is useful, but fails to bring the emerging criticism to the level of making defendable claims or the level of offering the conclusions to any sort of an audience who might then disagree.

Intermediate criticism, while still unconventional, moves in the direction of "making a case." Elementary, uncomplicated claims are made which are presented for approval or disapproval, acceptance or rejection based on the quick reasoning offered in the "analysis." Disagreement is assumed or hinted at in such a way as to acknowledge that other conclusions could be reached. Nevertheless, the writer asks the reader to participate in a quasi-analytic reasoning process about messages that form a part of human communication. That sort of analytic stance toward messages offered to audiences should be recognized and encouraged. We should not, however, equate such informal criticism as true, systematic criticism. So we need now to shift our attention to a brief description of what counts as systematic, meaningful rhetorical criticism as we make our way toward you writing in this tradition of analysis.

REAL RHETORICAL CRITICISM

To start the rookie process of writing rhetorical criticism, we must briefly note the requirements for actual practicing rhetorical critics as we discussed in Chapter 3. Academic rhetorical critics, you'll remember, start in a "place" not all that different from what we've described earlier as informal criticism. Suzanne Daughton notices a curious formal structure in *Groundhog Day* for which she has no immediate explanation,[11] Scult, McGee, and Kuntz were curious about the cultural narrative origins of the main story that sustained power taken by English kings,[12] and Pauley was curious about the power of political messages from the Truman presidency concerning civil rights.[13] In these cases the scholars involved began with something curious that caught their attention. Their curiosity, however, went far beyond merely turning it over in their mind for pleasure, distraction, or quick analysis. Instead they turned their attention to two tasks that form the next layer or steps in a process that took them (and will take you) toward writing serious criticism.

The next steps are to check on related research and to see if the question(s) raised by initial curiosity are worth spending substantial time, effort, and resources. Scholars such as Daughton, Scult et al., and Pauley comb their minds for related research (remember rhetoricians carry many different efforts of rhetorical criticism around with them in their heads in the same way a geologist knows about many different research efforts on different kinds of rock formations). Next, they would likely investigate all of the likely journals and books they could find that might carry primary or related research to the topic area suggested by their initial curiosity. Useful material found in this research could eventually help in building a strong justification for study (JFS) or help in the formulation of a solid method of analysis. We'll talk in a while about how you also can do these initial steps.

A related initial activity would be to discover any materials that help demonstrate the value, importance, or mystery of the study launched by the extension and development of the original curiosity.

Many things you discover in this part of your initial research could become part of an external JFS or a justification for artifact (JFA) in the set-up portion of your rhetorical analysis. So, for instance, if you were taking Spencer Heinz's intermediate analysis as a starting point for more serious analysis, one of your tasks would be to check any other scholars who had carefully examined phone books as a cultural message artifact. Another would be to document in a formal way the reach, power, exposure, or use held by phone books as wide-reaching, important messages in our culture. Since you are here involved in serious, systematic criticism, you would need to argue for your case by presenting evidence that the study would contribute to what we need to know about powerful cultural messages, and that you indeed have your critical focus on a powerful cultural message artifact. Remember, a rhetorical critic (much like many other members of a university community) is one of the few characters in our culture who are actually given *time* as a resource.

If you stop and think about it, human culture has given many professors time (of which almost no other profession has "enough") and expects them to do good things with it. Whereas political campaign workers, businesspeople, day laborers, and athletes are provided some time, university professors are some of the only people in the culture who are given substantial time to ponder, wonder, and research important matters. Giving professors time to think (including rhetorical critics) is a good thing because the ideas, innovations, and insights at which they arrive really are helpful to the rest of the culture. One of a thinking professor's responsibilities, then, is to establish solid foundations for useful studies. Finding the evidence for solid claims about messages under investigation is key in this process.

So, one of the things we see emerging as we move toward more serious, more valuable rhetorical criticism is the requirement that you create a sustained, compelling argument. Argument, in this case, is a very good thing.

Finding impressive evidence for the power or influence of your artifact(s) and building your case for the necessity for doing the research are two cornerstones of creating convincing reasons as to why you should do the research and why others should be interested to read the finished research.

After these initial steps, your next focus is on creating your research question and your actual steps of analysis. To those items we now turn.

Creating a solid research question is a challenging task. You must find the essence of what you seek in the rhetorical analysis and be able to place that in a clear, concise question that can be answered, but still have room for honest disagreement. Condit's research question on press coverage of reproductive technology was something like: What patterns of alliance and agreement do we see in news stories about reproductive technology advancements? And, what do any discovered patterns tell us about how power is used in a literate, affluent culture? (See Chapter 9.) Ivie's seeming question was: What are the sources of rhetorical invention that have undermined efforts so far to transcend the choice between chauvinism and pacifism in the messages of three Cold War idealists? (See Chapter 10.) Daughton's FDR question likely was: How did FDR deal with the dilemma of simultaneously trying to calm and activate the American people in his first inaugural address during the Great American Depression? (See Chapter 3.) Cloud's question seemed to be: How do media narrative biographies serve as a hegemonic tool to obscure tangible economic dislocation in a nation?[14] (See Chapter 9.) Olson wanted to find out: How do visual icons operate to create persuasion in political communication?[15] (See Chapter 7.) In each case the critic is searching for a response or answer to the source of their original curiosity about the message(s) involved. Later, in the workshop portion of this chapter, we'll ponder what makes a useful research question.

After finding a high-quality research question, the rhetorical critic needs to build a method (or set of analysis steps) that will help the investigation and answer (or solve) the research question.

We should note here that rhetorical critics could have very different scholarly motives for building a set of interpretive steps and for seeking the essence of the message(s) under scrutiny. One set of critics could be most interested in learning how a significant message operated in human experience and history. So, for instance, when Ronald Carpenter investigates the rhetoric of narrative in the writings of Admiral Mahan, his primary motive seems to be gauging the means and impact of a historian's writing on the military leaders of Japan prior to World War II and the attack on Pearl Harbor. Many solid pieces of rhetorical criticism move in exactly this direction.

On the other hand, some critics investigate messages in order to facilitate the building of rhetorical theory. For instance, John Lucaites goes out of his way in an analysis to demonstrate that the artifact he investigates (*Let Us Now Praise Famous Men*) was *not* a particularly powerful message upon its initial release.[16] Instead, he uses the compelling dynamics of the photos in Agee and Evan's book as a case example to better develop a rhetorical theory that addresses visual cultural persuasion. So, the motive of a rhetorical critic can be to best understand the contextual message sensation created by the artifact(s), or to use the study as a case example so as to build better, more useful, more insightful rhetorical theory (or both!).

Finding the right method steps is an objective or goal that has many different destinations. Among the possible routes open to a rhetorical critic are to build a new set of method steps, to borrow and revamp a set of existing method steps, or to combine two different sets of analysis steps as a method. In any of those cases the critic seeks to find or create the set of analysis devices that will allow her or him to answer the research question by seeking message analysis procedures that uncover the key dynamics operating in the message(s) artifact(s). Often critics will build on previous work (their own or related work of other critics) to select or design these steps of analysis, or the method.

So, critics build on their initial, unsolved curiosity about the cultural power of a message or set of messages. A critic then roughly follows the progression of analysis we've discussed. They are then prepared to actually perform the analysis and write about important discoveries and insights gained. A rhetorical critic so motivated goes about the strenuous work of building a JFS, finding the evidence that will support a strong JFA, discerning the core interest of investigation to construct a valuable research question, and designing a method (set of analysis steps) that will allow the analysis to proceed.

Most critics find that various aspects of each of these rhetorical criticism set-up elements may be subject to change and adaptation in the process

FIGURE 4.1 **Standard Rhetorical Criticism Setup Elements**

Source: Pierce Communication.

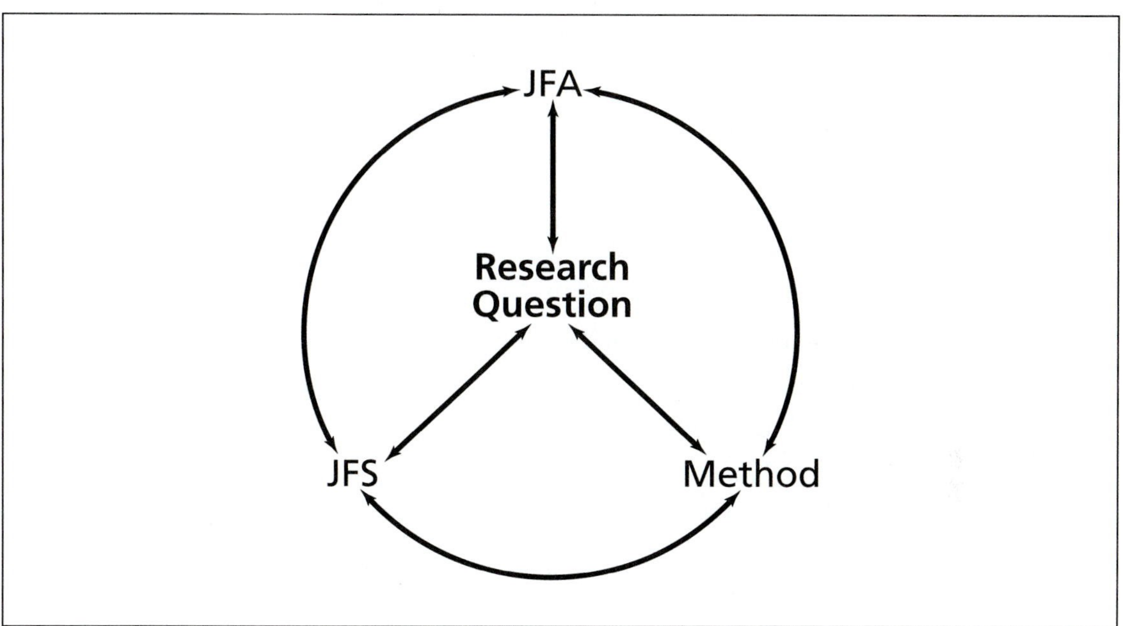

of analysis. Studies usually become more focused and stronger as the actual analysis goes forward because the critic may discover a better step of analysis, an even more compelling piece of JFA evidence, or an even more beneficial research question. So, the process is not necessarily one of being in lock step with the steps outlined earlier. Positive change, adaptation, and improvement are a regular part of any analysis project.

Your finished initial portion to an essay of rhetorical criticism will have four interlocking parts that mesh with each other to support and sustain your arguments presented later in your actual analysis and report of discoveries. Figure 4.1 shows these parts and their interaction.[17]

As you can see, the three areas of setup for a rhetorical criticism analysis influence one another. In each case the Research Question depends on the setup elements for its scope, authenticity, do-ability, and interest-level.

Let's talk first about where you as a novice, undergraduate rhetorical critic will want to start in building these set-up items.

After you think about an initial area of interest or message curiosity, (from TV news, political campaign speeches, political cartoons, newspaper editorials, persuasive websites, billboards, or movies), begin work on your Research Question and on the JFA section of your paper. We'll start first with your Research Question.

BUILDING YOUR RESEARCH QUESTION

A good rhetorical criticism Research Question is focused, doable, and interesting (and hasn't been answered before). To make your research question have all of those qualities, notice how your question interacts with the other three setup areas as shown in Figure 4.1.

A focused Research Question will make sure you have asked a question that will yield genuine tangible insights available from careful analysis of message characteristics. Let's look at four potential Research Questions and ask if they are focused.

1. Is *Lord of the Rings* a powerful movie?
2. Do politicians lie in their speeches?
3. What narrative characteristics made Admiral Mahan's book compelling to Japanese military leaders?
4. What are the means by which Ross Perot's messages of alternative political perspectives invited political reconsideration by voters?

You should be able to see a strong contrast in questions 1 and 2 compared to questions 3 and 4. The first question may be headed in the right direction because it seeks to analyze an important and influential message in our culture. Yet, it seems much too broad and vague. We would have to agree on what makes a movie powerful (probably with particular emphasis on that kind of movie) to even begin to pose and answer that question. While we would have plenty of room for disagreement with others, the question as it currently stands is just too indefinite to really help your analysis. You might be able to use items *related to* this question *later* in your JFA section, but for right now it would be a nightmare to build a method or JFS that would "hold" this huge question. You could, however, revamp the question.

Rather than ask a vague question about an undefined idea of "power" in the movie, why not go with something that sparked curiosity for you when you saw it the first (or twelfth) time? Focusing into a specific area that seems curious, or different, or inconsistent will help a great deal in creating a much stronger Research Question. So let's suppose that you noticed an interesting pattern in which *some* characters had hats (or other headgear) on in key scenes in the movie. Your new and improved Research Question might then become something like: What purpose do hats and other headgear serve in pivotal decision scenes in *Lord of the Rings?* While this question may or may not prove useful in the long run, it *is* very focused. It gives you a starting point and convergence point for selecting parts of a larger artifact and for possibly building a method of analysis.

The second question (Do politicians lie in their speeches?) also suffers from being too broad, but its most severe difficulty is elsewhere. Lying is probably easier to define (and perhaps to detect) in speeches than finding "power" in a movie might be. Nonetheless, think of the sheer scope of the current question. If properly addressed, you are actually asking (as currently stated) about all politicians, in all times, in all places in human history. Whew! Do you really want to take on a project that size?

Moreover, the history of finding some politicians caught in lies and others not suggests that the "do" portion of the Research Question is the weak link of the question. The most likely answer is yes *and* no (depending on the politician and circumstance in question). A number of changes will get us back on track.

Suppose we try, "How do state politicians in Florida lie when addressing state economic forecasts since 1996?" This more specific and focused question offers a number of improvements. By moving from a "do" question to a "how" question we've returned the focus back to specific messages and tactics we may find within them. Likewise, by specifying the state, the government level, the years, and a topic of concern, we have allowed a much more specific focus on items that can be examined and analyzed.

Of course, we would have to have prior evidence that politicians in a Florida might lie. Hence, the predicted interaction with your JFA and JFS sections would need to be strong and active.

Research Questions 3 and 4 are, of course, questions taken from existing, published studies.[18] They are focused, doable, interesting questions that served to help us discover elements and aspects about persuasive message use that we did not know before.

How can we make your Research Question a doable question? A doable Research Question will be able to be achieved given the resources, skill, and time you have available to propose, research, analyze, and write your study. Let's look at four potential Research Questions and ask if they are doable.

1. Does the hegemonic apologia on foreign policy in President Clinton's first State of the Union address indicate a weakening of the executive branch?

2. How did beverage ads during football bowl game broadcasts from 1998 to 2002 use indexical images to create narrative closure?

3. What function did archetypal metaphors serve in declaration speeches by major party candidates in the 2000 primaries?

4. How do haunted house films help audiences overcome feelings of cultural anomie and disorientation?

Research Questions 1 and 2 from this list are not doable simply because of degree of difficulty. You might be perfectly able (with a few key changes) to tackle these questions in a senior-level seminar class after you've had much more experience in analysis and writing. You might try to "slim down" either one of these questions to make them workable for you now. The question: "Does the hegemonic apologia on foreign policy in President Clinton's first State of the Union address indicate a weakening of the executive branch?" could be changed to: "How did President Clinton frame his foreign policy claims in his first State of the Union address?" Such a change, if supported with strong JFA and JFS and method sections, could become a strong rhetorical analysis project.

The second Research Question also assumes substantial background and experience in criticism; a talented, resourceful undergraduate could do it after some previous experience in analysis. Even then, however, it has some other distinct problems. Assuming you know, and could work out, all of the technical, analysis method, and critical perspectives challenges of answering this Research Question, you would still face an incredible task of collecting tapes and having time to watch them (let alone do thorough analysis). Let's see, a dozen bowl games times five years (60 games), times three hours each (180 hours) gives you the raw viewing time. Assuming you have access to such a tape or digital record of the games (maybe you've got an aunt and uncle who are football addicts), you would still have to have a sturdy remote and an iron bladder to endure the time necessary to examine the artifacts—even at a shallow level.

If you have a real interest in the *component parts* of the original research question, go for a more modest, doable range of analysis in your Research Question: "How did beverage ads during the 2001 Fiesta Bowl use indexical images to create narrative closure?" A Research Question of this type, when supported by a solid JFA, JFS, and method, will help you far more than one that is too wide-ranging.

Research Question 3 ("What function did archetypal metaphors serve in declaration speeches by major party candidates in the 2000 primaries?") is doable assuming you have access to legitimate transcripts or tapes (or both) of the speeches under consideration. Your other setup items would need to fit well and provide mutual support.

The final research question (Research Question 4) is from an existing study and fits all of the conditions we've been noting.[19]

One quick way to determine the value of your research question concerns prior research. Research that revolves around rhetorical criticism assumes that new ideas, approaches, and topics are being addressed. If someone else has already done an outstanding job on the specific topic you have in mind, you or I would be a bit foolish if we proposed doing it over again (unless we can do it better). Therefore, a solid JFS section of your paper (which we'll address later) should discover if previous research has already accomplished your proposed analysis.

Finally, if your Research Question is focused and doable (to your level of skill, preparation, and time limits), we must ask if it is interesting. The degree to which a Research Question is interesting to you is critical to the success of your research analysis and writing. You should have a genuine interest in discovering how a particular message or set of messages worked powerfully in our culture. If, on reflection, you have no such interest, you might need to reconsider your major or career plans. People who do well in the field of communication typically have a natural curiosity for human communication. That natural curiosity often prompts us to look deeper into public messages and their use in the first place.

If you have a number of messages, types of messages, or communication situations that have provoked your curiosity (or anger, zeal, etc.), then you will be fine when it comes to picking an analysis project. Go with your strong interests. Take something that has rung your intellectual bell in other chapters or exercises or projects and run with it. Realize, however, that personal excitement and curiosity (while important for crafting a solid Research Question) are not enough to carry the day in terms of an interesting Research Question. You must convince others that they should also be interested. You must make a convincing argument to others that your study and analysis are useful and necessary. For that we turn to developing your JFA section.

BUILDING YOUR JFA

The JFA section allows you to present evidence to the reader of your research paper that messages you have selected for analysis are worthy. A strong JFA section will gather and briefly discuss all of the pertinent reasons that the messages (or portions thereof) you will analyze are important. You can do so by presenting claims and evidence for the importance, influence, or significance of the message(s) you picked to analyze.

To show the importance of your selected messages, you might briefly address the historical moment involved as Daughton did with her study of FDR's speech in 1931.[20] (See Chapter 3.) Your selected message might be highly decorated with awards and honors, or highly successful in making money as Frentz and Rushing argued about the movie *Titanic*.[21] You might suggest that the selected artifacts are representative of a larger set of important messages, as did Mumby and Spitzack when they examined metaphors in news stories about politics.[22] In any case this third of your support triangle of setup material (the JFA) is the section that you are most capable of researching and writing as a beginning student of rhetorical criticism.

You are searching for valid *evidence* that your selected messages reached huge numbers of people, or used revolutionary message techniques, or created an unexpected reaction on the part of some audiences, or sold ancillary products, or reached a small but influential type of audience.

Sometimes JFA and JFS sections or material blend. Below I've put an example of evidence-based claims one of my colleagues used in his analysis of Rush Limbaugh. You can begin to see some of the range of possibilities when finding claims that when put together can form a strong JFA section to your research paper.

"Limbaugh is popular. Twenty million listen to Limbaugh's radio talk show. Three hundred and forty thousand subscribe to his newsletter. His books, *The Way Things Ought to Be* and *See, I Told You So* are best sellers. Limbaugh is [a] hero to people whose beliefs coincide with his."[23]

BUILDING YOUR JFS

Your JFS (justification for study) section will consist of pertinent historical or context background information and previous relevant studies from other rhetorical critics. You should seek the best quality sources you can find that will help you build a solid JFS section. Here your Research Question will be of great influence or aid. Your Research Question will guide you concerning whether we need to know more about the rhetor, the tactics within the message, the historical events surrounding the message, or the legacy of changes in the message.

In any of those possibilities (or others), you need to make cohesive claims supported by clear evidence.

So, if you claim that a certain mass protest was pivotal in revealing the political weakness of an influential senator, you'll need to find compelling evidence that the protest took place under the conditions reported by other scholars who have looked into the situation. You will need evidence that the senator in question was in fact influential (money raised? legislation passed? holder of important senate committee chair?). You will need evidence that the perceived weakness was tangible and influential (lower poll ratings? loss of election?). If those sorts of items are *not* important to your case, do not include them. If they are, work from primary sources (whenever possible) and from the best-related scholars in the area of interest.

Next, for a solid JFS, you will need to find other rhetorical scholars who have done related investigations. Rhetorical critics (as seen from articles available in other chapters) cite relevant studies that have preceded their study. You need to do the same. Do you want to do an analysis of the animated feature movie *Chicken Run?* Then you need to find other rhetorical scholars who have done analysis about animated comedy films that feature evil farmers and oppressed chickens. What if you find no scholar who has done analysis on other feature animated films about chickens and their oppressors? Then you'll need to come as close as possible.

Since *Chicken Run* is a message created in narrative form and is a feature animated film about agri-business, you need to find other studies that match significant portions of that description. Can you find other rhetorical analysis of animated films (concerning many other topics)? Can you find other rhetorical analysis of narrative tactics in feature films? Can you discover other pertinent studies about persuasion dealing with agri-business (even if about speeches or newspapers or barn art)?

Your task, then, is to find the most compelling, helpful, insightful research available that is close to your own selected artifacts and interests. You then weave brief descriptions about that research and key discoveries into your JFS section.

The final segment of your set-up items will be your description of the method steps you intend to use in your analysis.

BUILDING YOUR METHOD SECTION

Your method section will consist of a description of your steps of analysis combined with any background, history, or theory connections that would help your explanation of how you intend to accomplish your actual analysis. Rhetorical critics can create whole new methods of analysis, borrow a method from another critic/theorist and use it for their current analysis, or create a hybrid method by combining the steps of analysis from two or more other critic/theorists.

As an apprentice critic, you will most likely borrow a method from an existing critic, or you may adjust and adapt a method from one or more other critics. Your instructor will be of great help in making quality decisions about which method may best serve your needs.

Your borrowed, or adapted, method must at minimum give you a set of analysis steps, perspectives, and tools that will allow you to thoroughly examine and identify characteristics of the message(s) under investigation so that you can successfully respond to your research question.

In the workshop section of this chapter, you'll be able to see how a scholar specifies a rhetorical research method.

DOING YOUR ANALYSIS

Now that you have successfully done your groundwork for the analysis project by researching and writing your Research Question, JFA section, JFS section, and method section, you are ready to actually perform the analysis you addressed in your method section.

This part of your project will take the greatest amount of time. After you have all of the necessary message artifacts (transcripts, tapes, magazine

CHART 4.1

Sample Narrative Research Entry	
Speaker	Dawn Kennedy
Date of speech	17 June 1997
Story in speech sequence	First
Main character	Walter Morose
Secondary character	Timmy Blank (Walter's youngest son)
Secondary character	Glen Dull (Walter's oldest son)
Primary action in story[g]	Walter gives a bike to Timmy but not to Glen.
Secondary action in story[g]	Glen runs away from home.
Purpose of the story in the speech	To caution audience members

pages, DVDs, photos, etc.) gathered, you need to start your systematic analysis based on the steps of analysis you set up as your method.

As you start your analysis, be sure to have a system for keeping track of your discoveries or insights. You may wish to keep separate folders, files, notebooks, palm files, laptop files, or piles so as to keep an effective record of what you find in each of your analysis steps. Haphazard record keeping in this stage of analysis can come back to haunt you later if you are working against a time deadline.

For instance, if your are doing a narrative analysis of stories told by commencement speakers over the last 10 years at your college or university, you'll want a separate file (hardcopy or cyberfile) for each of the speakers. Then, you will need to keep track of your results as you examine each pertinent element that you've specified in your method. So, if you are keeping track of characters in each story and the function of the story in the speech by examining primary and secondary actions in each story, your entry for one story in one speech by one of the rhetors might look something like the one above (see Chart 4.1).

This chart, of course, does not count as analysis (you've not yet made any claims about how meaning is created in the speeches using narrative). It could stand, however, as the second or third step of your method. After you had collected all of the materials pertinent to your analysis from transcripts of each speech, you could begin the process of looking for patterns between and among the speeches. At that point your specified method steps would address actual propositions of analysis. For instance, do male characters in the speech narratives show up more often as primary or secondary characters? (You would have given definitions of who or what counts as a primary and secondary character in your JFS section of your paper by employing definitions drawn from previous research.) Or, how often is the purpose of the story to warn the audience compared to those stories designed to inspire and motivate audience members? (Again, your definitions and recognition markers for such categories would have been previously established in your JFS section.)

DESCRIBING YOUR ANALYSIS DISCOVERIES

Once you have used your method steps to accomplish your analysis, you need to explain what you have discovered in your study. You need to explain how and why your research question has been answered. Present any interesting insights that you've developed or encountered. You should also suggest where the discoveries of your research might now lead us in related research.

Let's look at two examples.

Lessl notes at the end of his study of stories that spread the Galileo legend signaled a *specific use* of the narrative for purposes of establishing a "perpetual" conflict situation:

> Perhaps the most suggestive feature of these stories [about Galileo and his "battle" with religion] is their tendency to reflect the master narrative of "warfare between science and religion" that has been such a prominent feature of scientific rhetoric during the past century.

Lessl notes that in the mid- to late-nineteenth century, "science" was one of several "voices" or groups vying for money and support:

> By the middle of the nineteenth century scientific growth could no longer be sustained by efforts of isolated amateurs. . . . Science had outgrown this cradle [of gentlemen scientists who "dabbled"]. It needed the wealth and ideological support of institutions that were specifically tailored to meet the needs of organized laboratory research. This meant universities that were allied with the interests of industry and secular governments. It also meant that advocates would need to foster an ideology that could justify the gradual usurpation of longstanding religious claims to authority in the education marketplace.
>
> An institutional transformation of such proportions requires a rhetoric that is similarly daring; thus the warfare narratives that spill across the pages of [Andrew Dickson] White's book [*History of the Warfare of Science with Theology,* 1976]. White constructs a historical vision of science as a noble but poorly understood activity that struggled for millennia against ecclesiastical interference and popular religious superstition before at last emerging triumphant in his own day. Like every other history constructed under the spell of powerful vested interests, this view had to be coerced from the historical record.[24]

So, Lessl argues for his discovery that perhaps a simple folktale about Galileo is not so simple after all. Perhaps "simple" folktales—and more specifically their use, by groups who wish to change the "formula" for funding and support from institutions such as universities—can tell us something about how stories are used in cultural competition for resources.

Lessl's discoveries are valuable information, of course, for all who have an interest in philosophical, economic, and support "splits" between scientists and other academic groups. His insights, however, are equally useful for those who want to know how stories (even small, simple ones) can wield great power in helping to frame cultural debate.

In a like manner, you need to help readers understand the real substance of your discoveries. Let's look at one more example of a critic specifying research discoveries. Harmeet Sawhney found a powerful connection between metaphor labels for communication technology and the eventual uses to which that technology was put.[25] His research indicates that often people who create powerful technology don't really know what to do with it and can't really anticipate how it will be used by large groups of people. This was true of the telegraph and telephone, true of radio and television, and continues to be true of computers and the Internet. Whereas Sawhney reports that AT&T once understood radio broadcasting as a "Phone Booth of the Air" (298), he digs deeply into whether we are well served by the metaphor of "the information superhighway":

> The accuracy of our forecasts about new technologies depends on our ability to detect new "liberties of action." This task is extremely difficult because we have to think within a conceptual vacuum. Even though we have no choice but to use metaphors based on the past to understand the future, we have to realize that these metaphors may have to be abandoned as the future reveals itself. The initial metaphors basically function as provisional hypotheses which can be held only as long as the facts permit. (300)

And:

> The "information superhighway" metaphor is perhaps one such construct [that tries very hard to describe the future by language from the past]. This metaphor does not necessarily capture the essence of what the future will ultimately be but merely provides a framework which we can relate to. Once we get a better understanding of the phenomenon we should be willing to abandon it if that is necessary. (301)

So, Sawhney reports to us that we should know that metaphors *will be* used when grappling with how to use, understand, and implement new things (whether technology, relationship styles, etc.). Therefore, with the resources presented by his research insight on metaphors (signaled in the title of his article where he depicts metaphors as "midwives"), we can make better plans about how to use language when we are confronted with new ways of doing life activities. We can also see some of the missteps taken by individuals and huge corporations in the past due to reliance on metaphors that turned out to be inaccurate.

Similarly, you need to both relate to your reader the essence of your critical research discoveries and suggest ways that such an awareness might make human communication processes and habits better.

We will now move into the workshop portion of this chapter in order to learn how to build a rhetorical criticism research proposal and how to initiate an actual project of rhetorical criticism.

Having seen other rhetorical critics at work (in other chapters or from class assigned readings), figuring out how to best analyze important cultural messages, you can now follow in those footsteps to discover your own talents and skills as a rookie rhetorical critic. The following workshop will provide you the tools to do just that.

In this Chapter 4 workshop, we will probe many of the concepts you discovered in this chapter. First, we will examine several possible research questions and ask if they are worth pursuing. Then, we will work on a step-by-step basis to first create a proposal paper for a rhetorical criticism project. That project proposal will serve as the foundation for your own research paper in which you become a rhetorical critic.

DEVELOPING A RESEARCH QUESTION

Remember that if the research question is *focused* it will yield genuine tangible insights available from careful analysis of message characteristics; if it is *doable* you'll be able accomplish the research with the resources, skill, and time *you* have available; and, if it is *interesting* it will pose and answer a question about human messages that will better our current understanding of communication processes and characteristics.

On the next page you'll find a dozen possible research questions to rate.

Discuss how you came to your conclusions. Make sure that the question cannot be answered in one word (for instance, the *Little Mermaid* question would be much better with a "how did" than just a "did"). Could you make minor changes and salvage any of these questions?

BUILDING A RHETORICAL CRITICISM PAPER PROPOSAL

In this workshop you will build the core parts of a rhetorical criticism analysis paper. You will be gathering and writing initial parts that will later be enlarged and enhanced to become the setup items in your study. You will write the following information as separate elements (for right now); some will be single words or phrases, but other sections of the proposal will be several pages long. At the end you will have specified your critical area of research interest, your artifact(s), your JFA, some core JFS studies, your research question, review of published scholarly materials, and your proposed method steps of analysis.

I. Critical area of research interest:

For this part of your proposal you need only one or two or several words. You specify *metaphors,* or *narrative,* or *presidential speeches,* or *visual persuasion,* or *language* and *ideology,* or similar areas of research interest as your base of analysis. If you know a specific sub-area (e.g., *archetypal metaphors,* or *visual synecdoches in* advertisements), you may add that designation.

	Ratings: Yes, No, Maybe		
Possible Research Question	**Focused**	**Doable**	**Interesting**
Did Bob Dole make wise use of narrative fidelity in his 1996 campaign?			
Which visual metaphors were most often used by political cartoonists to characterize actions and decisions made by the U.S. Congress in the past decade?			
What are the ideological functions of foundation narratives in large multinational companies?			
Did *mise en scene* contribute to important action events in the film *The Little Mermaid?*			
How do television narratives hinder our understanding of economic conditions?			
Did the new Ivory soap ad increase soap sales?			
What is the central action identified in narratives offered by print media concerning Colin Powell's possible run for a presidential nomination?			
How do presidents use metaphors during economic hard times?			
What are the persuasive functions of the metaphoric clusters in popular press coverage of American hostages?			
Do sermons use too many narratives to make theological points?			
How does clothing enhance the ethos of advocate spokespeople interviewed on TV news?			
How do editing techniques focus attention on character contrast in the film *Fargo?*			

II. Artifacts:

Here you need to specify the type, range, characteristics, and location of your artifacts. To make sure that you actually have access to the artifacts, it is helpful to make the first part of this entry as a bibliographical citation. If you were going to investigate editing tactics in influential sitcoms, you might specify:

Seinfeld. NBC. 23 May 1991; 21 Sept. 1995; 10 April 1997

Or, if you were going to investigate visual metaphors in ads in women's magazines, you might specify:

Cosmopolitan May; June; July 2001

Ladies Home Journal May; June; July 2001

Seventeen May; June; July 2001

Or, if you were going to investigate epideictic strategies in Rudolph Giuliani's speech to the United Nations, you might specify:

Giuliani, Rudolph W. "Eradication of Terrorism." *Vital Speeches of the Day* 68 (15 Oct. 2001): 3–6

III. JFA (Justification for Artifact):

Here you need to specify initial evidence that demonstrates the cultural power of your selected artifact or artifacts. You will eventually add to this material in your final paper, but for now you need two or three pieces of evidence that show the cultural influence or impact of your selected artifacts.

So, if you were going to investigate character depiction in animated feature films, you might specify:

Chicken Run earned $17.5 million in its first weekend release in America. The film had earned $50 million after two weeks in American theaters. It also earned almost 4 million pounds in England (£3.848m) in its opening weekend there (Internet Movie Database. <http://us.imdb.com/Business?0120630)>).

Or, if you were going to investigate press coverage of Michael Jordan's retirement announcement, you might specify:

Jordan's retirement press conference was carried by two of the three major networks, plus CNN, ESPN, and ESPN2. In contrast, Magic Johnson's 1991 retirement press conference was viewed over only one cable network: ESPN. CNN flipped between Jordan and Boris Yeltsin in Moscow, who was speaking for the first time since putting down the Russian revolt (Heisler 1). NBC anchor Tom Brokaw was at the press conference instead of covering the crisis in Moscow (Weir 2).[26]

Heisler, Mark. "Commentary; spotlight was too much for Jordan." *Los Angeles Times* 7 Oct. 1993: C1. Online. *Lexis-Nexis Academic Universe.* 9 Apr. 2000.

Weir, Tom. "'Goodbye to the Game'; Michael Jordan, One of a Kind, Retires." *USA Today* 7 Oct. 1993: 1A. Online. *Lexis-Nexis Academic Universe.* 9 Apr. 2000.

In each case you are giving evidence that the artifact or artifacts you wished to analyze did, in fact, have influence or substantial response within the culture. You are sure, also, to cite the location and source of your information.

IV. JFS (Justification for Study):

Here you need to specify the related sources and studies available to you that will help in framing or establishing the importance of your study. You should specify at least three related articles, books, or book chapters that are as close as possible to your investigation.

So if you were investigating the rhetorical power of satire in animated TV sitcoms, you might write:

> Numerous scholars have recognized the link between satire and rhetoric—some with a special eye toward visually-based satire in cartoons.[27] Others, typically writing in the appreciation of satiric literature, have also grappled with satiric practices.[28]

In each of the studies cited in the endnotes, the scholars writing have preceded you in the investigation of the area under consideration. They then act as "guides" to your research in terms of resources, perspectives, understanding, and terminology. This JFS section allows you to contextualize your proposed analysis project within a larger framework of available scholarship.

V. Research Question:

Here you need to specify your well-thought-out research question. Make sure that it is focused, doable, and interesting (to you and to others). (See previous workshop exercise for examples.)

VI. Review of Published Scholarly Method

Here you need to specify the actual steps of analysis used by a previous scholar to accomplish rhetorical criticism. You should specify all of the pertinent steps of analysis named or implied by a solid, useful scholar who did research similar to that you have in mind.

For example, Robert Ivie addresses his method steps in this way (this is an abridged paraphrased version of his steps; see the original article for his full treatment):[29]

First, familiarize yourself with the rhetor's text and context.

Second, select representative texts for a series of close readings undertaken to identify and mark metaphoric vehicles [metaphiers] employed by the rhetor.

Third, arrange the complete set of marked metaphoric vehicles [metaphiers] into subgroups by clustering those with similar entailments [paraphiers].

Fourth, compile a separate file of metaphoric vehicles [metaphiers] and their immediate contexts for each cluster of metaphoric terms.

Fifth, analyze the files compiled under step 4 one-by-one for patterns of usage within and between clusters, thereby revealing the rhetor's system of metaphoric concepts.

(Adapted from Ivie 1987:167–168)

Many critics will give method steps information that does *not* have this kind of specific detail. So, for instance, if a rhetorical critic says that "character traits in nighttime scenes were analyzed for fear appeals," you can assume that an original (but unstated) step was reviewing *all* scenes for the purpose of finding the nighttime scenes in the movie.

VII. Proposed Method Steps of Analysis

Here you need to specify *your* well-thought-out method steps of analysis. Make sure to specify each specific step. Recognize that these are *proposed* steps of analysis. You may well adapt or refine them as you do your actual analysis.

First, I will familiarize myself with the rhetor's text and context, discovering pertinent details about the rhetor and her/his contextual rhetorical challenges. I will also seek out responses to the message.

Second, I will secure a working transcript of the speech. I will compare the transcript to an audiotape copy of the speech. I will number each paragraph in the speech transcript.

Third, I will search each paragraph of the speech for archetypal, orientational, and novel metaphors. I will keep a chart of each type of metaphor with a notation as to the paragraph in which it appeared in the speech transcript.

Fourth, I will identify a recognizable function of each metaphor (e.g., warning, celebrating, informing, lamenting).

Fifth, I will identify any recognizable patterns of metaphor function based on the metaphiers used.

Sixth, I will specify any recognizable connection between selected metaphier, function of metaphor in speech, and the overall theme of the speech.

This example of planned method steps is the last item in a paper proposal.

If you do solid work on all seven elements of a paper proposal, you establish the groundwork for creating quality analysis.

Use your elements from your paper proposal, after getting feedback from your instructor, to start your actual process of analysis and writing. You'll learn a great deal from the process of proposing the study and then actually doing the analysis you've proposed.

Throughout this book I encourage you to benefit from the "gold" of insights gained from the research of other scholars. Here you will be able to have the satisfaction of beginning to create some of your own insight and discover "gold." Do good work!

Endnotes

1. Recognize the value of available artifacts as you think about doing rhetorical message analysis. You may remember that we talked about the difference between a message and a message artifact in Chapter 3. Access to a tangible artifact of the message in which you are interested is crucial to your analysis.
2. Stephanie Gaskell, "Critics Complain Statue of Sept. 11 Flag-Raising Distorts Event's Reality," *Oregonian* 12 Jan. 2002. A-6.
3. Gaskell 2002.
4. See Edwards and Winkler on the ideographic power of Iwo Jima images: Janis L. Edwards and Carol K. Winkler, "Representative Form and the Visual Ideograph: The Iwo Jima Image in Editorial Cartoons," *Quarterly Journal of Speech* 83 (1997): 289–310.
5. Gaskell 2002.
6. Many experienced instructors will be able to detect the influence of Wayne Brockriede in this list; for one of his hallmark articles on the basis for rhetorical criticism procedure see. "Rhetorical Criticism as Argument," *Quarterly Journal of Speech* 60 (1974) 165–174.
7. Spencer Heinz, "History in 3 Volumes," *Oregonian* 24 Dec. 1990. B-3.
8. Once again, note (even in a non-serious instance) the power and value of an artifact; Heinz could have in fact received many messages for which we have no record or artifact. See Chapter 3 for the discussion of what counts as an artifact.
9. Quentin Hardy, "If the Poky Truck Driver Wears a Bikini, Good Times Are Here," *Wall Street Journal* 20 June 1994. B-1.

10. Remember Kenneth Burke's instruction to us that language is not neutral. If someone is "investing" in a Third World economy, it sounds acceptable (if not admirable). If someone were "exploiting" others in a Third World economy, some would take exception to the activity.
11. Suzanne M. Daughton, "The Spiritual Power of Repetitive Form: Steps Toward Transcendence in *Groundhog Day*," *Critical Studies in Mass Communication* 13 (1996): 138–154.
12. Allen Scult, Michael Calvin McGee, and J. Kenneth Kuntz, "Genesis and Power: An Analysis of the Biblical Story of Creation," *Quarterly Journal of Speech* 72 (1986): 113–131.
13. Pauley, Garth E. "Harry Truman and the NAACP: A Case Study in Presidential Persuasion on Civil Rights," *Rhetoric and Public Affairs* 2 (1999): 211–241.
14. Dana L. Cloud, "Hegemony or Concordance? The Rhetoric of Tokenism in 'Oprah' Winfrey's Rags-to-Riches Biography," *Critical Studies in Mass Communication* 13 (1996): 115–137.
15. Remember that rhetorical critics often do *not* formally state a research question in their articles. Often the research question is *implicit,* based on the JFS and JFA material established in the early part of the article.
16. John Louis Lucaites, "Visualizing 'The People': Individualism vs. Collectivism in *Let Us Now Praise Famous Men*," *Quarterly Journal of Speech* 83 (1997): 269–288.
17. Diagram used with permission; © 1999 Pierce Communication.
18. See Ronald R. Carpenter, "Admiral Mahan, 'Narrative Fidelity,' and the Japanese Attack on Pearl Harbor," *Quarterly Journal of Speech* 72 (1986): 290–305; and Mari Boor Tonn and Valerie A. Endress, "Looking under the Hood and Tinkering with Voter Cynicism: Ross Perot and 'Perspective by Incongruity,'" *Rhetoric & Public Affairs* 4 (2001): 281–308.
19. See Barry Brummett, "Electric Literature as Equipment for Living: Haunted House Films," *Critical Studies in Mass Communication* 2 (1985): 247–261.
20. Suzanne M. Daughton, "Metaphorical Transcendence: Images of the Holy War in Franklin Roosevelt's First Inaugural," *Quarterly Journal of Speech* 79 (1993): 427–446.
21. Janice Hocker Rushing and Thomas S. Frentz. "Singing Over the Bones: James Cameron's *Titanic*," *Critical Studies in Mass Communication* 17 (2000): 1–27.
22. Dennis K. Mumby and Carole Spitzack, "Ideology and Television News: A Metaphoric Analysis of Political Stories," *Central States Speech Journal* 34 (1983): 162–171.

23. Bohn D. Lattin, "Rush to Praise and Blame: An Analysis of the Paranoid Ego-Function of Rush Limbaugh," *Journal of the Northwest Communication Association* 29 (2000): 1–11.
24. Thomas M. Lessl, "The Galileo Legend as Scientific Folklore," *Quarterly Journal of Speech* 85 (1999): 163.
25. Harmeet Sawhney, "Information Superhighway: Metaphors as Midwives," *Media, Culture & Society* 18 (1996): 291–314.
26. I'm indebted to Kristen Edwards for this example.
27. Donald C. Bryant, "Introduction—Uses of Rhetoric in Criticism," *Papers in Rhetoric and Poetic,* ed. Donald C. Bryant (Iowa City: University of Iowa Press, 1965), 1–14; and, "Persuasive Uses of Imaginative Literature in Certain Satires of Jonathan Swift," *Southern States Communication Journal* 46 (Winter 1981), 175–183; Edward A. Bloom and Lillian D. Bloom, *Satire's Persuasive Voice* (Ithaca, N.Y.: Cornell University Press, 1979); H. James Jensen, "Introduction," *The Satirist's Art,* eds. H. James Jensen and Malvin R. Sirker, Jr. (Bloomington: Indiana University Press, 1972), ix–xiv; Earl Miner, "Satire's Falling City," in *The Satirist's Art,* 3–27; Martin Price, *Swift's Rhetorical Act* (Carbondale: Southern Illinois University Press, 1953); James Sutherland, *English Satire* (London: Cambridge University Press, 1962); Robert C. Elliott, *The Power of Satire: Magic, Ritual, Art* (Princeton, N.J.: Princeton University Press, 1960); Matthew Hogart, *Satire* (New York: McGraw-Hill, 1969); Martin J. Medhurst and Michael A. DeSousa, "Political Cartoons as Rhetorical Form: A Taxonomy of Graphic Discourse," *Communication Monographs* 48 (1981): 197–236; Denise M. Bostdorff, "Making Light of James Watt: A Burkean Approach to the Form and Attitude of Political Cartoons," *Quarterly Journal of Speech* 73 (1987): 43–69; Marcus Wood, *Radical Satire and Print Culture, 1790–1822,* (New York: Oxford University Press, 1994); Margaret A. Rose, *Parody: Ancient, Modern, and Postmodern* (New York: Cambridge University Press, 1993); and Janis L. Edwards and Carol K. Winkler, "Representative Form and the Visual Ideograph: The Iwo Jima Image in Editorial Cartoons," *Quarterly Journal of Speech* 83 (1997), 289–310.
28. Lionel Duisit, *Satire, Pariodie, Calembour* (Saratoga, Calif.: Anma Libri, 1978); Northrop Frye, "The Nature of Satire," *University of Toronto Quarterly* 14 (1944–45), 75–89; and, *Anatomy of Criticism: Four Essays* (Princeton, N.J.: Princeton University Press, 1957), 223–239; W. O. S. Sutherland, Jr., *The Art of the Satirist* (Austin: University of Texas Press, 1965); Dustin Griffin, *Satire: A Critical Reintroduction* (Lexington, KY.: University of Kentucky Press, 1994); George A. Test, *Satire: Spirit and Art* (Tampa: University of South Florida Press, 1991); and James E. Gill, ed., *Cutting Edges: Postmodern Critical Essays on Eighteenth-Century Satire* (Knoxville: University of Tennessee Press, 1995).
29. Robert L. Ivie, "Metaphor and the Rhetorical Invention of Cold War 'Idealists,' " *Communication Monographs* 54 (1987): 165–182.

Chapter Five

Metaphors: Cultural Perception and Persuasion

Metaphors, or **non-literal comparisons**, are pervasive, provocative, and permanent devices used in human communication. When reading and listening to public or mass-media messages, we quickly find computer ID material left at Internet sites called digital "crumbs," or the performance of a new business CEO characterized as his first 15 months "on the mound," or a young tennis star described as being surrounded by a protective financial and educational "cocoon," or young lookouts at a drug house called "dixie cups." How (and why) are male sports teams easily designated in tournament play as "Cinderella" teams?

You may not realize how often you use metaphors, but you've probably tried something new by "getting your feet wet," or held a "dead end" job, or perhaps contributed money to a consumer "watchdog" group. I have a standing offer to my students: in the text portion of any general interest (non-technical) publication (e.g., *Time, Details, Essence, The Washington Post,* or *YM*), if we can find fewer than a dozen metaphors in a very few pages (for most magazines in three or fewer pages; for most newspapers in one or two pages) I'll buy the student a Baskin-Robbins triple ice cream cone. The same pace of metaphor use holds true for movies, TV shows, conversations, and travel brochures—really in almost any part of life where written or verbal messages are exchanged. In this chapter we will investigate why metaphors are so common, yet so powerful. We'll start with the type of non-literal comparison most easily recognized as a metaphor; later we'll discuss three other very important types of metaphors that may be less well known to you.

Our thinking in this chapter can only reflect a selected part of a much larger research program where scholars from a number of fields (including

Rhetoric, Communication Research, Linguistics, Psychology, English, and Cultural Studies) have sought a better understanding of use of metaphors. Ancient Western thinkers and contemporary postmodern theorists (and nearly everyone in between) have taken note of the power, potential, and impact of non-literal comparisons. Some scholars even hold that the human capacity and means for consciousness are grounded in metaphor.[1] As Lakoff and Johnson suggest:

> Metaphor is pervasive in everyday life, not just in language but in thought and action. Our ordinary conceptual system, in terms of which we both think and act, is fundamentally metaphorical in nature.[2]

Other cultural analysts argue that cultural phenomena—from declarations of war, to development of congregational self-image, to creation of political activism, and other practical instances—are influenced significantly by the use of specific metaphors or other non-literal comparisons.[3]

The philosophical, sociocultural, psycholinguistic, and rhetorical attention given to non-literal comparisons (especially to metaphors) in the past 20–30 years has been astounding. The insights we have gained have been substantial. We still, however, have work to do. Some scholars (e.g., philosophers of language and linguists) have contributed greatly to our understandings of cultural assumptions, structural design, generative capacity, and meaning capacity of comparisons.[4] Their discussions, however, are often dry and technical, and they often use artificial examples.

On the other hand, scholars within the Rhetorical Studies tradition have tended to investigate *real* comparisons as used within important messages (often speeches); for instance, Daughton studied the first inaugural of FDR (as we learned in Chapter 3) and Ivie speeches by President Truman.[5] These investigations have increased our understanding of pivotal examples of political and cultural communication. Rhetorical scholars Carpenter and Osborn have investigated the cultural impact of other key metaphors used over long spans of time. Carpenter, for instance, historically examined public expressions concerning America's involvement in wars from revolutionary times until the mid-1980s. He discovered a disconcerting thread of comparison-based discourse, which illicitly ties our perception of war activities together:

> Many people, particularly Americans, saw that combat [in World War I] metaphorically as an extension of our frontier experience. And after World War I that metaphor often characterized America's subsequent combat, tragically in Vietnam.[6] . . . This metaphor's tragedy is made manifest herein not only by demonstrating its lack of "truth" but also its "comparative worth" to "rival narratives." . . .[7]

Hence, Carpenter's careful research reveals in many American cultural messages a fixation that insisted on seeing the soldier as a "frontiersman." This metaphoric fixation set the stage for legislative, personal, and cultural disaster—lives lost and resources squandered.

Several examples help illustrate the depth and long use of this metaphoric imagery:

> In correspondence and speeches reaching wider audiences through newspaper publication in Chicago, Detroit, New York, and various western cities, President Theodore Roosevelt compared Filipinos in arms [in a late 1890s conflict with American troops] to "the Sioux, the Comanche, and the Apache Indians." (4)

Hence, by implication U.S. troops became the frontiersmen who were once again battling indigenous people.

Concerning World War II, Carpenter quotes John Steinbeck (of *Grapes of Wrath* fame) in a book Steinbeck wrote about bomber crews:

> . . . as springing from frontier traditions of "Kentucky hunter and the Western Indian-fighter," for when exchanging rifle for turret machine gun "the American boy simply changes the nature of his game. Instead of raiding Sioux or Apache, instead of buffalo or antelope, he lays his sights on Zero or Heinkel, on Stuka or Messerschmitt." (7)

Concerning early conflict in Vietnam Carpenter notes this observation from a book about special forces known as the Green Berets:

> By 1962, media images "crystallized into a portrayal of the Green Beret as a contemporary reincarnation of the western hero" with "wilderness skills" for any environment and superb physical conditioning. (11)

Carpenter argues that certain aspects of the "frontiersman" as a metaphoric figure became inauthentic as early as 1815 and have become even more greatly detached due to changes in warfare technology and practices since then. As we have moved into the warfare era of "Desert Shield," "Desert Storm," "Operation Infinite Justice," and "Operation Enduring Freedom," it is useful to inquire steadily as to which metaphors are acting as contemporary guideposts in our cultural talk about war and our participation in it.

Careful scholars, such as Ronald Carpenter, show us that metaphors are much more important in persuasion and language than in use as mere language decorations. Instead metaphors can become the framework within which we make life and death decisions for thousands of citizens.

Similarly, Michael Osborn has examined carefully **archetypal metaphors** that stubbornly transcend culture, time, and geography in political and cultural communication. He knows why politicians in ancient Athens as well as contemporary Washington, D.C., are likely to use images of light and dark, sickness and health, sailing and navigating, or the seasons as they try to persuade.

Osborn originally believed that archetypal metaphors had six characteristics:

1. Archetypal metaphors are selected and used more often than novel metaphors.

2. Archetypal metaphors stay the same across time, condition, and cultures.
3. Archetypal metaphors are grounded in direct, common human experience.
4. Archetypal metaphors are often based on basic human motivations.
5. Archetypal metaphors used in a message can often reach most audience members.
6. Archetypal metaphors often show up in the most important parts of the most important messages within any society.[8]

His initial study of archetypal metaphors concentrated on the speeches of Churchill, Edmund Burke, Douglas MacArthur, and John F. Kennedy. Speeches given by these rhetors at times of deep cultural importance clearly employed archetypal metaphors concerned with light–dark, the sun, heat and cold, and the seasonal cycles.

Osborn returned to archetypal metaphors a decade later to present his discovery that, while archetypal metaphors can be used by all cultures in all times, a culture can start to diminish use of a particular archetypal metaphor. Osborn studied 56 speeches from the nineteenth and twentieth centuries. He discovered that technological progress, historical expansion, and a turn toward the frontier revealed a sharp decline in use of sea imagery in public speaking. However, he found clear, changed remnants of sea and ocean metaphors, which had been popular in the nineteenth century, in metaphors that addressed river life (e.g., on the Mississippi) and that addressed sea language used in landlocked form (e.g., covered wagons as "prairie schooners"). Osborn's groundbreaking work in the discovery of archetypal metaphors signals to us the importance of metaphors in human argument and decision making.

Osborn's work with this type of metaphor has encouraged others to check his notion of widespread acceptance and use of archetypal images. While it is true that archetypal metaphors stubbornly transcend culture, time, and geography in political and cultural communication, some scholars have discovered interesting changes in use of such metaphors. For instance Lois Einhorn in her study of Native American speakers has found that "American speakers use archetypal metaphors in ways that promote a binary way of thinking characteristic of Western civilization and thought. Although Native American speakers often use the archetypal metaphors identified by Osborn, they do so in ways that encourage thoughts of wholeness and oneness, ideas . . . central to their worldview."[9]

Ronald Carpenter and Michael Osborn stand as examples of scholars who have helped us better understand the long-term patterns of metaphor use by individuals and groups within our society. We will return to research related to their work a bit later in this chapter.

By now understanding some of the focal points of interest by rhetoricians in metaphor, we are ready to move to the core of what makes a metaphor work.

NOVEL METAPHORS

Novel metaphors are the language devices most easy for us to recognize *as* metaphors. If someone says: "Heather is an oak tree," we do not think the person making this claim crazy or odd. Instead, our minds quickly go to work trying to formulate meaning associated with this odd claim about Heather. We know Heather is a human being and not an oak tree, yet we do not object because we know that the person describing Heather is using a novel metaphor. In a novel metaphor we conceptually join two dissimilar items (in this case a specific person and a type of tree) that nonetheless have a specific similarity that allows new perspective on Heather.

As we develop insight and awareness of the power of novel metaphors, we will focus initially on seven components. (Chart 5.1) Let's use our novel metaphor about Heather to see these elements at work.

Notice that we would have achieved a different meaning result if we had used any of these variations: Heather is a tree. Heather is a weeping

CHART 5.1

Heather is an oak tree.	
1. item or person described:	Heather
2. element of comparison:	oak tree
3. typical aspects or characteristics of the element of comparison:	strong, sturdy, old, wood, large, roots, branches, leaves, grow, acorn, grove, deciduous
4. aspects of comparison likely to carry over to the mind of an audience member due to the comparison linkage:	strong, sturdy
5. expected evaluation of the element of comparison (#2):	some neutral, some approval
6. evaluative component (often positive or negative) of the complete comparison (#1 and #2 combined):	to praise
7. the formal linguistic element(s) key to the comparison:	an adjective (oak) + noun (tree)

willow. Heather is a Douglas fir. Heather is an apple tree. Each of those sentences would still have been a novel metaphor, but each would have yielded different meaning.

How about Ned? Ned is a tiger. Is Ned really a tiger? No. Why do we say he is? Well, what do we know about tigers? Tigers live in India, have fur, are meat-eaters, and have cubs. Tigers are orange and black, have claws, climb trees, and are ferocious. Tigers are mammals, have tails, have great olfactory senses, and live in packs. Tigers hunt, prowl, stalk, chase, and sleep. You can see tigers in a zoo—or as a rug on someone's floor. Tigers are endangered. Tigers have four legs, can pounce, and can run faster than people. Whew! When we say Ned is a tiger, do we intend to point to *all* those attributes of a tiger? Of course not. The magic of a non-literal comparison (in this case a novel metaphor) guides our minds to the types of things that we really want to point out about Ned. See Chart 5.2.

Again notice that we would have achieved different meaning results if we had used any of these variations: Ned is a tiger at work. Ned is an old tiger. Ned is a crouching tiger. Ned is a tiger surrounded by elephants. Each of those sentences would still have been a novel metaphor, but each would have yielded much different meaning.

CHART 5.2

Ned is a tiger.	
1. item or person described:	Ned
2. element of comparison:	tiger
3. typical aspects or characteristics of the element of comparison:	tigers live in India, fur, meat-eaters, cubs, orange and black, claws, climb trees, fierce, mammals, tail, great olfactory senses, live in packs, hunt, prowl, stalk, chase, sleep, in zoo, a rug, endangered, four legs, pounce, run fast
4. aspect of comparison which is likely to carry over to the mind of an audience member due to the comparison linkage:	fierce
5. expected evaluation of the element of comparison (#2):	some some approval, some neutral, some approval
6. evaluative component (often positive or negative) of the complete comparison (#1 and #2 combined):	praise
7. the formal linguistic element(s) key to the comparison:	a noun

CHART 5.3

Writing songs is like a conceptual chiropractor for me—everything in my life straightens out.	
1. item or person described:	impact of writing songs on Alanis' life.
2. element(s) of comparison:	a chiropractor's work on a patient
3. typical aspects or characteristics of the element of comparison:	pain, discomfort, out of place, spine, manipulation, treatment, change, improvement, relief, comfort, straight, straighten out
4. aspects of comparison likely to carry over to the mind of an audience member due to the comparison linkage:	adjustment, straighten out, improvement
5. expected evaluation of the element of comparison (#2):	mixed; non-approval of apparent discomfort and approval of the change.
6. evaluative component (often positive or negative) of the complete comparison (#1 and #2 combined):	to praise.
7. the formal linguistic element(s) key to the comparison:	a noun (chiropractor) + a verb phrase (straightens out).

We've started our discussion of novel metaphors with these two quick examples. But, in using Ned and Heather, I'm guilty of using made-up examples (I earlier complained of philosophers of language doing just that). To correct this and to further enhance our understanding and mastery of non-literal comparisons, let's examine a couple of real-life examples from American mass-media messages.

We will allow this simple example of a non-literal comparison (in this case a **novel simile**) to help us through the seven elements we've learned. Singer Alanis Morissette has described songwriting as being a wonderful adjustment: "Writing songs is like a conceptual chiropractor for me—everything in my life straightens out (Chart 5.3)."[10] Let's take this example apart to better understand how all similes, metaphors, or other non-literal comparisons work.

While both ancient and modern scholars have recognized the intriguing chemistry that goes on between the item described (the number 1 component) and the element or means of the non-literal comparison (the number 2 component), few have given analytic names to all the parts and functions. Julian Jaynes, a professor at Princeton University, believed that metaphoric forms of language were at the root of how our minds understand our day-to-day worlds. He established helpful labels to aid our understanding of metaphors and other non-literal comparisons. The terms developed by Jaynes to characterize how a metaphor works are among the most insightful and helpful designations I've found. Several different sets of scholarly terms are used in the investigation of metaphors. Chart 5.7 lists equivalent terms in investigations of metaphors in human communication.

Jaynes sees such statements as the ones we've made about Heather and Ned, as well as the one that Alanis Morissette made about her songwriting, as working in this way: we understand the conceptual linking in the metaphor (or simile or other non-literal comparison) of two different things—the thing we wish to describe: the impact of Morissette's songwriting (Jaynes calls this a **metaphrand**) and the item we choose to create the non-literal comparison (he calls this a **metaphier**), in this case the need for, and the results of, a chiropractor's actions. Jaynes suggests that we are aware of various "associations or attributes of the metaphier which [he calls] **paraphiers.**"[11] Paraphiers for the need for, and the results of, a chiropractor's work include the items listed in number 3 in Chart 5.3. Note, however, that all paraphiers are *not* selected or joined to the metaphrand (in this case Morissette's songwriting and its results on her life). The "associations or attributes" that *are* selected or joined become what he would call paraphrands. Using these four key words allows us to see what human minds do when using metaphors or other non-literal comparisons.

Let's try using these terms with another example. Political commentator Molly Ivins once wrote: "Calling George Bush shallow is like calling a dwarf short (Chart 5.4)."[12] Note that the item described (the metaphrand)

CHART 5.4

"Calling George Bush shallow is like calling a dwarf short."		
1. item or person described:	calling George Bush shallow	metaphrand
2. element(s) of comparison:	calling a dwarf short	metaphier
3. typical aspects of the metaphier:	obvious, unnecessary, or pointing out the apparent	paraphiers
4. aspects of comparison which is likely to carry over and attach to the metaphrand in the mind of an audience member due to the comparison linkage:	obvious or unnecessary	paraphrand
5. expected evaluation of the metaphier:	non-approval	
6. evaluative component (often positive or negative) of the overall non-literal comparison (metaphrand + metaphier):	condemn	
7. the formal linguistic element(s) key to the comparison:	verb (calling) + noun (dwarf) +adjective (short)	

CHART 5.5

Decoding what he [Greenspan] says about the economy is like untangling a fishing line or untossing a salad.[13]		
1. item or person described:		metaphrand
2. element(s) of comparison:		metaphier
3. cultural aspects attached to the metaphier:		paraphiers
4. aspects of comparison likely to carry over to the mind of an audience member:		paraphrand
5. expected evaluation of the metaphier: (circle one)	approval non-approval neither/neutral both	
6. evaluative component (often positive or negative) of the overall non-literal comparison (metaphrand + metaphier): (circle one)	condemn praise	
7. the formal linguistic element(s) key to the comparison: (circle all that apply)	noun verb adjective adverb preposition	

is *not* George Bush; rather it is the *act of calling* the former president shallow. Our second component is the means of creating the non-literal comparison; in this case, calling a dwarf short (the metaphier). What do you suspect are the "associations or attributes" (the paraphiers) of "calling a dwarf short"? The answer of course has little to do with dwarfs *or* shortness, or even height. The paraphiers at work here are likely ideas, such as "unnecessary," "obvious," "apparent," or "evident." The most likely candidate for the paraphrand is "obvious." She *could* have said: "Calling George Bush shallow is unnecessary, because it is obviously true." But, by casting it in the terms of a non-literal comparison, Ivins provoked her readers in a much more captivating way.

With these examples we come much closer to being able to understand and use the magic of metaphors. If your mind is a bit overwhelmed right now as you try to remember the difference between a metaphrand and a paraphier, take heart. You are learning a technical vocabulary that will help you better discuss and understand one of the most important language devices ever invented. Remember that right now, medical students are studying the human circulatory system, law students are studying

CHART 5.6

This [bar] isn't the Taj Mahal we're visiting, after all, and I don't want to sell you the place.		
1. item or person described:		metaphrand
2. element(s) of comparison:		metaphier
3. cultural aspects attached to the metaphier:		paraphiers
4. aspects of comparison likely to carry over to the mind of an audience member:		paraphrand
5. expected evaluation of the metaphier: (circle one)	approval non-approval neither both	
6. evaluative component (often positive or negative) of the overall non-literal comparison (metaphrand + metaphier): (circle one)	condemn praise	
7. the formal linguistic element(s) key to the comparison: (circle all that apply)	noun verb adjective adverb preposition	

legal precedents, electrical engineers are studying load capacity—and you are studying the non-literal comparisons known as novel metaphors. Take a breath or two, sip a favorite beverage, and let's move ahead.

Use the statement made about Alan Greenspan in Chart 5.5 to test your understanding of our emerging system of analysis (in this case for a non-literal comparison known as a novel simile). Write in the appropriate entries. How did you do? Did having a double metaphier make the interpretation any different?

Now use the statement made by Stephen King about a bar he is going to write about as an example (Chart 5.6). How did you do? Did the use of a **negated metaphier** ("isn't the Taj Mahal") change your interpretation or understanding? A negated metaphier happens anytime a non-literal comparison suggests that someone or something has certain attributes by saying that the person or thing is *not* something or someone. So, someone being "no Einstein," or someone suggesting that their boss "doesn't walk on water," or someone claiming that their nurse in the hospital was "no Mother Teresa," all use a negated metaphier to make a point about a person.

Scrutinize exercise

If you wanted to make the following points about people and things, which negated metaphiers might you use to accomplish your meaning?

Use a negated metaphier to say that someone is very weak: Example: He's no Samson.

Use a negated metaphier to say that someone is very strong:

Use a negated metaphier to say that a train is very slow:

As we become familiar with examining novel metaphors and similes (and other similar non-literal comparisons) in greater detail, we will be able to discover many key elements to their power and persuasive potential. When we find a newspaper columnist telling us that "streetkids are the unsweepable litter of the urban landscape; theirs are the faces that stick like gum"[14] we can have a better understanding about the potential rhetorical power of such a statement. Additionally, we've begun to build a set of tools that will allow us to discover the meaning dynamics within a comparison.

If you enjoyed our discussion of novel metaphors (and similar non-literal comparisons), you will no doubt also enjoy our next stop: **systemic metaphors.**

SYSTEMIC METAPHORS

All of the metaphors we will discuss in the rest of this chapter started their "lives" as novel metaphors. For various reasons and due to the way we have used these metaphors (or other non-literal comparisons) they have taken on important, notable, and special characteristics.

Systemic metaphors (as the name suggests) are metaphors that work together within a system of human thought rather than as singular language devices. Systemic metaphors are in constant use, but we don't often realize we are using a metaphor (similar to **dead** or **buried metaphors,** discusses later).

Did you know that anger is a heated liquid held under pressure in a container? You did not? Well, consider the following phrases:

"My boss blew her stack last week."

"After I heard his sorry excuse I nearly exploded."

"My Dad just hit the roof when he saw our phone bill."

"Don't worry about her, she's just blowing off some steam."

"These prices just make my blood boil."

"I couldn't control it; I just felt the anger building up inside me."

"This argument has boiled over."

"Relax! Don't get hot under the collar."

"I was there when he flipped his lid."

Even though none of us has probably said: "Anger is a heated liquid held in a container," we often *talk* as if it is. When we have common ways of expressing the same topic (in this case how we talk about anger), we are using a systemic metaphor.

Lakoff and Johnson noticed that we often talk about time as if it were an economic resource—namely money.[15] Again, listen to the manner in which we often talk about time:

> "He's just living on borrowed time."
>
> "Quit wasting your time. Get a job."
>
> "Are you using your time wisely?"
>
> "Just what we need, another time-saving device in the kitchen."
>
> "I don't have enough time to deal with that project today."
>
> "Don't you dare squander your time in the islands."
>
> "I'm just counting the minutes until I'm outta here."
>
> "We lost a bunch of time on the last leg of the trip."

Is time really money? No. Do we often think about (and talk about) time as if it is money? Yes. When we do so we use a systemic metaphor.

Systemic metaphors (i.e., systems of language use in which a metaphoric idea is central) occur then when we have a more or less standard way of characterizing one part of human experience. If we only occasionally use a certain metaphoric expression to talk about a part of life *and* if we often use a variety of other metaphoric ideas to also talk about that part of life, we *do not* have a systemic metaphor.

Michael Reddy noticed this same process when he recognized that we often talk about human communication as if it were a physical process of moving a thing from one place to another. He called this characterization the "conduit metaphor."[16]

Here are five of his examples of this systemic metaphor:

1. "It's very hard to get that idea across in a hostile atmosphere." (189)
2. "Oh come on, let me have some of your great ideas about this." (190)
3. "The passage conveys a feeling of excitement." (191)
4. "He crammed the speech with subversive ideas." (191)
5. "They tossed your thoughts back and forth for over an hour, but still could not make sense of them." (196)

In each case, ideas, statements, or writing, when used in the process of communication, are talked about as if they were *physical objects* that could

Scrutinize exercise

What are some of the advantages of thinking about communication as a conduit or movement of physical objects or substances from one place to another? What are some of the disadvantages?

be moved from one place to another (typically from one mind to another). Such use, if it becomes the *standard* way we think and talk about communication, results in use of a systemic metaphor.

Can you think of five additional ways in which communication is characterized as a conduit, as a means of moving a physical object or substance from one place to another? List them on a sheet of paper.

If you can think about a part of life where we use a standard, interrelated set of metaphoric images (e.g., TIME IS MONEY or COMMUNICATION IS A CONDUIT) to talk or write about it, you have likely found a systemic metaphor. Hence, if you (off the top of your head), can name 10 or a dozen short sayings or typical phrases about some part of life, you likely have discovered or recognized a systemic metaphor. If you *cannot* easily think of ten or more examples, you may have a singular novel metaphor, or even a metaphoric cluster, but *not* a systemic metaphor.

Let's try this one out for practice. See if you can quickly think of 10 ways we commonly talk about romance, love, and human relationships using this central idea as a core image.

Romantic Relationships Are a Trip or a Journey

1. "Our relationship has come to a fork in the road."

(List 9 additional expressions on a sheet of paper.)

You may well be able to tell that systemic metaphors are powerful, and often unrecognized, parts of our use of language. If you enjoyed thinking about systemic metaphors, you may well also enjoy a similar kind of metaphor known as an orientational metaphor.

ORIENTATIONAL METAPHORS

Remember that systemic and orientational metaphors started their "lives" as novel metaphors. Whereas systemic metaphors become notable because we form systems of words to act as the standard way of talking about certain parts of life, **orientational metaphors** are notable because they center our perception on the way that *bodily experiences* become the metaphoric motif that allow us to express basic and interrelated ideas of human expression.

Again, a quick example will serve to introduce us to the idea:

Would you rather buy a high quality DVD player or a low quality DVD player?

No contest (if the right money is available), yes? But, turn your attention away from the DVD player for the moment and ask why did I not pose *this* question to you:

Would you rather buy a good quality DVD player or a poor quality DVD player?

Same question, right? Essentially, yes; the questions posed above are very similar. The first question, however, uses an orientational metaphor to accomplish its meaning making. Using the terms "high" and "low" make the first question a participant in form of metaphoric meaning creation.

Orientational metaphors (as the name suggests) are different metaphors from conventional novel metaphors in that they do not strictly take two unlike items (e.g., Ned and Tiger, or Time and Money) and relate them in metaphoric connection of terms connected to each other in time and space. Instead, orientational metaphors create a system of common reference points for things being positively or negatively evaluated using imagery ideas that are not directly accurate (hence, metaphoric).

Lakoff and Johnson put it this way:

> . . . most [orientational metaphors] . . . have to do with spatial orientation: up–down, in–out, front–back, on–off, deep–shallow, central–peripheral. These spatial orientations arise from the fact that we have bodies of the sort we have and that they function as they do in our physical environment. Orientational metaphors give a concept a spatial orientation[.] (14)

So, for example, Lakoff and Johnson claim that in our general way of speaking we support the claims that HAPPY IS UP and SAD IS DOWN. (15)

Let's see if you agree with them. First, consider the proposition "happy is up." Obviously this is not something that you would expect to hear in everyday conversation (in a way similar to the seldom heard statement, "Anger is a heated liquid held in a container"). You do not hear that "happy is up" or that "sad is down." Do you, however, hear statements such as these in everyday life: "I'm on *top* of my game today," "Things are really looking *up* around here," "I've just had a *mountain top* experience," "She's an *up* and coming executive," "You start this company and the *sky*'s the limit!" or "I'm going to spruce *up* my room." These common expressions suggest that happiness, satisfaction, joy, and good results are related to things *higher* rather than *lower, up* rather than *down.*[17] Hence, Lakoff and Johnson's formulation of HAPPY IS UP comes to us inductively when we recognize the number of phrases in our language that reflect this sentiment. See if you can quickly write five other statements on a sheet of paper that support the unspoken metaphoric proposition that HAPPY IS UP.

Now, can you come up with five statements that support the unspoken metaphoric proposition that SAD IS DOWN? (Hint: think of expressions that reflect or indicate "DOWN" such as "bottom," "low," "under.")

The essence, then, of orientational metaphors is *not* a one-for-one matching of a metaphrand to a metaphier. Instead, orientational metaphors suggest an evaluative angle (typically positive or negative) associated with saying that things are located in time and space when they actually have no physical location or object that would make that so.

If you think things are looking very *up* after our stop with orientational metaphors, you will no doubt also enjoy our next stop: **dead or buried metaphors.**

DEAD OR BURIED METAPHORS

Dead or **buried metaphors** have something in common with archetypal, orientational, and systemic metaphors: we don't tend to pay a great deal of attention to them. If you were to find the following three sentences in a typical week of media exposure, you would not likely pay the metaphors within them a great deal of attention:

"When I [Jon Spoelstra] started [as VP of marketing] with the New Jersey Nets, the owners recommended that I 'clean house.'"[18]

"He [Cleveland Amory] was the kind of guy who always swam upstream."[19]

"In fact, I think people are waiting for me [a person with sudden sight loss] to give them the green light to help."[20]

Chances are very great that you would automatically "get the point" of phrases such as "clean house," "swam upstream," and "give the green light." But how sharp would the point be? Metaphors such as these are *almost* dead metaphors. They have been buried under decades or centuries of language use, and are now so familiar that we hardly notice that they are metaphors at all. Obviously, these buried metaphors still serve a solid purpose in human communication. However, they are not *actual* dead metaphors because we can still recognize their metaphoric properties. If I read that Jon Spoelstra was ordered to "clean house" in his new job, I could raise the metaphor back to the level of full awareness by asking: "Should he use a broom or bleach?" If I can reestablish the metaphoric force of the metaphier (in this case by naming some of the paraphiers) by asking a silly question, I've demonstrated that a metaphor was being used in the first place. When we can raise audience member attention back to full awareness concerning a metaphor, we'll call it a buried metaphor.

If "buried" metaphors can be brought back into our awareness, then what is a "dead" metaphor? Scruples will help us answer that question.

Do you like people with scruples? Do you have scruples? If you are buying a car, would you rather deal with a scrupulous or unscrupulous salesperson? Why? Does the word "scruple" have any meaning to you other than a connection to ideas of ethics or honesty? Does the word scruple remind you of a rock? Probably not.

Stop now and look up the word "scruple" in the dictionary.

Now, take a closer look and examine the Latin root word *scrupulus* from which we take our English word "scruple." What does your dictionary say that *scrupulus* means?

You'll see that the Latin word meant a small sharp rock or stone. How do we get from a sharp stone to matters of honesty or ethics?

Have you ever had a small pebble or sharp stone in your sandal? How did it feel? Did you leave it in your sandal? What did you do with it?

Have you ever told a lie and then had your conscience bother you? How did it feel? Did you do anything about the lie? What did you do?

You might be able to see how an ancient person would have used the word *scrupulus* in a simile: "When I lie my mind (or my conscience) bothers me like having a sharp stone (a scrupulus) in my sandal." Hundreds of years later, after the idea and connection becomes conventional, one might have said (using a metaphor): "My lies have put a scrupulus in my brain." Many hundreds of years later, one might have said: "Have you a scrupulus?" (referring to the now frequent, understood metaphor connection between a bothersome thought and a bothersome sharp stone in life situations dealing with truth or lies). Hence, in our times the metaphoric connection is lost (except to those who read dictionary entries) and we find someone able to ask: "Do you have any scruples?" without *any* recognition that the word started out as a metaphoric reference. Who among us would see matters of bothersome conscious as connected to a bothersome sharp pebble in a shoe? When this happens (as is often the case with individual words), we have a genuinely dead metaphor. Without resorting to lengthy explanation or etymological investigation, few people would ever connect our word "scruple" with a bothersome rock. Truly dead metaphors are *unrecognizable as metaphors* because the metaphoric connection has been broken or lost through long centuries of language use. Therefore, the phrase "dead metaphor" is itself *not* a dead metaphor because we realize that metaphors cannot really die. (Don't think about that one for very long—at least not on an empty stomach.)

So, when we *cannot* so raise audience awareness, such as with the word "scruple," when we ask a simple related question ("what size is the rock in your shoe?") we'll call it a **dead metaphor.**

Congratulations! You now know (or are learning about) archetypal metaphors, novel metaphors, systemic metaphors, buried metaphors, dead metaphors, and orientational metaphors. Test your new insight and see how often you can recognize each type. Also, try to formulate why certain metaphors work better than others for you or for certain audiences. Next you will find a sample journal article by Hardy-Short and Short. Read the article in preparation for the Chapter 5 workshop.

We will see if we can put new understandings of metaphors to great use as we recognize the sheer power of these language devices to alter public perception. Then we'll launch on to Chapter 6 concerning the power of narrative communication.

Fire, Death, and Rebirth: A Metaphoric Analysis of the 1988 Yellowstone Fire Debate

Dayle C. Hardy-Short and C. Brant Short

This essay analyzes the public debate concerning management of the 1988 Yellowstone forest fires. Two primary archetypal metaphors—*death* and *rebirth*—emerged. These provided a conceptual worldview which helped observers define the situation and gave advocates an inventional tool for advancing their own agenda regarding fire policy and national park management. The crisis brought two competing views of public land management to the forefront of public discussion: the *ecological* view that public lands must be managed from a holistic view of resources and the *human-centered* view that resource use should recognize the preeminence of humans in policy-making.

During the late summer of 1988, Rocky Mountain newspaper headlines charted an impending crisis. "Epic Wildfires Alter Face of Yellowstone" (Jones A1). "Residents Leaving West Yellowstone as Fire Nears" (Foster A1). "Record High Temps Worsen West's Fire Situation" (Donnelly A1). "Flames Lick at Edge of Yellowstone Towns" (A1). "Giant Wildfire: Residents Flee as Fire Nears" (A1). "Outlook Grim for Saving Towns from Forest Fire" (Foster A1). And finally, "Cool, Wet Weather Calms Western Fires" (Oatis A2).

One of the more ominous headlines that summer appeared in the *Wall Street Journal:* "Yellowstone Burns as Park Managers Play Politics." Written by Donald R. Leal of the Political Economy Research Center, a conservative research center located in Bozeman, Montana, the editorial chastised federal land managers for allowing "natural" fires to burn out of control in the national forests and park areas (10). Leal used the Yellowstone crisis as a call to rethink the ecological worldview which had guided federal public land policy since the 1960s. "If the Yellowstone fires continue, and if controversy over the 'natural regulation' policy is sufficiently severe to arouse public opinion," argued Leal, "'natural regulation' may be curtailed" (10). This editorial represented one of the opening salvos

Source: *Western Journal of Communication* 59 (Spring 1995), 103–25.

Dayle C. Hardy-Short is an Assistant Professor in the Department of Communication and Theater, Idaho State University, Pocatello, ID 83209. C. Brant Short is an Associate Professor in the Department of Communication and Theater, Idaho State University.

in the national and regional debate that emerged during the severe fire season of 1988. Politicians, ranchers, journalists, and residents of fire-stricken areas claimed that the federal government's "natural fire" policy (called by many the "let burn" policy) was dangerous, short-sighted, and wasteful.

These claims illustrate historian Stephen Pyne's argument that fire is a "cultural phenomenon" (3). Calling the relationship between humans and fire "reciprocal," Pyne suggests that although fire alone "rarely devastate[s] a landscape," when coupled with human activity it can domesticate or ruin the land. He concludes that "fire itself takes on many particular characteristics because of the cultural environment in which it occurs" (4–5). However, only through rhetoric do these characteristics and the environment within which they occur become evident. The rhetorical construction of the (more or less) collective agreement about how humans should respond to fire allows us to describe and understand fire contextually. In the case of the Yellowstone fire controversy, an analysis of metaphor helps us understand how this agreement began to emerge.

As an organizing principle for rhetorical criticism, metaphor has enjoyed great attention in recent decades. Critics have used metaphor to investigate a number of rhetorical artifacts and in so doing have become comfortable theoretically with a broader view of metaphor than the classical Aristotelian conception of this figure of speech. "A number of theorists in various fields," writes Sonja Foss, "have helped transform the narrow view of metaphor into one in which it is seen as central to thought and to our knowledge and experience of reality" (188). In particular, Michael Osborn's work on the archetypal metaphor has been recognized by observers as important and "especially vital" (Brock, Scott, & Chesebro 286) for the practice of rhetorical criticism. Yet, only a few published studies attempt to refine and expand our understanding of the function of archetypal metaphors; most notably, these include Rickert's examination of Winston Churchill's war oratory, Perry's analysis of Hitler's rhetoric, and Jamieson's comparative study of Jerry Brown and Pope Paul.

Archetypal metaphors continue to have rhetorical power in contemporary public discourse and can offer an insightful critical tool. Moreover we agree with Robert Ivie's assumption that "metaphor is at the base of rhetorical invention" (198) and suggest that archetypal metaphors offer rhetors an inventional vehicle that is especially powerful in the context of crisis. In the following case study, we examine the debate surrounding the Yellowstone Park forest fires of 1988 and evaluate the function of archetypal metaphors in shaping public perceptions, actions and policy. Yellowstone, the first national park, is an especially important site for this kind of study because it has become the cultural yardstick against which all other set-aside areas are measured (Runte 212–214). National parks are ideological constructs and perceived in different ways than other forms of public lands. Public discussion of what happens in national parks is necessarily bound up in how we view ourselves and our relationship to nature—for many Americans, national parks *are* nature because they have no opportunity to experience other forms of the natural world. Our study focuses on the rhetoric of the crisis itself (from the beginning of the fires in July to their control in September 1988), and touches briefly on the aftermath of the fires in which the debate moved from the scene of the fires, the Rocky Mountain West, to the halls of Congress and the pages of scientific journals.[1]

To accomplish our goals in this study, we address three topics. Initially, we review the status of metaphor and its place as a tool for rhetorical criticism. Next, we review the rhetoric surrounding the fire debate, examining both local and national sources of public argument.[2] Finally, we draw conclusions and suggest implications for future studies of archetypal metaphor, especially in case studies dealing with environmental advocacy and natural resource rhetoric.

METAPHOR AND RHETORICAL CRITICISM

Metaphor allows us to describe the indescribable in a way that gives it meaning and makes it understandable to others. Michael Osborn and Douglas Ehninger suggest that metaphor functions as a "communicative stimulus" because it allows the user to identify "an idea or object through a sign which generally denotes an entirely different idea or object" (226). Metaphor also functions as a "mental response" because of the "interaction" between ideas suggested by the term's "usual denotation" and its "special denotation" in the particular context (Osborn & Ehninger 226). In resolving the apparent incompatibility of a metaphor's tenor and vehicle,[3] a listener relies on "qualifiers" or "forces" which "suggest or direct how the metaphor will be understood." Qualifiers may be "contextual" (based on the situation), "communal" (based in the common knowledge of a people), "private" (based in a listener's personal or subjective knowledge), or "archetypal" (based in experiences common to peoples across time) (Osborn & Ehninger 228–230).

George Lakoff and Mark Johnson suggest that within argumentation, metaphor helps to "structure our present reality." If a metaphor new to us enters our "conceptual system . . . it will alter that conceptual system and the perceptions and actions that the system gives rise to" (145). If the metaphor appears strongly enough to us, or we identify strongly enough with it, we will act on it.

Archetypal metaphors are powerful in part because of their ability to symbolize common human experiences that transcend time and culture. Because of their intrinsic connection to the human experience, archetypal metaphors may be called upon more often in crisis situations when people recall their most basic and fundamental experiences to understand a particular problem. Osborn explains that archetypal metaphors can be identified by their popularity in rhetorical discourse; their constancy through time and between cultures; their "ground[ing] in prominent features of experience"; their "embodiment of basic human motivations"; their universal appeal to audience members; and their appearance at "critical junctures" in discourse (116–117). In moments of "great crisis," writes Osborn, "when society is in upheaval and fashionable contemporary forms of symbolic cultural identity are swept away, the speaker must turn to the bedrock of symbolism, the archetype, which represents the unchanging essence of human identity" (120).

Several case studies have demonstrated that metaphors can be powerful sources of invention for rhetors. In her study of archetypal metaphors Jamieson finds that such metaphors "simultaneously create inventional possibilities and impose inventional constraints" (231). Ivie extends Jamieson's claim, demonstrating that identification of key metaphors helps reveal "their limits or untapped potential as sources of invention" (199). Significantly, speakers may "lose sight of alternatives when they become accustomed to routine extensions of images no longer serving their original purposes" (Ivie 199). In this way, the metaphor is literalized and becomes the essence of social reality for audiences and rhetors alike.

DEATH AND REBIRTH

Humans attach meaning to natural processes through language, often metaphorically, which in turn allows us to label, categorize, and discuss these processes. We contend that two essentially "pure" archetypal metaphors, *death* and *rebirth,* can be found at the center of the public debate regarding the Yellowstone fires and that such metaphors reveal the depth and scope of appeals used in the debate. Viewed in a larger context, death and rebirth are part of an overarching archetype of the human life cycle.[4] In this view, birth (whenever that is defined) occurs once and begins an endless process of life, death, and rebirth. Death and rebirth are forever tied to each other, as rebirth can occur *only* after some sort of death. Too, when rebirth is the metaphor paired with death (as opposed to life or birth), the pairing suggests a belief that all life is in flux.

Ecologist Daniel Botkin observes that metaphor has long been useful in describing nature as a whole. Until very recently, humans viewed nature as organic, either "*like* a living creature" or *as* "a living creature" (emphasis in original). Organisms pass through "major life stages" from birth to death, and their future depends not only on their present but their past state of existence (Botkin 92). The "development of modern sciences," Botkin explains, led to a shift from viewing nature as organic to viewing it as a machine (103). A machine is "predictable" with parts that may "age" but can be "replaced," thus ensuring that it will not die (Botkin 102). From this perspective, nature, left alone, would always reproduce itself; human involvement either "complete[s] the perfection of nature or . . . interfere[s] in its perfect processes" (Botkin 110). Death occurs when appropriate parts are not replaced.

Historically, the machine metaphor has been at the heart of national park and wilderness management, which mandated that responsible land managers should either prevent change or replace parts (which would also prevent change). Botkin suggests that we are now moving from a machine-like view of nature to viewing Earth as a biosphere, which is a "life-supporting and life-containing system with organic qualities" (151). This is a perspective that focuses on sustainability—or managing for change—and which combines the old organic view with a "new technological view" that understands nature as a more open than closed system (155–156). As an example of this shift, he describes how one scientist studying the Sequoia forests in the mid-1960s came to believe that change, in the form of fire, would actually be beneficial for the regeneration of the giant trees. Gradually, that belief influenced the National Park Service to allow controlled burns (Botkin 154).[5] The metaphor of rebirth is compatible with the view of Earth/nature as an open system, for while change may sufficiently alter something so that we no longer recognize it (a type of death), rebirth assumes the altering effects of change.

While we might see death and rebirth as part of a human-centered view of life, the ways in which these two metaphors were used when arguing about the Yellowstone fires places them more in opposition than such a view might suggest. When death dominates the talk, we might discover the view that things are permanent and that therefore change is value-laden, and that value can be measured only in human (and therefore economic) terms. The metaphor of rebirth *assumes* death. In cases where rebirth dominated the talk, we can find the view that life and all things in it are somehow transitory, that change is inevitable and we cannot judge it as good or bad. Rebirth suggests that the value in something can be both contemporary and delayed, and even that the greater value in something will be visible after its transformation by rebirth.

These two dominant metaphors both reflected and reinforced a conceptual worldview that helped observers define the situation and gave advocates an inventional tool for advancing specific arguments regarding fire policy and national park management. We do not suggest that advocates (of either side) consciously chose one archetype over another, but that at some point they did make conscious use of certain words that, when clustered, can be described by the archetype. At this point, language choice became strategic, and viewed largely, suggests an overall world view that allows observers to infer particular kinds of conclusions about similar uses of language in other situations.[6]

The crisis atmosphere surrounding the fire debate prompted metaphors that matched the visual images of a landscape being devoured in flames.

Appeals that furthered the sense of "crisis" were often based upon a deeply-rooted anti-government, anti-environmentalist core of opinion. Two competing views of public land management emerged at the forefront of public discussion: the *ecological* view that public lands must be managed from a holistic view of resources and a *human-centered* view that resource use should recognize the preeminence of humans in policy-making.

In the case of the Yellowstone forest fires, there is little doubt or surprise that public discourse emerged in the midst of a public crisis.[7] Describing and understanding the Yellowstone fires through the lens of death and/or rebirth created powerful metaphorical associations for audiences concerned with scenic beauty. Archetypal metaphors were important inventional devices for advocates and observers because they allowed a conceptual vision that provided a coherent and systematic form. As the crisis deepened, the metaphors used by opponents and supporters of the "let burn" policy to describe what was happening or going to happen in Yellowstone became more fixed to the public reality of what *had* happened in Yellowstone. The reliance on archetypal metaphors to conceptualize the fires and federal policy was based on the synergistic function of a mythic force (fire) altering a national/cultural icon (Yellowstone). Some members of the public became convinced that Yellowstone had been destroyed, while others were eager to see the transformation for themselves. The metaphorical reality of death or rebirth motivated specific action from members of the public who were conscious of the situation in Yellowstone.

NATIONAL PARKS AND FOREST FIRES

Before examining the events of 1988, it is helpful to understand the origins of the "natural fire" policy and how it evolved to become the standard mechanism for guiding federal land fire policy. In 1968, the National Park Service officially recognized the importance of fire in maintaining a healthy ecosystem.[8] By 1972, naturally-caused fires (often started by lightning) were usually allowed to burn. According to one federal study: "The purpose for this policy change was to restore fires to a more natural ecological role. 'Naturalness' is defined as those dynamic processes and components which would likely exist today, and go on functioning, if technological humankind had not altered them" (U.S. Dept. of Agriculture 7).

A typical account of the benefits of fire appeared in a 1986 feature story in the Boise *Idaho Statesman*. Commenting on a 25,000 acre burn in central Idaho, a Forest Service fire management officer observed, "That's a lot of acres to have burning with nobody on them. Ten years ago that was basically unheard of in the Forest Service. . . . Fire is a natural part of the ecosystem—it is a natural part of the wilderness. It's as natural as rainfall." The author of the story, the *Idaho Statesman*'s outdoors columnist, extended the management officer's claim by concluding, "Fire can be a tool in wilderness to clear old-growth timber, which shades the ground and limits the growth of new plants. Wildlife needs a diversity in vegetation for food and cover." To support this point, the columnist noted that the "recovery of burn comes faster than most believe" and that "new plants start to sprout in three or four weeks" (Zimowsky E1).

In Yellowstone Park, the natural burn area was limited to 300,000 acres until 1976 when it was expanded to include nearly the entire park. Since that year, 134 natural fires have been suppressed when officials determined they posed a potential threat to public facilities or could lead to much larger fires. Under the natural burn policy, Yellowstone's worst fire season prior to 1988 was 1981, when fifty-seven fires burned 20,000 acres of land (Barker, "Flame and Blame" 11).

1988 FIRE SEASON

Despite the Park Service's recognition of the benefits of fire in 1968, ecologically-minded critics might argue that the decision came too late. Unspent fuel had been accumulating for decades, and the pine beetle infestation of the late 1970s and early 1980s in Montana, Idaho, and Wyoming added an enormous number of dead and dying trees to the store of fuel. According to one of the co-authors of Yellowstone's 1972 fire management plan, Don Despain, "'fire is part of the system and therefore it causes no damage to the system. In fact, it is fire suppression that causes damage by destroying the natural frequency of fire in the ecosystem'" (quoted in Morrison 31). However, those who argued for preservation of the park and suppression of the fires would claim that the decision to let the fires burn in a severe drought year (coming at the end of several years of lower-than-normal precipitation) added a bad policy to a bad fuel situation. One group of advocates claimed the roots of the 1988 fire season lay in the historic policy of fire suppression, and another group suggested its roots were in the policy shift to let fires burn where they did not threaten humans and their possessions.

In 1988 the first fire near the Park started on June 25. Several fires ignited and throughout July the conditions worsened because multiple fires were burning and the weather was extremely dry. The first threat to tourists came on July 22 when fire approached the Grant Village area and the first fire evacuation occurred in the park. The fire changed course and no facilities were lost at Grant Village, although the danger prompted a visit by Secretary of the Interior Donald Hodel, who told *Good Morning America* on July 23, "Yellowstone is not in danger . . . We're not going to let Yellowstone be damaged by this" ("Hodel Says").

At this juncture, some fire experts believed the most severe fires were over. In a report to the park superintendent, a team of fire experts predicted that about 200,000 acres of the park would be burned by the end of the season. But they were wrong.

On August 20, the day many observers labeled as "Black Saturday," the fires exploded out of control. Winds of seventy to ninety miles per hour accelerated many fires and some officials believe over 165,000 new acres were set ablaze on this single day (Matthiessen 122). A crisis atmosphere gripped the region as the Montana communities of Silver Gate and Cooke City were threatened and residents of West Yellowstone saw fires on the outskirts of their community. National attention focused primarily on the threat to the historic Old Faithful Lodge and the evacuation of that area on September 8 added to the perceptions of a situation out of control. In rapid succession, President Reagan ordered over 5,000 military personnel to help fight the fires, most of the park was closed to the public after August 24, and Wyoming Senators Alan Simpson and Malcom Wallop demanded that National Park Superintendent William Mott be fired. All these factors combined to create a crisis which the public believed was caused by shortsighted and faulty management.

On September 10, a cold front approached and humid air pushed into the area. One day later rain and snow fell and the 1988 fire season was finally under control. Newspaper headlines after the snowfall reflected a lessening of crisis as Westerners began to debate the wisdom of a national "let burn" policy. "Sen. Wallop Finds Scapegoat for Tragic Yellowstone Fire" (10A). "Andrus Blasts Let-Burn Policy" (A4). "Fires Still Have Place in Forest Management, Chief Argues" (3). "Group Blasts Let-It-Burn Plan" {C1). "Environmental Groups Defend Administration's Firefighting Policies" (Darst). "Fire Policy Opens Way for Political Attacks" (A4). "Hodel Says Let-Burn Policy Must Be Changed" (LaMay C1). "Congress Will View Fire Policy" (4A). The crisis had passed, but Westerners (in particular) were deeply concerned about long-term policy affecting the national parks and forest systems.

COMPETING METAPHORS IN THE 1988 FIRE DEBATE

In the 1960s and 1970s a national "conservation consensus" emerged that legislated an ecological worldview in developing public land policies.[9] As a result, the public lands have been managed from a holistic perspective, displacing the historic view of a human-centered universe. The "natural burn" policy formulated by the Forest Service, the Bureau of Land Management, and the National Park Service reaffirmed the belief that public lands are a complex and diverse ecosystem with human needs representing only one factor in policy-making.

The arguments used by supporters and critics of the "natural burn" policy centered around the images associated with the archetypal metaphors of death and rebirth. The crisis atmosphere of August–September 1988 provided a window of opportunity for critics of public land management whose calls for a human-centered standard of allocating natural resources had lost support following James Watt's stormy tenure as Ronald Reagan's first Secretary of the Interior. For these individuals, the crisis of a national treasure burning to the ground could only be symbolized as "death." How could humans enjoy the wonders of Yellowstone in the midst of blackened ruins? On the other hand, supporters of a "natural burn" policy needed an alternative view of the fires that was consistent with an ecological perspective and, at the same time, countered the visions of "death" advanced by critics of the National Park Service and the U.S. Forest Service. In responding to their critics, supporters of the "natural burn" policy offered the metaphor of "rebirth."

In its most fundamental terms, the controversy over national park fire policy focused upon its proper name. The officially-designated term, "prescribed natural burn," implied a rational decision-making process that allowed some naturally-caused fires to burn while mandating that others be fought from their beginning. Opponents called the policy "let burn" management, a label used extensively by the news media, probably because of its brevity and color. In terms of public perceptions, "let burn" suggested a casual disregard toward fire and no concern for the economic ramifications of lost tourism and lost timber. Throughout the crisis phase of the fires, supporters of federal policies attempted to prove that "let burn" was a misleading label in describing the current policy.

Yellowstone officials attempted to reframe the impact of the fires beginning in August. Acknowledging that fires of "epic proportion" would "significantly alter the country's oldest national park, changing timberland into meadows," they also characterized the fire as an "ecological boon" to the Park which would result in the "first major regeneration of Yellowstone in as many as 400 years" (Jones A1). Despite their best efforts to discuss fires within an ecological framework, federal officials found themselves confronted by an increasing number of attacks as the fire crisis grew.

Visions of Death in the Fire Debate

Critics of the "natural burn" policy argued from a view of nature in which fire was acceptable only when created and managed by humans. For instance, fire has long been used as a cleansing element in land management—farmers and ranchers still burn stubble and rangeland to prepare for the next year's planting or growth. So, it was not the idea of fire itself or the function fire can serve when controlled that disturbed fire policy critics, but it was the idea and effects of "wild" fire that drew so much ire. One observer suggested that the fires had returned "wildness" to the so-called Yellowstone "wilderness" (Morrison 116), and it was this wildness that was so overwhelming. Presumably, had humans set the fires to help clear the accumulated fuel from the forest, they would have been able to control the consequences. The worldview that considers fire a human tool appears to contradict the belief that fire is part of nature and can have valuable effects even when not controlled. It is easy to see how a believer in managed fires could turn to a metaphor that equated wild fires with death.

The metaphor of death appeared in public arguments in various forms. For some advocates, the death of Yellowstone was the destruction of the forest lands and the animals; for others death appeared in the form of economic hardships and social consequences. Devastation, extinction, disease, ruin, murder, and waste were all terms used to evoke the greater image of death in its most horrific forms. Certainly, being burned alive is one of the most terrible forms of death we as humans can imagine, and critics of the fire policy invoked images closed associated with that: hell, mutilation, charring, burning to ash, charcoal grilling.

The *Idaho State Journal*[10] quoted David Hays, who watched the fires approach his home near the Park: "It looks like the surface of hell in Yellowstone. The sun and moon rise and set blood red. This is more like Mars than like Island Park anymore" (Rushforth A1). Residents of other communities confronted with fire expressed their outrage over fire management through the metaphor of death. In Gardiner, Montana, a local businessman argued, "I think the people here are primarily interested in another endangered species—the local businessman," while the owner of a local motel charged, "They've killed our business" ("Park Policy Under Fire" A2). In Dubois, Wyoming, merchants formed an association with other small communities demanding federal subsidies to replace business lost by the fire. They perceived the fires to be a direct result of poor federal land management, not the forces of nature. "They're the ones who created the policy," one merchant said. "They're responsible" ("Dubois Merchants" 9).

A group of citizens in Jackson, Wyoming, circulated a petition demanding a change in federal fire policy. The idea for the petition resulted from a comment made by visitors from New York: "They drove through Yellowstone and they said they were practically crying. . . . They asked us what we were doing about it." The petition noted that the "ill-timed Park Service policy allowing natural burns in Yellowstone Park has jeopardized, for future generations, both the use and enjoyment of our greatest national park." In attacking the existing policy, the petition noted that fires were causing pollution and contributing to economic hardship in Wyoming, Idaho, and Montana (Stump A16). Steve Fuller, who had lived near Yellowstone since 1972 observed "The desolation caused by this fire . . . it's a mutilation that I have never considered before. . . . My whole attitude on fire is changing. What I feel is gut-wrenching fear" (Wilkinson 11).

The death metaphor was pervasive in the editorial sections of Western newspapers. Attacking the "natural fire" policy, the *Jackson Hole [WY]*

News[11] claimed, "The immediate effects of the fires are clear and monumental. Homes were destroyed, lives threatened, businesses and local economies damaged, tons of pollutants thrown into the skies, hundreds of acres of forest blackened" ("Congress Should Investigate" A4). Writing in the *Salt Lake Tribune*, K. E. Grubbs attacked both the fire policy and the public information campaign to explain the benefits of fire:

> As we motored through acres of charred desolation to the orange skies surrounding the geyser basin—a scene that might have been described by Dante—the official perked up long enough to tell us how great it was to be alive now and to witness this magnificent event, the torching of Yellowstone. Never mind the human habitats and enterprises that have been ruined along with half of Yellowstone. And forget that goofy propaganda about how it will all be back to normal next year. It won't; not for years and years. Strike up the Twilight Zone theme. {Grubbs A21)

Some Westerners, particularly those in states bordering Yellowstone, reacted personally to the loss, claiming that the fires felt "like a death in the family" (Jones & Secter 1). And the Billings, Montana newspaper editorialized that "intellectually, of course, we know that Yellowstone is a national park. But deeper, we believe it is ours, these outsider experts have gambled with our treasure—and lost" (Jones & Secter 1, 15).

Various critics of the policy saw fire as a disease that had to be controlled to prevent death. "If forest fires are Nature's way of keeping balance, then is not disease similarly Nature's way of keeping population under control?" one editorialist wrote. "Should man, out of respect for Nature, decline to heal humans?" The writer concluded ominously, "If man lets Nature have its way, there soon may not be any Nature left" ("Fires Ravage West" 1016). Dave Flitner, a rancher and president of the Wyoming Farm Bureau, claimed that before "we invented vaccines to control historically-devastating diseases, nature destroyed humans in much the same manner as it destroyed trees. Surely environmentalists would not stretch their *c'est la vie* attitude toward nature to include man's 'unnatural' healing methods. Would they?" (Flitner A8).

In a guest editorial, a retired forester from Montana also used the fire as a vehicle to indict federal wilderness policies. Del Radtke attacked the Forest Service for being too closely aligned with environmental groups. Additionally, Radtke claimed that the problem with fire experts "is that they sometimes massage each other's egos to such an extent that they lose common sense." In a striking conclusion to his call for better land management, Radtke invoked the death—or murder—of an important symbol in previous fire publicity: "Like Smoky [sic] Bear said to children for years, before he was killed, 'Don't play with fire—you might burn a lot more than you figured'!" (5).

In the *Salt Lake Tribune*, nationally-syndicated columnist Joan Beck claimed that the "raging storms of fire" that turned Yellowstone Park to "acrid ashes" had also "scorched the National Park Service's ideological plan to let natural forest fires burn without interference." Attacking the rationale that fires promote growth and in fact support a healthy ecosystem, Beck concluded: "By the 23rd or 24th century, perhaps, those in charge of preserving our great national-park heritage will have figured out a more sensible way to protect and renew our national forests than by letting them burn down. However fascinating this untidy, blazing, spectacular climax of a forest cycle is, it is still extravagantly wasteful, dangerous and achingly sad" (13A). In a television interview, Wyoming Senator Malcom Wallop called for the resignation of National Park Service Director Mott because Mott "continues to find some reason to celebrate this event [the fires] while all the rest of us are suffering" ("Sen. Wallop Finds" 10A). Even sources who acknowledged the benefits of fire questioned the impact of allowing fires to burn large areas. The *Jackson Hole [WY] Guide* editorialized, "The damage is not permanent, but for some it might as well be. Regrowth will occur, but the long-term effects—impossible to measure—nonetheless are disturbing in their scope" ("Congress Should Investigate" A4).

Editorials in the national press also found more death than life in the fires. Most argued that, while there might be some merit in the let-burn policy, in certain years it should be abandoned, because, as the *St. Louis Post-Dispatch* claimed, "the danger is so great that fires will spread out of control, threatening property and lives and livelihoods" ("Fires Ravage West" 1017). Some, while admitting the overall wisdom of the policy, mourned the "charred disfigurement of Yellowstone National Park" (*Roanoke [VA] Times & World News* in "Fires Ravage West" 1015). The *Omaha World-Herald* suggested that "much of the park lies in ruin. Homes and businesses have been destroyed," and attacked the "defenders of the let-'em-burn policy" for allowing a "federal policy [to go] out of control, destroying millions of trees, leaving much of a major national park in ruin and fouling the air for hundreds of miles" ("Fires Ravage West" 1014). The *Billings [MT] Gazette* questioned why Yellowstone Park Superintendent Robert Barbee "blindly rode a dead policy into hell" ("Fires Ravage West" 1012). Perhaps one of the most vivid images came from the *Richmond [VA] News Leader:* "If you want to see the world's largest charcoal grill, just visit Yellowstone. Be sure to say, 'Thank you, environmentalists.' " The editorialist admitted that "Fires are Nature's way of dealing with thick forests, its way of thinning trees," but added that "Nature sometimes goes too far. While forests need periodic thinning, they don't need to be burned to ash" ("Fires Ravage West" 1016).

The tone of most of the editorials which appeared to reject the let-burn policy was "yes, but. . . ." In other words, most editorialists accepted the argument that regeneration would come from fire, but under certain weather conditions in certain years, the policy should be abandoned in order to avoid excessive damage—and nonabandonment was a mark of irresponsibility and lack of concern for humans *and* nature.

Visions of Rebirth in the Fire Debate

Supporters of the natural fire policy appealed to a metaphor of regeneration and rebirth, although the support was often tempered by the recommendation that the policy should be rethought for extreme drought years. Various natural resource-affiliated federal employees, environmentalists, and research biologists were especially prominent in using terms such as rebirth, renewal, greening, cycles, process, creation. Interestingly, consistent with the assumption of death within rebirth, many advocates used the image of a dead or dying forest in order to explain the effects of fire as rebirth, whereas opponents of the fire policy had spoken almost exclusively only of death. Forestry officials consistently argued that fires "prompt rebirth in the wilderness, clearing away the old, dead and overgrown while making way for new vegetation and new wildlife habitats" ("Park Policy Under Fire" A2). In fact, the *Jackson Hole Guide* reported on September 7 that "areas that burned a few weeks ago already have green shoots" (Kessler A1). This was *before* the snow fell.

Even during the most intense days of the fire Yellowstone Park officials were attempting to replace the death metaphor with that of rebirth. On September 4, the Idaho Falls *Post-Register*[12] reported that the Park Service had "launched an information blitz. It is trying to assure people that the fires will help the forest renew itself" (Huegel B1). The park had various displays created for tourist consumption, including a short film, "The Yellowstone Fires" which had been updated four times through September 4. Commenting on the ongoing fires, one ranger told the newspaper, "We're really hoping to use this as a way to teach the natural cycles of the forest" (Huegel B1).

The *Post-Register* suggested that because of the combination of severe drought and the pine beetle infestation which had devastated many Rocky Mountain forests from the late 1970s through the mid 1980s, "the forest was highly vulnerable to a devastating forest fire," so there was "no assurance that the fires could have been stopped, no matter what the policy." The editorial writer admitted that as a result of the fires, "the wildlife habitat in and around the park" might improve. The wisest course would be to study the policy further and, in the meantime, allow the professional forest managers to make decisions "based on available research, rather than impulsive reaction from critics or politicians" ("Natural Fire Policy" A4). The *Salt Lake Tribune* agreed that "fire is a natural process necessary for a healthy ecosystem in the park," and added that "natural forces sometimes conspire to create problems that, quite simply, are beyond the control of man" ("Sen. Wallop Finds" 10A). A Wyoming columnist put it more vividly. "The Yellowstone fires are a natural phenomenon akin to a flood or earthquake," Andrew Melnykovych wrote, "staggering in their scope and fundamentally beyond human control" (A8). Even some of those who appeared to oppose the policy admitted that fire was part of the natural process. An editorial in the *Idaho State Journal* argued that "in extreme drought years, the 'let it burn' policy ought to be abandoned," and then added, "even though such fires often bring regeneration and improve wildlife habitat in burned-out areas" ("What Have We Learned?" A4).

Scientists and their surrogates in environmental groups spent considerable time building the rebirth argument in the regional press. Lawson LaGate of the Sierra Club told the *Salt Lake Tribune,* "Ultimately, what is happening is going to be good for the park and the ecosystem. . . . From a wildlife standpoint, it will be a real boon for the elk. Frankly, I get very angry when I hear a congressman from Wyoming, in total ignorance, say these fires have sterilized everything" (Wharton 6B). Another environmentalist, Ed Lewis of the Greater Yellowstone Coalition, claimed that local economies would also be regenerated by the fires: "You may have a tremendous number of people coming to the park to see it after the fires. . . . Many people who have seen Yellowstone and have no reason to return are now looking forward to a different experience" (Wharton 6B). Donna Pinsof and Ralph Maughn of the Eastern Idaho chapter of the Sierra Club presented their chapter's views in an *Idaho State Journal* editorial:

> Of course, TV and press photos usually showed the public the worst, since that's more impressive. Nevertheless, new grass is already several inches high in many place burned in July. Next summer will bring an explosion of wildflowers amid the standing burned trees. . . . In a decade, new trees will hide most of the still standing snags. In a generation we think many will find the Park much more beautiful than before the fire with its dead trees and log-covered forest floor. (A5)

A group of five scientists from the University of Wyoming issued a press release on September 13 challenging the opponents of the natural fire policy. Calling Yellowstone a "living and dynamic entity," the scientists claimed that changes are inevitable, including those changes brought by fire. The report also noted that Yellowstone is "in no danger of being 'destroyed' by the fires since 'dead trees do not equate directly to dead forests'." The Wyoming scientists argued that economic losses of one summer season must be judged against the enormous economic benefits generated by communities being located near the park for so many years. Moreover, tourists would benefit ultimately from the fires because the newly opened meadows will allow greater opportunity to see wildlife in the park ("U.W. Scientists Say"). Two biologists from Idaho State University (Pocatello) also used local media to advance the ecological benefits of fire. Jay Anderson claimed that "most people seem unaware of the scientific evidence suggesting forests need fire to encourage new plant growth and create wildlife habitat." According to Wayne Minshall, another biologist at Idaho State, "We've oversown the Smokey the Bear syndrome and it's finally caught up to us" (Englert, "Environmentalists" A1).

Park officials were also quick to report the latest results of the fires. The *Riverton [WY] Ranger* reported the animals of the park actually preferred the burned out areas for food. One researcher noted that elk had migrated to the burned areas in search of ash, which had the attraction of a salt lick. The researcher also claimed that the fish population in the park would probably increase as the "nutrients left behind by the fires work their way into the streams and lakes and serve as a type of fertilizer for the food chain" ("Animals Prefer" 12). A park information officer told of animals grazing while fires blazed around them. "This is not a Bambi situation here," reported Jeff Selleck. "Even while the fire was burning, the animals seemed fairly serene" (McCabe 6A). An Associated Press report of September 19 illustrates the concerted effort of officials to report the park's rebirth: "During the three months Yellowstone National Park has burned, firefighters have struggled heroically, politicians have pointed fingers and the park has quietly gone about healing itself." The report noted that "just eight weeks after flames roared past the Grant Village complex . . . wildflowers already have sprouted from the blackened soil" ("Park Rebirth" A2).

In the national press, reports of the park's rebirth also appeared during the crisis stage. Jay Mathews of the *Washington Post* reported on September 12 that the "park has begun a remarkable regeneration. This surprising turnabout stems both from the natural cycle of fire and regrowth that renews all pine forests and from the destruction's stunning irregularity, of which the public remains largely unaware" (A1). A September 14 article in the *Christian Science Monitor* focused totally on the power of nature to regenerate itself after the fires. In describing a typical burned forest, the article listed the multiple benefits of fire for micro-organisms; plants, grasses, and trees; fish; and small and large mammals (Schierholz 1).

To help put the Yellowstone fires in perspective, some advocates reviewed the impact of other recent fires in the West. Recalling a 50,000 acre fire in the Boise National Forest in 1987, ranger Frank Carroll noted, "It 'a natural mosaic now, with open meadows and stands of timber. . . . A forest that was just getting older and deader has now been beautifully revived" ("Officials Cite Idaho Fire" A1). Tracey Trent of the Idaho Department of Fish and Game also emphasized the important benefits of fire: "When fire goes through an area and turns those trees into ash, one of the things that happens is that the minerals the tree has captured during its life are returned to the soil" ("Officials Cite Idaho Fire" A1–2).

Refuting the critics of the natural fire policy and their images of death and destruction, the *Los Angeles Times* observed:

> such complaints can fuel a Bambi syndrome among members of the public who see dramatic fire walls and smoke clouds on television news. They can envision helpless creatures of the forest fleeing the firestorms. They read of massive acreages 'destroyed' without understanding that fire is a necessary cog in the life cycle of a healthy forest, or that not every acre has been scorched. ("Fires Ravage West" 1010)

Other newspapers used similar visions of rebirth in supporting federal policy. The *Seattle Times* noted that when a forest is "aging, disease-ridden, insect-riddled and dry, it is ripe for natural fires that consume old, dead growth and make room for new plants and trees" ("Fires Ravage West" 1011). In a striking use of the rebirth metaphor, the *Burlington [VT] Free Press* observed:

> Fire is one of the midwives of life in the wilderness. The tight ranks of lodgepole pine that dominated Yellowstone shut out other species and provided a poor environment for wild animals. Fire swept them away, making room for a riotous variety of flowers, shrubs, and trees. ("Fires Ravage West" 1011)

In these editorials as well as others, the conception of fire as a means of achieving new life had been accepted as a fundamental part of national park and national forest policy.

LINKING THE METAPHORS PERMANENTLY

As the snows fell, the debate cooled and focused not on abandonment of the policy, but on revision of the policy to meet special circumstances, such as those present during acutely dry summers. Dale Robertson, chief of the U.S. Forest Service, argued that "natural fires should remain a part of national forest policy," but admitted that "'we're going to have to sharpen up our criteria on when it's applied and under what conditions'" ("Fires Still Have Place" 3). After touring Yellowstone, Interior Secretary Hodel promised "a new policy . . . before the beginning of the next fire year" (LaMay 10) . . . although major environmental groups such as the Wilderness Society and the National Parks and Conservation Association characterized the existing policy as "sound, flexible and scientifically based" (Darst). The Sierra Club claimed that "what is happening is going to be good for the park and the ecosystem" (Wharton 6B).

As snows continued to fall in 1988, newspaper articles began appearing which charted recovery of/in Yellowstone, and compared the fires in Yellowstone to earlier fires which had led to forest rebirth—as forest managers had been claiming. Headlines such as "What Fires? Large Animals in Yellowstone Grazed Serenely as Park Went Up in Smoke" (McCabe 6A); "Biologists Disagree on Fire Impact on Wildlife" (Kessler A1); "Animals 'Prefer Burned-Out'" (12); "Park Rebirth After Fire: Wildflowers Sprout from Blackened Soil" (A2); and "Analysts Begin Search Into Wildfires' Effects" (Nussbaum 10A); attest to the controversy surrounding effects of the fire but clearly juxtapose the metaphors of death and rebirth—perhaps giving the public the impression that death and rebirth might be inextricably linked. One article concerned the first fire to occur after the Forest Service natural fire policy had been adopted. The author described renewal of vegetation, new animals which had moved into the area, animals which had left and been replaced by others during the fourteen years since the fire, as well as the support for the policy which had grown after the fire had died (Thuermer 4). Timing the article for mid-September added support for the claim that the "let burn" policy was environmentally sound, and offered evidence that out of death could come new life.

During the "crisis aftermath" period, from early October to June 1989, the rebirth/regeneration argument assumed preeminence in public discussions of the fires. Removed from the daily televised images of flames, Army helicopters, and blackened areas, the rebirth metaphor could more rationally be coupled with scientific and ecological appeals. On October 5, for example, the *Jackson Hole Guide* reported that Wyoming Senators Simpson and Wallop had dropped their calls for the firing of National Park Superintendent Mott. In fact, Wallop called the existing fire policy "reasonable on its face" and said the government's task "was simply to discover what went wrong with the policy and make improvements" (Piccoli A1). In mid-October, Interior Secretary Hodel sent copies of a letter thanking firefighters for their efforts to newspaper editors in which he claimed "we are anticipating a great influx of tourists interested in seeing the extent of the damage and the progress of regrowth," and added "nature recovers from these events by rebirth of the old-growth forests and rejuvenation of forage and wildlife" ("Interior Secretary Hodel Praises"). In an editorial printed in both the *Jackson Hole Guide* and the *Salt Lake Tribune,* George Frampton, then President of the Wilderness Society, argued that the nation would marvel at the new life in Yellowstone: "Grass and brilliant wildflowers will spring up. Underrepresented, fast-growing aspen will take root. Birds that need dead-tree cavities for nests will colonize burned areas" (A5). At a forum in Idaho, sponsored by the League of Women Voters and a local Audubon chapter, two biologists stressed the benefits of fire and the worth of the "natural fire" policy. "If plant diversity and the patchwork pattern created by fire is any indicator," concluded one, "then the future of wildlife in Yellowstone is very bright" (Englert, "ISU Biologist Doubts" B1).[13]

In 1992, evidence of Yellowstone's ecological health continued to be reported. Observing that the fire had generated a huge increase in lodgepole pine seedlings, Dr. Jay Anderson found that in moderate-burn areas, from four to twenty-eight times as many seedlings were found. "In 10 to 20 years, Yellowstone will again have pretty, healthy forests as a result of the 1988 fires," concluded Anderson. Yellowstone's pristine condition before the fires, he concluded, "really was a consequence of previous fires." The biologist claimed that the lesson from the Yellowstone fires was simple: "when areas are ready to burn, they're going to. When the conditions are ripe, there isn't anything we can do about it" ("Thousands of Lodgepole" B3). Also in 1992 national park officials approved a new plan that allowed some natural fires to continue to burn and even permitted park officials to start fires for management purposes. The plan requires that park officials certify daily that "adequate firefighting sources are available to prevent [natural fires] from going out of control in the next 24 hours" (Barker, "Yellowstone OKs" D1).

CONCLUSIONS AND IMPLICATIONS

Although fires appear similar in power and scope to hurricanes, floods, and tornadoes, in fact fires are fundamentally different from other natural forces because of their mythic and cultural connotations. Noting that a fire environment is "as much cultural as natural," Pyne emphasizes the importance of human values in discussing fires:

> One can accurately speak about fire only in conjunction with something else—fire and flora, fire and fauna, fire and earth, fire and water. As an agency, fire can be as effective by its absence as by its applications. For this reason one is inevitably led back to that most fundamental of all associations with fire, the relationship between fire and man. (530)

Much of the debate over the Yellowstone fires reflects humankind's inherently dichotomous view of fire; while fire destroys and can be as devastating as any natural force, fire can also create, empower, and be managed. Because of its great power to create and destroy, Pyne explains, fire "had to be assimilated, explained, regulated. Time and again fire origin myths depict [us] as human only after [we have] acquired fire" (531). This duality may indicate why forest fire policy and public reaction to fire is so strained. Fifty years of Smokey Bear telling us that only *we* can prevent forest fires is one of the most deeply embedded messages in American culture.

The Yellowstone fire debate reveals that archetypal metaphors remain prominent in contemporary public discourse; that such metaphors have an inventional quality that provides observers a lens for describing and interpreting reality and gives advocates a foundation for rhetorical appeals; and that archetypal metaphors are especially powerful rhetorical devices in the context of a perceived crisis. Archetypal metaphors may be chosen less strategically than other rhetorical forms, but may be more intrinsic to a particular world view; analysis of such metaphors helps the critic to discover ways in which they reflect and/or reinforce one's world view. Jamieson's claim that archetypal metaphors have the ability to constrain rhetorical choices is also reflected by the choice of death versus rebirth in the fire debate. Advocates who perceived public land management from a *human-centered* perspective could only discuss fire in terms that related to human values and characteristics: fire destroys life if not managed; charred, blackened ruins can only be a sign of death, both literally and figuratively. On the other hand, those proponents of "natural fires" who saw the world from an *ecological* perspective, believing that all life forms live in a complex cycle of interdependence, found the archetypal metaphor of rebirth most meaningful from their world view. They could understand a world in which death was an essential step in the life-cycle and that ultimately fire would yield new life, regardless of its immediate consequences. This use of archetypal metaphors typify the human capacity—or need—to reconstruct chaotic images in fundamentally human terms. Environmental crises may be prone to archetypal imagery for this reason.

It appears that the archetypal metaphor of death pervaded media reports of the fires, both in reporter commentary and individuals selected to represent residents and tourists. In his study of media accounts of the Yellowstone fires, Conrad Smith found that cultural assumptions about forest fires inhibited accurate reporting. For example, he observed that the urban world view that fire "destroys" and leaves "victims" had a profound effect upon how the media reported the Yellowstone fires. We believe that such language choices, which emerge from a master metaphor of death, reinforced already powerful cultural assumptions and in turn helped construct a rhetorical climate of crisis. Smith reported that television crews consistently asked one question of park officials: "Where can I find reliable flames?" (50). In their quest to find an appropriate verbal symbol to match the visual images of flames, reporters could easily turn to the death metaphor. Out-of-control flames destroy, rather than create.

As the policy debate continued, it became clear that supporters of the prescribed natural burn policy were able to convince much of the public that "death" should be subsumed within "rebirth." This perspective of a life-cycle in which organisms are born, die, and are re-born—sometimes in different forms—appealed to members of the public who were sympathetic to an environmental perspective in which humans are part of nature, rather than to the perspective which suggests that humans are the center of nature. Acceptance of the rebirth metaphor created a picture of reality which allowed preservation of the natural fire management policy, despite the fact that the Interior Department chose to suppress all 1989 and 1990 fires. Had a significant number of members of the public and policy-makers embraced the death metaphor alone, inescapable pressure would have been exerted to return to the "Smokey the Bear" policy that *all* fires are bad. The perspective that prevailed was that, although parts of the policy may need to be more flexible in times of severe drought, "for the forests as a whole, the fires represent part of a cycle of death and renewal that occurred for many centuries until it was interrupted by man less than 100 years ago" (Melnykovych A8).

Reading Endnotes

1. For an extensive and highly critical account of the non-public discussion about the worthiness of the natural fire policy in Yellowstone, see Micah Morrison's *Fire in Paradise: The Yellowstone Fires and the Politics of Environmentalism*. Morrison examined the progress of each major fire in and around the Park, using diaries and interviews with many of the principals involved in the decision-making.
2. To facilitate this study, we examined approximately 150 newspaper articles in the Rocky Mountain region (Idaho, Montana, Utah, Wyoming) that were printed during the "crisis" period of late-August to late-September 1988. We also reviewed articles in the "crisis aftermath" period of October 1988 to June 1989.
3. Osborn and Ehninger describe the stimulus-response process created by metaphor as "error, puzzlement-recoil, and resolution." When we encounter a metaphor, our first impulse is to use the literal meaning for the terms (error). When we realize that the two terms are "inconsistent" (puzzlement-recoil), we search for a way to reconcile the two terms (resolution) (226–227).
4. We wish to acknowledge a *WSJ* reviewer for suggesting the concept of a dominant organic metaphor that includes death and rebirth.
5. See Alfred Runte, especially chapter 10, for a more lengthy discussion of the role the Sequoias played in development of the prescribed natural burn policy. See Pyne for a similar discussion, as well as a longer history of fire policy in federal agencies, especially pp. 260–326.
6. Edwin Black suggested, similarly, that when a speaker uses a single term associated with a particular ideology, the critic is "justified in suspecting that a general attitude—more, a whole set of general attitudes were being summoned" (112–113).
7. Crises are distinguished from other events, writes Dennis Gouran, by the "unexpectedness and sense of urgency their threatening qualities create for a speedy resolution" (174). A crisis situation, he continues, has three components: threat, time restrictions, and surprise. As will become evident in this study, national and regional audiences perceived all three features in the 1988 forest fires and reacted accordingly in their rhetoric.
8. An "ecosystem" can be thought of as "a set of interacting species and their local, nonbiological environment, functioning together to sustain life" (Botkin 230).
9. In *Ronald Reagan and the Public Lands*, Brant Short discusses evolution of the "conservation consensus." As is often the case with social movements, two factions of the conservation movement, one devoted to "orderly public land development" and the other committed to "preserving the wilderness intact," tried to dictate how the public ought to see the movement. Gradually, preservationist rhetoric and actions gained prominence and out of these roots grew the ecological movement (and worldview) with which we are more familiar today.

Although grounded in the same movement, in contemporary terms, "conservation" and "ecology" (or environmentalism) have acquired bi-polar meanings and are generally viewed as opposing movements. See especially ch. 1. In contrast with what we argue is the current domination by an environmental (or preservation) worldview Christine Oravec examines competing claims of conservationists and preservationists in her study of the Hetch-Hetchy dam controversy shortly after the turn of this century. She concludes that, as Short also points out, the preservationist view dominated public discussion about land management until recently.

10. The *Journal* is Pocatello's newspaper; Pocatello is located about three hours from Yellowstone.
11. Jackson Hole, Wyoming, is the southern entrance to Teton National Park, which borders Yellowstone at the south.
12. Idaho Falls is about two and a half hours away from Yellowstone.
13. In December 1988, a joint Agriculture and Interior Department Review Committee issued its final report regarding the "natural fire" policy and the Yellowstone fires. In answer to the question, "Is the policy allowing fire to play its natural ecological role in parks and wilderness under certain conditions flawed or inappropriate?", the report concluded that while there were some flaws in the implementation of the policy, it endorsed the concept of "natural fire" management and cited the benefits of fire (1–2, i). The report recommended a moratorium on the let-burn policy until the overall recommendations (including interagency cooperation, contingency plans for different categories of fires, use of planned burns, better fire personnel training, increase of public involvement, and more research on weather and fire behavior—see report, page ii) had been met (U.S. Dept. of Agriculture 16).

Reading Works Cited

"Andrus Blasts Let-Burn Policy." *Times-News* [Twin Falls, ID] 10 September 1988: A4.

"Animals 'Prefer Burned-Out.'" *Riverton Ranger* 13 September 1988: 12.

"Barker, Rocky. "Flame and Blame." *High Country News* 7 November 1988: 10–12.

Barker, Rocky. "Yellowstone OKs Natural-Burn Policy." *Post Register* 6 May 1992: D1.

Beck, Joan. "Park Service's Let-It-Burn Theory Backfires on an Innocent Victim." Editorial. *Salt Lake Tribune* 12 September 1988: 13A.

Black, Edwin. "The Second Persona." *Quarterly Journal of Speech* 56 (1970): 109–119.

Botkin, Daniel B. *Discordant Harmonies: A New Ecology for the Twenty-first Century.* New York: Oxford University Press, 1990.

Brock, Bernard L., Robert L. Scott, and James W. Chesebro. *Methods of Rhetorical Criticism: A Twentieth-Century Perspective.* 3rd ed., rev. Detroit, MI: Wayne State University Press, 1989.

"Congress Should Investigate Park Disaster." Editorial. *Jackson Hole Guide* 14 September 1988: A4.

"Congress Will View Fire Policy." *Idaho Statesman* 12 September 1988: 4A.

Darst, Guy. "Environmental Groups Defend Administration's Firefighting Policies." Dialogue Information Service, Inc. (AP News Wire Service Database, File 258.) Washington, D.C.: 10 September 1988.

Donnelly, John. "Record High Temps Worsen West's Fire Situation." *Idaho State Journal* 4 September 1988: A1+.

"Dubois Merchants Feeling Fires' Flame." *Riverton Ranger* 6 September 1988: 9+.

Englert, Stuart. "Environmentalists Still Embrace 'Let Burn.'" *Idaho State Journal,* 15 September 1988: A1+.

Englert, Stuart. "ISU Biologist Doubts Let-Burn Policy Doused." *Idaho State Journal,* 21 October 1988: B1.

"Fire Policy Opens Way for Political Attacks." Editorial. *Times-News* [Twin Falls, ID] 11 September 1988: A4.

"Fires Ravage West." *Editorials on File* 19.17 (1–15 September 1988): 1010–1017.

"Fires Still Have Place in Forest Management, Chief Argues." *Daily Spectrum*-Iron County Edition 11 September 1988: 3.

"Flames Lick at Edge of Yellowstone Towns." *Idaho Statesman* [Boise] 5 September 1988 A1+.

Flitner, David A. "Nixing Careful Harvest of Blowdown Backfires." Editorial. *Casper Star* 11 September 1988: A8.

Foss, Sonja K. *Rhetorical Criticism: Exploration and Practice.* Prospect Heights, IL: Waveland Press, 1989.

Foster, David. "Outlook Grim for Saving Towns from Forest Fire." *Idaho State Journal* 6 September 1988: A1+.

Foster, David. "Residents Leaving West Yellowstone As Fire Nears." *Idaho State Journal* 2 September 1988: A1.

Frampton, George, Jr. "We Can Push Nature So Far." *Jackson Hole Guide* 5 October 1988: A5.

"Giant Wildfire: Residents Flee as Fire Nears." *Idaho State Journal* 5 September 1988: Al+.

Gouran, Dennis. *Making Decisions in Groups: Choices and Consequences.* Glenview, IL: Scott, Foresman and Co., 1982.

"Group Blasts Let-It-Burn Plan." *Times-News* 11 September 1988: C1.

Grubbs, K. E., Jr. "Environmental Wisdom of Letting Fires Burn Goes Up in Smoke." *Salt Lake Tribune* 22 September 1988: A21.

"Hodel Says Interior Fighting Wildfires." Department of the Interior News Release. 28 July 1988.

Huegel, Tony. "Yellowstone Puts On New Face." *Post-Register* 4 September 1988. B1+.

"Interior Secretary Hodel Praises Forest Firefighters, Says Valiant Efforts Prevented Worse Destruction." Department of the Interior News Release. 13 October 1988.

Ivie, Robert. "Metaphor and the Rhetorical Invention of Cold War 'Idealists'." *Communication Monographs* 54 (1987): 165–182. Rpt. in *Rhetorical Criticism: Exploration and Practice.* Ed. Sonja K. Foss. Prospect Heights, IL: Waveland Press, 1989. 197–217.

Jamieson, Kathleen Hall. "The Metaphoric Cluster in the Rhetoric of Pope Paul VI and Edmund G. Brown, Jr." *Quarterly Journal of Speech* 66 (1980): 51–72 Rpt. in *The Practice of Rhetorical Criticism.* Ed. James R. Andrews. New York: Macmillan, 1983. 228–251.

Jones, Tamara. "Epic Wildfires Alter Face of Yellowstone." *Salt Lake Tribune* 24 August 1988: A1+.

Jones, Tamara and Bert Secter. "Yellowstone Crews Win First Battle." *Los Angeles Times* 12 September 1988, sec. I:, 1+.

Kessler, Nancy. "Biologists Disagree on Fire Impact on Wildlife." *Jackson Hole Guide* 7 September 1988: A1+.

Lakoff, George, and Mark Johnson. *Metaphors We Live By.* Chicago: University of Chicago Press, 1980.

LaMay, Colleen. "Hodel Says Let-Burn Policy Must Be Changed." *Idaho Statesman* 12 September 1988: C1+.

Leal, Donald R. "Yellowstone Burns As Park Managers Play Politics." *Wall Street Journal* 26 August 1988, natl. ed.: 10.

Matthews, Jay. "Yellowstone Begins Rebirth Amid Acres of Charred Earth." *Washington Post* 12 September 1988: A1+.

Matthiessen, Peter. "Our National Parks: The Case for Burning." *New York Times Magazine* 11 December 1988: 39–41+.

McCabe, Carol. "What Fire? Large Animals in Yellowstone Grazed Serenely as Park Went Up in Smoke." *Deseret News* [Salt Lake City, UT] 15–16 September 1988: 6A.

Melnykovych, Andrew. "Firing Mott Adds a Political Smokescreen." Editorial. *Star Tribune* 12 September 1988: A8.

Morrison, Micah. *Fire in Paradise: The Yellowstone Fires and the Politics of Environmentalism.* New York: Harper-Collins, 1993.

"Natural Fire Policy Change Takes Research." Editorial. *Post-Register* 31 August 1988: A4.

Nussbaum, Paul. "Analysts Begin Search Into Wildfires' Effects; Yellowstone's Small Animals Are Hardest Hit." *Salt Lake Tribune* 18 September 1988: 10A.

Oatis, Jonathan W. "Cool, Wet Weather Calms Western Fires." *Idaho State Journal* 14 September 1988: A2.

Oravec, Christine. "Conservationism vs. Preservationism: The 'Public Interest' in the Hetch Hetchy Controversy." *Quarterly Journal of Speech* 70 (1984): 444–458.

Osborn, Michael. "Archetypal Metaphor in Rhetoric: The Light-Dark Family." *Quarterly Journal of Speech* 53 (1967): 115–126.

Osborn, Michael M., and Douglas Ehninger. "The Metaphor in Public Address." *Speech Monographs* 26 (1962): 223–234.

"Park Policy Under Fire." *Idaho State Journal* 6 September 1988: A2.

"Park Rebirth After Fire: Wildflowers Sprout from Blackened Soil." *Idaho State Journal* 6 September 1988: A2.

Perry, S. "Rhetorical Functions of the Infestation Metaphor in Hitler's Rhetoric." *Central States Speech Journal* 34 (1983): 229–235.

Piccoli, Joseph. "Senators Mute Criticism of Fire Policy." *Jackson Hole Guide* 5 October 1988: A1+.

Pinsof, Donna, and Ralph Maughn. "Yellowstone Fires Were Inevitable in 1988." Editorial. *Idaho State Journal* 18 September 1988: A5.

Pyne, Stephen J. *Fire in America: A Cultural History of Wildland and Rural Fire.* Princeton, NJ: Princeton University Press, 1982.

Radtke, Del. "Letting Forests Burn is Folly." Editorial. *Missoulian* 4 September 1988: 5.

Rickert, W. "Winston Churchill's Archetypal Metaphors: A Mythopoetic Translation of World War II." *Central States Speech Journal* 28 (1977): 106–112.

Runte, Alfred. *National Parks: The American Experience.* 2nd ed., rev. Lincoln: University of Nebraska Press, 1987.

Rushforth, Desirai. "North Fork Fire Rapidly Closing on Island Park." *Idaho State Journal* 5 September 1988: A1+.

Schierholz, Tom. "Costly Forest Fires Can Still Carry Benefits." *Christian Science Monitor* 14 September 1988: 1+.

"Sen. Wallop Finds Scapegoat for Tragic Yellowstone Fire." Editorial. *Salt Lake Tribune* 10 September 1988: 10A.

Short, C. Brant. *Ronald Reagan and the Public Lands: America's Conservation Debate, 1979–1984.* The Environmental History Series 10. College Station, TX: Texas A&M Press, 1989.

Smith, Conrad. *Media and Apocalypse: News Coverage of the Yellowstone Forest Fires, Exxon-Valdez Oil Spill, and Loma Prieta Earthquake.* Westport, CT: Greenwood Press, 1992.

Stump, David. "Group Launches Petition to Change Park Fire Policy." *Jackson Hole Guide* 7 September 1988: A16.

"Thousands of Lodgepole Pine Seedlings Rejuvenate Yellowstone Park in Wake of 1988 Destructive Fires." *Idaho State Journal* 12 November 1992: B3.

Thuermer, Angus M., Jr. "The Waterfalls Fire Revisited." *Jackson Hole News* 28 September 1988: 4.

U. S. Dept. of Agriculture and Dept. of Interior. Forest Service. *Report on Fire Management Policy.* 14 December 1988.

"U.W. Scientists Say Yellowstone Not Wrecked." University of Wyoming News Service Release, 13 September 1988.

Wharton, Tom. "Wallop, Yellowstone Fire Critics Ignorant of the Facts." Editorial. *Salt Lake Tribune* 12 September 1988: 6B.

"What Have We Learned?" Editorial. *Idaho State Journal* 28 August 1988: A4.

Wilkinson, Todd. "Fuller Makes Last Stand at Canyon." *Jackson Hole News* 31 August 1988: 11.

Zimowsky, Pete. "Nature's Way of Reshaping Wildlife Habitat." *Idaho Statesman* 11 September 1986: E1.

In this Chapter 5 workshop, we will probe in focused workshop exercises many of the concepts you discovered in this chapter. Work at a pace by assignment, or by choice, that allows these various insights to "sink in" at an even deeper level for you.

As part of this Chapter 5 workshop, we will continue to probe several of the ways you can recognize and use the "gold" of academic, rhetorical criticism. Do you worry about forest fires? Some people are required by their jobs to do so. Moreover, reasonable people in our culture disagree—harshly—about how we should deal with forest fires. We can even see the issue pop up in popular entertainment; an episode of the hit TV drama *The West Wing* had Martin Sheen as President Josiah Bartlet in a dispute with a fictional governor of Wyoming about whether or not to allow an out of control forest fire to burn in his state.[21]

Dayle C. Hardy-Short and C. Brant Short have written an important and interesting study about an erupting public dispute over how to handle forest fires in Yellowstone National Park. Their deep understanding of archetypal metaphors should give governmental policymakers, journalists, and interested citizens pause when they think (as they should) about how language can guide and control a public debate and actions about vital issues.

You have already read the rhetorical criticism of public debate about forest fires in Yellowstone National Park by Hardy-Short and Short starting on page 146. Take careful notes on the justification for study (JFS), justification for artifact (JFA), method, and research question (RQ) items (about which you learned in Chapter 3) that Hardy-Short and Short use to establish the need for their research.

FINDING THE ANALYSIS SET-UP ITEMS

Find the various claims that serve as a JFS in this article.

Example:

Hardy-Short, Dayle C. and Brant C. Short. "Fire, Death, and Rebirth: A Metaphoric Analysis of the 1988 Yellowstone Fire Debate." *Western Journal of Communication* 59 (1995): 103–125.

(Page numbers in brackets indicate pages reprinted in this textbook.)

JFS	Page	Internal or External?
"Politicians, ranchers, journalists, and residents of fire-stricken areas claimed that the federal government's 'natural fire' policy (called by many the 'let burn' policy) was dangerous, short-sighted, and wasteful."	104 [147]	External
"Yet, only a few published studies attempt to refine and expand our understanding of the function of archetypal metaphors[.]"	104 [147]	Internal

FINDING THE ANALYSIS SET-UP ITEMS

Find the various claims that serve as a JFA in this article.

Example:

Hardy-Short, Dayle C. and Brant C. Short. "Fire, Death, and Rebirth: A Metaphoric Analysis of the 1988 Yellowstone Fire Debate." *Western Journal of Communication* 59 (1995): 103–125.

JFA	Page	Internal or External?
"This editorial [in the *Wall Street Journal* about federal forest fire policy] represented one of the opening salvos in the national and regional debate that emerged during the severe fire season of 1988."	103–104 [146–147]	External
"Next, we review the rhetoric surrounding the fire debate, examining both local and national sources of public argument."	105 [148]	External
"To facilitate this study, we examined approximately 150 newspaper articles in the Rocky Mountain region (Idaho, Montana, Utah, Wyoming) that were printed during the 'crisis' period of late-August to late-September 1988. We also reviewed articles in the 'crisis aftermath' period of October 1988 to June 1989.	(endnote 2 on page 121) [165]	External

FINDING THE GOLD

Next, re-read the chart on this page. See if you can notice how we moved from the original claim, insight, or discovery to the resulting "translations."

Next, use the blank chart on the following page to find more nuggets of "gold" in the article from your own reading. Be sure to keep track of the page on which you find the quotation and think about how you can best translate the insight or discovery to a practical translation you could use in preparing a message.

Discovering Application Ideas and Knowledge in Metaphoric Analysis Articles

Example:

Hardy-Short, Dayle C. and Brant C. Short. "Fire, Death, and Rebirth: A Metaphoric Analysis of the 1988 Yellowstone Fire Debate." *Western Journal of Communication* 59 (1995): 103–125.

Quotation	Page	Translated Idea or Insight
"Because of their intrinsic connection to the human experience, archetypal metaphors may be called upon more often in crisis situations when people recall their most basic and fundamental experiences to understand a particular problem."	105 [148–149]	Crisis situations should produce the use of archetypal metaphors in public messages about the crisis.
"We do not suggest that advocates (of either side) consciously chose one archetype over another, but that at some point they did make conscious use of certain words that, when clustered, can be described the archetype."	107 [150]	Rhetors often automatically choose metaphors without thinking. Selected words in a public dispute can be part of an archetypal metaphor without participants fully recognizing that they are using metaphors.
"Editorials in the national press also found more death than life in the fires."	114 [157]	National media messages may use different metaphors than do local or regional media messages concerning a public controversy.

Use the chart on the next page to find, identify, and chart the potential advantage of other observations on metaphors and public policy that Hardy-Short and Short make in their analysis.

Quotation	Page	Translated Idea or Insight

CREATING IMPLIED NON-LITERAL COMPARISONS

Implied metaphors can be very powerful rhetorical tools. Below you'll find several quick instances in which a metaphier is indicated by implication (i.e., indirectly) by using a specified paraphier to get an audience member to think of the metaphier. Once you get the idea, try to create your own specified paraphiers that will allow the creation of an implied non-literal comparison.

Indicate that you are shooting or aiming at someone or something:	"in the crosshairs"	
Indicate that someone or something is a dangerous spider:	"get caught in his deadly web"	
Indicate that someone or something is a dangerous jungle cat:		
Indicate that someone or something is a messy puppy:		
Indicate that a business is going down in quicksand:		
Indicate that a new law will do as much damage as a severe storm:		

ARCHETYPAL METAPHORS

Use the following archetypal metaphor types and create a series of specific metaphors that describe the success, or lack of success, of a favorite sports team.

House	"The foundation of the Tigers defense is crumbling."	
Weather	"The Eagles will roar into Dempsey stadium tomorrow like a series of twisters."	
Human Body		
Illness		
Seasons		
Food		

NOVEL METAPHORS

Examine the following three novel metaphors. Each one specifies or gives emphasis to a specific paraphier or set of paraphiers. Does this make the metaphor more effective? Why?

1. "The rush hour traffic is bleeding steadily out of all the city's major arteries this afternoon. Somebody better call a road doctor." [Without paraphier specification: Rush hour traffic is moving on the major arteries this afternoon.]
2. "Nothing great has happened in my life; if life is a roller coaster, then mine belongs in kiddieland." [Without paraphier specification: My life is a roller coaster.]
3. Sen. Wendell Ford (D-Kentucky): "If the Senate really wants a circus, we have all the ingredients right here, including the clowns." [Without paraphier specification: The Senate is a circus.]

Equivalent Key Terms Used in Metaphor Analysis

Chart 5.7 shows some of the central terms you have learned in this chapter. Listed with those terms are other equivalent terms that other rhetorical critics have used when doing metaphor analysis.

CHART 5.7

Metaphrand	Tenor	Target domain
Metaphier	Vehicle	Source domain
Paraphier	Entailment	Entailment
Paraphrand	Entailment	Entailment

Key Words

metaphor, *130–132*
novel simile, *136*
non-literal comparison, *130–132*
metaphrand, *137–139*
metaphier, *137–139*
paraphier, *137–139*
paraphrand, *137–139*
archetypal metaphor, *132–133*
novel metaphor, *134–140*
negated metaphier, *139–140*
systemic metaphor, *140–142*
orientational metaphor, *142–144*
buried metaphor, *144–145*
dead metaphor, *144–145*

Metaphor Analysis Articles

Below you will find a sample of rhetorical and cultural analysis articles that have investigated the power of metaphor in public messages.

Adams, John Charles. "Linguistic Values and Religious Experience: An Analysis of the Clothing Metaphors in Alexander Richardson's Ramist-Puritan Lectures on Speech, 'Speech is a Garment to Cloath Our Reason.'" *Quarterly Journal of Speech* 76 (1990) 58–68.

Black, Edwin. "The Second Persona." *Quarterly Journal of Speech* 53 (1970): 109–119.

Blankenship, Jane. "The Search for the 1972 Democratic Nomination: A Metaphorical Perspective." *Methods of Rhetorical Criticism.* 2nd ed. Eds. Bernard Brock and Robert L. Scott. Detroit, MI: Wayne State University Press, 1980. 321–345.

Brown, Richard Harvey. "Rhetoric and the Science of History: The Debate Between Evolutionism and Empiricism as a Conflict of Metaphors." *Quarterly Journal of Speech* 72 (1986). 148–161.

Campbell, Paul Newell. "Metaphor and Linguistic Theory." *Quarterly Journal of Speech* 61 (1975): 1–12.

Carpenter, Ronald H. "America's Tragic Metaphor: Our Twentieth-Century Combatants as Frontiersmen." *Quarterly Journal of Speech* 76 (1990): 1–22.

Colston, Herbert L. and Raymond W. Gibbs, Jr. "Analogy and Irony: Rebuttal to 'Rebuttal Analogy.'" *Metaphor and Symbol* 13 (1998): 69–75.

Daughton, Suzanne M. "Metaphorical Transcendence: Images of the Holy War in Franklin Roosevelt's First Inaugural." *Quarterly Journal of Speech* 79 (1993): 427–446.

Frentz, Thomas S. "Toward a Resolution of the Generative Semantic/Classical Theory Controversy: A Psycholinguistic Analysis of Metaphor." *Quarterly Journal of Speech* 60 (1974): 125–133.

Goodwin, Paul D. and Joseph W. Wenzel. "Proverbs and Practical Reasoning: A Study in Socio-logic." *Quarterly Journal of Speech* 65 (1979): 289–302.

Graves, Michael P. "Functions of Key Metaphors in Early Quaker Sermons, 1671–1700." *Quarterly Journal of Speech* 69 (1983) 364–378.

Gribbin, William. "The Juggernaut Metaphor in American Rhetoric." *Quarterly Journal of Speech* 59 (Oct. 1973): 297–303.

Ivie, Robert L. "The Metaphor of Force in Prowar Discourse: The Case of 1812." *Quarterly Journal of Speech* 68 (1982): 240–253.

Ivie, Robert L. "Literalizing the Metaphor of Soviet Savagery: President Truman's Plain Style." *Southern Speech Communication Journal* 51 (1986): 91–105.

Ivie, Robert L. "Metaphor and the Rhetorical Invention of Cold War 'Idealists.'" *Communication Monographs* 54 (1987): 165–182.

Jamieson, Kathleen Hall. "The Metaphoric Cluster in the Rhetoric of Pope Paul VI and Edmund G. Brown, Jr." *Quarterly Journal of Speech* 66 (1980): 51–72.

Jensen, J. Vernon. "British Voices on the Eve of the American Revolution: Trapped by the Family Metaphor." *Quarterly Journal of Speech* 63 (1977): 43–50.

Kaplan, Stuart Jay. "Visual Metaphors in the Representation of Communication Technology." *Critical Studies in Mass Communication* 7 (1990): 37–47.

Koch, S., & Deetz, S. (1981). Metaphor Analysis of Social Reality in Organizations. *Journal of Applied Communication Research*, 9, 1–15.

Leff, Michael. "Topical Invention and Metaphoric Interaction." *Southern Speech Communication Journal* 48 (1983): 214–229.

Mumby, Dennis K. and Carole Spitzack. "Ideology and Television News: A Metaphoric Analysis of Political Stories." *Central States Speech Journal* 34 (1983): 162–171.

Nilsen, Don L. F. "The Nature of Ground in Farfetched Metaphors." *Metaphor and Symbolic Activity* 1.2 (1986): 127–138.

Osborn, Michael M. and Douglas Ehninger. "The Metaphor in Public Address." *Communication Monographs [Speech Monographs]* 29 (1962): 223–234.

Osborn, Michael M. "Archetypal Metaphor in Rhetoric: The Light-Dark Family." *Quarterly Journal of Speech* 53 (1967): 115–126.

Osborn, Michael M. "The Evolution of the Archetypal Sea in Rhetoric and Poetic." *Quarterly Journal of Speech* 63 (1977): 347–363.

Perry, Steven. "Rhetorical Functions of the Infestation Metaphor in Hitler's Rhetoric." *Central States Speech Journal* 34 (1983): 229–235.

Scott, Robert L. and James F. Klumpp. "A Dear Searcher into Comparisons: The Rhetoric of Ellen Goodman." *Quarterly Journal of Speech* 70 (1984): 69–79.

Smith, Ruth C. and Eric M. Eisenberg. "Conflict at Disneyland: A Root-Metaphor Analysis." *Communication Monographs* 54 (1987): 367–380.

Stelzner, Hermann G. "Ford's War on Inflation: A Metaphor that Did Not Cross." *Communication Monographs* 44 (1977): 284–297.

Sawhney, Harmeet. "Information Superhighway: Metaphors as Midwives." *Media, Culture & Society* 18 (1996): 291–314.

Wolff, Janet. "On the Road Again: Metaphors of Travel in Cultural Criticism." *Cultural Studies* 7 (1993): 224–239.

Endnotes

1. Julian Jaynes, *The Origin of Consciousness in the Breakdown of the Bicameral Mind* (Boston: Houghton Mifflin, 1976); Paul Ricoeur, *The Rule of Metaphor: Multi-Disciplinary Studies of the Creation of Meaning in Language* (London: Routledge & Kegan Paul, 1978).
2. George Lakoff and Mark Johnson, *Metaphors We Live By* (Chicago: University of Chicago Press, 1980) 3.
3. Robert L. Ivie, "The Metaphor of Force in Prowar Discourse: The Case of 1812," *Quarterly Journal of Speech* 68 (1982): 240–253; Michael

P. Graves, "Functions of Key Metaphors in Early Quaker Sermons, 1671–1700," *Quarterly Journal of Speech* 69 (1983): 364–378; Jane Blankenship, "The Search for the 1972 Democratic Nomination: A Metaphorical Perspective," *Methods of Rhetorical Criticism*, 2nd ed. Eds. Bernard Brock and Robert L. Scott (Detroit: Wayne State University Press, 1980) 321–345.

4. Max Black, "Metaphor," *Models and Metaphors: Studies in Language and Philosophy* (Ithaca: Cornell University Press, 1962) 25–47; Paul Newell Campbell, "Metaphor and Linguistic Theory," *Quarterly Journal of Speech* 61 (1975): 1–12; Thomas S. Frentz, "Toward a Resolution of the Generative Semantic/Classical Theory Controversy: A Psychololinguistic Analysis of Metaphor," *Quarterly Journal of Speech* 60 (1974): 125–133; Ricoeur.
5. Suzanne M. Daughton, "Metaphorical Transcendence: Images of the Holy War in Franklin Roosevelt's First Inaugural," *Quarterly Journal of Speech* 79 (1993): 427–446; Robert L. Ivie, "Literalizing the Metaphor of Soviet Savagery: President Truman's Plain Style," *Southern Speech Communication Journal* 51 (1986): 91–105.
6. Ronald H. Carpenter, "America's Tragic Metaphor: Our Twentieth-Century Combatants as Frontiersmen," *Quarterly Journal of Speech* 76 (1990): 1.
7. Carpenter, 2.
8. Michael M. Osborn, "Archetypal Metaphor in Rhetoric: The Light-Dark Family," *Quarterly Journal of Speech* 53 (1967): 116.
9. Einhorn, Lois J. *The Native American Oral Tradition: Voices of the Spirit and Soul.* Westport, Connecticut: Praeger, 2000, 33. For an excellent examination of archetypal metaphors from Native American culture and nations see pages 32–54 of her book.
10. "Alanis is Cleaning House." *Newsweek* 4 March 2001. 60.
11. Jaynes, 56.
12. Molly Ivins, "Mimic Men," *Mother Jones* March 1990: 8. Remember that she was describing George Herbert Walker Bush (the former president), not necessarily his son (the current president).
13. Linton Weeks and John M. Berry. "The Fed's Alan Greenspan," *Washington Post* [Weekly Edition] 31 March 1997: 6.
14. Jonathon Nicholas, "The Faces That Stick Like Gum," *Oregonian* 8 Sept. 1991: L-2.
15. 1980. 7–9.
16. Michael Reddy, "The Conduit Metaphor," *Metaphor and Thought* 2nd ed. Ortony, Andrew, ed. (Cambridge: Cambridge University Press, 1993) 164–201.
17. While Lakoff and Johnson popularized the idea of an orientational metaphor, other scholars recognized, long before their formulation, the power of position in metaphors: "Vertical scale images, which project desirable objects about the listener and undesirable objects

below, often seem to express symbolically man's quest for power." Michael M. Osborn, "Archetypal Metaphor in Rhetoric: The Light-Dark Family," *Quarterly Journal of Speech* 53 (1967): 116.

18. Jon Spoelstra, *Ice to the Eskimos: How to Market a Product Nobody Wants* (New York: HarperCollins, 1997), 259.
19. "Humane Being." *People* 2 Nov. 1998: 62.
20. Jim Bobryk, "Navigating My Eerie Landscape Alone," *Newsweek* 8 March 1999: 14.
21. "Ways and Means," *The West Wing,* NBC 26 Oct. 2001.

Once Upon a Story: Narrative as Rhetoric

Storytelling has been central to all we know about human culture—for as many years as we have known about human culture. Stories help us tell a judge why we should not receive a speeding ticket. Tall tales have kept many of us entranced (whether around a campfire or a living room) when we were younger. We flock every week to theatres and multiplexes to watch De Niro, Streep, Affleck, Williams, Barrymore, Roberts, and Foster play in various cinematic stories. A story is the central means by which an American presidential candidate tells why she has the experience to be considered for the highest office in the land. Television news and entertainment programming would shrink to nothing if we took away the tools of storytelling. Fables allow us to employ human-like animals to teach youngsters wisdom that has held sway for centuries. It would be impossible for us to engage in normal communication over a 24-hour period without using the resources of narrative: "I'm not usually late to work, but you should have seen the wreck . . ." "What do you mean the shipment is going to be late because of a snowstorm?!" "Do you remember the last time we had lunch at the Cuban sandwich shop?" "He's going out with her—again?" "I've got to get to the dry cleaners before they close for spring vacation."

Scholars in many different disciplines have decided that narrative is *the* most important way in which all people take facts, events, characters, circumstances, and things, and then somehow connect all of those life-elements together in an understandable manner. Often we do not even notice our use of narratives (and that they are "using" us). Our unawareness suggests that we need to understand how widespread and convincing this system of human communication is to us.

This chapter covers the most indispensable aspects of narrative and how it creates meaning while provocatively reaching huge audiences. We will first cover some of the framework powers of narrative.

Basic analysis words and ideas we'll learn together will apply to all modes of storytelling used as communication or persuasion in our culture. Hence, the core ideas of how stories are created are the same for spoken stories (e.g., a story told by a Senate candidate or a newscaster reporting a political upheaval), for acted stories (e.g., on the stage or on TV), or for written stories (e.g., a novel or a children's book).

Once we have covered core narrative ideas, we'll shift our focus to the type of narrative that has become most influential for the largest number of people in the past century (as well as this one): Hollywood-style narrative. Next we'll consider how several key conceptual tools will allow us to look beneath the flashy surface of mass-mediated narratives. Finally, we will ponder how narrative creates cultural influence.

Read carefully. You must put the ideas and terms on the following pages to *daily* use if you are to be successful in influencing your critical understanding of story messages *daily* used to influence *you*.

THE FRAMEWORK OF "ONCE . . ."

We are very familiar with the signal "Once upon a time . . ." We know with no doubt that we are entering the realm and experience of storytelling. The word "once" can also serve us as we begin to discover the framework power of narrative. "Once" as a signal word holds for us at least three clues to the power of stories in human culture.

The first power of "once" is that of selection. By starting "Once upon a time . . ." or "There was once in Rome a slave named Androcles . . ." we signal to an audience member that we are telling of a particularly important part of life. At the moment of storytelling all other stories recede into the background of our awareness and mental focus. "Once" gives us the key signal that we are about to be informed or entertained (or both) with information, events and details presumably worth listening to. Hence, selecting one story (out of all possible stories) is a somewhat audacious move when you consider that we are promising audience members that we are about to use their time and attention. If "once" signals the starting of the story process, it also serves to remind us that we tend to use successful story *forms* over and over.

The second power of "once" is the power of repetition. Rarely do we see a sitcom, read a novel, watch a feature movie, or listen to a children's storybook and find a completely new *form* of story. Hence, quest myths, rags-to-riches stories, good vs. evil dramas, and fish-out-of-water comedies are but a few of the predictable forms of storytelling that seem very familiar to us. This power of "once" indicates that many different story elements can be made quickly recognizable by employing story forms that have been used for hundreds or thousands of years. Thus, repetition of familiar forms is the second clear power of "Once upon a time . . ." Familiar

FIGURE 6.1 **Concern for Life**
Change in life often finds us telling stories to address our concerns.

Source: Pierce Communication.

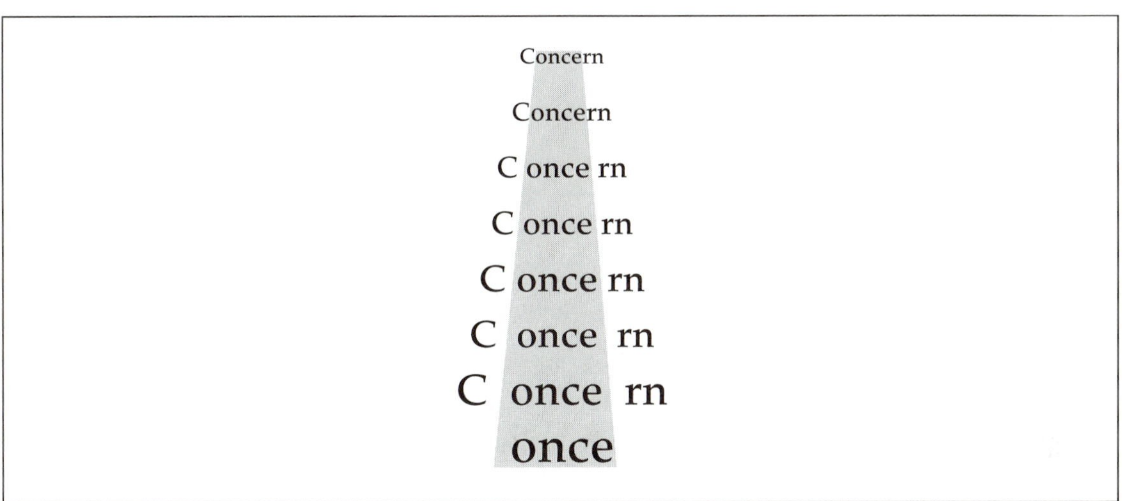

story patterns have often been used over the ages to help address change, and there we find the third power of "once."

The third power of "once" is the simple signal that notable change occurs and we want to communicate about that change. Think about how you would describe your hometown to a visitor. At least in part your description would include observations such as: "Once there was a bakery on that corner." "At one time we could drive from here to Billy's school in less than 10 minutes." "Once we had a choice of eight different bookstores in our neighborhood." In each case, the "once" comment refers to more than just selection; it also makes reference to important alterations to people, or buildings, or habits, or places. This power of "once" signals that we live in times, places, and communities that shift, swirl, and transform based on many different factors. When that change happens, we tell stories to each other to praise, follow, decry, complain, measure, or understand the alterations that have occurred. Change is constant, and so is our need to tell our stories of the experience of change. In fact it is no mystery that we find within the word "concern" our focal story word of "once." (see Figure 6.1)

When we are *concerned* about life matters, we often turn to stories to help address our worries and difficulties. This final power of "once" then helps us to understand that narrative is a crucial tool which we use to keep ourselves tuned to relevant alterations in our environment, culture, and relationships.

While stories permeate all aspects of our human use of language and communication, the focus held by many rhetorical and cultural critics concerns how stories told to mass audiences do their work within a culture. To those matters we now turn.

NARRATIVE: BASIC ELEMENTS

To best understand storytelling in American culture, we must first go to the very heart of what a story is and recognize the key parts of narrative that make it such a powerful communication apparatus. We will start with a working definition of narrative:

> Narrative is presenting, or more typically, re-presenting to an audience words, images, or sounds (at times in combination), and audience processing of those message elements. Narratives depict cause and effect relationships occurring in time and space between social actors in a form and sequence consistent with the storyteller's (or more accurately the story-evoker's) perspective and interests.

This definition points out that we are much more *active* participants in the *construction* of a story than we might first realize given our experience with most American mass-media narratives. Most of us think about films and television shows as finished products that we simply watch. This seemingly simple showing, or depiction, of stories requires from us more cooperation and work than we might first think. Contemporary film, television, and mass-media critics and theorists remind us that we are very active participants in the *creation* of story-based messages. Let's examine how this rhetorical process works.

Stories are really made up of two very different and significant parts. We will call them the **story given** (or **story^{g}**) and the **story constructed** (or **story^{c}**).[1] The story given (story^{g}) is made up of elements actually shown, spoken, or described in a medium used for story giving (e.g., film, radio, or a book). The story constructed (story^{c}) is what happens in the human mind once the story^{g} (story given) elements are received, organized, interpreted, and understood.

Whether you loved or hated the movie *Titanic,* we can use the opening sequence of scenes from that movie to understand this difference in story elements and processes. The opening minutes of *Titanic* depict two submersible research vessels approaching and investigating the wreck of the *Titanic* on the ocean floor. The audience is shown shots internal to the research vessels, external to those vessels and the *Titanic,* and shots that represent what a video camera was recording when the "boss" of the expedition is taping himself describing the voyage of discovery. The writers take pains to have the boss character say that they are two and a half miles down in the ocean.

FIGURE 6.2
Titanic Panic
Scenes we actually see in movies are part of the story given (story^{g}).

The entire first seven minutes of the film is depicted as happening in "real time." The seven minutes we watch take the same time as that needed to accomplish the actions depicted in the film. After discovering a safe in an interior room on the ship by means of a robot device, the leader of the expedition exults: "It's payday, boys." As the music swells, we next see a sweeping helicopter shot approaching the support surface ship; one research vessel is being lifted out of the water. So, in story^{g} (story given) terms, we are given many minutes of exploration, followed by activity on the surface of the ocean. But how did the research vessels get to the surface? To make sense of these two film segments, we must fill in story^{c} (story constructed) material that allows for the time and effort necessary to move the research vessels two and a half miles up through the frigid waters of the north Atlantic. Importantly, when watching the film in normal conditions, we do *not* see these first two segments of *Titanic* as unrelated or out of position. Instead our minds "fill in" the missing story material necessary for the second scene to make sense.

Of course, after years of training and practice we do this mental work without much conscious thought or effort. The "pace" of activity between story^{g} (story given) material and story^{c} (story constructed) work picks up slightly here as we are offered story^{g} elements that depict workers lifting a rope net out of the ocean while we are shown members of the exploration vessels embracing and shouting on deck. In real time the orange jumpsuited workers do *not* have enough time to hoist the net device holding the retrieved safe to the awaiting, celebrating explorers. The time necessary to move the net and the safe, and to release the net is removed (or "elided") from the sequence. Our minds fill in the necessary story^{c} information that allows the story to make sense. We do *not* perceive that we are jumping around in event sequence or time.

Instead our minds, working with the makers of the film, help create a story in our heads. That is the important point: the story *is* in actuality *created* in our minds—not just on a screen or on a page. The storyteller (or more accurately the story-evoker) only provides the raw materials that stimulate our mental story processes into action.

The process of receiving story^{g} information and using our minds to utilize story^{c} implications and connections results in a **diegesis,** or "world of the story," in our minds and understanding. We will extensively use the adjective form of that word (**diegetic**) to indicate those things that a moviemaker provides (story information) and those things we as audience members provide (story processes) that "fit" the story being created in the interchange. Hence, a diegetic sound will be one that "makes sense" within the story world (diegesis) that is being evoked for us.

Non-diegetic items, of course, can be given by a movie or inserted by audience members in the meaning making process. For instance, credits (most of the time) are information but don't really fit the "world of the story." Similarly when one of the characters in *Pulp Fiction* "draws" an animated square with her fingers—and the square actually appears on the screen—we recognize that such things don't really happen in perceived experience; hence, it would count as a non-diegetic element within the movie.

Diegetic elements are depicted as occurring somewhere and over some length of time. So our next focus will be on time and space in mass-media storytelling (or story-evoking).

Our working definition of narrative helps us to realize that the "relationships occurring in time and space" are never limited to one moment in time or one singular space. Since those who help us create stories in our minds do range across vast amounts of time, and boundless spaces, we must realize that time and space will always be presented or depicted in part and never in the whole. A brief example will help us sort this out.

When we systematically follow the activities and events of the Jamal Wallace character in *Finding Forrester,* we soon realize that the scenes are separated from each other by time and distance. When Jamal shows up on a rooftop basketball court at a prep school, we are left to imagine (create the appropriate connections) exactly how he arrived there. Our minds create or remember the connection points and provide the necessary story wholeness.

So, story^{g} and story^{c} work together to create a diegesis or story world in our minds. Diegetic elements in story^{g} are those that make sense as being in, or coming from, the world of the story. Obviously the diegetic elements (believable within the story world presented) in the movie *The Fifth Element* are quite different than story elements in *Saving Private Ryan.* If a blue, multi-tentacled diva appeared in a scene with Tom Hanks in *Saving Private Ryan*, she (it?) would not "fit" the story world of World War II. But the diva's appearance in *The Fifth Element* seems quite plausible given the other unusual things, places, and creatures depicted as occurring in a future time period. Non-diegetic elements are part of the story^{g} but do *not* fit

Scrutinize exercise

How are non-diegetic elements used differently in a comedy movie than in a dramatic movie? (Remember both have non-diegetic elements.) Which type of movie makes non-diegetic elements more noticeable?

the diegesis. Hence, sounds, music, titles, credits, and graphic devices, among other things, are presented to the audience but they do not fit the diegesis or story world.

As we move deeper into understanding narratives that reach millions, we will start with considerations of time and then move to considerations of space to better understand how moviemakers and other story-evokers reach audience members.

TIME DEPICTION IN NARRATIVE

Perception of time in stories is unsurprisingly created in both story[c] and story[g] parts of the story-making process. Let's start with how long it takes to watch a movie or TV show. **Screen time** is the amount of time it actually takes to show or display the movie or TV show. Screen time for most Hollywood movies is between 90 minutes and three and a half hours. Screen time for a typical sitcom is 20–22 minutes (without commercials). Of course, sitting through trailers for upcoming movies or commercials on TV (or worse yet at movie theatres!) can lengthen the process, but we are concerned here only with those minutes that actually present story[g] material.

Story[g] time is the length of time *actually depicted* in the story. Since movies and TV shows are depicted in scenes, we'll use that convention as a starting point to understand the narrative depiction of time. But what counts as a scene? Film scholars and theorists have wrestled with this question for some time. We will say (to keep the analytic waters non-muddy) that a scene exists in a film whenever the characters or action or scenic elements stay within one time and location framework. Therefore, a scene changes whenever there is a discernable change in time sequence or place from the previous scene. Therefore, **story[g] scene time** lasts as long as the scene seems to last to an audience member. If a scene takes seven minutes to show and seems to depict seven minutes, as with the opening minutes of *Titanic,* then you've discovered story[g] time for that scene. If a scene would take only seconds in real time, but is depicted, say, in slow motion (e.g., some of the Olympic sprinting scenes in *Chariots of Fire*), then the story[g] time is however long the slow motion takes to be depicted. If you take all of the scenes depicting story[g] time and add them together, they will come very close to equaling screen time.

Scrutinize exercise

For obvious reasons story^{c} time is often fuzzy or ambiguous. Pick a film and watch five scenes from the movie with a friend. Each person should estimate and write how much time has passed between scenes.

What are some of the standard story^{g} devices used by directors to mark passage of time or place? What are some of the unique or creative devices used to mark such passage?

On the other hand, the story^{c} time includes all of the story^{g} time, *plus* adds in all of the time removed for the convenience of story-evoking. So in the opening scenes of *Titanic,* the expedition leader finds, to his dismay, that the safe retrieved from the bottom of the ocean holds only waterlogged, ruined papers. The *next* scene depicts careful restoration work being done on some of those papers in a lab on the surface support ship. The time necessary to move the papers and the people (whether minutes or hours or days) to the lab was deemed unnecessary for depiction by the moviemakers. Once again our minds fill in the blanks and make the necessary time and space connections—used in the process story^{c} time. Human ability to make these time and space connections is very handy, so that depicting 7½ hours doesn't take 7½ hours of watching time in a theater.

In the next several scenes of *Titanic* the time removed between depicted scenes becomes more pronounced. An old woman is depicted working at a pottery wheel as she overhears an interview with the expedition leader on the surface support ship. We are neither told, nor shown, how much time has passed between the discovery of a drawing in the restoration lab and the interview with the expedition leader about finding that drawing. We can assume it took some time to arrange the media connections between the ship and the program or network depicted as performing the interview. We can also assume that no great amount of time has passed as the "interview" suggests a recent (and newsworthy) discovery. After an intervening scene where the old grandmother speaks with the expedition leader by phone, we next see a helicopter with the grandmother and her granddaughter on board flying over the ocean toward the surface support ship. How long did it take to arrange the trip? To pack? Where did the grandmother have to drive, or walk, or fly to reach the helicopter? Did anyone resist the idea of the trip? We'll never know because these *unnecessary* time and content components were removed from the string of scenes depicted. James Cameron and other filmmakers count on our minds to do the necessary connection work between story^{g} elements and the story^{c} results.

Of course, the story^{c} in response to this movie's story^{g} eventually covers from 1912 to the late 1990s (and probably beyond in both directions).

Scrutinize exercise

Story^g in the movie *Sleepless in Seattle* leaves the main characters on the top of the Empire State Building. Did your story^c also stop there? How far past the story^g elements did your mind go? Why?

Individual story^g elements, however, even when added together, last less than four hours. Our minds are quite talented and well trained to be able to leap all of the necessary time chasms and do most of the necessary time and concept connections.

Hence, story^g time elements are powerful markers in all forms of story-evoking as they provide audience members with the raw chronological framework within which we create the story^c time connections.

We will find that space as depicted and evoked in mass-media stories is quite similar to the manipulation and perception of time.

SPACE DEPICTION IN NARRATIVE

As is true with time, we have **story^g space** and **story^c space** used by moviemakers and other story-evokers. Space *given* in movies or TV (story^g space) is that space actually shown or depicted. Space constructed (story^c space) is all space that is "filled in" by our minds. The easiest way to recognize this is to think about a sitcom that is shot on a three-camera sound stage (e.g., *Married with Children*). We never see the famous "fourth wall" in rooms depicted, because there is no wall on that side of the set. Hence, we take story^g space that we *do* see and make story^c space that we are never shown. Drama shows such as *Ally McBeal* or *ER* (or even some sitcoms such as *Seinfeld*) shoot in single-camera style and therefore have much more varied story^g space information.

Since movies and television offer *motion*-oriented pictures to audience members, we need to be able to identify the directions and types of motion that can occur within the space of a movie or TV frame. Motion can occur horizontally, say a car depicted as driving from the left to the right across the screen; this is called movement along the **x-axis.**

Motion can occur vertically, say a rocket lifting off into the sky moving up into the picture frame; this is called movement along the **y-axis.**

Motion can occur as if it was coming toward your position as a viewer or away from you as a viewer; this is called movement along the **z-axis.**[2]

Motion can be created in three ways in film or television messages: **subject motion, camera motion,** or **cyber motion.**

Subject motion happens when an object or person moves in front of a camera and the motion is recorded on film, tape, or digital media.

Scrutinize exercise

Spend a few minutes looking back at four or five scenes in *Titanic, Clerks, The Hunt for Red October,* or *Clueless.* Recognize how often you are actually shown space elements (story^{g} space) within the movie and how often you are asked to *supply* space elements or conditions (story^{c} space) from within your mind.

Camera motion occurs when the camera moves, creating the sense of motion on the screen. When a camera does a pan, tilt, dolly, crane, or tracking move, the motion perceived by the audience is created by movement of the camera. So when cameras showed sprinters running at the Sydney summer Olympics, some of the shots were from cameras beside the track that moved at the same relative speed as the sprinters. In that case we were watching both subject motion (the runners running) and camera motion (the camera moving beside the track at the same pace as the runners).

Cyber motion is depicted whenever an object or person appears to move on the screen, but that movement has been created inside a computer.

Whether time or space is being depicted in a speech, movie, novel, TV show, or Internet site, we need to realize that key persuasive decisions were made about all of the elements presented to us. As much as most people may be unaware, someone had to make a decision for *each* item that is used to create a story^{g} so that a story^{c} fills our mind. We are now learning the process by which narrative is created.

Now that we've covered the basics of story elements given and story elements evoked in terms of time and space, we can turn our attention to three other core concepts that will help us better understand how Hollywood-style story-evoking has become powerful in the United States and around the world. Those three concepts will be ***mise-en-scene, in medias res,*** and **sound manipulation** in story-evoking.

MISE-EN-SCENE

Mise-en-scene is a French term that literally means "placed in a scene." True to a theater heritage, this phrase was in use long before movie scenes were invented. Various items were literally placed in scenes of plays. When the term was carried over to the study of movies, it became the covering phrase for all things that we see on a movie screen. So lighting, costumes, actors, props, scenery, location items, streetscapes, and so forth

FIGURE 6.3 **I see *mise-en-scene.*** Ties, hair, stairs, lighting, and clothes all can be part of *mise-en-scene.*

become part of the *mise-en-scene.* These elements become useful to consider as powerful visual devices used to prompt us to take story[g] visual elements and turn them into vivid story[c] results. Era-appropriate costumes and props let us construct a story[c] set in 1912 as *Titanic* unfolds as a movie. Lighting and color selection in films such as *The Sixth Sense* can profoundly influence how we feel and react to story[g] visual elements.

In *Thirteen Days,* a film concerning the Cuban Missile Crisis of 1962, we find a quick but telling example of the power of individual *mise-en-scene* elements.

The first scene of *Thirteen Days* depicts a U-2 spy plane flying over Cuba. That scene dissolves into the second scene which depicts Kevin Costner's character (Kenny O'Donnell, a special assistant to President Kennedy) waking up in bed and playing with his young children who have come to rouse their dad. The third scene finds the family at the breakfast table with the requisite commotion that would accompany a school day morning meal with parents and five kids. As his daughter proclaims that she can't find her shoes for school, audience attention is drawn to side-by-side phones mounted on the dining area wall. The phones are 60s style rotary-dial phones and, most strikingly, one is black, the other is red. The black phone would have looked like a standard-issue home phone of the era. But the red phone, especially in an era with no typical phone color choice, represents something very different. Even with Costner's character quizzing his older kids on federal cabinet members, the scene could have represented hundreds of government workers of the era having breakfast with family members—except for the multiple phones on the wall.

The double phone set, plus the red color of one of the phones, quickly marks this household as one different than most. The red "hotline" phone for the president of the United States has been a standard icon of the presidency for decades. Hence, the inclusion here of a similar red phone, in a home situation where double wall phones were never an option (let alone a norm), acts as a shorthand, *mise-en-scene* device that quickly allows an audience member a clue as to the status and position of this government official.

Taking the appropriate time to learn to notice and evaluate choices made for *mise-en-scene* elements should become a primary focus for you as

Scrutinize exercise

If you are from an era of American experience when multiple phones, multiple phone types, and multiple colors for phones are the norm rather than the exception, would you be as likely as your parents to see an extra red phone on the wall in the movie *Thirteen Days* as out of place? Can you think of other *mise-en-scene* items that change from generation to generation and therefore may be more or less useful as means of creating meaning in a movie scene?

you learn to evaluate and analyze the rhetorical power of film, TV, and Internet stories as mass-media messages.

Those items placed in the scene by directors, actors, writers, and cinematographers become *mise-en-scene* by specific decision and purpose. If we become aware that those items do not magically appear in front of a camera or on the page of a book, we will be much better equipped to make judgments as to the meaning impact of those selections. While regular audience members may be clueless about *mise-en-scene,* rhetorical critics cannot ignore the profound impact these items make on us. Who decided that Leeloo's hair should be orange in *The Fifth Element?* We may not care who made the decision, but by realizing that a decision *was made,* we are moving in the direction of recognizing the persuasion qualities of story-evoking in our culture. (Badda-Boom!)

IN MEDIAS RES

In medias res is a Latin phrase that means "in the middle of things." All Hollywood-style stories (and most others) start in the "middle" of something. Choice of that "middle" starting point is of considerable importance. How different would *The Matrix* have been if the writers had started depiction within the movie in Neo's childhood rather than showing him as an adult? What if, rather than starting with Trinity's run-in with agents, the director had started with the manufacturing process that created the red and blue pills? Writers and directors *always* have to make this critical choice. All stories have to start somewhere, and the choice of that "somewhere" and "somewhen"[3] is very important to what the movie is able to accomplish over an approximate two-hour time span.

If *The Sixth Sense* did not start with a post-award party, home discussion about the Willis character's achievements in helping children, the writer would have been forced to spend more time and effort in actually depicting that he helped and cared for children. The depicted "you won a great award" dialog quickly establishes his excellence, talent, and efforts, along with the result of all of those things. That occasion and dialog form a strong starting point in the "middle" of the depicted experience of an urban, professional couple.

Once started in the "middle of things," Hollywood-style movies move in a funnel-like fashion; in the beginning of such a movie all things seem possible (if you don't think so, check out *Bill & Ted's Excellent Adventure* again). By halfway through any Hollywood movie, most things are probable. By the end of most movies, all events and character actions seem necessary. The possibilities for character actions continually narrow as the movie unwinds. At the opening of *American Beauty* we are immediately told that the central character is going to be dead by the end of the film. However, the means, motives, and conditions of his death are open to hundreds of different possibilities. By the middle of that movie the number of people who are depicted as being upset with him is reduced to three or four. By the end of the film the depicted culprit seems the most obvious choice for the killer. So it is with the vast majority of films made in Hollywood, or that copy the dominant style adopted by American filmmakers. We will devote substantial energy later to recognizing what production decisions contribute to that dominant style of storytelling or story-evoking in film.

Starting points are critical to both initial impressions and believable extensions in story creation. Recognition of *in medias res,* then, is an invaluable tool to know and use. Awareness of initial starting points and the function of those decisions by media story-evokers allow us to recognize the rhetorical aspects of their choices.

If one hundred multiplex-weary movie patrons watch only with slack-jawed inattention to where the next Ben Affleck movie starts, you, on the other hand, will be keyed to begin (from the outset) to ask important questions about *why* the story starts at a particular place and time.

SOUND MANIPULATION

Many people systematically investigating narrative in movies for the first time forget how profoundly sound can influence our emotions, understanding, and sense making. We easily understand that *all* of the sounds in a movie like *Toy Story* must be produced from other sources. So when Tom Hanks gives Woody a voice to hold a "town meeting" with all of Andy's toys, we recognize at some level that *all* of the sound in the scene had to be borrowed or created. We may not so easily recognize or remember that exactly the same thing is true of *Braveheart* or *Face/Off.*

Sound in major release movies is *all* recreated. Hence, just as is true in decisions about *mise-en-scene,* or *in medias res,* some writer or director or editor had to make a decision about each element of sound we hear in a film. Since each decision is a rhetorical decision, we will do well to better understand the possibilities.

First, you will still see sound specialists recording sound on *sound stages* (can you hear the importance of sound even in the name of a primary place for creating a Hollywood movie?) or on location. The sound captured there is called **wild sound** or **scratch sound.** Wild sound is used as a reference point for later dialog replacement and other manipulations of the sound track in a movie.

On a conceptual side we need to recognize that sound we hear in a movie can either "fit" the space and context of the story (**diegetic sound**) or clearly (if we stop and think about it) be from "outside" the space and context of story (**non-diegetic sound**). If we can understand that the source of the sound is from within the story it is diegetic. The easiest way to recognize diegetic sound is to think about dialogue between characters. When we see lips moving and sound coming from a character it appears very natural; it "fits" the scene we are watching. If, on reflection, we recognize that the source of the sound could *not* come from within the story it is non-diegetic sound. When we remembered earlier in this chapter that music swelled in the movie *Titanic* as we watched the first shots of research vessels returning to the surface support ship, we recognize (on reflection) that the diegetic context at that moment has no "room" for an orchestra. We do *not* expect to see the source for that music depicted as coming from the deck of the support ship or on some separate vessel. Such sound is non-diegetic; it fits neither the space nor the context of the depicted story. Non-diegetic sound elements clearly help the message-process in movies; otherwise, directors would not use music, sound effects, and dialogue that otherwise "don't fit" the diegesis or world of the story.

Movie sound comes in three types: **spoken dialog, music,** or **sounds.** Each type can be diegetic or non-diegetic. Take a few minutes to watch scenes from *Toy Story* or any other animated movie. Pay special attention to decisions that have been made about sound. Then do the same with a feature, live-action movie and recognize that every sound in that movie *also* has been replaced or created. In fact, when you see the term **ADR** (or **automatic dialog replacement**) in the credits of a film, you see evidence that even all of the dialog is replaceable.

Similarly a **Foley artist** has the responsibility to use hundreds of different tricks and devices to reproduce sounds and noises that seem "natural" or realistic to the context of the story or the diegetic world created in the movie, or TV show, or commercial.

Scrutinize exercise

How many ADR talent people are listed in the credits for *Shakespeare in Love?* Which character's dialog (do you think) was replaced?

All of these different areas of insight about how story elements are offered, or evoked, so that our minds can build a story are of great worth. When we learn to use them to create initial analysis, we can begin to see how parts of a narrative are created that may have escaped us before. We still, however, need to think about how stories work as a whole message. To those concerns and insights we now turn.

NARRATIVE AND CULTURAL INFLUENCE

A variety of studies in interpersonal, group, organizational, and mass communication reveal that narrative in all of its many forms has six key functions for us:

- Narrative helps us organize information, places, people, and events into understandable messages.
- Narrative helps us evaluate (or size up) information, places, people, and events.
- Narrative helps us form indirect knowledge about things, places, people, and events about which we have no direct experience.
- Narrative helps us to reduce uncertainty about information, places, people, and events.
- Narrative helps us to work out conflicts.
- Narrative helps us make decisions.

Recognizing that narrative serves these functions for us, our key question is: How do mass-media stories contribute to our expectations for stories, and how can we best estimate their utility for us?

To better understand the answer to that question, we must characterize core expectations we have about how stories ought to work as message devices. A number of scholars in the last decade have been working hard to help us better understand those expectations. The two core expectations we hold for story messages are for **narrative cohesion** and **narrative fidelity.** We will explore both in turn.

NARRATIVE COHESION

Whenever we hear a story, see a movie, or listen to a story on the radio, we expect the story^{g} elements to make sense and work together as we create a story^{c} in our minds. All of the parts of a story^{g} that we've been discussing, then, have to work together to make a coherent whole. Let's look quickly at a story within a story to see how this works.

Stories or scenes based in courtroom events often play with how we have previously constructed our story^{g} elements. For instance, on

The Simpsons, when Bart Simpson goes on trial for the murder of Principal Skinner in the episode "Bart the Murderer," we have two good story^{g} elements on which to base our plausible belief that Bart is innocent.[4] First, we last see Principal Skinner being confronted in his office by three mob associates led by Fat Tony. The next scene has Edna Krabappel announcing to her fourth grade class that Principal Skinner is missing. Bart's class cheers as the program goes to a commercial break while Bart says: "Uh oh!" Second, Bart is tormented in a nightmare sequence with multiple Principal Skinners who accuse him of murder. But Bart, who only *complained* to Fat Tony about Skinner keeping him after school (setting in motion the mobsters' visit to the principal's office), questions Fat Tony about murdering the principal. Therefore, when Bart and the mobsters are all accused of the murder, the viewer has two distinct story^{g} elements that point to the mobsters as the true murderers: (1) the mobsters were last seen in a threatening posture in Skinner's office and (2) Bart's questioning of Fat Tony strongly suggests that Bart is innocent. Therefore, the narrative cohesion offered in story^{g} elements to convince the audience of Bart's guilt is weak, but the narrative cohesion in story^{g} elements for the guilt of the mobsters seems more and more plausible. The writers of this episode twist these expectations in a final farcical courtroom sequence. Bart seems to be framed by the mobsters, his father's testimony, and unseen but cited testimony from "emotionally shattered babysitters." Given the story^{g} elements, Bart seems ready to be convicted of a murder committed by mobsters. However, Principal Skinner dramatically bursts into the courtroom—alive—and relates a new series of story^{g} elements (which are simultaneously shown in visual flashback) that implausibly include an overly tall stack of newspapers, his mother's preserves, a basketball, a vacuum cord retractor, baking soda and lemon juice. The new story^{g} elements account for Skinner's disappearance and absence. However implausible, these story^{g} elements (as a story within a story) help build narrative cohesion that, when coupled with Principal Skinner's depicted living presence, becomes a story^{c} for the judge character who dismisses the charge of murder against Bart.

Obviously, when plausible connections in story^{g} material offered in a trial address the fate of O.J. Simpson (or Ted Kaczynski, Dan Rostenkowski, Timothy McVeigh, or Patty Hearst) rather than Bart Simpson, the importance of our ability to rightly judge the power of story elements becomes more than fun entertainment.

When you read a news account of a trial in a newspaper, or on the Web, you are often observing a story within a story. Trials in America and elsewhere revolve around the ability of prosecutors and defenders to tell effective stories to the judge or a jury. Whether a story offered in testimony "hangs together" and makes sense to a jury or a judge is critical to both prosecutors and defenders. If any piece, or detail, of the story offered in testimony (story^{g}) does not seem to make sense in light of other claims and testimony, the overall cohesion, and validity, of the story suffers.

Scrutinize exercise

Go to a movie (or watch a movie on tape or DVD) with a person who works daily at a job or profession depicted in the movie. After the movie (if the other person can wait that long), ask her or his evaluation of the characters, actions, and events depicted in the movie. Did he or she like the movie? Does he or she seem to have a different measure for narrative cohesion than you do? How much so?

So when story[g] elements do exhibit perceived narrative cohesion, the time, visual consistency, events, character traits, and locations depicted in the story[g] must make sense. You can easily test this by going to see a movie with someone who works at a profession depicted in the movie. A real life cop will have stronger standards for narrative cohesion in a police drama than do you or I. Due to professional training, experience, and expectations, a police officer will be able to pay attention to details of timing, procedure, and character action that are essentially unavailable to non-law enforcement people (most of the rest of us).

Successful and powerful stories as distributed in American mass media need to observe rules and conditions that lead to narrative cohesion. They also, however, need to exhibit narrative fidelity. We turn our attention in that direction now.

NARRATIVE FIDELITY

Walter Fisher argues that audience members check, and test, story[g] material to see if it "rings true" with "stories they know to be true in their own lives."[5] He calls such connection **narrative fidelity.**

If you've ever gone to four movies in a row with no really strong response, only to watch a fifth one that genuinely touches your heart, mind, or soul, you know the impact of narrative fidelity. Unlike narrative cohesion, which signals if story[g] elements makes sense and work well together, narrative fidelity addresses whether themes, values, and representations are close to what we believe and live.

If you or I feel oppressed, over-scrutinized, and manipulated at work, we may well respond with a strong narrative fidelity to a movie such as *The Matrix*. Without regard to the technical details about how plausible the depicted facts and relationships may be in the film, we can still feel a sense of identification with the film that is quite strong. If many people feel the same way, the filmmakers may well have a hit movie on their hands, and we may have a useful way to gauge the mood or disposition of the country in which the film is doing big box office.

Another set of ideas closely associated with narrative cohesion and narrative fidelity have been developed over the past 20 years by scholars interested in the power of stories. These ideas have to do with what mental framework an audience member uses to process, build, and understand story[g] elements. Since film and rhetorical scholars often refer to a movie as a "text," they also often discuss what kind of "reading" may be employed to understand and use that "text." Three main types of "reading" of mass-media movies have emerged: a **preferred reading,** a **negotiated reading,** and an **oppositional reading.** A preferred reading suggests that when an audience member creates a story[c] in her head that it is very close to what the production team had in mind. So, if you saw Tom Hanks in *Cast Away,* and understood the movie to be about the survival of the human spirit, tragic loss of love, and bittersweet recognition of the value of life and civilization, you would be close to a preferred reading of that movie. In other words, your "take" on the movie would be quite close to the understanding that the writers and director wanted you to have. If you understood the movie to be interesting in personal details about someone stranded on an island, but saw the love story as manipulative and full of schmaltz, you would be close to a negotiated reading of the movie. You might well discount the movie as being too contrived.

A negotiated reading of a story indicates that you do not "buy," understand, or accept the meaning likely intended by the creator(s) of the story. You "negotiate" a meaning by changing some of the factors or perspectives of evaluation of story[g] elements.

Your negotiated reading may well spring from a lack of narrative fidelity. Perhaps you've never won or lost love in life in such a dramatic fashion, hence you find it difficult to believe that it could happen for screen characters. If you understood the movie to be one big advertisement for FedEx and Wilson Sporting Goods, you would be in the territory of an oppositional reading. You might well question if all the trappings of a dramatic story are just an excuse to put FedEx logos on a huge screen for sustained periods of time and to make a Wilson Sporting Goods volleyball a sympathetic "character" in a big-budget Hollywood movie. Your skepticism would fuel an oppositional reading of the movie.

Scrutinize exercise

On the following page you find three cartoon strips from Bill Watterson's *Calvin and Hobbes.* As Calvin interacts with his bicycle, Watterson seems to give a preferred reading to Calvin's childlike notion that his bike may be out to get him. If that is the preferred reading, what does Calvin's father's comment in the final panel seem to represent? Can more than one type of reading be encouraged within a story message?

FIGURE 6.4 **The Evil Bike**
How does Calvin's version of events differ from his father's?

Knowing that we evaluate all stories for narrative cohesion and narrative fidelity allows us to begin to see the basis for both effective and ineffective stories offered in mass-media form. Further, knowing that we can take a stance toward understanding a mass-media story (in the form of a preferred reading, a negotiated reading, or an oppositional reading), allows us to detect some of the possible reasons that different people can understand media stories in such different ways.

In this chapter we have just begun to scratch the surface of how we can better understand and think about narrative as created and delivered to us as mass audience members. Carefully think about and use the new categories and designations you have learned by putting them into use to examine—with care—the stories that seek and demand your attention in our culture. Next you will find a sample journal article by Solomon and McMullen. Read the article in preparation for the Chapter 6 workshop.

We'll move now to the Chapter 6 workshop, and we can put several of your newfound ideas and analysis terms to work concerning the power of mass-media story messages in your life. Then we'll launch on to Chapter 7 concerning the power of visual communication.

Source: *Western Journal of Speech Communication* 55 (Fall 1991), 339–353.

Places in the Heart: The Rhetorical Force of an Open Text

Martha Solomon and Wayne J. McMullen

Approaching *Places in the Heart* as a text "open" to divergent ideological interpretations, this essay argues that the director's skillful manipulation of the romantic formula enhances the film's appeal to a broad audience. In particular, the essay suggests that the film offers complex messages about feminism and the farm crisis. These ambivalent messages sustain, rather than resolve, the tensions in viewers between the moralistic and materialistic dimension of the American Dream.

Places in the Heart, a film written and directed by Robert Benton, is the story of a Depression-era Texas housewife who is suddenly widowed and left to fend for herself and her family. She is at first reluctant to face the daunting new responsibilities and obstacles before her. With the help of a hired hand and a boarder, she summons the courage and wits to plant,

Martha Solomon (Ph.D., University of Texas, 1969) is Professor of Speech Communication at the University of Maryland. Wayne J. McMullen (Ph.D., Pennsylvania State University, 1989) is Assistant Professor at Pennsylvania State University, Delaware County. The authors gratefully acknowledge the comments of Peter Andersen, the editor of *WJSC*, the anonymous reviewers of this article, and Mary McCullough.

harvest, and sell a crop of cotton; thus, for the time being, she is able to make a payment on her farm's mortgage and keep her family together. The film received mixed reviews when it was released in the fall of 1984. Most critics acknowledged that Benton's semi-autobiographical movie effectively conveyed his emotional attachments to his boyhood during the Depression in Waxahachie, Texas, but their assessments of its emotional force varied from labeling it a "fastidious valentine" to "a tonic, a revivifying experience."[1] Stanley Kauffman voiced a common criticism: ". . . All the elements in his film move either to neat uplift or neat poignancy, and his very familiarity with film conventions makes him skid on triteness while he tries to travel toward truth."[2] Even sympathetic reviewers wondered if the film's "understated dignity . . . naturalistic approach lacking in dramatic punch" might "limit its commercial appeal," making "expansion beyond a core audience possible, but unlikely."[3]

Despite these critical reservations, *Places* fulfilled Richard Schickel's prediction that it would "find its place in many a heart this season."[4] It soon emerged as one of the leading films in box office receipts, garnering some fourteen million dollars in its first three months. Moreover, it earned Oscar awards for Sally Field, as best actress, and for Benton, as writer of the Best Original Screen Play, and was nominated for best picture of the year.[5] Clearly, audiences warmed to Benton's "personal vision."

Many factors help to account for the film's success. From one perspective, Benton's "sense of family, of community" made the film what one critic called an "idealized vision of hard times that brought out the best and redeemed the worst in people."[6] Many viewers undoubtedly found it "a full-hearted movie . . . a breath of pure air, a joyful glimpse into the true earthly paradise."[7] Its setting in rural America also corresponded to national nostalgia for the "pristine plains" and its theme testified "to the values of patience, hard work, faith, and the ability to forgive, values by which the heartland, in sentimental mythology, is supposed to function."[8] As Martha Wolfstein and Nathan Leite observe about popular films in general, the success of *Places* indicates that it "tapped . . . the reservoir of common day-dreams" in our culture.[9] The financial crises confronting American farmers during the Depression made the values reputedly underlying farm life especially salient. Gaylyn Studlar traces the lineage of such films to the pastoral soap opera, a staple in 1920s cinema. Since the plight of farmers in the 1980s resembles that in the 1920s, the similar social context, Studlar contends, accounts for the resurgence of "country films" in 1984, marked by the close release of *Places, Country,* and *The River.*[10]

Because of the complexities that a text such as *Places* presents to the viewer, we have chosen to use a collection of diverse critical approaches. Rhetorical criticism of film often calls upon critics to draw from a variety of critical bases in order to account for the film's rhetorical form. To this end, we draw from sources in both media theory and rhetorical theory. For example, touching upon cultural fantasies is one way that films function rhetorically to engage audiences. However, films can also dramatize symptoms of particular societal needs, help symbolize and reinforce societal trends, and express value changes in a culture.[11] For instance, Rushing and Frentz argue that the success of *Rocky,* a film with little initial promise, stemmed from its enabling viewers to resolve the tension between competing sets of values. They demonstrate how *Rocky* symbolized a dialectical synthesis of antithetical values of materialism and moralism present in the 1976 presidential campaign.

In a broader sense, commercial films can be discussed within a larger narrative paradigm recently articulated by Walter Fisher.[12] He proposes this paradigm to provide a way of seeing all forms of human communication as stories. Fisher argues that reasoning need not be limited to traditional conceptions of argumentation. Studies in argumentation by Stephen Toulmin, Chaim Perelman, Douglas Ehninger, and Wayne Brockreide show that formal logic inadequately explains informal rationality and human valuing.[13] Fisher's paradigm enhances our understanding of the realm of rhetoric by showing that narration, in all its forms, gives order to human experience, while *inducing* others to share in the common experience suggested by the narration. Historically, Hollywood films have shown their capacity to induce their auditors to share the symbols and signs of consubstantiation that are what Fisher calls the communicative expressions of social reality.[14]

A key presupposition of Fisher's narrative paradigm is his description of rationality in *homo narrans,* the narrative being, who is constituted by an awareness of narrative probability (does this story make sense?) and narrative fidelity (does this story ring true?). A film's coherence (narrative probability) and authenticity (fidelity) are vital to the rhetorical force of the text. However, "coherence" may be interpreted by some as singularity of meaning. Fisher's analysis of *Death of a Salesman,* for example, demonstrates that "the play 'argues' for a thesis: mistaken, unrealistic values yield unhappiness."[15] Some might even argue that *Places in the Heart* suggests a singular interpretation: the "heart" (caring relationships) provides the motivation to struggle against obstacles in order to preserve the family and one's roots ("places").

While some texts, such as *Death of a Salesman,* may invite a single interpretation from its auditors, scholars need to be wary of assigning a unitary meaning to a complex text. As Fiske has argued recently about television programs, many texts permit alternative, even contradictory, readings.[16] (Obviously the concept of the polysemity of texts did not originate with Fiske. For example, Northrop Frye holds that all literary texts are polysemous.[17]) Texts may reinforce divergent values by permitting viewers with disparate attitudes and ideologies to find very different meanings in it. Indeed, texts which permit or encourage such disparate readings may enjoy wider popularity because of their ideological ambivalence. Fiske argues that in order to reach a mass audience, television must be an "open" text. He notes that: "Central to this theory is the notion that all television texts must, in order to be popular, contain within them unresolved contradictions that the viewer can exploit in order to find within them structural similarities to his or her own social relationship and identities."[18] To explain popularity, then, critics should search for "contradictions and openness . . . not unity and closure" in a text.[19] Fiske deals almost entirely with television, only briefly discussing film.[20] While Fiske provides an important framework to account for both preferred and oppositional readings of television shows, film is also capable of generating an open text that may enjoy a wider audience appeal.

This essay will approach *Places in the Heart* as an open text, which sustains divergent interpretations of its ideological messages.[21] We will argue that while the film explores divergent attitudes toward capitalism and feminism, it provides complex, even ambiguous, answers to the issues involved. Because its ideology remains unclear, the film supports ideologically diverse readings which, in turn, sustain tensions between conflicting sets of American values. Its popularity, in part, stems not from its resolution through dialectical synthesis, as Frentz and Rushing observe in *Rocky*, but from its ability to sustain divergent interpretations.

PLACES IN THE HEART AS AN OPEN TEXT

In the following discussion, we will argue that Edna is involved in a quest that varies significantly from the usual narrative formula; the quest and its limited resolutions suggest a preferred reading to the viewers, but allows for alternative, subversive readings; and the fissures in the text broaden and enhance the film's appeal to American audiences.

Frye's concept of the romantic quest is essential to our argument, but we shall vary from the basic pattern he outlines. The romantic quest is fundamentally an adventure in which heros set out recurrently on perilous journeys in search of treasures, that may be wealth, wisdom, or power. Assisted by sympathetic characters, the hero confronts a villain in a death struggle, from which the hero emerges triumphant and as representative of the ideals of the society.[22] Since romances are "the nearest of all literary forms to the wish-fulfillment dream," variations in their typical patterns may reflect important changes in society from which they emerge.[23]

In the usual romantic quest, the motive of the hero is the attainment of a treasure, either wealth or its idealized counterparts, power and wisdom. The hero's reward often includes a bride, whom Frye suggests may be psychologically connected with the Oedipal fantasy. To attain these prizes, a hero may undergo mutilation or physical handicap.[24] Although the quest of Edna Spalding in *Places* reflects this pattern, the goal and focus of her efforts vary significantly.

The dramatic tension of *Places* develops from Edna's need to win a prize, $100, for the first bale of cotton ginned in a season. In a literal sense, her quest is for that monetary reward. But the prize is, in Edna's eyes, only a means to an end. Her real goal is to save the family farm from foreclosure and to keep her family together. Rather than gaining a new reward or treasure, Edna is striving to preserve the "good" in her life. The farm and family act as motives for belonging and roots (i.e., "places") and caring relationships (i.e., "the heart"). In contrast to the typical romantic hero who finds personal glory because of his daring deeds, Edna simply seeks security for those she loves.

As a protagonist, Edna differs from the usual hero in other ways as well. First, she undertakes her quest only when circumstances compel her; her husband's death mandates her action. Moreover, her first efforts to preserve her family reveal timidity and naivete: she will open a gift shop in her home or help her sister in her beauty parlor. Only when her overtures in these directions are rebuffed by the pragmatic banker and her practical, if sympathetic, sister does she realize she must consider other alternatives. Indeed, initially she resists the banker's suggestion to take in Mr. Will, his blind brother-in-law, as a boarder, presumably because it infringes on her privacy. She is, in contrast to traditional male heroes, quite reluctant to undertake any adventure. It is only later, when Edna comes to terms with the reality of the struggles facing her, that she undergoes the transformation into an empowered person.

If Edna differs from the usual hero, her helpers do as well. Moze, an itinerant farm worker, first denied work by Edna, steals her silver. Later, when the sheriff returns him and her silver, she lies to protect Moze, realizing his value as a farming assistant. Visibly uncomfortable with her prevarication, Edna protects Moze, only because he offers the key to her economic success. As a social outcast because of his race, Moze nonetheless reveals an amazing capitalistic shrewdness. He correctly assesses the potential of her land for cotton farming, alerts her to the gin owner's unscrupulous attempt to substitute inferior seed for the first quality she has purchased, and manages the farm. Through the course of the film, the viewer sees Moze's heroism through his behavior, in spite of the social and economic constraints placed on him because of his race.

Mr. Will, Edna's boarder, is another social misfit. Hostile to her at first, he comes to offer the moral support she requires as Moze provides the practical knowledge. A war hero, blinded by gas, Mr. Will is reduced to caning chairs and making brooms to support himself. Mr. Will's heroic role in Edna's quest is reflected quite clearly in two scenes. When a tornado threatens the farm, he gropes his way upstairs to rescue Possum, her daughter, who then assists him in making his way to the shelter. He thus helps Edna save her family. Unable to assist in picking the crucial cotton crop, Mr. Will makes his way to the kitchen, where Edna finds him snapping beans to prepare a meal for the workers. This reversal of traditional roles is both practically and symbolically important: Mr. Will assumes a supportive role that contributes to the maintenance of the family, while providing Edna with much needed moral support, in spite of his physical handicap.

The antagonists in Edna's struggle are all elements in the capitalistic system. The banker and the dishonest gin owner are eager to take advantage of her plight. The almost melodramatic depictions of these men make their villainy quite clear. But scenic elements also threaten Edna. The Depression, which forces down cotton prices, impels her to try to win the $100 prize to pay the mortgage. A tornado wrecks her property and increases her difficulties. Thus, Edna's foes are both materialistic (and sometimes murderous) men and natural forces.

Edna struggles against economic difficulties, however, as a means to an end: to keep her family together. Here too, the banker is a villain, for he immediately proposes that she send her children to more prosperous relatives. Her forceful refusal reflects her commitment to her family. Thus family entails another set of responsibilities for her. She must discipline and manage her children as she provides for them. The crucial episode in this struggle is a scene in which she must whip Frank for smoking. After asking his advice about how his father performed this task, Edna administers the "licks" with obvious pain and unhappiness. In a real sense, the punishment hurts her more than it does Frank but she realizes its necessity if she is to maintain control of her children.

This scene reflects another symbolic development. While she is in the kitchen whipping Frank, Mr. Will stands on the screened-in porch holding Possum's hand and listening. Moze enters and lifts Possum into his arms for comfort. The audience recognizes that in the process of saving her family Edna has welded together another family composed of a black man, a blind war hero, her children, and herself. As one critic noted, "In this beguiling scene, we witness the forging of a make-shift but authentic family."[25] Significantly, she has become the head of this family as well, for it is her farm that provides them a shelter, and her decisions that get implemented.

As this discussion has illustrated, in *Places* Edna develops the determination to win the prize so she can make the mortgage payment and save her family. As the central character, she undertakes this quest only when circumstances compel her to action; she initially displays naivete, reluctance, and timidity unusual for a hero. Her assistants, Moze and Mr. Will, are outcasts from an economic and social system, although Moze possesses the "secrets" necessary for capitalistic success and Mr. Will has sacrificed his sight in a war to preserve the established order. In her struggles, Edna relies on these men for moral support and practical advice. But as she grows in strength and matures in outlook, she becomes not only the savior of her family but the head of a new social unit, which is ruptured by racism to be reconstituted only in the final, utopian communion service. Significantly, at the end of the film Edna's quest is only partially successful. Because Edna's economic future is at best uncertain, her family is only temporarily secure. Her created family has sustained a major loss. Both her capitalistic prowess and her determination to protect her family make the film's conclusion bittersweet.

Much of the diegesis supports the reading of a woman struggling to overcome economic and natural forces that threaten her family's security. However, fissures in the text allow for resistance to this preferred reading. Contradictions in the text are centered largely around the sexual affair between Edna's brother-in-law, Wayne, and his best friend's wife, Viola. This subplot disrupts the Edna Spalding narrative at several junctures in the film, temporarily distracting the viewer's attention away from Edna's issues. First, the sexual affair expands the narrative scope of the film beyond the economic and interpersonal dilemmas of the Spalding farm, giving the viewer some emotional distance from those particular stresses.

Second, the affair reminds the viewer that Edna's story is placed in the context of the town of Waxahachie; Edna is only a part of a larger town/community. For example, the film begins and ends with the town: the opening credits are superimposed over images of town buildings, telephone poles, streets, etc.; the film ends with the selected townsfolk in Edna's vision. The Edna narrative, in fact, is set within the larger narrative of the town (though most of the screen time concerns itself with Edna's situation). Benton inserts frequent shots of the town center as ways of dividing and dating scenes. Within this visual context, the hymn, "Blessed Assurance" is heard on the sound track during the opening credits and final church service, suggesting hope through a conventional and religious faith that sustains the community through hard times. Those who are willing to remain through economic hard times (the Depression) and interpersonal difficulty (the aftermath of the sexual affair) are rewarded with a place in Edna's vision at the end of the film. Significantly, Viola and her husband depart during the church service for another town, and are denied a place in Edna's vision of community. In contrast, Wayne stays, admitting his guilt to his wife, who indicates forgiveness at the church service by placing her hand on his. Wayne is forgiven, and remains a part of the community.

Third, the affair suggests the potential within the community for moral imperfections that subvert the religious tone set by the opening scenes. The affair spoils the apparent moral correctness of the town. Wayne is portrayed as playful, even impish; his wife supports him financially while he pursues Viola. His irresponsibility clashes in juxtaposition to Edna's sober determination and hard work. Yet at no point does the film condemn him as a character, nor can the film be said even to condemn his actions. Wayne is ultimately remorseful, and his wife generously indicates her forgiveness in the final scene. The viewer is given an unusually wide range (for an American film) to respond to many of the characters in *Places.*

Thus, fissures are created within the text of *Places,* allowing for negotiation of meaning. Much of the text's disruption centers around the sexual affair. This subplot distracts the viewer from Edna's issues, providing temporary emotional distance from Edna. The affair draws the viewer's attention to a larger narrative about Waxahachie as a community struggling with external economic forces and internal interpersonal conflict. Finally, the subplot contradicts the apparent moral correctness of Edna and Waxahachie. Yet the film allows the viewer freedom to respond to characters' actions, while avoiding an explicit moral statement about sexual indiscretions.

RHETORICAL FUNCTION

Much of the film's appeal undoubtedly stems from its sometimes heartening story. But understanding its rhetorical impact requires examining its implicit messages and how these relate to issues salient for the audience. Because the film focuses on a woman's efforts to save her family's farm, it addresses two issues quite salient for contemporary Americans: the roles of women in society and the threatened demise of the family farm. On the surface the film's message seems simple: a spunky housewife resourcefully copes with economic reverses to save her farm and keep her family together; she becomes a competitor in the capitalistic system, acting as any man would be expected to. Thus, superficially, the film seems to endorse new, strong roles for women and present a hopeful future for those farm families faced with foreclosure. However, as we discuss below, this interpretation omits important elements in the film.

First, Edna remains essentially a traditional woman, initially yearning for the old roles and behaviors. Although some reviewers emphasized the significance of Edna as the protagonist, they also recognized that she was not a model of the liberated woman. Tom O'Brien in *Commonweal* noted that while the film is a "female Western," Edna is not a typical feminist.[26] Another critic pointed out that although Edna was "tough," she was also staying at home.[27] Indeed, Edna is depicted as a traditional female stereotype with few feminist values. If she can, as one critic commented, "roll up her sleeves and get down to work," she does so only under compulsion and only to preserve her home and family.[28] Even in the midst of her struggle, she yearns to return to the safety and tranquility of her life with her husband, as her reverie of dancing in his arms reveals. Her assertiveness and courage emerge only in the face of threatened ruin and only under the guidance of Moze, a shrewder man. After she whips Frank, she concludes she will never do that again, admitting in effect that she is emotionally unsuited to fill the role of a conventional disciplinarian. In essence, Edna emerges as a woman whose actions are liberated but whose emotions and psychology remain deeply rooted in traditional feminine roles.

From this purview, Edna reaffirms many societal stereotypes just as does the hero in the traditional romantic myth. She is the ideal for many persons in contemporary society. Frye notes that the romantic quest is "the search of the libido or desiring self for a fulfillment that will deliver it from the anxieties of reality but still contain that reality."[29] Edna's character in *Places* serves exactly that function for contemporary persons confused about the debate over women's roles: she is a strong woman who, in her time and place, still prefers the traditional patterns and values.

In this respect, Edna contrasts strongly with the central characters in *Country* and *The River,* who exhibit their strength as they preserve their relationships with their husbands. Because the husbands are less dynamic and resourceful than their wives, the females assume nontraditional leadership roles. Edna becomes strong only at her husband's death and her resourcefulness is drawn in large part from other male characters. Thus, the film presents a less controversial image of the acceptable role for women and does not examine the tensions created in marriages in which women assume control of the family.

Second, the film offers an inspiring, but unrealistic picture of the problems confronting modern farmers. Various reviewers were quick to compare *Places* with *Country,* a film starring Jessica Lange, which treats the contemporary financial plight of farmers through one family's struggle to fight off foreclosure.[30] A third film of the same season, *The River,* with Sissy Spacek, treated a related theme: saving the farm from financial peril created by a threatening flood. That the stars of these films were all asked to appear before a congressional committee considering the plight of the family farm indicates how salient the issue was for contemporary audiences. (Evidently, Jessica Lange was inspired to produce *Country* by a visit to her home in rural Minnesota, where she saw the problems firsthand.[31]) *Places* suggests that the answer to the crisis can be met with ingenuity, hard work, and some luck. Edna forestalls foreclosure simply by rolling up her sleeves, determining to win the prize, and persevering toward her goal. This depiction, of course, oversimplifies the problems facing modern farmers and the solutions to those difficulties. In this sense, it assuages our guilt about the plight of today's farmers by suggesting that they can triumph over their economic woes.

But Americans were concerned with more than the economic consequences of the demise of the family farm. The reaffirmation of patience, hard work, faith, and compassion, qualities associated with farm life, was compelling. Studlar, in reviewing *The River,* observed "a deep nostalgia for the values popularly associated with rural America. A new conservatism has gained strength by associating itself with an idealized, pre-urban America, defined primarily by the tight-knit family and by the heroism of individual labor. . . . In spite of the demography which shows the United States to be indisputably urban, Americans still like to think that the country ethic is the American norm; this ethic governs many people's perception of themselves and the national ideal."[32] The family farm is, thus, a powerful "summarizing" symbol of American life. As Sherry Ortner notes, such symbols represent for persons in a culture "in an emotionally powerful and relatively undifferentiated way, what the system means to them . . . they [summarizing symbols] operate to compound and synthesize a complex system of ideas, to 'summarize' them under a unitary form which, in an old-fashioned way, 'stands for' the system as a whole."[33] Thus, Edna's quest to save her farm was symbolically a struggle to preserve an important facet of American life. In a sense, Edna's experiences represented our efforts as a society to preserve and maintain not only our roots but the values which we feel have made us great. But, as Vincent Canby shrewdly observed in a column praising the film for enriching its genre, ". . . it's as much about what we'd like America to be as it's about what it actually was."[34]

In contrast to *Country* and *The River,* two films in contemporary settings, *Places* gains from its setting during the Depression. The other films, as indictments of policies within the Reagan administration, function to some extent as political criticism. This tendency is most obvious in the scrolling text at the end of *Country,* which summarized the financial plight of farmers. These films argue, at least implicitly, that there is a tragic contradiction between our valuing of the family farm and our neglect of real farmers. *Places* avoids this rhetorical risk, by calling up our nostalgic views of rural life while turning our attention away from the problems besetting modern farmers. Thus, *Places* speaks to a salient contemporary issue, while reaffirming traditional values. The viewer is enabled to exult with Edna's success and feel comfortable that traditional values are intact. *Places in the Heart* is not overtly political in the way that *Country* and *The River* are, but it is ideological in any case.

On another level, the film incorporates both sides of the American Dream which Fisher described.[35] The materialistic dimension had gained ascendance with Ronald Reagan's election. His appeals to initiative, self-reliance, and success found a strong response in Americans, who were weary of Carter's moralistic vision. The media, however, began to reveal the difficulties arising from Reagan's policies. Discussion of the "truly needy" and Reagan's insistence that he intended to provide a "safety net" for them disturbed many Americans, who still supported his policies. How to be both humane and practical perplexed many citizens. *Places* points out the gap between the ideal of caring/compassion and our inability always to realize it. The discrepancy creates guilt in us, though the film suggests the possibility of being both compassionate and competitive.[36]

If Edna's attitudes reflected the moralistic side of the American dream—allegiance to family, tolerance, charity, hard work, compassion—her actions embodied materialistic ideas. She succeeded not because of her innate "goodness," but because she used the tools of the system to overcome it. Competition to win the prize became the secret of her success. In a real sense, she reaffirmed the system which threatened her existence. Far from criticizing American practices, as *Country* did with the farmers' boycotting the foreclosure auction, *Places* indicated that capitalistic practices were still effective and, in the hands of good people, could be practiced humanely. Significantly, the film offers no hint about Edna's future. Viewers are left to speculate whether she can survive alone in the face of potentially threatening economic and natural forces.

Moze is a crucial figure in this respect. As a social and economic "outsider," he displays the very virtues necessary for success within the system. Symbolically, he suggests that initiative and hard work are keys to accomplishment. His departure at the end touches and angers the audience who despises the racism that robs Moze of his reward. This treatment of racism is, in itself, rhetorically adept. Because the film is set in the 1930s, the viewer can either feel comfortable that such blatant prejudice is now "history," or, transposing the events to the present, can be recommitted to creating social justice in our time. In either case, the treatment of racism, like that of capitalism and feminism, removes the "sting" for the audience.

Benton's final scene is a vision of a communion service, in which the participants share the sacramental bread and wine. This scene seems to offer a utopian view of a new kind of family. The vision selectively includes some of the living and the dead characters participating in a communal ritual. This scene is a key to understanding the film's rhetorical function. At first, the scene appears to be Edna's transcendent vision of her community. However, a closer examination of the scene reveals people with whom she does not share a supportive relationship (the banker), peripheral characters (the homeless woman who lived in a car), and suggests behavior that Edna may not have known about (her sister's forgiveness of Wayne). Rather, the characters are the ones the *viewer* has known and "shared a relationship" with throughout the film.

Even more significant here are those who are included and excluded from this scene. This points toward Benton's extension of the film's view of community. Wayne, for example, is included in the final scene. Though he has violated the standards of the community through his affair with Viola, Wayne atones for his sin and remains *in* Waxahachie. His wife forgives him, symbolized in a gesture depicted in close-up, in which she places her hand on his; Wayne is visibly, immensely relieved, and remains with the community. Viola, on the other hand, flees the town with her husband, despairing that Waxahachie's plight will never improve. She too has broken the rules, but she does not attempt reconciliation, and is excluded from the final vision. Similarly, Mr. Simmons, the dishonest seed vendor and KKK member, who threatens and attacks Moze, is also excluded. As a culmination of all that has preceded it, the final scene suggests that the film's center is the town/community, and the reinforcement of commonly shared values. These shared values, embodied in a dialectical reaffirmation of moralism and materialism, are set by the community. Though members may stray from and violate these codes, attempts at reconciliation are acknowledged. Only those who will not participate are excluded.

The affirmation suggested by the final scene is mitigated by its unreality. The presence of Wiley (the dead black man who had accidentally killed Edna's husband), Moze, and Edna's dead husband remind the viewer that this is a *vision*. The viewer is acutely aware that economic forces in the real world complicate the situation. The closest approach to this ideal in the film, Edna's created family with Moze and Mr. Will, was produced by economic necessity, saved by capitalistic shrewdness, and ruptured by racist jealousy of Moze's "uppitiness" in guiding Edna's successful farming efforts. Thus, viewers are left with a complex message about the relationship between moralism and materialism.

Perhaps what the film fails to accomplish is a coming-to-terms with its affirmation of the status quo. This refers to the film's portrayal of women who are ill-prepared by socially constrained roles to deal with life-rupturing events, such as the death of a spouse, and the consequences thereof. It also permits the bland acceptance of racism and Klan activities as a way of life. As a film made in 1984, it has the political advantage of hindsight, and the capacity to indict a social system that permits injustices. This is particularly true in the case of Moze, who is forced to leave by the Klan: Edna accepts his departure almost fatalistically, and the film does not encourage the viewer to question it (though the viewer is certainly enabled to feel outrage at the injustice and loss). While the film offers richness in its complex message, one cannot help but feel that *Places* is, to some extent, a missed opportunity to raise awareness on issues of gender and race.

CONCLUSION

As the above discussion has indicated, *Places* is not a unitary text with one clear message for its audiences. Indeed, depending on one's ideology, one can find quite disparate messages embedded in the film about such issues as feminism, capitalism, and the farm crisis. Far from aiding in the process of a dialectical synthesis of values, *Places* leaves unresolved the struggle within the audience about the two aspects of the American Dream as Fisher elaborated them.

This failure to offer a single answer to issues can be viewed as a source of richness in the film. Not only does the text sustain alternate interpretations of its messages (Edna is/is not a liberated woman, etc.), but it also suggests the complexity of real life. If Edna's success in saving the farm is an easy, appealing ending, the fate of Moze and her own future remain clouded. While we are satisfied with the short-term fulfillment of her quest, we also realize her future peril and, thanks to the utopian communion service, recognize how far she and we are from resolving knotty problems confronting our society. The final communion service lingers both as an inspiring ideal and an indictment of our failings.

The polysemity in this text depends in large part on Benton's skillful adaptation of the quest formula. While much research has confirmed the ambiguity of this narrative pattern, little attention has focused on the impact of skillful manipulation of the formula. In its more conservative, traditional form, the formula focuses almost entirely on the central character, who sets out to accomplish a quest successfully. Here Benton develops in the central character a mixture of traditional values and unorthodox behaviors, but leaves the quest only partially successful. Benton also introduces fissures into the central narrative structure, most obviously in the form of the sexual affair. The distractions distance the viewer from the quest, recasting it as one person's preoccupation in the midst of a larger social community where other dramas are being played out. While the basic formula retains its emotional appeal, Benton's manipulation of it "opens" the text to divergent readings. This film demonstrates, then, the importance of scholarly attention not only to general narrative structure, but to manipulation of such patterns.

The popularity of *Places* suggests that its themes tap into an integral part of American culture. The value systems depicted in this film have been identified in an earlier form by Tocqueville.[37] He suggested that Americans are a hard-working, but compassionate, people. Tocqueville argues that the principle of self-interest is a vital motivator of Americans; however, this self-interest is ennobled by an accompanying concern for their fellow countrymen.[38] Other observers of U.S. political/social systems have also identified tensions between value systems in American society. The paradox remains that Americans largely endorse a competitive system of capitalistic free enterprise, yet feel a compelling responsibility for the upholding of human dignity and social welfare of its people.[39] *Places* enacts these contradictions and affirms the experience of uncertainty generated by the dramatization of these issues. Because of the harsh reality depicted in the film, *Places* mitigates a compulsive American optimism for perennial happy endings. Instead, the film invites us to reflect on our cultural paradoxes.[40]

If the film does not help us move from one value orientation to another, it does remind us that solutions to social problems are often only temporary and that both new and traditional views have merit. While the film avoids dealing forcefully and clearly with major issues, it also suggests the ambivalence many of us feel about the roles of women, the family farm, and capitalism, though the film does not reveal the traps inherent in the capitalistic/patriarchal system. In one sense, however, it reveals that we are all, like Edna, an uneasy composite of conflicting views and attitudes. Also, like her, we draw on both our idealistic/moralistic and pragmatic/materialistic sides in gaining even temporary victories.

Reading Endnotes

1. J. Hoberman, "American, Right and Wrong," *Village Voice*, 3 October 1984: 52; Vincent Canby, "Film, *Places in the Heart*, Benton's Waxahachie in the Depression," *New York Times* 21 September 1984: C8.

2. "Native Lands," *The New Republic* 1 October 1984: 24; Cf. Pauline Kael, "The Current Cinema: Mirrors," *The New Yorker* 15 October 1984: 170–173.
3. A. Karp, Places in the Heart, *Boxoffice,* 19 November 1984: R-132; Jagr (Jeff Greenfield), "Places in the Heart," *Variety,* 19 September 1984: 20.
4. "A Search for Connections," *Time* 24 September 1984: 70–71.
5. Nick Roddick, *"Places in the Heart," Magill's Cinema Annual,* 1985 (Englewood Cliffs, N.J.: Salem Press, 1985), 371.
6. Lawrence Van Gelder, "At the Movies," *New York Times* 21 September 1984: C6; Jack Kroll, "The Best of Times, The Worst of Times," *Newsweek* 24 September 1984: 86; Roddick 372.
7. Kroll 89.
8. Kroll 86; Tom O'Brien, "All of Them: Catching up on Fall Releases," *Commonweal* 30 November 1984: 660–661.
9. *Movies: A Psychological Study* (Glencoe: Free Press, 1950) 13.
10. Gaylyn Studlar, *"The River," Magill's Cinema Review,* 1985, 416–420.
11. Janice Hocker Rushing and Thomas J. Frentz, "The Rhetoric of 'Rocky': A Social Value Model of Criticism," *Western Journal of Speech Communication,* 42:2 (1978), 63–72. Thomas J. Frentz and Janice Hocker Rushing, "The Rhetoric of 'Rocky': Part Two," *Western Journal of Speech Communication,* 42:3 (1978), 231–240.
12. Walter R. Fisher, *Human Communication as Narration: Toward a Philosophy of Reason, Value and Action* (Columbia, S.C.: University of South Carolina Press, 1989) 57–78.
13. Fisher ix.
14. Fisher 65.
15. Fisher 168.
16. Stanley [John] Fiske, "Television: Polysemy and Popularity," *Critical Studies in Mass Communication,* 1986, 3, 391–408.
17. Northrop Frye, *The Critical Path* (Bloomington: Indiana University Press, 1971) esp. 13–33. In his view that texts contain contradictory meanings, Fiske is clearly indebted to deconstruction theorists. For a brief discussion of this approach, see Terry Eagleton, *Literary Theory: An Introduction* (Minneapolis: University of Minnesota Press, 1983) esp. 127–150.
18. Fiske 392.
19. Fiske 391. Celeste Condit argues for a need to distinguish between polysemy and polyvalence. Condit suggests that audiences frequently share denotative understandings of a text, but may disagree about their evaluations of shared denotations, producing different interpretations of the same text. Condit calls this a polyvalence, which needs to be distinguished from genuine polysemy that occurs when a multiplicity or instability of textual meanings are available. Her distinction contributes to critical theory about television, though our view is that *Places* is indeed polysemous, because it makes available a multiplicity

of textual meaning. See Celeste Michelle Condit, "The Rhetorical Limits of Polysemy," *Critical Studies in Mass Communication* (1989): 6:2, 103–122, esp. 106–107.

20. Fiske argues that a text like a film "relies more on narrative sequence and cause and effect for its structuring principles, for these are agents of semiotic closure." Fiske's argument about film, however, apparently emerges from an assumption that films *necessarily* rely on narrative sequence and cause/effect, an argument that is weakened by historically notable instances which enjoyed critical and/or popular successes. For example, David Bordwell has argued that *Citizen Kane's* rich vision emerges largely from its ability to hold apparently irreconcilable contradictions in suspension. The film uses a highly segmented narrative structure to avoid closure. See David Bordwell, "*Citizen Kane*," *Film Comment* Vol. 7 (1971), rpt. in *Movies and Methods*, ed. Bill Nichols (Berkeley: University of California Press, 1976) 273–290. This is only one example of a successful film that invites divergent interpretations of reality. Thus, varying interpretations of an individual film indicate that the medium of film has access to segmented, associative structures such as those that Fiske claims exist in television.
21. Umberto Eco, *The Role of the Reader* (Bloomington: Indiana University Press, 1979).
22. Northrop Frye, *Anatomy of Criticism: Four Essays* (Princeton, N.J.: Princeton University Press, 1973) 186–206.
23. Frye, *Anatomy of Criticism* 193.
24. Frye, *Anatomy of Criticism* 193.
25. Kroll 89.
26. O'Brien 642.
27. Hoberman 52.
28. Greenfield, *Variety* 22.
29. Frye, *Anatomy of Criticism* 193.
30. John Simon, "Herstories," *National Review* 14 December 1984: 49–50; O'Brien 660; Hoberman 52; Kroll 86.
31. John Robert Kelly, "*Country*," *Magill's Cinema Annual* 1985, 156.
32. Gaylyn Studlar, "*The River*," *Magill's Cinema Annual* 1985, 417.
33. Sherry Ortner, "On Key Symbols," *American Anthropologist* 75 (October 1973) 1339–1340.
34. "Three New Movies Enrich Their Genre," *New York Times* 23 September 1984: 2:34.
35. Walter R. Fisher, "Reaffirmation and Subversion of the American Dream," *Quarterly Journal of Speech*, 59 (1973) (LIX): 160–167.
36. Two distinct patterns of change are suggested here. Janice Hocker Rushing has suggested that classic Westerns enacted a pattern of *dialectical reaffirmation*. In this rhetorical response, the tension between the opposing value system (in this case, moralism and materialism) is both acknowledged and reaffirmed. Given the ambiguous conclusion

of *Places*, however, this film may be seen as an enactment of a *dialectical disorientation*. In this pattern, the conflict between the opposed systems results in a paradoxical acceptance of the uncertainty of the human condition. See Janice Hocker Rushing, "The Rhetoric of the American Western Myth," *Communication Monographs*, (1983) 14–32; see also Karen Rasmussen and Sharon D. Downey, "Dialectical Disorientation in *Agnes of God*," *Western Journal of Speech Communication*, 52 (1989), 66–84.

37. Alexis de Tocqueville, *Democracy in America*, Vol. 2 (New York: Vintage Books, 1954).
38. Tocqueville 130–131.
39. John Gunther, *Inside U.S.A.* (New York: Harper and Brothers, 1947) 918–920.
40. Bellah et al. have recently examined the modern manifestations of individualism, warning that this American character trait may have evolved into a socially cancerous form. See Robert N. Bellah et al., *Habits of the Heart* (Berkeley: University of California Press, 1985) esp. vii–ix.

In this Chapter 6 workshop, we will probe in focused workshop exercises many of the concepts you discovered in this chapter. Work at a pace by assignment, or by choice, that allows these various insights to "sink in" at an even deeper level for you.

As part of this Chapter 6 workshop, we will continue to probe several of the ways you can recognize and use the "gold" of academic, rhetorical criticism. Read the rhetorical criticism of *Places in the Heart* by Solomon [Watson] and McMullen starting on page 202. Take careful notes on the JFS, JFA, Method, and RQ items (about which you learned in Chapter 3) that Solomon and McMullen used to establish the need for their research.

Next, re-read the chart on page 219. See if you can notice how we moved from the original claim, insight or discovery to the resulting "translation."

Next, use the blank chart on the following page to find more nuggets of "gold" in the article from your own reading. Be sure to keep track of the page on which you find the quotation and think about how you can best translate the insight or discovery to a practical translation you could use in preparing a message.

FINDING THE GOLD

Discovering Application Ideas and Knowledge in Narrative Analysis Articles

Example:

Solomon [Watson], Martha and Wayne J. McMullen. "*Places in the Heart:* The Rhetorical Force of an Open Text." *Western Journal of Speech Communication* 55 (Fall 1991): 339–353.

(Page numbers in brackets indicate pages reprinted in this textbook.)

Quotation	Page	Translated Idea or Insight
"Since the plight of farmers in the 1980s resembles that in the 1920s, the similar social context, Studlar contends, accounts for the resurgence of 'country films' in 1984, marked by the close release of *Places, Country,* and *The River.*"	340 [203]	Stories in popular Hollywood films tend to focus on themes and concerns facing America at the time.
"Texts may reinforce divergent values by permitting viewers with disparate attitudes and ideologies to find very different meanings in it. Indeed, texts which permit or encourage such disparate readings may enjoy wider popularity because of their ideological ambivalence."	341 [204]	The same movie characters and events may represent very different meanings to different audience members; allowing different audience members to "see" different meanings from the same characters in one movie may allow the filmmakers to sell more tickets.
"We will argue that while the film explores divergent attitudes toward capitalism and feminism, it provides complex, even ambiguous, answers to the issues involved. Because its ideology remains unclear, the film supports ideologically diverse readings which, in turn, sustain tensions between conflicting sets of American values."	341 [205]	Characters and events in a Hollywood movie can directly, or indirectly, address issues of concern to people in American culture. Filmmakers may, then, offer characters and actions that explore (and perhaps celebrate) different (even conflicting) values.

Use the chart on the next page to find, identify, and chart the potential advantage of other observations on narrative and culture that Solomon and McMullen make in their analysis.

Quotation	Page	Translated Idea or Insight

THE POWER OF SOUND

Get a videotape or DVD version of a popular release American film and listen to the first 10 minutes of the film with the picture turned off. Take notes about what you hear and to what you pay attention when the visual component of the film is removed.

NON-DIEGETIC ELEMENTS

Use a videotape or DVD version of a popular release American film and chart over the first hour of the movie all of the non-diegetic material in the film (sound or visual). Ask yourself the function of the non-diegetic elements within various scenes, that is, what was the purpose of including that material?

STORY^{G} AND STORY^{C}

Watch a videotape or DVD version of a popular release American film and stop the movie each time you are required as an audience member to "fill in" information. As you more clearly recognize the difference between story^{g} information and story^{c} processes, ask how different audience members might "fill in the blanks" differently.

THE POWER OF "ONCE . . ."

As you watch and listen to stories in the mass media over the next week keep a journal of times when you observe the three powers of "once." When do you notice that by offering a story to an audience, the rhetor is at that moment selecting one story to the exclusion of others that might be told? When do you notice that you've seen the same *form* of story used by someone else? When do you notice that a story is focusing on how something is now different than it used to be?

Try very hard to put your mind into the mode of analyzing stories offered to you rather than just accepting them.

IN MEDIAS RES

Carefully observe starting point of the next three sitcoms you watch over a week. Ask yourself what the impact might have been if you had the power to alter where and when and with whom the action started. What seems to guide those decisions for the writers and director of the sitcoms you watch?

Key Words

narrative, *183–184, 186*
story, *183*
first power of "once", *184*
second power of "once", *184–185*
third power of "once", *185*
story^{g}, *186–188*
story^{c}, *186–188*
diegesis, *188*
diegetic, *188*
non-diegetic, *188*
screen time, *189*
story^{g} scene time, *189*
story^{c} time, *190*
story^{g} space, *191*
story^{c} space, *191*
x-axis movement, *191*
y-axis movement, *191*
z-axis movement, *191*
subject motion, *191–192*
camera motion, *191–192*
cyber motion, *191–192*
mise en scene, *192–194*
in medias res, *194–195*
sound manipulation, *195*
wild or scratch sound, *196*
diegetic sound, *196*
non-diegetic sound, *196*
spoken dialog, *196*
music, *196*
sounds, *196*
ADR, *196*
Foley artist, *196*
narrative cohesion, *197–199*
narrative fidelity, *199*
preferred reading, *200*
negotiated reading, *200*
oppositional reading, *200*

Narrative Analysis Articles

Below you will find a sample of rhetorical and cultural analysis articles that have investigated the power of narrative in public messages.

Bennett, W. Lance. "Storytelling in Criminal Trials: A Model of Social Judgment." *Quarterly Journal of Speech* 64 (1978) 1–22.

Bennett, W. Lance and Martha S. Feldman. *Reconstructing Reality in the Courtroom.* New Brunswick, N.J.: Rutgers University Press, 1981.

Campbell, Richard and Jimmie Reeves. "Covering the Homeless: The Joyce Brown Story." *Critical Studies in Mass Communication* 6 (1989) 21–42.

Carpenter, Ronald R. "Admiral Mahan, 'Narrative Fidelity,' and the Japanese Attack on Pearl Harbor." *Quarterly Journal of Speech* 72 (1986): 290–305.

Collins, Catherine A. and Jeanne E. Clark. "A Structural Narrative Analysis of *Nightline's* 'This Week in the Holy Land.'" *Critical Studies in Mass Communication* 9 (1992) 25–43.

Condit, Celeste M. "The Rhetorical Limits of Polysemy." *Critical Studies in Mass Communication* 6 (1989): 103–122.

Condit, Celeste Michelle and J. Ann Selzer. "The Rhetoric of Objectivity in the Newspaper Coverage of a Murder Trial." *Critical Studies in Mass Communication* 2 (1985): 197–216.

Daughton, Suzanne M. "The Spiritual Power of Repetitive Form: Steps Toward Transcendence in *Groundhog Day.*" *Critical Studies in Mass Communication* 13 (1996): 138–154.

Deming, Caren J. "*Hill Street Blues* as Narrative." *Critical Studies in Mass Communication* 2 (1985): 1–22.

Dobkin, Bethami A. "Paper Tigers and Video Postcards: The Rhetorical Dimensions of Narrative Form in ABC News Coverage of Terrorism." *Western Journal of Communication* 56 (1992) 143–160.

Engnell, Richard A. "The Spiritual Potential of Otherness in Film: The Interplay of Scene and Narrative." *Critical Studies in Mass Communication* 12 (1995) 241–262.

Farrell, Thomas B. "Media Rhetoric as Social Drama: The Winter Olympics of 1984." *Critical Studies in Mass Communication* 6 (1989): 158–182.

Fisher, Walter R. "Narration as a Human Communication Paradigm: The Case of Public Moral Argument." *Communication Monographs* 51 (1984): 1–22.

Guerrero, Laura K. and George N. Dionisopoulos. "Enthymematic Solutions to the Lockshin Defection Story: A Case Study in the Repair of a Problematic Narrative." *Communication Studies* 41 (1990) 299–310.

Katriel, Tamar and Aliza Shenhar. "Tower and Stockade: Dialogic Narration in Israeli Settlement Ethos." *Quarterly Journal of Speech* 76 (1990): 359–380.

Kirkwood, William G. "Parables as Metaphors and Examples." *Quarterly Journal of Speech* 71 (1985): 422–440.

Lessl, Thomas M. "The Galileo Legend as Scientific Folklore." *Quarterly Journal of Speech* 85 (1999): 146–168.

Lewis, William F. "Telling America's Story: Narrative Form and the Reagan Presidency." *Quarterly Journal of Speech* 73 (1987): 280–302.

Medhurst, Martin J. "The Rhetorical Structure of Oliver Stone's *JFK*." *Critical Studies in Mass Communication* 10 (June 1993): 128–143.

Newcomb, Horace M. "On the Dialogic Aspects of Mass Communication." *Critical Studies in Mass Communication* 1 (1984): 34–50.

Olson, Scott R. "Meta-Television: Popular Postmodernism." *Critical Studies in Mass Communication* 4 (1987): 284–300.

Parry-Giles, Trevor and Paul Traudt. "The Depiction of Television Courtroom Drama: A Dialogic Criticism of *L.A. Law*." *Television Criticism: Approaches and Applications.* Eds. Leah R. Vande Berg and Lawrence A. Wenner. New York: Longman, 1991. 143–159.

Poulakos, Takis. "Isocrates's Use of Narrative in the *Evagoras:* Epideictic Rhetoric and Moral Action." *Quarterly Journal of Speech* 73 (1987): 317–328.

Rushing, Janice Hocker. "Mythic Evolution of the 'The New Frontier' in Mass Mediated Rhetoric." *Critical Studies in Mass Communication* 3 (1986): 265–296.

Scult, Allen, Michael Calvin McGee, and J. Kenneth Kuntz. "Genesis and Power: An Analysis of the Biblical Story of Creation." *Quarterly Journal of Speech* 72 (1986): 113–131.

Smith, Larry D. "Narrative Styles in Network Coverage of the 1984 Nominating Conventions." *Western Journal of Speech Communication* 52 (1988): 63–74.

Terrill, Robert E. "Put on a Happy Face: *Batman* as Schizophrenic Savior." *Quarterly Journal of Speech* 79 (1993): 319–335.

Trujillo, Nick and Leah R. Ekdom. "Sportswriting and American Cultural Values: The 1984 Chicago Cubs." *Critical Studies in Mass Communication* 2 (1985): 262–281.

Endnotes

1. Used with permission; © 1999 Pierce Communication.
2. Herbert Zettl, *Sight Sound Motion: Applied Media Aesthetics* 3rd ed. (Belmont, Calif.: Wadsworth 1999) 141–143.
3. Used with permission; © 1999 Pierce Communication.
4. "Bart the Murderer." *The Simpsons,* Episode 8F03, Fox Network 10 Oct. 1991.
5. Walter R. Fisher, "Narration as a Human Communication Paradigm: The Case of Public Moral Argument," *Communication Monographs* 51 (1984): 8.

Chapter Seven

Visual Messages: The Eyes Have It

You are part of the first generation in history to be raised in a media environment filled to overflowing with visual messages. Visual messages reach out to you from the far end of your grocery cart, from your computer screen, from your morning cereal box, and from the print pattern on your roommate's boxer shorts. The power represented in the creation and use of these visual messages is staggering. Much less complex to learn than any verbal language, visual messages circle the globe in nanoseconds, bringing information, persuasion, and perspective to millions each hour. While visual messages are less complex than word-based messages, they are nonetheless deeply influenced by the cultures, economies, and values of those who create them.

Clearly we must be hard at work to better understand how these visual messages work and are used. Visual rhetoric, or the study of visual persuasion, is the new kid on the block in academic areas of study. Since we've only had the ability to create visual messages that could reach a mass audience for the past 150 years or so, we understandably have had less time to think with care about visual rhetoric.

Have you ever lingered in a store for longer than 30 seconds looking at a particular poster? What about that image held your attention? Have you ever had a friend or family member yell: "Come here and *look* at this?" What image on the TV was so compelling as to provoke a special call for viewing? Do you have a set of images in your mind gained from the mass media that will be with you for your whole life? What images? Why were they memorable? For millions of people, images of JFK, the Challenger, Nazi death camps, Tiananmen Square, or the World Trade Center Towers will stick in their memories for as long as they live. In addition, we will all view millions of images from a variety of sources that do not stay in our conscious visual memory, but nevertheless have influence on our beliefs and life decisions.

In this chapter we'll investigate the terminology, perspectives, studies, and insights that have been gained over the past 50 to 100 years as various critics of our visual message culture have worked to better understand the rhetorical power of visual communication. As recently as the early 70s, scholars recognized the importance of visual messages and the necessity of our careful study of them:

> There is a level of sophistication necessary for the proper understanding of visual images. Pictures and film often convey misleading impressions of scale, distance, time, and relationship. By overcoming the limitations of space and time they may also fail to communicate the reality and importance of these dimensions. More importantly, perhaps, the images conveyed through these media may be deliberately or inadvertently false. The potential for misleading and dissembling, for confusing fiction and reality, is at least as great with photographs and films as with words and actions, and quite possibly much greater.[1]

We will divide this chapter into three segments. First we'll examine some basic conceptual tools to use for understanding and analysis of visual images. Next we will examine some standard tactics used by those who employ substantial amounts of visual material in their messages. Finally we'll examine some examples of visual messages in a primary visual persuasion arena: the American political cartoon.

BASIC TOOLS

Visual messages are substantially different than spoken or written messages in one fundamental way: they often look like the thing they are supposed to represent. Hence C-O-W, or *vache,* or *kuh* might serve us as written symbols for a four-legged, bovine animal in English, French, or German. But if we do not know the written code within a given language, we may not understand the reference. For instance, which of these sentences refers to a cow? 1. *Onde está minha vaca?* Or, 2. *Dove è la mia mucca?*[2] On the other hand, visual messages can recognizably represent the animal in question in many different ways. Which of the three pictures (Figs. 7–1 to 7–3) represents a cow?

Although these three pictures are vastly different, many English-speaking audience members upon seeing them would identify each of the animals depicted as a "cow."

The ability of a visual message to evoke that recognition and identification is called **iconicity.** An **icon** in semiotic terms is something that looks like the thing it resembles. Stop reading for a moment and pull out your driver's license or campus ID card. While the photo on the card or license may not be your favorite, it is there for a reason of iconic recognition. We know that the state police or various campus services would not accept a

FIGURE 7.1 Cow

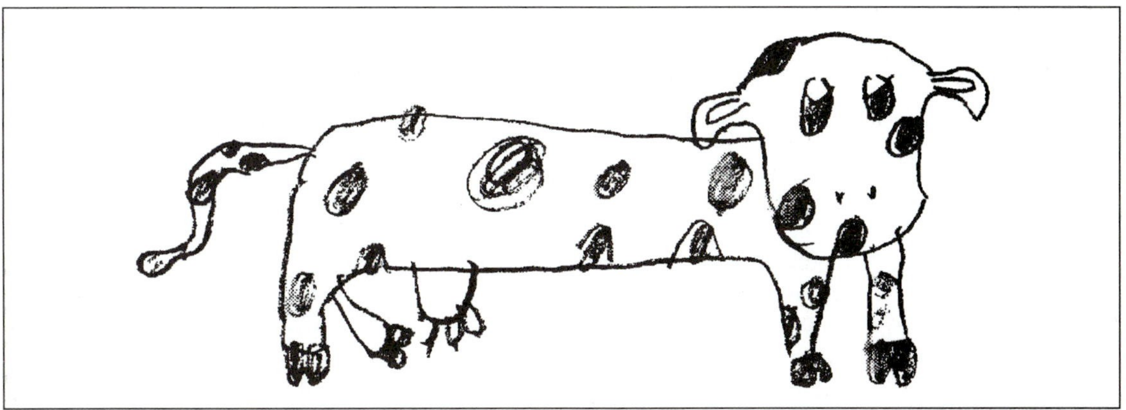

FIGURE 7.2 Cow

FIGURE 7.3 Cow

Picasso-style drawing of you or a stick figure likeness. The resemblance (or lack thereof) is precisely why a picture ID requires an iconic likeness of you that is recognizable and accurate. If we mailed your license or campus ID to Denver or Tallahassee and asked someone who did not know you to use the photo on the ID to find you getting off an airplane, would the resemblance be strong enough to allow the person to pick you out of a crowd of hundreds in an airport terminal? If so, we have identified the core aspect of an iconic visual message. (If not, perhaps you need a new ID or license.)

Icon, iconic, and iconicity are three terms that have become associated with a system of investigating meaning creation called **semiotics** (or by some people in some places as **semiology**). Swiss linguist Ferdinand de Saussure, American philosopher Charles Sanders Peirce, and French thinker Roland Barthes are often given the greatest credit for giving us a basic set of ideas and terms that help us see language (both verbal and visual) as a set of **signs.**[3]

I will briefly cover basic semiotic terms borrowed from these three scholars for visual analysis before continuing our discussion of basic tools of rhetorical visual analysis.

From de Saussure we learned that a sign (i.e., any message or element within a message) is made up of a **signifier** and a **signified.**[4] A signifier is the physical image we observe in the ad, or family photo, or television screen. The signified is the mental connection called up for us as prompted by the signifier. So when we look at a picture of someone from our *own* family, the signifier would be the actual picture. The signified for one person might be "Aunt Ellie from Albuquerque," or if we have no aunt in Albuquerque, the signified might simply be "a female person."

From Barthes, and de Saussure, we learned that a sign has a **denotation** meaning and a **connotation** meaning.[5]

The McAfee ad (Fig. 7.4) prominently features a picture signifier of a porcupine. Our minds quickly move to a signified of "porcupine" (as opposed to "dog" or "hamster" or "pin cushion") which is the denotation meaning that we've learned. But, in a fraction of a second we also create a connotation meaning that might include "danger," "pain," "beware," or "prickly." The McAfee copywriters make sure you get the right connotation. They mention "your unfriendly side" that may be wise to use when dealing with hackers.

From C. S. Peirce we learned that a sign can appear in one of three forms.[6] A sign can be an **iconic sign,** an **indexical sign,** or a **symbolic sign.** An iconic sign, as we've discussed concerning your license or campus ID, is an image that looks like the thing or person it represents. An indexical sign is a sign that some process or activity has taken place. So the picture of dirty dishes (Fig. 7.5) indicates (or is an **index**) that eating and stacking have gone on.

FIGURE 7.4 Porcupine Signifier

SHOW HACKERS YOUR UNFRIENDLY SIDE.

EVEN ON THE RUN.

www.mcafee.com/wireless or viruscenter.lycos.com

Scrutinize exercise

If you were working for the ad agency that created the McAffee ad, and you decided *not* to use the image of a porcupine, what would have been an acceptable alternative? Remember, you are trying to visually signal (rapidly) that hackers who encounter your protection software will be compelled to back off. What other animal besides a porcupine would work? Could you use an image that was not an animal? What would you use?

FIGURE 7.5
Dirty Dishes as Indexical Sign

A symbolic sign is arbitrary and created. Do you recognize the image in Figure 7.6?

FIGURE 7.6
Mazda Emblem as Symbolic Sign

The people at Mazda *hope* you recognize it. They have spent substantial sums of money to include it in print and electronic media ads. The Mazda emblem is a good example of what Peirce would call a symbolic sign. It is not iconic in the same way your picture on an ID card resembles you. It is not an indexical sign in the same way that a stack of dirty dishes signals that someone has eaten food. Instead, a symbolic sign is a visual sign that could just as easily been designed in a very different way.

So, we've learned that visual signs, or messages, are created from a signifier that causes our minds to create a mental connection to a signified. Moreover, a signifier can create meaning that is denotative or connotative. Signs come in three types: iconic, indexical, and symbolic.

Visual messages, whether held on a card in your wallet or presented on a mega-screen display at a sports arena, are important for us to consider because contemporary rhetors as often as not will be working with pictures as well as words. Just as we know words can go well beyond simple (iconic) identification, we recognize as well that visual messages can also go far beyond simple mental identification of people, places, and critters.

Let's explore several other examples of visual communication and persuasion as you gain experience with these designations of visual analysis and ideas of how visual messages create meaning. We'll start with some indexical examples.

Examine the Cheney cartoon below (Fig. 7.7).

Notice that the cigarette butt in the drawing suggests something more than mere presence in the picture of the desert. If the butt had been a cactus, or a cow skeleton head, or a palm tree, we might have thought little of its specific meaning in the drawing. The cigarette butt in this picture is an indexical visual message in that it signals something beyond its presence in the picture. Part of the humor that Cheney, the artist, aimed for was to call up your memories of when a smoker has extinguished a cigarette in a

FIGURE 7.7
Cigarette butt as indexical sign. What does your mind tell you about how the cigarette butt got in this scene?

sand-like substance. Hence the butt in this drawing becomes not just an image, but also an indication that something else (not pictured) has happened. So we recognize this as an indexical image within a cartoon message: one that points beyond to other actions or events.

Likewise, when you see visual messages that contain images of bullet holes, or lipstick marks on a glass, or tire tracks in the snow, or a hole in the ground with freshly dug dirt, you are interpreting images that use indexicality to help make visual meaning.

Look at the pencils depicted in the Majestic ad in Figure 7.8.

Since you cannot go to your local office supply store and buy pencils that look like the ones in this ad, we must assume that some process has changed the appearance of the pencils. While the denotation meaning indicates pencils that have somehow been indented, the connotation meaning of chewed pencils being a by-product of nerves, anxiety, distress, or confusion can come from personal or observed experience. Hence the pencils depicted serve as an indexical visual message element that point beyond its sheer representation to a behavior that produced the tooth marks on the pencils.

We can recognize how powerful indexical visual messages are by noticing when they *cannot* be used. For instance, look at the Ford truck ad (Fig. 7.9). Notice that various word labels have been blocked out. What meaning do you attribute to the various marks, mud, and grass? The helmet depicted is certainly an index of collisions with other players and contact with grass turf. Now flip to Figure 7.10 and read the word labels that appeared in the original ad. Can you see the meaning-creation limitation of a visual index?

While the visual index elements on the helmet can clearly indicate activity on the football field (complete with collisions and turf connections), those same elements need word-based help to create more specific meaning. Specific marks on a helmet might tell us about a collision with another player; they cannot—on their own—tell us that a defensive player knocked the wind out of a running back.

Of course visual index images also participate in iconicity. Whatever we see in the picture that points to something else, nonetheless it is what it appears to be.

Scrutinize exercise

Look at Figure 7.11. This picture comes from the *second* page of a two-page ad. If you recognize the bicycle and the helmet, it is because you can decode the images by their iconic attributes. When you see these items at this depicted stone wall, what comes to your mind? If you knew a person was going to be shown in page one of this ad, what kind of person would you guess?

FIGURE 7.8 Chew marks as Indexical Sign

FIGURE 7.9 Ford Ad (Labels Removed)

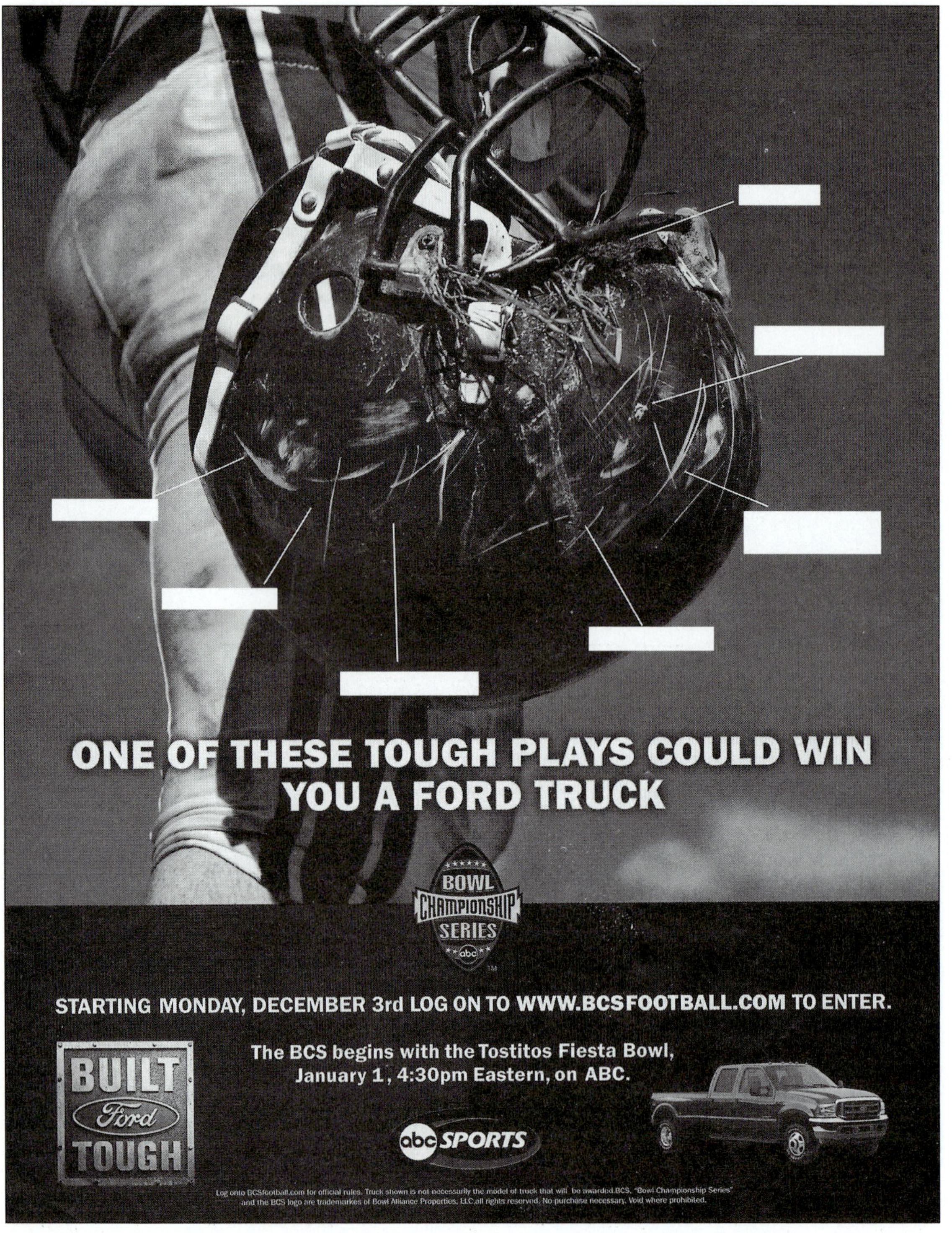

FIGURE 7.10 Ford Ad with Original Labels

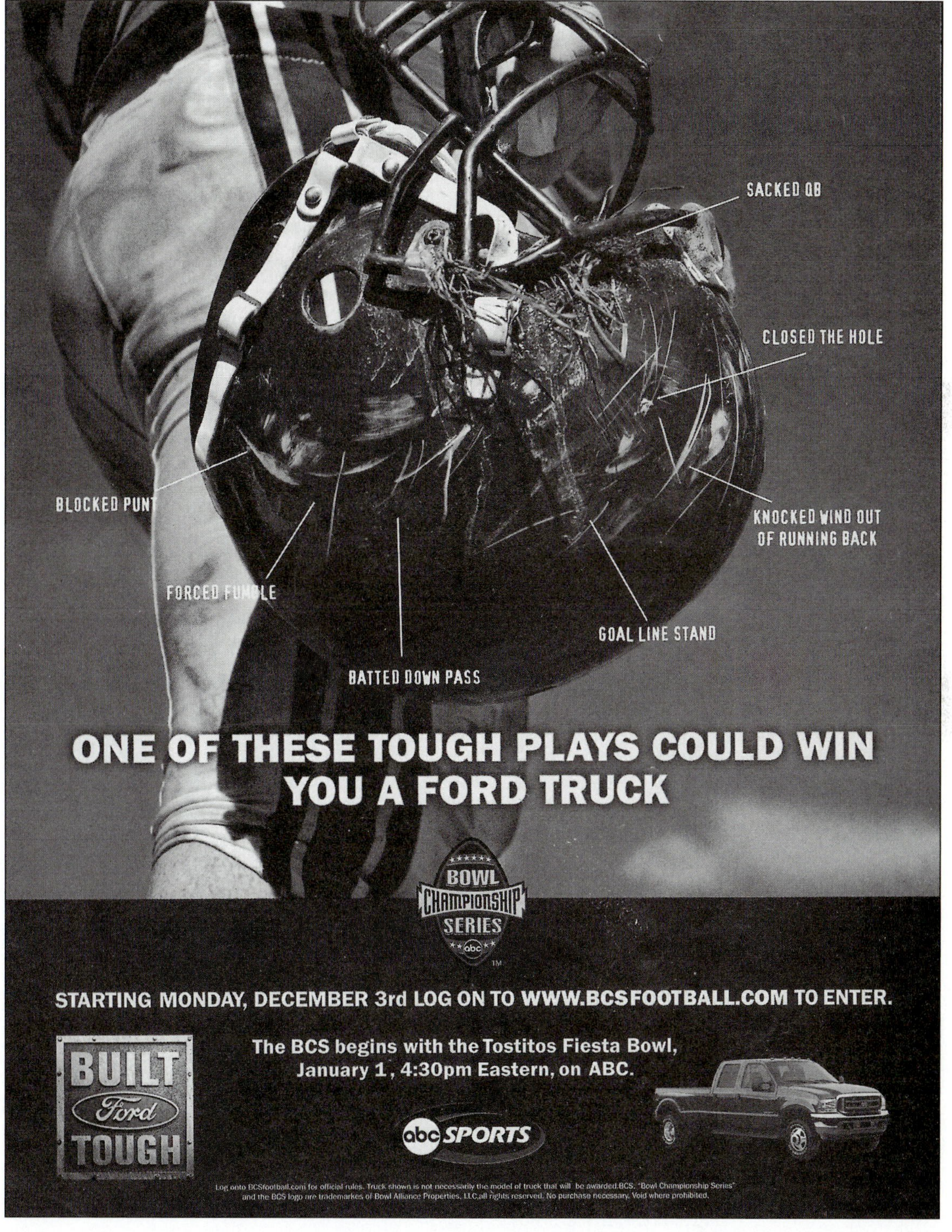

FIGURE 7.11 Lucent Ad (Second Page)

Now look at the picture on the next page and you see the lead, or first, page of the Lucent ad.

FIGURE 7.12 Lucent Ad (First Page)

Did you anticipate seeing a kid? Based on the bicycle and the helmet, what kind of person did you anticipate? Did you anticipate a boy or a girl? In any case we can see how the bike and the helmet functioned as a visual index for you to create meaning.

Finally, you have experienced many visual images that do *not* make direct reference to something (as with a picture of a cow or porcupine), and that do *not* make indirect reference to something implied, but not shown (as with dirty dishes, a chewed pencil, or a bike and helmet); yet these visual images have significant meaning.

Have you ever seen this shape before?

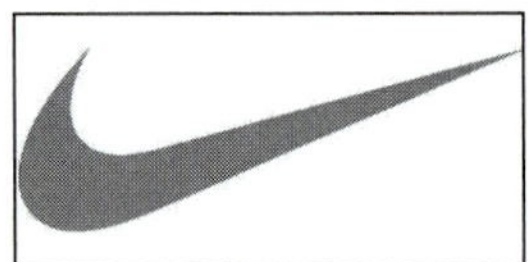

FIGURE 7.13
Nike Swoosh Design

If not, you likely have not been near a TV, athletic contest, newspaper, billboard, shoe store, or movie in the past 25 years.

The Nike Swoosh Design trademark is but one of hundreds of corporate emblems that have visual meaning, but not icon meaning or index meaning. Instead, we have to learn by experience what the Swoosh Design (or any other visual message) might mean in terms of reference or expectation. As we've learned, such visual messages are symbolic visual messages. Since Swoosh Designs don't appear in nature we cannot recognize them as we do a cow picture (icon) and since Swoosh Designs don't call up automatic, direct connections to specific behavior as do lipstick marks on a glass we cannot recognize them as an index; nonetheless, we do readily recognize the Swoosh Design mark as a visual message that *represents* Nike, Inc. It serves well as an example of a *learned* visual message: a symbolic visual message.

With these three basic types of visual messages in hand (icon, index, and symbol) we can go much farther in our quest to better understand the rhetorical implication and practices of those who make visual messages.

Our basic designations are detailed in Chart 7.1.

CHART 7.1
Visual Rhetorical Messages

Type	Characteristic	Message Result	Question Answered by Image
Icon/Iconic	Direct Resemblance	Recognition by Resemblance	What or who is it?
Index/ Indexical	Indirect Indication	Recognition of Unseen Elements	To what does it point or what does it indicate?
Symbol/ Symbolic	Learned Resemblance	Recognition by Experience and Training	To what does it refer?

FIGURE 7.14 **Visually Clamming Up**
What visual tactic allows the comic rhetors to depict the son's non-reaction?

Source: © Zits Partnerships. Reprinted with Special Permission of Kings Feature Syndicate.

You have likely already begun to ask questions about visual messages that seem to span or occupy more than one of these categories as we actually use pictures, drawings, and images to make meaning. You are correct to assume that many visual messages fit more than one of these designations. For instance, although we've said that Cheney's representation of a giant cigarette butt in the desert (Fig. 7.7) is an indexical visual message, it obviously must resemble a real cigarette butt (i.e., it must have iconic characteristics) to allow its indexical message to be created. Moreover, for some audience members it may be a symbolic visual message that carries a *learned* resemblance to death, or cancer, or a loved one's hacking cough.

So we must take care in assigning these categories and realize that they may overlap and coordinate with each other to make rhetorical meaning for audience members.

Let's try these terms on one more message with strong visual components. The Scott and Borgman strip (Fig. 7.14) uses comic-style drawing to depict a common family social relationship situation. Our visual rhetorical analysis terms should allow us to specify the means by which they create comic meaning. Nearly all of the identifiable elements in the two panels of this strip (e.g., hands, glasses, chairs, table, hair, elbows) have message resemblance properties we would label as iconic. So far, so good. Nothing in either of the panels seems to stand out as a distinctive visual index sign. While liquid in glasses or food on plates may well visually signal prior events of cooking or pouring (hence creating a visually-driven narrative framework), no visual element seems the message equivalent of tire tracks in mud indicating the likely prior presence of a vehicle. Nor does the clamshell in panel two (while recognizable by iconic properties) seem to fit our working definition of a visual symbol. We don't often see a clam sitting atop a comic human neck (whereas we regularly expect to see the Nike Swoosh mark in ads and on merchandise, or we regularly expect to see a skull and crossbones on a pirate flag). Yet we find these two comic rhetors playing with the visual equivalent of a verbal phrase about non-communication ("he's clamming up"). In the following section covering some standard tactics of visual rhetoric, we'll discover yet another layer of analysis terms that can work together with those we've developed thus far.

STANDARD TACTICS

Visual persuasive tactics, fully covered, could fill three books this size. We will examine four of the most frequently used tactics as we enlarge your working visual analysis vocabulary and create new awareness of visual meaning possibilities for those of you who will enter message making professions that substantially use visual messages. The four most frequently used visual tactics are: visual metaphors, visual metonymys, visual synecdoches, and visual replacement. Whenever possible we will use the language terms already established (icon, index, and symbol) when describing these tactics so we can build your visual persuasion knowledge base.

VISUAL METAPHORS

Visual metaphors have some similarity with word-based metaphors in that they combine two things that are not alike to create perspective or awareness. Hence, we'll continue to use Julian Jaynes's terms developed in Chapter 5 as we discuss visual metaphors. Can you see a visual metaphor in the ad in Figure 7.15?

In this ad the image of a turtle replaces that of a modem; a DSL provider is visually depicted as a rocket strapped to the turtle's back. Talented artists or graphics technicians (rhetors) can create almost any combination of two different things or people that we might be able to imagine. When doing so they are taking a metaphrand (the thing or item or person they wish to depict) and visually combining it with a visual metaphier (the means of creating the perspective). We have a series of beliefs about the visual metaphier that we will call the paraphiers of the visual metaphier; in the case of this ad, all the things we think we know about turtles (paraphiers)—they are slow, they are reptiles, they hatch from eggs, they have four legs, and so forth—are accessed by our brains. However, just as with word-based metaphors, not all of those paraphiers become attached to the metaphrand (in this case your modem as an Internet provider); the paraphrand (conventional attachment) of slowness is doubly enhanced here by the contrast between the speed of the rocket compared to the culturally known slowness of the turtle.

FIGURE 7.15 Turtle and Rocket as Visual Metaphor

CHART 7.2
Base Metaphor

METAPHRAND: A current modem connection to the Internet	+	VISUAL ***METAPHIER:*** A turtle
Paraphrand: Slow		***Paraphiers:*** Slow, reptile, four legs, retractable head and legs, two eyes, scaly skin, hatches from egg, etc.

CHART 7.3
Adapted Metaphor

METAPHRAND: A current modem connection to the Internet replaced by a DSL line	+	VISUAL ***METAPHIER:*** A turtle with a rocket strapped to its back
Paraphrand: Slow changed to fast		***Paraphiers:*** Turtle: Slow, reptile, four legs, retractable head and legs, two eyes, scaly skin, hatch from eggs, etc. Strapped to: Rocket: Fast, fuel, burn, cylinder, nosecone, etc.

A chart of this visual metaphoric exchange suggests how we make sense of such ads.

Recognize that visual metaphors have several key differences from verbal metaphors. First, since a visual metaphier is *depicted* or shown rather than spoken or written, we have *less* latitude for different audience members to see or perceive different things. So, in a written metaphor, if we call a child a "flower," an audience member might read that metaphier and think of a rose, a daisy, a lily, or a tulip. If, on the other hand, we used *a picture of a rose* as a visual metaphor for a child, audience members would be encouraged or compelled to think *only* of the rose. So we can say that visual metaphiers are often more specific than their verbal or written counterparts. Second, a visual metaphor can depict, emphasize, or focus on specific paraphiers that can be perceived as quickly as can the visual metaphier. Hence, in our example, the advertising agency for Flashcom placed goggles on the turtle. Those goggles are much easier to see, perceive, and understand as a visual item than they would be to express in speaking or writing. (Imagine the difficulty of writing: "Your new DSL line will change your current turtle modem into a rocket-powered turtle who moves so fast as to appear against a blurred background while needing goggles to deal with the wind from the speed of the rocket.") Pictures can be more specific and move more quickly into meaning for audience members. Finally, visual metaphors can be set up with either visual or non-visual metaphrands. In the Flashcom ad the modem and the DSL service are written metaphrands. They could have been depicted, but the writers and ad designers decided not to do so.

FIGURE 7.16 **Spider Webs as Visual Metonymy**
Notice that spider webs can help indicate passage of time.

VISUAL METONYMY

Verbal or written **metonymys** are a language device where one part of something stands for the whole by convention or association. So when a news reporter says "The White House said today . . ." we know that no one actually held a microphone up to the physical building we call the White House. Instead, the "White House" has become a verbal metonymy for the executive branch of American government and usually more specifically for the administration of the current president.

Visual metonymys operate when a visual item represents something else with which it is strongly associated. In (Figs. 7.16 and 7.17) two examples you can see instances when a spider web (or cobweb) is used as a visual metonymy for the passage of time. We recognize that in real life cobwebs only appear after time has passed and after an area or object has been untouched or ignored. Likewise, drawn or photographed cobwebs are visual markers (that we will call metonymys) that indicate the passage of time, neglect, or inactivity.

Visual metonymys have rhetorical power because they can indicate processes, history, development, awareness, or change that has taken weeks, months, decades, or centuries to develop by use of a single, specific visual icon. Well-known structures or statues or monuments often serve as visual metonymys for a specific city or region. Hence, it's difficult to see a photo of the Statue of Liberty without thinking about New York City or a picture of the Golden Gate Bridge without thinking about San Francisco. Can you think of a visual metonymy that would quickly cause an audience member to think of Paris? Human memory, experience with specific visual messages, and cultural agreement about "what stands for what" all play a part in the creation and understanding of visual metonymys.

FIGURE 7.17 Cob Webs as Visual Metonymy

Scrutinize exercise

Look through a week's worth of pictures, ads, comics, and other messages from a favorite publication of yours. Make sure your selected publication has strong visual components. Can you discover the use of visual metaphors or visual metonymys? What purpose did the rhetor(s) have when selecting these visual tactics? What meaning did the rhetor(s) wish to create?

VISUAL SYNECDOCHE

Verbal or written **synecdoches** are similar to metonymys because both are language devices where one part of something stands for the whole. However, where a metonymy uses convention or association as the basis for a part standing for the whole, synecdoche uses actual connection. So when a sixteenth century sailor called out: "I see three sails on the horizon!" The sailor's crewmates knew that real ships (not just sails) had been spotted. Likewise when we hear that a friend has purchased a "new set of wheels," we know that she has an entire car and not just the wheels. When we use "sails" to mean ships or "wheels" to mean a car, we are using a verbal synecdoche.

Scrutinize exercise

Tape five music videos. Use a remote and a check pad to count the number of times you detect a director or cinematographer using various visual synecdoches. Pick one or two of your favorite examples; show the examples in class and discuss what purpose and function the use of the visual synecdoche had on the message(s) offered in the video.

Visual synecdoches operate when a visual item represents a portion of something else to which it belongs or is actually attached. Figure 7.18 is a Rockport ad that shows no shoes (Rockport's product), but does depict a close photographic view of a head, neck, hand, and foot. In this ad we see only a portion of each body part. Hence the head and neck, the hand, and the foot each act as a visual synecdoche. The part stands for the whole. We need not see all of the body to which the portion is attached to make appropriate meaning.

Visual synecdoches are powerful as rhetorical devices because they can encourage the mind to "fill in the blank" by completing the picture, scene, or image that has only been partially depicted. The benefits of using visual synecdoches are many. Advertisers, filmmakers, music video makers, and many others save money and effort by only using a visible part of an item or person. Moreover, audience involvement in recreating the whole from the display of the part creates a level of cognitive involvement not available if the entire item or person is depicted.

VISUAL REPLACEMENT

We know that we can violate expectations in verbal or written messages when we substitute one word or phrase for another that we strongly expect. So if you read "'Twas the night before . . ." at the opening of a children's book, you likely expect "Christmas" as the next word. A writer wanting to play on that expectation could write: "'Twas the night before Labor Day and all through the house . . ." We also can replace expected visual items for others and create a set of visually driven meanings. Examine Figure 7.19 and ask yourself what you normally expect to see between two trees.

When the Chrysler ad agency team decided to visually suspend their convertible between two palm trees, was that a good decision? By using **visual replacement,** the ad designer and copywriter suspected that you would see the incongruity of the substitution and visually connect the car to a hammock. Visual replacement is powerful as a meaning-making device for the same reason that we've seen with several of the other visual tactics: your mind is put in action to make a special participatory meaning based on visual icons. In this case the visual replacement created a visual

FIGURE 7.18 **Face, Foot, Hand**
Visual synecdoches allow a part to stand for the whole.

FIGURE 7.19 **Car as Visual Replacement**
What did you expect to see between the trees?

Scrutinize exercise

Does visual replacement always create a visual metaphor? As a class find 10 or 15 examples where an advertiser or other visual rhetor uses visual replacement as a meaning creation tactic. Look for "out of place" items or people and in situations or circumstances where you would normally expect something, or someone, else. In each case do you recognize and process the resulting image as a visual metaphor? If not, what other meaning creation is established for you?

metaphor, if you "got" the reference to the hammock. What paraphiers (characteristics) of a hammock located in a tropical setting did the ad designers hope that your mind would remember? Did it work?

We have now learned about iconic messages, indexical messages, and symbolic messages as basic conceptual tools for visual analysis and about how visual metaphors, metonymys, synecdoches and replacement are some of the most common visual tactics found in visual rhetoric. We can now turn our focus to the use of these and other rhetorical tactics in American political cartoons. The rhetors we know as Ohman, Oliphant, Toles, Wright, and Auth daily create political drawings designed to provoke humor and ire. Their work is of great interest to those who seek to better understand visual rhetoric because they, perhaps more than any single other type of rhetor, have to regularly use the tools of visual persuasion.

POLITICAL CARTOONS

Political persuasion has been the focus of various kinds of artwork for nearly all of human history. Political cartoons, however, are a relatively recent persuasion form.

Thomas Nast, who began his work for *Harper's Weekly* as a Civil War battlefield illustrator, is typically acknowledged as the first person in American history to be employed and paid as a political cartoon artist.[7] Figure 7.20 is a reproduction of one of his famous drawings. The drawings that launched Nast's worldwide fame concerned the political corruption of a New York City administration known as the Tweed Ring. The ring was accused of stealing vast amounts of money in a variety of schemes. The construction of a new courthouse resulted in some padded charges: 40 chairs and three tables "cost" the Tweed Ring almost $180,000; thermometers were $7,500; a plasterer earned $138,187 (in two days!).[8] Nast continued a venerable tradition of satirists and humorists by infusing the satiric rhetoric with graphic pictorial force. The accuracy of his caricatures and the force of his graphic persuasion were primary in bringing down one of the most powerful political groups in New York City history. We need to pay heed to the resources used by Nast and other visual rhetors so as to understand, and anticipate, where the power of their rhetoric may reside.

FIGURE 7.20 A Group of Vultures Waiting for the Storm to "Blow Over"—"Let Us Prey"

What gives a political cartoon such as Nast's "A Group of Vultures Waiting for the Storm to 'Blow Over'—'Let Us Prey'" drawing (Fig. 7.20) its persuasive force? Nast, and political cartoonists drawing in his rhetorical lineage, use four primary graphic stylistic tools that I've identified as reduction and simplification, regular character depiction, non-narrative hyperbole, and narrative hyperbole.[9] Note that we are not leaving behind our previous sets of basic analysis terms. Finding indexical message components or visual metaphors (or other examples of our previous analysis terms) in political cartoons is highly likely. However, a discussion of additional tools used by specific rhetors will help us better understand how this one type of graphic persuasion is constructed.[10]

Reduction and Simplification

A graphic rhetor like Thomas Nast could create startlingly realistic images of his political subjects. Yet his drawings gained power from a radical reduction and simplification of the issues and persons at hand. Whereas the *New York Times* or other newspapers and magazines had to adhere to some norms of public message making, evidence, and logical argument, Nast was free to create utterly simple and provocative drawings. Thus, "Nast's political cartoons appear as the product of some odd peripatetic photographer who happens onto very strange situations. That such situations are imbued with political over-and undertones simply underscores the talent of the 'photographer'" (Pierce 68). The strong crosshatching and visual composition of a drawing such as "Let Us Prey" take incredibly complex alleged crimes by politicians and swiftly reduce them to utter simplicity: Tweed Ring politicians are vultures. Since we don't normally like for our elected officials to be vultures picking over the bones of "law," "justice," and "suffrage," the message is clear: stop them!

Similarly, in Figure 7.21 graphic rhetor Jack Ohman juxtaposes familiar images of grocery shopping with issues from genetics in human reproduction as he creates a provocative comment on changes in how we create humans.

The quick power of these messages is built in large measure on simplification of very complex issues and the visual reduction of pertinent issues to a razor's edge of cutting satire. The older woman represented in this cartoon, however, is an exception to the next stylistic tool used by most political cartoonists: regular characters.

Regular Characters

A very predictable set of characters show up in most political cartoons. The president (of course), certain congressional leaders, the Supreme Court, celebrities of the moment (Elian Gonzales, Monica Lewinsky), heroes (e.g., astronauts, sports figures, firefighters, police officers), and villains (Hitler, Castro, Saddam Hussein, Osama bin Laden) are but a few of

FIGURE 7.21 Ohman Cartoon (28 Nov. 2001); Reduction and Simplification

FIGURE 7.22 Toles Cartoon (9 Dec. 2001); Regular Characters

the standard characters who most often show up within the inked square of a political cartoon. Other standard characters such as the Republican elephant and the Democratic donkey—which were initiated by Thomas Nast—continue to show up in contemporary cartoons as in the Tom Toles cartoon reproduced in Figure 7.22.

Scrutinize exercise

Use a microform reader in your library and look over three months of political cartoons in a large newspaper. Which real life characters show up repeatedly? (Think of mayors, presidents, heads of large software firms, etc.) Which symbolic life characters keep showing up? (Think of the Russian Bear, Uncle Sam, Statue of Liberty, etc.) What benefit does a continuing cast of characters have for political cartoonists? Do you find certain graphic figures more compelling or persuasive than others? Why?

FIGURE 7.23
Nast Cartoon (21 Oct. 1871)

By using regular characters, political artists ensure that we will recognize, respond to, and remember the depicted characters better than if they chose a wider group of subjects. In the five years that Nast attacked the Tweed Ring (1868–1872), he used people other than Tweed, Sweeney, Connolly, Hall, and Hoffman (the primary identified corrupt politicians) only seven times.[11] Repetition of images by these graphic rhetors also allows a level of persuasive comfort to sneak into our recognition of visual devices associated with these regular characters (Bill Clinton's hair, Richard Nixon's nose, or bin Laden's beard). So familiar do we become with these attributes of repeated characters that rhetors who draw at the level of Thomas Nast can even forego one of their strengths (facial caricature) as seen in the drawing that Nast labeled "The 'Brains' " (Fig. 7.23).

By 1871 Nast had drawn Boss Tweed so often and so well that he could replace his face with a bag of money and allow recognition via Tweed's body characteristics and a visual metonymy (a diamond stick pin; notice that the stick pin is on the Vulture Tweed in the drawing in Figure 7.20 as well); such are the payoffs of visual persuasion done with regular characters.

We should remember that "[r]epetitive depiction is a powerful rhetorical tool. Once a normative perception is established in the minds of a readership . . . it often establishes beliefs and expectations about the depicted individuals."[12]

If cartoonists acting as graphic rhetors use regular characters in highly simplified and reduced images to create political humor and critique, we must also note that they are not shy of using extreme exaggeration.

Non-Narrative Hyperbole

Non-narrative hyperbole (or extreme exaggeration) is a standard stylistic tool of all political cartoonists. The Tweed "Brains" cartoon in Figure 7.23 is a model of this type of cartoon. People don't often have bags of money in place of their heads. "Hyperbole based in image relies on instant recognition of the propositional value of iconic and symbolic elements" (Pierce 80–81). Visually "proposing" that money is wrongly creating political influence for Boss Tweed is to suggest that most citizens would prefer something other than money to control political decision making (e.g., a money bag for a head/brains), whereas the essence of non-narrative hyperbole "is to assert that a certain condition or state of affairs exists" (Pierce 84–85).

As you may have guessed, if we find graphic political rhetors using non-narrative hyperbole as a tool of persuasion, we must by reversal be able to find them using narrative hyperbole—and we do.

Narrative Hyperbole

Narrative hyperbole occurs in those cartoons where "a modicum of storytelling [is used] . . . to understand the meaning" (Pierce 79). Specific story scene elements, specific character actions, and perceived story sequence are all visual signals to an audience member that we should understand that we are observing a story frozen in a single frame. For instance, in Figure 7.24, "Can the Law Reach Him? The Dwarf and the Giant Thief," we do not need a coherent story logic to guide our understanding of Nast's attempted persuasion. The sheer size difference between Boss Tweed, the police officer, and a "normal," controllable criminal is enough to suggest (using non-narrative hyperbole) that Tweed is beyond the reach of the law. In Figure 7.25, however (in a rare double panel Nast drawing), you see reproduced a cartoon "Wholesale and Retail" which needs a story frame to make sense of the suggested contrast.

Drawings such as "Wholesale and Retail" provide audience members what we called in Chapter 6 story^{g} (story given) elements. In the lower picture Nast helps us observe a ragged man apprehended by the police while stealing bread for his wife and children who hide at the corner of the bakery. In the upper picture, similar police officers salute as Boss Tweed and his cronies walk—without restraint—out of the New York City Treasury. By placing us in the middle of two contrasting story sequences, Nast was no doubt using the simplification and hyperbole we've already identified as stylistic tools of a strong political cartoonist. But, he was also invoking our power to understand two related stories-in-progress to help make his persuasive point. So the "Brains" drawing in Figure 7.23 merely pokes fun at Boss Tweed for his use of money for political influence, but requires no story frame to "get" the point of the drawing. On the other hand, one would be hard-pressed to understand the dual images in the

FIGURE 7.24 Nast Cartoon (6 Jan. 1872)

CAN THE LAW REACH HIM?—THE DWARF AND THE GIANT THIEF.

FIGURE 7.25 Nast Cartoon (16 Sept. 1871)

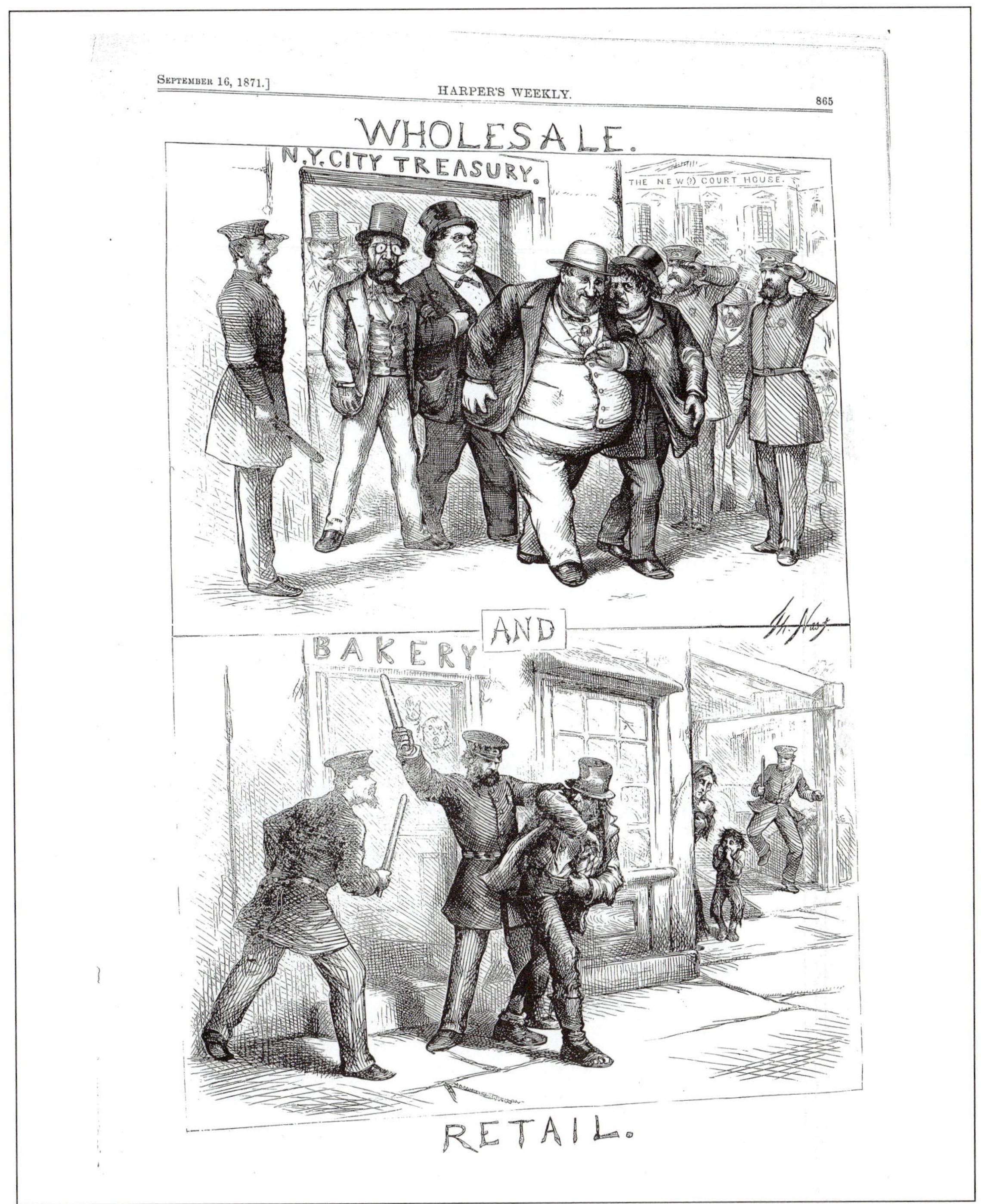

"Wholesale and Retail" without the resources of putting together a story sequence complete with characters and motives.

Interestingly, Nast used narrative hyperbole by more than a 4-to-1 ratio over non-narrative hyperbole during his graphic political campaign against the Tweed Ring. My informal observation of contemporary political cartoons suggests that the ratio may now be just the opposite (i.e., many more cartoons using sheer visual hyperbole with little story format).

This quick tour through the work of a tiny fraction of what political cartoonists create each day gives us a glimpse of tactics employed by such graphic rhetors. No other group of rhetors must so consistently create persuasive messages that rely so much on visual elements. Their work can give us strong hints about both the power, and most oft-used tactics, employed in visual communication that seeks to persuade.

In this chapter we have given you some rudimentary tools to begin creating analysis of visual messages you find in your media environment. As a culture we've moved from Thomas Nast's provocative Boss Tweed drawings to Matt Groening's creation of Bart Simpson; our continued pursuit of how visual meaning is created in public messages will continue to be worthwhile.

Next we'll enter the Chapter 7 workshop where we'll investigate more of the power of persuasive images to influence our lives. Below you will find a sample journal article by Olson. Read the article in preparation for the Chapter 7 workshop. That workshop material will be followed by Chapter 8 where we will initiate our consideration of language and Ideology.

Source: *Quarterly Journal of Speech* 69 (1983), 15–24.

Portraits in Praise of a People: A Rhetorical Analysis of Norman Rockwell's Icons in Franklin D. Roosevelt's "Four Freedoms" Campaign

Lester C. Olson

Norman Rockwell's posters, "The Four Freedoms For Which We Fight," were an integral part of Franklin D. Roosevelt's "Four Freedoms" campaign which generated support for the allied war effort by articulating national ideals. About Rockwell's illustrations, Thomas Buechner wrote

Mr. Olson is a candidate for the Ph.D., Department of Communication Arts, University of Wisconsin, Madison, WI 53706. He gratefully acknowledges advice from Richard B. Gregg, Michael Leff, Edwin Black, Diane Dowdey, and Keith Rosemore.

that "millions of copies were printed and distributed by the government and private agencies all over the world; the Treasury department toured the four originals to sixteen cities where they were seen by 1,222,000 people and used in selling $132,999,537 worth of war bonds. For many Americans World War II made sense because of the goals depicted in the 'Four Freedoms.'"[1] Thus, Rockwell's illustrations provide an ideal opportunity to study the suasory role of icons in political communication.

By examining Norman Rockwell's "Four Freedoms" posters, and then considering the particular historical circumstances during which they were mass-distributed first by the *Saturday Evening Post* and later by the government, we will observe how epideictic icons that present an idealized view of the United States become deliberative icons which urge support of the United States' participation in World War II. The icons primarily praise the political and religious values of Americans rather than detail a particular policy. However, within the context of Roosevelt's campaign to educate Americans on behalf of participation in the war, the posters exemplify what Americans should strive to protect and preserve, thereby serving a deliberative function that was explicitly amplified by the slogans on the posters, by the accompanying texts in the *Post*, and, implicitly, by the Roosevelt administration's pro-war campaign. The texts in the *Post* emphasize that the values depicted in the posters are American in character and are antithetical to the values of the Axis powers. Roosevelt's speeches express similar antitheses.

Rockwell's posters conveyed a simple, but ambiguous, message. Americans could readily understand the ideals that Rockwell's posters portrayed because he selected images which represented a simple, American way of living based upon fundamental institutions: the church, the work ethic, the family, the community, the educational system, and the democratic processes. Very broadly, then, the posters promoted identifications which constitute the tenets of a conjoined religious and political perspective. Yet, more importantly, this direct message was effective largely through productive ambiguities that broadened the posters' appeal for unity. Rockwell fused symbols from diverse American populace, situations, and actions into each of the paintings. Although Rockwell's meticulous attention to exact detail was well-known, perhaps not so well-known was his ability to omit detail so as to promote varied identifications.

THE VISUAL RHETORIC OF NORMAN ROCKWELL'S "FOUR FREEDOMS"

"Freedom of Speech," published in the *Post* on February 20, 1943, was the first of Rockwell's four illustrations. We can see Rockwell's skillful use of strategic equivocation especially in this illustration where he represented no fewer than seven American institutions: the church, the work ethic, the educational and judicial systems, the political process, the community, and the family. For example, the possible meanings attached to the white-collared shirts refer to at least two institutions. On the one hand, Americans may associate the white-collared shirts with their particular religious values, since a white shirt and tie are appropriate dress for church or synagogue. On the other hand, American viewers may associate the white-collared shirts with a particular class commonly called "white collar" workers. The religious interpretation of the white shirts is supported by the pews, while the socioeconomic interpretation is supported by a laborer wearing a blue-collared shirt. To the extent that religious values and the work ethic both served Rockwell's purpose, such an equivocation is productive in that it provides alternative bases for identification.

In "Freedom of Speech," the principle of productive ambiguity also characterizes the setting. The town meeting apparently occurs in a school room, since the background is a blackboard, a symbol of education. That the listeners hold copies of the annual report—a document that requires literacy to be understood—reinforces this education interpretation. Yet, alternatively, the meeting may take place in a church or courthouse, since the people sit in pew-like forms.[2] Rockwell combines educational, judicial, and religious symbols into one equivocal scene, thereby broadening the potential bases for identification.

Various meanings may also arise from the action in "Freedom of Speech." While some words on the blue pamphlet in the foreground are missing, cut off at the edge of the poster, the visible portion reads "_nnual Report of the—Town of _ermont," indicating that the scene is a town meeting. Many Americans associate such meetings with public debates vital to a democratic process. Town meetings are also social gatherings which allow Rockwell to appeal broadly to values associated with the community, the "human family." In addition, since the speaker at this town meeting is a worker—he wears a tattered jacket, a blue-collared shirt, and his hands are brown and weathered from outdoor labor—"Freedom of Speech" emphasizes that the political system is one under which the worker's voice is heard. His listeners represent differing ages, marital statuses, and genders providing a spectrum of people with whom the viewer might identify. Yet, despite the spectrum of backgrounds, Rockwell stresses the unifying purpose of the gathering: the official pamphlet appears in the workman's pocket, the married man's hand, and the elderly man's hand.

In the other illustrations, Rockwell repeats his appeal to values associated with most of these institutions. For example, Rockwell may appeal to education in "Freedom from Fear" since the father holds a newspaper and reading glasses. Similarly, in "Freedom of Worship," the Greek Orthodox churchman holds a black book, a symbol of education and religion. Rockwell appeals again to values associated with the work ethic, since an apron in "Freedom from Want" expresses the notion of labor. Rockwell repeats the appeal to values associated with the community: like "Freedom of Speech," "Freedom of Worship" depicts individuals of apparently divergent backgrounds respecting the others in the scene, possibly indicating their interdependence, possibly recognizing the dignity of the individual who participates in his or her own way to benefit the community as a whole.

Although the only suggestion of the family in "Freedom of Speech" is a wedding ring in the foreground, another pervasive appeal in these posters centers on the family. Obviously, "Freedom from Want" and "Freedom from Fear" portray family scenes—one at mealtime and the other at bedtime. "Freedom from Want" features a family gathering on Thanksgiving as indicated by a huge turkey and festive food. A grandmother "places a turkey, that most American of birds, on a white table cloth before her children and grandchildren. Her husband, an approving look on his face, waits to demonstrate his skill with the carving knife."[3] Thanksgiving is a national holiday when many people thank God for his bountiful gifts, and the folded hands in the lower left corner evoke the ritual of prayer. "Freedom from Want" fuses family, country, and God into a celebration. As Robert Bellah claims, Thanksgiving "serves to integrate the family into the civil religion."[4]

Quiet and intimate, "Freedom from Fear" focuses upon the children's bedroom upstairs in a family's home. The children's toys—a doll and a building block—are scattered on the floor, revealing their busy day at play and reminding some viewers of similar scenes in their own homes. The mother tucks the children into bed, while father looks on, holding his newspaper and glasses. The scene is peaceful, except for the unsettling headline on the newspaper: "Bombing Ki—Horror Hit—," and in smaller print: "Women and Children Slaughtered by Raids." These words reveal a threat to the tranquil family life. The newspaper strategically omits the location of the bombing, ambiguously allowing the viewers to bring the threat into the home in the painting and into their own homes as well.

The appeal to family in these paintings entails additional features. The children in the paintings symbolize dependence upon the present generation to preserve the American way of living. The children also represent hope for the future, and continuity in American traditions, as suggested in "Freedom from Want" by the placement of the youngest granddaughter nearest to the grandfather and opposite the grandmother. Implicit in both "Freedom from Fear" and "Freedom from Want" is a definite family structure, characteristic of the time, with father as breadwinner and mother tending to family needs; mother cooks food and tucks children into bed while father looks on approvingly and presides at the head of the table. The other paintings also contain a symbol of family, a wedding ring. The central figure in "Freedom of Worship," an elderly woman, wears a simple gold band as does the father in "Freedom from Fear" and the man in the foreground, lower right of "Freedom of Speech." These rings also may implicitly express a belief in God, since to many Americans marriage is ordained by God.

Values associated with the church and the fundamental belief in God are central in the posters, though the posters are clearly nondenominational. In particular, "Freedom of Worship" portrays "people of different faiths joined in the act of prayer. Heads, seen in profile, and hands fill the canvas."[5] One woman clasps a rosary; a man holds a black book and wears the clothing of a Greek Orthodox church member. An elderly woman presses the palms of her hands together, touching them to her lips. Another person rests his chin on his hand, perhaps listening to a sermon, perhaps thinking intently, perhaps representing the agnostic. The rosary, the book, the clothing, and the folded hands are all images that evoke people, situations, and acts within the church. The poster presents hands folded in different ways, and this may encourage viewers to identify with the image most similar to their own position for prayer.

More important, the poster emphasizes variety itself as a salient feature of American religious expression. In "Freedom of Worship," Rockwell portrays representatives from different faiths, different racial backgrounds, different ages, and both genders, providing a spectrum of people with whom most Americans might identify. Despite the divergent backgrounds and views represented in the painting, Rockwell presents a view of religious unity rather than religious squabbling, by depicting them in a monochromatic gold light and by portraying them in a similar act. Furthermore, he fuses these symbols into an ambiguous scene; nothing in the painting indicates a location beyond a community of religious expression sharing in common faith in the existence of God. Such an omission of detail is a productive ambiguity in the sense that Rockwell avoids selecting one religious setting which consequently might be construed as more preeminent than the other religions. In gold lettering, similar to that found in many religious settings, Rockwell states: "Each According to the Dictates of His Own Conscience."[6]

THE VERBAL RHETORIC OF THE TEXTS IN THE *POST*

During World War II, Rockwell's version of the "Four Freedoms" was circulated in three forms: paintings, magazine illustrations, and posters. In 1941, when Rockwell first offered the "Four Freedoms" to the government, Secretary of the Treasury Henry Morganthal refused the gift, because the Treasury did not dabble in art. Subsequently, the four paintings were published originally inside the *Post* in four consecutive issues between February 20 and March 13, 1943, under the heading "Number __ in a Series Depicting the Four Freedoms For Which We Fight."[7] Because the posters were first submitted to the government, they were developed before the texts that eventually accompanied them in the *Post*. Yet the texts probably contributed to securing the overwhelmingly favorable response from readers that convinced the government to request the right to use the posters in the drive for war bond sales.[8] The government then toured the four originals in sixteen cities, and reproduced the series without the texts, printing and distributing over four million copies.

In the *Post*, each illustration was accompanied by a text by one of four well-known authors: Will Durant, Booth Tarkington, Carlos Bulosan, and Stephen Vincent Benét. These texts all followed a similar form. They focused first upon the meaning of the freedom in the United States, then upon the Axis antithesis, and finally upon a call to battle. For example, Will Durant wrote about freedom of worship that "this little church is the first and final symbol of America. For men came across the sea not merely to find new soil for their plows but to win freedom for their souls, to think and speak and worship as they would."[9] He stressed that the worshipers "do not demand that others should worship as they do, or even that others should worship at all." He added that "mutely these worshipers understand that faith takes many forms, and that men name with diverse words the hope that in their hearts is one."

To these writers for the *Post*, the Axis powers represented the destruction of such values. Durant commented that "now suddenly, through some paranoiac mania of racial superiority, or some obscene sadism of political strategy, persecution is renewed. . . ." He referred to the German leaders as men who "seem to delight in human misery, who openly pledge themselves to destroy Christianity, who seem resolved to leave their people no religion but war, and no God but the state." To preserve American institutions, Durant called for personal sacrifice, stressing that when "we yield our sons to war, it is in the trust that their sacrifice will bring to us and our allies no inch of alien soil, no selfish monopoly of the world's resources or trade, but only the privilege of winning for all peoples the most precious gifts in the orbit of life—freedom and body and soul, of movement and enterprise, of thought and utterance, of faith and worship, of hope and charity, of a humane fellowship with all men."

Because the Axis powers threatened cherished American values, they became the evil which had to be punished. Although the paintings themselves did not explicitly depict the Axis threat, the accompanying texts in the *Post* did describe them as threatening the Four Freedoms, thereby articulating the need to protect America. Carlos Bulosan captured the essential antithesis between American values and the Axis threat in his text on "Freedom from Want" when he wrote that "the totalitarian nations hate democracy. They hate us, because we ask for a definite guaranty of freedom of religion, freedom of expression, and freedom from fear and want. Our challenge to tyranny is the depth of our faith in a democracy worth defending."[10]

FDR'S "FOUR FREEDOMS" CAMPAIGN

Conflict between isolationists and interventionists heightened disunity over national purpose at the beginning of World War II. Consequently, the Roosevelt administration faced a need to educate the public on behalf of supporting the war effort. As an integral part of that educational campaign, the ideal of the "Four Freedoms" became a dominant theme of the administration. The "Four Freedoms" first gained widespread public attention on January 6, 1941, when Roosevelt gave his "Annual Message to Congress," better known as the "Four Freedoms" speech. The statement on the Four Freedoms justified increased financial support of Britain and seemed to strike a common chord in American values by echoing sentiments of the American constitution.

> In future days, which we seek to make secure, we look forward to a world founded upon four essential human freedoms.
>
> The first is freedom of speech and expression—everywhere in the world.
>
> The second is freedom of every person to worship God in his own way—everywhere in the world.
>
> The third is freedom from want—which, translated into world terms, means economic understanding which will secure to every nation a healthy peacetime life for its inhabitants—everywhere in the world.
>
> The fourth is freedom from fear—which, translated into world terms, means a world-wide reduction of armaments to such a point and in such a thorough fashion that no nation will be in a position to commit an act of physical aggression against any neighbor—anywhere in the world.[11]

Subsequently, the Four Freedoms became a theme in several of Roosevelt's speeches.[12] He associated the Four Freedoms with the religious ideals of Americans by comparing them to the Ten Commandments, by referring to them as blessings, and by describing them as "the Christian Ideal." He equated them with such major historical accomplishments as the Magna Carta, the Emancipation Proclamation, and the Atlantic Charter. He also identified the Four Freedoms with the essence of American political ideology by identifying them with the political process and with the "very life of this nation." He linked them with survival by relating them to sustenance and with life itself. He connected them with idealism in general by calling them the means to achieving the "greatest age of man" and by affirming that they are "glorious ideals which have figured into every milestone in human progress."

Roosevelt placed this wide-ranging conception of the Four Freedoms in direct opposition to the Axis powers. Whereas the Roosevelt administration's Four Freedoms represented religious ideals, the Axis governments represented "pagan brutality." Whereas FDR's Four Freedoms represented freedom and democratic processes, the Axis governments represented "slavery." Whereas FDR's Four Freedoms were gifts to humankind, the Axis countries offered only deprivation. While FDR's Four Freedoms represented sustenance and life itself, the Axis governments represented brutality, withering, and death. Roosevelt went a step further in the early speeches by identifying the Axis countries and these consequences of Axis domination with the counterproductive stance of "unwitting appeasers" such as the isolationists.

These equations and oppositions in Roosevelt's rhetoric filtered into numerous speeches, essays, stories, paintings, conversations, press reports, and generally into the public awareness, so that by the time the *Saturday Evening Post* first distributed Norman Rockwell's version of the "Four Freedoms" in February and March of 1943, the Four Freedoms already were serving several functions in Roosevelt's campaign.[13] Initially, in 1941, they justified increased financial support of Britain and virtually silenced the isolationists.[14] The Four Freedoms also educated and unified American citizens by articulating clear ideals for the country. After the Japanese attacked Pearl Harbor on December 7, 1941, the Four Freedoms provided an additional justification for American entry into the war. During the war, they boosted American morale, and in February 1943 the Post Office issued a Four Freedoms postage stamp "to impress upon the public the necessity of spreading the Four Freedoms throughout the world. . . ."[15] Eventually, with the government-sponsored tour of Rockwell's "Four Freedoms" paintings and the mass-distribution of the four posters, the "Four Freedoms" functioned to raise money by promoting the sale of war bonds during the final war years.

The values associated with the Four Freedoms in Rockwell's paintings correspond to the associations in Roosevelt's speeches, so Roosevelt's speeches implicitly supplied the contents for Rockwell's appeal. Thus these paintings and posters were a positive example of what America should strive to protect and preserve. Even the titles of the paintings—"Freedom from Fear," "Freedom from Want," "Freedom of Speech," and "Freedom of Worship"—are rhetorically functional. They are framing devices that evoke what the historian Robert Bellah called the "sacred scripture" of civil religion.[16]

The antitheses between the American and Axis governments in the texts from the *Post* correspond to the antitheses in Roosevelt's speeches. Perhaps to allow another antithesis to function between the American and German governments, Rockwell's posters conspicuously omit any men resembling the blond-haired, blue-eyed Aryan male so idealized in Nazi Germany. They also omit any stereotypical Italian or Oriental individuals. In addition, the original title of the poster series—"The Four Freedoms For Which We Fight"—suggests that combating the Axis powers was vital to preserving the Four Freedoms. Accordingly, Americans were urged to sacrifice.

The plentiful food on the table in "Freedom from Want" no doubt reminded the public both of a past which victory would return and a sense of personal sacrifice for the country, since by 1943 the government was rationing food. Roosevelt's speeches and the accompanying texts in the *Post* reinforced the idea that the Four Freedoms meant fighting the Axis countries, sacrificing self for country and freedom. The support-the-war-effort conclusions of the texts in the *Post* and "Buy War Bonds" on the posters asked Americans to sacrifice to ensure the reward of American virtue as manifest in their institutions and to endorse the punishment of the Axis countries' evil. Since the end of the war, the title of Rockwell's poster series has been shortened to the "Four Freedoms," partially no doubt because the new title is simpler than the original, partially because the immediate need for combative support of the Four Freedoms ended with World War II.

CONCLUSION

Rockwell's "Four Freedoms" illustrate how political and religious values can be conjoined in icons and how such portraits in praise of a people can motivate political action. Both of these principles have been observed in discursive communication as well. The American manner in which political and religious values are often joined has been described variously by Robert Bellah as American civil religion, by John F. Wilson as civic piety, and by Roderick P. Hart as the political pulpit.[17] The transformation of epideictic messages into deliberative ones has been observed by Aristotle, who affirmed in the *Rhetoric* that "to praise a man is in one respect akin to urging a course of action."[18] Similarly, Kenneth Burke has stressed in *A Rhetoric of Motives:* "[If] in the opinion of a given audience, a certain kind of conduct is admirable, then a speaker might persuade the audience by using ideas and images that identify his cause with that kind of conduct."[19] In other words, to the extent that people act according to virtuous motives, epideictic discourses are inherently deliberative.

Rockwell was not the first illustrator to use American values to inspire wartime commitment. Similarly, during the Civil War, Thomas Nast's illustrations such as "Christmas Eve, 1862," "Thanksgiving Day, 1863," and "The War in the West" mediated a predominantly religious and political view of Americans.[20] Like Rockwell's posters, Nast's illustrations appealed primarily to values associated with the church, the family, and the political system. According to Morton Keller, Nast's "series of allegorical celebrations of national holidays caught—and heightened—the mix of patriotism, religiousity, and elevated moral purpose that gave important elements of Northern opinion the will to see the war through to its bloodied, weary end."[21] But unlike Rockwell's posters, Nast's illustrations also present images of war: death, destruction, and mourning. Because Rockwell's posters omitted such war imagery, they have transcended the particular circumstances surrounding World War II.

The visual rhetoric of Rockwell's "Four Freedoms" sums up many ideals of the American political system. Thanksgiving as stressed in "Freedom from Want" represents a time when the family gathers together to thank God and country for their bountiful gifts, and these gifts are typically regarded as a reward for the virtue of Americans who are hard-working, faithful, active citizens. "Freedom of Worship" celebrates religious diversity that is made possible by the separation of church and state in American political ideology. "Freedom from Fear" portrays family safety and security as dependent upon the preservation of the American political system. Finally, "Freedom of Speech" stresses the vital contribution of open and public debate for the betterment of American society. Rockwell's "Four Freedoms" consist, then, of epideictic icons which signify an idealized view of the United States' political and religious values.

Since Roosevelt already had identified the Four Freedoms with various national ideals, the Roosevelt administration's verbal rhetoric had created a context in which the essential ideas of Rockwell's appeal were already articulated. In light of the administration's rhetoric, Rockwell's posters exemplified enduring ideals rather than an ephemeral period in American life. Yet, the administration's rhetoric implicitly stressed a deliberative function of Rockwell's works by placing them in fully articulated antitheses to the Axis governments and by calling for personal resolve and self-sacrifice to preserve the Four Freedoms. These rhetorical functions of Rockwell's "Four Freedoms," as examples and antithetical principles, recurred explicitly in the texts which accompanied Rockwell's illustrations in the *Post*. Thus, the essential conjoinment of political and religious values became amplified in a manner which enabled Roosevelt's administration to use Rockwell's portraits in praise of a people to advance political policy.

The ability of the Roosevelt administration to use Rockwell's "Four Freedoms" to affect political action proves that a people's aesthetic sensibilities can be manipulated for pragmatic ends. Visualization of the praiseworthy or the blameworthy allows for the union of aesthetics and society, since a people's aesthetic artifacts can both reflect and reform social action. Similar principles operate in other cultures as well, sometimes in benign and sometimes in sinister forms. For example, during the Nazi years in Germany, the Nazis conjoined religious and political imagery to generate fanatical support. Such use of visual symbols can be seen in *The Dream that Was No More a Dream* in which Bill Kinser and Neil Kleinman affirm that: "we discovered not only that a translation between German history and art was possible, but that the Nazis had deliberately intensified the feedback between the two."[22] Perhaps, then, the political uses of icons merit additional attention in rhetorical studies.

Reading Endnotes

1. Thomas Buechner, *Norman Rockwell: A Sixty Year Retrospective,* Catalogue of an Exhibition Organized by Gernard Daneberg Galleries (New York: Harry N. Abrams, 1972), p. 85. For additional information about Norman Rockwell, the following may be helpful: Norman Rockwell, *102 Favorite Paintings by Norman Rockwell,* intro. Christopher Finch (New York: Crown Publishers, 1978); *50 Favorite Paintings by Norman Rockwell,* intro. Christopher Finch (New York: Crown Publishers, 1977); Arthur L. Guptill, *Norman Rockwell Illustrator,* preface by Dorothy Canfield Fisher, biographical introduction by Jack Alexander (New York: Watson-Guptill Publications, 1975); Christopher Finch, *Norman Rockwell's America,* opening photographic essay by John Bryson (New York: Harry N. Abrams, 1975); Thomas S. Buechner, *Norman Rockwell, Artist and Illustrator* (New York: Harry N. Abrams, 1970). Any of the above works can be consulted for reproductions of the "Four Freedoms." Buechner's *Norman Rockwell: A Sixty Year Retrospective* contains a second version of "Freedom of Speech," especially created for the Metropolitan Museum and different from the version used in the *Post* and for the posters.

   According to *New Yorker* magazine, reproductions of the "Four Freedoms" posters were displayed in a wide variety of settings, such as "schools, post offices, Elks clubs, ration-board offices, Sunday schools, and railroad stations." R. Jarman, "Profiles: U. S. Artist," *New Yorker,* 21 (March 17, 1945), 41.

   For an example of a different approach to the rhetorical analysis of icons, see Robert Scott, "Diego Rivera at Rockefeller Center: Fresco Painting and Rhetoric," *Western Journal of Speech Communication,* 41 (1977), 70–82.
2. George Kennedy suggests that the pew-like icons in this illustration are known as "forms," which were used in one-room schoolhouses in New England. Kennedy adds that "a form is a bench which runs across the room. Usually it had cast iron legs and is made of pine boards. On the back of each bench is a writing surface for the students in the row behind." Letter received from George Kennedy, 26 June 1981.

   Although such forms may have been well-known in New England, Rockwell was working for a national periodical and a national campaign, and he probably recognized that many people would see such forms as pews.
3. Norman Rockwell, *102 Favorite Paintings by Norman Rockwell,* p. 70. It is difficult to know how to interpret Rockwell's decision to place himself in "Freedom from Want." One interpretation is simply that he placed an image of himself in the painting as a product of his own vanity. Another interpretation is that he is symbolically looking at the viewer as though expecting a response. A third possibility is that he is looking at a door in response to a welcome, or perhaps an unwelcome, intruder.

4. Robert N. Bellab, "Civil Religion in America," *Daedalus,* 96 (1967), 11.
5. Rockwell, *102 Favorite Paintings,* p. 68.
6. Several ideas in this paragraph on the icons associated with the church were, at least in part, based upon a personal interview with Conrad Cherry, 27 October 1978.
7. Norman Rockwell, "Four Freedoms; Painting," *Saturday Evening Post* (February 20 and 27, 1943, March 6 and 13, 1943), pp. 12–13 in each issue.
8. In response to his posters, Rockwell received over sixty thousand letters, most of them commenting favorably on the posters. According to *Time* magazine, few of the letters objected to the painting, and "most of the adverse criticism pointed out that one particular religion (or another,—always that particular critic's) was not strongly enough plugged." See both "I Like To Please People," *Time* (June 21, 1943), pp. 41–42 and R. Jarman, p. 41. The background information in this paragraph is based upon a telephone interview with Marshall Stoltz, curator of the Norman Rockwell Museum in Philadelphia, Pennsylvania, 23 October 1978.
9. All quotations are from Will Durant, "Freedom of Worship," *Saturday Evening Post* (February 27, 1943), p. 12.
10. Carlos Bulosan, "Freedom from Want," *Saturday Evening Post* (March 6, 1943), p. 12.
11. Franklin D. Roosevelt, *The Public Papers and Addresses of Franklin D. Roosevelt,* intro. Franklin Roosevelt, compiled and collated, Samuel I. Rosenman (New York: MacMillan Company, 1950), IX, 672. For information about the preparation and revision of FDR's "Four Freedoms" speech, see Laura Crowell, "Building the 'Four Freedoms' Speech," *Speech Monographs,* 22 (1955), 266–283.
12. In the following two paragraphs, all comments in quotation marks were drawn from *The Public Papers and Addresses of Frank/in D. Roosevelt.* For examples of the domestic speeches in which Roosevelt alludes to the Four Freedoms, see Roosevelt, X, 66, 192–193, 334, and 498; XI, 161 and 287; and XII, 30. For an example of an address in a foreign country in which Roosevelt alludes to the Four Freedoms, see Roosevelt, XII, 368. Roosevelt also emphasized the Four Freedoms in international policy-making. Three of the Four Freedoms were incorporated into the Atlantic Charter; through an oversight, freedom of religion was not mentioned. "So severe was the criticism," writes Robert Sherwood "that when the Atlantic Charter was incorporated into the first Proclamation of the United Nations on January 1, 1942, Roosevelt was careful to see to it that Freedom of Religion was included (and with Russian agreement)." From Robert E. Sherwood, *Roosevelt and Hopkins: An Intimate History* (New York: Grosset and Dunlap, 1950), p. 361.
13. Numerous spokesmen elaborated upon the Four Freedoms. Among them were Under Secretary of State Sumner Welles and President of

Columbia University Nicholas Murray Butler. Sumner Welles, "The Free World: Requirements for the Four Freedoms," *Vital Speeches of the Day*, 9 (December 1, 1942), 114–116; Nicho1as Murray Butler, "What Does Freedom Mean?" *Vital Speeches of the Day*, 10 (September 15, 1943), 710–713.

A brief sampling of magazines might include: "Cultivating the Four Freedoms: Children Must Learn Their Meaning at Home," *Parents Magazine*, 17 (January 1942), 17; "United States Peace Aims," *Catholic World* (September 1942), p. 745; "Contributions of the English to the Four Freedoms," *Education* (September 1944) pp. 45–56; "The Four Freedoms Are an Ideal," *Saturday Evening Post* (September 25, 1943), p. 112; "Symbols of National Solidarity: The Four Freedoms," *Annals of the American Academy*, 23 (September 1942), 157–161.

Hugo Ballin's California mural was "the first endeavor of an artist to recognize the potentialities of the four values of life for painterly expression," "Hugo Ballin Interprets the Four Freedoms in California Mural," *Art Digest*, 17 (August 1943), 10. At the suggestion of Roosevelt, Walter Russell sculpted a monument depicting the Four Freedoms, complete with four angels, one for each freedom. Russell commented: "last summer at Hyde Park the President suggested to me that through the medium of the arts, a far greater number of people could be brought to understand the concept of the Four Freedoms." "Artists Interpret the Four Freedoms," *Art Digest*, 17 (March 1943), 10; Betty Woodworth designed five panels for the children's room—one panel for each of the Four Freedoms and a fifth panel of children raising the American flag. Carolyn Crawford, "Democracy and the Four Freedoms—Panels for the Children's Room," paintings by Betty Ruth Woodworth, *Library Journal*, 69 (February 1, 1944), 106–108.

14. "There could no longer be any doubt," writes Geoffrey Perrett, "that isolationists were in the thick of a losing fight and would be lucky if they could keep from being routed. Roosevelt's fireside chat at the end of 1940, followed by the assertive, popular Four Freedoms, had thrown them more than ever on the defensive. Isolationists were openly, and often, branded 'appeasers.'" Geoffrey Perrett, *Days of Sadness, Years of Triumph* (New York: Coward, McCann and Geoghegan, 1973), p. 157.
15. United States Post Office Department, *Postage Stamps of the United States* (Washington, D.C.: United States Government Printing Office, 1968), p. 107. Carlos Stoetzer also mentions the Four Freedoms stamp in *Postage Stamps as Propaganda* (Washington, D.C.: Public Affairs Press, 1953), p. 17.
16. Roberi N. Bellah, "Civil Religion in America," p. 9.
17. "Although matters of personal religious belief, worship, and association are considered to be strictly private affairs, there are, at the same

time, certain common elements of religious orientation that the great majority of Americans share." Bellah, p. 3. From similarity in beliefs, rituals, and religious symbols arises a feature of American political life that Bellah calls civil religion. According to Bellah (p. 5), Rousseau "outlines the simple dogmas of civil religion: the existence of God, the life to come, the reward of virtue, and the punishment of vice, and the exclusion of religious intolerance." To Bellah (p. 10), civil religion evolved with the history of America, and it eventually came to include a "new theme of death, sacrifice, and rebirth." Through civil rituals, beliefs, and symbols, the American civil religion became "powerful symbols of national solidarity" that could "mobilize deep levels of personal motivation for the attainment of national goals" (Bellah, p. 13).

Although John F. Wilson and Roderick P. Hart, among others, have challenged Bellah's conceptualization, arguing that civil religion is a misnomer for a phenomenon that should more accurately be labeled as "civil piety," for our purposes, we need not become entangled in that controversy, because all parties concerned agree that the phenomenon is essentially characterized by a conjoining of political and religious values in a distinctly American manner. For more information about the debate, the following essays may be most helpful: John F. Wilson, "The Status of 'Civil Religion' in America," *The Religion of the Republic,* ed. Elwyn A. Smith (Philadelphia: Fortress Press, 1971), pp. 1–21; Donald G. Jones and Russell E. Richey, "The Civil Religion Debate," *American Civil Religion,* ed. Russell E. Richey and Donald G. Jones (New York: Harper and Row, 1974), pp. 3–20; Robert Bellah, "American Civil Religion in the 1970's," *American Civil Religion,* 255–272; Roderick P. Hart, *The Political Pulpit* (West Lafayette, Indiana: Purdue University Press, 1977), see esp. pp. 29–42.

18. Aristotle, *Rhetoric,* trans. W. Rhys Roberts (New York: The Modern Library, 1954), 1367b.
19. Kenneth Burke, *A Rhetoric of Motives* (Berkeley: University of California Press, 1969), p. 55.
20. Thomas Nast St. Hill, *Thomas Nast: Cartoons and Illustrations* (New York: Dover Publications, 1974), pp. 6–7 and 12–13 for "Christmas Eve, 1862" and "The War in the West" respectively. Morton Keller, *The Art and Politics of Thomas Nast* (New York: Oxford University Press, 1968), pp. 14–15 and 20–21 for "The War in the West" and for "Thanksgiving Day, 1863" respectively.
21. Keller, p. 13.
22. Bill Kinser and Neil Kleinman, *The Dream that Was No More a Dream: A Search for Aesthetic Reality in Germany, 1890–1945,* coordinated by Lynn Musgrave (Cambridge, MA: Schenkman Publishing Company, 1969), p. 6.

In this Chapter 7 workshop, we will probe in focused workshop exercises many of the concepts you discovered in this chapter. Work at a pace by assignment, or by choice, that allows these various insights to "sink in" at an even deeper level for you.

Having read the rhetorical criticism article by Lester C. Olson entitled "Portraits in Praise of a People: A Rhetorical Analysis of Norman Rockwell's Icons in Franklin D. Roosevelt's 'Four Freedoms' Campaign" on page 256. Use the chart on the next page to start a careful notes on the JFS and JFA items (about which you learned in Chapter 3) that Olson used to establish the need for this research. Make other notations in the margin of the reproduced article.

FINDING THE SET-UP ITEMS

Discovering JFS and JFS items

Olson, Lester C. "Portraits in Praise of a People: A Rhetorical Analysis of Norman Rockwell's Icons in Franklin D. Roosevelt's 'Four Freedoms' Campaign." *Quarterly Journal of Speech* 69 (1983): 15–24.

(Page numbers in brackets indicate pages reprinted in this textbook.)

Item	Page	
JFS	15 [257]	"Thus, Rockwell's illustrations provide an ideal opportunity to study the suasory role of icons in political communication."
JFS		
JFS		
JFA	15 [256–257]	"About Rockwell's illustrations, Thomas Buechner wrote that 'millions of copies were printed and distributed by the government and private agencies all over the world[.]"
JFA		
JFA		

As part of this Chapter 7 workshop, we will continue to probe several of the ways you can recognize and use the "gold" of academic, rhetorical criticism. Re-read the chart on the next page. See if you can notice how we moved from the original claim, insight or discovery to the resulting "translation."

Next, use the blank chart below to find more nuggets of "gold" in the article from your own reading. Be sure to keep track of the page on which you find the quotation and think about how you can best translate the insight or discovery to a practical translation you could use in preparing a message.

Item	Page	

FINDING THE GOLD

Discovering Application Ideas and Knowledge in Visual Messages Analysis Articles

Example:

Olson, Lester C. "Portraits in Praise of a People: A Rhetorical Analysis of Norman Rockwell's Icons in Franklin D. Roosevelt's 'Four Freedoms' Campaign." *Quarterly Journal of Speech* 69 (1983): 15–24.

(Page numbers in brackets indicate pages reprinted in this textbook.)

Quotation	Page	Translated Idea or Insight
"Although Rockwell's meticulous attention to exact detail was well-known, perhaps not so well-known was his ability to omit detail so as to promote varied identifications."	16 [257]	What's left out of a persuasive picture can function to give audience members more common ground.
"The children also represent hope for the future, and continuity in American traditions, as suggested in 'Freedom from Want' by placement of the youngest granddaughter to the grandfather and opposite the grandmother."	18 [259]	Generations represented in a picture can suggest connection and continuation of tradition; and, placement of characters in a picture can strongly suggest relationship.
"The poster presents hands folded in different ways, and this may encourage viewers to identify with the image most similar to their own position for prayer."	18 [260]	Varied images in a picture may raise evocative connections at a personal level with a greater number of people.

Use the chart on the next page to find, identify, and chart the potential advantage of other observations on narrative and culture that Olson makes in his analysis.

Quotation	Page	Translated Idea or Insight

THE POWER OF REMEMBERED IMAGES

People with a couple of decades of life under their belt have seen, literally, millions of images. What makes you remember some images rather than others? Working *only* from memory, try to think of the funniest image you've ever seen. (Remember to recall, for our purposes, only images you've seen from the mass media.) What's the saddest image you've ever seen? The most stupid? The most frightening? Do your "most remembered" images have any thing in common with each other? Do they tend to be iconic, indexical, or symbolic images?

MANIPULATED IMAGES

What clues do you have that someone is manipulating the mass-media images you see? (Hint: all mass-media images are manipulated.) You are much more likely to see the people "behind" the scenes of media productions (say, on Leno or Letterman), than would have been true 20 years ago, hence potentially raising your awareness that someone is making decisions about the images you see.

For the next week keep a log for 10 minutes each day when you are in a media-rich visual environment (watching TV, watching a movie on DVD, reading magazines at the laundromat, seeing bus billboards passing on a busy city street). Pay careful attention to the "unseen" people responsible for the images crossing your path as an audience member. What were *they* thinking about *you?* What tactics do you observe them using to visually attract or reach you? Do you see evidence of visual metaphors, or metonymys, or synecdoches, or replacements being used? Which seem most powerful to you? Why?

THE POWER OF LEARNED CONNECTIONS

Look through a magazine thick with glossy ads (it shouldn't be hard to find; the tough part is finding the articles among the glossy ads). Try to find individual image elements within each ad and attempt to mentally separate their denotation meaning from a perceived connotation meaning (what it is versus what it "means").

Try to find five image elements within five ads that have a strongly negative connotation. Try to find five image elements that have strongly positive connotation. And, try to find five image elements in five ads that have a neutral connotation.

Do certain types of denotated items or people seem better "fit" creating negative, positive, or neutral connotations? What might influence such perception? Do you know of any image (denotation message element) that previously had strong negative connotations for you but now is positive?

ICONS, INDEXES, AND SYMBOLS, OH MY!

Icons are images of what they are, right?

Indexes are images of what was there, right?

Symbols are "created" images (not found in nature) and are not a "trace" of something else, right?

Try to find five print or electronic ads that have *all three* types of visual message within each ad. How does each of the elements interact? What function does each one seem to serve? Is it possible to say that one type is more important or prevalent than the other two? Why?

THE POWER OF POLITICAL CARTOONS

Find 10 political cartoons that use visual metaphors. (Hint: The *Washington Post* (Weekly Edition) usually has multiple political cartoons within it; check your library.)

Do the visual metaphors use both visual metaphrands and visual metaphiers? Or, do you find visual metaphors that use only a visual metaphier?

What types of metaphrands (whether visual or in words) become linked in a metaphoric bond with a metaphier?

Do the visual metaphors create useful perspective for you (as any strong metaphor should)?

Say the visual metaphor in spoken words (e.g., "the congressman is a clown"). Does the metaphor seem stronger in visual or verbal form? Why?

Key Words

semiotic, *228*
sign, *228*
signifier, *228*
signified, *228*
denotation, *228*
connotation, *228*
iconic sign, *228*
indexical sign, *228, 230–231*
symbolic sign, *228, 230, 238*
icon, *226*
iconic, *238*
iconicity, *226*
index, *238*
indexical, *238*
symbol, *238*
symbolic, *238*
visual metaphor, *240*
visual metaphier, *240*
paraphier, *242*
paraphrand, *242*
visual metonymy, *243–244*
visual synecdoche, *244, 245*
visual replacement, *245, 248*
reduction and simplification, *250*
regular characters, *250–252*
non-narrative hyperbole, *253*
narrative hyperbole, *253*

Visual Analysis Articles and Books

Below you will find a sample of rhetorical and cultural analysis articles and books that have investigated the power of visual public messages.

Barker, David. "Television Production Techniques as Communication." *Critical Studies in Mass Communication* 2 (1985) 234–246.

'Barker, David. " 'It's Been Real': Forms of Television Representation." *Critical Studies in Mass Communication* 5 (1988) 42–56.

Bostdorff, Denise M. "Making Light of James Watt: A Burkean Approach to the Form and Attitude of Political Cartoons." *Quarterly Journal of Speech* 73 (1987) 43–69.

Byer, Robert H. "Words, Monuments, Beholders: The Visual Arts in Hawthorne's *The Marble Faun*." *American Iconology: New Approaches to Nineteenth-Century Art and Literature.* New Haven: Yale University Press, 1993. 163–185.

Curtis, L. Perry, Jr., *Apes and Angels: The Irishman in Victorian Caricature.* Washington, D.C.: Smithsonian Institution Press, 1971.

Dabydeen, David. *Hogarth's Blacks: Images of Blacks in Eighteenth Century English Art.* Surrey, England: Dangaroo Press, 1985.

DeSousa, Michael A. and Martin J. Medhurst. "The Editorial Cartoon as Visual Rhetoric: Rethinking Boss Tweed." *Journal of Visual Verbal Languaging* 9 (Fall 1982) 52–59.

DeSousa, Michael A. "Symbolic Action and Pretended Insight: The Ayatollah Khomeini in U.S. Editorial Cartoons." *Rhetorical Dimensions in Media: A Critical Casebook.* Rev. ed. Eds. Martin J. Medhurst and Thomas W. Benson. Dubuque, Iowa: Kendall/Hunt, 1984. 204–230.

Edwards, Janis L. and Carol K. Winkler. "Representative Form and the Visual Ideograph: The Iwo Jima Image in Editorial Cartoons." *Quarterly Journal of Speech* 83 (1997): 289–310.

Entman, Robert. "Modern Racism and the Images of Blacks in Local Television News." *Critical Studies in Mass Communication* 7 (1990) 332–345.

Ferguson, Marjorie. "Images of Power and the Feminist Fallacy." *Critical Studies in Mass Communication* 7 (1990) 215–230.

Fiske, John. "The Discourses of TV Quiz Shows or, School + Luck = Success + Sex." *Central States Speech Journal* 34 (Fall 1983) 139–150.

Foss, Sonja K. "Ambiguity as Persuasion: The Vietnam Veterans Memorial." *Communication Quarterly* 34 (Summer 1986): 326–340.

Foss, Sonja K. "Body Art: Insanity as Communication." *Communication Studies [Central States Speech Journal]* 38/2 (Summer 1987) 122–131.

Fox, Celina. "The Development of Social Reportage in English Periodical Illustration During the 1840s and Early 1850s." *Past and Present* 74 (Feb. 1977) 90–111.

Gilman, Sander L. "Black Bodies, White Bodies: Toward an Iconography of Female Sexuality in Late Nineteenth-Century Art, Medicine, and Literature." *Critical Inquiry* 12 (Autumn 1985): 204–242.

Goldman, Robert, Deborah Heath, and Sharon L. Smith. "Commodity Feminism." *Critical Studies in Mass Communication* 8 (1991) 333–351.

Goodstein, Ethel S. "Southern Belles and Southern Buildings: The Built Environment as Text and Context in Designing Women." *Critical Studies in Mass Communication* 9 (June 1992) 170–185.

Haines, Harry W. "'What Kind of War?': An Analysis of the Vietnam Veterans Memorial." *Critical Studies in Mass Communication* 3 (March 1986) 1–20.

Hall, Stuart. "The Social Eye of the Picture Post." *Working Papers in Cultural Studies* 2 (1972) 71–120.

Kaplan, Stuart Jay. "Visual Metaphors in the Representation of Communication Technology." *Critical Studies in Mass Communication* 7 (1990): 37–47.

Kaplan, Stuart Jay. "A Conceptual Analysis of Form and Content in Visual Metaphors." *Communication* 13 (1992): 197–209.

Kervin, Denise. "Gender Ideology in Television Commercials." *Television Criticism: Approaches and Applications.* Eds. Leah R. Vande Berg and Lawrence A. Wenner. New York: Longman, 1991. 235–253.

Lemon, Judith. "Women and Blacks on Prime-Time Television." *Journal of Communication* 27 (1977) 70–79.

Lucaites, John Louis. "Visualizing 'The People': Individualism vs. Collectivism in *Let Us Now Praise Famous Men.*" *Quarterly Journal of Speech* 83 (1997) 269–288.

Medhurst, Martin J. "Hiroshima, Mon Amore: From Iconography to Rhetoric." *Quarterly Journal of Speech* 68 (1982) 345–370.

Medhurst, Martin J. and Michael A. DeSousa. "Political Cartoons as Rhetorical Form: A Taxonomy of Graphic Discourse." *Communication Monographs* 48 (1981) 197–236.

Messaris, Paul and Jisuk Woo. "Image vs. Reality in Korean-Americans' Responses to Mass-Mediated Depictions of the United States." *Critical Studies in Mass Communication* 8 (1991): 74–90.

Messaris, Paul. "Visual Literacy vs. Visual Manipulation." *Critical Studies in Mass Communication* 11 (1994): 181–203.

Messaris, Paul. *Visual Literacy: Image, Mind and Reality.* Boulder, Colorado: Westview Press, 1994.

Messaris, Paul. *Visual Persuasion: The Role of Images in Advertising.* Thousand Oaks: Calif.: Sage, 1997.

Miller, David C., ed. *American Iconology.* New Haven: Yale University Press, 1993.

Miller, David C. "The Iconology of Wrecked or Stranded Boats in Mid- to Late Nineteenth-Century American Culture." *American Iconology: New Approaches to Nineteenth-Century Art and Literature.* New Haven: Yale University Press, 1993. 186–208.

Mitchell, W.J.T., ed. *Language of Images.* Chicago: University of Chicago Press, 1980.

Mitchell, W.J.T., ed. *Iconology: Image, Text, Ideology.* Chicago: University of Chicago Press, 1986.

Olson, Lester. "Benjamin Franklin's Pictorial Representations of the British Colonies in America: A Study in Rhetorical Iconology." *Quarterly Journal of Speech* 73 (1987) 18–42.

Olson, Lester. "Benjamin Franklin's Commemorative Medal *Libertas Americana:* A Study in Rhetorical Iconology." *Quarterly Journal of Speech* 76 (1990) 23–45.

Olson, Lester C. *Emblems of American Community in the Revolutionary Era: A Study in Rhetorical Iconology.* Washington, D.C.: Smithsonian Institution Press, 1991.

Olson, Scott R. "Meta-Television: Popular Postmodernism." *Critical Studies in Mass Communication* 4 (Sept. 1987): 284–300.

Pierce, Dann L. "Cultural Molding of a Provocative Rhetor: Thomas Nast and Graphic Persuasion." *Journal of the Northwest Communication Association* 26 (Spring 1998) 47–62.

Pierce, Dann L. "Stylistic Devices in Graphic Rhetoric: Thomas Nast's Persuasive Tools," *Virginia Journal of Communication* 11 (1998) 63–92.

Poynton, Beverley and John Hartley. "Male-Gazing: Australian Rules Football, Gender and Television." In *Television and Women's Culture: The Politics of the Popular.* Ed. Mary Ellen Brown. Newbury Park, Calif.: Sage, 1990, 144–157.

Roeder, George H. *The Censored War: American Visual Experience During World War Two.* New Haven: Yale University Press, 1993.

Scott, Robert L. "Diego Rivera at Rockefeller Center: Fresco Painting and Rhetoric." *Western Journal of Speech Communication* 41 (1977) 70–82.

Sontag, Susan. "The Image-World." *On Photography.* New York: Farrar, Straus and Giroux, 1977. 153–180.

Steiner, Linda. "Oppositional Decoding as an Act of Resistance." *Critical Studies in Mass Communication* 5 (1988) 1–15.

Tufte, Edward R. *Visual Explanations: Images and Quantities, Evidence and Narrative.* Cheshire, Connecticut: Graphics Press, 1997.

Worth, Sol. *Studying Visual Communication.* Ed. Larry Gross. Philadelphia: University of Pennsylvania Press, 1981.

Endnotes

1. Larry P. Gross, "Modes of Communication and the Acquisition of Symbolic Competence," *Communication Technology and Social Policy,* Eds. George Gerbner, et. al. New York: John Wiley and Sons, 1973, 204–205.
2. Both sentence 1 and sentence 2 ask "Where is my cow?" (in Portuguese and in Italian, respectively).
3. While scholars writing in the semiotics tradition see all human messages as a semiotic or sign system, rhetorical scholars have in practice use semiotic terms for the analysis of visual messages rather than for all messages.
4. Ferdinand de Saussure, *Course in General Linguistics* (New York: McGraw-Hill, 1966).
5. de Saussure 1966; Roland Barthes, *Image Music Text* (New York: Hill and Wang, 1977).
6. Charles Sanders Peirce, *Philosophical Writings of Peirce* (New York: Dover, 1955).
7. Dann L. Pierce, "Cultural Molding of a Provocative Rhetor: Thomas Nast and Graphic Persuasion," *Journal of the Northwest Communication Association* 26 (Spring 1998) 47–62.

8. Albert Bigelow Paine, *Th. Nast: His Period and His Pictures* (New York Macmillian, 1904) 175–176.
9. Dann L. Pierce, "Stylistic Devices in Graphic Rhetoric: Thomas Nast's Persuasive Tools," *Virginia Journal of Communication* 11 (1998) 63–92.
10. For other overarching discussions on tactics used by political cartoonists see: Denise M. Bostdorff, "Making Light of James Watt: A Burkean Approach to the Form and Attitude of Political Cartoons," *Quarterly Journal of Speech* 73 (1987) 43-69; and, Martin J. Medhurst and Michael A. DeSousa, "Political Cartoons as Rhetorical Form: A Taxonomy of Graphic Discourse," *Communication Monographs* 48 (1981) 197–236.
11. Pierce, 70.
12. Pierce, 78.

Chapter Eight

Language and Ideology: Twins Separated at Birth?

Does language have power? If language has little or no power, then what does have power? (Careful, this is a trick question; in order to talk about power, you must use language.) Where *does* power reside? Does nature, or human behavior, or language have greater power? You may recognize that this question parallels the three "worlds" we discussed in Chapter 1 (the physical world, the social world, and the symbol world). We obviously can find "power" in all three "worlds." Hence, it would be somewhat silly to debate which world has more "power." For starters, power comes in different forms (you can't pick up two quarts of "power" at your local grocery store). If power were uniform and recognizable, we would still find that power (and its use) are interactive between and among the three worlds.

For instance, genetic research in many forms has been in the news lately. Stem cell research, cloning, insurance screening, crop varieties, and human fertility (among many other concerns and issues) form the focus of countless reports, policies, investigations, debates, and news reports. Genetic research obviously is beholden to the "power" of the physical world. The ability to detect, manipulate, and use parts of genetic codes (including those of humans) obviously depends on physical materials, tools, devices, places, and subject matter. We can accomplish no more than the capacities and characteristics of physical devices and places used to perform genetic research and engineering.

Moreover, scientists and others concerned with genetic issues live, create, and work within many social relationships. They communicate with peer professionals, family members, critics, and administrative staff (to name but a few types of people who share social "power" with them at various social levels). The very desire to do genetic research is no doubt born within the matrix of expectations that a scientist has learned from his or her social connections and norms.[1]

But, like all professionals, scientists concerned with genetic research eventually must communicate. Their messages will depend on languages that were given to them—languages that, in some ways, they will help to change and modify. The "power" of language is very important to consider. Effective use of the physical world and the social world in which scientists (and all the rest of us) operate depends on the qualities of the language(s) available to them. Choices they make about how to represent their work to themselves and others will have profound impact for many years.

Let's examine some of the many characteristics and mysteries of human language and its uses.

To start, humans began communication activities that we would recognize as "language" with sounds. Many generations (or millennia) later those sounds have grown in number, complexity, and utility. We know them as "words" in either verbal or written form. Once we begin to use multiple words in cooperation with each other, we recognize that in spoken expression or written expression we can communicate in three basic ways.

We communicate first by statement of proposition, next by metaphors, and finally by stories. All three basic forms of word-based communication (propositional, metaphoric, and narrative) are used extensively in contemporary life to accomplish our goals and desires. We've initially explored these communication forms in previous chapters.

In this chapter, however, we need to recognize that *all* three basic forms depend on some common characteristics of word-based language as people around the globe use it.

While we often recognize that word-based language is a tool or device (otherwise why learn fifth grade grammar?), we don't often probe under the hood to see how that tool or device works. Let's start.

Word-based language as learned in your native culture is first and foremost a filter for perception and experience. A talented scholar of rhetoric named Kenneth Burke famously told us that language "selects," "deflects," and "reflects" in all three of the "worlds" we've identified together.[2] If you have ever tried to have a discussion with someone who does not share your native language (either as a host, or as a visitor), you know how quickly you recognize that that person is using different sounds, words, and concepts to understand *his or her* three worlds. Let's use a couple of examples to quickly demonstrate this idea of filtering perception and experience.

On my campus we've had trouble within our "social world" over the years deciding on what to call students who fall *outside* the range of an 18–22 year old student who comes to college immediately after finishing high school. Are such people "returning" students, "non-traditional" students, "adult" students, "older-than-average" students, "independent" students, or what? Each word or label we apply to them holds some accuracy, yet encourages us to pay special attention to some leading characteristic of that word, or designation, for the person. What happens when some of the "returning" students aren't returning at all? (Perhaps they never started college in the first place.) What if one of the "non-traditional" students proves to be *very* traditional in his or her outlook or behavior? What if some of the "adult" students are much more immature than some of their younger counterparts in the classroom? Each word or phrase we try holds some advantages and some liabilities. If we use Burke's idea of language acting as a screen or filter, we recognize that calling a returning 36-year-old student an "independent" student *selects* certain attributes (e.g., living alone, responsible for own expenses), *deflects* attention from other life attributes (her love of Coen brothers movies and monster truck events), and *reflects* cultural values of how we think older-than-22-year-old people should live and act.

If words we use to name or deal with older-than-22-year-olds who want to pursue college degrees were the *only* place that posed this human language challenge, we could dismiss it as odd. Instead, we find on careful examination that this dilemma is the very *essence* of the human use of language. We often act as if words, descriptions, labels, names, and designations are natural and normal. We often don't realize that words are selected, interactive, and (to some degree) arbitrary.

Instead of thinking of a word as a label that you were given to use, think of it instead as a highly compressed set of instructions—instructions as to how you (or I) are *supposed to act* toward the object, person, place, or process we are naming.

If you were a manager or a vice president at a huge corporation that builds cars, would you pick up (much less read) a book entitled: *10 Ways to Slightly Change Your Management Team for Partial Results?* Of course not. Darrell Rigby noticed the opposite of this strategy when he wrote in the *Wall Street Journal:*

> An estimated 10,000 business books have been published worldwide over the past three years, many touting management "tools" promising to make their users incredibly successful by showing them new ways of doing business. Beware. . . . Gurus ridicule modest course corrections, clamoring for radical revolutions that will turn conventional wisdom on its head. Check the titles among Amazon's most popular business books: *Leading the Revolution, The Customer Revolution, New Rules For the New Economy: 10 Radical Strategies for a Connected World.* And who could forget *Reengineering the Corporation: A Manifesto for Business Revolution.*[3]

Why did these various authors (and their publishers) use words so closely linked to revolution, radical change, and substantial transformation? At least one reason revolves around our *expectations* when we want

Scrutinize exercise

If you were a business decision maker (manager, vice president, CEO, or other) who wanted substantial change in your corporation management style, would you be more prone to "revolutionary" or "radical" change or "slight" or "incremental" change? Why? Where did you get the idea or inclination that one would be better than the other? Have you ever purchased or used a device, program, or process that was labeled "revolutionary" only to find that the claim was not true? When do we want or see the need for "revolution" (in management or any other part of life)? What words (other than the term "revolution") prepare us to *want* dramatic change?

to change and improve something (in this case, a business over which we have substantial control). Speaking of "revolution" allows us to justify and expect *substantial* change in procedure, products, and sales. If we are attracted to such a book in the first place, we are given a signal that the "instructions" for substantial (not partial) change and improvement may well rest in this management book.

"Revolution" in the title may sell the book (or the workshop, or the college class), but it may also create the sort of resentment that Rigby also notes in the same article:

> Most [management] tools set unrealistic expectations. They overstate benefits and understate costs. Over time, employees grow fatigued as they are whipsawed from one tool to the next. As one weary store manager recently sighed to me, "If I'm told to jump on one more bandwagon, I'm jumping ship."

Clearly, what we call something or someone has much to do with our reaction to that thing or person.

Examine the advertisement from Informatica reproduced in Figure 8.1. The person holding his nose while wearing skin diving flippers is just that, "a person holding his nose while wearing skin diving flippers," until we apply one of the labels that the ad writer cleverly placed over the image. Is he a marine biologist? A pearl diver? A company sports day leader? Or an employee on "disability" leave?

Each of those names or labels calls up a different set of expectations. The seeds of our behavior are in the language choices we use or accept.[4] A marine biologist probably ought to be appreciated for using diving gear. An employee on disability leave probably ought not be skin diving (or so would think the insurance companies to which the software ad is aimed).

In these various examples we see that what we *call* something or someone is both a designation and a call for action. Notice that you probably

FIGURE 8.1 Language Sets Expectations
Which label will get this guy in the most trouble?

recognize the word "designation," but would not recognize the word "deaction." "Designation" comes from Latin and literally means "to mark out." When we designate one student to represent our college at an international conference, we "mark" that person out for special responsibility. If we "deaction" someone, what would happen? "Deaction" is a term I just invented that might mean "to act out" (invented from Latin terms: *de-* = out and *actio* = action). We are familiar with thinking of words being used to "mark out" things or people. We are less familiar with thinking about words as instructions for action. Could "deaction" serve that purpose? Let's see.

Would you care greatly if a livestock farmer was called a "hog farmer" or a "pork producer"? Paul Willis reportedly cares a great deal. He raises hogs in Iowa and believes that his old-fashioned methods (which include free-range pasture instead of scientific, industrial confinement systems) are better than contemporary industry standards.[5] Farmer Willis is not alone in his estimation. Upscale, white-linen restaurants have chefs who make statements such as: "'It actually tastes like pork, [rather] than like the package it came in,' says [Kurt] Friese. 'It's much richer, and more complex than pork from hogs raised in confinements.'" So for at least one Iowa farmer and one chef, the 12 letters that make up "pork producer" (cdekoopprru) and the nine letters that make up "hog farmer" (aefghmorr) make a world of difference. (Farmer Willis prefers "hog farmer.")

Again, the most important point for us: we are taught and conditioned to "hear" or understand words as sets of instructions. You and I might not *care* whether *we* call a person who raises hogs for slaughter a "pork producer" or a "hog farmer," but a talented chef at an upscale restaurant might find great meaning in the difference between the two. Hence, for the chef, the "instructions" contained in the two designations would cause a decision to buy from one but not the other. Of course the power of such naming is precisely the moment when the language strongly suggests a *best* appropriate action. If you were a member of PETA (People for the Ethical Treatment of Animals), you would not call the Iowa farmer a "pork producer" *or* a "hog farmer." You would likely opt for "murderer." If *you* agreed, by whatever means, that the Iowa farmer was a murderer, would it cause you to change your behavior? PETA hopes so. Consequently, when we see the bumper sticker

Meat is Murder

we are encouraged to see all people who raise animals for slaughter as murderers (or at least accomplices to murder). We assume that our language guides us to act differently toward people who raise hogs (**murderer!**) than we do toward people who raise hogs (**pork producer!**), which is different yet from how we should act toward people who raise hogs (**hog farmer!**). Get the picture? Word-based language in all its forms is very powerful in this way. Language (and our response to language) guides our behavior, our evaluation of our behavior, and our evaluation of the behavior of others.

We should also note that not all designations are meaningful to the level of action (i.e., not all designations become instructions for actions). We may miss shades or nuances of meaning that may jump off the page or into the ear of another person to whom the words have special meaning. (If you don't believe this, find someone who served in the U.S. Navy on a submarine and ask him[6] which "ship" he served on.)

Words then, in a word-based language, serve to both "mark out" (designate) and to "instruct to action" (could we use "deaction"?). However, since we inherit the language(s) we use from previous generations of language users and modifiers, we also run up against the problem you may have already recognized with my proposed "Latin" term "deaction." Other than using it briefly in this chapter, I doubt that it will receive very much use because we have too many other English words starting with "de-" that can indicate that something is being stopped or reversed (e.g., deactivate, decommission, decay, or decompress). Thus, we notice that words have history, sound quality, and experience with which they must contend when trying to create meaning. We need another word! Do we have one?

While we are looking for another word to help us better understand words, let's examine a few silly examples of how words help to designate, instruct, and guide our actions.

Scrutinize exercise

Can you, using root words from another language (Greek? French? Spanish? Latin? Italian? Swahili? Norwegian?), create a word that helps us create an awareness that words lead us to what we believe is appropriate action (in the same way that the word "designate" leads us to understand that words "mark out" certain things and people)? What are some of the difficulties in creating such a word or modifying an existing word? What are the potential difficulties of meaning creation for people who read or hear the new or adapted word?

FIGURE 8.2 Garfield Cartoon

Jim Davis helps us understand that we have different feelings and understandings about "gluttons" than we do about "performance artists" (Fig. 8.2). To see his cartoon character Garfield as a *glutton* is to invoke a whole series of evaluations and judgments about overeating; whereas, to see Garfield (or anyone else) as an *artist* suggests skill and laudable behavior. Recognized words in language use strongly suggest to us an appropriate response or action.

Several years ago, I arrived at my home to find the front door standing open and a substantial amount of electronic gear and family valuables missing. Calling the police, I reported a "robbery." The police, the insurance company, and the homeowner (me) all agreed that I was a victim of a "burglary." (Check a legal dictionary for the difference between a "robbery" and a "burglary.") By giving the physical world evidence this name, we all agreed to set in motion a whole series of paperwork, agreements, and purchases designed to address this event in my life. When telling this story to some friends a few days later, one friend gasped (a couple of sentences into the story): "You were robbed!!" To which my other friend replied: "No, no, no. Dann was simply selected for an urban economic redistribution program." Well, any evaluations of my friend's wit or humor aside, which was it? Was I "robbed" or a participant in an "urban economic redistribution program"? To use one set of words rather than the other is to give privilege to a certain set of assumptions about how to evaluate the event. We'll discuss later in this chapter how this giving of "privilege" to certain words helps us spot the most important words in any culture.

The cartoon in Figure 8.3 uses the terms "Antiques," "Collectibles," "Bric-a-brac," and "Garbage" to make a point about how we respond to certain things offered to us for sale.

The cartoonist quickly establishes that the title of a store both designates and gives cultural instruction as to how we might act (including possible purchase price!) toward items we might find in these various businesses. Ponder, for a few minutes, that some people will pay

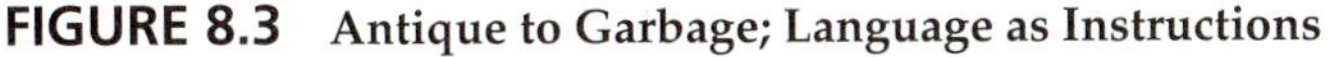
FIGURE 8.3 Antique to Garbage; Language as Instructions

hundreds of thousands of dollars for something called an "antique," but would not do so for something called "bric-a-brac" or "knick-knacks." At what point does a dresser, or car, or picture frame move from being merely "old" to being an "antique?"

While you may not have recently been in an antique shop wondering if you held in your hand a very valuable object or if it was merely bric-a-brac, you probably *have* had some interaction with someone who cared which labels you use for people or other weighty considerations. Should you call the vacation-days-season in December "Christmas," "the holiday season," "Xmas," or what? Should you call your supervisor at work "Ms.," "Mrs.," or "Miss" Arganal? Are people in wheelchairs "handicapped" or "differently abled"? Are people who hail from south of the U.S. border (from Mexico, Central America, and South America) "Latinos," "Hispanics," or what? These general social and language dilemmas have been given the general label of the problem of "politically correctness" (or is calling it a dilemma or a "problem" also pre-setting our response?).

Being "politically correct" is seen by some as being courteous, civil, and sensitive to the feelings and traditions of others. For some, however, expectations of using "politically correct" speech seem artificial, unnecessary, and oppressive to "free speech." Carol Tavris recalls the following verbal mix-up:

> During a recent dinner party, a friend of mine got himself into a charming verbal muddle. In his desire to use the encompassing "he or she" instead of the generic male "he," my friend found himself referring to the "pregnant person"—he "or she. . . ." Surely, we all agree, this was carrying equality too far![7]

Tavris, however, develops in her book how language, culture, laws, "typical" practices (e.g., in medicine), and social expectations have placed women in a dilemma (at best) and at risk of death (at worst). For instance, should women and men be treated symmetrically or asymmetrically under the law? She cites legal experts on both sides of this issue. Should laws "protect" women in ways different from men? Should laws "account for" the social, economic, or employment circumstances faced by many women? Legal definitions for terms such as "no-fault divorce," "displaced homemakers," "battered woman's syndrome," "marital sex," "property rights," "emotional harm," and "parental leave" have profound impact on court cases and people's lives as guided by those cases. In our legal system (as well as in many other forms of social, institutional life) what we call people, processes, and things is worth our thoughtful consideration.

Now let's examine a few other sobering examples of how words help to designate, instruct, and guide our actions.

Carl T. Rowan wrote:

> Leaders here [in Washington, D.C.], as in the rest of the world, are agonizing over the epidemic of terrorism that afflicts world society.
>
> We hear of plans for special anti-terrorist commando units, special FBI teams, new international agreements and other schemes for foiling the hijackers, kidnappers, bombers and others who spread fear and death across the political landscape.[8]

Sounds very much like today's headlines, yes? Rowan wrote the column in which these sentences appear in April of 1978. His point was to recognize that *our* "freedom fighter" may well be their "terrorist." And, *their* "freedom fighter" will very likely be our "terrorist":

> Those who do violence in support of causes that we like we call "freedom fighters"; those who fight and kill in disputes where we are not

Scrutinize exercise

Make a list of five "politically correct" words or phrases that "make sense" to you. Make a parallel list of five "politically correct" words that seem silly or unnecessary. Compare your two lists with someone else in your class. What similarities or differences do you find? On what basis did you decide what was "sensible" and what was "silly"?

Scrutinize exercise

If you were the head of your campus programming or activities board, and you needed to find a speaker for the spring term, would you rather invite a "freedom fighter" to address students on your campus or a "known terrorist"? What would help you make a decision in either case?

emotionally committed we call "guerrillas"; those whose causes we detest are "terrorists" and "murderers."

The events of September 11, 2001, of course, brought all of these problems and perspectives crashing to America's doorstep in ways that have clearly heightened our interest in terrorist organizations. Moreover, many have begun trying to understand those people and groups who would applaud those we perceive as terrorists. For instance, Thomas L. Friedman traveled to Pakistan and discovered that other points of view might hold for some citizens there:

> You need only spend an afternoon walking through the Storytellers' Bazaar here in Peshawar, a few miles from the Afghan border, to understand that America needs to do its business in Afghanistan—eliminate Osama bin Laden and his Taliban protectors—as quickly as possible and get out of here. This is not a neighborhood where we should linger. This is not Mr. Rogers' neighborhood.
>
> What makes me say that? I don't know, maybe it was the street vendor who asked me exactly what color Osama bin Laden T-shirt I wanted—the yellow one with his picture on it or the white one simply extolling him as the hero of the Muslim nation and vowing "Jihad Is Our Mission."[9]

We need not go to Afghanistan chasing al Qaeda to find instances of language guiding and suggesting appropriate (and necessary) action; we can find the same language dynamic as close as our homes and daily activities. The point in all cases: what we call someone or something with a name or word often gives us the clues we need to decide how to evaluate and act.

The focus we must keep is the part *language* plays in the formation of political positions and understanding. The Pakistani street vendor is operating within a language structure that makes perfect sense to him—as is the American reporter who tells us about his activities. To such language structures we now turn our attention.

LANGUAGE, STRUCTURE, POWER

Look around your reading environment right now. What do you see? Sand, desks, ocean, lamp, blue sky, computer, birds, books? If you are reading this book while on spring break at the beach, you might have a better chance of seeing sand than if you are in the library (or a dorm room) in November. In either case, take a moment to reflect on how little control you have over what you call things. You did not choose the words *sand, ocean, blue, sky, birds,* or *surfboard.* Yet you would feel very comfortable using those words to designate objects, situations, or conditions that seemed to match them. We need to recognize that we *inherit* a word-based language and we use that language—extensively—long before we become aware of the deep power that it has over our lives.

We've been discussing how individual words and phrases have power to guide our perception and actions. We need to also realize that languages are *systems* of word usage that encourage certain types of behavior. If you are reading this book as part of a class, you might feel comfortable calling yourself a "student." But where does "student" fit within the larger usage of the English language? Is being a student a good thing or a bad thing? Do we pay students huge salaries? Do students attract the attention of police officials? How do students treat their parents? Is a young student better than an old student? Can students rock and roll? Do students deserve respect? Can you depend on a student?

What would happen if we substituted the terms "pro basketball player," "American," "drug dealer," or "toddler" for "student"? Let's try.

> Is being a *pro basketball player* a good thing or a bad thing? Do we pay *pro basketball players* huge salaries? Do *pro basketball players* attract the attention of police officials? How do *pro basketball players* treat their parents? Is a young *pro basketball player* better than an old *pro basketball player?* Can *pro basketball players* rock and roll? Do *pro basketball players* deserve respect? Can you depend on a *pro basketball player?*
>
> Is being an *American* a good thing or a bad thing? Do we pay *Americans* huge salaries? Do *Americans* attract the attention of police officials? How do *Americans* treat their parents? Is a young *American* better than an old *American?* Can *Americans* rock and roll? Do *Americans* deserve respect? Can you depend on an *American?*
>
> Is being a *drug dealer* a good thing or a bad thing? Do we pay *drug dealers* huge salaries? Do *drug dealers* attract the attention of police officials? How do *drug dealers* treat their parents? Is a young *drug dealer* better than an old *drug dealer?* Can *drug dealers* rock and roll? Do *drug dealers* deserve respect? Can you depend on a *drug dealer?*
>
> Is being a *toddler* a good thing or a bad thing? Do we pay *toddlers* huge salaries? Do *toddlers* attract the attention of police officials? How do *toddlers* treat their parents? Is a young *toddler* better than an old *toddler?* Can *toddlers* rock and roll? Do *toddlers* deserve respect? Can you depend on a *toddler?*

Can you see how your understanding of life (and your place in it) is positioned within designations given by language? We have certain expectations of Americans. We have certain expectations of toddlers. We also

FIGURE 8.4 Hagar Cartoon

Reprinted with Special Permission of King Features Syndicate.

recognize that we could combine word designations (and therefore expectations): a pro basketball player who is an American. And we recognize that certain combinations would not make much sense: few of us know a toddler who is also a drug dealer. So who you are, where you are, what you are, how you are, and what you are supposed to do are all bound up in word-based systems of language over which you have little choice or control (or do you?).

As we see Hagar the Horrible and Lucky Eddie toast in the cartoon above (Fig. 8.4), we can see that Hagar isn't too sure of Lucky Eddie's understanding of "the Viking thing."

But, what *is* "the Viking thing," "the pro basketball player thing," "the toddler thing," "the American thing," "the drug dealer thing," or "the student thing"? How can Hagar be *so* certain that cuddly puppies don't go with raiding and looting?

Rhetorical scholars and others working over the past thirty years would say that Hagar can be sure that cuddly puppies don't "fit" because he is a participant in Viking ideology.

Ideology has become one of the main terms contemporary scholars have used to identify and recognize the power of language to structure entire countries, civilizations, or eras.

We were recognizing earlier the power of individual words within a language to guide individual perception and behavior. The notion of ideology takes that same idea to the level of large groups of people working together with the power of language to define and guide entire cultures.

Have you ever felt constrained, hemmed in, heavily influenced, or controlled by your culture? Or by individuals, or institutions, within the culture? If so, you probably were feeling the result of language tied to the physical means and social practices that guide individual behavior within a culture. Let me offer an ordinary, personal example.

I live in the Pacific Northwest where winters on the Western side of the Cascades can be quite wet (*quite* wet!). So, in the summer (when things dry

FIGURE 8.5
No Outlet Sign
Who controls the power of signs?

out a bit), I, like many Northwesterners, enjoy being outdoors. Summers allow me the opportunity to ride a mountain bike to campus from my home (about a 10 mile ride). One part of that ride takes me through an urban wilderness park that rises to about 800 feet.[10] My return bike commute crosses a small residential area before entering the park area. A sign at the base of a long hill entering the residential area simply states: NO OUTLET.

That sign is a lie. True, the residential street leads to a gravel road that is secured by a large tubular gate. There *is* no outlet, *if* you are driving a car (hence, partial accuracy for the sign). But, *free and complete* access is available for hikers, runners, horseback riders, or people on bikes. I mention this less to tell you about my summer commuting patterns than to describe the ideological presence and power of that road sign (NO OUTLET). That sign is a marker of a culture that promotes an ideology of vehicular, motorized, automobile culture. Now, I'm not deeply opposed to vehicular, motorized, automotive transportation; like most Americans, I frequently travel by car. The inaccuracy, however, of that one sign is an indicator of how cultural messages (including road signs) can be an indication of who holds and uses power in human cultures. Of course, most language use that points to power tensions within a culture are much larger, much more weighty, and *much* more important than whether or not you can ride a bike through a neighborhood and into a park. Let's look at a couple.

In 1992, many different cultural groups noted the 500 year anniversary of the arrival of Christopher Columbus to islands close to the North American continent. To successfully describe this event we need to use a verb. What is it that Columbus *did?* Did he discover America? Did he invade America? *Discover* or **INVADE**—these are starkly different possible ways of designating his activity. Which should we choose? If we pick "discover," we would join with most primary school teaching done in America for over 200 years. American schoolchildren have long learned that European explorers sailed to North, South, and Central America in the years between 1492 and 1673 to *discover* lands in the "new" world.

If we pick "invade," we would join with many groups in the late twentieth century that think European acquisition of land in the "new" world was an illegal, immoral, unjustified attack. Both groups, indigenous peoples to what we know as the Americas and European explorers, used language and ideology to guide their respective cultures. But due to the military and cultural successes of European peoples, American citizens tend to hear more about the "winning" group than about the vanquished group. As someone once sagely said: "Winners get to write the history books."

The language components that convinced European explorers to sail thousands of miles away from their homelands and explore (or invade) other lands is part of the English language set that Americans still use today. Government officials in Spain, Portugal, England, France, Holland (and elsewhere) funded and supported the expeditions that brought European people to the shores of the Americas. Do government officials still fund expeditions of "exploration"? If so, for what purpose? A culture, language, and ideology that supports such ventures would see value in providing funding and support for exploration. Do you see signs that our culture is currently funding exploration?

To seek or support exploration, we must be convinced that there is something to explore. Often in American culture, we have called that "something" to explore the "frontier." (A bit later in this chapter we will investigate how frontier ideology was exchanged between indigenous natives and European settlers.) At first, the entire North American continent was a "frontier" (e.g., a place unexplored and uninhabited by Europeans.) As Stephen Ambrose points out:

> When Thomas Jefferson took the Oath of Office as the third president of the United States on March 4, 1801, the nation contained 5,308,483 persons. . . . Although the boundaries stretched from the Atlantic to the Mississippi River, from the Great Lakes nearly to the Gulf of Mexico (roughly a thousand miles by a thousand miles), only a relatively small area was occupied. Two-thirds of the people lived within fifty miles of tidewater.[11]

When Jefferson sent Lewis and Clark to explore the Louisiana Purchase, many competing European interests claimed parts of North American land. The British, Russians, French, and Spanish had explored (invaded?) parts of North America, and all wanted to control it in whole, or in part. What compelled Jefferson and European leaders to explore and control the land they found? According to one scholar, Thomas Jefferson envisioned the creation of government control that would have peoples living from the Atlantic to the Pacific "speaking the same language, governed in similar forms, and by similar laws."[12]

Jefferson was on the mark in terms of recognizing that language is central to culture and governance. He clearly understood that the language inherited by English (and other) settlers was geared to an ideology that would support the way of life established and promoted in the American revolution. The ideology or worldview formed and promoted by language and used by former British citizens promoted government, commerce, culture, and habits that featured individual liberty and freely elected representatives.

But, as you know, various people and groups through the history of the United States have questioned parts (or all) of that ideology. Coxey's "Army" in 1894 questioned what type of government control ought to exist over citizen farmers. Trade unions questioned Republican and Democratic party support of the NAFTA treaty in 1993. American orator Victoria Claflin Woodhull thought culture in the United States should promote "free love" in 1870.

In other words, although the predominant language used in America from 1690 until now has been American English, the ideology or worldview promoted by that language has constantly been under discussion, dispute, and reconsideration. Below you'll find a series of academic definitions of "ideology."

DEFINITIONS OF, AND OBSERVATIONS ABOUT, IDEOLOGY

"A system of shared meaning [that] represents the world for us; it gives us a common picture of reality[.]" (Grossberg, Wartella, and Whitney 1998:21)

"The social relations of signification (knowledge and consciousness) in class societies" (O'Sullivan, Hartley, Saunders, Montgomery, and Fiske 1994:139).

". . . ideology is the means by which ruling economic classes generalize and extend their supremacy across the whole range of social activity, and naturalize it in the process, so their rule is accepted as natural and inevitable; and therefore legitimate and binding" (O'Sullivan et al 1994:141).

"Ideology cannot be deduced from economic considerations alone. It also derives from man's nature as a 'symbol-using animal.'" (Burke 1969:146)

While these definitions and observations have differing understandings and points of emphasis, all hold that language is key in the process of creating the personal, social, economic, and governmental structures that guide, promote, and constrain life. Our habits and behaviors are created and refined, rewarded and punished, changed or sustained through our use of language.

Let's briefly look at how three very different pieces of rhetorical criticism have investigated this relationship between language, cultural messages, and ideology. We will then return to a reconsideration of word-based ideology that asks what the most important words in a culture might be.

Our first example comes from an analysis of Steven Speilberg's movie *Jaws*. Frentz and Rushing argue that the movie left "an indelible mark on the American psyche[.]"[13]

Frentz and Rushing build their study on, and as a response to, the cultural criticism written by two other scholars (Frederic Jameson and Jane Caputi, respectively). (We will return to the idea of scholars building on each other's work when we discuss rhetorical theory in Chapter 9.) They believe that *Jaws* represents popular movie storytelling that was built on a well-known American myth about frontier hunters: "the relationship between class and gender in *Jaws* is best explained by situating it within the context of the American myth of the frontier hunter—specifically, the white man's adaptation of the holistic hunting rituals of the American Indian" (62).[14]

Frentz and Rushing trace how the myth of the hunter moved from use within the culture and language structure (the ideology) of Native Americans to an altered version in the use of frontier settlers. They explain that the Native American version of the hunter myth emphasized the hunter's connection with the game animals sought and with the wilderness in which the hunting took place. The Anglo-American settler version of the myth presents the wilderness as something wild (if not evil) that needs to be tamed and controlled.[15] They argue, "The hero of the [white settler] hunter myth represents the demand that the wilderness frontier submit to his knowledge and control" (64). Frentz and Rushing then suggest that Ahab and his pursuit of Moby Dick is an intermediate step in cultural storytelling from eighteenth century American frontier hunter stories to Spielberg's *Jaws* story. The prey in *Jaws* is seen by these critics as a challenge to individual males and their economic/political system: "This Leviathan [the shark in *Jaws*] is a fitting prey for the hunters, for it challenges both their manhood and their political system" (69). Frentz and Rushing trace characteristics (and cultural reflections) of the three main male characters and see their pursuit of the threatening shark as both an initiation rite (of the Brody and Hooper characters) and a cultural representation of how society should deal with threats.

So, rhetorical critics, examining and analyzing wildly popular cultural messages (like *Jaws*) seek to recognize and trace the implications of the ideological beliefs represented in the film. Even if you do not accept their entire analytic project, you can see that they have recognized important connections in cultural belief structures as represented in important messages.

It seems a great distance from a fictional New England beach town to the halls of government power in Washington, D.C. We will find, however, that ideological constructions in mass-media messages come not only from the pens of authors (Benchley) or the cameras and editing tables of directors (Spielberg), but also from those who seek to influence what we know within our home culture.

Shawn J. Parry-Giles sought to better understand the relationship between propaganda and news when he investigated internal media documents from the Truman and Eisenhower administrations. He argues that "the domestic news media willingly and unwittingly served as another branch of America's propaganda program in the 1940s and 1950s."[16]

Think about the number of decisions and influences that go into whether or not a newspaper story is researched, written, and offered to readers. Some laws control message content in media coverage. Economic considerations are present in nearly all forms of mass-media news. Audience desires and conditions have impact on news coverage. Literacy levels within a community concern those who write the news. Governments, businesses, and institutions have whole staffs that are concerned with providing reporters with "raw" material. These matters are even more pronounced now than in the era investigated by Parry-Giles in this article.

All of this is of interest to us in our tour through considerations of language and ideology because news media are primary sources of messages that either challenge or reinforce ideological constructs within a society. Parry-Giles cites Fiske as recognizing that "meanings of texts are produced through the 'intersection [of a] socially situated reader [with the] social forces structured into the text' "(148).[17] How *are* social forces (especially governmental sources) structured into texts? In other words, how do those who hold power in a culture construct (or support the construction of) messages that support their hold on power? How *are* readers socially situated or positioned? (In the same way that the "NO OUTLET" sign I wrote about earlier "positioned" me as a "driver" rather than as a "bike rider.") In other words, how do messages "position" members of the audience? The first questions, those concerning social forces, address what Parry-Giles sought to discover in his research. He argues that mainstream journalists (as a whole) were horrified at U.S. government attempts in the World War I era to manipulate or control news. But, journalists were heavily recruited during World War II to operate U.S. propaganda and war information programs. As you may be able to guess, this raises concerns for many people at the very intersection of language and ideology. The very essence of political, national ideology during a war is support for deeply held cultural values, and, for support of the fighting effort. Hence, propaganda (in a negative sense of manipulation of the news) is seen as useful and necessary. But, because the essence of the professional ideology of journalists since the early twentieth century is to provide "fair" and "objective" news reporting, you may detect a storm brewing between the two ideologies.

Indeed, Parry-Giles, while covering historical, legislative, and economic aspects of news coverage in the 50s and 60s in America, is clearly most concerned about the ease with which journalists cooperated with government sources. He argues that "the Truman administration, like its successor, constructed sophisticated strategies in order to win the news media's support for America's propaganda program. Such strategies involved the subsidization of the private media as well as the construction of veiled tactics designed to influence coverage" (152).

Scrutinize exercise

Do current presidential administrations seek to influence media news coverage? Is C.J. on *The West Wing,* as a presidential press secretary, a good character or a bad character? Why? Do any other institutions in the government attempt to influence media news coverage?

Parry-Giles's research reveals that the U.S. government used everything from assistance on passports to direct money subsidies (for overseas distribution of publications), from aid in finding housing in international countries to arranging interviews with international leaders, in order to influence international and domestic news coverage.

Parry-Giles's concern in this research addresses ideology and language at two levels. One level concerns professional ideology—in this case for journalists—and how those norms, beliefs, and values might be strained or violated when manipulated. The other level is a national or cultural ideology which seeks to inform people within a nation as to who they are, what they are doing, and whether their actions are good or bad. He believes that compelling evidence exists as to direct government efforts to influence news coverage so as to burnish the image of the United States and the presidential administrations in power. News, or information, is then seen by officials in government as important enough to influence; that influence attempt then indicates the importance of particular messages that conform with the ideology of the culture that produces it.

We have seen that ideological messages can address national image as seen in mythic figures (the hunter as quintessential American character), whether a frontiersman fighting a bear [Daniel Boone], or a sea captain fighting a whale [Captain Ahab], or a small town police chief fighting a shark [Chief Martin Brody]). Other ideological messages can address national image as influenced by government institutions seeking to engineer favorable news coverage, or can address the perceived role of a profession (journalist). (Both are addressed in the study by Parry-Giles about the Truman and Eisenhower administrations.) A third rhetorical analysis will remind us that mass-mediated, ideological messages can cover intensely personal areas of life.

Nick Trujillo's study of media coverage of a baseball star addressed over 25 years of print and electronic media coverage focused on Nolan Ryan, a pitcher. Trujillo discovered some very telling trends in the coverage of Nolan Ryan. He believes that how writers celebrate the achievements of a male sports star can in turn create rhetorical control if people in the culture accept the ideological assumptions contained in the mass-media messages. Trujillo, extending from analysis done by Connell, and by Hanke, uses the term hegemony in this study to mean cultural control via language. He is particularly interested in tactics used when gender characteristics for men are celebrated in mass-media messages. Ideology then, as represented by cultural messages designed to encourage certain male gender roles, is called "hegemonic masculinity." Trujillo cites Hanke's definition of that term: "Hegemonic masculinity refers to the social ascendancy of a particular version or model of masculinity that, operating on the terrain of 'common sense' and conventional morality, defines 'what it means to be a man.'"[18] In other words, media coverage about male sports stars implicitly tells audience members how a man ought to be a man in America.

Let's look at a couple of insights from the following analysis. Nolan Ryan has been represented as a valuable commodity with instrumental impacts on his teams. Yankee owner George Steinbrenner, quoted in *Sports Illustrated,* called Ryan "one of the most desirable quantities in baseball" (Keith, 1979, p. 34). Reporters bragged about Ryan when he signed with the Astros as the first million dollar free agent. They bragged about Ryan and his earning power in part because they represented him as a "humble, honest man who was not preoccupied with money, unlike many other athletes who have been depicted as greedy, selfish men" (297). Hence, if you read the stories celebrating Ryan after his earnings became substantial, you would learn an implicit, ideological lesson: Men who earn substantial sums of money should care more about other things.

Likewise, off the baseball field, stories of Ryan's family life were found to reaffirm gender-related family roles: "The media have reaffirmed hegemonic representations of male–female relations in the family as they have described the relationship between, and respective roles of, Nolan and Ruth Ryan. Predictably, the media chose to present Nolan as the breadwinner. . . . Additionally, the media reaffirmed the hegemony of family patriarchy by glorifying Nolan's role as actual and symbolic father. The media have emphasized Ryan's relationships with his two sons while they have deemphasized his relationship with his daughter" (297–298). Thus, according to Trujillo's analysis, if you read the stories celebrating Ryan as a family person, you would learn another implicit, ideological lesson: Men should marry, earn a worthwhile living for their family, and favor their sons in relationships between father and children.

Trujillo, then, finds that attainment coverage (say, of achieving a baseball record), general sports coverage, off-season coverage, and participation in product ads *all* find writers and producers focusing on a very narrow range of characteristics about Nolan Ryan. This would be insightful if the amount of publication and broadcast time covered was three or four years; it is all the more impressive when you realize that Trujillo's research shows that 25 years of stories and ads stay in some very predictable zones of coverage. He concludes: "Nolan Ryan represents a white, middle-aged, upper-class, banker-athlete, with working-class cowboy values, who was raised by a middle-class family in a small rural town, and who is a strong father and devoted heterosexual husband" (303).

Scrutinize exercise

Can you recall sports coverage of an athletic hero who is black, young, lower-class, with unusual values, who was raised by an upper-class family in a huge city, and who is a weak, single, lesbian? Why not? I've reversed Trujillo's description of the Nolan Ryan media stories' character in this string of characteristics. Can you think of any celebrated sports star who matches four or five of the characteristics? If you built on Trujillo's analysis for such a celebrated sports star, would you find any other kinds of hegemonic, implicit instructions on how to be a person in American culture? Why, or why not?

Trujillo's analysis represents a large body of scholarship that has actively been investigating the ideological instructions given to us by powerful media messages. Moreover, he recognizes that decades of coverage of people, institutions, or groups can have powerful built-up cumulative messages that subtly suggest the "right" path for development of personal, professional, or cultural characteristics.

We've seen how language can invoke ideological meanings at a national, professional, and personal level. Ideology and language mutually reinforce each other in all cultures. We'll now investigate key words in such a dynamic.

IDEOGRAPHS, LANGUAGE, AND PUBLIC PERSUASION

What are the 18 most important words in the English language? A decision on an answer to such an audacious question would seem to be very difficult. Yet history, experience, investigation, and perspective in the use of language in American culture suggests that an answer is not that far away.

One of the clues you might use in making a decision on such a word would be: is it used as a "pivot" word to settle disputes? Any word that could act to settle arguments might prove a very valuable language tool. If the word, in addition, could hold many of the cherished values in a given culture, it would be more valuable yet.

One scholar with a deep interest in language and ideology recognized that certain words seemed to be used in public, political disputes with unnerving frequency. Michael Calvin McGee recognized that competing sides in a public debate, leaders seeking a following, or politicians seeking to justify an action would all use a very limited set of value terms. He named such terms *ideographs*.[19] He defined an **ideograph** as "an ordinary language term found in political discourse. It is a high-order abstraction representing collective commitment to a particular but equivocal and ill-defined normative goal" (15).

Let's see if we can walk through one ideograph that McGee used in his first essay naming this essential language device: *Liberty.*

<Liberty>[20] is but seven English letters (beilrty), but hearing the word "liberty" doesn't set your ear on edge like the word "egalitarian" might; hence, it is an "ordinary language term." (Chevron marks are used by some scholars to indicate use of an ideograph.) While we might say "I'm not at liberty to discuss that right now," we'd be much more likely to find <liberty> in a chatroom discussion about public policy on Web censorship at the library; hence, it is regularly "found in political discourse." It is a "high-order" abstraction, in that we've probably never seen a "liberty" while walking in the mall. It is not a tangible thing, but rather a term we use to try to express certain conditions in life experience. It "represents a collective commitment," in that most Americans would claim to be "for" it rather than "against" it. But, do we have "it"? (Or, enough of it?) We must recognize that often it is a goal (perhaps especially for teens), that might be in dispute with whomever, or whatever, is preventing or withholding <liberty> from a person or a group. McGee sees this as "a particular but equivocal and ill-defined normative goal." That is, not everyone will see the use, necessity, or appropriate application of <liberty> in exactly the same way. Chances are very strong that in the next two years on your campus some person or group will claim that they have too little (or someone else too much) <liberty>. Yet, we cannot buy two liters of <liberty> (or "liberty") at the store. Yet, millions of dollars will be spent to send troops, weapons, and material halfway around the world to defend <liberty>. Note that we would not do the same for "enjoyment," even though we probably deeply relish all the moments of "enjoyment" we can get.

The number, use, and visibility of ideographs within American culture (or any other) changes from time to time as various issues and concerns seem to seize our attention.

Over the years, various scholars have pursued the study of ideographs from French-Canadian politics to timber industry disputes, from political bosses fraud to midwife legislation.[21] As these case studies in public argument add up, we gain a much clearer picture of the ways in which ideographs are used to promote or defend political decisions.

In popular news coverage you can usually discover ideographs used by opposing sides in disputes before the U.S. Supreme Court. Hence, <privacy> will be argued against the <right to know>, or <freedom> will be set against <safety>, or <freedom of expression> will be argued against <family values>. In each case the core, or pivot point, of the public argument comes down to one special word or phrase that seems to capture our most deeply held values.

Studies of ideographs will continue to be a strong part of the ongoing investigation of how language and ideology interact within human cultures.

In this chapter we have opened the door to important concepts that inform and guide our use of language in human culture. We started by discovering that any selected word within a language can serve to guide our perception (Selection! Deflection! Reflection!). Moreover, words in language give us clues about expected appropriate behavior (is he a preacher, or a riverboat gambler?). When language is used for hundreds of years, certain power relationships and preferred characters become woven into the language. People and groups then have to accept, reject, or try to modify resulting cultural ideology. Finally, ideographs, are selected terms that become the focal point of public disputes.

Let's proceed to the Chapter 8 workshop where we can work to better understand how language and ideology have power in your experience. Below you will find a sample journal article by Cloud. Use the article to prepare for the workshop. After the workshop we'll begin Chapter 9 to learn the power of rhetorical theory.

Hegemony or Concordance? The Rhetoric of Tokenism in "Oprah" Winfrey's Rags-to-Riches Biography

Dana L. Cloud

□—*This article examines television and print biographies of television talk show host and producer Oprah Winfrey. Conventional biographical narratives construct a token "Oprah" persona whose life story resonates with and reinforces the ideology of the American Dream, implying the accessibility of this dream to black Americans despite the structural economic and political barriers posed in a racist society to achievement and survival. The article develops theories of tokenism, biography, autobiography, and hegemony to analyze both racial and gendered dimensions of tokenist biography. It describes tokenism as a rhetorical mechanism of liberal hegemony with regard to race and class. The essay challenges recent redefinitions of hegemony as happy "concordance" and suggests that critics cannot assume that black stars and texts automatically represent difference and resistance in popular culture.*

Source: *Critical Studies in Mass Communication* 13 (1996), 115–137.

Dana L. Cloud is Assistant Professor of Speech Communication at the University of Texas, Austin. She thanks Lauren Rabinovitz at the University of Iowa, Keith Hutchinson, and several anonymous reviewers whose helpful remarks guided revision of this article.

> A black person has to ask herself, "If Oprah Winfrey can make it, what does it say about me?" They no longer have any excuse.
>
> —Oprah Winfrey, quoted in Mair (1994, p. 183)

> The journey of Oprah Gail Winfrey from Hattie Mae's pig farm in Mississippi to the pinnacle of wealth, power, and success in American television is a journey we must all admire. . . . She is the ultimate American success story. That a tiny, illegitimate black girl from dirt-poor Mississippi can transform herself into the richest and most powerful black woman in the world is a triumph of the human spirit and the American dream.
>
> (Mair 1994, p. 349)

The story of individual triumph over humble beginnings is a staple of a culture steeped in Horatio Alger mythology, in the service of an inegalitarian economic order buttressed by an ideology of individual achievement and responsibility. As Weiss (1996) summarizes in his book on the Horatio Alger myth,

The idea that ours is an open society, where birth, family, and class do not significantly circumscribe individual possibilities, has a strong hold on the popular imagination. The belief that all men, in accordance with certain rules, but exclusively by their own efforts, can make of their lives what they will has been widely popularized for well over a century. (p. 3)

Rooted in the Protestant ethic and popularized in novels and self-help literature, the success myth is continually belied by the realities of class, race, and gender stratification in capitalist society.

Recent communication scholarship on Bill Cosby and the *Cosby Show* has suggested that popular discourse about black family life often deploys assumptions of liberalism that interpret poverty and hardship as individual or family failures, and success exclusively as individual triumph (Gray, 1989; Jhally and Lewis, 1992). This work argues that *Cosby* perpetuates self-blame among African-Americans for failure and complacency in the dominant culture regarding the fight against racism. Even when black people produce their own images, as Cosby and Oprah Winfrey do, secondary texts, including the news, star discourse, and biographical profiles work to frame those images and build the personae of black stars in hegemonic ways that escape the stars' control.

McMullen and Solomon (1994) make a similar argument about Steven Spielberg's appropriation and adaptation of Alice Walker's novel *The Color Purple*. They argue that the film turned the book, which was a powerful account of racism, sexism, and poverty from the vantage of its protagonist Celie, into

> the *melodramatic* narrative of an individual who successfully triumphs over interpersonal and economic adversity. Like other melodramas, the heroine's success results not only in personal glory, but also in the restoration and reaffirmation of the social order. (p. 163)

This strategy of appropriation and adaptation marks the proliferation of popular biographies of Oprah Winfrey. This article examines these narratives in order to understand how they construct an "Oprah" persona whose life story as it is appropriated in popular biographies resonates with and reinforces the ideology of the American Dream, implying the accessibility of this dream to black Americans despite the structural economic and political obstacles to achievement and survival posed in a racist society. I do not mean to indict Oprah Winfrey herself, but rather challenge her persona as it is constructed and performed both with and without her direct participation. In referring to "Oprah," a first name bracketed by quotation marks, rather than to Oprah Winfrey the "real" person, I mean to aim my criticisms at the way in which popular culture appropriates and uses the images and stories of black Americans. Popular biographers of Winfrey almost exclusively use only her first name, in the rhetorical construction of a persona who is not necessarily coterminous with the person. McMullen and Solomon (1994) write that popularizations function as "terministic screens" or filters that foreground some features of reality and obscure others, and that produce conventional, ideological narratives out of complex experience.

This article argues that the content, pervasiveness, and popularity of the "Oprah" narratives warrant the recognition of a "terministic screen" or genre of discourse called tokenist biography, defined as biographical narratives that authorize a person from a marginalized or oppressed group to speak as a culture hero *on the condition* that the person's life story be framed in liberal-capitalist terms. Like Clarence Thomas during his Supreme Court confirmation hearings (see Morrison, 1992), "Oprah" is constructed in the biographical narratives that frame her rise to stardom in the late 1980s as a black person who, refusing identification with the politics of black liberation, "proves" that the American Dream is possible for all black Americans.

The article theorizes the concepts of hegemony, tokenism, star personae, and biographical narrative, arguing against Condit's (1994) reframing of hegemony as an acceptable cultural negotiation or compromise. Then I summarize the generic Oprah Winfrey biography, drawing out its constituent elements, and describe how this narrative represents a rhetoric of tokenism. Third, the essay analyzes specific instances of biographical tribute to Oprah Winfrey, focusing on a televised video biography of Oprah aired in 1990. Finally, I challenge the assumption of identity politics that representatives of oppressed groups automatically speak in an authentic oppositional voice.

Although texts like the television tribute to Oprah Winfrey invoke histories of race- and gender-based oppression, they recuperate and neutralize these histories in the liberal discourse of individual success. This bootstraps philosophy obscures the collective nature of oppression and the need for collective social action, exemplified in the sit-ins, marches, demonstrations, strikes, and other collective challenges of the civil rights movement, to remedy social injustice. Often, such discourse takes the form of biographical narratives glorifying a person for overcoming hardship. My examination of television and magazine biographies of "Oprah" reveals the hegemonic effect of elements of these narratives. This essay explores how the rags-to-riches narrative of much popular biography serves the hegemony of liberal individualism in U.S. popular and political culture.

LIBERAL HEGEMONY: CONCORDANCE OR CONTAINMENT?

By hegemony, I refer to the process by which a social order remains stable by generating consent to its parameters through the production and distribution of ideological texts that define social reality for the majority of the people. Condit (1994) has challenged this notion of hegemony, arguing that critics should take "hegemony" to mean "concordance," or the emergence of tenable compromise out of multicultural conflict, "the best that can be negotiated under the given conditions" (p. 210). Condit accuses feminist and Marxist critics of overestimating the forces of domination and oversimplifying the process of cultural negotiation. Even so, I maintain that an understanding of hegemony as concordance is an appropriate critical model only if one is satisfied with the compromises allowed within and by the "given conditions." Indeed, an analysis of "Oprah" biographies as an example of a kind of cultural compromise will test Condit's assumptions.

Condit's reworking of Gramsci's (1971/1936) theory depends upon her argument that economic relations of contemporary Western society are no longer based on prominent class divisions; rather, she suggests, contemporary U.S. society runs on a "mixed economy" that provides an adequate safety net for the poor and a large measure of material equality. For this reason, her purpose is to give the term "hegemony"—previously associated with a negative critique of a dominant and dominating culture—a more positive valence with the term "concordance." However, Condit's assumption that domination and division are longer primary features of contemporary Western society is fundamentally mistaken. While affluent nations, in times of economic growth, do provide jobs and some measure of security to wage laborers (the majority of the population), that security by no means negates the fundamental class relations of the society. In other words, the relative prosperity of some sectors of the working class does not mean that those workers are "amalgamated with capitalists" (Condit, 1994, p. 208) in their long-term interests. The erosion of prosperity during the protracted periods of economic recession in the world economy over the last two decades makes class divisions easier to see.

While Condit points out that the United States is a society of relative affluence, she fails to note that fully one-third of black Americans (and nearly half of all black children; see Edmonds & Udansky, 1994) live in poverty. Further, real wages overall in the United States have declined twenty percent in the past two decades. An October, 1994, census report showed that from 1989 to 1993, the typical American household lost $2,344 in annual income, a decline of seven percent. Further, the number of Americans living in poverty was up sharply in 1994 from 1989. The *New York Times* reported,

> While average per capita income was up, by 1.8 percent, most of the benefits flowed to the wealthiest Americans. The Census report showed record levels of inequality, with the top fifth of American households earning 48.2 percent of the nation's income, while the bottom fifth earned just 3.6 percent. (DeParle, 1994, p. A16)

This report confirmed what Bartlett and Steele (1992) and Phillips (1990) have noted, namely that class divisions in the United States have become more, not less, pronounced in recent decades, as CEO incomes average more than 150 times the average worker's salary, and the minimum wage is, in real terms, worth less than it was in the 1930s. And because of ongoing racism and sexism, black Americans and women are overrepresented among the working poor. Clearly, the United States (indeed, the world) is still a society divided not only by class but also by race and gender.

In this context, classical hegemony theory usefully calls attention to the limits of compromises within the available conditions. It is crucial to understand how a rhetorically crafted concordance presents the facade of democratic compromise while obscuring the conservative effects of such a compromise. Gramsci (1971/1936) and later writers on hegemony (see Gitlin, 1980; Hall, 1986a; Lears, 1985; Murphy, 1992; Williams, 1973) understood that capitalist societies produce relations of power not only in structures of commodity production and exchange, but also through structures of ideas, or ideologies, that become the taken-for-granted common sense of the society. Cultural texts win the adherence of the mass audience to "the values, norms, perceptions, beliefs, sentiments, and prejudices that support and define the existing distribution of goods, the institutions that decide how this distribution occurs, and the permissible range of disagreement about those processes" (Lears, 1985, p. 569).

However, because social systems and their prevailing ideological justifications (capitalism and liberalism in the United States) are always contested, social stability depends on the ability of the ideology to absorb and re-frame challenges (see also Hall, 1986a). For this reason, contradiction, rupture, and multivocality are taken by the hegemony theorist not as signs that a democratic compromise has been achieved, but that a few token voices are allowed to speak within the "permissible range of disagreement." This critical emphasis is important if we are to guard against overplaying small moments of contradiction, rupture, or textual play in a social system and ideological frame that has been relatively effective at containing the impact of those moments. The rhetoric of tokenism, as it will be defined below, participates in the hegemony of liberal capitalism in so far as it acknowledges black voices, but redefines oppression as personal suffering and success as individual accomplishment.

This individualism is central to liberalism, the ideological counterpart to modern capitalist economics. As Hall (1986b) explains, liberalism varies between conservative, "laissez-faire" libertarianism (Reaganism, Thatcherism) and a social-democratic liberalism that favors state moderation of the effects of capitalism and tempers radical individualism with notions of social justice, as in the New Deal. Regardless of its variations, however, liberalism's core is its notion of the autonomous individual who is ostensibly free from structural or economic barriers to fortune. In his essay "A Liberal Legacy: Blacks Blaming Themselves for Economic Failures," Wayne Parent defines liberalism as the belief in America as a land of abundant opportunity and resources for everyone, and "a common belief in the propriety of individual labors producing individual rewards" (1985, pp. 3–4). Parent adds, "Blacks have been the most glaring exception to the uniquely American experience" (p. 5). An analysis of the Oprah Winfrey biography reveals how liberal individualism requires the "rags-to-riches" story as "proof" that the dream of individual achievement against all odds is real. This dream, in turn, justifies continuing inattention to structural factors, like race, gender, and class, that pose barriers to the dream for some Americans.

BIOGRAPHY, AUTOBIOGRAPHY, AND STAR DISCOURSE

One way in which biographical and autobiographical narratives encode the American Dream is through the invention of the classical liberal self who is the hero of the story, which is presented as "true." For example, Mair (1994) gives his biography of "Oprah" the title *Oprah Winfrey: The Real Story*, as if editing, selection of narratives, framing, chapter organization, and so forth were not rhetorical choices on the part of the biographer. As a realist form of narrative, biography naturalizes its rhetorical strategies and ideological motives (Nadel, 1984, p. 6). Recent scholarship on autobiographical writing and performance has suggested that even (self-authored) autobiographies construct selves and narrate lives as "critical fictions" (Smith, 1987, p. 6) rather than as expositions of "authentic" life experience. Smith (1987) writes that in autobiography, "the narrative 'I' becomes a fictive persona" (p. 46). Oprah Winfrey's autobiography, originally due out from Knopf in 1993, has been put on hold. However, it follows that what is true of self-constructs in autobiography—that they *are* constructs—is even more evident in the practice of biography, which reveals more about cultural ideologies than about its purported objects, the personalities of popular heroes.

Although "Oprah" herself participates in the construction of her persona (in interviews and so forth), the invention of "Oprah" has assumed dimensions beyond "Oprah's"—or any single agent's—direct control. Because race, gender, and other dimensions of identity are products of cultural definition rather than essential characteristics of a person, popular culture heroes, more than most people, "speak the culture" and are not the sole agents in the creation of their selves and social roles. Hall (1981) writes, "We have to 'speak through' the ideologies which are active in our society and which provide us a means of 'making sense' of social relations and our place in them" (p. 32). So even when "Oprah" is speaking on her show or to reporters, her persona has a cultural life of its own.

More to the point is how biographers appropriate the lives of celebrities to create a public persona that works within "the permissible range of disagreement" of liberal society. Richard Dyer's (1986) study of how "stars function as media texts" (p. ix) notes that "stars are involved in making themselves into commodities. . . . They do not produce themselves alone" (p. 5). Dyer goes on to describe how "the star him/herself as well as make-up artists, hairdressers, . . . body-building coaches, . . . publicists" and others perform the labor of transforming the raw material of a person into a star—a publicly held icon of fame and fortune (p. 6). Dyer argues that because individualism is at the heart of both the liberal ideology and the making of a star, "protest about the lack of control over the outcome of one's labor can remain within the logic of individualism" (p. 7). "Oprah" herself provides an example of this containment mechanism.

In a recent *People* profile (Dale, Fisher, & McFarland, 1994), "Oprah" expresses frustration with and resistance to audience expectations regarding her weight, her engagement to Stedman Graham, or her show's topics and style. It is clear from her statements that she, like the stars in Dyer's study, resents her lack of control over her image and her lack of privacy: "You reach the point where you're not willing to accept the bull that you used to . . . . I don't feel the pressure now to make sure people like me" (quoted in Dale, Fisher, & McFarland, 1994, p. 87). Most recent profiles of "Oprah" emphasize her new "to-hell-with-what-the-world-thinks attitude" (Kanner, 1994). The cancellation of her autobiography, a last-minute decision, is hailed as a demonstration of "Oprah" 's independent will (see Randolph, 1993). Dyer (1986) explains that the tension between the sometimes incongruent private and public "selves" of a celebrity can generate moments of reflexivity about the production of a public persona. In other words, "Oprah" 's self-authorizing in an autobiography may have been at odds with public expectations about her persona and role. But resistance to expectations in the form of the assertion of individual autonomy (rather than criticizing the ideological uses to which one's life has been put) is acceptable within the frame of a larger, entrepreneurial ethos.

The Oprah Biography

Dyer's point that stars do not make themselves alone provides insight into the production of discourses about Oprah Winfrey. Biographical profiles framing "Oprah" as liberal hero have proliferated and continue to appear in a wide range of popular outlets, from *Reader's Digest* (Culhane, 1989) and *People* (Dale, Fisher, & McFarland, 1994; Levitt, Fisher, & Mills, 1993; Rosen & Fisher, 1994; Richman, 1987) to *Ebony* (Randolph, 1993; Whitaker, 1987), *Essence* (Edwards, 1986; Noel, 1985; Taylor, 1987), *Redbook* (Rogers, 1993), *Cosmopolitan* (Cameron, 1989), *Ladies Home Journal* (Brashler, 1991; Gerosa, 1994; Gross, 1988; Kanner, 1994), *Good Housekeeping* (Anderson, 1986; Ebert, 1991), *Time* (Zoglin, 1986 & 1988), *Ms.* (Angelou, 1989; Barthel, 1986; Gillespie, 1988), and *Working Woman* (Goodman, 1991; Noglows, 1994).[1] In addition, there have been at least four popular book-length "Oprah" biographies (Bly, 1993; King, 1987; Mair, 1994; Waldron, 1987) and a television tribute (*America's All Star Tribute,* 1990) to Oprah Winfrey. The book-length biographies, all "unauthorized" by Winfrey, routinely appear on national bestseller lists. Bly (1993), for example, sold more than one million copies in its first year, and was one of only six mass-marketed non-fiction books to become a best-seller in that year, according to *Publisher's Weekly* (McEvoy, 1994, p. 36). Bly's "Oprah" biography also made the mass market best-seller lists in 1994 (Simson, 1994 & 1995).

Despite the cultural and political range of the periodicals represented (*Reader's Digest* to *Ms.*), the "Oprah" biography is generic. Without exception, these narratives, reaching audiences of millions in major popular periodicals, deal exhaustively with "Oprah" 's struggle to control her eating and her weight, her shopping sprees and exotic vacations, her on-and-off engagement to Stedman Graham, her ongoing confrontation with memories of childhood sexual abuse, and her subsequent campaign to educate her audiences about child sexual abuse.

But most consistently (with the exception of Harrison, 1989, discussed below), the narratives of "Oprah" 's life begin with stories of her humble and difficult childhood, which included episodes of physical and sexual abuse as well as poverty and racism, trace her life through her college years during which she rejected the claims and politics of the civil rights movement, and celebrate her rise to fame and her philanthropic spirit during her film and television career.

In *Redbook,* Rogers (1993) proclaims,

> Oprah Winfrey's life is a modern-day Horatio Alger story of a poor, illegitimate black girl who went from rags to incredible riches while challenging all the rules. (p. 94)

Similarly, the flyleaf to Robert Waldron's best-selling biography of "Oprah" (1987) reads,

> Here's the COMPLETE story of the life of the incredible Oprah Winfrey . . . a woman who beat the traumas of a downtrodden childhood and the racial barriers put up by society—a woman who has gone on to become a gifted and acclaimed actress, and a TV personality whose bonds of trust and warmth with her guests and her audience have made her one of the nation's most beloved personalities.

In addition to narrating Oprah Winfrey's life as an incredible individual triumph over adversity, another generic convention of "Oprah" biographies is an emphasis on "Oprah" 's refusal to participate in the civil rights movement. Waldron quotes "Oprah" on her college years:

> "Everybody was angry for four years. . . . Whenever there was any conversation on race, I was on the other side, maybe because I never felt the kind of repression other black people are exposed to." (quoted in Waldron, 1987, p. 63)

Likewise, Mair (1994) notes that

> When she was in college, she worked in broadcasting during the burgeoning civil rights movement and didn't have either time or sympathy for black militants on campus. To Oprah this was an enormous waste of time and it still is. *She think you have to make it on your own and be answerable for your own success or failure.* (p. 174, emphasis added)

The mythos of the self-made person, in concert with the rejection of structural critique of racism and sexism, resonates throughout all of the biographies. "Oprah" 's refusal of civil rights agitation and repeated assertion that she was not oppressed contradict other stories she has told countless reporters about growing up with cockroaches for pets, living with the shame of a mother who cleaned the houses of her white schoolmates, and so on. Paradoxically, Winfrey's sister, Patricia Lee, denies "Oprah" 's tales of hardship, claiming a difficult but not desperately poor childhood. Why might "Oprah" invent herself—and be invented by her biographers—in terms of a childhood of oppression and suffering? Perhaps a starker contrast between past and present makes for a compelling narrative documentation of the rise from penury to profit.

The contrast between past and present, and the contradiction between oppression and triumph, is a central tension of tokenist biography, which must pry into and recognize oppression while at the same time disclaiming its salience with regard to an individual's success or failure. The motion in the narratives is always from a linguistic emphasis on "Oprah" 's difference and her collective group identification, to individualistic themes of self-determination and success: Oprah goes from being a self-described "little nappyhaired colored girl" (quoted in Bly, 1994, p. 376) to "the world's highest paid entertainer" (Bly, p. 376) unmarked by race or gender difference in the generic narrative.

Tokenism and Liberal Hegemony

The rhetoric of tokenism is one strategy by which texts authorize people whose difference (along the axes of race, class, gender, sexual orientation, or other category) if politicized and collectively articulated might pose a threat to a dominant order in which some groups are kept subordinate to others. A token is the cultural construction of a successful persona who metonymically represents a larger cultural grouping. Tokens, as the word implies, are a medium of exchange, through which group identity, politics, and resistance are traded for economic and cultural capital within popular cultural spaces. Tokenism glorifies the exception in order to obscure the rules of the game of success in capitalist society.

But tokenism is not one-sided. For someone to be constructed as a token, she or he must by definition have overcome the oppression resulting from membership in a subordinate group. For this reason, texts that make tokens out of figures like Bill Cosby or Oprah Winfrey always acknowledge the dire straits from which they rose. In the sociological literature on organizations, tokens are women and/or racial minorities, recruited in small numbers, who are "hired, admitted, or appointed to a group *because* of their differences from other members, perhaps to serve as 'proof' that the group does not discriminate against such members" (Zimmer, 1988, p. 65) when in fact discrimination remains ongoing and systematic (see Pettigrew & Martin, 1987; Yoder, 1991 & 1994). Laws (1975) provides a definition of tokenism with particular bearing on my argument:

> Tokenism is likely to be found wherever a dominant group is under pressure to share privilege, power, or other desirable commodities with a group which is excluded. Tokenism is the means by which the dominant group advertises a promise of mobility between the dominant and excluded classes. By definition, however, tokenism involves mobility which is severely restricted in quantity, and the quality of mobility is severely restricted as well. . . . The Token is a member of an underrepresented group, who is operating on the turf of the dominant group, under license from it. The institution of tokenism has advantages both for the dominant group and for the individual who is chosen to serve as Token. These advantages obtain, however, only when the defining constraints are respected: the flow of outsiders into the dominant group must be restricted numerically, and they must not change the system they enter. (pp. 51–52)

This passage highlights the rhetorical processes by which tokenism operates. According to Laws, tokenism "advertises a promise of mobility" that pays lip service to multiculturalism and difference, and to opportunity for previously excluded groups. But that promise, a concordance between the token and the group licensing or authorizing the token, serves to obscure the limits of mobility. Laws also notes that one condition regulating the participation of tokens in an organization or culture is that they be exceptional, and that their exceptionalism "bolsters the premises of meritocracy and individualism" (p. 57).

Of course, to describe tokenism as a rhetorical and ideological process is not by any means to underestimate the real talent and effort required on the part of women and minorities in racist, sexist society in order to attain positions of relative power and prominence. Nor do I mean that persons filling token positions are present only by virtue of their race or gender; indeed, in my experience representatives of oppressed groups often must be more qualified and hardworking than members of dominant groups in the same positions. My point is simply that once someone has struggled through the barriers of discrimination to achieve power or prominence, her persona is appropriated by the dominant ideology of liberalism and inscribed in public texts in such a way as to perpetuate individualist myths and lessons necessary to liberalism and capitalism.

Laws' analysis also suggests a connection between tokenism and hegemony: Tokenism is the calculated, negotiated response of a "dominant group under pressure to share privilege," just as hegemony refers to the attempts of the dominant culture to incorporate challenges without having to change substantially itself. Laws' essay, like most of the research on tokenism, refers to this process as it occurs in corporate organizations. But this literature sheds some light on how a culture hero can become a token not in an organization but in the culture at large. In popular culture, therefore, a token can be defined as a persona who is constructed from the character and life of a member of a subordinated group, and then celebrated, authorized to speak as proof that the society at large does not discriminate against members of that group. Narratives about the culture token "advertise a promise of mobility" by emphasizing the exceptional qualities of the token in a rhetorical justification of liberal meritocracy. In this way, a cultural persona is created and authorized to testify on behalf of the dominant culture.

TRIBUTE AND BIOGRAPHY AS TOKEN MACHINES

Biographical narratives of token personae acknowledge the subordinate positions of the oppressed, giving members of a subordinate group opportunities to identify with the hero of the story. The narratives dramatize extreme suffering and dejection, situations with which oppressed audiences can easily identify. For example, Waldron (1987) describes the "terrible obstacles" (p. 30) facing "Oprah" 's mother, a single black parent on welfare. But the texts always re-frame suffering in individualist terms, chronicling individual faith, work, and determination to make it through hard times to wild success. Again, Waldron (1986) writes, "Oprah believes a more positive approach is to accept the responsibility not for what happened but for *overcoming* what happened" (p. 36). Ironically the texts work by affirming oppression, then neutralizing that affirmation in an individualistic rhetoric. For example, Nellie Bly (1993) includes the following among the "six keys to Oprah's success" (p. 310): persistence, self-discipline, and "faith in yourself."

The motion from awareness of structural barriers, on the one hand, to exhortation toward individual transcendence of those obstacles, on the other, is a key strategy of the texts constituting "Oprah" Winfrey as a liberal hero. In 1990, Oprah Winfrey was the third recipient (after Bob Hope and Elizabeth Taylor) of the "America's Hope" award, honoring "outstanding individuals who exemplify the spirit of America" (*TV Guide,* 1990, p. 216). The video of the *America's All Star Tribute* ceremony (1990) is one example that reveals several aspects of the rhetoric of tokenism: unquestioned faith in the American Dream and its accessibility to all people, the belief in a universal human nature, celebration of philanthropy as an appropriate means of social change (in contradistinction to political activism), and above all the exhortation to transcend racial or cultural conflict. The tribute spectacle is divided into segments of "Oprah" biography, speeches applauding "Oprah" 's success and contributions to American society, and comic and musical performances. On the face of it, these segments are performed by an odd assortment of public figures: Sinbad and Lily Tomlin, Bob Hope and Whoopi Goldberg, Roseanne Barr and the voices of Calvary Choir, among others.

On this night, "Oprah" provides a shining example of someone who made it. Her gown, of black satin and sequins, glitters like a thousand points of light as she mugs for the camera and takes her seat. This image of "Oprah" in the frame of her box seat is a significant one, because she is the object of these proceedings, framed by an allstar gala that defines her and her role in popular culture as it celebrates her. She is a cultural persona constructed by this text, a self-conscious curtsey to the camera indicating that she does not feel quite "herself" here. As Dyer (1986) notes, the tension between public image and private self is a site of constant negotiation for the star, regardless of the extent to which the star has participated in the construction of her public image. In the tribute, "Oprah" must witness with (real or feigned) pleasure the appropriations of her life story, as it is told by personages ranging the gamut from M.C. Hammer to then-First Lady Barbara Bush.

Here she is defined as an American hero, someone in charge of her life and her discourse. But even as these definitions take shape, "Oprah" becomes (as she does in all of the discourse surrounding her in the popular media) part of the larger story of liberal individualism in capitalist society. The authorization of "Oprah" also occurs through the gendering of her persona with regard to children, represented by the child stars featured in the tribute, Fred Savage and Neil Patrick Harris. The tribute program explores the theme "Help Our Children" in a song by this title performed by M.C. Hammer, and in its continual emphasis on "Oprah" 's philanthropic projects such as literacy campaigns and big-sister programs. Here "Oprah" is constituted as mother-figure to the children of the world, and more specifically as the mammy, benevolent black guardian of white children everywhere (and on her talk show, of the women in her audience).

This racist stereotype has its roots in slavery, when demeaning images of slaves happy to serve white people served to justify the practice of slavery (see Riggs, 1986; 1991). In popular culture, Hattie McDaniel performed the role of mammy in films of the 1930s. Film scholar Donald Bogle describes the mammy as "big, fat, and cantankerous," and "firmly wedged into the dominant white culture" (Bogle, 1989, p. 9). Bogle explains that the mammy image "of the jolly black cook was completely manufactured and presented for mass consumption" (p. 63). The function of the mammy, like all of the "servant-figures" popular in racist culture since slavery, is to provide an unthreatening, subservient fantasy role for blacks to fill in American popular culture (see Cloud, 1992; Hall, 1981). So "Oprah" is authorized to speak only if first, her life story is told as an allegory of the American Dream, and second, she is sufficiently feminine in the mammy mold, giving to society in traditionally feminine ways to children and adults regardless of race.

"Oprah" 's battle with her weight and the obsessive reporting in the tabloid press of her eating habits, exercise regimens, and clothes size are related to the mammy image, which is traditionally fat; Louise Beavers had to struggle to *gain* weight to play the mammy in the 1934 film *Imitation of Life*. In this light, "Oprah" 's weight loss regimens might be read as a partial, though atomized and limited, refusal of the mammy role. The slimmer "Oprah" body better fits the needs of the liberal entrepreneurial ideology. As Susan Bordo (1993) argues, the "hard bodies" sought by men and women in 1980s American culture represent mastery and control in the economic and political realm. "The ability of the (working-class) heroine and hero to pare, prune, tighten, and master the body operates as a clear symbol of successful upward aspiration, of the penetrability of class boundaries to those who have 'the right stuff' " (Bordo, 1993, p. 195). In this light it is possible to read "Oprah" 's current grueling daily workout as an attempt to emulate and embody entrepreneurial success: "She says she is in the process of becoming an all-new Oprah" (Reynolds, 1993, p. 86), with a lean political show to match her remade body (see also Gerosa, 1994; Rosen & Fisher, 1994).

The structure of the video tribute to Oprah Winfrey portrays "Oprah" as the success-object of white adoration. The program features white stars, both child and adult, whose performances frame the black performers as if to embrace them, claiming the token successes for the dominant culture and the ideology of liberalism. But first the program, like the print biographies, must acknowledge oppression based on race and gender. This acknowledgment happens in the segment narrated by film and television actress Whoopi Goldberg. In a series of racial jokes, Goldberg articulates her awareness that she and "Oprah" share in common an experience that excludes the majority of the audience. Explaining that the Palm Springs auditorium was difficult to find, she jokes, "I'm not the first black Jew to wander in the desert. Moses made it, and here I am." Later she refers to "Oprah" as a "sister," mocking the white audience for paying $500 a head to participate in the glorification of a black woman. But the politically charged language of difference and mutual empowerment is immediately recovered in her introduction to the generic "Oprah" biography. Goldberg says, "You can win the race no matter how far behind you start out." With the emphasis placed on "Oprah" 's individual ability to come from behind (and implicitly, Goldberg's own ability to do the same), the possibility of a structural critique of American racism is undermined.

Goldberg's remarks introduce a video version of the same narrative of "Oprah" 's life that one finds everywhere: the hard childhood under her grandmother's iron rule, the early and repeated sexual abuse at the hands of various male relatives, abject poverty and adolescent rebellion, and her miraculous turnaround under the tutelage of her father (in a gesture toward the ideological significance of black fatherhood in the popular imagination). Finally we see images of "Oprah" 's current success, the history of her broadcast career, her ratings triumph over Phil Donahue during the 1986 fall television season, and her assertion that it can only get better. The segment ends on an interesting reflexive note. Looking up at "Oprah" 's box, Whoopi Goldberg says, "If we didn't have an Oprah Winfrey, we'd have to invent one." Is Goldberg calling our attention to the process of invention at hand? For the popular culture *has* invented an "Oprah" persona whose biography undermines a critique of racism, sexism, and class exploitation. In the words of a *New York Times Magazine* article, "Her audiences are co-creators of the self and the persona she crafts. . . . Here she is, an icon, speaking" (Harrison, 1989, p. 28).

"Oprah" 's iconic status allows both Whoopi Goldberg and Barbara Bush, at extremes of any cultural or political spectrum, to claim "Oprah" as a friend in this text. On a theory of hegemony as concordance, one might applaud the construction of an "Oprah" who can bring together liberal and conservative, black and white, in liberal harmony. However, attending to what is obscured or dismissed in Bush's narrative reveals a darker side to the concordance that is established. In his introduction to Barbara Bush's speech, Fred Savage emphasizes "Oprah" 's triumph over an "unhappy" (notably, not an "oppressed") childhood and her contributions to generic "children," unmarked by race or gender. Bush reinforces Savage's emphases, writing "Oprah" into the Bush administration's "thousand points of light" rhetoric, a political philosophy that places the burden of change and the blame for failure squarely on the shoulders of individuals. Bush says,

> Tonight we honor the third recipient of America's Hope Award, given each year to an individual who exemplifies the spirit of America through their words, actions, and deeds. You've made a superb choice in Oprah Winfrey. She overcame her own personal adversity through education, inner strength, and faith. Today she shares that success in so many ways, giving millions of dollars and hundreds of hours to the cause of literacy, to historically black colleges, to help abused and battered women. The list goes on and on. Tonight, Oprah my dear friend, we salute you as an educator, entrepreneur, actress, humanitarian, philanthropist, and all around wonderful woman. Thank you for helping make America a kinder and gentler place.

Again, the stress is on individual accomplishment. Bush redefines "Oprah" 's oppression, arguably a product of racist and sexist power structures shared by women and blacks, as "her own personal adversity" that requires only individual efforts toward education, inner strength, and faith in the entrepreneurial dream. Bush also applauds "Oprah" 's contributions to charity. Philanthropy, as part of the rhetoric of tokenism, shares in its contradictions. One is supposed to acknowledge that in this country, many people are hungry, homeless, abused, and illiterate. Yet one is required to overlook the collective nature and structural sources of this suffering and call for individual giving as the solution.

This text's emphases on philanthropy as the agency of social change, the narrative of "Oprah" 's exceptional triumph over collective adversity, and the stress on the importance of individual responsibility firmly place "Oprah" (as a product of this text) within the realm of the liberal ideology. In absorbing "Oprah" 's experience into the "thousand points of light" theme, Bush makes a political argument to replace social programs with the voluntarism of individuals.

Predictably, the structure of this televisual tribute to "Oprah" appears over and over again in the mass of material on "Oprah" in the popular press. Yet these narratives are not seamless. In particular, two sites in the print texts expose interesting contradictions in the narrative of tokenism. The ways in which the biographies foreground issues of race and gender briefly acknowledge the reality of oppression, only to elide and naturalize the structural origins of racism, sexism, and poverty.

RACE AND GENDER IN THE RHETORIC OF TOKENISM

Many writers and interviewers call attention to "Oprah" 's blackness. In *Cosmopolitan,* Markey (1986) writes, "No ma'am, there is nothing blonde, white bread, or benign about Oprah Winfrey. There she sits, 175 pounds of brass, sass, and candor . . . , something of a cross between a puppy and Pearl Bailey, nuzzling her audiences one minute and then knocking them breathless the next." The article's definition of black womanhood as brash and aggressive, animal-like, and extravagant reinforces questionable racial stereotypes. And, the article shifts its focus from racial difference to mainstream success and to "Oprah" 's distance from the black political struggle during her college years. Similarly, Norman King (1987) in his book-length biography of "Oprah" describes her as "brassy," "soulful," "taunting," and "sassy" (1987, p. 10). In these ways, Oprah's race is highlighted as a salient feature of her identity.

In a 1987 interview with *Essence* (Taylor, 1987), "Oprah" explicitly identifies herself with the black community: "As black people we all share the same kind of emotional roots," she says. She also tells a story of feeling oppressed because she was bused to a white, upper-middle class school while her own mother worked a maid in the homes of the other students. Later in the same interview she says, "I know and understand that I am where I am because of the bridges that I crossed over to get here. Sojourner Truth was a bridge. Harriet Tubman was a bridge. . . . I feel very strongly about black womanhood." Although her experience of hardship is so rooted in her identity as a black woman, she also comments, "But I am where I am because I believed in my possibilities. Everything in your world is created by what you think." Or, in *People Weekly* (Richman, 1987), "I never felt the kind of repression other black people are exposed to . . . Blackness is something I just am. I'm black. I'm a woman. I wear a size ten shoe. It's all the same to me." It is her willingness to deny the importance of her difference that endears her to biographers, who make choices in deciding which quotations and details to foreground. Because a key point here is that biographers work as filters or screens, producing life stories that are ideological fictions, it is interesting to note that both Waldron (1987) and King (1987) write glowingly about "Oprah" 's willingness to leave racial antagonism behind.

"Oprah" simultaneously identifies herself with black culture and the legacy of oppression faced by many black Americans, as she does in some of her show topics and in the film projects she chooses, and she distances herself from that history. Of course, "Oprah" does move, if minutely, toward critique before backtracking. Although one can hardly fault Winfrey as an individual for hedging (her refusal of collective identification has earned her millions of dollars), those small moments should not be read as emancipatory. For "Oprah" 's ambivalence is replicated in the culture at large, which features simultaneous acknowledgment and denial of race- and gender-based oppression. The discourse of tokenism must acknowledge difference, because it is difference that allows for exploitation. One cannot exploit a group unless one dehumanizes its members and distinguishes them from oneself. But the discourse must also mask that process of dehumanization and distancing in order to prevent serious resistance. In a 1989 speech to an American Woman's Economic Development Corporation conference, Winfrey herself mixed acknowledgment of oppression with denial of it, saying both that the "notion that you can do and be anything you want to be" is "a very false notion we are fed in this country," *and* that "The life I lead is good. All things are possible" (quoted in Harrison, 1989, p. 46). This contradiction, between the critique of individual success as a "false notion" and the faith that "all things are possible," is the foundation of the rhetoric of racial tokenism.

However, tokenism does not work in exactly this way with regard to gender difference. "Oprah" 's biographical trajectory as it is chronicled in popular texts takes her from a racially marked position to an e-raced position, but emphasizes rather than negates her femininity. The construction of a feminine persona is nowhere more evident than in the contrasts noted in the popular press between "Oprah" and Donahue. "They have different styles, of course," writes Richman (1987), "Donahue coming at you hard and smart and Winfrey sidling up soft and accessible . . . 'He'd do nuclear disarmament much better than I would,' she says." Here and elsewhere, "Oprah" is characterized as soft, empathic, emotional, instinctive, mystical, and sensuous rather than smart, in contrast to a hard, smart, and politically astute masculine position. Carbaugh (1988; see also Zoglin, 1986) describes Donahue as the quintessential liberal individual, committed to a discourse of political rights, "talking American." Reviewers note that "Oprah," by contrast, touches her audiences, loves them, caring for and reaching out to them in a traditionally feminine mode (Zoglin, 1988). As King (1987, p. 9) puts it, "You are aware of a sense of . . . pervasive human warmth, an enveloping hug of empathy." Or, "She'll hug anyone who happens by. She'll sing to herself. She'll fling her arms out exuberantly . . . or she'll break out into a hip-swinging, arms-extended shimmy" (Reynolds, 1993). Haag (1992/93) argues that on her program and in interviews, "Oprah" is constructed as "every viewer's favorite girlfriend" (Kanner, 1994, p. 96), approachable, warm, and empathetic. It is her culturally feminine qualities of warmth, empathy, and connection that give "Oprah"—to a greater degree than Phil Donahue—authority to talk with people about their emotional lives.

On her show "Oprah" is expected to appeal to and empathize with women, to talk about women's concerns, their abusive relationships and their self-esteem problems. Often she does deal with problems that have as their cause systemic, gender-based oppression (divorce, battering, incest, relationships). "She is a giggling best friend, inspiring older sister, and stern mother" (Rogers, 1993, p. 130). In this way, "Oprah" is caught in the double bind of having to continue to stress empathy, emotion, and identification with women on her show while endorsing a therapeutic discourse that blames individuals, extracted from their social context, for their problems. She can never admit the need for systematic structural change and collective political activity. Thus the contradictory statement: "The message is, you're responsible for your life. People watch our show and realize they're not alone" (Taylor, 1987).

The apparent contradiction between collective consciousness ("they're not alone") and individual responsibility ("you're responsible for your life") is resolved through narrative emphasis on "Oprah" 's substantial philanthropic giving and individual hard work. Through philanthropy, individuals, especially women, are allowed the expression of their caring for transformations that make great hero stories but oversimplify the process of overcoming hardship.

TOKENISM, CLASS POLITICS, AND CULTURAL CRITICISM

Oprah Winfrey has taken some criticism in the popular press, most notably in a *New York Times Magazine* article that accuses her candor and goodwill of being "more apparent than real" (Harrison, 1989, p. 54). The author lambastes Winfrey as an individual for contriving her own Horatio Alger story, embracing wealth as a God-ordained reward, and rejecting any political civil rights discourse in order to become popular and successful. "In a racist society," Harrison writes,

> the majority needs, and seeks, from time to time, proof that they are loved by the minority whom they have so long been accustomed to oppress, to fear, or to treat with real or assumed disdain. . . . Oprah Winfrey—a one-person demilitarized zone—serves that purpose. (p. 46)

In particular, Oprah has been criticized for giving white supremacists air time (in a 1987 episode featuring a town in Forsyth County, Georgia). I have been interested less in this article in accusing Oprah Winfrey herself of bad faith or false consciousness than in why and how popular culture iconizes characters whose stories enact liberal success myths and provide the society at large with easy tokens of good faith toward black Americans. As the title of one biography suggests, "Everybody Loves Oprah!" (King, 1987). But should "everybody"—including critics of popular culture—love "Oprah"?

There is a tendency among critics of racism, sexism, and capitalism to muffle criticism of popular figures who represent socially marginalized groups simply because they are women, or black women, or black lesbian women, and so on. This tendency is often labeled a politics of difference or identity. Its representatives maintain that a person's voice is automatically distinctive and politically charged if that person comes from the ranks of the oppressed (and, conversely, that someone from outside those ranks has a less legitimate critical voice). An analysis from this perspective would seek some authentic aspect of the "Oprah" phenomenon, some word or gesture that is not mired in the dominant ideology and its contradictions. Although the oppressed have had sometimes to adopt the mannerisms of the dominant culture in order to survive, Lorde (1984) argues, black women retain a distinctive and liberating voice (p. 114). Henry Louis Gates' (1988) theory of Signifyin(g) suggests that black people create their own vernacular structures in relation to the dominant white culture, producing a double-voiced set of texts that mimic and participate in the canonical, dominant culture but always with meaningful differences signifying resistance and transgressive appropriation. Lorde and Gates might hail the contradictory sides of "Oprah" 's persona as evidence of such double-voiced vernacular structures.

One can question the extent to which The *Oprah Winfrey Show* or any of the texts constructing "Oprah" 's persona constitutes a "vernacular" discourse, if one defines "vernacular" as "discourse that resonates in and from historically oppressed communities" (Ono & Sloop, 1995, p. 20). Ono and Sloop suggest that black vernacular discourse "constitutes African American communities, constructs social relations, and protests representations of African Americans circulating in dominant culture" (p. 22). Although Oprah Winfrey is a black woman whose voice and experience clearly resonate not only with blacks and women but with men and women of all races, the texts surrounding her and constructing her as a star are located firmly in the dominant culture, in the ways I have described. Ono and Sloop suggest that critical scholars turn our attention away from the discourses of the dominant culture and toward the "subaltern" expressions and self-constitutions of marginalized and subordinated groups. Yet at the very least an examination of "Oprah" texts troubles the distinction between "dominant" and "vernacular" in so far as it is difficult to locate these texts squarely in one or the other category. Further, the popularity and pervasiveness of the "Oprah" biography, as with other mainstream mediated texts, is what makes it a necessary target of critique. Contrary to Ono and Sloop, I wish to suggest that critics continue to attend carefully to the most persuasive, most popular, and most widely-available dominant culture narratives and icons in order to understand and critique—not to reify, as Ono and Sloop fear—the continuing force of racism, sexism, and class-based exploitation in our society.

Some media critics have emphasized the complexity, ambivalence and potential oppositional nature of the relationship of even dominant-culture television representations of racial difference to black viewers (Gray, 1993; hooks, 1992). Analyses of stereotypes often point out that stereotypes occur in binary oppositions that have their roots in slavery: happy slave *vs.* wild and dangerous savage (Dates and Barlow, 1990; Cloud, 1992; Morrison, 1992). Herman Gray (1993, 1995) argues that while television is primarily a medium of normalization, commodification, and absorption of difference, the process of incorporation of difference is "not always uniform or effective" (1993, p. 191; 1995, p. 3). Gray warns critics against excessive, pessimistic structuralism with regard to televisual constructions of "blackness," but also against "uncritical celebrations of the practices of collective and individual subjects . . . as resistance" (1995, p. 3).

An example of celebratory criticism is Masciarotte's (1991) argument that Oprah Winfrey's show is a complex, empowering site of consciousness-raising that has been wrongly attacked by ideology critics. Masciarotte attempts to dispel what she sees as "wholesale disregard" of the talk show genre, arguing that Winfrey "begins to articulate a significantly different politics of the subject which re-inscribe the 'making of a self'" (p. 83). In pointing out how the *Oprah Winfrey Show* gives voice to difference, Masciarotte credits the show with oppositional potential. However, this kind of rehabilitation of a demonstrably conventional set of texts risks overlooking the role popular appropriations and constructions of racial difference play in reinforcing hegemonic assumptions about social reality.

On the other hand, critics of hegemony have noted the limitations of talking about social problems in the therapeutic frame of the talk show, which locates responsibility for problems with the individual and mitigates against political awareness or action (Peck, 1992; Banks and Tankel, 1992). Peck (1992) details the ways in which the *Oprah Winfrey Show* itself deploys "liberal, therapeutic, and religious frames of meaning" (p. 91) in order to blunt a critique of racism. Peck describes how the definition of racism as an individual psychological problem and a religious discourse of love work against the efforts of some guests on the show to call attention to the appropriateness of anger and collective action in the face of structural racism. Given the ideological limits of "Oprah" 's discourse in her own program, Peck argues against a valorization of difference that "vacates space from which arguments for intercollective struggle, identification, and empathy might be formulated" (p. 118).

Dates and Barlow (1990, p. 296) argue that representations of African Americans in the mass media are schizoid or split, between those created by and for white culture and those produced by blacks themselves. With regard to Oprah Winfrey, who owns her own production company, chooses her own projects, and has some autonomy and control over her representations of race, the matter is not so simple. For no matter whether "Oprah" or her biographers or publicists are the agents of persona construction, "Oprah" 's identity is articulated within a liberal frame that guarantees continued high ratings and profits. It is not enough that in the *Oprah Winfrey Show* and in the biographies under consideration here, constructions of black identity, language, and culture proliferate—so long as articulation of difference remains at the level of identity and does not imply political opposition or activity against the system that produces racism and sexism. No doubt Oprah Winfrey, the person, transgresses a "social and cultural order that has historically stereotyped, excluded, objectified, and silenced black subjects" (Gray, 1993, p. 191). She is neither silent nor excluded, although she is often stereotyped and objectified. In her film and television projects, she has celebrated black women, and for this reason Angelou (1989) hails her as a "roadmaker" for black women.

Yet, to hail the simple presence of a black woman on television risks ignoring the conditions imposed on that presence and the political inflections of those voices chosen to speak. Indeed, it is necessary to set aside the problematic of "difference" if we are to understand how popular culture texts and personae participate in the maintenance of economic and political power in racist, capitalist society. More crucial than representations of "difference" are the ideological uses to which difference is put in popular texts.

Framing biographies like the America's Hope award ceremony and the other profiles are significant cultural texts at work in this process of cultural authorization. Although "Oprah" is a member of an oppressed group, her life story is appropriated by the dominant culture for the construction of meanings that recover any threatening implications of "Oprah" 's racial difference. We cannot "discover" "Oprah" as an authentic black woman. To take such a position is to risk falling into unhelpful identity politics, emphasizing issues of identity and textual play at the expense of attention to material (economic and physical) aspects of oppression and the possibility of collective political resistance to systemic injustice (see Adams, 1989; Bordo, 1990; Briskin, 1990; Clarke, 1991; Escoffier, 1991; Kauffman, 1990; Smith, 1994).

"Oprah" 's identity and her politics are securely located by framing narratives within liberal individualism and an oppressively gendered meaning system. My analysis of biographical narratives about Oprah Winfrey reveals that a patterned, generic narrative constituting a rhetoric of tokenism pervades popular discourse about "Oprah." These biographical narratives inflate the persona of "Oprah" so that she becomes a larger-than-life cultural icon of racial harmony and opportunity. Further work might examine biographical. narratives of other popular black Americans, women, and other minorities. For example, the dust jacket to Howard Means' *Colin Powell* (1992), a biography of the prominent black U. S. military leader, claims, "General Powell emerges as *the embodiment of the American Dream:* the son of Jamaican immigrants, he rose from the hard life of the South Bronx to become the most talked about military leader since World War II" (emphasis added). This example once again suggests that in general, the rhetoric of tokenism, while internally contradictory regarding the existence of inequality, serves to interpret success and failure as a matter of individual responsibility regardless of one's structural location in systems of power and privilege; it provides the dominant culture a defense against charges of racism while continuing to naturalize and justify racism; it makes heroes out of blacks willing to abnegate political resistance in favor of speaking on behalf of the system.

This conclusion challenges Condit's (1994) (re)definition of hegemony as acceptable compromise. The concordance established in the rhetoric of tokenism obviously benefits a class based, racist social order dependent upon the ideals of meritocracy. Further, in the context of bipartisan attacks on the American social safety net, narratives of "Oprah" 's heroic life story lend persuasive weight to those who wish to accelerate the erosion of social services like welfare and indigent health care. Biographies like the ones of "Oprah" acknowledge difference, giving the appearance of negotiation and compromise. But the implication of those narratives is that because there are no structural barriers to individual advancement, blacks (and other oppressed groups) must blame themselves for failure to thrive.

Of course, many African Americans do make it through the persistent barriers of racism and injustice. This does not mean that those barriers have dissolved. According to census data, the proportion of black households earning at least $50,000 a year rose between 1967 and 1991 from 5.2 to 12.1 percent (reported in Cose, 1993, pp. 36–37). On the other hand, The Milton S. Eisenhower Foundation (1993) recently reported on a study showing that the number of blacks living in poverty and the degree of *de facto* racial segregation in the U.S. have changed little or grown worse since the 1960s. Despite a continuing legacy of racism felt by black Americans of all economic classes, Cose (1993) writes,

> America likes success stories. We also prefer to believe that our country—give or take a David Duke or two—is well on the road to being color-blind. And since the predicament of the black underclass seems so hopeless, many find it comforting to concentrate on those who are doing well. (pp. 37–38)

Cose goes on to argue that while success stories may be comforting, they have a double edge: They hold up "paragons of middle-class virtue" (p. 37) as ideological lessons to blacks who are still struggling in a society that is still far from color-blind or racially just. Ideological constructions of race and power in texts like biographies of Oprah Winfrey correspond to and legitimate ongoing oppression by holding up representatives of the black élite as "proof" that the system is just and that racism is a thing of the past.

White respondents to a Los Angeles survey in the wake of the videotaped police beating of black motorist Rodney King expressed beliefs in a ratio of two to one that joblessness and poverty were the result of moral failures of individual black and Latino people (Mydans, 1993). The respondents could not see the structures of racism and exploitation as contexts of individual hardship. Such attitudes are the product of persuasion, of rhetorics that systematically obscure structure and system in favor of individualistic explanations of poverty and despair. The rhetoric of tokenism, exemplified in the Oprah Winfrey profiles, is one such rhetoric. Although it is contradictory, tokenist biography serves to blame the oppressed for their failures and to uphold a meritocratic vision of the American Dream that justifies and sustains a more troubling American reality.

Reading Endnote

1. The patterns I describe are replicated in the tabloid press. In order to make this project manageable, I have limited my analysis to glossy trade magazine and book-length writings that feature Oprah Winfrey's life story (as opposed to her riches, her chef, or her weight).

Reading References

Adams, M. L. (1989). There's no place like home: On the place of identity in femimst politics. *Feminist Review,* 31, 22–33.

America's all-star tribute to Oprah Winfrey (1990, September 18). [Television program]. ABC.

Anderson, C. (1986, August). Meet Oprah Winfrey. *Good Housekeeping.*

Angelou, M. (1989, January/February). Women of the year: Oprah Winfrey. *Ms.,* p. 88.

Barthel, J. (1986, August). Here Comes Oprah. *Ms.*

Bartlett, D. L and J. B. Steele (1992). *America: What went wrong?* Kansas City: Andrews and McMeel.

Banks, J. and J. D. Tankel (1992). Constructions of sexuality on television talk shows. Paper presented to the 42nd Annual conference of the International Communication Association, Miami, FL.

Bly, N. (1993). *Oprah! Up close and down home.* Zebra Books.

Bogle, D. (1989). *Toms, coons, mulattos. mammies, and bucks: An interpretive history of blacks in American films.* New York: Continuum.

Bordo, S. (1990). Feminism, postmodernism, and gender-skepticism." In L. J. Nicholson (Ed.), *Feminism/Postmodernism* (pp. 133–156). New York and London: Routledge.

Bordo, S. (1993). *Unbearable weight: Feminism, Western culture, and the body.* Berkeley: University of California Press.

Brashler, B. (1991, August). Next on Oprah . . . *Ladies Home Journal,* no page given (Lexis/Nexis).

Briskin, L. (1990). Identity politics and the hierarchy of oppression. *Feminist Review,* 35, 102–108.

Cameron, J. (1989, February). Simply . . . Oprah! *Cosmopolitan,* no page given.

Carbaugh, D. (1988). *Talking American: Cultural discourses on Donahue.* Norwood, NJ: Ablex.

Clarke, S. A. (1991). Fear of a black planet. *Socialist Review,* 21 (3), 38–59.

Cloud, D. (1992). The limits of interpretation: Ambivalence and the stereotype in *Spenser: For Hire. Critical Studies in Mass Communication,* 9, 311–324.

Condit, C. M. (1994). Hegemony in a mass-mediated society: Concordance about reproductive technologies. *Critical Studies in Mass Communication,* 11, 205–230

Cose, E. (1993). Rage *of a privileged class.* New York: HarperCollins.

Culhane, J. (1989, February). Oprah Winfrey: How truth changed her life. *Reader's Digest*, pp. 101–105.

Dale, S., L. Fisher, and S. McFarland (1994, Sept. 12). In full stride. *People Weekly.* pp. 84–90.

Dates, J. L. and W. Barlow, Eds. (1990). *Split image: African Americans in the mass media.* Washington, D.C.: Howard University Press.

DeParle, J. (1994, October 7). Census sees falling income and more poor. *New York Times*, p. A16.

Dyer, R. (1986). *Heavenly bodies: Film stars and society.* New York: St. Martin's Press.

Ebert, A. (1991, September). Oprah Winfrey talks openly about Oprah. *Good Housekeeping.* No page given (Lexis/Nexis).

Edmonds, P. and M. L. Usdansky (1994, November 14). Children get poorer, nation gets richer. *USA Today*, p. 1A.

Edwards, A. (1986, October). Oprah Winfrey Stealing the Show. *Essence.*

Escoffier, J. (1991). The limits of multiculturalism. *Socialist Review*, 21 (3), 61–73.

Gates, H. L. (1988). *The signifyin(g) monkey: A theory of Afro-American literary criticism.* New York, Oxford: Oxford University Press.

Gillespie, M. A. (1988, November). Winfrey takes all. *Ms.*, pp. 50–54.

Gitlin, T. (1980). *The whole world is watching: Mass media in the making and unmaking of the new left.* Berkeley, Los Angeles: University of California Press.

Gerosa, M. (1994, November). What makes Oprah run? *Ladies Home Journal*, pp. 200 ff.

Goodman, F. (1991, December). The companies they keep [on Oprah Winfrey and Madonna]. *Working Woman*, pp. 52ff.

Gramsci, A. (1971). *Selections from the prison notebooks.* (Q. Hoare and G. N. Smith, Trans.). New York: International Publishers. (Work originally written in 1936–37.)

Gray, H. (1989). Television, black Americans, and the American dream. *Critical Studies in Mass Communication*, 6, 376–386.

Gray, H. (1993). The endless slide of difference. Critical television studies, television and the question of race. *Critical Studies in Mass Communication*, 10, 190–197.

Gray, H. (1995). *Watching race: Television and the struggle for "blackness."* Minneapolis: University of Minnesota Press.

Gross, L. (1988, December). Oprah Winfrey, Wonder Woman. *Ladies Home Journal.*

Haag, L. (1992/93). Oprah Winfrey: The construction of intimacy in the talk show setting. *Journal of Popular Culture,* 26, 115–121.

Hall, S. (1981). The whites of their eyes: Racist ideologies and the media. In G. Bridges and R. Brunt (Eds.), *Silver linings* (pp. 28–52). London: Lawrence and Wishart.

Hall, S. (1986a). Gramsci's relevance for the study of race and ethnicity. *Journal of Communication Inquiry,* 10, 5–27.

Hall, S. (1986b). Variants of liberalism. In J. Donald and S. Hall (Eds.), *Politics and Ideology* (pp. 34–69). Philadelphia: Open University Press.

Harrison, B. G. (1989, June 11). The importance of being Oprah. *New York Times Magazine,* pp. 28–29ff.

hooks, b. (1992). *Black looks.* Boston: South End Press.

Jhally, S., & J. Lewis (1992). *Enlightened racism: The Cosby Show, racism, and the myth of the American dream.* Boulder, CO: Westview Press.

Kauffman, L. A. (1990). The anti-politics of identity. *Socialist Review,* 20 (1), 67–80.

Kanner, M. (1994, February). Oprah at 40. *Ladies Home Journal,* pp. 96ff.

King, N. (1987). *Everybody loves Oprah.* New York: William Morrow and Co.

Laws, J. L. (1975). The psychology of tokenism. *Sex Roles,* 1, 51–67.

Lears, T. J. J. (1985). The concept of cultural hegemony: Problems and possibilities. *American Historical Review,* 90, 567–593.

Levitt, S., L. Fisher, and B. K. Mills (1993, November 29). Oprah's mission. *People,* p. 106.

Lorde, A. (1984). *Sister outsider: Essays and speeches.* Trumansburg, NY: Crossing Press.

Mair, G. (1994). *Oprah Winfrey: The real story.* Secaucus, NJ: Carol Publishing.

Mann, B. (1986, September 8). Oprah Winfrey: A refreshingly different TV host. Oakland, CA *Tribune* [Newsbank microfiche].

Means, H. (1992). *Colin Powell.* New York: Donald I. Fine.

Markey, J. (1986, September). Brassy, sassy Oprah Winfrey. *Cosmopolitan*, pp. 94–100.

Masciarotte, G. (1991, Fall). C'mon girl: Oprah Winfrey and the discourse of feminine talk. *Genders*, 11, 81–110.

McEvoy, D. K. (1994, Sept. 25). Fighting for mass market space. *Publishers' Weekly*, p. 36.

McMullen, W. J. and Solomon, M. (1994). The politics of adaptation: Steven Spielberg's appropriation of *The Color Purple. Text and Performance Quarterly*, 14, 158–174.

Milton S. Eisenhower Foundation. (1993). *Investing in children and youth, reconstructing our cities: Doing what works to reverse the betrayal of American democracy.* Washington, D.C.

Morrison, T., Ed. (1992). *Race-ing justice, En-gendering power: Essays on Anita Hill, Clarence Thomas, and the Construction of Social Reality.* New York: Pantheon.

Murphy, J. M. (1992). Domesticating dissent: The Kennedys and the Freedom Rides. *Communication Monographs*, 59, 61–78.

Mydans, S. (1993, June 10). Los Angeles elects a conservative as mayor and turns to a new era. *New York Times* [National Edition], pp. A1ff.

Nadel, I. B. (1984). *Biography: Fiction, fact, and form.* New York: St. Martin's Press.

Noel, P. (1985, April). Lights, Camera, Oprah! *Ebony*.

Noglows, P. (1994, May). Oprah: the year of living dangerously. *Working Woman*, pp. 52ff.

Ono, K. and J. M. Sloop (1995). The critique of vernacular discourse. *Communication Monographs*, 62, 19–46.

Parent, W. (1985). A liberal legacy: Blacks blaming themselves for economic failures. *Journal of Black Studies*, 16, 3–20.

Peck, J. (1994, Spring). Talk about racism: Framing a popular discourse of race on *Oprah Winfrey. Cultural Critique*, pp. 89–125.

Pettigrew, T. F. and J. Martin (1987). Shaping the organizational context for Black American inclusion. *Journal of Social Issues*, 43, 41–78.

Phillips, K (1990). *Politics of rich and poor.* New York: Random House.

Randolph, L. B. (1993, October). Oprah opens up about her weight, her wedding and why she withheld the book. *Ebony*, pp. 130–132.

Reynolds, G. (1993, November). Oprah unbound. *Chicago Magazine*, pp. 86ff.

Richman, A. (1987, January 12). Oprah. *People Weekly,* pp. 48ff.

Riggs, M. (1986). *Ethnic notions* [documentary film]. San Francisco: California Newsreel.

Riggs, M. (1991). *Color adjustment* [documentary film]. San Francisco: California Newsreel.

Rogers, J. (1993, September). Understanding Oprah. *Redbook,* pp. 94ff.

Rosen, M. and L. Fisher (1994, January 10). Oprah overcomes. *People,* pp. 42ff.

Rubenstein, L. (1987, August). Oprah! Thriving on Faith! *McCall's.*

Simson, M. (1994, March 7). The red and the black: Tallying the books '93. *Publishers' Weekly,* p. S21.

Simson, M. (1995, March 20). The red and the black: Paperback bestsellers. *Publishers' Weekly,* p. S24.

Smith, S. (1987). *A poetics of women's autobiography.* Bloomington: Indiana University Press.

Smith, S. (1994). Mistaken identity. *International Socialism,* 62, 1–49.

Taylor, S. (1987, August). An intimate talk With Oprah. *Essence,* pp. 57–59ff.

TV Guide (1990, September 14–21). [Television schedule listings].

Waldron, R. (1987). *Oprah!* New York: St. Martin's Press.

Weiss, R. (1969). *The American myth of success: From Horatio Alger to Norman Vincent Peale.* New York: Basic Books.

Whitaker, C. (1987, March). Oprah Winfrey: The most talked about TV talk show host. *Ebony.*

Williams, R. (1973). Base and superstructure in Marxist cultural theory. *New Left Review,* 82, 3–16.

Yoder, J. D. (1991). Rethinking tokenism: Looking beyond numbers. *Gender and Society,* 5, 178–192.

Yoder, J. D. (1994). Looking beyond numbers: The effects of gender status, job prestige, and occupational gender-typing on tokenism processes. *Social Psychology Quarterly, 57,* 150–159.

Zimmer, L. (1988). Tokenism and women in the workplace. *Social Problems,* 35 (1), 64–77.

Zoglin, R. (1986, September 15). "People sense the realness." *Time,* p. 99.

Zoglin, R. (1988, August 8). Lady with a calling. *Time,* pp. 62–64.

In this Chapter 8 workshop, we will probe in focused workshop exercises many of the concepts you discovered in this chapter. Work at a pace by assignment, or by choice, that allows these various insights to "sink in" at an even deeper level for you.

You have read the rhetorical criticism by Dana L. Cloud entitled "Hegemony or Concordance? The Rhetoric of Tokenism in 'Oprah' Winfrey's Rags-to-Riches Biography." Use the chart below to start careful notes on the JFS and JFA items (about which you learned in Chapter 3) that Cloud used to establish the need for this research. Make other notations in the margin of the reproduced article.

FINDING THE SET-UP ITEMS

Discovering JFS and JFS items

Cloud, Dana L. "Hegemony or Concordance? The Rhetoric of Tokenism in "Oprah" Winfrey's Rags-to-Riches Biography." *Critical Studies in Mass Communication* 13 (1996): 115–137.

(Page numbers in brackets indicate pages reprinted in this textbook.)

Item	Page	
JFS	116 [304]	"Recent communication scholarship on Bill Cosby and *The Cosby Show* has suggested that popular discourse about black family life often deploys assumptions of liberalism that interpret poverty and hardship as individual or family failures, and success as exclusively an individual triumph." (Gray, 1989; Jhally and Lewis, 1992)
JFS	118 [307]	"While Condit points out that the United States is a society of relative affluence, she fails to note that fully one-third of black Americans (and nearly half of all black children; see Edmonds & Udansky, 1994) live in poverty."
JFS		
JFS		
JFA	120 [310]	"Biographical profiles framing 'Oprah' as liberal hero have proliferated and continue to appear in a wide range of popular outlets . . ."
JFA		

FINDING THE GOLD

Discovering Application Ideas and Knowledge in Language and Ideology Analysis Articles

As part of this Chapter 8 workshop, we will continue to probe several of the ways you can recognize and use the "gold" of academic, rhetorical criticism. Re-read the chart below. See if you can notice how we moved from the original claim, insight or discovery to the resulting "translation."

Example:

Cloud, Dana L. "Hegemony or Concordance? The Rhetoric of Tokenism in 'Oprah' Winfrey's Rags-to-Riches Biography." *Critical Studies in Mass Communication* 13 (1996): 115–137.

(Page numbers in brackets indicate pages reprinted in this textbook.)

Quotation	Page	Translated Idea or Insight
"The mythos of the self-made person, in concert with the rejection of structural critique of racism and sexism, resonates throughout all of the biographies."	122 [311]	Key story themes in biographies may interact to reinforce each other.
"My point is simply that once someone has struggled through the barriers of discrimination to achieve power or prominence, her persona is appropriated by the dominant ideology of liberalism and inscribed in public texts in such a way as to perpetuate individualist myths and lessons necessary to liberalism and capitalism."	123 [313]	When a minority status person achieves strong success in American culture, popular messages about her will celebrate her individualism, and thus support the status quo.
"One cannot exploit a group unless one dehumanizes its members and distinguishes them from oneself. But the discourse must also mask that process of dehumanization and distancing in order to prevent serious resistance."	128 [318]	Using members of a less powerful group in a culture requires not treating them as fully human. However, cultural messages must seem to treat people from that group as fully human, so as to prevent fighting back.

Use the chart on the next page to find, identify, and chart the potential advantage of other observations on narrative and culture that Cloud makes in her analysis.

Quotation	Page	Translated Idea or Insight

THE POWER OF INDIVIDUAL EVERYDAY WORDS

Which of the following everyday words is most important?

Drive Thru Window	Drink	Sell	Styrofoam	Sugar
Hot	Lid	Grandson	Hazard	Absorb
Scald	Burn	Holding Temperature	Coffee	Cream
Car	Sweatpants	McDonald's	Passenger	Spill

All of these are words we might use in a regular week (well, perhaps with the exception of "holding temperature"). You might also recognize them as words that were key parts of a lawsuit filed for Stella Liebeck of Albuquerque, New Mexico, when she received third-degree burns after spilling a coffee from McDonald's in her lap. Which of the words seem most important to you right now? Take a few minutes to look up a rendition of the story on the Web (search with Key Words: coffee, McDonald's, grandmother, Liebeck). After reading (or re-reading and recalling) the story and the outcome of the case, which of the words in the grid now seem most important? Why? Discuss how words often function to give us "instructions" for living.

DEFINING OUR ACTIONS

A 1971 college textbook claims: "Neither Columbus nor any of his men suspected it, but the discovery of San Salvador [the name Columbus gave the island on which he first landed] was probably the most important event in the history of western civilization since the birth of Christ. Besides unleashing a series of events that improved man's material prospects, the discovery also advanced man's spiritual prospects enormously."[22] An elementary textbook from 1995, however, sidesteps the Columbus "verb" issue by naming the section on Columbus: "Columbus Reaches America" (although a later chart of French and English explorers has them variously "sailing," "reaching," "claiming," and "exploring").[23]

Do you have a preference for what Columbus did (Explored? Discovered? Invaded? Reached?)? What should we teach elementary schoolchildren when they first learn this part of American history? Should we celebrate or condemn the Columbus Day holiday? Do we usually have holidays for people who "reach" a destination? On the Web, or in other sources, find arguments made on both sides of this issue. What key verbs do people use concerning Columbus' voyages? Do they give reasons or argument for their choice?

THE POWER OF CULTURAL HEROES

Can you think of a current movie that places a main character in the position of being an actual frontier hunter (or the modern equivalent? a future equivalent?). Do you agree with Frentz and Rushing that finding such characters in a popular movie demonstrates an extension of ideological power structures within American culture? Can you think of such a hunter character in a widely-available film who is played by a female character? Can you think of such a hunter character who fails to capture or kill his or her prey?

What other "stock" cultural characters can you discover in movies over a sustained period of time? How do you rate yourself in comparison to those characters? Or, is rating itself an ideologically charged activity?

LANGUAGE AS "FILTER"

If someone on your campus was called the "Robin Hood" of campus, what would you think of that person? Why?

Write two lists under the heading of "Addicted." Include on first list things that would be bad if you had such an addiction. Make the second list a list of things that would be good if you were so addicted. Is it acceptable to be an addict? Do we have a synonym to use?

Have you ever seen a "full cranial prosthesis"? A federal appeals court in March 1993 rejected a woman's claim that her insurance company should provide her with a $400 full cranial prosthesis. The answer to what we commonly call a full cranial prosthesis is on the bottom of the next page. Before you look, can you guess what it is? After you look, ask yourself which term would look more impressive on an insurance claim form.

THE POWER OF HEGEMONIC LANGUAGE

"Anthropologists and archaeologists say they are indispensable to the study of the history of man, and that to lose them would be to lose a valuable scientific tool."

"Native Americans say that to keep them here is to desecrate their ancestors, defile their religions and denigrate Indians by treating them as curios rather than as human beings."

"They are the remains of more than 14,000 American Indians, part of the Smithsonian's collection of nearly 33,000 skeletal human remains that are stored here and used for research."[24]

Who should decide if the human bones held by the Smithsonian are a "valuable scientific tool" or sacred body parts being treated as "curios"?

IDEOGRAPHS

Join with one other person in your class and draw up a list of ten ideographs. Start with <freedom> and <choice> and go from there. Divide the list into two groups of five and then put each of the ideographs into a superior value match with an ideograph from your partner's list. Is <privacy> more or less important than <family values>? Is <freedom> better than <life>? Chart your discussion and see which real life situations and disputes become the examples on which you base your argument.

Answer from previous page:

Full Cranial Prosthesis	OR	Wig

Key Words

language selects, *282*
language deflects, *282*
language reflects, *282*
words as instructions for action, *283*
ideology, *293, 296*
socially situated audience member, *298*
professional ideology, *299*
national ideology, *299*
cultural ideology, *299*
hegemony, *300*
ideograph, *301*

Language and Ideology Analysis Articles

Below you will find a sample of rhetorical and cultural analysis articles and books that have investigated the power of language and ideology in public messages.

Bineham, Jeffery L. "Theological Hegemony and Oppositional Interpretive Codes: The Case of Evangelical Christian Feminism." *Western Journal of Communication* 57 (1993): 515–529.

Brown, William R. "Ideology as Communication Process." *Quarterly Journal of Speech* 64 (1978): 123–140.

Charland, Maurice. "Constitutive Rhetoric: The Case of the *Peuple Quebecois*." *Quarterly Journal of Speech* 73 (1987): 133–150.

Condit, Celeste M. *Decoding Abortion Rhetoric: Communicating Social Change*. Urbana: University of Illinois Press, 1990.

Condit, Celeste M. and John Louis Lucaites. *Crafting Equality: America's Anglo-African Word*. Chicago: University of Chicago Press, 1993.

McGee, Michael C. "In Search of 'The People': A Rhetorical Alternative." *Quarterly Journal of Speech* 61 (1975): 235–249.

McGee, Michael Calvin. "The Origins of 'Liberty': A Feminization of Power." *Communication Monographs* 47 (1980): 22–46.

McGee, Michael C. "The 'Ideograph': A Link Between Rhetoric and Social Theory." *Quarterly Journal of Speech* 66 (1980): 1–16.

McGee, Michael Calvin and Martha Anne Miller. "Public Knowledge and Ideological Argumentation." *Communication Monographs* 50 (1983): 47–65.

Miller, M. Linda, "Public Argument and Legislative Debate in the Rhetorical Construction of Public Policy: The Case of Florida Midwifery Legislation." *Quarterly Journal of Speech* 85 (1999), 361–379.

Moore, Mark P. "Constructing Irreconcilable Conflict: The Function of Synecdoche in the Spotted Owl Controversy." *Communication Monographs* 60 (1993): 258–274.

Endnotes

1. See Lessl's article about one part of how scientists become scientists: Thomas M. Lessl, "The Galileo Legend as Scientific Folklore." *Quarterly Journal of Speech* 85 (1999): 146–168.
2. Kenneth Burke, *Language as Symbolic Action* (Berkeley: University of California Press, 1966), 45.
3. Darrell Rigby, "Don't Get Hammered by Management Fads," *Wall Street Journal* 21 May 2001, A–22.
4. Used with permission; © 1999 Pierce Communication.
5. Dan Zinkand, "Of Pigs and Prairies," *Iowa Alumni Magazine* August 2001, 16–19.
6. According to William Kenny, public affairs officer at the U.S. Naval Submarine School at Groton, Connecticut, women are not permitted to serve on U.S. Navy submarines; personal correspondence, 27 Oct. 2001.
7. Carol Tavris, *The Mismeasure of Woman* (New York: Simon & Schuster, 1992), 106.
8. Carl T. Rowan, "Shoe of 'Terrorism' Fits Too Many Feet," *Oregonian* 12 April 1978, C–8.
9. Thomas L. Friedman, "In Pakistan, It's Jihad 101," *New York Times* 13 Nov. 2001.
   http: //www.nytimes. com/2001/11/13/opinion/13FRIE.html
10. Marcy Cottrell Houle, *One City's Wilderness: Portland's Forest Park* (Portland, Oregon: Oregon Historical Society Press, 1987).
11. Stephen E. Ambrose, *Undaunted Courage: Meriwether Lewis, Thomas Jefferson, and the Opening of the American West* (New York: Simon & Schuster, 1996), 51.
12. John Chester Miller, *The Wolf by the Ears: Thomas Jefferson and Slavery* (New York: Free Press, 1977), 226.
13. Thomas S. Frentz and Janice Hocker Rushing, "Integrating Ideology and Archetype in Rhetorical Criticism, Part II: A Case Study of Jaws," *Quarterly Journal of Speech* 79 (1993): 61–81.
14. Frentz and Rushing point out in endnote 7 (p. 80) that they "employ the term 'Indian' rather than the more accurate 'Native American' in their discussion of the frontier hunter myth "because this is the term of currency within the myth itself."
15. Their analysis is much more detailed than this brief summary; they include elements of gender, myth, critical reflection, moral duty, and marriage ritual in this analysis.
16. Shawn J. Parry-Giles, "'Camouflaged' Propaganda: The Truman and Eisenhower Administrations' Covert Manipulation of the News," *Western Journal of Communication* 60 (1996): 147.
17. He is citing John Fiske, *Television Culture* (London: Methuen), 80–81; brackets are from Parry-Giles.
18. Nick Trujillo, "Hegemonic Masculinity on the Mound: Media Representations of Nolan Ryan and American Sports Culture," *Critical Studies in Mass Communication* 8 (1991): 291. He is citing Robert Hanke,

"Hegemonic Masculinity in *thirtysomething*," *Critical Studies in Mass Communication* 7 (1990): 232.

19. Michael Calvin McGee, "The 'Ideograph': A Link Between Rhetoric and Ideology," *Quarterly Journal of Speech*, 66 (1980), 1–16.
20. I'm adopting the practice established by Condit and Lucaites to indicate an ideograph by setting it within chevron emblems. See John Louis Lucaites, and Celeste Michelle Condit, "Reconstructing <Equality>: Culturetypal and Counter-Cultural Rhetorics in the Martyred Black Vision," *Communication Monographs* 57 (1990): 5–24.
21. See, respectively, Maurice Charland, "Constitutive Rhetoric: The Case of the Peuple Quebecois," *Quarterly Journal of Speech* 73 (1987), 133–150; Mark P. Moore, "Constructing Irreconcilable Conflict: The Function of Synecdoche in the Spotted Owl Controversy," *Communication Monographs* 60 (1993), 258–274; Michael Calvin McGee and Martha Anne Martin, "Public Knowledge and Ideological Argumentation," *Communication Monographs* 50 (1983), 47–65; M. Linda Miller, "Public Argument and Legislative Debate in the Rhetorical Construction of Public Policy: The Case of Florida Midwifery Legislation," *Quarterly Journal of Speech* 85 (1999), 361–379.
22. John A. Garraty, *The American Nation*, 2nd ed. (New York: Harper and Row, 1971), 15.
23. James A. Banks, Jean Craven, Barry K. Beyer, Gloria Ladson-Billings, Gloria Contreras, Mary A. McFarland, and Walter C. Parker, *United States and Its Neighbors* (New York: Macmillian/McGraw-Hill School Publishing Company, 1995), 144 and 183.
24. Ron Martz, "Scientists Call It Archaeology; Indians Call It Grave Robbing," *Atlanta Journal and Constitution* 16 November 1986, A–15.

Rhetorical Theory: Saying Something Profound about No *One* Thing

Without realizing it, you have been working with rhetorical theory in each of the previous chapters. Theory is the way we attempt to use words and ideas to better understand something that is important to us. We need theories to make our best attempt to capture the essence of how messages work in human communication. Rhetorical theory, then, is a set of specialized words developed by rhetoricians as they attempt to explain the nature, functions, and characteristics of messages that reach public audiences. Theory is always "under development," and rhetorical theorists are always willing to change, adapt, or reject theories if a better theory is developed and offered that explains how messages operate in human experience.

A wise person once said, "Any tyro can talk about something. But it takes a really profound thinker to say profound things about nothing."[1] What could that possibly mean? If you think about it, you'll agree that a person who builds a theory is someone who says "profound things about nothing" or actually "profound things about no (one) thing." Since the purpose of any theory is to give a solid explanation about the item or process under investigation, theory (by definition) must be about no *one thing,* but rather about all of the "things" it seeks to study. For instance, if you were an early biologist studying frogs, you would study *individual* frogs in an attempt to better understand *all* frogs. But your purpose in trying to build a "frog theory" would be to find all of those characteristics, habits, and responses that were true for *any* frog.

FIGURE 9.1
(Aren't you glad you study language, messages, and communication instead of frogs?)

So, if in your study of frogs you discovered three frogs out of a thousand that had a red spot on their right hind foot, you would *not* make that a necessary characteristic for being a frog. On the other hand, if you discovered that *all* the individual frogs you studied had no teeth on their lower jaw, had external eardrums, and began life as an egg in water, you might build into your frog theory a section that attempted to include and explain each of these "frog" characteristics.

In this chapter we will examine sets of terminology that represent the most commonly used theories in Rhetorical Criticism. Your practice and understanding of these specialized words of theory will give you the beginning basis for reading many articles and books written by rhetorical critics and rhetorical theorists. You will also be able to launch (see Chapter 4) into initial rhetorical criticism with a solid array of terms, ideas, concepts, and frameworks that come from theory terms you've learned in this chapter and in previous chapters.

This chapter will be in a format quite different from previous chapters. Since we have a number of theories and perspectives to cover, each set will be in a module that is only several pages long. We will not have time to give in-depth background for each set of theory terms, so a set of suggested readings will accompany each module, should you choose to follow the background readings into a deeper understanding of the theory terms. Before we actually start these theory term modules, I will briefly discuss some of the characteristics of rhetorical theories and some of the potential pitfalls of theory building.

Rhetorical theorists, like scholars in many other fields, want to give themselves and others the most valuable tools possible for understanding an item or process. As you recognize by now, rhetorical theorists examine message artifacts used in human communication that are directed to public audiences. They want to better understand how those messages work and the key characteristics of those messages. Let's first discuss some characteristics of building a theory about rhetorical messages.

People who have studied human communication over thousands of years recognize the genuine power messages have to move individuals and groups of people to specific behaviors. Due to the profound power in words (and now images) to change people, scholars who have built rhetorical theory have always been sensitive to the ethical or moral component in human communication. Since the time of the early Greeks attempting to use democracy in city-states, scholars have worried over the misuse and abuse of human messages. The temptation, then, is to build a theory of human communication based on what we think *ought* to happen in human communication. The first thing we need to note about theory building in rhetoric, then, is that rhetorical theorists need to build theory on what *actually* happens within messages and *not* on what we think *ought* to happen in human messages.

This is not to suggest that we can drop ethical, moral, or ideological concerns as we study human messages—we cannot pretend that human communication is value free. But, we do need to build theory on what we actually *find* in human message creation, not on what we *wish* we would find.

Imagine if a hydrologist (an expert in how water operates in various conditions) built hydrological theory on how she *wanted* water to operate rather than on how it actually operated.[2] The resulting theory would be flawed from the outset. Our first notation about rhetorical theory, then, is that we must study messages in their "natural habitat," and we must strive to accurately describe, categorize, and analyze characteristics as they actually happen. If we wish to evaluate those messages from a moral, ethical, or political stance, our time for doing so must be *after* we've given the most accurate theoretical account possible of the messages under investigation. Unlike a hydrologist, however, a rhetorical theorist is analyzing messages which are much more readily influenced by human desires, values, and beliefs than are the basic properties of water. Rhetorical critics, then, must wrestle actively with the responsibility to guide the practice of message creation and use *after* quality theory building has helped create useful understanding.

The second aspect of theory building we need to note is that theory building is a collaborative (or community) building project. No theorist working and writing today can afford to work on his or her own. We, by definition and necessity, build on the theory ideas and frameworks that have been developed before by people over the ages who have seriously, and systematically, investigated the power of human messages in communication.

Finally, you should be aware that, as an early apprentice in the study of human public communication, you are not expected to build or develop theory. That may come later for some of you who so love the investigation of human communication that you devote a substantial part of your professional career to a better understanding of how messages work. On the other hand, you should readily recognize key components in rhetorical theory that will help you make better decisions about the messages you will create, mold, or influence as you move into one of hundreds of different occupations that have message creation as a core responsibility.

Let's briefly discuss three pitfalls in rhetorical theory building and then launch into our coverage of key theory terms that you will find in scholarly writing in rhetorical criticism.

The first potential pitfall is the belief that something new is better than something old. In all parts of human life we can fall prey to this fallacy. New-fangled theory is not necessarily better than older, shopworn theory just because it is new. New terms, ideas, and frameworks should do more than create new labels for old concepts. New theory should contribute something different and previously unknown about how messages work. Many "old" theory words are still perfectly functional today, thousands of years after their creation, because they still help us understand important aspects about how we create and use messages.

The second potential pitfall we face in theory building is the problem of exclusivism. Theories, like any other human construction, are going to have strengths and weaknesses. If we build a rhetorical theory and expect that it is the *only* valid, valuable theory, we run the risk of *not* noticing how other (perhaps rival) theories might be of aid to us in understanding some part of human messages. We need to be flexible in recognizing the strengths, and weaknesses, that theories may exhibit.

The third potential pitfall we face is one we've already talked about briefly: the temptation to favor *ought* over *is*. This pitfall suggests that we will be foolish if we build a theory based on how we believe messages *should* (or *ought*) operate. If we believe that a public speaker *ought* to do certain things to build credibility with an audience (and if we build a rhetorical theory based on that *ought*), we may well miss strategies that *real* public speakers are using in actual speaking situations to build credibility. In other words, we cannot allow what we would like to be true about humans making messages fog our understanding about practices, habits, and choices evident in *actual* use of rhetoric in artifacts of human public communication.

With these preliminary considerations established, let's examine a series of key theory word modules. Remember that your understanding of these terms (and the ideas behind them) is at the very center of your development as a communication professional, or as any professional who extensively uses communication. Recall that as you work to establish your credentials as an expert in human communication, law students are beginning their study of how laws are formulated, dental students are beginning the study of the human mouth, and engineering students are beginning to learn terms that help them understand decisions that they will later make in building computers, bridges, or buildings.

Learning these terms is critical to your development as a professional. You must make these terms and ideas part of your everyday professional vocabulary. You would not want to be sitting in a dentist's chair a few years from now while your dentist fumbled through instruction manuals of how to "do" dentistry. Similarly, individuals, campaigns, groups, and businesses will be relying on you, years from now, to make *expert* decisions about how to construct messages that will be crucial to desired goals. Will you be ready?

If you have seriously absorbed the previous chapters in this book, and if you diligently learn the terms offered in this chapter, you will be prepared to really help accomplish important persuasion and information goals using messages that will be informed with insights gained from serious, systematic study of rhetorical practices in human messages. Moreover, mastering this material will allow you to have a solid foundation as you approach upper-division classes in your course of study in your degree program. In some classes you can afford to use what I call a "parade" strategy of study. In the "parade" strategy, you examine the ideas within the class as if they were beautiful floats in a parade. You see them. You enjoy them. You remember enough about them to be accountable on a final test. And, then, you forget them. (To test this idea, see if you can describe in detail a float you saw in a Fourth of July parade two years ago. Can you do it?) You must *not* use the "parade" strategy in early classes in communication study degree programs if you seek to be a communication professional. Your future company, clients, bosses, or constituents cannot afford your lack of insight if you learn these ideas for a short time only. Take your study seriously and learn these ideas as if your success and future depended upon it. (They do.)

Each definition offered in this chapter will be my "paraphrase" of a much more technical definition. Nearly all of these theoretical terms have rich histories and much more complex definitions than I offer here. Likewise, not everyone agrees with many of these theoretical definitions (even in their more complex forms in their original documents and secondary discussions). Hence, these definitions should be taken as a starting point—not as a final destination. As you learn more about theory and specialized words that support rhetorical theory building, you will recognize shades of meaning and definitional disputes about key words unavailable here. At the end of this chapter you will see two scholars at work trying to resolve just such a dispute. These paraphrased definitions are intended as a "doorway" into quick use of these terms. Further reading and lecture material from your class will broaden, sharpen, or change these initial definitions.

In most cases my paraphrase definition will be used to capture a simplified, straightforward understanding of more technical definitions originally used by the rhetorical theorists and critics. When I *do* directly use all, or part, of a definition from an original source, I will give credit to that source via an endnote. When I cross-reference terms or ideas covered in the previous chapters, I will place the term cross-referenced in brackets with the chapter number. Quick examples will be provided as needed. These definitions are in approximate chronological order of their development and use. I have also included a chart listing the definitions by theorist's last name and one by key theory word.

Theory Terms by Theorist

Theory Terms by Key Word

Theory Terms by Key Word *(Continued)*

TERM EXPLANATIONS

THEORIST:
Longinus

Term:
Sublime

Sublime:

A quality of a message that connects with an audience in a manner or mode of bliss, inspiration, or beauty that seems beyond explanation, but not beyond invention by a rhetor.

Quick Example:

Think of the last time you heard a concert, or read a book, or saw a movie, or listened to a speech and, seemingly, time stood still (i.e., you were so involved in the message or performance that you were temporarily unaware of mundane markers of time and space). If you can't think of such a time, perhaps you need to look into a different set of concerts, books, movies or speeches.

For more information see:
Longinus. *On the Sublime.* Trans. James A. Arieti and John M. Crossett. New York: E. Mellen Press, 1985.

THEORIST:
Many People

Terms:
Metaphor
(also: Novel Metaphor)
Dead Metaphor
(Really) Dead Metaphor:
Buried Metaphor
Metaphoric Entailment

Metaphor:

A message component where one item, person, or process is described by suggesting that it is another (unlike) item, person, or process.

Quick Example:

When an EPA administrator calls statues in a central-city area "the canary in the coal mine" for detection of acid-rain damage, she is using a metaphor.

Dead Metaphor:

A metaphor where the metaphier (see Chapter 5) is so often used that we (unless prompted) don't recognize it as a metaphor. (I prefer to call this a buried metaphor.)

Quick Example:

When a friend has had a difficult week and says: "My week's been a roller coaster." While we would recognize a week with "ups and downs " quite readily, we might not even notice that a roller coaster had been used as a metaphier.

(Really) Dead Metaphor:

A metaphor where the metaphier (see Chapter 5) has been so often used that we *cannot* recognize it as a metaphor without being introduced to some word history that points out a once, but now lost, metaphor connection.

Quick Example:

While you probably recognize that a turbine is a machine that uses a wheel or cylinder to convert energy, you probably don't have memory of the Latin root of that word (*turbo*) that refers to a spinning top; hence, the original metaphor connection is lost (really dead) until explained.

Buried Metaphor:

A metaphor where the metaphier (see Chapter 5) is so often used that we (unless prompted) don't recognize it as a metaphor.

Quick Example:

A store manager tells you that demand for a certain type of digital camera has "mushroomed." You typically think about increase in sales and not about the plants that grow well on damp forest floors.

Metaphoric Entailment(s):

Recognized characteristics about metaphiers (see Chapter 5) and paraphiers that "go along" with the expressed part of the metaphor.

Quick Example:

If we say that a parent's approach with a loan officer was velvet, a baby's bottom, silk, or cream, we might in each case be reaching for (or trying to evoke) the entailment of "smooth."

For more information see:

Black, Max. "Metaphor." *Models and Metaphors: Studies in Language and Philosophy.* Ithaca, N.Y.: Cornell University Press, 1962. 25–47.

Campbell, Paul Newell. "Metaphor and Linguistic Theory." *Quarterly Journal of Speech* 61 (1975): 1–12.

Jaynes, Julian. *The Origin of Consciousness in the Breakdown of the Bicameral Mind.* Boston: Houghton Mifflin Co., 1976.

Kittay, Eva Feder. *Metaphor: Its Cognitive Force and Linguistic Structure.* New York: Oxford University Press, 1987.

Lakoff, George and Mark Johnson. *Metaphors We Live By.* Chicago: University of Chicago Press, 1980.

Ortony, Andrew, ed. *Metaphor and Thought.* 2nd ed. Cambridge: Cambridge University Press, 1993.

Richards, I. A. *The Philosophy of Rhetoric.* London: Oxford University Press, 1981.

Stern, Josef. *Metaphor in Context.* Cambridge, Mass.: MIT Press, 2000.

Wheelwright, Philip. *Metaphor and Reality.* Bloomington: Indiana University Press, 1962.

THEORIST:
Aristotle

Terms:
Rhetoric
Ethos
Pathos
Logos
Deliberative Rhetoric
Judicial Rhetoric
Epideictic Rhetoric
Enthymeme

Rhetoric:

Finding, in any given case of creating a message, the available means of persuasion.

Quick Example:

If you want to convince your city council to build new softball fields, and you need to build and deliver a speech to persuade them, rhetoric would be the process of finding all of the necessary parts, practices, and aspects of the message necessary to persuade them.

Ethos:

Character or reputation of a rhetor, especially as developed within a message to influence an audience.

Quick Example:

When you explain to an audience (that does not know you) your background, education, experiences, and expertise, you are attempting to strengthen reasons for them to find you as having good character or reputation (hence, developing ethos).

Pathos:

Appeals to emotions as developed within a message to influence an audience.

Quick Example:

If you tell a scary story in a speech to create fear in your audience, you are appealing to their emotions to make a point. You are using pathos.

Logos:

Language used to appeal to reason as developed within a message to influence an audience.

Quick Example:

If you make clear claims, offer evidence, and employ clear warrants in your speech, you are attempting to appeal to the rational decision making capacity of the audience (hence, using logos).

Deliberative Rhetoric:

Messages used to argue for the best course of action for a group often focused on the future (What will we do concerning "X"?).

Quick Example:

Legislators who create laws often argue for the best course of action for the future (hence, use deliberative rhetoric).

Judicial Rhetoric:

Messages used to argue about matters of justice typically focused on past events.

Quick Example:

Lawyers who represent clients often argue for evaluation of past events so as to accomplish justice (hence, use judicial rhetoric).

Epideictic Rhetoric:

Messages used on ceremonial occasions typically to celebrate the identity or accomplishments of individuals or groups within a community.

Quick Example:

Graduation speakers celebrate the accomplishments of the graduates (hence, use epideictic rhetoric).

Enthymeme:

A message that uses a deductive argument in a full or partial syllogistic form to reach a conclusion that will influence audience members.

Quick Example:

If you say: "Andalusians are often high-spirited horses; Cindy owns an Andalusian; Cindy's horse is probably high-spirited," you have used an enthymeme.

Quick Example:

If you say: "People who wear red socks are highly intelligent; Cindy wears red socks," you have used an enthymeme.

For more information see:

Aristotle. *Rhetoric*. In *The Complete Works of Aristotle*. Vol. 2. Ed. Jonathan Barnes. Princeton, N.J.: Princeton University Press, 1984.

Bitzer, Lloyd F. "Aristotle's Enthymeme Revisited." *Quarterly Journal of Speech* 45 (1959): 399–408.

Condit, Celeste M. "The Functions of Epideictic: The Boston Massacre Orations as Exemplar." *Communication Quarterly* 33 (1985): 284–299.

Conley, Thomas M. "The Enthymeme in Perspective." *Quarterly Journal of Speech* 70 (1984): 168–187.

Kennedy, George A. *Classical Rhetoric and Its Christian and Secular Tradition from Ancient to Modern Times*. Chapel Hill: University of North Carolina Press, 1980.

THEORIST:

Unknown [Author of Rhetorica Ad Herennium]

Terms:

Canons of Rhetoric:
Invention
Disposition
Style
Memory
Delivery

Canons of Rhetoric:

Five segments of rhetoric used in ancient Greece and Rome for development of a message, also in rhetorical education.

Invention:

Early stage in development of a message where a rhetor gathers, remembers, or solicits elements that may be used in a message.

Disposition:

Secondary stage in development of a message where a rhetor decides how to sequence and coordinate segments of a message.

Style:

Secondary stage in development of a message where a rhetor decides on the mode of words (or equivalent elements) to use in the message with special attention given to expectations of the audience.

Memory:

Tertiary stage in development of a message where a rhetor uses specialized techniques to lodge message in memory to facilitate delivery; especially important in public speaking in oral cultures.

Delivery:

Tertiary stage in development of a message where a rhetor develops the encoded elements of articulation and emphasis pertinent to the medium in use.

For more information see:

Corbett, Edward P. J. and Robert J. Connors. *Classical Rhetoric for the Modern Student.* 4th ed. New York: Oxford University Press, 1999.

Kennedy, George A. *Classical Rhetoric and Its Christian and Secular Tradition from Ancient to Modern Times.* Chapel Hill: University of North Carolina Press, 1980.

THEORIST: Marcus Tullius Cicero

Terms:
Plain Style
Middle Style
Grand Style
Stasis
Question of Fact
Question of Definition
Question of Quality
Question of Jurisdiction

Plain Style:

A message designed for instruction by a rhetor who uses the easily understood language of common people.

Middle Style:

A message designed to give pleasure to an audience by a rhetor who uses devices and tactics of language that use a recognizable flair and panache.

Grand Style:

A message designed for persuasion by a rhetor who uses devices and tactics of language that indicate a deeply important occasion or subject.

Stasis:

A point in an argument where a rhetor can find the means to "arrest," "stop," or "intercept" the force of an opponent's argument; a resource sought by the rhetor at the stage of *invention.*

Question of Fact:

A stance taken by a rhetor when defending an accused person where the rhetor challenges the accusation at the point of whether or not the accused actually did the crime; a resource sought by the rhetor at the stage of *invention.*

Question of Definition:

A stance taken by a rhetor when defending an accused person where the rhetor challenges the accusation at the point of whether or not the alleged crime fits the appropriate legal definition; a resource sought by the rhetor at the stage of *invention.*

Question of Quality:

A stance taken by a rhetor when defending an accused person where the rhetor challenges the accusation at the point of whether or not unusual circumstances were in play when the accused did the crime; a resource sought by the rhetor at the stage of *invention.*

Question of Jurisdiction:

A stance taken by a rhetor when defending an accused person where the rhetor challenges the accusation at the point of whether or not the trial for the defendant is taking place in the appropriate court; a resource sought by the rhetor at the stage of *invention.*

For more information see:
Cicero, Marcus Tullius. *De Inventione.* Trans. H. M. Hubbell. Cambridge, Mass: Harvard University Press, 1976.
Cicero, Marcus Tullius. *De Orator.* Trans. James M. May and Jakob Wisse. New York: Oxford University Press, 2001.

THEORIST:
Kenneth Burke

Terms:
Motion/Action
  Language Is Symbolic Action
Terministic Screen
Pentad
Identification
  Equipment for Living

Motion/Action:

Things move; people act. Actions taken by people are based in language and hence are motivated. Seeing people as taking motivated action encourages moral, ethical, and legal decisions. Movements are done by things with no basis in language and are unmotivated.

Quick Example:

If a bear savagely attacks a person, human response may include counterattacking, banishing, or killing the bear. (Note: no use of language to "work out the situation.") The bear, while "motivated" by hunger or territory protection or protection of cubs, has no range of choice permitted by language.[3] If a person savagely attacks a person, human response typically will include arrest and prosecution in a court of law. (Note the use of language to "work out the situation.") The attacking person is seen as having a wide range of choice permitted by language and cultural training; hence, the person is held responsible for action taken in a fashion that would not be true in response to the bear's attack.

Language Is Symbolic Action:

Language sets our understanding of conditions, expectations, and circumstances of our behavior. The seeds of our behavior in any circumstance are found in our language-based understanding of that life situation.

Quick Example:

The next time you walk into a fast-food restaurant to order a juicy, delicious ___________ (fill in the blank: Whopper, Big Mac, Classic, Sourdough Bacon Cheeseburger), order instead "your best dead cow meat burger." In either case you'll get the top-of-the line burger served there. Your enjoyment of the burger, however, will be better served by the expectations created by the names given by the burger selling establishment.

Terministic Screen:

Language acts as a screen or filter as we experience life. Language reflects our belief structures by selecting certain attributes to which we pay attention and by deflecting our attention from other attributes of people, things, and situations.

Quick Example:

If we call a shirt a "garment," we will most likely see it as an article of clothing to be worn. If we call the same shirt a "rag," we may select its ability to absorb or clean more than its size or fit. If we call the same shirt a "life saving device," we may pay attention to its capacity to be tied together with other pieces of cloth to form a device to escape out the window of a burning building.

Pentad:

A tool that aids in understanding how rhetors *explain* the primary relationship between five parts (scene, act, agent, agency, and purpose) of a typical narrative explanation about any human action. This tool addresses *explanations* of human action and *not* a direct labeling of human action.

Quick Example:

If you are arrested for driving 97 mph on a straight stretch of road in Montana, the report in the local paper the next day could give a variety of explanations for your action: "Pat was exceeding the speed limit in an attempt to outrun a forest fire that was engulfing the roadway." (A scene:act explanation) "Pat was exceeding the speed limit because she says she has speed in her blood." (An agent:act explanation) "Pat was exceeding the speed limit because her new BMW just begged to be let go." (An agency:act explanation) "Pat was exceeding the speed limit as she was racing to Kalispell to a family reunion." (A purpose:act explanation)

Identification:

A condition of mutually perceived similarity and connection between individuals or groups based on the resources of language. Association is built or undone by words or phrases that point out sameness or dissimilarity.

Quick Example:

In the movie *Independence Day* (1996), people from various nations (who might normally be seen as adversaries or opponents) were depicted as rallying and fighting together as "earthlings" in the face of a supposed attack from malevolent aliens. The movie depicted how language in messages might establish identification (as earth dwellers) between and among groups that would normally not be seen as the same.

Equipment for Living:

Messages created for audiences (ranging from comic strips to novels, from web-zines to Hollywood blockbuster films, from T-shirts to opera) are a means to provide a certain attitude toward recurring life situations.

Quick Example:

People watching *Seinfeld* could observe (and copy if they wanted to) an approach to life that highlighted detachment, personal needs, irony, friendship, unmerited success, and changing relationships in a 1990s urban setting. Using the sitcom in that way would be to see it as an aid or as equipment for living.

For more information see:

Burke, Kenneth. *The Philosophy of Literary Form: Studies in Symbolic Action.* 3rd ed. Berkeley: University of California Press, 1973.
Burke, Kenneth. *Language as Symbolic Action: Essays on Life, Literature, and Method.* Berkeley: University of California Press, 1966.
Burke, Kenneth. *A Grammar of Motives.* Berkeley: University of California Press, 1969.
Burke, Kenneth. *A Rhetoric of Motives.* New York: Prentice Hall, 1950.

THEORIST:
I. A. Richards

Terms:
Metaphor
Tenor
Vehicle

Metaphor:

A message component where one item, person, or process is described by suggesting that it is another (unlike) item, person, or process.

Quick Example:

If you say "Democracy is three wolfs and a lamb deciding on what to have for lunch," you have used a metaphor to try to explain what "democracy" is. You have attempted to create perspective by describing democracy as something it is not.

Tenor: [Ch. 5: *metaphrand*]

In a metaphor, the item, person, or process that is being described or characterized by attaching a vehicle.

Quick Example:

If a sportswriter called Lisa Fernandez "the Babe Ruth of women's softball," the person being described (Lisa Fernandez) would be the tenor of the metaphor.

Vehicle: [Ch. 5: *metaphier*]

In a metaphor, the item, person, or process that provides the means of creating the metaphor insight about the tenor.

Quick Example:

If a sportswriter called Lisa Fernandez "the Babe Ruth of women's softball," the means of creating the positive description (Babe Ruth) would be the vehicle of the metaphor.

For more information see:

Richards, I. A. *The Philosophy of Rhetoric.* London: Oxford University Press, 1981.

THEORIST:
Stephen E. Toulmin

Term:
Toulmin's Model of Argument

Toulmin's Model of Argument:

Rhetors make claims which they support with evidence; the claim and evidence are linked conceptually by a warrant. The claim may be limited by a qualifying clause. The warrant may be supported by backing.

Quick Example:

Republicans will lose seats in the midterm elections in 2002 (claim) unless they can find unusually strong wedge issues (qualifying clause) based on trends seen in elections over the past 50 years (evidence). The warrant that would link the claim to the evidence would be: consistent past events help predict similar future events.

For more information see:
Toulmin, Stephen Edelston. *The Uses of Argument*. Cambridge: Cambridge University Press, 1958.

THEORIST:
Michael Osborn

Term:
Archetypal Metaphor

Archetypal Metaphor:

A metaphor where the *metaphier* [Ch. 5] is grounded in an item, experience, or process that is known across cultures and across human history.

Quick Example:

When a singer says that his former lover is a disease without a cure, he is using a metaphor that could be understood by most people in most cultures in most periods of human history. We all experience illness and usually know about someone (or ourselves) with an incurable illness.

For more information see:
Osborn, Michael. "Archetypal Metaphor in Rhetoric: The Light-Dark Family." *Quarterly Journal of Speech* 53 (1967): 115–126.
Osborn, Michael. "The Evolution of the Archetypal Sea in Rhetoric and Poetic." *Quarterly Journal of Speech* 63 (1977): 347–363.
Hardy-Short, Dayle C. and Brant C. Short. "Fire, Death, and Rebirth: A Metaphoric Analysis of the 1988 Yellowstone Fire Debate." *Western Journal of Communication* 59 (1995): 103–125.

THEORIST:
Lloyd F. Bitzer

Terms:
Rhetorical situation
Exigence
Audience
Constraints

Rhetorical Situation:

A problem experienced in life where a rhetor can make and deliver a message designed to respond to the circumstance by gaining audience cooperation in solving or addressing the problem.

Quick Example:

If a parent of a missing child makes a plea on the evening news for help in searching a national park for his lost child, he would be involved in a rhetorical situation—one that could possibly be solved by gaining cooperation from others to solve the problem.

Exigence:

"an imperfection marked by urgency; it is a defect, an obstacle, something waiting to be done, a thing which is other than it should be."[4]

Quick Example:

A child missing in a national park area. Imperfect because children should not be lost in dangerous circumstances. A defect because parents prefer their children to be safe and in the company of their caregivers.

Audience:

People who can be influenced by a rhetorical message and who can respond to help change the rhetorical situation.

Quick Example:

People who, upon hearing a plea on the evening news for help in searching a national park for a parent's lost child, respond and help search.

Constraints:

"persons, events, objects, and relations which are parts of the situation because they have the power to constrain decision and action need to modify the exigence."[5]

Quick Example:

If a parent of a missing child makes a plea on the evening news for help in searching a national park for his lost child, a constraint could be anyone or anything that could have impact on reception of the message or response to it; e.g., if a scout leader thought the weather was too dangerous to send a scout troop out in support of the search, that belief could be a constraint.

For more information see:
Bitzer, Lloyd F. "The Rhetorical Situation." *Philosophy and Rhetoric* 1 (1968): 1–14.
Vatz, Richard E. "The Myth of the Rhetorical Situation." *Philosophy and Rhetoric* 6 (1973): 154–161.

THEORIST:
Edwin Black

Term:
Second Persona

Second Persona:

Audience as discoverable in implications found within the message artifact.

Quick Example:

A bumper sticker seen on a car parked outside of a hair styling salon states:

I cut hair—I don't do magic

At which audience do you think this bumper sticker is aimed? If you can "detect" haircut patrons who, perhaps, expect too much of the haircutter *and* the haircut, then you've discovered the essence of a "second persona." The message seems to suggest, or point to, the intended audience.

For more information see:
Black, Edwin. "The Second Persona." *Quarterly Journal of Speech* 56 (1970): 109–119.

THEORIST:
Louis Althusser

Term:
Interpelation (Hailing)

Interpellation (Hailing):

When a message appears to make certain assumptions about you, thereby inducing or demanding that you take a recognizable stance or response.

Quick Example:

An ad in a Los Angeles newspaper (in October) offers to sell you a fake "Alaskan Fir" Christmas tree; the ad promises a perfect "look of nature."[6] The ad "positions" you as someone who would be interested in buying a holiday tree in the fall season, someone who would be interested in a fake tree, someone who would want the fake tree to be associated with Alaska, someone who would want your "Alaskan" fake tree to look as if it came from "nature."

For more information see:

Althusser, Louis. "Ideology and Ideological State Apparatuses." *Lenin and Philosophy and Other Essays*. Trans. Ben Brewster. New York: Monthly Review Press, 1971.

Condit, Celeste Michelle. "Introduction—Interpellating Rhetoric, Politics and Culture: 'Hail' or 'Greetings.'" *Communication* 11 (1990): 241–252.

THEORIST:
Antonio Gramsci

Term:
Hegemony

Hegemony:

Control exhibited through language and social practices that favors certain life stances, activities, and legal arrangements.

Quick Example:

Many businesses now encourage, require, or demand that you contact them by a World Wide Web address for ordering, information, product registration, or consumer contact. Such expectations repeated over and over in the media strongly suggest that you must own (or have access to) a computer to be a participant in the marketplace of the 2000s. Such technological expectations indicate a hegemony by those who have the power, funds, and inclination to do business by computer. While you can obviously participate in contemporary life without a computer, the implicit and explicit "message" from the culture at large suggests that you are somehow deficient if you have no computer or web access.

For more information see:

Gramsci, Antonio. *Selections from the Prison Notebooks of Antonio Gramsci*. Eds. and Trans. Quintin Hoare and Geoffrey Nowell Smith. New York: International Publishers, 1971.

Pierce, Dann. "The Oregonian and the Japanese: Stereotypical Depiction as an Aspect of Rhetorical Hegemony, Circa 1906." Thesis. University of Portland, 1979.

Gitlin, Todd. "Prime Time Ideology: The Hegemonic Process in Television Entertainment." *Television: The Critical View*. 4th ed. Ed. Horace Newcomb. New York: Oxford University Press, 1987. 507–532.

Trujillo, Nick. "Hegemonic Masculinity on the Mound: Media Representations of Nolan Ryan and American Sports Culture." *Critical Studies in Mass Communication* 8 (1991): 290–308.

Condit, Celeste Michelle. "Hegemony in a Mass-Mediated Society: Concordance about Reproductive Technologies." *Critical Studies in Mass Communication* 11 (1994): 205–230.

Cloud, Dana L. "Hegemony or Concordance? The Rhetoric of Tokenism in 'Oprah' Winfrey's Rags-to-Riches Biography." *Critical Studies in Mass Communication* 13 (1996): 115–137.

Condit, Celeste Michelle. "Hegemony, Concordance, and Capitalism: A Reply to Cloud." *Critical Studies in Mass Communication* 13 (1996): 382–384.

Cloud, Dana L. "Concordance, Complexity, and Conservatism: Rejoinder to Condit." *Critical Studies in Mass Communication* 14 (1997): 192–197.

Condit, Celeste Michelle. "Clouding the Issues? The Ideal and the Material in Human Communication." *Critical Studies in Mass Communication* 14 (1997): 197–200.

THEORIST:
Julian Jaynes

Terms:
Metaphor
Metaphrand
Metaphier
Paraphier
Paraphrand

Metaphor:
A message component where one item, person, or process is described by suggesting that it is another (unlike) item, person, or process.

Quick Example:
If someone says, "Our senator is just digging herself a deeper hole," in reference to renewed support of some failed legislation, she or he is using a metaphor to characterize the senator's activity.

Metaphrand:
In a metaphor, the item, person, or process that is being described or characterized by attaching a metaphier.

Quick Example:
If someone says about your mayor, "His statement on water rates had the effect of a blowtorch on a snow cone," the metaphrand would be the mayor's statement on water rates.

Metaphier:
In a metaphor, the item, person, or process that is creating the description or characterization or perspective by being attached to a metaphrand.

Quick Example:
If someone says about your mayor, "His statement on water rates had the effect of a blowtorch on a snow cone," the metaphier would be the effect of a blowtorch on a snow cone.

Paraphier:
In a metaphor, the characteristics, aspects, or attributes remembered about the metaphier.

Quick Example:
If someone says about your mayor, "His statement on water rates had the effect of a blowtorch on a snow cone," the paraphiers would be: impact, hot, melt, destroy, eliminate, ruin, hot/cold, temperature, difference.

Paraphrand:
In a metaphor, the characteristics, aspects, or attributes from the metaphier that get mentally attached to the metaphrand.

Quick Example:
If someone says about your mayor, "His statement on water rates had the effect of a blowtorch on a snow cone," the paraphrands would be: impact, destroy, eliminate, ruin.

For more information see:
Jaynes, Julian. *The Origin of Consciousness in the Breakdown of the Bicameral Mind.* Boston: Houghton Mifflin Co., 1976.

THEORIST:
Many People

Term:
Metonymy
Synecdoche

Metonymy

A figure of verbal communication or visual communication where an *associated* part stands for the whole.

Quick Example:

(In verbal message:) Someone announces: "The suits are here for the meeting." "Suits" in this case can stand for businesspeople or lawyers who are associated with wearing a certain kind of attire.

Quick Example:

(In visual message:) In a movie, a character seen on a subway wearing a certain kind of long paper hat could be associated with employment at a fast-food shop (especially a hot-dog stand). The long paper hat has no absolute or necessary connection with selling fast food, but we've come to associate it with that line of work.

Synecdoche:

A figure of verbal communication or visual communication where an *integral* part stands for the whole.

Quick Example:

(In verbal message:) Sign seen at many fast-food eateries: Now hiring smiling faces. (We assume that the restaurant wants to hire more than just the face!)

Quick Example:

(In visual message:) In food ad: you can see only a hand and a butcher knife. (Seeing the hand and the butcher knife encourages you to think of the rest of the person wielding the knife.)

For more information see:

Corbett, Edward P. J. and Robert J. Connors. *Classical Rhetoric for the Modern Student*. 4th ed. New York: Oxford University Press, 1999.
Osborn, Michael. *Orientations to Rhetorical Style*. Chicago: SRA, 1976.

THEORISTS:
George Lakoff and Mark Johnson

Terms:
Ontological Metaphor
Orientational Metaphor
Systemic Metaphor[7]
Metaphorical Coherence

Ontological Metaphor:

A message component where one item, person, or process is described by *indirectly* suggesting that it is another (unlike) item, person, or process.

Quick Example:

If someone says, "He is emerging from his cocoon," in reference to a sports superstar who was devastated by a loss in a championship game, they are *indirectly* suggesting that the superstar is a butterfly (or other creature) who emerges from a cocoon.

Orientational Metaphor:

In a metaphor, an item, person, or process that is being described or characterized by attaching a spatial, body-positioned paraphier whose complete *metaphier* (see Chapter 5) is hidden or obscured.

Quick Example:

If someone claims, "This quarter's earning statement puts us sky high," the person is noting, in essence, that upward trends or movements are good; hence, "up is good" becomes the orientational metaphor that supports the positive value of this statement.

Systemic Metaphor:

In a metaphor, the item, person, or process that is being described or characterized is most often addressed within a systematic and predictable set of *metaphiers* (see Chapter 5). (Note that systemic metaphors use ontological metaphors.)

Quick Example:

If someone says that a love relationship of a famous singer is "going off the tracks," we can recognize that we regularly talk about personal relationships as if they were part of a journey or trip or transportation. Hence, the transportation or trip set of *metaphiers* becomes the system by which we metaphorically talk about human relationships.

Metaphorical Coherence:

In a metaphor, the characteristics, aspects, or attributes remembered about the *metaphier* (see Chapter 5) fit together in an acceptable, coherent way with other possible extensions of the metaphor.

Quick Example:

If someone says that a love relationship of a famous singer is "going off the tracks," we can stay within metaphorical coherence if we maintain the focus on language that uses a journey or trip or transportation image. Hence, we could talk about putting the relationship "back on track," or talk about it being "sidetracked," or talk about it "climbing a mountain," all of which would stay coherent with the original metaphoric expression.

For more information see:
Lakoff, George and Mark Johnson. *Metaphors We Live By*. Chicago: University of Chicago Press, 1980.

THEORIST:
Ernest Bormann

Terms:
Fantasy Theme
Chaining Out
Fantasy Type
Rhetorical Vision

Fantasy Theme:

A message, or message segment, that offers a fictional or dramatized version of life (or a portion of it) that meets the needs of the rhetor who creates the message; fantasy themes can incorporate actual events and people as well as fictional ones.

Quick Example:

The movie *The Matrix* creates a fantasy theme about how computers might be able to manipulate human minds so as to simulate living in reality.

Chaining Out:

The process that occurs when one audience member selects a fantasy theme from another rhetor and extends, shares, or modifies that fantasy theme.

Quick Example:

When a Saturday Night Live "news" program takes message form and content in different directions via modification and extension.

Fantasy Type:

A fantasy theme that becomes common in a culture by repeated and differential use.

Quick Example:

When we think we know about "scam artists" who would dupe us out of money via standard schemes of deception—even if we've never been so approached.

Rhetorical Vision:

A complex understanding of cultural processes or events as seen in messages that contain and coordinate many fantasy themes and fantasy types.

Quick Example:

A "recession economy" becomes the title for a series of expectations, actions, activities, policies, and norms when we have a rhetorical vision of certain economic conditions.

For more information see:

Bormann, Ernest G. "Fantasy and Rhetorical Vision: The Rhetorical Criticism of Social Reality." *Quarterly Journal of Speech* 59 (1972): 396–407.
Bormann, Ernest G. "A Fantasy Theme Analysis of the Television Coverage of the Hostage Release and the Reagan Inaugural." *Quarterly Journal of Speech* 68 (1982): 133–145.
Mohrmann, Gerald P. "An Essay on Fantasy Theme Criticism." *Quarterly Journal of Speech* 68 (1982): 109–132.
Bormann, Ernest G. "Fantasy and Rhetorical Vision: Ten Years Later." *Quarterly Journal of Speech* 68 (1982): 288–305.
Mohrmann, Gerald P. "Fantasy Theme Criticism: A Peroration." *Quarterly Journal of Speech* 68 (1982): 306–313.
Bormann, Ernest G. "Symbolic Convergence Theory: A Communication Formulation." *Journal of Communication* 35 (1985): 128–138.

THEORIST:
Michael Calvin McGee

Term:
Ideograph

Ideograph:

A highly abstract word or phrase taken from shared cultural history that serves as a primary value term, especially in disputes between rhetors in a given culture. Seen to have material force within a language-based community.

Quick Example:

When Bill Clinton claimed a right to <privacy> concerning his personal activities, whereas his opponents claimed that he must yield to the <rule of law> and cooperate with court orders, we observed two ideographs used by rhetors in American political culture.

For more information see:

McGee, Michael Calvin. "The 'Ideograph': A Link Between Rhetoric and Social Theory." *Quarterly Journal of Speech* 66 (1980): 1–16.

McGee, Michael Calvin. "In Search of the 'People': A Rhetorical Alternative." *Quarterly Journal of Speech* 66 (1975): 235–249.

Condit, Celeste Michelle and John Louis Lucaites. *Crafting Equality: America's Anglo-African Word.* Chicago: University of Chicago Press, 1993.

THEORIST:
Walter R. Fisher

Terms:
Narrative Coherence
Narrative Fidelity

Narrative Coherence: [Ch. 6]

Degree to which the characters, actions, and scenes in a narrative are plausible or believable. Believable characters, actions, and scenes are "coherent," whereas characters, actions, or scenes that violate likelihood or credibility standards are not "coherent."

Quick Example:

In older western movies some audience members found it implausible that a six-shooter pistol could be fired many more than six times without apparent reloading; hence the narrative coherence of the movie was damaged for some viewers.

Quick Example:

When news reports indicate that a professional entertainment wrestler is running for the office of governor in a prominent state, many people saw the emerging story as implausible, unbelievable, or incoherent.

Narrative Fidelity: [Ch. 6]

Degree to which the characters, actions, and scenes in a narrative seem to resonate with life experiences held by an audience member. Characters, actions, or scenes match personal experience, expectations, or values to create connection and fidelity. Others that do not create that matching can be observed, but seem distant or only indirectly connected.

Quick Example:

Primary female characters in *Sleepless in Seattle* are depicted "connecting" with the movie *An Affair to Remember.* The presumed narrative fidelity between that movie and those characters show that the movie connects beyond the level of mere entertainment.

For more information see:

Fisher, Walter R. "Public Moral Argument: The Nuclear Controversy." *Argument in Transition: Proceedings of the Third Summer Conference on Argumentation.* Ed. David Zarefsky, Malcolm O. Sillars, and Jack Rhodes. Annandale, Va.: Speech Communication Association, 1983. 441–462.

Fisher, Walter R. *Human Communication as Narration: Toward a Philosophy of Reason, Value, and Action.* Columbia: University of South Carolina Press, 1989.

Fisher, Walter R. and Robert F. Goodman, eds. *Rethinking Knowledge: Reflections Across the Disciplines.* Albany: State University of New York Press, 1995.

THEORIST:
Many People

Terms:
Feminist Rhetoric
Feminist Rhetorical Theories

Feminist Rhetoric:

Public and private messages often created by female rhetors. A critique and awareness of how cultural messages have framed and motivated women in human culture.

Quick Example:

Mary Daly's written and spoken messages. Cindy L. Griffin's analysis of Daly's rhetoric. Janice A. Radway's analysis of women and popular romance literature.

Feminist Rhetorical Theories:

Systematic concepts of the dynamics of messages for and about women in human culture. "[P]lausible, valid, and important explanations of how rhetoric works in the world."[8] These theories of human communication and meaning making often focus on equality, marginalization, or oppression of people; they may promote an activist stance for using theory to promote social change.

Quick Examples:

Foss and Griffin's theory of a feminist rhetoric. Sharon D. Downey's feminist rhetorical theory.

For more information see:
Campbell, Karlyn Kohrs. "The Rhetoric of Women's Liberation: An Oxymoron." *Quarterly Journal of Speech* 59 (1973): 74–86.
Campbell, Karlyn Kohrs. *Man Cannot Speak for Her: A Critical Study of Early Feminist Speakers.* Westport, Conn.: Greenwood Press, 1989.
Donawerth, Jane, ed. *Rhetorical Theory by Women before 1900.* New York: Rowman and Littlefield, 2002.
Downey, Sharon D. "Rhetoric as Balance: A Dialectical Feminist Perspective." *Women's Studies in Communication* 20 (1997): 137–150.
Foss, Sonja K. and Cindy L. Griffin. "A Feminist Perspective on Rhetorical Theory: Toward a Clarification of Boundaries." *Western Journal of Communication* 56 (1992): 330–349.
Foss, Sonja K. and Cindy L. Griffin. "Beyond Persuasion: A Proposal for an Invitational Rhetoric." *Communication Monographs* 62 (1995): 2–17.
Griffin, Cindy L., Sonja K. Foss, and Karen A. Foss. *Feminist Rhetorical Theories.* Thousand Oaks, Calif.: Sage, 1999.
Biesecker, Barbara. "Coming to Terms with Recent Attempts to Write Women into the History of Rhetoric." *Philosophy and Rhetoric* 25 (1992): 140–161.
Griffin, Cindy L. "Women as Communicators: Mary Daly's Hagography as Rhetoric." *Communication Monographs* 60 (1993): 158–177.
Campbell, Karlyn Kohrs. "Biesecker Cannot Speak for Her Either." *Philosophy and Rhetoric* 26 (1993): 153–159.
Radway, Janice A. *Reading the Romance: Women, Patriarchy, and Popular Literature.* Chapel Hill: University of North Carolina Press, 1984.
Rakow, Lana F., ed. *Women Making Meaning: New Feminist Directions in Communication.* New York: Routledge, 1992.

THEORISTS:
David Bordwell and Kristin Thompson

Terms:
Plot
Story

Plot: [Ch. 6: *story*[g]]

Elements of depiction actually provided for an audience member. In print narrative, words that depict; in visual narrative (movies or television or Internet) items actually seen or heard.

Quick Examples:

In a novel when the writer depicts by saying, "The breadbox was bright, radiant red," we are being given a plot item.

In a movie when the director depicts by showing us a bright, radiantly red breadbox, we are being given a plot item.

Story: [Ch. 6: *story*[c]]

Elements of depiction *not* actually provided for an audience member; items that the audience imagines or fills in based on *story*[g] elements. In print narrative, filling in time, space, or physical characteristics not directly depicted; in visual narrative (movies or television or internet) filling in time, space, or physical characteristics not directly depicted.

Quick Example:

In a novel when the writer depicts by saying, "After her surgery, and a three week stay in the hospital, she was desperate for a home-cooked meal." We are left to fill in the unstated *story*[c] information about the experiences and food offered in a three week hospital stay.

In a movie when the director depicts by showing us a character slowly waking up in a sun-streaked barn loft and picking straw out of his hair when we last saw him hitchhiking on a country road late at night. We are expected to fill in the unstated *story*[c] events that allowed the character to get from the country road the night before to the hay loft the next morning.

For more information see:

Bordwell, David and Kristin Thompson. *Film Art: An Introduction.* 5th ed. New York: McGraw-Hill, 1997.
Sternberg, Meir. *Expositional Modes and Temporal Ordering in Fiction.* Baltimore: Johns Hopkins University Press, 1978.

THEORIST:
John Fiske

Term:
Polysemy

Polysemy:

Flexibility of messages to be understood in different ways by different individuals and groups.

Quick Example:

When one audience member might see *Titanic* (the movie) as a love story, another might see it as a critique of wealth, another might see it as a coming of age story, etc.

For more information see:

Fiske, John. "Television and Popularity." *Critical Studies in Mass Communication* 3 (1986): 391–408.
Condit, Celeste Michelle. "The Rhetorical Limits of Polysemy." *Critical Studies in Mass Communication* 6 (1989): 103–122.

THEORIST:
Celeste M. Condit

Term:
Polyvalence

Polyvalance:

Flexibility of messages to be understood in the same way as to what they depict, but in different ways as to the meaning or value of the message.

Quick Example:

When two audience members see the same young women "competing" for the title of Miss America, but one person sees the contest as a good opportunity for a girl and the other sees the "contest" as an outrage to young women.

For more information see:
Condit, Celeste Michelle. "The Rhetorical Limits of Polysemy." *Critical Studies in Mass Communication* 6 (1989): 103–122.

THEORIST:
Many People

Terms:
Narrative
Diegesis
Diegetic
Non-Diegetic
Screen Time
Story^{g} Time
Story^{c} Time

Narrative:

Presenting, or more typically, re-presenting to an audience words, images, or sounds (at times in combination), and audience processing of those message elements. Narratives depict cause and effect relationships occurring in time and space between social actors in a form and sequence consistent with the storyteller's (or more accurately the story-evoker's) perspective and interests.

Quick Examples:

A kindergarten teacher reading *The Little Engine that Could* to a class.
A person watching *O Brother, Where Art Thou?* on DVD.

Diegesis:

The world of the story evoked (*story*^{c}) by presentation by a rhetor of *story*^{g} elements in a narrative process.

Quick Example:

When we watch Tom Hanks in *Cast Away* for several hours and a story of several years of experience in the lives of the depicted characters is created in our minds.

Diegetic:

When a *story*^{g} element "fits" in the overall "world of the story" being depicted by a rhetor in a narrative process.

Quick Example:

When we watch Tom Hanks in *Cast Away* and he has ice skates on a tropical island, yet we understand how the ice skates got to the island.

Non-Diegetic:

When a *story*^{g} element does not "fit" in the overall "world of the story" being depicted by a rhetor in a narrative process.

Quick Example:

When we hear music accompany George C. Scott scenes in *Patton* and there is no place "within" the world of the story for an orchestra.

Screen time:

The amount of time it takes for a narrative to be presented on a movie or television screen.

Quick Example:

Screen time for *The Big Lebowski* is 117 minutes.

Story^{g} **time:**

The amount of time it takes to depict all of the diegetic *story^{g}* elements for a narrative on a movie or television.

Quick Example:

Story^{g} time for *Sleepless in Seattle* is less than 105 minutes.

Story^{c} **time:**

The amount of time it takes for all of the depicted *story^{g}* elements to "play out" chronologically for a narrative on a movie or television.

Quick Example:

Story^{c} time for *Sleepless in Seattle* is many months.

For more information see:
Bordwell, David. *Narrative in Fiction Film.* Madison: University of Wisconsin Press, 1985.
Chatman, Seymour. *Story and Discourse: Narrative Structure in Fiction and Film.* Ithaca: Cornell University Press, 1978.
Chatman, Seymour. *Coming to Terms: The Rhetoric of Narrative in Fiction and Film.* Ithaca: Cornell University Press, 1990.
Sternberg, Meir. *Expositional Modes and Temporal Ordering in Fiction.* Baltimore: Johns Hopkins University Press, 1978.
Thompson, Kristin. *Storytelling in the New Hollywood: Understanding Classical Narrative Technique.* Cambridge, Mass.: Harvard University Press, 1999.

THEORIST:
Herbert Zettl

Terms:
X-axis
Y-axis
Z-axis

X-axis:

Any point on a screen on a horizontal plane from right to left or left to right.

Quick Example:

When an airplane is shown flying across the sky (from right to left or left to right on the screen) the airplane is moving on the x-axis.

Y-axis:

Any point on a screen on a vertical plane from top to bottom or bottom to top.

Quick Example:

When a rocket is shown taking off from a launch pad (from bottom to top on the screen) the rocket is moving on the y-axis.

Z-axis:

Any point on a screen on an imaginary plane from screen surface to an infinity point at a vanishing point that appears to be "in the far distance" from the screen surface.

Quick Example:

When a person seems to walk directly toward you in a camera shot, he or she is walking on z-axis.

For more information see:
Zettl, Herbert. *Sight, Sound, and Motion*. 3rd ed. Belmont, CA: Wadsworth, 1999.

THEORISTS:
Many People

Term:
Subject Motion
Camera Motion
Cyber Motion
Mise-en-scene
In medias res
Wild (scratch) sound
ADR
Diegetic sound
Non-Diegetic sound

Subject Motion:

When an object or person moves in front of a camera and the motion is recorded on film, tape, or digital media.

Quick Examples:

A bank robber's movement is captured on a surveillance camera at a bank.

Camera Motion:

When the camera moves, creating the sense of motion on the screen—such as a pan, tilt, dolly, crane, or track move—the motion perceived by the audience is created by movement by the camera.

Quick Example:

When we watch the camera "circle" around Nicolas Cage in *Face Off* as he is constrained, the perceived motion is from camera motion.

Cyber Motion:

When an object or person appears to move on the screen, but that movement has been created inside a computer.

Quick Example:

When we watch Woody or Buzz Lightyear move in *Toy Story,* we are watching cyber motion created inside a computer for display on a movie screen.

Mise-en-scene:
Any element visible in a directed movie or television program including lighting, costumes, actors, props, scenery, location items, streetscapes, landscapes, seascapes, and spacescapes.
Quick Example:
When you observe the hat worn by Gandalf the Grey in *Lord of the Rings,* the stark lighting in *Blood Simple,* the bridge in *Free Willy,* or Robin Williams's face in *Good Morning Vietnam,* you are observing elements of *mise-en-scene.*
In medias res:
The starting point (in the middle of things) for most narratives (except for some creation stories) with events that are assumed to precede the current tale and with event assumed to follow it.
Quick Example:
When *Rocky* opens in a run-down Philadelphia gym, we are joining the characters depicted in a mid-point of their lives.
Wild (or scratch) Sound:
Sound originally recorded on a sound stage or on location that is later used as a reference point for re-recording dialog in feature films.
Quick Example:
The sound you never hear unless the movie is a documentary, a very low budget film, or a show on the "making of" a feature film.
ADR:
Automatic dialog replacement: recording vocal talent's dialog over the scratch sound dialog originally recorded on location or on a sound stage (sometimes the actual voice of the actor whose face you see, but—many times not [especially for non-stars]).
Quick Example:
Dialog heard in most feature films released from Hollywood.
Diegetic Sound:
Sound that "fits" in the overall "world of the story" being depicted by a rhetor in a narrative process.
Quick Example:
Squealing tires heard from cars being stolen in *Gone in 60 Seconds* fit the "world of the story" being depicted.

Non-Diegetic Sound:

Sound that does not "fit" in the overall "world of the story" being depicted by a rhetor in a narrative process.

Quick Example:

When we hear odd sounds coming from characters' mouths in certain scenes from *Me, Myself & Irene,* we can be sure that they do not "fit" any known world of human experience.

For more information see:
Gross, Lynne S. and Larry W. Ward. *Electronic Moviemaking*. 4th ed. Belmont, Calif.: Wadsworth, 2000.
Rabiger, Michael. *Directing: Film Techniques and Aesthetics*. 2nd ed. Boston: Focal Press, 1997.
Stewart, Garrett. *Between Film and Screen: Modernism's Photo*. Chicago: University of Chicago Press, 1999.

Below you will find a series of journal articles written by Condit and by Cloud. Use these articles to prepare for the Chapter 9 workshop.

Source: *Critical Studies in Mass Communication* 13 (1996), 382–384.

Hegemony, Concordance, and Capitalism: Reply to Cloud

Celeste M. Condit

In her essay of June 1996 in this journal, Dana Cloud misrepresented my statement of the theory of concordance (*CSMC*, September 1994). To avoid any assumption by the readership of *CSMC* that I agree with her characterization of the theory, the Editor has graciously allowed me to respond to her misrepresentations. Professor Cloud does both scholarship and progressive politics a disservice by her reductive and misleading representation of my essay. I am eager to argue with anyone about what the best possible course might be for progressive social change to take. In such a conversation, however, we need to argue with each other's position, not with some chimera. Therefore, I seek to make it clear where Cloud misconstrues my position.

1. Cloud says that my article claimed that "contemporary U.S. society runs on a 'mixed economy' that provides an adequate safety net for the poor and a large measure of material equality" (p. 117). My essay did not say that there is an adequate safety net, and I do not believe there is one. Complicated revisions would be needed in the U.S. social system

Celeste M. Condit is professor of speech communication at the University of Georgia and Review and Criticism editor of *Critical Studies in Mass Communication.* She wishes to thank Bonnie Dow, John Lucaites, and Bruce Railsback for helpful comments on a previous draft of this essay.

to make an adequate minimal support system, and I support such revisions. I do believe it to be factually obvious that the U.S. society runs on a "mixed economy." As I said in the essay, "the economy itself is not a purely capitalist one, but a mixed economy in which over a third of the gross national product is redistributed by governments at various levels" (p. 208). Such a factual claim hardly seems to imply satisfaction with the particular arrangements that exist. In a nation where basketball players and auto company executives pull down multimillion dollar annual salaries, it would seem odd to claim that there is a "large measure of material equality." My essay didn't say that, and my analysis of the meaning of the word "equality" is far more complicated than Cloud suggests (see Condit & Lucaites, 1993).

2. Cloud says that I support a "happy concordance" (p. 115). I never typified concord as happy. I described concordance in our society as "less than ideal, but materially tenable," and said that "This does not mean that an ideal, fair, or just concordance is produced, because some groups have disproportionate rhetorical advantage and some groups are not invited by the mediators into the concordance at all" (p. 226). I believe that in general concord is reluctant, disgruntled, and often angry. After the Civil War, for example, black leaders such as Booker T. Washington adapted to the conditions of lynching and zero-economic opportunity for blacks through an industrial education program. Washington's adaptation did not mean that he was satisfied with political conditions, but merely that he was doing what he was able to do for his people in the context of the times.

3. Cloud further indicates that I say that class conflict no longer exists. She says "Condit's assumption that domination and division are no longer primary features of contemporary Western society is fundamentally mistaken" (p. 117). She says further that Condit "fails to note that fully one-third of black Americans . . . live in poverty," and that "because of ongoing racism and sexism, black Americans and women are overrepresented among the working poor" (p. 118). In contrast, what I wrote was:

> Recent analyses indicate that cultural factors such as race, gender, and religion have their own determinate influence "in the last instance." (Or more appropriately, that there is never a "last instance.") In light of contemporary multicultural conditions, economic universalism must give way to less totalized assumptions about the ability of one class adequately to represent or speak for any others. . . . This produces models of political process that incorporate multiple contesting groups rather than a simple bivalent opposition between a unified, homogeneous capitalist class and a unified, universal working class. (pp. 209–210)

The obvious thrust of my essay was not to argue that the U.S. has achieved an ideal and happy democracy, but rather to suggest that models employed for analysis of social division and contestation must incorporate more factors than simplistic models based solely on class have included. I believe that I am following Gramsci faithfully when I say that we need to recognize the material state of the current populace and formulate our theories and actions (our praxis) based on those conditions. In our context, that means turning the mixed economy to the advantage of those who are less advantaged, protecting the environment in all feasible ways, and understanding and protecting gender, racial, and ethnic diversity.

In summary, Cloud has tried to reduce my position to a stick-figure version of happy capitalism. That kind of reduction serves no one well. My theoretical formulations are as sensitive to the problems of racism, sexism, and capitalism as is Cloud's 19th century Marxism (rather, more so). The pressing political question is how to deal with these problems. To deal with them adequately, one must understand the world in which we live. Ours is not a world in which a simple homogeneous working class opposes a simple, homogeneous capitalist class. We live no longer in the 19th century. The interests of a black woman employed in a poultry factory in the South are in important ways different from those of a male, white skilled laborer employed in a high-tech automobile plant in the North, which are again different from those of a Chicano school teacher in the West (who may be the only union member among the three). Classical Marxist dogma held that the best way to produce social change was to efface these differences in the name of a single "working class." Such a rhetorical strategy does violence to the particularity of different groups. It ignores the unique reproductive concerns of women, it effaces the problems of cultural diversity (not merely race), and it does not come to grips with the complexity of the alliances among different social groups.

The theory of concordance does not seek to efface class issues, but rather to provide a methodology for exploring a broader set of discursive forces active in public media. I invite the readership to return to my essay and make their own assessments about the utility of the methodology for this purpose. As my original essay noted, "hegemony functions differently in different times and places. Hence, this is neither a universal model nor a prescriptive one" (p. 211). The model I employed pertained to press representations of *in vitro* fertilization technologies. If we are to judge the appropriateness of our competing models, therefore, we must ask how Cloud's theoretical model would treat that original case. For those who have easily borne children, it might seem tempting to employ Cloud's classical dominant ideology critique to portray women who use infertility technologies as either simple oppressors of other women or as dupes of a unified capitalist class. I hope that more of us will be able, however, to see the complexities embedded in such social practices. Whether or not the methodology of concordance might also provide insight about figures in mass entertainment such as Oprah Winfrey, I leave to others to explore. I have offered a critique of concordance simply as one means for probing the often wrenching complexities of our contemporary social life.

Reading References

Cloud, D. L. (1996). Hegemony or concordance? The rhetoric of tokenism in 'Oprah' Winfrey's rags-to-riches biography. *Critical Studies in Mass Communication,* 13, 115–137.

Condit, C. M. (1994). Hegemony in a mass-mediated society: Concordance about reproductive technologies. *Critical Studies in Mass Communication,* 11, 205–230.

Condit, C. M. & Lucaites, J. L. (1993). *Crafting equality: America's Anglo-African word.* Chicago: University of Chicago Press.

Source: From *Critical Studies in Mass Communication* 14 (1997), 192.

A June 1996, *Critical Studies in Mass Communication* article by Dana L. Cloud ("Hegemony or Concordance? The Rhetoric of Tokenism in Oprah Winfrey's Rags-to-Riches Biography"), prompted a reply from Celeste M. Condit, some of whose work Cloud had reviewed in her article, which we published in December 1996 ("Hegemony, Concordance, and Capitalism: Reply to Cloud"). This correspondence in turn has prompted an additional response from Cloud, and a reply from Condit.

Dana Cloud is an assistant professor in the Department of Speech Communication at the University of Texas at Austin, and Celeste Condit is a professor in the Department of Speech Communication at the University of Georgia.

Source: *Critical Studies in Mass Communication* 14 (1997), 193–200.

Concordance, Complexity, and Conservatism: Rejoinder to Condit

Dana L. Cloud

In a response to my essay "Hegemony or Concordance? The Rhetoric of Tokenism in the Rags-to-Riches Biography of 'Oprah' Winfrey" (Cloud, 1996), Celeste Condit (1997) charges me with misrepresenting her theory of hegemony as concordance (Condit, 1994). Unfortunately, Condit's *ad feminem* attack on me diverts attention from the most productive and interesting loci of debate about hegemony theory. Further, her essay builds

For their close readings of and excellent advice about an earlier version of this essay, I thank Keith Hutchinson and Carol Stabile. Readers should refer to Stabile's essay "Resistance, Recuperation, and Reflexivity: The Limits of a Paradigm" (1995) which also takes issue with Condit's reformulation of hegemony theory.

and burns a straw version—reliant upon the god term "complexity" and the devil term "dogma"—of ideology critique. Her article and her response both reveal a series of fundamental misunderstandings: of the Gramscian theory of hegemony, of Marxist approaches to the interplay of race- and gender-based oppressions in capitalism, and of the purposes of ideology criticism.

Ironically, Condit accuses me of dogmatic Marxist reductionism while herself reducing class-based critique to an ill-informed straw person. Her original essay and her response to my article ignore a wide range of influential critiques of hegemony as a strategy of domination—Marxist, feminist, and otherwise—by authors such as Terry Eagleton (1991), Collette Guillaumin (1995), Todd Gitlin (1980), Stuart Hall (1986), Raymond Williams (1973), Herman Gray (1995), Mary Poovey (1986), bell hooks (1996), and others (see Dow, 1992; Murphy, 1990). More specifically, the work of materialist feminists does a superb job of explaining how class bears directly on the lives of women and on their gendered identities and oppressions. For example, Stephanie Coontz's *The Way We Never Were* (1992) offers a materialist history of the normative nuclear family, and discusses how common sense understandings of "family values" and gender are interwoven with class position. All of this literature provides complex analyses of gender, race, class, and culture that defy Condit's strawwoman and challenge Condit's ungrounded claim that race, gender, and religion have their own determining influence independent of class.[1]

Yet Condit's opposition of the god term "complexity" (along with recency or newness as spurious criteria for theoretical relevance) against the devil terms "orthodox," "19th-century," and "dogmatic" is made to bear the weight of her unsubstantiated assertion that materialist approaches do violence to difference and complexity. In addition, there are serious problems with elevating "difference" and "complexity" to the status of god terms. These problems include a refusal to confront economic structures of power in favor of examining, deconstructing, and reconstructing discourses about identity; and, on the other hand, the near-impossibility of building a cohesive movement in the absence of any notion of collective interests across race, gender, culture, religion, sexuality, etc. (see Kauffman, 1990; Smith, 1994; Wood, 1986). In addition to generating fragmented and ineffectual movements, the politics of difference or identity is idealist, in the philosophical sense of an overemphasis on ideas and consciousness in producing social change. An emphasis on class challenges the discursive hubris or rhetorical idealism of our field (Cloud, 1994).

Condit condemns my critical approach for failing to acknowledge her "complex" (read, "textualist" or "discourse-oriented") definition of equality, advanced in the book *Crafting Equality* (Condit and Lucaites, 1993). Yet I am interested less in how concordances about equality and freedom emerge in discourse as in how those rhetorics obscure or belie material conditions of unfreedom and inequality in the everyday world of work and struggle for the poor and disenfranchised. This was the point of my article on "Oprah" biographies, which noted how the pronounced celebration of one woman's success corresponds with growing structural racial inequality. In this context, the retreat from class as an analytical category of social explanation is less a progressive gesture toward diversity and multiculturalism than it is a concession to existing political fragmentation and the erosion of material gains made by strong collective, antagonistic movements in the past.

It is imperative to read Gramsci in the context of such movements. Indeed, there is a stark difference between what Gramsci meant by the winning of consent and Condit's "concordance," defined in her article as "simply the best that can be done under the circumstances" (p. 210). Although Condit is correct in noting that she never put the word "happy" before the word "concordance" (meaning "state of agreement") in her article, the word "concordance" itself has a positive connotation that, if adopted as a substitute for hegemony, renders the contemporary hegemony of liberal capitalism less amenable to critique. Indeed, Condit stresses that her new, positive emphasis is on how women and other groups can be better regarded as "active constructors of their own interests" (p. 219) in the concordance model. As Carol Stabile notes in an analysis of *Roseanne,* this perspective de-emphasizes the constraining role of economic and dominant political interests in cultural production and negotiation over controversial texts (Stabile, 1995).

Gramsci's original understanding of hegemony, developed in the fight against fascism, stands in contrast to Condit's redefinition of hegemony as concordance. Early in the *Prison Notebooks,* Gramsci defines hegemony as

> the "spontaneous" consent given by the great masses of the population to the general direction imposed on social life by the dominant fundamental group; this consent is "historically" caused by the prestige (and consequent confidence) which the dominant group enjoys because of its position and function in the world of production. (1971, p. 12)

The placement of the word "spontaneous" in quotations marks suggests Gramsci's ironic awareness that the perception of active participation or concordance from below in the dominant ideas of a culture is illusory. Further, Gramsci is careful to point out that the persuasive function of hegemony is backed up by force, "the apparatus of state coercive power which 'legally' enforces discipline on those groups who do not 'consent' " (p. 12). Again the selective use of ironic quotation marks indicates that we are to understand the legality of the state's power as problematic, constructed as part of a reigning common sense by those in power (see pp. 235, 263, 285, and 328 for passages with similar emphasis).

Of course, Gramsci does complicate the economism of earlier Marxists in two ways, first by emphasizing the possibility and the necessity of building democratic socialist counterhegemonic blocs to confront capitalist power and the totalitarian state. Second, Gramsci emphasizes the importance of ideas, persuasion, and consciousness in the formation of a counterhegemonic movement (Gramsci, 1971, pp. 333 and 377; see also Zompetti, 1997). However, these amendments do not warrant stripping the concept of hegemony of its critical political valence.

Critical scholars today should retain Gramsci's materialist understanding of hegemony in order to explain persuasive rhetorics that carry heavy material penalities for those scapegoated in them. For example, meritocratic rhetorics justify penalizing welfare recipients and some immigrants for their failure to thrive despite rhetorical lip service to "opportunity" and "choice." Likewise, the current crime wave hype is matched by repressive police violence in urban areas against black youth who have been discursively criminalized. Another crucial question from the perspective of an ideology critic is whether the "choices" offered in the rhetorics of the marketplace and liberalism are real for the majority of the people. We should extend the concept "choice" in order to challenge its liberal-capitalist inflections with regard to the inaccessibility of some choices (including both abortion and fertility and pregnancy specialists) to poor women, disproportionately women of color. This material backdrop for "choice" calls into question the possibility of a true "concordance" under capitalism, which limits "choice"—in terms of reproduction as well as cultural and political representation—to those who can pay.

Such critique of how ideas, system, and structure work together does not necessarily entail personal indictment of people who, out of necessity, participate in the real world of contemporary capitalism. For example, I would never condemn any individual woman invested in new reproductive technologies as a "dupe" or "oppressor" as Condit suggests I would (1997, p. 384). However, I think it is crucial for socialists, progressives, feminists, and other critical rhetoricians to ask why and how many American women are persuaded that nothing is more important in their life than bearing children. As Coontz (1992) points out, the motherhood imperative has long served ideologically to privatize social responsibility for the care of citizens and workers, with most of the burden of care falling on women's shoulders. This set of questions targets for critique the ideologies sustaining prevailing social relations—not ordinary people negotiating their way through daily life.

Thus I believe that what is at stake between Condit and me with regard to the concept of hegemony is not the particular semantic weight of "mixed" vs. "pure capitalist" economies, "adequate" vs. merely "materially tenable" safety nets, or liberal "truth" and Marxist "dogma." The issue is whether one's purposes in performing criticism are to critique a system fundamentally based on exploitation and oppression and to expose the limits of its justificatory rhetorics, or to settle for the limited personal agency, tokenist representation, and consumer choice market capitalism will allow. As Condit (1994) admits, "Social concord is based on an accommodationist model of discourse . . . Concord is neither harmonious nor inevitably fair or equitable, it is simply the best that can be done under the circumstances" (p. 210).

I and other materialist scholars have been and will be held accountable to Condit's "accomodationist model of discourse" when we use the word "hegemony," unless we challenge the concordance model directly. For this reason, I reserve Gramsci's concept of hegemony, a product of class struggle and anti-capitalist critique, for a critical project emphasizing the continuing salience of concepts of structure, domination, and class antagonism. And I ask that we conduct this argument about critical practice and its attendant theories around significant loci of debate rather than around spurious and defensive charges of distortion and dogma.

Note

A few words are in order about another dimension of Condit's misunderstanding of the Marxist tradition: the confusion of state control or "big government" with socialism. If state control of the economy equaled socialism, then fascist states would have to be considered socialist in nature; socialists, however, are among the most vociferous anti-fascists in Europe and the United States. In addition, most Marxists active today in the academy and in social movements recognize that the Soviet Union after Stalin's rise to power and the Eastern bloc under Stalinism represented not socialism (which would include both political and economic democracy) but totalitarian state capitalism, run in the interests of a bureaucratic elite (see Cliff, 1996). In the contemporary United States, the active intervention of the government in the economy has represented less a move toward a mixed economy (in Condit's terms), than toward the greater investment of the American state in protecting corporate interests, as the recent campaign finance scandals revealing the peddling of influence might suggest.

Reading References

Cliff, T. (1996). *Russia: From workers' state to state capitalism.* London: Bookmarks.

Cloud, D. L. (1994). The materiality of discourse as oxymoron: A challenge to critical rhetoric. *Western Journal of Communication,* 58, 141–163.

Cloud, D. L. (1996). Hegemony or concordance? The rhetoric of tokenism in 'Oprah' Winfrey's rags-to-riches biography. *Critical Studies in Mass Communication,* 13, 115–137.

Condit, C. M. & Lucaites, J. L. (1993). *Crafting equality: America's Anglo-African word.* Chicago: University of Chicago Press.

Condit, C. M. (1994). Hegemony in a mass-mediated society: Concordance about reproductive technologies. *Critical Studies in Mass Communication,* 11, 205–230.

Condit, C. M. (1997). Hegemony, concordance, and capitalism: Reply to Cloud. *Critical Studies in Mass Communication*, 13, 382–384.

Coontz, S. (1992). *The way we never were: American families and the nostalgia trap.* New York: HarperCollins.

Dow, B. (1990). Hegemony, feminist criticism, and *The Mary Tyler Moore Show. Critical Studies in Mass Communication*, 7, 261–274.

Gramsci, A. (1971). *Selections from the prison notebooks.* Trans. Q. Hoare and G. Nowell Smith. New York: International Publishers. (Work first written in 1936–37.)

Eagleton, T. (1991). *Ideology: An introduction.* London: Verso.

Gitlin, T. (1980). *The whole world is watching: Mass media in the making and unmaking of the new left.* Berkeley: University of California Press.

Gray, H. (1995). *Watching race: Television and the struggle for "blackness."* Minneapolis: University of Minnesota Press.

Guillaumin, C. (1995). *Racism, sexism, power, and ideology.* London: Routledge.

Hall, S. (1986). Gramsci's relevance for the study of race and ethnicity. *Journal of Communication Inquiry,* 10, 5–27.

hooks, b. (1994). *Outlaw Culture.* New York: Routledge.

Kauffman, L. A. (1990). The anti-politics of identity. *Socialist Review,* 20, 67–80.

Murphy, J. (1992). Domesticating dissent: The Kennedys and the Freedom Rides. *Communication Monographs*, 59, 61–78.

Poovey, M. (1986). Scenes of an indelicate character: The medical treatment of Victorian women. *Representations,* 14, 137–167.

Smith, S. (1994). Mistaken identity. *International Socialism,* 62, 1–49.

Stabile, C. (1995). Resistance, recuperation, and reflexivity: The limits of a paradigm. *Critical Studies in Mass Communication,* 12, 403–422.

Williams, R. (1973). Base and superstructure in Marxist cultural theory. *New Left Review,* 82, 3–16.

Wood, E. M. (1986). The retreat from class. London: Verso.

Zompetti, J. (1997). Toward a Gramscian critical rhetoric. *Western Journal of Communication*, 61, 66–86.

Clouding the Issues? The Ideal and the Material in Human Communication

Celeste M. Condit

What scholarly projects ought critical media scholars to prefer? My own work has sought to understand how linguistically material discursive formations come in to being. Cloud insists instead that we should expend our efforts in demonstrating that these formations "obscure or belie material conditions of unfreedom or inequality." These two projects are not inherently incompatible. They are made incompatible at the level of critical procedure, however, by our differing epistemological assumptions and political scope. Cloud's project presumes that it is self-evident what social formations are constituted by the ideals of "freedom" and "equality" and that these could be readily articulated both in the academy and in the mass media. Contemporary media products are therefore simply to be condemned for their failure to represent these utopian ideals.

In contrast, while I find it easy to endorse the ideals of "freedom" and "equality," I feel bewildered and ignorant about the ways in which these abstract ideals can be materially instantiated in any universal fashion. I do not believe that there is an *a priori* meaning to such terms, but rather that their meanings are produced in particular social formations through situated human discourse (McGee, 1980). In our own time, there are two major material barriers between these ideals and our material realities. First, to the extent that we now understand language, culture, and identity not as ideals, but as material in substantive ways, it seems unclear what "economic equality" should mean in a culturally diverse population of four billion people. As an example, consider the migratory groups of Native American plains people. To sustain their culture materially would require reestablishing their hegemony over thousands of acres of land so that they might once again engage in the seasonal movement from camas digging grounds to salmon fishing streams to hunting and wintering lands. How can such a set of material requirements be "equalized" with the material conditions of traditional Japanese culture or South American jungle peoples? Or the Amish? Or the Mormons? With four billion people and thousands of cultural groups, every culture's claimed material needs cannot be met and any mathematical formula for "equality" necessarily impinges on the ways of life of some of these groups.

Hence, because culture is material, any commitment to cultural diversity makes us rethink what economic equality might mean. As long as we do not come to grips with the conflicting values and needs of different peoples it is the easy part of scholarship to "critique a system fundamentally based on exploitation and oppression:" and it remains the hidden challenge of our scholarship to understand how we might materialize other values in a just social concordance.

Second, because the nature of "economic equality" is not simple and self-evident, it seems impossible to produce "economic equality" without a dictatorial social entity prescribing fundamental behaviors for members of diverse cultures, against their will. Cloud assumes that a true "political and economic democracy" can arise to fulfill this need, and she seems to think that the will of the majority by definition is non-coercive. As a model of such a utopia, Cloud (1992) recommends Marge Piercy's *Woman on the Edge of Time.* In Piercy's world, culture is mostly decorative, and there is no apparent struggle over resources between the various "cultural" groups that have all agreed to live on a similar model of small, high-tech townships. Furthermore, the deficiencies Cloud attacks in the equality of reproductive choices in our own social formation are remedied in Piercy's world by prohibiting everyone's right to reproduce. A people's board (of unclear membership, but apparently majoritarian democratic sentiments) dictates which humans will be cloned to enter the next generation. This seems to be a blatant instantiation of "unfreedom" (and to fit many definitions of fascism). At the least, this disregard for reproductive freedom fails to attend seriously to the values of most of the world's cultures, and it does so because it fails to understand the centrality of human reproduction as the material process by which culture and identity are reinstantiated. Perhaps we might conclude some day that the elimination of reproductive freedom is essential to vanquish other forms of oppression, but what could be the epistemological warrant for presuming as self-evident that this trade-off is either sufficient or desirable? The fact that the child-rearing arrangements in most cultures are not optimal for women does not justify the elimination of child-bearing.

Because human life is material all the way through, the ideal of "economic equality" is not the only one that must be treasured in order to avoid violence and oppression. Culture, language, and identity are as significant and as real as economics, though they are interwoven with economic structures. Consequently, I have begun to play with terms such as "care" and "health" as alternatives or supplements to our earlier vocabulary of mathematical equality, and I am pondering feminist metaphors like gardening and child raising to replace our manly use of "revolution" as the ideal model for social change.

I am still frequently stirred by the rousing rhetoric that calls us to march against oppression. But I am now critical of the murky directions and routes that the vanguard party would lead us in. If we are to achieve a more democratic polity and economy we need to understand more about how it is that people, materially situated in culture, language, ideology, and economic institutions, come to social "concord."[1] If there are no self-evident, *a priori* meanings to our cherished abstract ideals, then we need to understand how it is that we produce and materially instantiate better ideographic configurations than those we currently have.[2]

In destroying the Enlightenment dream of universality, cultural diversity has also destroyed the possibility of an easy reckoning of economic equality. To the extent that Cloud understands "identity" as an immaterial factor that gets in the way of the important work of class organizing, she has not accepted this lesson.[3] To the extent that she feels free to castigate women (or even their cultures) for their desire to bear children, she has not internalized its implications. I find her critique frighteningly presumptuous. I do not have the answers as to how we are to integrate the needs and desires of the four billion persons on this planet in the best possible fashion, but I am quite sure that Cloud does not either. Thus, I urge that we direct our critical goals toward understanding how it is that diverse groups, situated by cultural and economic materialities, might come to better, if always imperfect, concordances. I urge a critical practice that elicits contextualized judgments rather than mere condemnation of the status quo in the name of abstract and presumptive universal ideals that can be neither effectively articulated nor materially instantiated within the current conditions of human diversity.

Notes

1. Note that I borrowed this term directly from Gramsci's texts. Cloud's complaints about its connotations should be tempered by the realization that the translation between English and Italian (a material process) necessarily produces difficulties of connotations; moreover, such connotations are open to change in the process of the development of new social and technical vocabularies.
2. This does not require the acceptance of "limited personal agency, tokenist representation, and consumer choice," and I find it difficult to see how one would read my original essay as endorsing such positions.
3. This is not true of all of the parties in the substantial bibliography Cloud lists in her rejoinder, but my original reply was directed against Cloud and not all materialists, especially since I see myself as a linguistic materialist. If I am building a straw person, it wears the visage of Cloud, not of all materialists or even all Marxists.

Reading References

Cloud, D. L. (1992). The possibility of a liberating narrative: Woman on the Edge of Time as radical, mythic, moral argument. In L. A. M. Perry, L. H. Turner & H. M. Sterk (Eds.), *Constructing and reconstructing gender: The links among communication, language, and gender* (pp. 5–15). Albany, NY: SUNY Press.

McGee, M. C. (1980). The origins of "liberty": A feminization of power. *Communication Monographs*, 47, 23–45.

In this Chapter Nine workshop, we will probe in focused workshop exercises some of the concepts you discovered in this chapter. Work at a pace by assignment, or by choice, that allows these various insights to "sink in" at an even deeper level for you.

You have read the exchange of articles concerning rhetorical theory and criticism by Cloud and Celeste M. Condit starting with Condit's reply "Hegemony, Concordance, and Capitalism: Reply to Cloud," and the colloquy from 1997 that includes Cloud's "Concordance, Complexity, and Conservatism: Rejoinder to Condit" and Condit's "Clouding the Issues? The Ideal and the Material in Human Communication." Now re-read Dana L. Cloud's article, "Hegemony or Concordance? The Rhetoric of Tokenism in 'Oprah' Winfrey's Rags-to-Riches Biography," reprinted at the end of Chapter Eight.

Since this is an extended exchange about matters of criticism and theory, we will *not* find JFS and JFA items (about which you learned in Chapter 3) that are typical for most rhetorical criticism articles; instead we will track the key points of exchange (agreement and disagreement) between Cloud and Condit as they use scholarly repartee to advance a better understanding of how to accomplish rhetorical criticism and the building of rhetorical theory.

Realize that you are reading the complex, difficult, involved communication between two highly trained, deeply intelligent, passionate people who are superb critics and theorists. They are seeking to find qualified ways to best create rhetorical criticism of important cultural messages. In this workshop we'll track their connections and disconnections, their agreements and disagreements, their assumptions and conclusions at a basic level. We cannot presume to (at this time in your development as a communication professional) understand and utilize their extensive bases of research and insight (which have taken decades to develop). Instead, we *can* find the direction, expectations, and implications of their theory building as each seeks to better understand the point of view of the other critic/theorist.

To start we must realize that both Cloud and Condit are concerned with how messages in the society have impact on individuals and groups within that society. Both critic/theorists realize that complex processes of history, economics, personhood, media, and government create the conditions in which Americans live. Both Condit and Cloud are talented rhetors (i.e., they can argue persuasively). And, both are committed to types of criticism purpose and key theory terms that they believe are valuable for accurate and forceful analysis of cultural messages to take place. Let's see where their theory dispute takes them.

First we will briefly examine key portions of an initiating article by Condit ("Hegemony in a Mass-Mediated Society: Concordance about Reproductive Technologies") that sets the stage for key theory terms to which Cloud responds in her rhetorical

FIGURE 9.2

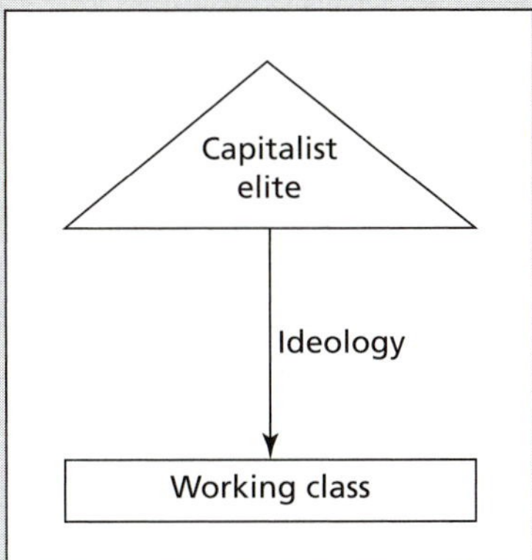

FIGURE 9.3

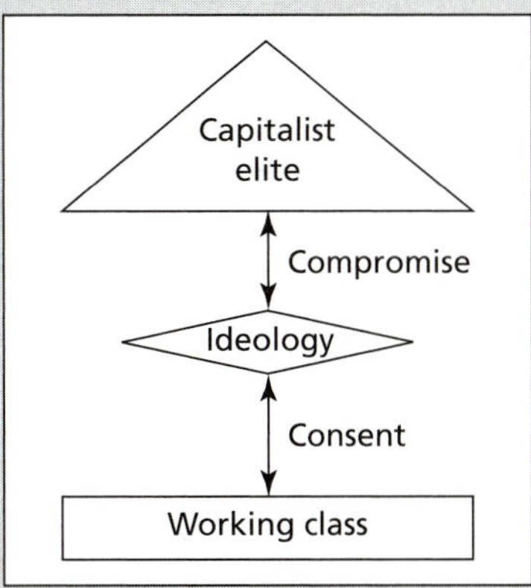

criticism concerning Oprah Winfrey's biographies. Next, we will look for points of agreement and disagreement in each of their follow-up exchanges. I will give several examples and you can search for other possible points contained in their arguments.

In the September 1994 essay, "Hegemony in a Mass-Mediated Society: Concordance about Reproductive Technologies," Condit seeks to better understand how press coverage of reproductive technologies illustrates how certain groups in American society gain more message power than do others. To accomplish that critique Condit offers a method of analysis that extends then-current theories of hegemony in mass-media messages within a political culture (the U.S.). Figures 9.2 and 9.3 illustrate her understanding of a transition from older Marxist-based culture and language critiques to a refined model.[9] She believes that initial work by Marxist scholars proposed a model of communication (Fig. 9.2) in society where a minority elite used language and cultural messages to create an ideology that was used to control and manipulate working class people.

This control was understood as influence by the resources of a "dominant ideology" and also, when necessary, by direct physical power (such as in the form of police or an army).

Condit estimates that the term "hegemony" came to be substituted for "dominant ideology" when Marxist cultural critics began to use the theories of Antonio Gramsci. "Hegemony," it seems, was a less rigid term that suggested that a minority elite in a capitalist economy could control the working class in a country, but by using language and cultural messages as a buffer to create an ideology that would require some compromise from the minority elite and some consent and cooperation from the oppressed working classes.

Condit, then, saw cultural critics (who were working from the lineage of Marxist criticism) as having three typical steps in cultural critique as they sought to discover, and uncover, hegemony:[10]

1. The critic should do an oppositional reading (as an adversary) of the artifact by analyzing it with care and doubt with a goal to undercut the ethos of the elite group that created or supported the creation of the message.
2. The critic should describe the main themes of the artifact and show how those themes hide the ways of manipulation and control by the economic elite who created (or supported the creation of) the message artifact.
3. The critic should locate and reveal the inconsistencies within the artifact analyzed that prove the value of the original oppositional stance.

Condit then explained the steps necessary for a critic to accomplish analysis based on her critique of concordance model which she sees as an extension and improvement on the dominant ideology critique:

1. The critic should do a judgmental reading (as an arbitrator) of the artifact by analyzing it with care and doubt with a goal to evaluate the accommodation reached between competing sides on an issue or controversy based on multiple available criteria for judgment.
2. The critic should estimate how one or more of the competing positions gained relative dominance by exploring alliances and interests created when the messages of multiple groups has some overlap and agreement.
3. The critic should seek to maximize the different categories discovered in the messages; then those categories should be recontextualized by cross-checking the merits and liabilities of the value stances offered by opposing sides in the controversy (especially against the ideological stance(s) favored by the critic).

As seen by Figure 9.4, Condit believes that her critique of concordance model offers a more accurate view of cultural messages and persuasive impact of hegemony than the simpler view held by those doing criticism from a model of a hegemony created by a dominant ideology.[11]

Condit closes her article with a detailed and thorough analysis of press coverage of advances in reproductive technology. Using her critique of concordance model, her tally analysis reveals that three interest groups (doctors and researchers in reproductive technology and the medical community that benefits from that research, middle class couples seeking reproductive assistance, and news reporters) form an informal alliance that celebrates and holds as generally positive the intent and results of research and developments in reproductive technology. In following the outlines of

FIGURE 9.4

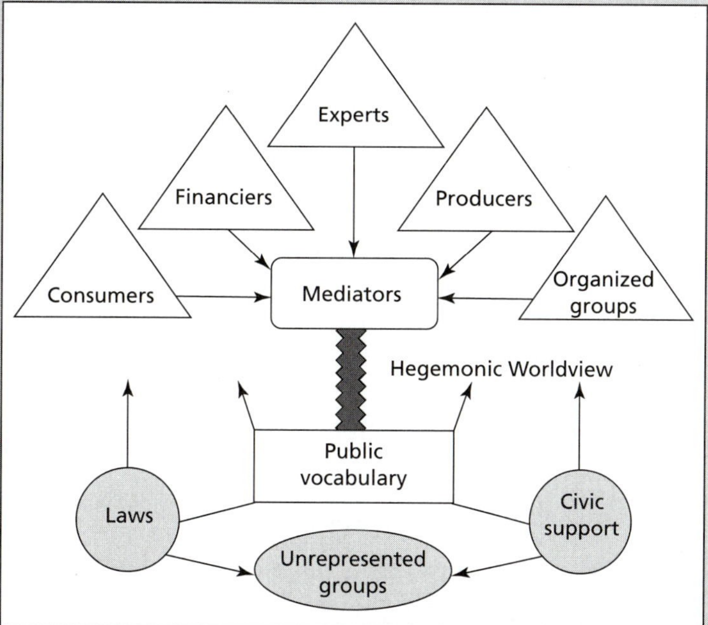

her suggested method steps, Condit ponders the unheard "voices" or "voices" without power representing groups in the culture who may receive little or no coverage in popular press accounts of these cultural issues; she includes working women, poor women, lesbians, and the Catholic Church as being left out of a cultural dialog that positions reproductive technology as a consumer choice rather than a social policy choice. She notes minor impact by these three groups in public debate on reproductive technologies because of a presumed lack of overlap, connection, and coordination of values, interests, and access to means of influence within the culture.

Condit's understanding of her contribution to building theory then is seen in one of her final observations:

> The hegemonic worldview that arises [in this case analysis a positive and affirming press coverage of advances in reproductive technology and the necessity of supporting research] does so on the basis of a plurivocal set of interests [many sides being represented in press coverage], not a single dominant interest [as with a dominant economic elite].
>
> Hence, a critique of concord should not simply deconstruct the ideology from an oppositional stance. Instead, it should account for both the plurivocal contents of the public discourse and for the particular features of the hegemonic accord. . . . This will make hegemony more than simply a synonym for dominant ideology as it opens up new forms of critical reading as well. (226)

In summary, then, Condit has reviewed the critical theory of rhetorical culture critics who have used the term "hegemony" to mean overt control of public messages (and other cultural resources and institutions). She finds that theory too simplistic and proposes a change and extension of Gramsci's term "hegemony" to a revised theory model she calls a critique of concordance. In this model different groups of social power "voice" their issues and arguments and certain overlap and common interests informally combine to create the appearance, and force, of social agreement (concord) on issues of controversy in public media messages. She argues that economic control and power still operate in the social, political, and communication systems ("an interlocking set of minimally and moderately well to do groups amalgamated with capitalists oppress a minority" [208]), but that control and power are not concentrated or uniform ("a small capitalist elite does not oppress a majority").

With this review of Condit's initiating article we can move on to Cloud's initial, direct response in her study of a media personality.

FINDING THE KEY EXCHANGE POINTS

Discovering Agreement and Disagreement Items

Cloud, Dana L. "Hegemony or Concordance? The Rhetoric of Tokenism in 'Oprah' Winfrey's Rags-to-Riches Biography." *Critical Studies in Mass Communication* 13 (1996): 115–137.

Cloud makes a detailed study of multiple biographies of Oprah Winfrey that result in an "Oprah" persona offered to American culture. She argues that "Oprah" becomes a token figure whose life story is specifically used to celebrate the values of individual achievement in a capitalist system. In turn, that cultural celebration acts, Cloud argues, as a mask to hide or distract Americans from hard facts of poverty, achievement barriers, and little economic mobility for large numbers of people in America. Hence, the *story* of a racial minority person, as an individual achiever who has won great economic success and power in American culture, becomes a tool of oppression.

Along the way, Cloud also takes strong exception to Condit's proposed critique of concord model: "Th[is] article theorizes the concepts of hegemony, tokenism, star personae, and biographical narrative, arguing against Condit's (1994) reframing of hegemony as an acceptable cultural negotiation or compromise. . . . [A]n analysis of 'Oprah' biographies as an example of a kind of cultural compromise will test Condit's assumptions" (117).

To track the development of theory between these two scholars, read the rest of Cloud's article and search for points of agreement and disagreement with Condit.[12] List your found items on the chart below.

Discovering Agreement and Disagreement Items

(Page numbers in brackets indicate pages reprinted in this textbook.)

Item	Page	
Agreement	117 [306]	"Condit accuses feminist and Marxist critics of overestimating the forces of domination and oversimplifying the process of cultural negotiation."
Agreement		
Agreement		
Disagreement	117 [306]	"understanding hegemony as concordance is an appropriate model only if one is satisfied with the compromises allowed within and by the 'given conditions.' "
Disagreement	117–118 [306]	"Condit's assumption that domination and division are no longer primary features of contemporary Western society is fundamentally mistaken."
Disagreement		
Agreement	118 [307]	"social systems and their prevailing ideological justifications (capitalism and liberalism in the United States) are always contested."
Agreement		
Agreement		
Disagreement	118 [307]	"a rhetorically crafted concordance presents the façade of democratic compromise while obscuring the conservative effects of such a compromise."
Disagreement	118–119 [307]	"contradiction, rupture, and multivocality are taken by the hegemony theorist not as signs that a democratic compromise has been achieved, but that a few token voices are allowed to speak within the 'permissible range of disagreement.' "
Disagreement		
Disagreement		

What other points of agreement or disagreement did you find in Cloud's theory and criticism? Be careful to watch for these as the dialog unfolds in other responses between the two critic/theorists.

Cloud discovers in her analysis that celebration of *one* "token" minority person who has "hit it big" based on her individual achievement and working within the capitalist system is a strategy of cultural containment:

> The rhetoric of tokenism is one strategy by which texts [e.g., "Oprah" being made a hero in the culture and her story being widely (and uniformly) celebrated] authorize people whose difference (along the axes of race, class, gender, sexual orientation, or other category) if politicized and collectively articulated might pose a threat to a dominant order in which some groups are kept subordinate to others. (122)

In other words, if the media production system in America weren't so busy celebrating the achievements of a single, wildly successful minority woman who has "played by the rules" of the dominant economic system, it might have to pay attention to large numbers of deprived people, if they could become a political force and find a powerful means to express their discontent. Cloud argues that the biographical celebration of public personas like "Oprah" retards and discourages millions of people by suggesting, falsely, that if they were only like "Oprah" (or like "Mike" or "Colin") they too could be substantially successful within the economic system when economic and social oppression makes that impossible, or unlikely:

> . . . tokenism "advertises a promise of mobility" that pays lip service to multiculturalism and difference, and to opportunity for previously excluded groups. But that promise, a concordance between the token and the group licensing or authorizing the token, serves to obscure the limits of mobility. . . . [A] token can be defined as a persona who is constructed from the character and life of a member of a subordinated group, and then celebrated, authorized to speak as proof that the society at large does not discriminate against members of that group. (123–124)

Hence, in disputing Condit's reconstruction of "hegemony" as a theory term that should account for exchange, interaction, and alliances formed within public disputes, Cloud strongly suggests that whole groups within the society are held down, or back, by a hegemony of a specific economic, political, social system. She argues that the *appearance* of participation in the economic system does indeed take place, but only in forms such as the biographical celebration of "Oprah" that serve to hide true economic conditions for millions while simultaneously building a false, saving explanation for any failure ("they" could all be like "Oprah" if they only tried). That process, Cloud argues, deflects attention from social and economic practices that indicate great misery and failure to "achieve" within the dominant system that clearly rewards certain groups with great economic prosperity.

The theoretic "ball" is now back in Condit's court.

FINDING THE KEY EXCHANGE POINTS

Discovering Agreement and Disagreement Items

Condit, Celeste M. "Hegemony, Concordance, and Capitalism: Reply to Cloud" *Critical Studies in Mass Communication* 13 (1996): 382–384.

Condit responds in this essay to Cloud's overt challenge to her proposed change in understanding the theory term "hegemony." She claims Cloud has misrepresented her theory of concordance and seeks to re-outline her actual proposed changes.

Let's again look for points of actual, eventual, and perceived agreement and disagreement.

(Page numbers in brackets indicate pages reprinted in this textbook.)

Item	Page	
Agreement	382 [368]	(No safety net for poor.) "My essay did not say that there is an adequate safety net, and I do not believe there is one."
Agreement	382 [369]	(No real material equality in U.S.) "My essay didn't say . . . that there is a large measure of material equality."
Agreement		
Agreement		
Disagreement	382 [369]	(Concordance means happy or indicates a positive arrangement.) "I never typified concord as happy. . . . I believe that in general concord is reluctant, disgruntled, and often angry."
Disagreement		
Disagreement		
Agreement	383 [370]	Pierce paraphrase: We need to create a mixed economy where those who are less advantaged have a fair chance, we protect the environment in all feasible ways, and we understand as well as protect gender, racial, and ethnic diversity.
Disagreement		

Item	Page	
Disagreement	383 [370]	"Ours is not a world in which a simple homogeneous working class opposes a simple, homogeneous capitalist class."
Disagreement		
Disagreement		
Disagreement	383 [370]	Pierce paraphrase: Producing social change by lumping all non-elite-capitalists together into a single "working class" ignores the particular, unique concerns of certain cultural groups and does not address complex alliances formed in messages by different social groups in American society.
Disagreement		

Condit in her reply argues that she was misunderstood and misrepresented; she also claims that her position was made more simple than it really was ("a stick-figure version"). This is a complaint we'll hear from both scholars. She defends her theory by saying that the "theory of concordance does not seek to efface class issues [an item obviously important to Cloud], but rather to provide a methodology for exploring a broader set of discursive forces [meaning made from messages] active in public media" (383–384).

Let's now turn to a colloquy enabled by the editor of *Critical Studies in Mass Communication* between these two scholars. First is Cloud's rejoinder to Condit's reply. Look again for points of agreement and disagreement.

FINDING THE KEY EXCHANGE POINTS

Discovering Agreement and Disagreement Items

Cloud, Dana L. "Concordance, Complexity, and Conservatism: Rejoinder to Condit." *Critical Studies in Mass Communication* 14 (1997): 193–200.

Cloud claims, as did Condit, that her essay must respond to an oversimplification of her position (Condit's essay "builds and burns a straw version" of her version of hegemony theory).

Item	Page	
Agreement	193 [372]	Pierce paraphrase: Social, political, economic, and communication problems in America are complex and include a great diversity of types of people. These problems need a theory that is able to address inequality and complexity.
Agreement		
Agreement	195 [374]	Pierce paraphrase: Choices are offered in messages about participation in American political and economic life.
Disagreement	193–194–195 [372–374]	Pierce paraphrase: Condit misunderstands Gramacian theory of hegemony and ideological criticism done by scholars working in a Marxist tradition.
Disagreement	193 [372]	"Materalist approaches [critical analysis using Marxist-oriented theories of hegemony] do [not] do violence to difference and complexity."
Agreement		
Agreement		
Agreement	194 [372]	Pierce paraphrase: Condit's theory of concordance fails to "confront economic structures of power in favor of examining, deconstructing, and reconstructing discourses about identity[.]"
Disagreement		
Disagreement	194 [372–373]	Pierce paraphrase: Condit's approach to concordance as a substitute for Marxist notions of hegemony presents a more positive spin on economic and political conditions than is acceptable; it would actually hinder critique of economic and political practices through messages in America.
Disagreement		
Disagreement		

Cloud in her rejoinder defends her theory by saying that oppression and exploitation based on class really *do* exist in America. Moreover, she claims that Marxist-oriented analysis really can deal with complexity and significant differences of groups in American culture (an item obviously important for Condit). She wonders whether the choices that Condit's theory of concordance seems to champion are real: "[are] the 'choices' offered in the rhetorics of the marketplace and liberalism . . . real for the majority of the people[?]" (195).

Condit's reply to the rejoinder to the reply to the challenge to her concordance theory proposal is next. Are you ready?

FINDING THE KEY EXCHANGE POINTS

Discovering Agreement and Disagreement Items

Condit, Celeste M. "Clouding the Issues? The Ideal and the Material in Human Communication." *Critical Studies in Mass Communication* 14 (1997): 197–200.

After three previous exchanges, Condit is able to narrow the focus of the discussion to a handful of key issues while giving repetition to her main claims and arguments.

(Page numbers in brackets indicate pages reprinted in this textbook.)

Item	Page	
Agreement	197 [377]	Pierce paraphrase: Media messages are worth analyzing.
Agreement		
Agreement		
Disagreement	197 [377]	Pierce paraphrase: Creating equality and freedom in actual human society is exceedingly difficult and out of reach in any full or absolute manner. Moreover, "equality" or "freedom" do not have clear, univocal (completely agreed upon) meanings that can guide real life practices and experiences.
Disagreement	198–199 [377]	Pierce paraphrase: Sheer cultural diversity across any culture or across the globe makes full equality an unattainable ideal.
Disagreement	198 [377]	"'Equality' [for any specific cultural group] necessarily impinges on the ways of life of some . . . [other group]."

Item	Page	
Disagreement	198 [378]	"The will of the majority [in] a . . . true 'political and economic democracy' . . . [could well be coercive]."
Disagreement	199 [378]	Pierce paraphrase: Marxist critics who call for economic and political equality for the masses do not know how to actually accomplish that goal in a way that is equitable and non-coercive.
Disagreement	199 [379]	Pierce paraphrase: Cloud may not understand Gramsci's connotations in translation any better than other critic-scholars; Gramsci's formulations are, in any case, open to further development and change.
Disagreement	199 [379]	Pierce paraphrase: A theorist using the critique of concord theory would not endorse or support overt individualism that limits group action, use of minority token people to oppress others, or consumer choice that creates oppression.
Disagreement	199 [379]	Pierce paraphrase: Call for universal economic justice, and the oppositional criticism it engenders, is less well suited to current social and political conditions than a concordance criticism that uses contextualized judgments.

Five essays later do we know any more about "hegemony" than before this exchange began? Yes.

The two critic/theorists involved clearly have strong points of disagreement. Both are clearly committed to criticism of public messages that makes a difference. Both clearly think that they have the better means of accomplishing that criticism. Note, however, that through the exchange each critic/theorist was expected to re-examine her assumptions, evidence, definitions, and perspectives.

Other critics who read this exchange have a much better idea of some of the core issues involved in attempting to discover how social, economic, and political power is used in messages that influence millions of people. We are better acquainted with potential difficulties and hazards should we wish to build criticism on either of the models offered. We can also think about ways to resolve or bypass some of the points that seem to arrest agreement between these two talented scholars. Remember, we said in the beginning of this chapter that theory development is to find effective ways to say something (useful and insightful) about no one thing (in this case about how public messages can best be analyzed). Scholars such as Condit and Cloud show the courage, and we hope patience, necessary to do the hard thinking required to discover the dynamics of how human public communication works. The rest of the workshop exercises in this chapter will deal with finding the real worth of what you've just read and thought about.

THE POWER OF THEORY DEVELOPMENT

Celeste Condit had the "final word" in this particular five-part exchange. If you were Dana Cloud (and knowing how the flow of this exchange has gone), how would you respond if you had a sixth essay and the "final word"?

Use the chart below to list potential agreements and disagreements.

Item	
Agreement	
Agreement	
Agreement	
Disagreement	
Disagreement	
Disagreement	
Disagreement	
Disagreement	

THEORY DEVELOPMENT AND EVIDENCE

Reexamine the most significant points of disagreement that I identified and that you discovered in these theoretical exchanges. Play the role of each critic/theorist and suggest to yourself what *you* (as Cloud or Condit) would take as adequate evidence that the *other* critic/theorist was *right* on a given point of disagreement.

For instance, in Cloud's 1997 essay (her rejoinder to Condit), she suggests that (Pierce paraphrase) Condit's theory of concordance fails to "confront economic structures of power in favor of examining, deconstructing, and reconstructing discourses about identity[.]" What would Cloud take as adequate evidence that the theory of concordance *does* confront economic structures of power?

Likewise, in Condit's 1996 reply to Cloud, she suggests that (Pierce paraphrase): Cloud lumps all non-elite-capitalists together into a single "working class;" ignores the particular, unique concerns of certain cultural groups; and does not address complex alliances formed in messages by different social groups in American society. What would Condit take as adequate evidence that Cloud's understanding of hegemony *did* address unique concerns and address complex alliances?

THE POWER OF THEORY DEVELOPMENT

Think about your own experiences and observations about the mass-media messages in America. Which theory model (of the two offered) more closely matches your experience and insights? Why?

Then, think of yourself as the *opposite* of what you are (or believe yourself to be); if you are a member of the working class fooled by the hegemony messages offered to you, then think of yourself as a member of the capitalist elite; if you are a member of the capitalist elite, then think of yourself as a member of the working class fooled by the hegemony messages offered to you (in Cloud's terms). If you are a member of a privileged group that has power and access to making your message heard in disputes of public importance, then think of yourself as a member of a powerless group that has no voice in the cultural discussion or dispute. If you are a member of a powerless group, then think of yourself as a member of a privileged group that has power and access to making your message heard (in Condit's terms). Which theory makes more sense to you now? Is it easy or hard to think of yourself in an opposite position to your current status? Why? Is it easy or hard to place yourself in one position or the other? Are there other positions for which Condit or Cloud do not allow? Can a third or fourth or fifth position be established or argued? Remember that you are trying to create a theory about cultural messages and society that will explain power, inequality, habits of message creation, and issue development about situations of political, social, economic, or religious dislocation or dispute.

Endnotes

1. Kenneth Burke, *A Grammar of Motives* (Berkeley: University of California Press, 1969), 189.
2. I borrow the idea of a hydrologist from Donald C. Bryant who wrote: ". . . the relationship of rhetoric to the subject matters of economics, or public health, or theology, or chemistry, or agriculture is like the relation of hydraulic engineering to water, under the specific circumstances in which the engineer is to construct his dam or his pumping station or his sewage system, and in view of the specific results he is to obtain. He develops a method for determining what questions to ask and answer from all which can be known about water." "Rhetoric: Its Functions and Scope," *Quarterly Journal of Speech* 39 (1953): 409.
3. For a range of examples see Larry Kaniut, *Alaska Bear Tales* (Anchorage: Alaska Northwest Publishing, 1983) and *Bear Tales for the Ages from Alaska and Beyond* (Anchorage: Paper Talk, 2001).
4. Lloyd Bitzer, "The Rhetorical Situation," *Philosophy and Rhetoric* 1 (1968): 6.
5. Bitzer, 8.
6. Gibsons ad. *Los Angeles Times* 21 Oct. 2001, A-5.
7. Lakoff and Johnson never employ the actual term "systemic" metaphor, yet they thoroughly talk about systems, systematicity, and so forth, such that a "systemic" metaphor seems the closest correct adjective that matches their theory.
8. Cindy L. Griffin, Sonja K. Foss, and Karen A. Foss, Feminist *Rhetorical Theories* (Thousand Oaks, Calif.: Sage, 1999), 10.
9. These diagrams appeared in Condit's article on page 209.
10. These are my paraphrases of Condit's original three noted steps.
11. This diagram appeared in Condit's article on page 211.
12. I'm including in these lists both *direct* agreement or disagreement and statements that I believe represent a point of agreement or disagreement given the overall context of their theoretical exchange.

Using Rhetorical Criticism

As a degree-holding communication professional or as a professional who uses communication extensively, you will eventually be involved in the creation, management, critique, or investigation of messages. You very likely will be a message maker or co-creator. We have many different names for such a person in our culture. Writer, speaker, motivational specialist, producer, director, cinematographer, design expert, speech writer, editor, diplomat, campaign manager, and copywriter are but a few of the names we use for people who design, create, or approve messages that reach mass or public audiences. Messages (and the influence they can create), then, are likely at the center of why you became interested in the study of human communication in the first place. Messages, and the influence they *will* create, then, need to be the focal point of your education and professional development.

We call people who create or deliver messages to audiences "rhetors." People who *research* the patterns, habits, conditions, resources, and characteristics of messages that reach large groups of people are called "rhetoricians." Our purpose in this chapter will be to investigate with care how rhetors can use the work of rhetoricians to make their work easier, more influential, and more likely to accomplish desired goals. In Chapter 2 you were introduced to a rhetorician we called a rhetorical critic. In Chapter 3 you learned, in an initial sense, how to read one of the most common forms of research produced by rhetorical critics: the analytic journal article. If you have been using the Workshop material in Chapters 5, 6, 7, 8, and 9 to discover both how the sample journal articles were set up, and how to find good insights discovered by the rhetorical critic(s), you are likely ready to move on to the next level: *using* existing rhetorical criticism.

In this chapter we will seek to show how you can best reach into existing research to find telltale insights that will help you create stronger, more professional, more thoughtful, more effective messages. Rereading the materials in Chapter 9 may help even more in establishing the vocabulary and frameworks that will allow you to use material in this chapter; or, you may feel sufficiently primed by the preceding chapters on metaphor, narrative, visual persuasion, and language/ideology to launch into this material. In either case we'll be building on the hard work you have already put into building the foundation of your professional "house."

Remember that while we continue to focus on a few foundational areas (e.g., metaphor or narrative) that are central to your ability to create quality messages, these by no means exhaust the types of language or messages that are worthy of rhetorical criticism. Even a quick glance at recent journals reveals quality analytic criticism on topics or areas such as religious witnessing, public opinion, antislavery petitions, haunting protests, or post-feminist depiction of professionals.[1]

All people, in all cultures, in all times of human history have created messages. For the most part, they learned how to adapt those messages by trial and error. Trial and error is a tool we *all* use to create human communication, but it will not be enough for someone who wishes to create messages based on systematic, thorough, analytic, investigation of *how* messages work. In a few cultures in human history, including Greek culture in the fourth and fifth century B.C. and the Roman culture in the first through the fourth centuries A.D. rhetoricians began to look *beyond* trial and error experience to a more systematic means of understanding how messages reach audience members.

Hence, Isocrates and Aristotle in ancient Athens, Cicero in ancient Rome, and a political campaign manager in Washington, D.C., in the early 2000s have very much in common. They all want to know how the design and delivery of messages can reach people who can make a difference.

USING RHETORICAL CRITICISM: METAPHOR ANALYSIS

Let's start our investigation of how to best use the work of rhetorical critics by examining the work of a rhetorician named Robert Ivie. Professor Ivie has spent a substantial amount of time investigating the characteristics of metaphors used in political messages.[2]

By the mid-1980s Americans had lived for more than 30 years under the threat of nuclear annihilation from foes of America in the Cold War. Ivie wondered why opponents of nuclear arms had failed to produce any sustained political effort to create peace and reduce the number of threatening nuclear weapons.[3] As he put it, ". . . fear of total annihilation has failed so far to produce public pressure sufficient even to slow the arms race, let alone to reverse it" (165). Ivie knew that specific groups and individual rhetors had been working for many years to convince the American people and U.S. government to reduce nuclear weapons and to seek peace with global adversaries. So he selected three of the most influential rhetors, whom he called "Cold War idealists," and he investigated why their rhetoric may have *failed* to reach audiences—even though audience members' lives, culture, and planet were at risk.

Ivie saw that American audiences were confronted with two radically different visions of political "reality" in the Cold War era: "One view [of the Soviet Union] advocated by 'realists,' threatens them with extermination should the arms race touch off a nuclear war. The other view, advanced by 'idealists,' threatens them with loss of national power and personal freedom should the Russians take advantage of a disarmed America" (166). Was nuclear disarmament the only rational approach to a world threatened by military mechanisms set to create mass, unthinkable destruction of places and people (the idealists' argument)? Or, was a strong nuclear arms buildup and threat of mutually assured destruction (MAD) the only way to keep the Soviets at bay (the realists' argument)? Professor Ivie saw this "choice" of views as no choice at all. He believed that Americans were being "forced to choose between two radically opposing and potentially disastrous views of the Russians" (166).

He selected messages created by Henry Wallace, J. William Fulbright, and Helen Caldicott for his investigation. His purpose was to "identify sources of rhetorical invention that have undermined efforts so far to transcend the choice between chauvinism [the 'realist' desire to be strong against the Russians] and pacifism [the 'idealist' desire to eliminate the threat of nuclear weapons]" (166). When he writes about "rhetorical invention," Ivie is discussing the resources open to rhetors to create persuasive messages. (Remember that we addressed "invention" and other parts of the rhetorical process first in Chapter 9.) Note that Ivie is proposing to study how important, influential rhetors in our culture *failed* to accomplish their persuasive goals: "By examining the structure of metaphor, primarily in the rhetoric of Wallace, Fulbright, and Caldicott, I intend to show the roots of their collective failure" (166). Professor Ivie's excellent study of these rhetors and their message decisions stands as a solid reminder that we can learn as much from rhetorical efforts that fail as from ones that have great success.

Professor Ivie decided that the key to investigating the messages of these three influential rhetors in one of the most important controversies of the twentieth century was their choice of metaphors: "I begin with the premise that metaphor is at the base of rhetorical invention. Elaborating a primary image into a well formed argument produces a motive, or interpretation of reality, with which the intended audience is invited to identify" (166). Hence, he believes that when an influential writer or speaker seeks to persuade an audience that person will naturally use metaphors as she or he selects images, arguments, and ideas devoted to changing the audience or their actions. Ivie believes that finding the most important of these metaphors will allow us (as critics and interested rhetoricians) to see the primary choices made by important rhetors engaged in public persuasion about crucial issues of human culture and governmental policy.

Finding core metaphors within the messages investigated allows us to see that "[t]his kind of metaphor serves as a nomenclature that 'necessarily directs the attention into some channels rather than others' and thus establishes what Kenneth Burke has called a 'terministic incentive' (1969, p. 45)" (166) [see Chapter 9 and "terministic screen"]. In other words, when rhetors create persuasive messages, they often use metaphors; those metaphors create a framework of motivation and evaluation about the issues or policies they represent. Let's use a couple of examples to quickly demonstrate this idea of how metaphors can guide and direct human decisions.

If I am an opponent of a new city tax being proposed for owners of pets, I might call that tax a "trap." Moreover, I might suggest that people who support the tax are trying to distract citizens while they "lure" unsuspecting pet owners to their "doom." None of the terms "trap," "lure," or "doom" (or related metaphor terms that a rhetor might use) is *literally* true. They do, however, seek to convince audience members that the proposed tax is unacceptable, threatening, and to be avoided. The embedded metaphors encourage, or route, the audience's perception in the desired direction.

Similarly, if you are trying to convince the administration on your campus to transform some underutilized offices into a center for student groups on campus, you might suggest that with proper "cultivation" the misused space could become a "garden" of fresh life and "growth" on your campus. "Garden, "cultivation," "growth," and related metaphor images would not be literally true, but would be an attempt to frame the request and related issues as something that would need work (as would creation of any garden), but that would produce wonderful results (the "fruits" of student activism). The metaphors, then, attempt to frame the request as positive and productive.

In a similar way Professor Ivie wanted to discover what metaphor choices were evident in the persuasion crafted by the "idealist" rhetors whose messages he studied. Ivie argues: "The value of locating underlying metaphors is in revealing their limits or untapped potential as sources of invention [see Chapter 9 and "invention"], something that is far more difficult to accomplish when a generating term is allowed to operate without being explicitly acknowledged as such. Speakers lose sight of alternatives when they become accustomed to routine extensions of images no longer serving their original purposes. Stripping away the outer layers of literalized metaphors exposes them to closer scrutiny and possible reconstruction . . ." (167). So, Ivie believes that once a rhetor begins to use a framework based in a metaphor image, that rhetor may well lose sight of the implications of the metaphor, and of available, useful alternatives.

Let's turn our attention now to his discoveries in the messages of Wallace, Fulbright, and Caldicott.

We'll start with his investigation of messages produced by Henry A. Wallace. Wallace was an editor, agriculture researcher, cabinet member (agriculture and commerce) for two presidents, and vice president of the United States from 1941 to 1945. He also ran for president in 1948 under the Progressive party banner. Ivie picked two speeches, a book, a memo, and a radio broadcast made by Wallace between 1946 and 1948 as representative of Wallace's views and persuasion concerning Cold War foreign policy and the need for peace. Ivie found that Wallace used metaphor references that clustered around two primary core metaphors: "GAME" and "FORCE."

In the "GAME" cluster, Wallace was seen to use images such as a card game to describe, identify, and provide a critique of American policy toward the U.S.S.R. in the nuclear arms race. Whereas the "FORCE" cluster was split between metaphor images that praised "positive" force and ones that were critical of "negative" force: "Negative force was that which violated rules and laws and consequently was destructive" (e.g., "bully," "stampede," "mob," "slam"). "Positive force, on the other hand, was the constructive force of the Lord. It was active, renewing, and full of fight but blessed with love, joy, and hope" (170) (e.g., "sell their souls or stand up and fight," or "unleash [a] creative force").

In addition to the primary or core metaphor clusters of "GAME" and "FORCE" (and the interplay between them), Ivie discovered Wallace using five reinforcing metaphor clusters: "DARK-LIGHT," "SICK," "MONEY," "BREED-PLANT," and "PREACH." For instance, in the cluster of metaphor images that Ivie designated the "SICK" cluster, he found Wallace using images of both mental illness and physical, body illness. So terms such as "festering," "infection," or "psychopathic" became the means of focusing on the element of public policy with which Wallace had

Scrutinize exercise

See if you can discover metaphors from within the "GAME" cluster still operating in political disputes today (similar to the ones Ivie found in the rhetorical messages of Henry A. Wallace). Find a database for popular news coverage and search the database for key ideas involved in the core metaphor of "GAME." Search for phrases such as "cards," "dealt cards," "bet," "ante," "card game," or "stack the deck." Are post-2000 rhetors still using a card game (probably poker) as a means to create perspective or persuasion? What are the advantages of using such metaphors? What are the disadvantages? If you encountered an *opponent* using a card game as an important persuasive image, what could you do to counter that imagery?

substantial disagreement. Ivie summarizes his discoveries from within Wallace's persuasive messages as:

> Wallace's critique of the Cold War was driven by an ideal image, or metaphorical concept, of a spiritually awakened America engaging the Soviet Union in peaceful competition to heal an economically sick world and eventually to win the allegiance of humankind. His metaphors placed the blame for the problem and the responsibility for its solution almost exclusively on the United States, which was associated with a sick, dark, and deceitful 'get tough' policy designed to overpower the Russians and serve the evil interests of 'reactionary capitalism' . . . (172).

Ivie wisely notes the problems with such a metaphoric strategy (whether intended or unintended): "Not surprisingly, the public simply was unwilling to accept any such analysis that focused the guilt on their nation alone. Thus Wallace was easily dismissed as Russia's naive apologist" (172). Ivie also notes other difficulties with the metaphoric framework selected and used by Wallace:

> Wallace ultimately fell victim to the inadequacies of his own rhetorical invention. His system of metaphorical concepts proved to be self-defeating because it did not enable him to explain [hostile, aggressive] Soviet initiatives without *either* continuing to blame the United States for creating the conditions that forced the Soviets to compete unfairly *or* deciding eventually that the Soviets were actually Satan's surrogates. As the vehicles [Ch. 5: *metaphiers*] of light and darkness, breeding and planting, sickness and greed, and ministering and crusading combined to reinforce Wallace's faith in peaceful competition, they undermined his ability to perceive the rhetorical limits of a vision that failed both to account for Soviet imperialism and to characterize the Russians as good sportsmen in the game of power politics. The only alternative, finally, was to adopt the opposing metaphor of Soviet savagery that (within Wallace's metaphoric system) made communism itself a dark, degenerative, negative force—the source of all evil (173).

As we turn our attention from Henry Wallace to the second rhetor investigated by Ivie (J. William Fulbright), we can begin to ask if we can learn (and use) information *today* from the words and strategies of an *unsuccessful* politician from 1946. Our intent is not to learn a dusty history lesson about the Cold War and nuclear disarmament disputes; instead, we want to ask if we can learn and use practical carryover lessons from Professor Ivie's investigation. At first blush, we learn that using metaphors to create strong negative characterizations of a community, people, or nation is often unwise. Lest we think, however, that *we* would never be so foolish to use "SICK" metaphors, or unfair "GAME" metaphors, we should remind ourselves that Henry Wallace was a successful, accomplished politician who served as a presidential cabinet member and as vice president of the United States. If he was capable of making profound metaphoric mistakes, so are we. Let us be forewarned. We can also learn that, over time, metaphors selected and used in political disputes can prevent (or prohibit) our ability to see alternatives. The force of the metaphors used multiple times is enough to make us unwilling to see behaviors or actions that don't "fit" the metaphor scheme we've established. In other words, we need to be able to see the advantages and *limitations* of our own metaphor characterizations. In the spirit of continued discovery, we'll now turn our attention to Ivie's second "idealist" rhetor.

J. William Fulbright was an influential senator who wrote several books on U.S. foreign policy and political culture in the 60s and 70s. Professor Ivie uses two of Fulbright's books (*The Arrogance of Power* and *The Crippled Giant*) as artifacts for his rhetorical criticism. Ivie found that Fulbright explicitly rejected the "GAME" metaphor that had been a strong part of Wallace's persuasive message strategy. Fulbright also stayed away from use of a "CRUSADE" or religious metaphor cluster that had been a clear part of Wallace's inventional formula. Professor Ivie did find some overlap between the two rhetors who were separated by two decades of Cold War hostility and provocative activity. Senator Fulbright substantially used a set of metaphors that highlighted psychological illness:

> The senator's principal concept, however, was similar to the SICK cluster used by Wallace to denigrate negative force. Just as Wallace had emphasized "neurosis," "obsession," "suicide," and "psychopathology" among the various forms of physical and mental sickness, Fulbright primarily drew upon a cluster of PSYCHOLOGY vehicles [Ch. 5: *metaphiers*], including essentially negative terms such as "psychotic," "delusions of grandeur," "projection," "pathology," "confuse," "arrogance," "irrational pressures," "drive," "instinct," "insane," "nervous breakdown," "paranoid fears," and "inferiority complex," as well as more positive terms such as "rehabilitation," "grow up," "empathy," "reconciliation," "mature," and "come of age." (174)

Clearly, Ivie has discovered in another influential rhetor a formula of metaphor use that holds some advantage for critique, but also many negative characteristics:

> Although Fulbright's system of metaphorical concepts differed significantly from Wallace's, it suffered from some of the same flaws. More importantly, the senator's metaphoric system stressed the culpability of the United States almost exclusively, accusing it of an anti-Communist obsession, an underlying lack of confidence in itself, an exaggerated fear of failure, an arrogance of power, and a crusading puritan spirit manifested as ideological warfare. . . . (175)

Professor Ivie's analysis of Fulbright's metaphor use finds that he too is hedged in by his own metaphors:

> [Fulbright's] idealism hardly took into account any better than Wallace's game metaphor the sources of Soviet behavior that could be expected to promote accommodation over confrontation, cooperation over subversion,

> or tolerance over totalitarianism. . . . [Fulbright's] dependence on PSYCHOLOGY as the dominant metaphorical concept was, at best, overdeveloped for the United States and underdeveloped for the Soviets. (175)

And,

> [Fulbright's] metaphorical system could [not] yield arguments that might pacify the fear of a barbarian foe. Again, Americans were expected to accept the full burden of guilt for the Cold War and to take on faith that the enemy would respond in kind to their leadership by example and acts of friendship. (176)

Here again Professor Ivie identifies for us that an influential rhetor may build a system of metaphor images in his persuasive writing that severely limits possible alternatives for a national foreign policy. He also reminds us that metaphor expressions may place us in a static relationship mode with an enemy that exhibits characteristics not noted in the metaphor system under use.

As a communication professional or other professional rhetor, you may never be called upon to create a speech that characterizes an enemy who has at their disposal the military weapon means to destroy you and the rest of the world. (Although, remember that *some* communication professional *will* have that specific job.) You may need to represent "enemies" of your state, or community, or educational plan, or ballot initiative, or company in rhetorical messages that will influence decision makers within your community or region. Since you know that your messages will almost certainly use metaphors of some type, how can you use Professor Ivie's investigation of Wallace and Fulbright's rhetorical messages to your own best advantage? Remember that you will be characterizing both your "enemy" and your own group stance. Ivie's research reminds us that whatever metaphors we use will hold *both* advantages and disadvantages. Moreover, we've learned from his investigation of the first two "idealist" rhetors that characterizations over many pages in a book, or over many speeches and proclamations, will typically fall into recognizable "clusters" of metaphor. Many writers or speakers, who work only from the resource of conventional wisdom and trial and error, may not even be aware (at a direct conscious level) that they are consistently using metaphor images from a certain cluster. You, on the other hand, will not only be aware of such characteristics, but will be equipped to anticipate metaphor use by your own causes and purposes—and also by those of your political, economic, or ideological opponents. We turn now to Ivie's analysis of a third "idealist" rhetor, the "mother" of the nuclear freeze movement: Dr. Helen Caldicott.

Helen Caldicott represented a vigorous, influential voice for nuclear disarmament in the 1980s that came as the next extension of resistance that we've seen in the rhetorical messages of Wallace and Fulbright in previous decades. As a former faculty member of the Harvard Medical School, a pediatrician, and a founder of Physicians for Social Responsibility,

Caldicott represented a high profile rhetor who commanded much attention and who held substantial cultural power. Professor Ivie used two of her books (*Nuclear Madness: What You Can Do!* and *Missile Envy: The Arms Race and Nuclear War*), a movie (*If You Love This Planet: Dr. Helen Caldicott on Nuclear War*), and her standard stump speech or lecture as artifacts for his rhetorical analysis.

Professor Ivie's analysis of Caldicott's messages reveals deep dependence on one central core metaphor:

> MADNESS vehicles [Ch. 4: *metaphiers*] have pervaded Caldicott's rhetoric to a fault. Her favorites have been "crazy," "deranged," "madness," "insane," "pathogenesis," "pathological," "mad lust," "paranoia," "anxiety," "indignation," "anger," "frustration," "projection," "fantasy," "mental masturbation," "disease," "etiology," "psychic numbing," "missile envy," "suicide," "mental illness," "frantic desperation," "emotional cripple," "power-hungry," "egocentric," and "killing animus." As the list suggests, she has elaborated the concept well beyond Wallace's SICK cluster and even pursued more vehicles [Ch. 4: *metaphiers*] than were featured in Fulbright's PSYCHOLOGY cluster. So complete a commitment has magnified the concept's limitations. (176)

Ivie also finds extensions of this core metaphor in Caldicott's answer to the inevitable question about whether or not the Russians are trustworthy: "the pattern has been to associate the United States with MADNESS, focusing attention on the sources of American culpability and dismissing fear of the Russians as a pathological condition, 'the primitive mechanism of blaming the Russians,' (1985, p. 348). The Soviet Union has been presented essentially as the victim of America's craziness. In Caldicott's view, 'As America has led the arms race, so Russia has inevitably and inexorably copied and followed.' Russian fears are justified; their leaders 'have every cause to be realistically frightened and perhaps a little paranoid.' The culprit is America who 'has engineered her own suicide' through the mechanism of 'paranoid projection' (1985, pp. 103, 308, 313)." (177)

Hence, Ivie believes that Caldicott's choice of a core MADNESS metaphor focus in her persuasive messages has placed a complex, international military and diplomatic problem within a very personal, relationship metaphor structure. If someone in your family were suffering from MADNESS, what would be the appropriate response on your part (or on the part of your family and community)? At minimum most people would work within a medical metaphor to search for the appropriate cause and opportunity for a cure or for a reasonable, loving response of medical care. Is it fair for an influential rhetor to propose essentially the same model for an entire nation as it attempts difficult international diplomacy? As with the Wallace metaphors and the Fulbright metaphors, Caldicott's core metaphor seems to lay responsibility at America's doorstep and seems to leave the U.S.S.R. depicted as a potentially nice but misunderstood foe. Ivie cites several scholars in his article that suggest the Soviets in the 1980s were anything but friendly and misunderstood.

Scrutinize exercise

Have you ever heard an advocate rhetor call an opponent (or an opponent's position on an issue) crazy? Look in news accounts of various political or cultural conflicts and search for words that depict someone or some group as crazy, mentally unhinged, or nuts (or dozens of other possible indicator words for mental problems). Given Ivie's negative evaluation of Caldicott's use of a core MADNESS metaphor, do you think *all* uses of a CRAZY or MADNESS metaphor are bad or unacceptable? Could they ever work to motivate positive social, economic, or governmental change?

Ivie's analysis reveals some of the key reasons that audiences may not have responded to Wallace, Fulbright, or Caldicott as they attempted to change U.S. foreign policy and nuclear arms policy:

> Contrary to tradition, Cold War "idealists" have attempted to decivilize America's image rather than the enemy's by relying upon metaphorical concepts such as MAD, PATHOLOGY, SICK, and FORCE, they have portrayed the United States as the irrational, coercive, and aggressive agent of extermination, urging Americans to follow instead the path of love, friendship, trust and empathy. (178)

Most Americans who were the intended audience of Henry A. Wallace, J. William Fulbright, and Dr. Helen Caldicott did not wish themselves as citizens (or their nation) to be seen as sick, crazy, deranged, or a manipulative user of power (even in a game context). Yet, Wallace, Fulbright, and Caldicott were bright, capable, sincere, concerned public rhetors who genuinely wanted change that they thought would make the world a safer place to live.

Let's not minimize the difficulty of rhetorical invention that Ivie is addressing here. Ivie outlines the concepts that a worthwhile core metaphor would have to cover:

> The replacement metaphor must take into account the evidence that both parties are rational and irrational, aggressive and pacific, competitive and cooperative, independent and interdependent. It cannot ignore, for instance, established perceptions that the Soviets are obsessed with a paranoid desire for security, that they are secretive, xenophobic, and distrustful, that they suffer from an inferiority complex and are ruthless, imperialistic, authoritarian (even totalitarian), militaristic, and anti-capitalistic. It cannot deflect attention, though, from other less threatening observations about the Soviets: that they possess a rich culture, suffer from limited resources and an inefficient economy, are basically conservative managers and technologists; that their revolutionary climate is localized (not a symptom of or inspiration for world revolution), that they are a patriotic people and a stable society, that they share with America a frontier heritage, and that they are officially atheistic but culturally religious . . . .

> The replacement metaphor must serve the goal of co-existence by redefining the ideal of global freedom (or world communism) to one of mutual security and continued competition. A replacement metaphor is needed to integrate mixed images of both superpowers in a manner that will promote arms reduction and manage conflict between them (180).

WHEW!! That's asking a bunch from *any* metaphor. Since, however, most students reading this book will have been born during a time of power transition across the globe, you are in a unique place to make a judgment about how we do talk about Russia (or any other world power). It has become popular since the fall of Soviet communism to suggest that America is the sole remaining "superpower" in the world. Even with dramatic changes in the geo-political power structure of the world, we still hear disputes about nuclear arms, space-based defensive "shields," and potential threats from "rogue states." Do we still use metaphors to describe and position the United States in terms of policy options? In the ever-changing post-9/11 world we inhabit, are we possibly using deficient metaphors to guide our decision-making? Or, have we found the right mix of metaphor images that capture the difficulties faced in the 2000s?

Returning for a moment to Ivie's study of Wallace, Fulbright, and Caldicott, can we *still* learn from their apparent mistakes? What if we really believe that a national policy is sick, or deranged, or manipulative? Must we change our tune in order to reach audience members capable of creating necessary change? This article is one example of how we can *anticipate* probable audience response to specific rhetorical message decisions. If you attend 10 speaker sessions held on your campus this year where the speaker (*rhetor*) is addressing a difficult or controversial issue, you will likely hear more than one of them characterizing their opponents or their opponent's policies as CRAZY or SICK (even if the rhetor doesn't use those exact terms, but uses metaphor terms that invite our interpretation of those core metaphors). If you were the speechwriter for one of those guest speakers, how would you advise them to *change* their appeal to avoid the pitfalls discovered by Robert Ivie? You should be much better equipped now to think about how metaphors may cluster into core representations that may or may not be to the rhetor's advantage. This illustrates how you as a communication professional, or other professional rhetor, can *use* the discoveries of rhetorical critics to make better judgments about messages over which you have some degree of control or influence.

By examining Robert Ivie's investigation about metaphors used by rhetors trying to change national policy across 40 years of American difficulties with the former Soviet Union, we have discovered some possible ways to extract key lessons about how rhetors use metaphors. Moreover, we've seen some of the potential difficulties of finding viable alternatives. Let's see if we can discover some of the same extended value with an examination of some research that addresses the power of stories in American culture.

Scrutinize exercise

Obtain and read Robert Ivie's article on Cold War idealists. Pay special attention to his call for stronger alternatives (on pages 178–181) that would transcend the limited core metaphors he discovered with Wallace, Fulbright, and Caldicott. (Also read one of his prior journal articles [listed in the "References" section at the end of his article] as background for an enhanced understanding of previous rhetorical decisions by national leaders when talking about enemies, or war, or threats.) What does he think would make a better core metaphor? Do you agree with him? Can you think of a metaphor image that would meet his requirements?

USING RHETORICAL CRITICISM: NARRATIVE ANALYSIS

Have you ever noticed that your best friendships are very flexible and resilient even through difficult times and problems? Have you ever noticed that your favorite films are ones that allow you to participate in facing and resolving problems very similar (or parallel) to difficulties you face? Have you ever noticed that politicians are involved in an ongoing set of changing friendships and alliances that permit agreements on legislation and public policy? If you think these three questions are somewhat odd when posed one after another, you are correct. However, one professor has discovered an interrelationship among these questions that has helped him better understand popular American films, political culture, and human decision-making. We'll next turn to his work as we seek to better understand how working communication professionals can learn from, and use, rhetorical criticism about how stories are told and used in our culture.

In the late 1980s and the early 1990s James Jasinski noticed that a very popular 1983 film (*The Big Chill*) had been uniformly trashed by conservative *and* radical/progressive popular critics.[4] Beyond this oddity of vastly different critics objecting to a very successful film, Professor Jasinski also noticed that the characters in the film addressed some key issues that stand at the heart of political communication, community, and action (continuing areas of research and interest to him). He set out to discover how a specified interpretation of the film might help us to better understand these puzzles of human relationships and politics.

We will face at least two challenges as we seek to examine his discoveries: 1) he is discussing a non-written artifact that he (and we) are trying to talk about in written form, and 2) he (as did Professor Ivie previously) covers insights and observations in a depth all of which we will be unable to use. With those two cautions we can proceed to "dock" with his article to gain perspective on narrative, politics, and human communication. (It would be a very good idea to rent or borrow a video or DVD copy of *The Big Chill* to view [or re-view] prior to reading the rest of this chapter. How

FIGURE 10.1 **With which of these characters do you most identify? Which character is more likely to be a part of a community?**

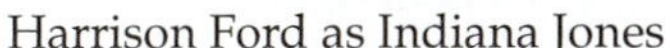

Harrison Ford as Indiana Jones

Harrison Ford as Bob Falfa

many textbooks request that you put them down to engage in a couple of hours of movie watching?)

Professor Jasinski thinks that films form "friendships" with viewers by encouraging them to identify with various characters or groups of characters in a movie. He uses an interpretive framework devised from the separate works of Hannah Arendt and James Boyd White that allows him to see how audience members are encouraged to "comprehend a narrative by imaginatively entering and participating in the constructed world which enables them to learn, and eventually judge, the norms of each community inscribed in the narrative" (469). In other words, in popular movies (often) various groups of people (sometimes only a pair, or a "team," or a community of people) are shown pursuing a goal (or goals) that produces conflict, problems, and difficulties. We as viewers are invited to watch and "think through" the depicted strategies, values, and understandings those groups use. Obviously writers and directors will have some depicted values and actions that they present as more favorable or desirable than others. The depicted community (whether a couple or a town) will be shown to have an emerging set of norms and understandings that guide their depicted behavior and decisions.

So, before we even think about Jasinski's specific rhetorical criticism of the movie *The Big Chill*, we can note that as a communication professional the *story*^{g} elements you learned about in Chapter 6 form a *story*^{c} that includes characters and groups with whom you feel some identification.

Professor Jasinski explores the difference between depicted eros (romantic, intense, intimate) relationships and philia (friendly, open, connected) relationships as he examines the plot structure and character actions in *The Big Chill*.

Characters in *The Big Chill* are posed as old college friends from the 60s who are gathered together for a weekend after the funeral of a common friend who has committed suicide. Relationships (old and new), career and life choices, values, and life perspectives become the focal point of discussion in the film. As more than half of the film is in sessions of group dialog, *The Big Chill* stands in a long line of creative or philosophical efforts that use group dialog as a rhetorical means of exploring important issues (e.g., Plato's *Gorgias,* Wilde's *The Importance of Being Earnest,* Stoppard's *Arcadia,* Hughes's *The Breakfast Club*).

Jasinski sees in the film that: "The group's challenge (articulated most directly in the minister's funeral speech) is to rediscover hope by (re)constitution of their community." (470) He detects that "communities" form around the three main male characters in the film (Nick, Harold, and Sam). Further, he notes that recurring "topics within the narrative (judging character, temporal orientation, and the possibility of providing assistance to others) function as cues to help uncover communal norms" (470). Hence, knowing how to judge others, knowing how to reflect on the differences between the "good ol' days" and now, and knowing how (and when) to help others are discovered focal points within this movie.

Jasinski sees one function of popular movies such as *The Big Chill* as giving advice: "Like many of our human friends, *The Big Chill* gives us advice and instruction on both the necessity of, and the criteria for, judging character" (479). Using Jasinski's analysis as a springboard, we can see that many different kinds of narratives depict people making decisions about matters of importance to them. Detected themes of this sort can serve *you* as a communication professional, or other professional rhetor, in at least two ways.

First, if you know ahead of time that character interaction in movies can help us sort out difficult issues, you can use the most popular movies of a given year as a rough detection device to determine which issues seem to be on the "mind" of the nation (as least as far as movie attendance can reveal that).

The second way you can use Jasinski's insight is to detect *how* the filmmaker made these themes or issues come to life in the building of *story*[g] elements. For instance, Jasinski several times discovers characters within the narrative of the movie telling a story about themselves: "Nick's story [one of personal and professional failure and disillusionment] reflects the same

Scrutinize exercise

Five 2001 movies earned more than 200 million dollars (*Shrek, Monsters, Inc., Rush Hour 2, The Mummy Returns,* and *Harry Potter and the Sorcerer's Stone*). Pick two of the movies and decide what key issues seem to occupy the main characters. What are they trying to "work out"? Can the popular appeal of these movies be traced back to the issues that seem to be highlighted by character action and dialog? Or, are there other reasons for the popularity of these particular films?

kind of scepticism that marked his response to Harold's earlier offer, but in this instance Nick's scepticism is immediately countered by Chloe [the only "outsider" character in the movie who is younger and not part of the original "old college friends" group]. She responds by telling a story that complements, and—in a way very different from Karen's response to Sam—also 'corrects,' Nick ['s story] . . ." (473). So, whether you intend to make Hollywood feature films, 30 second commercial spots, or radio news in the future, you can recognize that having characters within your narrative "tell" a story about themselves (rather than show it as an enacted part of the narrative) is a powerful device for "proving" or demonstrating a point that the character wishes to make.

Jasinski discovers that by the end of the film we have been "encouraged to compare and contrast the community created between Sam and Karen with that constituted by Meg, Sarah, and Harold" (476). He sees the Sam character [a TV actor] and Karen [an unhappy housewife and mother of two] as forming a couple based on *eros* while Meg [an attorney], Sarah and Harold [a physician and businessperson as well as wife and husband] form a "community" based on *philia.* As Jasinski's analysis reveals: "In the end, Harold, Meg, and Sarah come to embody an alternative communal possibility—one capable of restoring (if only on a small scale) lost hope—constituted by the values, practices, and norms of philia" (470). Hence, in *The Big Chill,* one type of human relationship is "featured" as more successful and worthwhile than another. Again, Jasinski detects this not only in themes but in recognizable production decisions within the film:

> Toward the very end of the film, we are issued one of the strongest invitations possible to contrast the two principal relationships. Despite his earlier decision, Sam ends the evening making love with Karen. The film cross cuts between the two acts of love making. Sam and Karen make love outdoors. It is dark. They grapple with each other's clothes, struggling to get them off. They settle on the essentials. The only sounds we hear are grunts. Harold and Meg make love indoors [with Sarah's approval so as to help Meg become pregnant and have a child] in a softly lit room on a bed that has been "lucky" for Harold and Sarah (so even though Sarah cannot be there to help, she is nevertheless "present" in a sense). They are nervous, but they also retain a sense of humor (Meg tells Harold that she feels like she got a great deal on a used car). They talk to each other about their feelings. They are naked. The following morning, Sarah joins Meg in the bedroom as Harold goes out for his regular run; the previous evening seems to have brought them closer together. At some point during the evening Sam and Karen moved indoors and now we see them packing for their respective trips home. In a way they act as if nothing has happened, but the scene is ripe with tension. . . . Given what we know about the characters and their relationships, we are invited to see Sam and Karen's lovemaking as an ardent, intense fulfillment of a lurking passion from the past that results in the irony of intimacy: in their effort to forge a relationship around the norms of intimacy Sam and Karen have in fact

> grown further apart. Their intimacy has exhausted the possibility of future action; there is nothing left for them to do. On the other hand, we are encouraged to view Harold and Meg's love making as an act of friendship with a collaborative "end" (Meg's hope to have a child in the future) beyond the immediacy of the moment. Rather than exhausting future possibilities, Harold and Meg preserve a sense of incompleteness that nurtures continued action (477).

One can be forgiven for wondering if people interviewed outside any theater mega-plex in 1983, after having seen the Sam and Karen characters in *The Big Chill,* would have known that they had just seen a couple trying to "forge a relationship around the norms of intimacy" in contrast to the *philia* norms exhibited by Harold, Meg, and Sarah. But, we must recall that a rhetorical critic looks at an artifact (in this case a film) as an integrated whole; that is, the critic carefully examines how the filmmakers' decisions allowed the different narrative parts to function together. Whereas a typical movie audience member understands the film at a surface, entertainment level without (perhaps) thinking about the deeper philosophical or ideological implications of the character actions and decisions in the film.

Jasinski presents compelling evidence for his understanding that two different kinds of relationship (intimacy or *eros* and friendship or *philia*) are central to the meaning structure of this movie. As he concludes: "Through its disjunctive structure, *The Big Chill* reveals the limitations of communities based on either estrangement [represented in the film by cynical, unconnected characters] or intimacy [represented by Sam and Karen and their furtive, ultimately temporary lovemaking] and affirms the norms of *philia*—a revitalized form of friendship—as the substance of community life [as seen in the sharing of sperm in joined effort to produce a baby by Harold and Meg (with Sarah's approval)]" (477).

To recap our discoveries to this point: Using Professor Jasinski's analysis of *The Big Chill* as a resource, a communication professional can discover how certain characters (and their decisions) form a type of "community" within a movie to which an audience member may feel some connection [Chs. 6 and 9: *narrative fidelity*]. Moreover, those who create narratives that reach huge audiences (including filmmakers) typically favor or feature certain characters or groups of characters as being more admirable than others within the narrative. By understanding that story-building dynamic, we can discover through Jasinski's skilled critical eye the norms for the created "communities" within this movie are designed to contrast the liabilities of intimacy with the advantages of friendship. We should be aware of how such core messages within films arouse within us, as movie patrons, enough interest to make the movie a strong economic success. We also saw how certain tactics of movie production (what we called in Chapter 6 development of *story*^{g} elements), such as characters telling verbal stories within the narrative of the movie, or intercutting scenes between two rival groups in a film, can help nudge an audience member toward what we have called a *preferred reading* of the movie (one intended and encouraged by the story-evoker). Such insights can become initial building blocks for people like you who will be rhetors creating messages for mass or public audiences in the future.

As a communication professional, you will want to have the ability to create the strongest stories possible. By finding these (and other) insights from an in-depth rhetorical analysis such as Professor Jasinski's, you can begin to assemble a much more sophisticated understanding about how movies (and other narrative forms) are built and implemented.

Jasinski goes one step further in his analysis of *The Big Chill*. The discoveries he made about different sets of characters offering "competing" sets of values and life philosophies to audience members are valuable within themselves. However, Professor Jasinski takes the interpretation to another level as he sees the competing groups depicted in the film as offering two versions of appropriate communities (understood more broadly):

> Narratives remind us that politics involves more than institutional arrangements and policy formation. Our experience of a narrative can recall, if we engage it in its fullness, a sense of politics as an ongoing project of communal (re)construction: a continual process of shaping and reshaping our possibilities of collective action. The final question to consider, then, is how does *The Big Chill* speak to the larger relationship of communal norms and political possibilities? (480)

Here Jasinski is suggesting that the relationships we see depicted in a hit movie can serve as a teacher, if we but see the broader political implications of the relationships celebrated and besmirched in the movie. As he puts it:

> The film presents intimacy and a revitalized sense of friendship as alternatives to the fragmented and ultimately vacuous experience of community promoted by our liberal, emotivist political culture. As rival responses, intimacy and friendship share important presuppositions and move in a similar direction, thus making a precise delineation of their political implications difficult. Despite this difficulty, I believe the film encourages reflective extension of the norms of intimacy and friendship thereby rendering their political possibilities perceptible. (480)

For instance, one of the characters in *The Big Chill* (Sam) is shown struggling again and again between the intensity of intimacy and the tedium of boredom. Jasinski sees this dilemma as not so different from what we experience as citizens within a political culture:

> like Sam's relationship with his first wife, the politics of intimacy is constantly plagued by the problem of boredom. . . . Sam's vacillation between intensity and boredom illustrates a key tension in certain forms of contemporary cultural politics. . . . Adherents to the politics of intimacy [Jasinski would include events such as music concerts designed as one-shot

Scrutinize exercise

Obtain and read James Jasinski's analysis of *The Big Chill*. (Be sure to watch the movie on tape or DVD prior to reading his whole article.) He claims in his essay that "*The Big Chill* counsels us that recognizing the limits of politics does not entail political resignation." Have you ever felt bored with, or helpless within, the ordinary political processes (at the local, state, or national level)? Assuming that you had not seen *The Big Chill* before reading this book, can you think of other films with which you are more familiar that celebrate friendship over intimacy? Can you think of the opposite: films that celebrate (or feature) intimacy over friendship? Does either type of depiction within a movie reinforce or have any impact on your desire (or lack of desire) to participate in the political process?

> solutions to complex problems as part of the politics of intimacy] strive to transcend the mundane world of traditional politics. This world lacks the intensity, the instant gratification provided by our contemporary politics. Participation in zoning hearings, political canvassing, or community organizations, by comparison, is boring. (480)

So, while movie patrons in 1983 were *not* likely to be making connections between the characters in *The Big Chill* and activities in their local city council, Professor Jasinski makes a compelling case that striking parallels exist between the frustrations and inactivity depicted for characters within the movie and habits and patterns of inactivity seen in citizens in a democracy.

By reviewing James Jasinski's analysis of this movie that was one of the first to grapple with and depict baby-boomers as changed from their own college days in the 1960s and 70s to different life experiences in the 1980s, we have discovered how a communication professional (*rhetor*) can employ some of the lessons about how movie-making rhetors use narrative tactics and themes. Furthermore, we've seen how it is possible to find stark parallels between the depiction of fiction characters on the silver screen and political processes within a community. We'll finish this chapter on using rhetorical analysis with an examination of some research that addresses the power of visual persuasion directed at mass viewing audiences.

USING RHETORICAL CRITICISM: VISUAL ANALYSIS

Television made its mark in American culture by adding pictures to sound (whereas radio broadcasts had been only sound). Ever since, we've been trying to figure out how exactly the production decisions that result in what we see on television have an impact on the meaning we create.

David Barker studied two famous television situation comedies (*All in the Family* and *M*A*S*H*) to better understand how visual encoding decisions might have impact on the characters, actions, and situations covered by sitcom material.[5] He realized that what we see on the screen doesn't happen by accident or happenstance. Equipment selection, crew size, budget, staging area, historical production practices, and visual medium choice all have a substantial impact on what eventually shows up on a movie or television screen.

Hence, even though we've had fewer years to study visual rhetorical practices, available current research can begin to encourage us to understand in greater depth the practices and norms of creating visual persuasion.

For his study Professor Barker randomly selected 20 episodes of each sitcom series. Each episode was analyzed for use of specific production techniques and then one episode of each series was randomly selected and subjected to a shot by shot analysis.

He discovered that the producers of *All in the Family* (Norman Lear) and *M*A*S*H* (Larry Gelbart) had picked significantly different styles of using **camera space.** For Barker, *camera space* [Ch. 6: *screen space*] (the area that the camera makes visible to us watching the result on a screen) is made up of a horizontal field of view (i.e., different type of shots: close-up, head and shoulders, medium shot, wide shot); what Barker terms **camera proximity** (location of the camera in relation to performers) (e.g., from the front, side, back, above, below) constitutes the distance between the camera and the character(s).

Barker also paid close attention to what he called **performer space** (positioning and movement along the *x-axis* or along the *z-axis*) [Ch. 9] for characters in both sitcoms.

Professor Barker discovered that all of the selected *All in the Family* episodes were shot in proscenium. This style of shooting is very recognizable in many situation comedies shot on a sound stage. Three cameras sit adjacent to a set where the camera view provides an image of three walls (the ones to the right and left of the camera and the back wall). See Figure 10.2. So sitcoms like *All in the Family* resemble a traditional theater stage with cameras standing in for the audience.

*M*A*S*H,* on the other hand was shot in single-camera, film style. The camera could be anywhere on the set so long as what it was "observing" was consistent with the situation and characters in the scene.

Barker's analysis revealed that more than 90 percent of the shots in *All in the Family* had character blocking and movement along the *x-axis.* Whereas, *M*A*S*H* had more than 75 percent of the character blocking along a *z-axis:*

> In *AITF,* performers were blocked almost exclusively along the x-axis as they moved from the front door through the living and dining rooms to the kitchen and back again. The only time there was a real potential for

FIGURE 10.2 Proscenium Staging for Taping
Cameras become the "fourth wall"

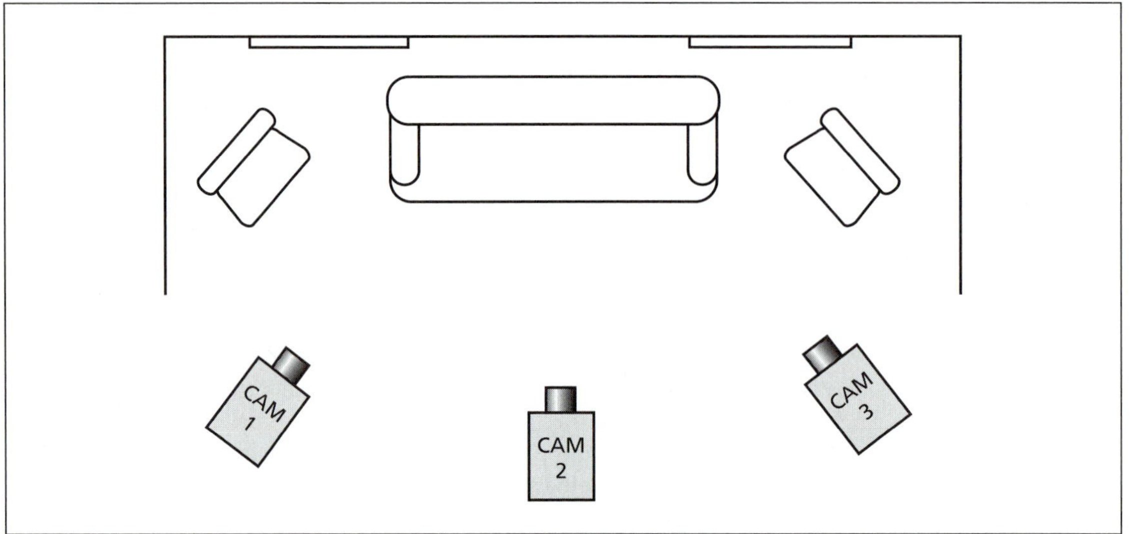

> movement toward or away from the cameras [along the *z-axis*] occurred when a character moved upstage to the stairway or downstage to the television set. *M*A*S*H*, on the other hand, utilized a great deal of movement along z-axis motion vectors. Because the camera was free to move into the performer's space for shot-reverse-shot sequences, performers could move toward and away from the camera as easily as they could move perpendicular to it. (238)

Barker discovered that the relative static and constrained camera shot view in *All in the Family* led to a reinforcement of Archie (the main male character) as a patriarch of his family: "the proscenium technique . . . utilized in *AITF* would seem to favor an axial, somewhat patriarchal narrative structure in that it allows the viewer to only look at a character rather than with them [as would be true if point of view shots had been used]" (238).

In other words, since the cameras had to stay at a distance from the central character, and since most of the character movement was in a highly predictable direction, it was easier to maintain the persona of a character who expected, and thought he deserved, control and authority.

Professor Barker's research allows you, as a communication professional in development, to learn that camera placement is as much a rhetorical device as any configuration of words has ever been. Production people have to make decisions every day that fundamentally alter our perception of what (or whom) we think we are seeing. Visual persuasion can be enhanced or ruined by decisions such as lighting, set design, character blocking, and camera placement.

Scrutinize exercise

Watch two episodes of *The Drew Carey Show* and two episodes of *Malcolm in the Middle.* You can see the same dynamic at work in these two programs as David Barker found in comparing *All in the Family* and *M*A*S*H.* Since the producers of *Malcolm* shoot most (if not all) of the program in single-camera, film style, you should see much more character action along the *z-axis* (toward or away from you) than you do along an *x-axis.* Whereas characters on *Drew Carey* should move primarily at the "back" of the set from left to right or right to left on an *x-axis.* How does the regular placement of cameras in a static or fixed position have impact on your perception of the characters? How does the placement of a single mobile camera have impact on your perception of characters?

Barker also finds that lighting in the two sitcoms under investigation is fundamentally different. Since light is a primary tool for changing a two-dimensional medium (either television or film) into a perceived three-dimensional experience, it only makes sense that it would become a focal point for the rhetorical analysis of television. Barker uses two terms borrowed from Zettl, *chiaroscuro lighting* and *flat lighting,* to describe the two types of lighting he found in *M*A*S*H* and *All in the Family,* respectively. *Chiaroscuro* lighting in *M*A*S*H* was "primarily in the form of source-directed lighting: during the day the sets were bright with 'sunlight' streaming through windows while, at night, shadows increased markedly, the sets becoming dimmer, with darkened windows and light [seemingly] provided by lamps or overhead fixtures" (241). Whereas, in *All in the Family* "the set was lit flatly and evenly. There was no regard for time of day—it was as bright inside the Bunker house at night as it was during the day. Similarly, there was no regard for light source . . . . Most importantly, shadows were virtually nonexistent" (241).

Set design followed the pattern that Barker has discovered concerning camera placement and lighting; it too is used in vastly different ways between the two sitcoms.

Barker found that depth cues (including **overlapping planes, relative size,** and **height in plane**) "were all missing from the particular episode of *AITF* under discussion . . . and were comparatively rare in any of the episodes analyzed in preparation for [Barker's research]" (242). Whereas, "*M*A*S*H* utilized sets of great depth, and these three depth cues were all conspicuously evident" (242). "The great use of depth in the set designs for *M*A*S*H* stands in sharp contrast to the designs for *AITF,* where sets tended to be long and shallow. But because there was comparatively little movement toward or away from the camera [*z-axis* motion], sets with any degree of real depth were unnecessary . . ." (242). Related to set design and lighting, Professor Barker notes that *All in the Family* showed little of the world outside the Bunker house whereas *M*A*S*H* consistently showed outside activity through doors and windows of tents. All of which leads him to observe: "The two dimensional treatment of the outside world in *AITF* led to little or no sense of space beyond the confines of the Bunker home. . . . The basically two-dimensional set design of *AITF*—drab and nondescript—and the minimal visual information provided concerning the outside world, encouraged the viewer to focus attention on those things inside the Bunker house that were three-dimensional: the characters and their confrontations" (243).

Hence, if we are thinking about which one of these sitcoms was "better," we miss Barker's insight completely. Remember that both of these sitcoms were award-winning shows with huge ratings. So, when Barker suggests that the *All in the Family* sets were "drab and nondescript," he is not making a negative style judgment; instead, he is asking the appropriate rhetorical question: what *function* does a drab and nondescript set serve in a hit situation comedy?

If you are seeking insight from this research on visual persuasion (and you should be), you might ask why *anyone* would want to have a disconnected, plain set with flat (uninteresting) lighting where a great distance is maintained most of the time between the cameras and the primary character. The answer, of course, is that you would want that set up when you have great writing, focused characters, and a desire to keep audience focus on the confrontational interaction between the characters. So if you are ever faced with covering a weakness in a video or film production (say, a poor script, a poor actor, or an uninspiring theme), you might want to try to distract the audience with wild lighting, wacky sets, or unusual character movement schemes. Come to think of it, that describes a substantial amount of advertising on television now!

Likewise, *M*A*S*H* has left its mark on how television (both comedy and drama) are taped or filmed. Barker traces some of the look and style of the single-camera, film-style shooting from *M*A*S*H* to *Lou Grant*, to *Hill Street Blues*, to *St. Elsewhere*, (and we could add *L.A. Law*, *NYPD Blue*, etc.). Hence, ensemble casts with "realistic" lighting, overlapping storylines, cameras following character movement, and sets with substantial planes of depth (foreground, middleground, and background) are now "required" rhetorical production components for many successful series.

Barker recognized early on how both (very different) visual rhetorical styles of production could have great value:

> Inasmuch as *AITF* revolved about an axial character, the true essence of the program was that the world began and ended with Archie [the father/husband character in the series]. It was essential, then, that *AITF* employ the narrative gestalt to a much greater degree than *M*A*S*H*, and a great part of that narrative gestalt was the creation through specific set design and lighting techniques of a physical environment that was itself a complete, self-contained unit, apart from the outside world.
>
> The need for narrative gestalt in *AITF* made it very much a drama [even in a sitcom!] of interiors. But in *M*A*S*H*, as much of the outside world as possible was included. I would argue that . . . unlike those in *AITF*, the

> characters in *M*A*S*H* were very closely tied to the outside world. So much of what happened in their lives was dictated by the ebb and flow of conflicts beyond their compound and beyond their control. Thus, a narrative heavily dependent on external realities was reflected in set designs that were open and emphasized the outside world. (243)

So, are the characters in your TV spot, documentary, or website animation intended to be seen as connected or disconnected to the world about them? Are they speaking well-written scripts or mediocre scripts? Are they focused on one central character or do they feature an ensemble cast? Professor Barker has reminded you that many different visual rhetorical decisions concerning camera placement, lighting, set design, and character movement can either help your characters or hurt them. Choose wisely.

In this chapter we have seen Robert Ivie offer to you an absorbing caution about metaphors that would be rejected by audience members when attached to fiercely contested issues. James Jasinski suggests that narrative as seen in a very popular movie is likely to use age-old themes that are recognizable (if one looks with care) on a personal, social, and community/political level. David Barker examines two of the most successful television sitcoms of all time only to find out that each found success with dramatically different production design decisions. All of these scholars have demonstrated that careful, systematic, thoughtful analysis of rhetorical messages in our culture bears much fruit. You have been gaining the ability through various chapters to "find the gold" of insights offered by scholarly critics. In this chapter we've pointed to a few ways in which you can anticipate using those insights to your best advantage when constructing messages that will reach large audiences that count.

The Chapter 10 workshop will offer you another chance to move deeply into scholarly writing (now we hope with greater experience and ability to seek insights) as you more fully recognize the power of using existing rhetorical criticism. On the next page you will find a journal article by Carpenter. Use the article to prepare for the workshop.

Scrutinize exercise

Obtain and read David Barker's study of *M*A*S*H* and *All in the Family.* If you can, watch re-runs of each series on cable or on a local channel that carries the programs (you'll probably find more reruns of *M*A*S*H* than *All in the Family.* If you cannot watch either of these programs choose a sitcom that is shot in proscenium style with three studio cameras and a studio audience (e.g., *That 70's Show* or *Will and Grace*) and watch a show shot in single-camera, film style that features an ensemble cast (e.g., *The West Wing* or *Ally McBeal*). Do you find continuing similarities with Barker's discoveries? Differences? Barker explains that viewers did "encroach" on the main character, Archie, in one way (even if most other rhetorical production tactics were designed to keep the viewer's distance from him). How did the producers create the encroachment? Why, according to Barker, did they bring the audience close? Do sitcoms today use this (or other tactics) to create spatial closeness with sitcom characters?

Source: Quarterly Journal of Speech 72 (1986), 290–305.

Admiral Mahan, "Narrative Fidelity," and the Japanese Attack on Pearl Harbor

Ronald H. Carpenter

The name recurs in analyses of America's emergence as a world power as well as the course of international affairs generally: Alfred Thayer Mahan. In the United States, this naval historian's discourse influenced decisions favoring imperialism: Germany and Great Britain used his doctrine to justify naval growth, colonial expansion, and actions during both World Wars; and recent Russian naval building "might almost have been inspired by the prophetic writings of . . . Alfred Thayer Mahan."[1] To Theodore Roosevelt, "he was one of those men who leave a permanent mark on history and literature, aside from their profound and far reaching influence on contemporary thought."[2] For many people, Mahan articulated "man's role in society" during "widening uncertainty and chronic stress" when "the historian's voice is most needed, the moreso as the others seem inadequate, often absurd."[3] His message was part of the "communication mosaic" about military might during the turn of the century.[4] But, Mahan was heeded because he made compelling historical sense to guide future action.[5]

While nominally a United States Navy officer and Naval War College lecturer, Mahan contributed prolifically to periodicals and wrote several volumes on naval history. His reputation rests most securely, though, on *The Influence of Sea Power Upon History*, published in 1890. The book won acclaim not only for its content but also for its form and style.[6] Letters from his readers pointed to a persuasive "paramessage" from his style in discourse "*quite apart from the representational meaning of the message itself.*"[7] For readers of English, carefully qualified periodic sentences evinced a prudent cautious writer not given to rash assertions or overstatement; and a stylistic counterpoint of epigrammatic generalizations projected exceptional wisdom and powers of insight.[8]

My concern here is with Japanese readers of translations who praised "the great principles herein set forth by your forcible pen." With Japan's "Naval and Military College having adopted it as their textbook," *The Influence of Sea Power Upon History* also was in "every middle, higher middle and normal school in Japan."[9] Ronald H. Spector identifies sources of

Ronald Carpenter is professor of English, University of Florida. A version of this essay was presented to the Naval History Symposium at the United States Naval Academy in 1985. He wishes to express appreciation to Ed Johnson, Robert Newman, and Herman Stelzner for helpful readings of early drafts of the essay.

Japanese decisions about Pearl Harbor as ranging from "the British Royal Navy to the histories of Alfred Thayer Mahan."[10] And other historical research offers diaries, interviews, and correspondence indicating that Admiral Yamamoto, his planning staff, and attack commanders were "true disciples of Mahan."[11] Those rich primary sources facilitate rhetorical analysis of how the course of Japanese strategy and tactics at Pearl Harbor were vectored in part by an American's historical narrative.

I

Characterizing historians as "rhetorical agents" who "are always in search of those proofs that are able to explain the past to the present in the most persuasive terms," E. Culpepper Clark asks: "What makes certain explanations more satisfactory than others?" For him, historical writing is an analog of an oration's *narratio* or "statement of facts" wherein "stylistic devices are to employ the story . . . transform the warrant from its status as a general inferential rule to a connector between thought and action that is grounded in experience and appeals to common sense."[12] It is true that discourse does not function in isolation from other discourses.[13] But in Japan, Mahan's historical narrative superseded other stories about sea power.

My thesis is that for Japanese naval personnel who planned and executed the Pearl Harbor raid, Mahan's writing became increasingly influential as its message became doctrine as it was corroborated by events. To help account for decisions by planners of the Pearl Harbor attack and commanders at sea and in the air on 7 December 1941, I will employ Walter R. Fisher's concept of "narrative fidelity." His narrative paradigm construct is appropriate here because it views human communication "as historical as well as situational, as stories competing with other stories; . . . and as rational when they satisfy the demands of narrative probability and fidelity."[14] Thus, I shall explicate those events which made Mahan's story "ring true" for the Japanese prior to the attack on Pearl Harbor.

Although rhetorical interaction between discourse and corroborating events is integral to attaining narrative fidelity, Mahan's credibility complemented the process as his reputation among Westerners caused the Japanese to read him initially as they entered the twentieth century with a "catch up" mentality about naval warfare. They found enticing statements from a distinguished historian who seemed to write directly about their nation and to advocate models of behavior. Readers so persuaded are drawn to such models initially because they perceive real or imagined similarities to people whose behavior should be emulated.[15] To Kenneth Burke such identification is *"acting together."*[16] But, as Fisher also observes, "any story, any form of rhetorical communication, not only says something about the world, it also implies an audience, persons who conceive of themselves in very specific ways. If a story denies a person's self-conception, it does not matter what it says about the world. . . . The only way to bridge this gap, if it can be bridged through discourse, is by telling stories that do not negate the self-conceptions people hold of themselves."[17] Mahan's "story" appealed forcefully to Japan's self-conceptions.

II

The most significant portion in *The Influence of Sea Power Upon History*, was the opening chapter, "Discussion of the Elements of Sea Power." Preceding 421 pages of historical narrative about naval engagements between 1660 to 1783—typically won by British naval prowess—these 55 pages identified and explained six sources of a nation's greatness at sea and thereby in the world: geographical position, physical conformation, extent of territory, population, national character, and character of government.[18] Mahan's model was the British Islands (rather than continental France or Holland), but he could have been writing about Japan! That island nation shared several of Great Britain's sources of sea power.[19] Perceiving bases of similarity with Great Britain, Japanese naval personnel also read Mahan's extensive, patent praise for "men and deeds of the British Navy."[20]

Great Britain's naval prowess was emulated by Japan. During the Russo-Japanese War of 1904–05, Captain William C. Pakenham of the Royal Navy was with Admiral Togo throughout the war as an observer and firm friend. He was aboard ship for fourteen months, during which Togo consulted Pakenham and another British naval attache, Captain Thomas Jackson. Samuel Eliot Morison observes that Japanese naval "training methods and organization were on British models."[21] And after Pearl Harbor, Navy Day in Japan (May 27, 1942) was celebrated with parades, ceremonies, and this proclamation published in English:

> This year, Navy Day is not a day of mere remembrance, not a mere reminder; it is a day of *fulfillment*. The Japanese Navy has not only duplicated the exploits of 37 years ago, but it has repeated it [sic] time and time again and on an unbelievably greater scale. . . . This is the moment of culmination, the moment of *fulfillment*.
>
> Today, *Britain's control over the seas has vanished*, thanks to the work of the German and Italian submarines and more to the work of the Japanese Navy. Britain's auxiliary, the United States, has likewise had her navy practically destroyed by the Japanese Navy. As a result, *Japan stands today as the premier naval power of the world*. It may well presage *the rise of Japan in the future history of the world to a position comparable to that which Britain has occupied in the past*.[22]

Japan's success in emulating Britain's Royal Navy was made possible by learning the lessons taught in story after story within Mahan's broader historical narrative. That success was also made possible by an interaction between Mahan's discourse and an event which helped endow his stories with "narrative fidelity" for the Japanese: the battle of Tsushima.

In his "Introductory," Mahan argued that "at a very conspicuous and momentous period of the world's history, Sea Power had a strategic bearing and weight." He immediately provided a supporting "story" of Rome's victory over Hannibal in the Second Punic War.[23] Mahan's autobiography summarized his conception (in 1885 while reading Mommsen's *History of Rome*) and how it led him to "investigate coincidentally the general history and naval history of the past two centuries, with a view to demonstrating the influence of events of the one upon the other"; for "It suddenly struck me, whether by some chance phrase of the author I do not know, how different things might have been could Hannibal have invaded Italy by sea, as the Romans often had Africa, instead of by the long land route; or could he, after arrival, have been in free communication with Carthage by water."[24]

Here was the historical analog of Japan and Russia at Tsushima in 1905. After Japan's surprise attack on Russia's fleet at Port Arthur ("the first Pearl Harbor"), their mainland war was one of sieges, frontal assaults, and massive bodies of troops (at Mukden no larger forces ever had met in war's history). Hampered by a long, overland supply route for which the TransSiberia Railroad was inadequate, Russia sent an armada from Europe to interdict Japanese supplies and reinforcements to mainland operations. In the Straits of Tsushima between Korea and Japan, that fleet was destroyed decisively by Admiral Togo (with Captain Pakenham on the flagship *Mikasa* and preparations "according to the best British traditions"). According to Togo, "the fate of our empire was really settled within the first half hour" on 27 May 1905 (hence the date of Navy Day).[25] Tsushima brought Russia earnestly to the conference table.[26] Japanese naval planning thereafter favored a "statutory Great All-Out Battle" because such "decisive victory" allowed the winner "to 'control the seas,' to cut off the enemy's seaborne supplies and reinforcements, and to ensure the arrival of one's own."[27] Rome against Hannibal paralleled Japan's experience with Russia, and Mahan's detailed chronicles of other "decisive" sea battles won by "men and deeds of the British Navy" corroborated extensively and authoritatively what Japan believed already.

Mahan's eminence in Japan also is explained as "opinion leadership." For groups, some people's opinions expressed outside the group are especially potent. As described by Klapper, their influence is "expended often in favor of reinforcement" of group norms *because* the opinion leader is perceived as "characteristically more competent, within his specialty, than are his fellows," with "access to wider information," and "like everyone else only moreso." From such a "*super-representative*," that "guidance seems to be sought or accepted in specific areas partly—or perhaps largely—because it provides his followers with the sort of satisfaction they seek in those areas.[28] Mahan's credibility in Western eyes demonstrated competence to the Japanese; his book's scope of detail evinced "access to wider information"; and the historian's praise of "elements of sea power"—which Japan *shared* with Britain—displayed similarity in values with Japanese naval personnel. And by "predicting" in 1890 the impact of Togo's naval victory at Tsushima in 1905, Mahan's narrative about the past offered guidance for those who planned and executed the attack on Pearl Harbor. The experience confirmed the veracity of Mahan's narrative and fulfilled the early expectation of Japanese leaders that his work could "awaken our nation and as in Moses time may be the pillar of fire leading our nation in the century to come."[29]

III

Another persuasive aspect of Mahan's story was his terminology. "Sea Power" was such a term.[30] However, it was the expression *"fleet in being"* that had a decisive impact on Japanese minds and military strategy and tactics. This term referred to a concentration of warships sufficient to ensure offensive success. The narrative fidelity to the concept was confirmed for Japanese by events that occurred during the Spanish-American War, which lasted 113 days.

First there was the battle of Manila Bay. Two months before formal outbreak of hostilities on 22 April 1898, Assistant Secretary of the Navy, Theodore Roosevelt, cabled Commodore Dewey, commanding the U.S. Navy's Asiatic Squadron, to be ready at Hong Kong for "offensive operations in Philippine Islands" upon the declaration of war against Spain. So in Manila Bay at 5:40 A.M. on 1 May, Dewey said to the *Olympia's* commander, "You may fire when you are ready Gridley"; at 7:35 A.M., after five passes at Spain's ships, the squadron withdrew to redistribute ammunition and have breakfast; at 11:16 A.M. Dewey resumed the attack; at 12:30 P.M. the Spanish surrendered. American casualties were "none killed and but six slightly wounded."[31] In a few hours—including a break for breakfast—America acquired a forward Philippine naval base from which the United States Fleet could "dominate the Far East."[32] Second, consider America's naval triumph at Santiago de Cuba. Spain's fleet under Admiral Cervera left harbor shortly before 10:00 A.M. on 3 July 1898 to battle the blockading Americans; by 1:15 P.M. its last vessel was destroyed; one American was killed. With morale shattered, Spanish troops there surrendered and peace was proclaimed on 12 August. Moreover, triumph at Santiago was witnessed by Lt. Akiyama Saneyuki, Imperial Japanese Navy, as an observer aboard Admiral Sampson's flagship.[33]

Saneyuki became a pivotal figure who between 1900 and 1912 exerted a "dramatic and comprehensive impact on Japanese naval thinking."[34] During duty in America (1897–99), he conferred with Mahan, who received him cordially and recommended readings for his professional education. Although denied admissions to the United States Naval Academy and the Naval War College, Saneyuki's assignment on Admiral Sampson's flagship allowed him to be the *first* Japanese naval officer to witness Western sea power in action. His observations about Sampson's "bold initiatives" using modern battleships became Secret Intelligence Report 108, the "classic source of information on the U.S. Navy for Japanese planners," and his analysis of America's blockade at Santiago guided Japan's successful blockade of Port Arthur six years later—which Mahan described in *Naval Strategy* (1911) as a model of a "fleet in being" engaged in offensive operations.[35] Assigned to Japan's Naval Staff College in 1900, Saneyuki "brought a sense of authority to his lectures" founded upon readings and status as Japan's only direct witness to what America's battleships could do.[36] Reflecting medieval Japanese treatises, such as *The Ancient Corsair Tactics of the Yashima School* written in the 14th century, his doctrine (like Mahan's) advocated "concentration of forces" but added destroying the enemy's "will" as equally important, if not moreso, than ships. By 1904, as his navy's "unrivaled tactical genius," Saneyuki was aboard Togo's flagship drafting the battle plan for Tsushima and subsequently writing the report of the engagement, thus being both architect and scribe of victory. So impressions during the Spanish-American War helped shape tactics for Japan's naval triumphs against Russia and resultant doctrine favoring "concentrated fleets of battleships" to win "command of the sea" in decisive battles.[37]

Still another of Mahan's ideas ultimately helped shape Japanese naval planning. Two and one-half weeks before formal hostilities, Admiral Cervera's fleet sailed from Cadiz for the Western hemisphere (the *Maine* disaster in Havana preordained war). While its location was unknown, that "fleet in being" caused panic along America's eastern seacoast. A Georgia congressman asked the Navy Department for a ship to defend Jekyll Island "because it contained the winter homes of certain millionaires," and an influential woman insisted that "a ship should be anchored off a huge sea-side hotel because she had a house in the neighborhood." The Atlantic Fleet remained concentrated, though, for *offensive* operations to blockade Cuba and then "force Spain to surrender by threatening a naval attack on her coasts."[38] In *Lessons of the War With Spain*, Mahan explained why American battleships must not be detached as single units to be overwhelmed by larger forces:

> The Navy Department had . . . to keep in mind . . . that we had not a battleship in the home ports that could in *six months* be made ready to replace one lost or seriously disabled. . . . *If we lost ten thousand men, the country could replace them; if we lost a battleship, it could not be replaced.* The issue of the war, as a whole and in every locality to which it extended, depended upon naval force. . . . A million of the best soldiers would have been powerless in the face of hostile control of the sea.[39]

And in *The Influence of Sea Power Upon History,* Mahan quoted "a most accomplished French officer of the day" about another war: "Behind the squadron of twenty-one ships-of-the-line . . . there was no reserve; not another ship could have been commissioned within *six months*."[40] For Japanese readers, "six months" became a potent frame of reference; it later constrained decisions about America's "fleet in being" of battleships. Again, events made Mahan persuasive.

The Washington Naval Conference Treaty of 1922 did not favor Japan. Great Britain, the United States, and Japan could build battleships in a 5-5-3 ratio, respectively, for a 40 percent American superiority over the Japanese (and the London Naval Treaty of 1930 specified 10-10-7, respectively, for cruisers). Japan experienced a "ratio neurosis" about being outgunned in the Pacific.[41] Two "super battleships," *Yamato* and *Musashi,* were secretly built to offset the imbalance. With eighteen-inch guns and displacing 70,000 tons, these behemoths substituted "striking power per ship for number of vessels"; and faith in "huge battleships and big guns" constituted "mainstream" and "conservative" thought in Japan's Navy.[42] Even after the successful carrier air strike against Pearl Harbor, the Japanese Naval General Staff still said that "The battleship constitutes the nucleus of naval power."[43] As O'Conner concluded, "Japan, in keeping with her program of Westernization, emulated Great Britain and the United States in embracing the fleet concept with the battleship as the ultimate arbiter."[44] That battleship mentality was maintained by Rear Admiral Matome Ukagi, for instance, who as Combined Fleet Chief of Staff "had almost reverent faith in the lessons taught in the Naval General Staff College and in the concept of the Great All-Out Battle"; and Admiral Yamamoto, despite his pioneering efforts to foster development of aircraft carriers and naval aviation, was said to be "under the influence of Alfred Thayer Mahan" and "visualized the battleship as the queen of the fleet."[45] That orthodoxy became more significant, however, as Japan moved inexorably closer to attacking Pearl Harbor.

Bogged down since 1937 in war with China, Japan sought expansion in Southeast Asia for raw materials, especially oil. Holland and France were defeated by Nazi Germany in 1940; Great Britain seemingly awaited only Hitler's final blow; their Asian empire was vulnerable. In July 1941, Japanese troops entered French Indo-China and secured the flank for a drive to obtain oil in the Dutch East Indies. Although many Americans were isolationists, despite Franklin Roosevelt's appeal in 1937 to "quarantine" aggressors, sentiment was turning against Japan due to pro-Chinese propaganda, including the widely published photograph of a Chinese baby crying amid rubble after a Japanese air raid.[46] The French Indo-China incursion prompted a stern warning from Roosevelt and an embargo on America's shipments of strategic materials to Japan, including high octane gasoline and crude oil. Time was running out. Japan could not meet extensive oil needs with synthetics or purchases abroad; its Navy "would be disabled in two years, and important industries paralyzed in less than half that time" (in another estimate, the navy "had enough oil for only eighteen months of operations under war conditions"); and military seizure of oil and raw materials in Southeast Asia "would almost certainly precipitate war with the United States."[47]

One American force was, in Yamamoto's words, a "dagger being pointed at our throat": the U.S. Navy's Pacific Fleet.[48] Formerly based on America's West Coast, those ships were sent to Hawaii in May 1940 as a "putative deterrent to Japanese aggression against British or Dutch possessions in Southeast Asia."[49] Their maneuvers were regarded in Tokyo as a "brandishing of the big sword," calling forth "vigorous protests," for those ninety-six vessels—including eight battleships—constituted a "fleet in being" which "created a *strategical* situation incomparably more tense and threatening to the Japanese than had existed when it was based on the Pacific coast."[50] An attack on Pearl Harbor, once only a possibility in Japanese planning, became a probability.

IV

Japan thought about war with the United States as early as 1907 because of tensions over American discrimination against Japanese immigrants. The early plan was to seize Guam and the Philippines. Ships sent to recover United States possessions would be intercepted near Japan and destroyed in decisive battle. For thirty years, the Japanese Navy's "long-cherished" posture was "conservative," *defensive* one of "calmly remaining in waiting" in "seas adjacent to Japan" for "its sole imaginary enemy," the United States Navy.[51] In 1936, however, Japan's Naval War College produced an *offensive* view of "Strategy and Tactics in Operations Against the United States," the surprise attack on Pearl Harbor.[52] At Japan's Naval Academy, cadets soon learned about "sudden attack" against "the United States fleet, the strongest in the world."[53] By 7 January 1941, events—and the factor of time—led Admiral Yamamoto as Combined Fleet Commander to write to Navy Minister Admiral Koshiro Oikawa that "a conflict with the United States and Great Britain is inevitable." Therefore, Japan's Navy should "fiercely attack and destroy the U.S. main fleet at the outset of the war, so that the morale of the U.S. Navy and her people" would "sink to the extent that it could not be recovered." Moreover, "we should do our very best at the outset . . . to decide the fate of the war on the very first day" with aircraft carriers launching a "surprise attack . . . on a moonlight night or at dawn" against Pearl Harbor. In late January, Yamamoto and Rear Admiral Takijiro Onishi agreed on "smashing the morale of the American people by sinking as many battleships as possible," for "most Americans—like most Japanese—still believed battleships to be the mightiest weapons of war. The sinking of one or, better yet, a number of these giant vessels would be considered a most appalling thing, akin to a disaster of nature."[54] So Mahanism, favoring bold, offensive applications of sea power against battleships, complemented traditional doctrine from Saneyuki advocating a decisive blow at the enemy's will; and together the two viewpoints began to modify Japan's conservative, defensive naval posture toward the United States.

In February 1941, an air officer on the carrier *Kaga* was ordered to develop the mission's operational concept. As "one of the most brilliant 'Young Turks' of naval aviation in Japan," Commander Minoru Genda completed his assignment quickly; and while differing from Yamamoto in that the main objective was America's two aircraft carriers at Hawaii, Genda saw the raid as "difficult but not impossible."[55] Furthermore, "if Yamamoto was the father of the Pearl Harbor plan," Genda was "spiritual and intellectual mother, coaxing it to life, nourishing it from the well springs of his own heart and mind, defending it against all comers."[56] As of April, however, the Naval General Staff felt that "Hawaii Operation" planning should be abandoned, but Yamamoto's staff of "very loyal" and "powerful supporters" now included Captain Kameto Kuroshima, who authored that pivotal 1936 Naval War College paper.[57]

Yamamoto's forceful personality and his planners' loyalty resembled "groupthink" wherein "members use their collective resources to develop rationalizations supporting shared illusions about the invulnerability of their organization or nation." Along with their willingness to take extreme risks and collective discounting of warnings to reconsider assumptions, such groups often achieve conformity by stifling counter arguments and adverse information that might undermine faith in their decision.[58] Yamamoto, whose "position and influence in the Japanese Navy were unique," threatened to resign if the Pearl Harbor raid was not approved by the Naval General Staff.[59] Illusions about invulnerability were evident in the planners' table-top war games (as practiced at the United States Naval War College and introduced to Japan by Saneyuki).[60] During September 1941, Yamamoto stood "over the table" and "dominated" exercises wherein one team executed his plan "as faithfully as possible" and another team simulated various American responses. When attackers suffered heavy losses, games were replayed with new dice; or umpires decreed the Japanese fleet "was divinely aided by a squall just in time to permit it to leave the Pearl Harbor area without serious damage." In postwar interviews, participants characterized their procedures as "unrealistic" and "self-indulgent thinking" wherein umpires would "slant their decisions" to favor the attackers.[61]

Despite the planners' conformity and illusions of invulnerability, however, Japan wavered. By October 1941, torpedoes still were not perfected for Pearl Harbor's shallow waters (when dropped from aircraft they nosed down too sharply and hit bottom); practice bombing results still left doubts in planners' minds; and Admiral Nagumo, who would command at sea, remained unconvinced about the attack.[62] Serious reservations about the attack's feasibility also were held by Commander Mitsuo Fuchida, who would lead aircraft over Pearl Harbor.[63] Air crews stepped up training and increased proficiency, however. As of 18 October, though, the Navy General Staff remained unconvinced about launching the raid; for, as Admiral Shigeru Fukudome recalled in 1950, "we in Tokyo were against the Pearl Harbor plan." Nevertheless, because of Yamamoto's threatened resignation if his plan was not accepted, the Navy General Staff acquiesced on 21 October, with Admiral Nagano as Chief of Staff saying, "If he has that much confidence, it's better to let Yamamoto go ahead."[64] But the Naval General Staff was not ready yet to endorse the plan forward for Imperial sanction!

Japan could not attack Pearl Harbor because Yamamoto threatened resignation. In the psychology of groups, even those characterized by "groupthink," decisions often required "bolstering" before final implementation. "*Bolstering* is an umbrella term that includes a number of different psychological tactics that contribute to creating and maintaining the decision maker's image of a successful outcome with high gains and tolerable losses"; and when fostered by "strong deadline pressures along with little or no opportunity to shift responsibility," the "classic pattern of *selective exposure* becomes dominant, marked by active search and preference for supportive information and avoidance of discrepant information."[65] That "supportive information" was obtained promptly on 23 October 1941 when Lieutenant Commander Takeshi Naito lectured to Yamamoto's planning staff, which now included Fuchida. In 1940, Naito was Assistant Naval Attache in Berlin when British carrier aircraft launched a torpedo raid against the Italian fleet in Taranto Harbor. The Germans flew him to Taranto to appraise the damage. Back in Japan, Naito reported his direct observations to the planners, and Fuchida as a good friend "interrogated him extensively all the next day."[66] To bolster a group's decision in the face of "strong deadline pressures," Naito's news was superb.

On the evening of 11 November 1940, the British aircraft carrier HMS *Illustrious* was 170 miles from Taranto and Italy's six battleships and three of its cruisers. She launched twenty-one aircraft, eleven of which carried torpedoes (the other carried bombs and flares to light targets and help pilots avoid barrage balloons and their steel cables). The first planes attached at 10:56 PM; within 65 minutes the last planes turned back to their aircraft carrier. Two battleships were so heavily damaged they were beached; another battleship and two cruisers were severely damaged; two destroyers were damaged and two auxiliary vessels sunk. Losing only two aircraft, *Illustrious* escaped unscathed. Italy withdrew remaining major warships to safer harbors from which they never again conducted offensive operations. Just as Japanese supplies could flow unmolested to Asia's mainland after Tsushima, British convoys to Malta, Egypt, the Suez Canal, and India beyond were no longer interdicted by Italy's "fleet in being." British naval prowess praised by Mahan again attained decisive victory, this time with aircraft carrier operations which Japan began imitating shortly after World War One.[67] But Britain's Fleet Air Arm used twenty-one Fairey Swordfish aircraft—fabric covered, open cockpit biplanes, affectionately known as "Stringbags," with a top speed of 138 miles per hour.[68] If Britain accomplished so much at Taranto with obsolescent biplanes, Japan should attain more by surprise on a Sunday morning, against Pearl Harbor at peace, with six aircraft carriers and three hundred and fifty-three superior aircraft.

In late 1940, Genda was still Assistant Naval Attache in London, reading British releases about Taranto which undoubtedly influenced his subsequent operational plan for Pearl Harbor.[69] But in late October 1941, Naito's eyewitness report about Britain's naval success was more pertinent as Japan's Naval General Staff moved closer to its *final* decision, which was not reached until 5 November 1941. Saneyuki's earlier eyewitness analyses stood the test of time and contributed to Japan's "self conception" of its own naval prowess. In making a final decision, Naito's eyewitness report about a corroborative event was an important addition to interact with other input, including orthodox attitudes about Mahan's "fleet in being"—particularly when Yamamoto's plan was *so pragmatic* in its ultimate goals.

Despite bravado about deciding "the fate of the war on the very first day," Yamamoto really wanted six months. As a man who would avoid war with America if possible, he did not anticipate landing troops in California, fighting across a continent, and capturing Washington, D.C. Yamamoto's primary goals were (1) protecting the drive south for oil and other raw materials and (2) securing sea lanes by which these resources came home; for "the southern operations, unlike the operations in China, will determine the nation's rise or fall." By destroying or crippling America's "fleet in being" threatening those operations, and taking away its forward base in Manila Bay (won by Dewey's "fleet in being" in six and one-half hours, including a break for breakfast), Japan obtained time to seize and strengthen forward island bases behind which its new empire would be secure until America's rebuilt fleet advanced to the "Great All-Out" naval engagement far in the western Pacific. Thus in January 1941, as he wrote to Navy Minister Oikawa, Yamamoto saw the Pearl Harbor attack gaining "approximately six months" and thereby assuring success for Japan's primary objectives.[70] And to Premier Konoye, Yamamoto boasted that "in the first six months to a year of war against the U.S. and England I will run wild, and I will show you an uninterrupted succession of victories."[71] For, as Mahan proclaimed in *Lessons of the War With Spain*, America "had not a battleship in the home ports that could in six months be made ready to replace one lost or seriously disabled."

America's "fleet in being" was Japan's target at Pearl Harbor. As Prange attests, "the Japanese were after the U.S. Pacific Fleet and Oahu's air power—not the military installations, the tank farms, the dry docks, the machine shops, or the submarine base." On 23 November, Admiral Nagumo convened taskforce commanders and finally announced "our mission is to attack Pearl Harbor"; having solved the problem with their torpedoes, the raiders departed on 26 November. On the way Fuchida's airmen "drilled incessantly" on recognizing ships that were their targets, for Yamamoto's direct order was to "operate in such a manner as to destroy the U.S. Fleet at the outset of the war."[72] So strategy dominated Japanese naval planning. But tactics deserve consideration, too. As "a word which perhaps better than any other indicates the dividing line between tactics and strategy," Mahan recommended "*contact*."[73] Once the attackers made contact in the air over Pearl Harbor, decision making shifted from Yamamoto in Tokyo to Nagumo on his flagship *Akagi* about 200 miles north of Oahu.

V

In Tokyo, as reports came in, the Naval General Staff felt "intense joy and relief" as the attack "greatly exceeded its most optimistic expectations."[74] In under two hours, Pearl Harbor's "Battleship Row" became a disaster scene. *Arizona* and *Oklahoma* were totally lost (as well as the target ship *Utah* and two destroyers); *West Virginia, California,* and *Nevada* were sunk or beached (but salvageable); *Tennessee, Maryland, and Pennsylvania* were damaged (as well as three cruisers and a destroyer). America's airpower in Hawaii was shattered. One hundred and eighty-eight Army and Navy planes were destroyed and one hundred and fifty-nine damaged. Japan lost twenty-nine planes and their sixty-four crewmen (although seventy-four other planes suffered some damage).[75] Japanese pilots returned to aircraft carriers "wild with joy." Upon landing, Fuchida hurried to Admiral Nagumo. As he reported "four battleships sunk" and "four battleships damaged," the taskforce commander interrupted with the question uppermost in his mind: "Do you think that the U.S. Fleet could come out from Pearl Harbor within six months?" Fuchida replied: "The main force of the U.S. Pacific Fleet will not be able to come out within six months." Then, although Fuchida pressed for a second strike against "dockyards, the fuel tanks, and an occasional ship," Nagumo dismissed him with a "few words of praise."[76] In battle's heat, while making a tactical decision, Nagumo was constrained by "six months" as a criterion for judgment.

A second strike was within Nagumo's capability. Despite higher seas, aircraft landed without incident, and over two hundred planes could have been refueled, rearmed, and launched again. Fuchida's plea for the return was endorsed by Lt. Jinichi Goto (commanding *Akagi's* torpedo planes), Lt. Saburo Shindo (commanding fighter aircraft), and Genda (who wanted to find and destroy the two American aircraft carriers, *Lexington* and *Enterprise,* not in the harbor that morning); for Pearl Harbor was "the chance of a lifetime." After weighing alternatives, including possibilities that Japanese submarines also sent to Hawaii would sink America's carriers, Nagumo ordered "Preparations for attack cancelled." Upon seeing *Akagi*'s signal flags sending the armada homeward, Fuchida rushed to the bridge and protested "why are we not attacking again?" Before Nagumo could speak, his chief of staff, Rear Admiral Ryunosuke Kusaka, replied "The objective of the Pearl Harbor operation has been achieved." Fuchica saluted, turned on his heel, and stalked out "a bitter and angry man."[77]

A second strike would have altered the course of the war. In retrospect, Admiral Chester Nimitz "knew what a close thing Pearl Harbor had been" because the Japanese did not "complete the job" and destroy "the oil supply," which "would have prolonged the war another two years." Admiral Raymond Spruance agreed that "the Japanese could have done much more damage. . . . So long as anything was left, they had not completed the job."[78] Amid the disaster scene, even Admiral Kimmel saw "some positive aspects to his situation. His precious oil tanks had escaped destruction; so had his machine ships, his 'Navy behind the Navy.'" Indeed, he fully expected another strike against shipyards and docks still "relatively undamaged, and above all, the tank farms," for "if they had destroyed the oil which was all above ground at that time . . . it would have forced the withdrawal of the fleet to the coast because there wasn't any oil anywhere else out there to keep the fleet operating."[79] Now America's naval war in the Pacific would not be fought from the West Coast.[80]

Nagumo's tactical decision reflected several factors. He was not absolutely sure Hawaii's land based airpower was shattered (it was) and feared counterattack.[81] More important were American aircraft carriers whose location was unknown. Nagumo need not have worried. Japanese *Zeros* were superior to Grumman F4F *Wildcat* fighters or any naval aircraft Americans could put in the sky, and the U.S. Navy's torpedo bomber, the Douglas TBD-1 *Devastator,* was inadequate as a frontline aircraft (at Midway *all* of Torpedo Squadron 8 was destroyed by *Zeros* or antiaircraft fire before achieving a single hit). Japanese pilots then were "among the best in the world," many with years of combat experience in China.[82] Aviators from *Lexington* and *Enterprise* likely could not have found and hurt Japan's ships appreciably, particularly when they believed the raid was launched from south of Oahu.[83] But the most significant factor affecting Nagumo's *tactical* decision was commitment to a strategic goal. As a doctrinaire, Nagumo from the outset insisted "One attack only! One attack only!"[84] He even considered aborting the raid as late as 6 December when intelligence from the Japanese consul in Hawaii (relayed through Tokyo) reported America's aircraft carriers absent from Pearl Harbor. But his chief of staff Admiral Kusaka argued "We can't do anything about carriers that are not there. I think we should attack Pearl Harbor tomorrow."[85] As Admiral William Furlong concluded in 1962, "Nagumo followed classic naval doctrine in staying within the established boundaries of his task and refusing to be tempted into alluring side paths"; and although "that mission may have been wrong," the tactical commander "stuck with it."[86] He gained "six months" by destroying battleships, the core of America's "fleet in being." Mahanism could not have been served better, particularly when Nagumo's "fleet in being" remained intact for subsequent, "decisive" engagements and that statutory "Great All-Out Battle."

But Mahan did identify shore installations as contributing to sea power. While discussing "the making and repairing of naval material," the historian lauded that "staying power, or reserve force, which is even greater than appears on the surface." The topic was treated, though, under "Number of Population," and the importance of destroying an enemy's dockyards was buried in commentary about "Character of Government."[87] Thus, clues to tactical targets were subordinated to strategic conceptualizations. As a reader suggested in 1892, "it seemed to me that there loomed up through the account of various naval engagements a vague suggestion of a right way and a wrong way to do the thing and I wondered whether anyone is looking up the question of tactics"; and for that specific advice from the world's authority on sea power, people needed "careful" reading, even "two or three" times to find "anything that suggests itself," exercising "patience and comprehensiveness" coupled with "time and iteration" to find "true meaning" for tactical consideration.[88]

In conclusion, Pearl Harbor served Japanese strategy. In addition to gaining time deemed essential for success of the "southern operations," naval treaties under which Japan suffered a "neurosis" no longer mattered. By destroying America's battleship "fleet in being," the Japanese navy was no longer "outgunned" in the Pacific, and Yamamoto believed the "balance of power" was tipped in "in our favor."[89] That orthodox view was shaped in part by Mahan's historical narrative. In final decisions about and at Pearl Harbor, however, that discourse could remain influential only as it told "stories that do not negate the self-conceptions people hold of themselves." Mahan had corroborated Tsushima and in turn was corroborated by Taranto. Within a narrative paradigm, that interaction between events and discourse had advantage to be rhetorically potent. And the magic of Mahan's "six months" remained evident to Japan as its own formidable "fleet in being" roamed with impunity from Pearl Harbor on 7 December 1941 until America's decisive naval victory at Midway on 4 June 1942, as history repeated itself for the Japanese—for a while.

VI

In the predawn of 7 December 1941, as *Akagi* turned into the wind to launch aircraft, an unique flag flew from her mast: Admiral Togo's banner from Tsushima.[90] In attacking Pearl Harbor, Japan's navy demonstrated faith in history. What Japanese naval planners knew as history, however, evolved from interaction between their nation's experiences and an American admiral's discourse. And because Mahan's narrative of sea power achieved fidelity from real events, his rhetoric about the past guided Japan's future, briefly but momentously.

Reading Endnotes

1. See Barbara Tuchman, *The Proud Tower: A Portrait of the World Before the War—1900–1914* (New York: Macmillan Company, 1962), pp. 130–37, 148–49, 248–53; Howard K. Beale, *Theodore Roosevelt and the Rise of America to World Power* (Baltimore: The Johns Hopkins University Press, 1956); W. D. Puleston, *Mahan* (New Haven: Yale University Press, 1939), pp. 106–09, 159; William Livezey, *Mahan on Sea Power* (Norman: University of Oklahoma Press, 1947), p. 70; Louis Hacker's Introduction to Alfred Thayer Mahan, *The Influence of Sea Power Upon History, 1660–1783* (New York: Hill and Wang, 1957), p. vi; and "Reaching for Supremacy at Sea," *Time,* 31 January 1972, p. 29.
2. Theodore Roosevelt to Mahan's wife, 5 December 1914, Box 2, Alfred Thayer Mahan Collection in the Library of Congress, hereafter cited as ATM. I was able to work with these papers as well as the Naval Historical Foundation Collection, hereafter cited as NHFC, through a Social Sciences Institute Grant from the University of Florida.
3. See Barbara Tuchman, "The Historian's Opportunity," Address, American Historical Association, December 1966. This address is published in the *Saturday Review,* 25 February 1967 as well as in Tuchman, *Practicing History: Selected Essays* (New York: Alfred Knopf, 1981), pp. 51–64. See in particular pp. 51–2.
4. Samuel Becker, "Rhetorical Studies for the Modern World," in *The Prospect of Rhetoric,* ed. Lloyd Bitzer and Edwin Black (Englewood Cliffs, N.J.: Prentice Hall, 1971), p. 33.
5. For other discussions of persuasion through history, see Ronald H. Carpenter, "America's Opinion Leader Historians on Behalf of Success," *Quarterly Journal of Speech,* 69 (1983), 111–26; "Carl Becker and the Epigrammatic Force of Style in History," *Communication Monographs,* 48 (1981), 318–39; and *The Eloquence of Frederick Jackson Turner* (San Marino, Calif.: The Huntington Library, 1983).
6. My dichotomy between style and content, or how a person talks about something rather than what he talks about, reflects a viewpoint expressed in Rulon Wells, "Nominal and Verbal Style" and Charles E. Osgood, "Some Effects of Motivation on Style of Encoding," both in *Style in Language,* ed. Thomas A. Sebeok (Cambridge, Mass.: MIT Press, 1960), pp. 215 and 293.
7. See Paul I. Rosenthal, "The Concept of the Paramessage in Persuasive Communication," *Quarterly Journal of Speech,* 58 (1972), 15–17.
8. See my "Alfred Thayer Mahan's Style on Sea Power: A Paramessage Conducing to *Ethos,*" *Speech Monographs,* 42 (1975), 190–202.
9. To Mahan from M. Minikami, Naval Commanding Staff Imperial Japanese Navy Department, 15 July 1899, and from the Secretary of the Oriental Association, Tokyo, 1 April 1897, both in Box 3 ATM. See also Puleston, pp. 106–109 and Livezey, p. 70.
10. Ronald H. Spector, *Eagle Against the Sun: The American War With Japan* (New York: The Free Press, 1985), p. 33.

11. Spector, p. 293. In addition to other helpful sources, I refer in particular to Gordon W. Prange, *At Dawn We Slept: The Untold Story of Pearl Harbor* (New York: McGraw-Hill, 1981) as well as his *Miracle at Midway* (New York: McGraw-Hill, 1982).
12. E. Culpepper Clark, "Argument and Historical Analysis," in *Advances in Argumentation Theory and Research,* ed. J. Robert Cox and Charles A. Willard (Carbondale: University of Southern Illinois Press, 1982), pp. 298–317.
13. Stephen Lucas. "The Schism in Rhetorical Scholarship," *Quarterly Journal of Speech,* 67 (1981), 7.
14. Walter R. Risher, "Narration as a Human Communication Paradigm: The Case of Public Moral Argument," *Communication Monographs,* 51 (1984), 1–22. See in particular pp. 2, 6–8, 10 and 15. For another view of rhetorical narration, see Thomas S. Frentz, "Mass Media as Rhetorical Narration," The Van Zelst Lecture in Communication, Northwestern University (Evanston: Northwestern University, 1985). See in particular pp. 6–7, 15.
15. See Jerome Kagan, "The Concept of Identification," *Psychological Review,* 65 (1958), 304; and Walter Weiss, "Effects of the Mass Media of Communication," in the *Handbook of Social Psychology,* 2nd ed., by Gardner Lindzey and Elliot Aronson (Reading, Mass.: 1969), pp. 98–100.
16. Kenneth Burke, *A Rhetoric of Motives* (New York: George Braziller, Inc., 1955), pp. 19–23, 55–59.
17. Fisher, p. 14.
18. For other indices of the potency of Mahan's generalizations, see Carpenter, "Style on Sea Power," especially pp. 195–99.
19. See Theodore H. White, "The Danger from Japan," *New York Times Magazine,* 28 July 1985, pp. 19ff.
20. For further discussion of Mahan's praise of British naval prowess, and Lord Nelson specifically, see Julius W. Pratt, "Alfred Thayer Mahan," in *The Marcus W. Jernigan Essays in American Historiography,* ed. William T. Hutchinson (Chicago: University of Chicago Press, 1937), pp. 221–22. Or, see Carpenter, "Mahan's Style on Sea Power," pp. 195 and 201.
21. Samuel Eliot Morison, *History of United States Naval Operations in World War II,* Volume Three, *The Rising Sun in the Pacific 1931–April 1942* (Boston: Little, Brown and Company, 1948), p. 21. See also Denis Warner and Peggy Warner, *The Tide at Sunrise: A History of the Russo-Japanese War 1904–1905* (New York: Charterhouse, 1974), p. 184.
22. *Japan Times and Advertiser,* 27 May 1942, in Prange, *Midway,* p. 88. Italics are mine.
23. Mahan, *Influence,* pp. 11–18.
24. Mahan, *From Sail to Steam* (New York: Harper and Brothers, 1907), p. 277.

25. This discussion is based on Warner and Warner, particularly pp. 494–520 about Tsushima. See also pp. 3–20 on "the first Pearl Harbor" and p. 513 about Togo and Mahan.
26. For discussion of the impact of the Japanese victory at Tsushima, see Eugene P. Trani, *The Treaty of Portsmouth: An Adventure in American Diplomacy* (Lexington: University of Kentucky Press, 1969), pp. 46, 56, and 110. Trani also found evidence that the Japanese sought advice from Admiral Mahan for the final terms of settlement in the Treaty of Portsmouth. See p. 92.
27. Prange, *Midway*, p. 116 and Spector, p. 511.
28. Joseph T. Klapper, *The Effects of Mass Communication* (New York: The Free Press, 1960), pp. 34–35. See also my application of this construct to historical discourse in "America's Opinion Leader Historians on Behalf of Success."
29. To Mahan from M. Minikami, Naval Commanding Staff, Imperial Japanese Navy Department, 15 July 1899, Box 3 ATM.
30. See reactions in the *Boston Evening Transcript*, 14 May 1890; *New York Daily Tribune*, 18 May 1890; *Louisville Courier Journal*, 24 May 1890; *San Francisco Chronicle*, 1 June 1890; *Chicago Daily Inter-Ocean*, 7 June 1890; *Literary World*, 5 July 1890; *Royal United Service Institution Journal*, 34 (1890–91), 1067; *London Times*, 23 October 1893; and *Le Journal* (Paris), 3 December 1914. Actually, Mahan predicted his evolving statement would be less about tactics and more about "great moral lessons" upon which sea power and thereby international strength were based, Mahan to Luce, 22 January 1886, Box 3 ATM.
31. G. J. A. O'Toole, *The Spanish War: An American Epic* 1898 (New York: W. W. Norton, 1984), pp. 102–03, 136–37, and 174–93. Dewey then held Manila under seige, not attacking the city itself and forcing its surrender until 13 August, the day *after* the peace protocol was signed by both countries.
32. See the discussion of Japan's concerns in Asada Sadao, "The Japanese Navy and the United States," in *Pearl Harbor as History: Japanese-American Relations 1931–1941*, ed. Dorothy Borg and Shumpei Okamoto (New York: Columbia University Press, 1973), pp. 243–44. See pp. 650–63 for an indication of the extensive primary sources used in this analysis. Naval presence in the Philippines *still* is important to the United States. See analyses in the *New York Times*, 23 February 1986, pp. E1 and E3.
33. For an account of the battle of Santiago de Cuba, see O'Toole, pp. 328–339. Saneyuki's role as observer also is noted in Spector, p. 43.
34. Mark R. Peattie, "Akiyama Saneyuki and the Emergence of Modern Japanese Naval Doctrine," *U.S. Naval Institute Proceedings*, 103 (1977), pp. 62–5.
35. Mahan's chapter on "Fleet in Being and Fortress Fleet: The Port Arthur Squadron in the Russo-Japanese War" is reprinted in *Mahan on*

Naval Warfare: Selections from the Writings of Rear Admiral Alfred T. Mahan, ed. Allan Westcott (Boston: Little, Brown and Company, 1920), pp. 256–75.

36. Prior to Saneyuki's experience, a few Japanese officers had visited sites of naval battles in the Sino-French War of 1884 and the Greco-Turkish War of 1897, but they only interviewed participants after the encounters. See Peattie, p. 69. For other noting of Saneyuki as a student of Mahan, see Warner and Warner, p. 500.
37. Spector, pp. 18–19.
38. O'Toole, pp. 194–95, 209, 223, and 325.
39. Mahan, *Lessons of the War With Spain* (New York, 1899), p. 185. Italics are mine. As an indication of American commitment to a concentrated "fleet in being," Britain asked in the spring of 1941 that the United States divide its Pacific Fleet and detach some of those ships to help defend Singapore, but the request was denied because "it was fundamental that the Pacific Fleet be held intact." See Morison, p. 50.
40. Mahan, *Influence,* p. 39. Italics are mine.
41. See the discussion, based on Japanese naval documents, in Sadao, pp. 240–43. See also Spector, pp. 20–1 and 39–40.
42. Sadao, pp. 238–42; Spector, p. 47; and Prange, *Midway,* p. 15.
43. Captain Hideo Hiraide, in the *Japan Times and Advertiser,* 27 May 1942, in Prange, *Midway,* p. 89.
44. See Raymond O'Connor's "Commentary" in *The Japanese Navy in World War Two: An Anthology of Articles by Former Officers of the Imperial Japanese Navy and Air Defense Force* (Annapolis: United States Naval Institute, 1971), p. 136.
45. Prange, *Midway,* pp. 305 and 34. For discussion of Yamamoto's efforts on behalf of naval aviation and aircraft carriers, see Sadao, p. 238.
46. For public opinion poll data at this time, see Morison, pp. 39 and 58–61.
47. Prange, *At Dawn,* pp. 169 and 191 as well as Shigeru Fukudome (Rear Admiral and Chief of Staff under Yamamoto at the time of Pearl Harbor), "Hawaii Operation," in *The Japanese Navy in World War II,* pp. 8–9. The Japanese Navy wanted 500,000 tons of oil on reserve "for the Great All-Out Battle" but peacetime consumption was 300,000 tons every month. For similar conclusions based on the United States Strategic Bombing Survey, see Morison, pp. 36, 62–63, 70 and 78. See also Spector, pp. 75–76.
48. In Fukudome, pp. 5 and 8.
49. Spector, p. 1. In ordering those ships to Hawaii, the President reflected is own Mahanism, for "ever since his school days at Groton. Roosevelt had been convinced of Japan's long-range plans of conquest. He pored over Admiral Mahan's *The Influence of Sea Power Upon History* until, according to his mother, he had 'practically memorized the book.' Later he corresponded with Mahan and learned that the

admiral shared with him a strong concern over Japan as a major threat in the Pacific." See John Toland, *The Rising Sun: The Decline and Fall of the Japanese Empire 1936–1945* (New York: Random House, 1970), p. 47. Toland also notes that "at Harvard, in 1920 [sic], a Japanese student told Roosevelt in confidence about his nation's hundred-year plan for conquest, drafted in 1889" which included Manchuria, China, and British and American possessions in the Pacific including Hawaii. In 1934 Roosevelt informed Henry L. Stimson of this "plot" and pointed out how "many of its particulars had already been verified."

50. Fukudome, p. 5. Italics are mine. See also Morison, pp. 42–3 as well as O'Conner, p. vi.
51. Fukudome, pp. 4–5. See also the postwar testimony of Admiral Osami Nagano, Chief of the Naval General Staff in *What Happened at Pearl Harbor: Documents Pertaining to the Japanese Attack of December 7, 1941, and Its Background*, ed. Hans Louis Trefousse (New York: Twayne Publishers, 1958), pp. 254ff.
52. Spector, pp. 44 and 79. The Americans also devised their corresponding "Orange Plan" for war in the Pacific.
53. Kazuo Sakamaki, *I Attacked Pearl Harbor* (New York: Association Press, 1949), p. 28. He had entered the Academy in 1937 and graduated in 1940.
54. From Prange's interviews with Juji Enomoto and Shuichi Mizota, respectively the legal advisor to the Japanese Navy and Yamamoto's translator, in Prange, *At Dawn*, pp. 16–7 and 19–21. According to Prange, the first time Yamamoto spoke about attacking Pearl Harbor was in March or April 1940, to Fukudome. See p. 14. For discussion of Onishi's role in planning the attack, see Fukudome, p. 6.
55. See Spector, pp. 79–80 as well as several primary sources cited in Prange, *At Dawn*, pp. 20–7.
56. Prange, *Midway*, p. 136.
57. See Fukudome, p. 6 and Prange, *At Dawn*, pp. 226 and 98 as well as p. 235 on Admiral Matome Ukagi's "shatterproof convictions of the loyalty a chief of staff owed to his commander in chief," Yamamoto. See also Prange, *Midway*, p. 69.
58. Irving L. Janis and Leon Mann, *Decision Making: A Psychological Analysis of Conflict, Choice, and Commitment* (New York: The Free Press, 1977), pp. 129–31. For analysis of American unpreparedness at Pearl Harbor, see Janis, *Groupthink: Psychological Studies of Policy Decisions and Fiascos*, 2nd ed. (Boston: Houghton Mifflin, 1983).
59. Prange, *At Dawn*, pp. 297–303; Spector, pp. 81–2; and Prange, *Midway*, p. 23 about Yamamoto "threatening to resign if he did not get his way, and the Naval General Staff yielding to his polite blackmail."
60. Peattie, pp. 63–64. See also Spector, pp. 43–44.
61. See especially Prange, *At Dawn*, pp. 223–31 and 234. See also Spector, pp. 81–82.

62. Spector, pp. 81–82, and Prange, *At Dawn,* pp. 225, 236, 258–60.
63. Mitsuo Fuchida, "The Attack on Pearl Harbor," in *The Japanese Navy in World War II,* p. 18.
64. Fukudome, pp. 8–9 as well as Prange, *At Dawn,* pp. 295–303.
65. Janis and Mann, pp. 91, 205–06.
66. Prange, *At Dawn,* p. 320.
67. O'Conner, p. vii. The success of the British air strike against Taranto had not gone unnoticed by U.S. Navy personnel, including Admiral Stark at Pearl Harbor. See Prange, pp. 40, 45, 47 and 159. But inertia worked to the Americans' disadvantage. As Spector concludes, "naval aircraft were improving rapidly during the late 1930s; they had performed impressively on maneuvers, but they had also proven to be highly dependent on good weather and visibility. Their carriers, meanwhile, had proven highly vulnerable to both surface and air attack. Tactics that were to prove decisive in the air-sea battles of the 1940s appeared impossible with the aircraft available in the 1930s. 'There was just not enough evidence [yet] that aircraft carriers had become the dominant ship type' to convince most of the navy's senior command to abandon the battleship as the basis of the combat fleet." See Spector, p. 23.
68. Ian G. Stott, *The Fairey Swordfish Mks. I-IV: Profile #212* (Windsor, England: Profile Publications Ltd., no date), pp. 34–37, 43. See also A. B. C. Whipple, *The Mediterranean* (Chicago: Time-Life Books, 1981), pp. 63–71.
69. John Deane Potter, *Yamamoto: The Man Who Menaced America* (New York: Viking Press, 1965), p. 55.
70. Prange, *At Dawn,* pp. 10–12, 18, and 549. A copy of the letter was obtained by Prange from Rear Admiral Teikichi Hori, close friend and confident of Yamamoto. See also Morison, pp. 80–81.
71. From Prince Konoye's Memoirs, quoted in Morison, p. 46 and in Roberta Wohlstetter, *Pearl Harbor: Warning and Decision* (Stanford, Calif.: Stanford University Press, 1962), p. 350.
72. Fukudome, p. 11; and Prange, *At Dawn,* pp. 27, 373–79, and 415. During September 1941, the Yokosuka Air Group experimented with torpedoes to which a special stabilizing fin had been added. These proved satisfactory in tests conducted in shallow waters similar to those of Pearl Harbor. The Mitsubishi firm quickly adapted its Mark II torpedoes with this fin and delivered a sufficient quantity to the striking force just in time for their departure. Prange, pp. 321–23.
73. Mahan, p. 7.
74. Prange, *At Dawn,* pp. 548–49.
75. Arthur Zich, *The Rising Sun* (Chicago: Time-Life Books, 1977), p. 72. See also Prange, *At Dawn,* pp. 544–45.
76. Prange, *At Dawn,* pp. 541–43. Quotations from the Fuchica-Nagumo interchange are from Fuchida's recollections during an interview in

1963. In Fuchida's published account for the U.S. Naval Institute, "six months" is not included as part of the dialogue. But after the report of the number of battleships sunk, Nagumo is quoted as saying "We may then conclude that anticipated results have been achieved." Fuchida, p. 27.

77. Prange, *At Dawn*, pp. 543–47. See also Fukudome, pp. 12–14.
78. Prange, *Midway*, p. 9 (from an interview with Nimitz on 4 September 1964) and Prange, *At Dawn*, p. 550 (from an interview with Spruance on 5 September 1964).
79. Prange, *At Dawn*, pp. 549–50, 563, 575, and 587. Even during the subsequent Naval Court of Inquiry into the Pearl Harbor disaster, Admiral Kimmel asserted his *dis*belief that the Pacific Fleet "would constitute the Prime target." He testified "I thought it was much more probable that the Japs would attempt a raid on Pearl Harbor if the Fleet were away than if it were there." See p. 627.
80. See Spector, p. 83–84 as well as Morison, pp. 125–26.
81. Prange, *At Dawn*, p. 546.
82. Spector, pp. 46–47.
83. Morison, pp. 214–15, 218. Even when the Americans expected the Japanese at Midway, U.S. naval aviators almost missed finding the enemy's fleet (this was a time before airborne radar and its search capabilities).
84. Prange, pp. 426 and 545.
85. Fuchida, p. 21. See also Wohlstetter, p. 378. For further discussion of Japan's battleship mentality, see Spector, pp. 34, 88, 167, and 319.
86. In Prange, *At Dawn*, pp. 549–50. For the subsequent defense of Nagumo's decision, see Fukudome, p. 15.
87. Mahan, *Influence*, pp. 40, 55, and 62–63.
88. To Mahan from Captain C. F. Goodrich, 14 May 1892 and from Thomas G. Bowles, 14 January 1893, both in Box 3 ATM. See also an unidentified newspaper analysis of 2 December 1914, in Box 1 ATM (although the date is evident, the name of the newspaper was cut off).
89. Prange, *At Dawn*, p. 202.
90. That *beau geste* is noted in several sources. See Fuchida, p. 22; Prange, *At Dawn*, p. 472; Morison, p. 93; or Warner and Warner, p. 20.

In this Chapter 10 workshop, we will further examine how you can gain insight from articles of rhetorical criticism. Work at a pace by assignment, or by choice, that allows these various insights to sink in at an even deeper level for you. Begin to ponder how you might best use the insights in real life situations.

Having read the rhetorical criticism by Ronald H. Carpenter, "Admiral Mahan, 'Narrative Fidelity,' and the Japanese Attack on Pearl Harbor," use the chart on the next page to start careful notes on the JFS and JFA items (about which you learned in Chapter 3) that Carpenter used to establish the need for this research. Make other notations in the margin of the reproduced article.

FINDING THE SET-UP ITEMS

Discovering JFS and JFS Items

Carpenter, Ronald R. "Admiral Mahan, 'Narrative Fidelity,' and the Japanese Attack on Pearl Harbor." *Quarterly Journal of Speech* 72 (1986): 290–305.

(Page numbers in brackets indicate pages reprinted in this textbook.)

Item	Page	
JFS	290 [419]	"And other historical research offers diaries, interviews, and correspondence indicating that Admiral Yamamoto, his planning staff, and attack commanders were 'true disciples of Mahan.' "
JFS	290–291 [419]	"Those rich primary sources facilitate rhetorical analysis of how the course of Japanese strategy and tactics at Pearl Harbor was vectored in part by an American's historical narrative."
JFS		
JFS		
JFA	290 [418]	"His reputation rests most securely, though, on *The Influence of Sea Power Upon History,* published in 1890. The book won acclaim not only for its content but also for its form and style."
JFA		

Item	Page	

As part of this Chapter 10 workshop, we will continue to probe several of the ways you can recognize and use the "gold" of academic, rhetorical criticism. Re-read the chart on the next page. See if you can notice how we moved from the original claim, insight or discovery to the resulting "translation."

Next, use the blank chart on the following page to find more nuggets of "gold" in the article from your own reading. Be sure to keep track of the page on which you find the quotation and think about how you can best translate the insight or discovery to a practical translation you could use in preparing a message.

FINDING THE GOLD

Discovering Application Ideas and Knowledge in Rhetorical Criticism Articles

Example:

Carpenter, Ronald R. "Admiral Mahan, 'Narrative Fidelity,' and the Japanese Attack on Pearl Harbor." *Quarterly Journal of Speech* 72 (1986): 290–305.

Quotation	Page	Translated Idea or Insight
"They [the Japanese military] found enticing statements from a distinguished historian who seemed to write directly about their nation and to advocate models of behavior. Readers so persuaded are drawn to such models initially because they perceive real or imagined similarities to people whose behavior should be emulated."	291 [419]	Storytellers (or evokers) can create stories that seem so parallel, so close, so similar to the audience receiving the story that it has profound impact on the audience's future actions, which imitate what they've seen in story form.
"In attacking Pearl Harbor, Japan's navy demonstrated faith in history. What Japanese naval planners knew as history, however, evolved from interaction between their nation's experiences and an American admiral's discourse."	301 [431]	Stories drawn from understood history can have profound influence when they seem to match the direct experience of those receiving the stories. Direct experience that seems to match historical stories mutually reinforces the "truth" of the story from history.

Use the chart on the next page to find, identify, and chart the potential advantage of other observations on narrative and culture that Carpenter makes in his analysis.

Quotation	Page	Translated Idea or Insight

THE POWER OF HISTORICAL NARRATIVES

After thoroughly reading and understanding Ronald Carpenter's article on Admiral Mahan's influence on the Japanese military prior to World War II, affirm and defend one of these two propositions:

1. A dusty military history about the British Royal Navy written by an American admiral was substantially responsible for the attack on Pearl Harbor, Dec. 7, 1941.
2. A dusty military history about the British Royal Navy written by an American admiral could never have substantially caused the attack on Pearl Harbor, Dec. 7, 1941.

Have any of your life decisions ever been deeply influenced by a story about someone else who seemed very similar to you? (i.e., have you ever personally seen the impact of *narrative fidelity?*).

NARRATIVE ARCHITECTURE

Obtain and seriously read this article:

Goodstein, Ethel S. "Southern Belles and Southern Buildings: The Built Environment as Text and Context in Designing Women." *Critical Studies in Mass Communication* 9 (June 1992): 170–185.

Make margin notations (only on a xerox copy!) concerning your identification of JFS and JFA claims made by Goodstein. Identify the specific artifact(s) under investigation. Identify the method used to accomplish the analysis of the artifacts. Identify the working Research Question that guides inquiry in the article.

Next collect a series of at least six insights that you can gain about depicted architecture in a television series.

Write down how you think you might use the insights gathered to increase your awareness about possibilities of creating visual persuasion.

How does Goodstein think that the architectural imagery used in *Designing Women* might encourage a "post-feminist" understanding of the series characters?

THE POWER OF WRITTEN COMPARISONS

Obtain and seriously read this article:

Scott, Robert L. and James F. Klumpp. "A Dear Searcher into Comparisons: The Rhetoric of Ellen Goodman." *Quarterly Journal of Speech* 70 (Feb. 1984): 69–79.

Make margin notations (only on a xerox copy!) concerning your identification of JFS and JFA claims made by Scott and Klumpp. Identify the specific artifact(s) under investigation. Identify the method used to accomplish the analysis of the artifact(s). Identify the working Research Question that guides inquiry in the article.

Next collect a series of at least six insights that you can gain about how a comparison can set the tone for persuasive messages (such as a columnist might write).

Write down how you think you might use the insights gathered to increase your awareness about possibilities of creating and using potent comparisons.

Why do Scott and Klumpp think that columnists may be similar to preachers? Do you feel as if you are "in church" when reading a columnist?

LEGEND NARRATIVE AND SOCIAL TRAINING

Obtain and seriously read this article:

Lessl, Thomas M. "The Galileo Legend as Scientific Folklore." *Quarterly Journal of Speech* 85 (1999): 146–168.

Make margin notations (only on a xerox copy!) concerning your identification of JFS and JFA claims made by Lessl. Identify the specific artifact(s) under investigation. Identify the method used to accomplish the analysis of the artifact(s). Identify the working Research Question that guides inquiry in the article.

Next, collect a series of at least six insights that you can gain about how a short folklore story can help establish a professional image and understanding.

Write down how you think you might use the insights gathered to increase your awareness about possibilities of using short tales of legend.

Lessl argues that short, legend stories about historical events may leave out key details. How long must a historical story be to *not* leave out key details?